Growing Consensus II

THE ECUMENICAL DOCUMENTS SERIES

From Paulist Press

Volume I: *Doing the Truth in Charity: Statements of Pope Paul VI, Popes John Paul I, John Paul II, and the Secretariat for Promoting Christian Unity, 1964-1980* (1982)

Volume II: *Growth in Agreement: Reports and Agreed Statements of Ecumenical Conversations on a World Level* (1984)

Volume III: *Towards the Healing of Schism: The Sees of Rome and Constantinople: Public Statements and Correspondence Between the Holy See and the Ecumenical Patriarchate, 1958-1984* (1987)

Volume IV: *Building Unity: Ecumenical Dialogues with Roman Catholic Participation in the United States* (1989)

Volume V: *Growing Consensus I: Church Dialogues in the United States, 1962-1991* (1995)

From the United States Conference of Catholic Bishops

Volume VI: *Deepening Communion: International Ecumenical Documents with Roman Catholic Participation* (1998)

From the World Council of Churches

Growth in Agreement II: Reports and Agreed Statements of Ecumenical Conversations on a World Level, 1982-1998 (2000)

ECUMENICAL DOCUMENTS VII

Growing Consensus II

CHURCH DIALOGUES IN THE UNITED STATES, 1992-2004

Edited by
LYDIA VELIKO AND JEFFREY GROS, FSC

with Preface by
BISHOP THOMAS HOYT AND BISHOP WILLIAM SKYLSTAD

Bishop's Committee for Ecumenical and Interreligious Affairs
United States Conference of Catholic Bishops

Washington, D.C.

The document *Growing Consensus II* was developed as a resource by the Bishop's Committee for Ecumenical and Interreligious Affairs of the United States Conference of Catholic Bishops (USCCB). It was reviewed by the committee chairman, Bishop Stephen E. Blaire, and has been authorized for publication by the undersigned.

Monsignor William P. Fay
General Secretary
USCCB

First Printing, April 2005

ISBN 1–57455–557–X

Dedicated to

Fr. Thomas Stransky, CSP,
ecumenical pioneer, mentor to many,
and founder of this ecumenical documents series

and to

The Reverend Thomas Earl Dipko,
dedicated ecumenical scholar and visionary,
whose imagination has paved the way
for unimaginable progress

Table of Contents

PART 2. BILATERAL DOCUMENTS

Abbreviations

Entities

AELC	Association of Evangelical Lutheran Churches
ALC	American Lutheran Church
ARCIC	Anglican Roman Catholic International Commission
ARC-USA	Anglican Roman Catholic Dialogue in the USA
BWA	Baptist World Alliance
CDF	Congregation for the Doctrine of the Faith
COCU	Consultation on Church Union
CRC	Christian Reformed Church in North America
CUIC	Churches Uniting in Christ
CWC	Christian World Communions
ELCA	Evangelical Lutheran Church in America
GCM	General Conference Mennonite Church
JCG	Joint Consultative Group
JPIC	Justice, Peace, and Integrity of Creation
JWG	Joint Working Group: World Council of Churches and Catholic Church
LCA	Lutheran Church in America
LCMS	Lutheran Church—Missouri Synod
LCWE	Lausanne Committee on World Evangelization
LED	Lutheran Episcopal Dialogue in the USA
L/RC	U.S. Lutheran–Roman Catholic dialogues (cited by the dialogue's number: 1-9)

LWF/RC	International Lutheran World Federation–Roman Catholic dialogues (cited by the dialogue's number: 1-9)
LWF	Lutheran World Federation
MC	Mennonite Church
NADEO	National Association of Diocesan Ecumenical Officers
NAE	National Association of Evangelicals
NCCB	National Conference of Catholic Bishops (now USCCB)
NCC	National Council of the Churches of Christ in the USA
PCPCU	Pontifical Council for Promoting Christian Unity (formerly "Secretariat")
PCFNA	Pentecostal Charismatic Fellowship of North America
PCID	Pontifical Council for Interreligious Dialogue
RCA	Reformed Church in America
SBC	Southern Baptist Convention
SPCU	Secretariat for Promoting Christian Unity (now Pontifical Council)
USCC	United States Catholic Conference (now USCCB)
USCCB	United States Conference of Catholic Bishops (formerly NCCB/USCC)
WARC	World Alliance of Reformed Churches
WCC	World Council of Churches
WEF	World Evangelical Fellowship (now "Alliance")

Documents

AAS	*Acta Apostolica Sedis: Commentarium officiale.* Vatican City: Vatican Polyglot Press, 1909-.
AA	Second Vatican Council. *Apostolicam Actuositatem (Decree on the Apostolate of the Laity)* (November 18, 1965).
AC	*Augsburg Confession.* In BC.
ACC	Lutheran-Reformed Committee for Theological Conversations. *A Common Calling: The Witness of Our Reformation Churches in*

	North American Today. Eds. Keith Nickle and Timothy Lull. Minneapolis: Augsburg, 1993.
AG	Second Vatican Council. *Ad Gentes Divinitus (Decree on the Church's Missionary Activity)* (December 7, 1965).
Apol	Apology of the Augsburg Confession (1531). In BC.
AS	WCC, Faith and Order, *Towards a Common Date for Easter* (the "Aleppo Statement") (March 1997), http://wcc-coe.org/wcc/what/faith/easter.html (accessed June 21, 2004).
Balamand	Joint International Commission for the Theological Dialogue Between the Roman Catholic Church and the Orthodox Church, "Uniatism: Method of Union of the Past, and the Present Search for Full Communion" (Balamand, Lebanon, June 17-24, 1993). In GA II.
BC	*The Book of Concord: The Confessions of the Evangelical Lutheran Church.* Eds. Robert Kolb and Timothy J. Wengert; trans. Charles Arand et al. Minneapolis: Fortress Press, 2000.
BCO	Reformed Church in America. *Book of Church Order.*
BCP	Anglican Church. *Book of Common Prayer.*
BDAG	*A Greek-English Lexicon of the New Testament and other Early Christian Literature*, 3rd ed. Rev. and ed. F. W. Danker. Chicago: University of Chicago Press, 2000.
BEM	WCC, Faith and Order. *Baptism, Eucharist and Ministry.* Geneva: WCC, 1982. In GA I.
BU	Joseph A. Burgess and Br. Jeffrey Gros, FSC, eds. *Building Unity: Ecumenical Dialogues with Roman Catholic Participation in the United States.* New York: Paulist Press, 1989.
CA	*Confessio Augustana (Augsburg Confession).* In BC.
CBCR	*Constitution, Bylaws, and Continuing Resolutions of the Evangelical Lutheran Church in America.* Chicago: ELCA, 2001.
CC	ARCIC II. "Church as Communion: An Agreed Statement by the Second Anglican Roman Catholic International Commission" (Dublin, Ireland, August 28–September 6, 1990). In GA II.

CCC	*Catechism of the Catholic Church*, 2nd. ed. Washington, DC: Libreria Editrice Vaticana–USCCB, 2000.
CD	Second Vatican Council. *Christus Dominus (Decree on the Pastoral Office of Bishops in the Church)* (October 28, 1965).
CIC	*Code of Canon Law.* Washington, DC: Canon Law Society of America, 1983.
CCEO	*Code of Canons for the Eastern Churches.* Washington, DC: Canon Law Society of America, 1991.
CN	CDF. *Communionis notio (Letter to the Bishops of the Catholic Church on Some Aspects of the Church Understood as Communion)* (May 28, 1992). http://www.vatican.va/roman_curia/congregations/cfaith/documents/rc_con_cfaith_doc_28051992_communionis-notio_en.html (accessed on June 17, 2004).
CWP	"Common Witness and Proselytism: A Study Document," *Ecumenical Review* 23 (1971).
Directory	PCPCU. *Directory for the Application of Principles and Norms on Ecumenism.* Washington, DC: USCCB, 1993.
DH	Second Vatican Council. *Dignitatis Humanae (Declaration on Religious Liberty)* (December 7, 1965).
DHn	Heinrich Denzinger. *Enchiridion symbolorum definitionum et declarationum de rebus fidei et morum*, 37th ed. Ed. Peter Huenermann. Freiburg, i.B.: Herder, 1991.
DS	H. Denzinger and A. Schönmetzer, eds. *Enchiridion symbolorum*, 33rd ed.
DV	Second Vatican Council. *Dei Verbum (Dogmatic Constitution on Divine Revelation)* (November 18, 1965).
EN	Pope Paul VI. *Evangelii Nuntiandi (On Evangelization in the Modern World)*. Washington, DC: USCCB, 1975.
ER	*The Emmaus Report: A Report of the Anglican Ecumenical Consultation.* Cincinnati: Forward Movement, 1987.
ERCDOM	*Evangelical–Roman Catholic Dialogue on Mission* (1984). In GA II.
ES	Extraordinary Session of the Synod of Bishops. "Final Report." *Origins* 15:27 (December 19, 1985): 444-450.

EV	Pope John Paul II. *Evangelium Vitae (The Gospel of Life: On the Value and Inviolability of Human Life)*. Washington, DC: USCCB, 1995.
FC Ep	*Formula of Concord* (1577), "Epitome." In BC.
FC SD	*Formula of Concord* (1577), "Solid Declaration." In BC.
FR	ARCIC I. "Final Report" (1982). In GA I.
FU	LWF/RC. *Facing Unity* (1984). In GA II.
GofA	ARCIC I. *The Gift of Authority: An Agreed Statement.* New York: Church Publishing, Inc., 1999.
GA I	Meyer, Harding, and Vischer, Lukas, eds. *Growth in Agreement: Reports and Agreed Statements of Ecumenical Conversations on a World Level.* New York: Paulist Press, 1984.
GA II	Gros, Jeffrey, Meyer, Harding, and Rusch, William G., eds. *Growth in Agreement II: Reports and Agreed Statements of Ecumenical Conversations on a World Level, 1982-1998.* Geneva: WCC Publications, 2000.
GC I	Burgess, Joseph A., and Gros, Jeffrey, eds. *Growing Consensus [I]: Church Dialogues in the United States, 1962-1991.* Ecumenical Documents 5. New York: Paulist Press, 1995.
GS	Second Vatican Council. *Gaudium et Spes (Pastoral Constitution on the Church in the Modern World)* (December 7, 1965).
HC	*Heidelberg Catechism.*
JDDJ	LWF/R. *Joint Declaration on the Doctrine of Justification.* 1999. In GA II.
JWG-LC	JWG. *The Church: Local and Universal: A Study Document Commissioned and Received by the JWG* (1990). In GA II.
LA	*The Leuenberg Agreement.*
LBW	*Lutheran Book of Worship.*
LC	Martin Luther. *Large Catechism.* In BC.
LC 20	"An Appeal to All Christian People," Resolution 9, Lambeth Conference, 1920.
LC 78	"The Anglican Communion in the Worldwide Church." Document 22, Lambeth Conference, 1978.

LD	*Lectio Divina.*
LG	Second Vatican Council. *Lumen Gentium (Dogmatic Constitution on the Church)* (November 21, 1964).
LinC	ARCIC II. *Life in Christ* (1993). In GA II.
MBW	*Moravian Book of Worship.*
MR	"Report of the Anglican/Roman Catholic Joint Preparatory Commission" (The Malta Report) (1968). In GA I.
NA	Second Vatican Council. *Nostra Aetate (Declaration on the Church's Relations with Non-Christian Religions)* (October 28, 1965).
NAB	*New American Bible.* Washington, DC: Confraternity for Christian Doctrine.
NABRNT	NAB Revised New Testament.
NJBC	*New Jerome Biblical Commentary.*
NPC	WCC. *The Nature and Purpose of the Church* (1998).
NR	Anglican–Lutheran Dialogue. "Niagara Report" (1984). In GA II.
NRSV	New Revised Standard Version.
OE	Second Vatican Council. *Orientalium Ecclesiarum (Decree on the Catholic Eastern Churches)* (November 21, 1964).
OL	Pope John Paul II. *Orientale Lumen (The Light of the East: To Mark the Centenary of Orientalium Dignitas of Pope Leo XIII).* Washington, DC: USCCB, 1995.
PA	First Vatican Council, *Pastor Aeternus (Dogmatic Constitution on the Church of Christ)* (July 18, 1870). DS 3053-3064.
PCCW	Reformed-Catholic Dialogue. *The Presence of Christ in the Church and World* (1977). In GA I.
PG	Migne, J.-P., ed., *Patrologia Graeca* (Paris: 1857-1866).
PL	Migne, J.-P., ed., *Patrologia Latina* (Paris: 1844-1855).
PO	Second Vatican Council. *Presbyterorum Ordinis (Decree on the Life and Ministry of Priests)* (December 7, 1965).
Porvoo	Anglican-Lutheran Northern European Dialogue. *Together in Mission and Ministry: The Porvoo Common Statement with Essays on Church and Ministry in Northern Europe* (1993).

PU	General Convention of the Episcopal Church. "Principles of Unity": Resolution A47A (1982).
RBEM	PCPCU. "Vatican Response to BEM." *Origins* 17:23 (November 19, 1987): 401-416.
RFR	The Official Roman Catholic Response to the Final Report of ARCIC I (1991).
RSV	Revised Standard Version.
SA	Anglican–Roman Catholic Consultation in the United States. "How Can We Recognize 'Substantial Agreement'?" (1993). See Document 12 in this volume.
Santiago	WCC, Faith and Order. *On the Way to Fuller Koinonia: Official Report of the Fifth World Conference on Faith and Order.* Eds. Thomas F. Best and Günther Gassmann. Geneva: WCC, 1994.
SC	Second Vatican Council. *Sacrosanctum Concilium (Constitution on the Sacred Liturgy)* (December 4, 1963).
SES	Commentary on "Standards for Eucharistic Sharing." Resolution A43, the General Convention of the Episcopal Church, 1979.
Str.-B	Strack, H. L., and P. Billerbeck. *Kommentar zum Neuen Testament aus Talmud und Midrasch*, 6 vols. Munich, 1922-1961.
TBC	*The Belgic Confession.*
TFC	Lutheran-Episcopal Dialogue III. *Toward Full Communion* (1991). In GC I.
TMA	Pope John Paul II. *Tertio Millennio Adveniente (On the Coming of the Third Millennium)*. Washington, DC: USCCB, 1994.
TPPP	*Treatise on the Power and Primacy of the Pope.* In BC.
UR	Second Vatican Council. *Unitatis Redintegratio (Decree on Ecumenism)* (November 21, 1964).
UUS	Pope John Paul II. *Ut Unum Sint (That They May Be One)*. Washington, DC: USCCB, 1995.
VR	"The Report of the Inter-Anglican Theological and Doctrinal Commission" (*The Virginia Report*), 1996.

VS	Pope John Paul II. *Veritatis Splendor (The Splendor of Truth: Regarding Certain Fundamental Questions of the Church's Moral Teaching)*. Washington, DC: USCCB, 1993.
WC	Roman Catholic–Lutheran Commission. *Ways to Community* (1980). In GA II.

Preface

The twentieth century, often called "the ecumenical century," saw the dawning of an ecumenical consciousness born in significant degree from missionary commitments, the birth of major ecumenical institutions, and unprecedented modern ecumenical engagement of Roman Catholic, Orthodox, Anglican, and Protestant churches in local, national, and international settings. Its last decade saw both steady ecumenical commitment and dramatic strides in agreement. The end of the century also saw contentious debate, as long-standing partners deliberated on the precise shape of agreements, the character and depth of the proposed commitment, the criteria with which churches were judged to be acceptable partners, and the range of activity characterizing permissible ecumenical engagement.

The final years of the "ecumenical century" and the first years of the next have seen the emergence of both anxiety and hope as the landscape for ecumenical relationships began to shift. Church leaders and ecumenical practitioners have begun to take note of the ways in which the Christian landscape has changed in the years since many dialogues—the fruits of which are evidenced in this volume—first emerged. No longer is it possible to rely entirely on the constructs formulated by an ecumenism dominated by the traditions of the western and northern hemispheres.

Dozens of ecumenical relationships and consensus agreements have in fact emerged in the latter decade of the twentieth century and the first years of the twenty-first, supported substantially by the premises and commitments of previous decades. Simultaneously, however, leaders from all sectors of the Christian family have begun to recognize the way in which emerging parts of the global church—notably the communities of the southern and eastern hemispheres, and those from burgeoning communities such as Pentecostal and evangelical traditions—have increasingly shaped the discourse. Christians in ecumenical dialogue and relationship have become aware of the ways in which the issues brought by these churches, historically not strongly represented in ecumenical engagement, have begun to shape the agenda and challenge the assumptions on which the earlier century's discourse was predicated. Church leaders, both in the United States and around the globe, from Orthodox, Protestant, Anglican, and Roman Catholic traditions have begun to talk of "larger forums" and "expanded tables," seeking to craft arenas where the agendas of a much broader spectrum of the Church of Jesus Christ could be considered. In the midst of this development, issues of social justice, seen to be church-dividing not only *among* the churches but *within* them, have stridden to the fore and influenced ecumenical relationship and agendas. In the United States, racial and ethnic reconciliation has become a central, no longer an incidental, aspect of what it means to be in ecumenical relationship.

The end of the twentieth century has been an era where numerous consensus agreements, themselves the fulfillment of decades of theological deliberation, have been imagined and formed. In this time, churches dedicated themselves to closer relationship. The documents in this volume bear witness to that commitment and dedication, born of vision and hope grounded in Jesus' prayer "that they may all be one": not as an end in and of itself, but rather in service to the mission and ministry of the Church of Jesus Christ, "that the world might believe that you sent me."

Bishop Thomas Hoyt
Christian Methodist Episcopal Church
President of the National Council of Churches, USA

Bishop William Skylstad
President, United States Conference of Catholic Bishops

General Introduction

The Holy Spirit has richly blessed the churches in the United States in the last decades of the twentieth century, with signs and stages pointing the way to that unity for which Christ prayed. In this volume—the third volume to chronicle dialogues among the churches in the United States[1]—are texts documenting major shifts in the relationships with the Christian Churches. This and the previous two volumes need to be seen against the background of the international bilaterals and of the contributions of Faith and Order.[2] These dialogues are only one of the many dimensions of the movement for unity in the United States.[3]

In addition to the dialogues in this volume, the churches—Evangelical and Pentecostal, African American and ethnic, Orthodox, historic Protestant and Catholic, Roman and Eastern—are considering a proposal for a new ecumenical structure for dialogue and collaboration: Christian Churches Together in the United States of America.[4] Whatever the outcome, this process will provide new opportunities for Christian reconciliation in this country.

In the last decade of the twentieth century, Pentecostal, Holiness, and evangelical scholars have continued their commitments to reconciliation, and their churches have shown an increased openness to be in conversation with fellow Christians.[5]

This decade has demonstrated some dramatic, positive steps by the churches in response to Christ's prayer for the churches: that they all may be one. On an international scale, the *Joint Declaration on the Doctrine of Justification*[6] as well as full communion agreements in other places in the world have both built on the U.S. contribution and provided an impulse for deeper unity among churches in this nation. There is much more to the ecumenical movement than these dialogues, just as there is much more to the Church's mission of restoring unity among Christians: "Ecumenical renewal is indeed a pivotal aspect of comprehensive ecclesial renewal, but there is much more to ecclesial renewal than resolving the problem of disunity."[7]

The texts gathered here arise from a variety of sources and serve a variety of reconciling purposes. The reader will need to attend to their sources and particular purposes. In introducing them, we would like to note three elements: (1) the image of unity, full communion, emerging among the churches; (2) the journey of reception on which the churches are embarked; and (3) the challenge of ecumenical formation before the churches.

The present volume is intended as a resource to be utilized with other documents in this series and with the documents, processes, or church decisions with which they are associated. Introductory material has been kept to a minimum, except when the text itself does not clarify its origin, purpose, and contribution to the unity of the churches. (Unless otherwise indicated, such editorial notes are provided by the editors of this volume.)

Thus, these documents, to be read effectively, should be linked by the reader to the documents on which they comment (12-14, 16, 18-20, 26, 32, 35), the predecessor documents in previous volumes (4-5, 7-14, 17, 21, 24, 27, 30-34), the international dialogues with which they are linked (1, 10, 12-14, 16, 18-20, 25-26, 30, 32), the process of dialogue to which they contribute (1, 8, 20, 26, 30-34), or the churches' actions that they support (1, 2-8, 28). If any of these documents is used independently, it will be necessary to draw on the introductory material provided in the previous volumes in this series. Those earlier introductions outlined the origin and development of the relationships that have produced the texts in this volume.

I. Emerging Vision of Full Communion

For the churches traditionally involved in ecumenical dialogue—Orthodox, historic Protestant, Anglican, and Catholic—the goal of the ecumenical movement remains steadfastly the full, visible, sacramental unity of the Church. The shape of that unity emerges only in dialogue among the churches, with the varieties of their perspectives on ecclesiology, tradition, and authority.

On the pilgrimage to Christian unity in a conciliar fellowship of all in each place, the particular models the churches have found preferable for realizing this biblical understanding of organic union have varied over the centuries. Full communion has meant, for some churches, institutional unity in a merged fellowship: creating a new structure and church order, and incorporating the gifts of the predecessor bodies.

Today, the churches' preference seems to be for a full communion of churches united in all those things deemed necessary for a visible Church, with less concern about cultural and institutional coherence. However, as the churches together continue the pilgrimage together toward that unity for which Christ prayed, the gifts and struggles and, above all, the theological foundations of united churches that characterized twentieth-century unions dare not be lost.[8]

"Full communion" is an expression used in common religious discourse as well as in technical canonical and theological senses. In the ecumenical sense, "full communion" is an analogous term applied differently according to the two or more ecclesial bodies in communion. Different "models" or proposals for visible unity come before different sets of churches. Because of the ease with which communion ecclesiology can be used in a variety of ways, it has been important to be clear about its ecumenical usage. For this reason, the churches together have tried to clarify these meanings and to be in dialogue with churches who do not share the same ecumenical goal (Document 1).[9]

Communion is among the many images of the Church in the New Testament. It is used not directly as a definition of Church, but rather as a more general description of community or of the relationships among Christians and between Christians and God.[10] The 1991 Canberra text, "The Unity of the Church as Koinonia: Gift and Calling," which was also the basis for the 1993 World Conference on Faith and Order, provides the most detailed ecclesiological description yet produced by the churches together. In this World Council Canberra text, a brief theological statement on the nature of the Church as communion is given, following Ephesians 1. However, it also lays out the elements of full communion, both as a common theological affirmation of the nature of the Church, and as an agenda before the churches in their work toward visible unity:

- The unity of the church to which we are called is a koinonia given and expressed in
  - the common confession of the apostolic faith;
  - a common sacramental life entered by the one baptism and celebrated together in one eucharistic fellowship;
  - a common life in which members and ministries are mutually recognized and reconciled; and

    - a common mission witnessing to the gospel of God's grace to all people and serving the whole of creation.
- The goal of the search for full communion is realized when all the churches are able to recognize in one another the one, holy, catholic and apostolic church in its fullness.
- This full communion will be expressed on the local level and the universal levels through conciliar forms of life and action.
- In such communion churches are bound in all aspects of life together at all levels in confessing the one faith and engaging in worship and witness, deliberation and action.[11]

It is within this spare ecclesiological framework that the rich detail of the texts included here can be assessed.

Previous assemblies of the World Council also articulated levels of unity upon which the churches could agree. The "Conciliar Fellowship" vision articulated in Nairobi in 1975[12] and the "All in Each Place" text of New Delhi in 1961[13] are foundations on which this more detailed vision of unity has been built.

Communion ecclesiology has also been used in contextual theologies.[14] That is, it is applied to relationships that take different forms and provide different challenges in the variety of cultures in which the Church is incarnated. It has served to give attention to the link between communion and ethics, especially in World Council circles, with the wide variety of priorities for these diverse churches working together on many areas of mission in addition to the theological pilgrimage toward visible unity.[15] These U.S. texts also reflect some of these contextual concerns (see Documents 8, 14, 31, 33, and 34).

The ability to share the elements of full communion is grounded in the 1952 methodological shifts and the convergences on Scripture, Tradition, and the traditions developed in the fourth World Conference on Faith and Order at Montreal in 1963. One of the texts represents full communion proposed (Document 7); one represents union within one confessional family (Document 2); and others represent full communion achieved between particular partners (Documents 3 through 6).

II. Reception

The earlier volumes have addressed this theme.[16] Since that time, more studies and dissertations have been done on the theme and on particular agreements. Three more fora have been sponsored on the bilaterals since *Growing Consensus I*.[17]

One can identify three stages in ecumenical encounter. These are not chronological or sequential but rather reflect a deepening in the relationships between particular churches and among the churches together. They can be simplified as (1) an openness to relationship, collaboration, and recognition of one another as fellow Christians; (2) the more intentional relationship that is entailed in the commitment to dialogue, to mutual understanding, and to taking up the path toward unity together; and (3) the beginning and culmination of decisions that move the dialogues into the commitment of the churches together to a new stage of unity.[18]

Reception is a dialectical, not linear, process. There are often moments of rejection, evaluation, and reformulation as the interaction moves forward. The churches learn from their own processes of reception and from one another (Documents 11 through 14, 16, 18 through 20, 26, 30, and 32). Reception—into the spiritual and liturgical life of the churches, and into the decision making of the Church—of the expressions of faith enunciated by the Church or by an ecumenical dialogue brings institutional change.

These are all elements of the complex and multidimensional process by which Christian truth informs the ecclesial life of a community.[19] Texts in this volume illustrate the dramatic movement from dialogue to decision encountered in the last decade of the twentieth century (Documents 2 through 6, 10, 12, and 13). Other texts demonstrate the dialectical nature of reception, as texts are evaluated by national dialogues (Documents 14, 16, 18 through 20, 26, and 30 through 32) or by dialogues that take up different partners (Documents 30 and 33 through 35).

New issues are entertained and are therefore received as topics to be discussed or issues to be resolved (Documents 21, 31, and 33 through 35). Evaluations of a particular dialogue may stimulate the need for clarification by one or more partners (Documents 12, 14, 28, and 29). In some cases, confessions or creeds have to be re-evaluated and re-received as a result of the dialogue with the partner against whom the original affirmation was professed (Documents 13, 28, 29, 30, 34, and 35). The success of initial dialogues illuminate methodological issues that need exploration

(Documents 9, 12, 14, 28, and 35). Responses to dialogue results clarify other areas where agreement is necessary and where more theological and historical work may be needed (Documents 10, 21, 24, 28, 32, 34, and 35).

In response to all of the work on the positive nature of the Church, sacraments, mission, and authority, the World Council has been impelled to provide an important study for scrutiny and feedback: *The Nature and Purpose of the Church.*[20] As we have learned more about the responses of the churches, the variety of interpretive principles at work has required a study on hermeneutics.[21]

It is particularly important in the North American context, whose history is so recent, to be prepared to re-receive and review the tradition, both classical and ecumenical.[22]

III. Ecumenical Formation

With the rich harvest of theological results and new theological and ecclesial relations, the churches and their people have before them a major challenge. These gifts of the Holy Spirit can only be fruitful in ecclesial life—for the deepening of relations with Christ and one another, and for enhancement of the mission of the Church in the world—if they move beyond the theoretical and juridical.

These texts provide important resources for parish membership classes: rites for initiating adults, for preaching, for religious education programs in congregations held for young people and adults, for seminaries and lay ministry training programs, and for the writing of religious education text materials.

However, these texts will need to be edited, excerpted, and adapted for the audiences for whom they are intended. Furthermore, they will need to be placed into a context where they will inform the whole life of the Christian and his or her community. This means that the goal of Christian unity and the method of dialogue will be essential in forming the identity of all members of the community, not just its leaders or specialists. A faith in Christ's prayer for the unity of the Church and a zeal for the realization of that goal will be at the core of Christian formation.[23]

We need ecumenical companions for Sunday school and church school teachers, specifically to accompany their teachers' guides, which have distillations of the content of these texts and their implications for the faith and life of church members. These agreements are meant to change lives and transform churches. Concern must be given to the audiences in our churches, to their learning styles and the factors that motivate them in deepening their identity with the Church in Jesus Christ. The quest for visible unity and reconciliation must become central to the identity of each Christian in our churches. Conversion to Christ's will for the Church's unity must be seen as essential to belonging to him.

Some summaries of particular dialogues have been produced,[24] as well as a study guide for the World Council commentary on the Nicene Creed.[25] Some churches include study materials on their relationships in the resources prepared for congregations.[26] Some churches make available a few guides for religious educators.[27]

Among the principles to be kept in mind are (1) the interpretive attitude we bring to the Church and to one another, (2) the hierarchy of truths, and (3) the results of the dialogues. These texts and other dialogue results provide a context for a change of heart and mind among our people. Not only are the biblical texts and the faith of the Church through the ages now able to be interpreted together. We also can learn to interpret the institutions, rituals, and spiritualities of communities in a more positive light, recognizing the gifts of the Spirit wherever they may be found. Christian education assists in moving from an "us/them" approach to fellow Christians and other churches and toward a "we" approach: fundamentally united in faith, but on a pilgrimage toward that unity for which Christ prayed.

This interpretive view requires a conversion of heart. First is an openness of love and reconciliation. Then this basis in Christian charity makes it possible to face the serious church-dividing issues, together in a dialogue of truth. As scholars pursue the biblical and traditional content of the faith together, they come deeper into Christ's truth, enabling convergence and even consensus to come forth. For those faithful not formed in theological detail, a receptive spirituality provides the ground for responding positively in faith and love to the new reconciling insights that emerge from these dialogues.

In the formation of the Christian people for the ecumenical challenge, it is important to keep in mind the hierarchy of truths.[28] On the one hand, we dare not lose any of the insights of the Christian faith that the churches have received from the Holy Spirit in their separation. On the other hand, in ordering the truths of the Gospel, our Christian formation needs to be clear on what is central—what is related to our central Christian faith and is, therefore, seen as necessary doctrine—and on what are particular traditions, interpretations, emphases, or devotional practices that may be important to the individual believer or the community but that are not church-dividing.

The work of the Faith and Order movement to order the elements of agreement and disagreement around the central truths necessary for the common confession of the Apostolic Faith today has been an important contribution to a common understanding of the hierarchy of truths together.[29]

Finally, a way must be found to make the results of these dialogues an integral part of all religious formation at every level of church life, if they are to truly become a "common heritage" that can inform our pilgrimage toward full communion at every stage in the Christian journey and in every program of our churches.

NOTES

1. The previous two volumes are Jeffrey Gros and Joseph Burgess, eds., *Building Unity* (BU) (New York: Paulist Press, 1989); and Joseph Burgess and Jeffrey Gros, eds., *Growing Consensus* (GC I) (New York: Paulist Press, 1995).
2. Lukas Vischer and Harding Meyer, eds., *Growth in Agreement Reports and Agreed Statements of Ecumenical Conversations on a World Level* (GA I) (New York: Paulist Press, 1984); William Rusch, Harding Meyer, and Jeffrey Gros, eds., *Growth in Agreement II* (GA II) (Geneva: World Council of Churches; Grand Rapids: Wm. B. Eerdmans, 2000).
3. Arleon Kelley, ed., *A Tapestry of Justice, Service, and Unity: Local Ecumenism in the United States, 1950-2000* (Tacoma, WA: National Association of Ecumenical and Interreligious Staff Press, 2004).
4. National Council of Churches USA, "Plans for 'Christian Churches Together in the USA' Move From Vision Toward Reality," http://www.ncccusa.org/about/cctusa.html (accessed on May 1, 2004).
5. Ted Campbell, Ann Riggs, and Gilbert Stafford, eds., *Ancient Faith and American Born Churches* (New York: Paulist Press, 2004). Jeffrey Gros, "A Pilgrimage in the Spirit: Pentecostal Testimony in the Faith and Order Movement," *Pneuma* 25:1 (Spring 2003): 29-53.
6. *Joint Declaration on Justification by Faith* (JDOJ) (Grand Rapids: Wm. B. Eerdmans, 2000). Cf. William Rusch, ed., *Justification and the Future of the Ecumenical Movement* (Collegeville: Liturgical Press, 2003).
7. William Abraham, "Ecumenism and the Rocky Road to Renewal," in *The Ecumenical Future*, eds. C. Braaten and R. Jenson (Grand Rapids: Eerdmans, 2004), 187.

8. Cf. Elsabeth Slaughter Hilke, ed., *Growing Toward Unity*, vol. 6: *The Living Theological Heritage of the United Church of Christ* (Cleveland: The Pilgrim Press, 2001).
9. See also Jeffrey Gros, "Toward Full Communion: Faith and Order and Catholic Ecumenism," *Theological Studies* 65:1 (March 2004): 23-43; Lorelei Fuchs, *Koinonia and the Quest for an Ecumenical Ecclesiology: From Foundations through Dialogue to Symbolic Competence for Communionality* (Leuven: Katholieke Universiteit Leuven, 2003).
10. John Reumann, "Koinonia in Scripture: Survey of Biblical Texts," in *On the Way to Fuller Koinonia* (Santiago), eds. Thomas Best and Gunther Gassmann (Geneva: World Council of Churches, 1993), 37-69.
11. Santiago, no. 2.1, 269-271.
12. David Paton, ed., *Breaking Barriers: Nairobi 1975* (London: SPCK, 1976), 60; "Ecumenical Chronicle," *The Ecumenical Review* 26 (1974): 291-298; "Conciliar Fellowship," in BU, 458-484.
13. Harding Meyer, *That All May Be One* (Grand Rapids: Eerdmans, 1999). William Rusch, "A Survey of Ecumenical Reflection about Unity," in *The Ecumenical Future*, eds. Carl Braaten and Robert Jenson (Grand Rapids: Eerdmans, 2004), 1-10.
14. Jamie Phelps, "Communion Ecclesiology and Black Liberation," *Theological Studies* 61 (2000): 672-699; Jeffrey Gros, "The Synod for America, 1997: A Contribution to Koinonia Ecclesiology," *One in Christ* (2000): 167-175; Francis Hadisumarta, "The Church as Communion," in *The Asian Synod: Texts and Commentaries*, ed. Peter Phan (Maryknoll: Orbis, 2002), 119-121; Dennis Doyle, *Communion Ecclesiology* (Maryknoll: Orbis Books, 2000), 119-150.
15. Thomas Best and Wesley Granberg-Michaelson, eds., *Costly Unity: Koinonia and Justice, Peace and Creation* (Geneva: World Council of Churches, 1993); Gennadios Limouris, ed., *Church, Kingdom, World* (Geneva: World Council of Churches, 1986); *Church and World: The Unity and the Church and the Renewal of Human Community*, Geneva: World Council of Churches, 1991.
16. BU, 5-8.
17. Günther Gaßmann, *International Bilateral Dialogues 1992-1994* (Geneva: World Council of Churches Publications, 1995); Alan Falconer, ed., *Emerging Visions of Visible Unity in the Canberra Statement and the Bilateral Dialogues: Seventh Forum on Bilateral Dialogues* (Geneva: World Council of Churches, 1997); Faith and Order, *Eighth Forum on Bilateral Dialogues: Implications of Regional Agreements for the Internatinal Dialogues of Christian World Communions* (Geneva: World Council of Churches, 2002).
18. John Hotchkin, "The Ecumenical Movement's Third Stage," *Origins* 25:21 (November 9, 1995): 353-361.
19. Hervé Legrand, Julio Manzanares, and Antonio García y García, eds., *Reception and Communion Among the Churches* (Washington, DC: Catholic University of America, 1997); Ormond Rush, *The Reception of Doctrine: An Appropriation of Hans Robert Jauss' Reception Aesthetics and Literary Hermeneutics* (Rome: Editrice Pontificia

Universita–Gregoriana, 1997); William Rusch, "The Journey to Reception—A Progress Report," *Ecumenical Trends* 32:6 (June 2003): 1-8; María del Carmen Márquez Beunza, "Hermenéutica, eclesiología, contextualidad: cuestiones emergentes in el proceso de recepción de BEM," *Diálogo Ecuménico* 37:120 (2003): 7-54; Angel Antón, "La 'recepción' en relación con la eclesiología," I and II, in *Gregorianum* (1996), 57-96, 437-469; Henry Chadwick, "Reception," in *Christian Life and Witness*, eds. C. Sugden and V. Samuel (London: SPCK, 1997); R. Greenacre, "Two Aspects of Reception," in *Christian Authority: Essays in Honour of Henry Chadwick*, ed. G. R. Evans (Oxford: Clarendon Press, 1998); Jaroslav Pelikan, "Reception of Creeds, Councils, and Confessions as Ratification," in *Credo* (New Haven: Yale University Press, 2003), 255-260; Paul Avis, ed., *Seeking the Truth of Change in the Church: Reception, Communion and the Ordination of Women* (London: T & T Clark, 2004), 172; K. Bloomquist and W. Greive, eds., *The Doctrine of Justification: Its Reception and Meaning Today* (Geneva: Lutheran World Federation, 2003).

20. World Council of Churches, "The Nature and Purpose of the Church: A Stage on the Way to a Common Statement" (NPC) (Geneva: World Council of Churches, 1998) http://wcc-coe.org/wcc/what/faith/nature1.html (accessed on May 1, 2004).
21. Faith and Order Commission, *A Treasure in Earthen Vessels: An Instrument for an Ecumenical Reflection on Hermeneutics* (Geneva: World Council of Churches, 1998).
22. Barbara Brown Zikmund, series editor, *The Living Theological Heritage of the United Church of Christ*, vols. I-VII (Cleveland: Pilgrim Press, 1995-1999).
23. Joint Working Group, Roman Catholic Church–World Council of Churches, *Ecumenical Formation: Ecumenical Reflections and Suggestions* (Geneva: World Council of Churches, 1993), in GA II, 884-890.
24. *The Lutheran-Catholic Quest for Visible Unity: Harvesting Thirty Years of Dialogue* (Chicago: Evangelical Lutheran Church in America; Washington, DC: United States Catholic Conference, 1998); *Thirty Years of Mission and Witness: United Methodist Roman Catholic Dialogue* (Washington, DC: United States Catholic Conference; Nashville: United Methodist Commission on Christian Unity and Interreligious Concerns, 2001); John Radano, *Catholic and Reformed*, Occasional Paper 8 (Louisville: Office of Theology and Worship, Presbyterian Church, 1996); *Journey in Faith: Forty Years of Reformed Catholic Dialogue: 1965-2005* (Washington, DC: United States Conference of Catholic Bishops, in press).
25. *Toward Sharing the One Faith: A Study Guide for Discussion Groups* (Geneva, World Council of Churches, 1996).
26. I.e., Evangelical Lutheran Church of America, "Ecumenical Approaches/General Resources" http://www.elca.org/ea/Resources/genrsce.html (accessed on June 10, 2004); United Church of Christ, "Ecumenical Affairs" http://www.ucc.org/ecumenical/resources.htm (accessed on June 10, 2004); Centro Pro Unione "Interconfessional Dialogues" http://www.prounione.urbe.it/dia-int/e_dialogues.html (accessed on May 1, 2004).

27. Jeffrey Gros, *That All May Be One: Ecumenism* (Chicago: Loyola University Press, 2000).
28. Joint Working Group, Roman Catholic Church–World Council of Churches, *Ecumenical Formation: Ecumenical Reflections and Suggestions* (Geneva: World Council of Churches, 1993), in GA II, 884-890.
29. Faith and Order, *Confessing the One Faith: Towards an Ecumenical Explication of the Apostolic Faith as Expressed in the Nicene Constantinopolitan Creed* (381) Study Document (Geneva: World Council of Churches, 1991). A compendium of creeds and confessions has recently become available, with a valuable, ecumenically attuned overview: Pelikan, "Reception"; Jaroslav Pelikan and Valerie Hotchkiss, *Creeds and Confessions of Faith in the Christian Tradition*, vols. I-III (New Haven, CT: Yale University Press, 2003).

Textual Note

Some of these texts are the product of the dialogue members as they report to the churches, while others are statements of the churches themselves. Therefore, very little has been done to edit them for grammatical style, capitalization, or documentation. The paragraph numbers remain intact, as do the footnote sequences when excerpts have been included. Since these texts are published in a variety of places and formats, paragraph numbering is an easier guide than pagination, which may vary widely. Other than the addition of abbreviations, which have been used to standardize the volume, and bracketed source information, when needed for clarity, no other attempts have been made to alter or enhance references and citations.

Growing Consensus II

PART ONE

Full Communion Documents

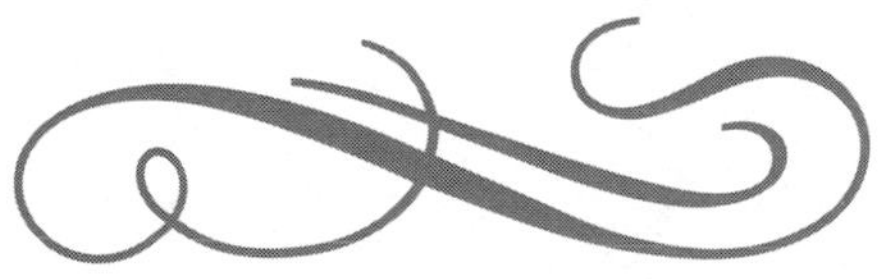

Editors' Note: *As noted in the Introduction, the last decade of the twentieth century has produced a rich harvest of agreements among churches and theological advances. This section gathers three types of texts.*

This first text (Document 1) is an appraisal of the vision of visible unity articulated by the member churches of the Faith and Order movement, including theologians representing churches whose vision of unity does not include visible communion in the same way. It also explores the different ways the communion/koinonia language is used in different agreements. By this study, churches' theologians who have not been involved in full communion agreements, or even in the commitments and discussions that have made them possible, participate in the common effort to understand the biblical and theological foundations for the nature and mission of the Church. Document 1 is O. C. Edwards Jr.'s summary of four years of intensive study and analysis; the full report is to be released elsewhere.

This critical analysis is followed by five texts (Documents 2 through 6) that demonstrate, in different ways, the concrete actions of churches moving beyond dialogue into full communion. Finally, this section includes two texts (Documents 7 and 8) from the nine members of Churches Uniting in Christ, which marks a stage on the way to full communion.

Full Communion Analysis

Document 1

PROBLEMS WITH THE MEANING OF FULL COMMUNION: FAITH AND ORDER REPORT, 2003

by O. C. Edwards, Jr.

When the group of American Faith and Order commissioners assigned to study "full communion" during the new quadrennium first met in March 2000, our task seemed simple enough. It soon became evident, however, that we were not dealing with a clear term that had a simple meaning which only needed to be observed in its various manifestations. Instead, a number of traditions use the term "full communion" but do so in different ways, while others do not use it at all, having terms of their own to express the closest relation Christian bodies can have to one another. And even in the churches that use the term, it does not always reach the heart of the matter, it does not always touch what for those traditions is the essence of life in the Body of Christ, the criterion by which they recognize authentic Christian faith and life in their own and other groups.

This awareness made us conscious of the great danger of talking past one another when we use this heavily freighted term as though we all mean the same thing by it and we all know what that is. Nor is this danger limited to our group; it is, if anything, greater in the ecumenical world at large, and the possible damage of such misunderstanding is proportionate to the levels of discussions in which it might occur.

As a result, our work for the four years took a different turn. We decided that our time together would be well spent if we could produce a typology, a taxonomy, a roadmap of the different ways in which "full communion" is used by different traditions, what terms are used instead by other bodies, and what aspects of life in the Body are of the essence of authentic Christian identity for them. While this is a more modest goal than the one we started out with, it seemed to us that it might be of greater service to the churches if it could help them avoid misunderstandings in the future. It is in hope of providing such a service that this report is offered.

Before our group realized the lack of clarity in the term, we tried to discover its meaning by considering full communion agreements that are in operation. We had two papers on each of the ones examined: one by someone from one of the traditions that was party to the agreement and the other by someone outside it. Each paper was to do two things. First it was to see if agreement could be phrased in the language of "The Unity of the Church: Gift and Calling," the Faith and Order document adopted by the Seventh Assembly of the World Council of Churches held in Canberra, Australia, in 1991. The second was to discuss how the agreement is actually being lived out by the churches that are party to it.

The key term in the Canberra document was the Greek word *koinonia*, a term used in the New Testament to embrace a range of meanings, including fellowship, close mutual relationship, participation, sharing-in, partnership, contribution, and gift. Perhaps the nearest English equivalent to *koinonia* is "communion."

We knew at the time that full communion was not just a matter of eucharistic sharing, that it included sharing in a number of other elements in the life of the church as well. The way the term is used in the Canberra Statement was appropriate to this understanding. Canberra speaks of a *koinonia* given and expressed in

1. the common confession of apostolic faith
2. a common sacramental life entered by the one baptism and celebrated together in one eucharistic fellowship
3. a common life in which members and ministries are mutually recognized and reconciled

4. a common mission witnessing to the Gospel of God's grace to all people and serving the whole creation.

The Statement then goes on to offer a strategy for achieving full communion embodying those elements.

I. Glitches in the Canberra Model

At first we found no difficulty analyzing full communion agreements in terms of the Canberra elements of *koinonia* because many churches can achieve full communion that way without distorting the essence of the life of the Body of Christ as they perceive it. That can be seen in the full communion agreements that the Evangelical Lutheran Church in America (ELCA) has reached with the Episcopal Church, on the one hand, and a group of churches in the Reformed tradition, on the other.

The ELCA, for instance, has a list of the "theological and missiological implications of the Gospel" that they regard as the "characteristics of full communion." This list is the Canberra list with two differences. The first is a provision for joint decision-making that gives reality to the other commitments, and the second is a mutual lifting of condemnations that reflects Lutheran history in which anathemas were given and received.

One of ELCA's dialogue partners, the Episcopal Church, has had a list since the late 1880s of the common elements needed for it to unite with other Christian bodies, the Chicago-Lambeth Quadrilateral. These are the Bible, the ancient creeds, baptism and eucharist, and the historic episcopate. While neither Canberra nor the ELCA list specifies the historic episcopate, Canberra was based on the recommendations of the WCC Faith and Order document *Baptism, Eucharist and Ministry* that included it, and ELCA accepted it as the way ministries of the two churches would be reconciled. Since the acceptance of the Bible could go without saying for Canberra and ELCA, the three lists would seem functional equivalents of one another.

That is, it would until the agreement between ELCA with the Episcopalians is compared to the one they made with the Presbyterian Church, USA, the United Church of Christ, and the Reformed Church in America. None of those churches has the historic episcopate, and nothing was said about their acquiring it. Thus, for all their apparent similarity, these lists of the conditions for full communion are not quite the same.

This problem of similarity obscuring deep differences can be seen by looking at another list that sounds very much like those already discussed.

Roman Catholics speak of three bonds of unity in the church: unity in faith, in worship, and in ministry. As one of their members of our commission pointed out, unity in ministry involves the Petrine ministry of papal primacy.

This recognition that the Episcopal Church makes the historic episcopate a prerequisite for full communion and that the Roman Catholic Church does the same with the Petrine ministry demanded our attention. It showed that while both churches can employ the *koinonia* language of Canberra to talk about full communion, each reserves an additional element that is for them a sine qua non for such a relation. The recognition that each of these traditions has an element that for them is a non-negotiable condition for full unity opened the possibility that *koinonia* language does not always get to the heart of the matter, that different churches have their individual commitments to what for them is the essence of life in the Body of Christ.

II. The Essence of Life in the Body

The possibility became a certainty when our group looked at some other churches for whom the Canberra categories are appropriate descriptions of much of their life. Our Orthodox commissioner, for instance, said that the principle of church organization for his tradition is territorial, and that it would reject any denominational model that allowed parallel church bodies in the same geographical area. He went on to admit that, since the rise of Communism in Eastern Europe, the situation of Orthodoxy in North America has not followed that territorial principle; but he said that all recognize that situation to be an anomaly and a scandal.

Alerted by this discovery, our group went on to identify such non-negotiable elements in other communions. Our Presbyterian commissioner suggested that a de facto one, if not a theoretical one, for his church could be their belief that ruling elders are not just ministers of governance. Rather, they are ordained presbyters as truly as the teaching elders who are ministers of word and sacrament. It was that conviction, he said, as well as opposition to the historic episcopate, that caused 104 out of 170 presbyteries to vote against approving the original proposal of the Consultation on Church Union (COCU). This principle did not deter the United Church of Christ, the other Reformed body in the original consultation, from giving the proposal full support. Nor does it seem to be an issue for the Reformed Church in America, the third Reformed church in the full communion agreement with ELCA.

Since a number of references have been made to COCU, something needs to be said about that group and its relation to full communion. In 1962 the Presbyterian Church in the USA, the Episcopal Church, the Methodist Church, and the United Church of Christ formed the Council on Church Union to begin discussing the possibility of uniting with one another to form a church that would be "truly catholic, truly reformed, and truly evangelical." In time five other churches joined them. A *Plan of Union* was drawn up by 1970 and another in 1985, but both were rejected, largely because of disagreements about ministry. Since then, the goal has changed from organic unity to a covenant relation among separate churches. In 1999 the member churches made a provisional agreement that left the issues concerning ministry to be settled later. This agreement was consummated in 2002, and COCU was succeeded by CUIC (Churches Uniting in Christ).

Three of the five churches that joined the initial four were historic black churches in the Wesleyan tradition: the African Methodist Episcopal Church, the African Methodist Episcopal Church Zion, and the Christian Methodist Episcopal Church. Understandably, then, the Report of the Eighteenth Plenary of COCU includes among the "visible marks" of CUIC that it sets forth the pledge to combat systematic white privilege. This could be a "heart of the matter" issue for the black churches involved. Having been disappointed so often by the white churches' lack of persistence in combating racism, they could feel that this is a "put up or shut up" situation.

A communion that is quite explicit about its own *sine qua non* is the Lutheran Church–Missouri Synod (LCMS). Believing, as Luther did, that there is only one church of all the faithful but that this has to be distinguished from "visible Christendom," LCMS says that external fellowship may be shared only with bodies in which the gospel is preached purely and the sacraments are rightly administered. To make sure that the gospel is preached purely, churches entering into altar and pulpit fellowship must share the same confession of faith that is embodied in the historic Lutheran documents.

From all this it can be seen that for a number of churches, although some have an additional element that for them is the key to full communion, the elements of *koinonia* listed by Canberra nevertheless serve as entrée into the way they understand the essence of life in the body of Christ. The remaining churches to be looked at, however, have basic understandings of what it means to be church that have very little in common with the elements of *koinonia* listed in the Canberra statement.

III. Churches the Canberra Pattern Does Not Fit

Baptists are a good case in point. They think that the local congregation (the real locus of church for them) is made up of believers who have been born again: indeed, they are not baptized until they can demonstrate their condition. Their task is to discern the will of God for them as it is revealed in scripture, and they do that by coming to agreement over the meaning of what is said in the Bible. They thus constitute a priesthood of believers and need no authority beyond themselves. To exercise that priesthood, their freedom of conscience must be recognized. This process of discernment happens in congregations that are autonomous, and freedom of religion is a presupposition of it. In the perspective of such congregationalism, the concept of full communion between denominations is alien. Association is based on shared mission rather than any sacramental or organic relation.

Another instance is the Churches of Christ. These churches grew out of the Second Great Awakening in the nineteenth century in movements founded by Barton Stone and Alexander Campbell, who sought to restore Christianity to its New Testament purity. While their generic name originally was an effort not to distance themselves from other Christians, the Churches of Christ over time came to see themselves as the only Christians. Thus for them, full communion with another body would be apostasy. They interpreted 2 John 9-11 to mean that they had to accept every statement attributed to Jesus in the New Testament, understanding it in the sense in which their leaders interpreted it. Since people in other churches interpret the statements differently, fellowship with them would be fellowship with error. While this exclusivist position is no longer absolutely uniform among the Churches of Christ, it will probably take time before the issue of full communion occupies much attention in most Churches of Christ.

A third tradition for which the *koinonia* categories of Canberra simply do not fit is that of the Church of God, Anderson, Indiana. This group grew out of the Holiness movement of the nineteenth century and thus talks of two experiences or "works of grace," conversion, and "entire perfection" or "sanctification." New birth makes one a member of the one and only universal church. Thus, the Church of God has no formal procedures for the admission of members; one becomes a member of a congregation by participating in its life. And it is within the life of the congregation that sanctification occurs. This second work of grace is understood not as the achievement of moral perfection but precisely as being overcome with love for God, for God's people, and for God's world. It is especially an awareness of the unity of the church that can be described as "seeing the church." This awareness comes upon the sanctified especially in worship and times of spiritual sharing. And if "full communion" were a term used in this network of churches, it would refer to this experience. Yet the experience is not limited to the particular network of churches; one can have it across denominational lines. But formal negotiations between bodies are not necessary for it and cannot guarantee the experience.

Similar to the Holiness perspective of the Church of God, Anderson, is the Pentecostal one of the Assemblies of God. They see no need to establish formal relations of full communion with other Pentecostal churches because they are already one in the Spirit. Or, more precisely, those who have received the gifts of the Spirit in any of these churches are already at one with each other. The commissioner from the Assemblies of God admitted that there are limits to this perspective, in that it restricts rapprochement with non-Pentecostal churches, but insists as well that there is an understanding here of what it really means to be one in Christ that formal negotiations for full communion cannot guarantee.

Most of the churches for whom the Canberra model does not fit have an emphasis on religious experience that focuses on inward spiritual change brought about by the Holy Spirit. The presentation by our commissioner from the Evangelical Friends International showed that Quaker belief fits that pattern in many ways. His way of stating their position was that full communion or *koinonia* is a spiritual reality that is experienced by all who respond to the grace of God and try to live in faithfulness. He also said that, while Friends do not use outward and visible signs to convey the grace of sacraments, they are nevertheless sacramentalists. Indeed, he seemed to feel that the grace of sacraments can be experienced more fully apart from outward signs. Thus Friends do not have John the Baptist's water baptism but have instead Jesus' baptism of fire and the Holy Spirit. And they feel that they experience communion of the Real Presence of Christ in their unprogrammed meetings for worship.

This situation of groups like Quakers who do not use the matter of sacraments, is addressed in the Canberra statement in its discussion of the forms of eucharistic hospitality that could be appropriate in the light of convergence in faith, and in baptism, eucharist, and ministry. There it says that "we gladly acknowledge that some who do not observe these rites share in the spiritual experience of life in Christ."

Our full communion study group also took cognizance of a growing phenomenon in American Christianity, the mega-churches, and consulted through the mail Dr. Gilbert Bilezekian of Trinity Evangelical University, whose thought is the inspiration of Willow Creek Church in South Barrington, Illinois. At first he was reluctant to respond, saying, "I would be at a loss to find enough coherence among them to describe their practice of full communion when their very *raison d'être* is often the rejection of inter-church communion." He went on to say, however,

> Such churches may indeed interrelate among themselves at the level of associative networks designed for sharing information and resources. But their fellowship protocols are generally confined to the internal life of congregations that view themselves as self-contained and self-sufficient entities.

This represents one end of the spectrum of degrees to which the Canberra pattern of *koinonia* applies. The experience of these congregations of what it means to be church does not include any need for wider fellowship. Instead, some mega-churches suggest new and different directions toward full communion that transcend denominational structures.

IV. Conclusion

This brings us to the end of our consideration of the various approaches and alternatives to full communion in the thought of the Christian bodies surveyed. The main result of this study has been to see that many of the churches that use the Canberra model find their own sense of the essence of in the Body of Christ to lie in a sine qua non that the *koinonia* categories really do not touch. Either that, or the churches belong to traditions that find the entire Canberra mode of stating things to be foreign to their way of thinking.

Phrased this way, our conclusions sound rather pessimistic. Yet it is at least possible that what appears so negative may be one of the most promising aspects of our study. A way forward seems indicated by something in the Canberra statement, a suggestion that there is value in diversity. That suggestion was picked up by one of our older members, who said,

> When I first began to glimpse something of the ecumenical vision in the early sixties, it occurred to me that in our separation God was allowing each tradition to explore one or more facets of the divine glory, and the results of their exploration

> would be what each brought to the reunited church so that we could all profit from one another's experience and be mutually enriched by one another's gifts. About the time this occurred to me, I came across H. Richard Niebuhr's *Christ and Culture*. One of the important principles of this book is an expression that Niebuhr attributed to the nineteenth-century Anglican theologian, Frederick Dennison Maurice, that people are "generally right in what they affirmed and wrong in what they denied." The use of this hermeneutical principle could make it possible for the way that each tradition has experienced the essence of life in the Body to become the common treasure of all.

That would be full communion indeed.

Full Communion Agreements

DOCUMENT 2

CONFESSION OF FAITH IN A MENNONITE PERSPECTIVE, 1995

Mennonite Church

Editors' Note: *The following introduction and commentaries throughout these selections from the document have been provided by Dr. Helmut Harder, Emeritus Professor of Theology at Canadian Mennonite University:*

"In July 1995 the two largest Mennonite churches in North America, the Mennonite Church (MC) and the General Conference Mennonite Church (GC), met in joint assembly at the convention centre in Wichita, Kansas. The joint meeting, not the first of its kind, became historic when on the fifth day each of the delegate bodies, meeting separately, gave full assent to a jointly prepared statement of faith, entitled 'Confession of Faith in a Mennonite Perspective' [henceforth CFMP].

"For nine years, since fall 1986, a committee of twelve persons, six MCs and six GCs, had met together to prepare the CFMP. It was hoped that a joint confession would facilitate the projected merger of the MCs and the GCs into one church body. Indeed, at the Wichita meeting the two churches made the resolute decision to unite as one church, bringing to culmination a process of exploration that had begun in the early 1980s. Full integration was accomplished a few years later at a joint meeting in July 1999 at St. Louis, Missouri. The process of preparing a joint Confession of Faith Committee and the final product played a

significant role in the healing of a schism that had occurred among North American Mennonites in 1860, almost 140 years before.

"While the main purpose of the CFMP was to provide a theological basis and rationale for the integration of the MCs and the GCs, its significance extends beyond that inner-Mennonite function. The CFMP was also intended as a word from the Mennonites to the wider Christian church. The inclusion of the word 'Perspective' in the title was meant, at least in part, to imply that the CFMP commends itself as a contribution to a common understanding of the Christian Gospel. There was a time when Mennonite theological discussion was carried on essentially within Mennonite circles. But you could say that Mennonites are 'coming of age.' There is among them a sense of confidence that they have something to offer the ecumenical world, and certainly also that they have something to receive from other Christian traditions. Of the twenty-four articles that compose the CFMP, those selected here provide illustrations of how the CFMP has sought to unite MCs and GCs under a common confessional umbrella, and also of how the CFMP helps to set the stage for discerning dialogue between Mennonites and Christians of other traditions.

"For a complete text of the 'Confession of Faith in a Mennonite Perspective,' visit www.mennolink.org/doc/cof *(accessed on September 20, 2004). Printed copies can be ordered from Herald Press, Scottdale, PA 15683 or Waterloo, Ont., N2L 6H7."*

Selected Texts

Article 1. God

Harder: *To say that the sixteenth-century Anabaptists, forerunners of the Mennonites, were judged as heretics rather than as orthodox Christians, is to state the obvious. However, since that time this judgment has been reversed, and today the Mennonite Church is included as one of the Christian churches, despite lingering statements to the contrary in some sixteenth-century confessional statements. In its Introduction, the CFMP acknowledges its ecumenical orientation by affirming the historic ecumenical creeds. Furthermore, in its first article, on "God," the CFMP is forthright and clear about its Trinitarian faith. At the same time, Article 1 casts its statements about God mainly in biblical terms.*

We believe that God exists and is pleased with all who draw near by faith (Exod. 3:13-14; Heb. 11:6). We worship the one holy and loving God who is Father, Son, and Holy Spirit eternally (Exod. 20:1-6; Deut. 6:4; Matt.

28:19; 2 Cor. 13:13[14]). We believe that God has created all things visible and invisible, has brought salvation and new life to humanity through Jesus Christ, and continues to sustain the church and all things until the end of the age.

Beginning with Abraham and Sarah, God has called forth a people of faith to worship God alone, to witness to the divine purposes for human beings and all of creation, and to love their neighbors as themselves (Gen. 12:2-3; Lev. 19:18; Rom. 4:11-25; 1 Pet. 3:9-11). We have been joined to this people through the faithfulness of Jesus Christ and by confessing him to be Savior and Lord as the Holy Spirit has moved us (Gal. 2:20; Rom. 3:22). We humbly recognize that God far surpasses human comprehension and understanding (Exod. 3:13-14; Job 37; Isa. 40:18-25; Rom. 11:33-36). We also gratefully acknowledge that God has spoken to humanity and related to us in many and various ways. We believe that God has spoken above all in the only Son, the Word who became flesh and revealed the divine being and character (John 1:14,18; Heb. 1:1-4).

God's awesome glory and enduring compassion are perfect in holy love. God's sovereign power and unending mercy are perfect in almighty love. God's knowledge of all things and care for creation are perfect in preserving love. God's abounding grace and wrath against sinfulness are perfect in righteous love. God's readiness to forgive and power to transform are perfect in redemptive love. God's unlimited justice and continuing patience with humankind are perfect in suffering love. God's infinite freedom and constant self-giving are perfect in faithful love (Exod. 20:4-6; 34:5-7; Ps. 25:4-10; Isa. 6; 54:10; Matt. 5:48; Rom. 2:5-11; 3:21-26; 1 John 4:8, 16). To the one holy and ever-loving triune God be glory for ever and ever!

Article 8. Salvation

Harder: *Originally, Anabaptist-Mennonite confessions of faith included discipleship (German:* Nachfolge*) as an essential component of salvation, thus referencing the entire way of Christ—birth, life, death, and resurrection—as the theological and practical basis of salvation. In later centuries Mennonite confessions sometimes chose one or another of the classic theories of atonement as their primary point of reference for an understanding of salvation. At times the MCs favored the "moral influence" theory while the GCs favored the "substitution" theory. The CFMP overrides these preferences by recognizing all three theories as useful, and by favoring a holistic view of salvation that incorporates the way of* *discipleship within its purview. The CFMP article on salvation was embraced by both MCs and GCs as a uniting statement.*

We believe that, through the life, death, and resurrection of Jesus Christ, God offers salvation from sin and a new way of life to all people. We receive God's salvation when we repent of sin and accept Jesus Christ as Savior and Lord. In Christ, we are reconciled with God and brought into the reconciling community of God's people. We place our faith in God that, by the same power that raised Christ from the dead, we may be saved from sin to follow Christ in this life and to know the fullness of salvation in the age to come.

From the beginning, God has acted with grace and mercy to bring about salvation—through signs and wonders, by delivering God's people, and by making a covenant with Israel (Ps. 74:12; Deut. 6:20-25; Exod. 20: 1-17). God so loved the world that, in the fullness of time, God sent his Son, whose faithfulness unto death on the cross has provided the way of salvation for all people (John 3:16; Gal. 4:4; Heb. 1:1-2). By his blood shed for us, Christ inaugurated the new covenant (Matt. 26:28; 1 Cor. 11:25). He heals us, forgives our sins, and delivers us from the bondage of evil and from those who do evil against us (Rom. 5:1-5; Mark 2:1-12). By his death and resurrection, he breaks the powers of sin and death (Rom. 8:2; Heb. 2:14-15), cancels our debt of sin (Rom. 3:24-25; Col. 2:13-14; Mark 10:45), and opens the way to new life (Rom. 6:4). We are saved by God's grace, not by our own merits (Eph. 2:8-9).

When we hear the good news of the love of God, the Holy Spirit moves us to accept the gift of salvation. God brings us into right relationship without coercion. Our response includes yielding to God's grace, placing full trust in God alone, repenting of sin, turning from evil, joining the fellowship of the redeemed, and showing forth the obedience of faith in word and deed (Rom. 1:5; Luke 19:8-10). When we who once were God's enemies are reconciled with God through Christ, we also experience reconciliation with others, especially within the church (Rom. 5:6-10). In baptism we publicly testify to our salvation and pledge allegiance to the one true God and to the people of God, the church. As we experience grace and the new birth, we are adopted into the family of God and become more and more transformed into the image of Christ (Rom. 12:2; 2 Cor. 3:18). We thus respond in faith to Christ and seek to walk faithfully in the way of Christ.

We believe that the salvation we already experience is but a foretaste of the salvation yet to come, when Christ will vanquish sin and death, and the redeemed will live in eternal communion with God.

Article 14. Discipline in the Church

Harder: *Ever since the Anabaptists of the sixteenth century indicated that they preferred to discipline erring brothers and sisters in their own redemptive way in the church rather than to have heretics subjected to the state's trial by fire, Mennonites have given concerted attention to matters of internal discipline. Of late, some MCs have shied away from discipline, against the background of its sometimes harsh application. Some GCs have neglected the practice altogether, under the influence of a liberalizing trend in the church. Thus the practice of discipline has fallen into disrepair. The CFMP intends to recover the intent of the tradition for a postmodern church. Both MCs and GCs have embraced Article 14 wholeheartedly.*

We believe that the practice of discipline in the church is a sign of God's offer of forgiveness and transforming grace to believers who are moving away from faithful discipleship or who have been overtaken by sin. Discipline is intended to liberate erring brothers and sisters from sin, to enable them to return to a right relationship with God, and to restore them to fellowship in the church. It also gives integrity to the church's witness and contributes to the credibility of the gospel message in the world.

According to the teaching of Jesus Christ and the apostles, all believers participate in the church's mutual care and discipline as appropriate. Jesus gave the church authority to discern right and wrong and to forgive sins when there is repentance or to retain sins when there is no repentance (Matt. 18:15-22; Jn 20:21-23; Gal. 6:1-2; Deut. 19:15). When becoming members of the church, believers therefore commit themselves to give and receive counsel within the faith community on important matters of doctrine and conduct.

Mutual encouragement, pastoral care, and discipline should normally lead to confession, forgiveness, and reconciliation. Corrective discipline in the church should be exercised in a redemptive manner. The basic pattern begins with "speaking the truth in love," in direct conversation between the erring person and another member (Eph. 4:15; Matt. 18:15). Depending on the person's response, admonition may continue within a broader circle. This usually includes a pastor or congregational leader. If necessary, the matter may finally be brought to the congregation. A brother or sister who repents is to be forgiven and encouraged in making the needed change.

If the erring member persists in sin without repentance and rejects even the admonition of the congregation, membership may be suspended. Suspension of membership is the recognition that persons have separated themselves from the body of Christ (1 Cor. 5:3-5). When this occurs, the church continues to pray for them and seeks to restore them to its fellowship (2 Cor. 2:5-11).

We acknowledge that discipline, rightly understood and practiced, undergirds the integrity of the church's witness in word and deed. Persistent and uncorrected false teaching and sinful conduct among Christians undermine the proclamation and credibility of the gospel in the world (Matt. 5: 14-18; Rom. 2:21ff). As a sign of forgiveness and transforming grace, discipline exemplifies the message of forgiveness and new life in Christ through the power of the Holy Spirit. As a means of strengthening good teaching and sustaining moral conduct, it helps to build faithfulness in understanding and practice.

Article 17. Discipleship and the Christian Life

Harder: *The MCs have traditionally specified boundaries of belief and practice, such as religious dress codes and patterns of behavior. From its very beginning in 1860, this was not the GC practice. GC confessions tended to concentrate on core principles of Christian ethics rather than on setting boundaries. The CFMP tends to follow the GC emphasis, a direction that the MCs have increasingly assumed over the past several decades.*

We believe that Jesus Christ calls us to take up our cross and follow him. Through the gift of God's saving grace, we are empowered to be disciples of Jesus, filled with his Spirit, following his teachings and his path through suffering to new life. As by faith we walk in Christ's way, we are being transformed into his image. We become conformed to Christ, faithful to the will of God, and separated from the evil in the world.

The experience of God through the Holy Spirit, prayer, Scripture, and the church empowers us and teaches us how to follow Christ. Likewise, as we follow Christ in our lives, we are brought into closer relationship with God, and Christ dwells in us (Phil. 3:10). Through grace, God works in us to recreate us in the image of Christ, himself the image of the invisible God. Wherever Christian faith is active in love and truth, there is the new creation. By the new birth, we are adopted into God's family, becoming children of God (Rom. 8:12-17). Our participation in Christ includes both salvation and discipleship.

Conformity to Christ necessarily implies nonconformity to the world (Rom. 12:1-2). True faith in Christ means willingness to do the will of God, rather than willful pursuit of individual happiness (Matt. 26:39). True faith means seeking first the reign of God in simplicity, rather than pursuing materialism (Matt. 5:3; 6:25-33). True faith means acting in peace and justice, rather than with violence or military means (Zech. 4:6; Matt. 5:6, 9, 38-48). True faith means giving first loyalty to God's kingdom, rather than to any nation-state or ethnic group that claims our allegiance (Josh. 24; Ps. 47; Acts 5:29). True faith means honest affirmation of the truth, rather than reliance on oaths to guarantee our truth telling (Matt. 5:33-37). True faith means chastity and loving faithfulness to marriage vows, rather than the distortion of sexual relationships, contrary to God's intention (Matt. 5:27-30). True faith means treating our bodies as God's temples, rather than allowing addictive behaviors to take hold. True faith means performing deeds of compassion and reconciliation, in holiness of life, instead of letting sin rule over us (Mic. 6:8; Rom. 6:12-14). Our faithfulness to Christ is lived out in the loving life and witness of the church community, which is to be a separated people, holy to God.

In all areas of life, we are called to be Jesus' disciples. Jesus is our example, especially in his suffering for the right without retaliation (1 Pet. 2:21-23; Rom. 12:9-21), in his love for enemies, and in his forgiveness of those who persecuted him. Yet as we follow Jesus, we look not only to the cross, but through the cross, to the joy of the resurrection. We place our hope in God's vindication of those who take the narrow way that leads to life (Matt. 7:13-14). "If we have died with him, we will also live with him. If we endure, we will also reign with him" (2 Tim. 2:11-12).

Article 22. Peace, Justice, and Nonresistance

Harder: *From the beginning of the Anabaptist-Mennonite movement, confessions of faith have typically included statements on peace and nonresistance. Only recently has justice been added explicitly as an element in the confessions. The entire Article 22 serves not only to unite the Mennonite Church in its faith and witness to the gospel of peace. The article intends as well to invite dialogue with and among all Christians concerning what Mennonites, and a growing chorus of other Christian communions, believe to be an essential component of the Gospel.*

We believe that peace is the will of God. God created the world in peace, and God's peace is most fully revealed in Jesus Christ, who is our peace and the peace of the whole world. Led by the Holy Spirit, we follow Christ in the way of peace, doing justice, bringing reconciliation, and practicing nonresistance even in the face of violence and warfare.

Although God created a peaceable world, humanity chose the way of unrighteousness and violence (Gen. 1-11). The spirit of revenge increased, and violence multiplied, yet the original vision of peace and justice did not die (Isa. 2:2-4). Prophets and other messengers of God continued to point the people of Israel toward trust in God rather than in weapons and military force (Lev. 26:6; Isa. 31:1; Hos. 2:18).

The peace God intends for humanity and creation was revealed most fully in Jesus Christ. A joyous song of peace announced Jesus' birth (Lk. 2:14). Jesus taught love of enemies, forgave wrongdoers, and called for right relationships (Matt. 5:44; 6:14-15). When threatened, he chose not to resist, but gave his life freely (Matt. 26:52-53; 1 Pet. 2:21-24). By his death and resurrection, he has removed the dominion of death and given us peace with God (1 Cor. 15:54-55; Rom. 5:10-11). Thus he has reconciled us to God and has entrusted to us the ministry of reconciliation (2 Cor. 5:18-21).

As followers of Jesus, we participate in his ministry of peace and justice. He has called us to find our blessing in making peace and seeking justice. We do so in a spirit of gentleness, willing to be persecuted for righteousness' sake (Matt. 5:3-12). As disciples of Christ, we do not prepare for war, or participate in war or military service. The same Spirit that empowered Jesus also empowers us to love enemies, to forgive rather than to seek revenge, to practice right relationships, to rely on the community of faith to settle disputes, and to resist evil without violence (Matt. 5:39; 1 Cor. 6:1-16; Rom. 12:14-21).

Led by the Spirit, and beginning in the church, we witness to all people that violence is not the will of God. We witness against all forms of violence, including war among nations, hostility among races and classes, abuse of children and women, violence between men and women, abortion, and capital punishment.

We give our ultimate loyalty to the God of grace and peace, who guides the church daily in overcoming evil with good, who empowers us to do justice, and who sustains us in the glorious hope of the peaceable reign of God (Isa. 11:1-9).

Document 3

ECUMENICAL PARTNERSHIP: ESTABLISHING FULL COMMUNION BETWEEN THE CHRISTIAN CHURCH (DISCIPLES OF CHRIST) AND THE UNITED CHURCH OF CHRIST, 1989

Editors' Note: *Conversations between the Christian Church (Disciples of Christ) and the United Church of Christ began first in 1911 between the predecessor bodies of the two present-day communions, and then officially in 1961 between the two current communions. This Ecumenical Partnership moves one step beyond the recognition of ordained ministries, thereby enabling the orderly exchange of ministers of word and sacrament, to a full reconciliation. As the two churches define it, full reconciliation means that, after demonstrating proficiency in the theology, ecclesiology, and history of the partner church, an ordained minister of word and sacrament with valid standing in one of the churches can obtain lifetime "ordained ministerial partner standing" in the other church, so long as the original ordination credential remain valid. This contrasts this full communion agreement with others where "standing" in a partner church ordinarily is granted and lasts for only for the period of pastoral service in the partner church's congregation or other valid ministry.*

In addition, as a further expression of full communion, in 1995 the two denominations effected a full merger of their global ministries functions; and now the missionaries from both the United Church of Christ and the Christian Church (Disciples of Christ) serve on behalf of both denominations, the programs and priorities are overseen by a Common Global Ministries Board, and the staff are employed in common by both denominations.

Background

The Christian Church (Disciples of Christ) and the United Church of Christ affirm the New Testament understanding of the essential unity of Christ's church. Recognizing that there is a need for visible unity, the churches have turned to each other and to other churches to speak of how this unity can be realized.

This biblical understanding of our essential unity has led both churches into other ecumenical settings as well. The churches' efforts to heed the gospel call to overcome the separations that early beset the church of Jesus Christ have given birth to the Consultation on Church Union, the World Council of Churches, the National Council of Churches and other expressions of the ecumenical movement.

In 1911 the United Church of Christ predecessor bodies and the Christian Church (Disciples of Christ) held their first conversations. Since 1961, official conversations have be aimed at achieving a deeper and more visible unity.

The declaration of an Ecumenical Partnership and establishment of an Ecumenical Partnership Committee by the 15th General Synod of the United Church of Christ (1985) and the General Assembly of the Christian Church (Disciples of Christ) (1985) followed six years of work by a joint steering committee. A responsibility of the Ecumenical Partnership Committee was to take to the General Synod and the General Assembly in 1989 proposals for action that would lead to full communion between the two churches.

Editors' Note: *Following the text of the resolutions that were passed both by the General Synod of the United Church of Christ and by the General Assembly of the Christian Church (Disciples of Christ), the commentary below was affirmed by both bodies as explication of the meaning of full communion in this context.*

Commentary

We envision full communion as a dynamic and growing relationship that is more than just accepting one another as we now are. It is a mutual commitment to grow together toward a vision of the church that enriches our theological traditions, enhances service and mission, and deepens worship. We will find diverse expressions of what it means to live in full communion in Christ as we experience life together.

There follows a commentary on the five aspects of the meaning of full communion. It must be understood within the context of our wider ecumenical commitments, especially the World Council of Churches (including its text, *Baptism, Eucharist and Ministry*) and the Consultation on Church Union. The Christian Church (Disciples of Christ) and the United Church of Christ, along with seven other churches in the USA that are in the Consultation on Church Union, are laboring to achieve covenant communion in faith, sacraments, ministry, and mission.

> After more than two decades of theological work by officially designated persons responsible to the most authoritative bodies in the several churches, it is now evident that an essential core of theological agreement exists and continues to grow among these churches in matters of faith, worship, sacrament, membership, ministry, and mission.
>
> —*Churches in Covenant Communion, approved by the 17th Plenary of the Consultation on Church Union (December 1988) and sent to member churches for formal action*

1. Common Confession of Christ

Early Christians declared Jesus to be the Christ (Peter in Matthew 16:16 and Martha in John 11:27). Although the church has developed more extensive statements of faith, the Christian community finds its fundamental identity in this confession. In this resolution we begin by proclaiming our common devotion to the God who was in Christ reconciling the world to God's self (2 Cor. 5:19), the One in whom "we live and move and have our being" (Acts 17:28). By it we also declare our rejection of the distortions both of the gospel and of the cultural idols that constantly tempt us.

2. Mutual Recognition of Members

Baptism and membership in the church are inseparably linked. To be baptized into Christ is to become a member of the body of Christ, the church. For two churches mutually to recognize each other's members implies the recognition that the baptism administered by the partner church is a valid sacramental act. Baptism involves the gift of God's grace and the response of faith. Through baptism, all Christians are united by the Holy Spirit in the one universal church. Mutual recognition does not commit either church to give up its normative practices (for Disciples, the dedication of infants and baptism by immersion of those who make a personal confession of faith; for the United Church of Christ, the sprinkling of the children of believing parents, normally followed, at an appropriate age, by confirmation) or the baptism by the sprinkling or immersion of adults. Mutual recognition of members allows for transfer of membership between Disciples and United Church of Christ local churches by letter.

This declaration is a testimony to the growing theological agreement on baptism among the churches, achieved through the ecumenical movement. It is an affirmation that differences of practice need no longer divide the churches. Partnership is therefore a process for moving beyond divisive disagreements and renewing our understanding of baptism, the sacrament of unity.

3. Common Celebration of the Lord's Supper/Holy Communion

The most powerful sign of Christian unity is the common sharing at the Lord's Supper/Holy Communion. Through the life, death, and resurrection of Jesus Christ, God has reconciled us to God's self and offered us a new relationship of love and unity with one another. Celebrating the sacrament together, we are responding as one family with thanksgiving to what Christ has done for us, praying as one people that the Holy Spirit will lead us into deeper truth and unity, and remembering as one pilgrim people the promises of hope and salvation.

While it is already possible for these two churches to celebrate the Lord's Supper/Holy Communion together, this declaration of full communion encourages such common celebration more regularly and intentionally. Congregations that are geographically near each other are urged to find ways to share in the sacred meal together at least once or twice a year, and to consider more frequent eucharistic services. Conferences and regions, associations and areas are encouraged to plan opportunities to join around the Table regularly and so to bear witness to the conviction that the Lord's Supper/Holy Communion is the central event in the church's life. From it all things flow—engaging in mission, caring for the poor, struggling for justice and peace, making real an inclusive life in Christ, yearning for unity.

The United Church of Christ and the Disciples traditionally have had different eucharistic practices in two respects. Disciples congregations make the Lord's Supper the central point of each Sunday's worship, while most United Church of Christ local churches observe the sacrament monthly or quarterly. Nearly all United Church of Christ local churches have ordained or licensed ministers preside at the Table, whereas elders or ordained ministers preside among Disciples. Neither of these differences, however, need divide our two churches at the Table. The theological issues they raise are being explored in our churches and in the wider ecumenical dialogue in the Consultation on Church Union and in the World Council of Churches.

4. Mutual Recognition and Reconciliation of Ordained Ministries

Mutual recognition of ordained ministries (ministers of word and sacrament of the United Church of Christ; ordained elders and ministers of word and sacrament of the Disciples) is intended to acknowledge in the ministries of the partner church the manifest blessing of God and the fruit of the Spirit, and therefore to affirm them as true ministries of the one, holy Church of Jesus Christ. Reconciliation of ordained ministries is intended to refer to future actions by the churches, both separately and together, whereby their ordained ministries become one ministry of Jesus Christ.

Reconciliation is not intended to mean either that the standard of ministerial training and certification or differences in ministerial practice and placement process must become the same for both churches. Reconciliation means that an ordained minister of one partner church may function, whenever invited, and as established procedures permit, as a minister to the other. Such action of recognition and reconciliation of these ordained ministries is in harmony with the wider ecumenical understandings.

Ordained ministry in these two partner churches is sufficiently similar in form and substance to pose no serious theological obstacle to the mutual recognition and reconciliation of these ordained ministries in subsequent liturgical celebrations.

5. Common Commitment to Mission

Unity and mission are inseparable. If we imagine ourselves to be sacramentally one and do not engage together in mission, we deceive ourselves. Christ calls us to unite in one mission in and to a suffering and divided world. The church is called to visible oneness as a sign, instrument and foretaste of God's saving reconciliation of all things in Christ. In declaring full communion, these two churches acknowledge that they are partners together in God's mission to and for the whole world.

The mission of the church takes many forms. The church engages in mission through worship, through proclamation of the gospel, and through action. In worship, the church recalls and celebrates the mighty acts of God in creation, redemption, and providence. Thus graciously renewed in faith, hope, and love, its people are sent out in the power of the Holy Spirit to be ambassadors, witnesses, and servants of Christ in the world. In proclamation, the church tells the story by which its own life is defined. As it confesses unambiguously the Christ in whom it lives; the church invites all who will to enter its fellowship of life in Christ. In its action, the church embodies God's justice, peace, and love. As the church reaches out to others, both individually and systemically, it manifests God's reconciling purpose and saving reign in all the earth.

In partnership, the Christian Church (Disciples of Christ) and the United Church of Christ fully claim the mission and make deliberate commitment to engage in mission together, wherever and whenever possible.

DOCUMENT 4

CALLED TO COMMON MISSION, 1999

Editors' Note: *In 1997 the Episcopal Church and the Evangelical Lutheran Church in America proposed a Concordat of Agreement (see GC I, 153-338) that did not reach the necessary two-thirds agreement in the ELCA Churchwide Assembly. In 1999 this text was approved by both churches, effecting full communion between them.*

Introduction

Our churches have discovered afresh our unity in the gospel and our commitment to the mission to which God calls the church of Jesus Christ in every generation. Unity and mission are organically linked in the Body of Christ, the church. All baptized people are called to lives of faithful witness and service in the name of Jesus. Indeed, the baptized are nourished and sustained by Christ as encountered in Word and Sacrament. Our search for a fuller expression of visible unity is for the sake of living and sharing the gospel. Unity and mission are at the heart of the church's life, reflecting thereby an obedient response to the call of our Lord Jesus Christ.

Many years of thorough and conscientious dialogue have brought our churches to this moment. The history of how far our churches have already traveled together is significant. It guides us on a common path toward the unity for which Christ prayed.

The purpose of this Concordat of Agreement is to achieve full communion between the Evangelical Lutheran Church in America and The Episcopal Church. Our churches have set this goal in response to our Lord's prayer that all may be one. Our growing unity is urgently required so that our churches will be empowered to engage more fully and more faithfully the mission of God in the world. "I ask not only on behalf of these, but also on behalf of those who will believe in me through their word, that they may all be one. As you, Father, are in me and I am in you, may they also be in us, so that the world may believe that you have sent me" (Jn 17:20-21).

The Concordat is the latest stage in a long history of ecumenical dialogue between the two churches. Although the issues that gave rise to the Protestant Reformation in England and on the European continent were dissimilar in some respects, Anglicans and Lutherans have long recognized something of themselves in each other, and our churches have never issued condemnations against one another. Liturgical and sacramental worship has always figured largely in the identity and character of each tradition.

Moreover, the architects of reformation, both in England and on the continent, were concerned to uphold the catholic faith. Thus it is no surprise that official ecumenical conversations between Lutherans and Anglicans date back to the late nineteenth century.

The first official conversation in this century involving Anglicans and Lutherans in the USA took place in December 1935, between The Episcopal Church and The Augustana Evangelical Lutheran Church, a church with roots in Sweden. In 1969, the first of three rounds of Lutheran-Episcopal Dialogue began. Periodic reports were submitted to the Evangelical Lutheran Church in America and its predecessor bodies and to The Episcopal Church. Two final reports, *Implications of the Gospel* and "*Toward Full Communion*" and "*Concordat of Agreement*," were submitted in 1988 and 1991, respectively.

Lutheran-Episcopal Dialogue was coordinated through the Lutheran World Federation and the Anglican Consultative Council with the Anglican-Lutheran International Conversations, the European Regional Commission, and the other national and local dialogues. Consultations were held as well with other churches and traditions in dialogue with Lutherans and Anglicans.

In 1996, the Nordic and Baltic Lutheran and the British and Irish Anglican churches entered communion on the basis of agreement in the Porvoo Common Statement. Earlier, in 1988, the Evangelical Lutheran Church in Germany and the Church of England agreed on steps to closer relations on the basis of the Meissen Declaration. Anglican and Lutheran churches in Canada, in southern and eastern Africa, and in Asia have initiated dialogue and begun to share in mission. These actions, and those that follow, help to prepare us and, indeed, other churches committed to the ecumenical movement, to move from our present separation into a relationship of full communion.

CALLED TO COMMON MISSION

A Lutheran Proposal for a Revision of the Concordat of Agreement

As Amended by the 1999 Churchwide Assembly of the Evangelical Lutheran Church in America (August 19, 1999)

1. The Lutheran-Episcopal Agreement of 1982 identified as its goal the establishment of "full communion (*communio in sacris*/altar and pulpit fellowship)" between The Episcopal Church and the churches that united to form the Evangelical Lutheran Church in America. As the meaning of "full communion" for purposes of this Concordat of Agreement, both churches endorse in principle the definitions agreed to by the (international) Anglican-Lutheran Joint Working Group at Cold Ash, Berkshire, England, in 1983, which they deem to be in full accord with their own definitions given in the Evangelical Lutheran Church in America's policy statement *Ecumenism: The Vision of the Evangelical Lutheran Church in America* (1991), and in the "Declaration on Unity" of The Episcopal Church (1979). This agreement describes the relationship between our two church bodies. It does not define the Church, which is a gift of God's grace.

2. We therefore understand full communion to be a relation between distinct churches in which each recognizes the other as a catholic and apostolic church holding the essentials of the Christian faith. Within this new relation, churches become interdependent while remaining autonomous. Full communion includes the establishment locally and nationally of recognized organs of regular consultation and communication, including episcopal collegiality, to express and strengthen the fellowship and enable common witness, life, and service. Diversity is preserved, but this diversity is not static. Neither church seeks to remake the other in its own image, but each is open to the gifts of the other as it seeks to be faithful to Christ and his mission. They are together committed to a visible unity in the church's mission to proclaim the Word and administer the Sacraments.

3. The Episcopal Church agrees that in its General Convention, and the Evangelical Lutheran Church in America agrees that in its Churchwide Assembly, there shall be one vote to accept or reject, as a matter of verbal content as well as in principle, the full set of agreements to follow. If they are adopted by both churches, each church agrees to make those legislative, canonical, constitutional, and liturgical changes that are needed and appro-

priate for the full communion between the churches. In adopting this document, the Evangelical Lutheran Church in America and The Episcopal Church specifically acknowledge and declare that it has been correctly interpreted by the resolution of the Conference of Bishops of the Evangelical Lutheran Church in America, adopted at Tucson, Arizona, March 8, 1999.

A. Agreements

Agreement in the Doctrine of the Faith

4. The Evangelical Lutheran Church in America and The Episcopal Church recognize in each other the essentials of the one catholic and apostolic faith as it is witnessed in the unaltered Augsburg Confession, the Small Catechism, and *The Book of Common Prayer* of 1979 (including "Ordination Rites" and "An Outline of the Faith"), and also as it is summarized in part in *Implications of the Gospel* and *"Toward Full Communion" and "Concordat of Agreement,"* (containing the reports of Lutheran-Episcopal Dialogue III), the papers and official conversations of Lutheran-Episcopal Dialogue III, and the statements formulated by Lutheran–Episcopal Dialogues I and II. Each church also promises to encourage its people to study each other's basic documents.

5. We endorse the international Anglican–Lutheran doctrinal consensus which was summarized in *The Niagara Report* (1989) as follows:

> We accept the authority of the canonical Scriptures of the Old and New Testaments. We read the Scriptures liturgically in the course of the church's year. . . . We accept the Niceno-Constantinopolitan and Apostles' Creeds and confess the basic Trinitarian and Christological Dogmas to which these creeds testify. That is, we believe that Jesus of Nazareth is true God and true Man, and that God is authentically identified as Father, Son, and Holy Spirit.

Anglicans and Lutherans use very similar orders of service for the Eucharist, for the Prayer Offices, for the administration of Baptism, for the rites of Marriage, Burial, and Confession and Absolution. We acknowledge in the liturgy both a celebration of salvation through Christ and a significant factor in forming the *consensus fidelium* [consensus of the faithful]. We have many hymns, canticles, and collects in common.

We believe that baptism with water in the name of the Triune God unites the one baptized with the death and resurrection of Jesus Christ, initiates into the one, holy, catholic and apostolic church, and confers the gracious gift of new life.

We believe that the Body and Blood of Christ are truly present, distributed, and received under the forms of bread and wine in the Lord's Supper. We also believe that the grace of divine forgiveness offered in the sacrament is received with the thankful offering of ourselves for God's service.

We believe and proclaim the gospel, that in Jesus Christ God loves and redeems the world. We share a common understanding of God's justifying grace, i.e., that we are accounted righteous and are made righteous before God only by grace through faith because of the merits of our Lord and Savior Jesus Christ, and not on account of our works or merit. Both our traditions affirm that justification leads and must lead to "good works": authentic faith issues in love.

Anglicans and Lutherans believe that the church is not the creation of individual believers, but that it is constituted and sustained by the Triune God through God's saving action in Word and Sacraments. We believe that the church is sent into the world as sign, instrument, and foretaste of the kingdom of God. But we also recognize that the church stands in constant need of reform and renewal.

We believe that all members of the church are called to participate in its apostolic mission. They are therefore given various ministries by the Holy Spirit. Within the community of the church the ordained ministry exists to serve the ministry of the whole people of God. We hold the ordained ministry of Word and Sacrament to be a gift of God to his church and therefore an office of divine institution.

We believe that a ministry of pastoral oversight (*episkope*), exercised in personal, collegial, and communal ways, is necessary to witness to and safeguard the unity and apostolicity of the church.

> We share a common hope in the final consummation of the kingdom of God and believe that we are compelled to work for the establishment of justice and peace. The obligations of the kingdom are to govern our life in the church and our concern for the world. The Christian faith is that God has made peace through Jesus "by the blood of his cross" (Col 1:20) so establishing the one valid center for the unity of the whole human family. [NR]

Agreement in Ministry

6. The ministry of the whole people of God forms the context for what is said here about all forms of ministry. We together affirm that all members of Christ's church are commissioned for ministry through baptism. All are called to represent Christ and his church; to bear witness to him wherever they may be; to carry on Christ's work of reconciliation in the world; and to participate in the life, worship, and governance of the church. We give thanks for a renewed discovery of the centrality of the ministry of all the baptized in both our churches. Our witness to the gospel and pursuit of peace, justice, and reconciliation in the world have been immeasurably strengthened. Because both our churches affirm this ministry which has already been treated in our previous dialogues, it is not here extensively addressed. Both churches need more adequately to realize the ministry of the baptized through discernment of gifts, education, equipping the saints for ministry, and seeking and serving Christ in all persons.

7. We acknowledge that one another's ordained ministries are and have been given by God to be instruments of God's grace in the service of God's people and possess not only the inward call of the Spirit, but also Christ's commission through his body, the church. We acknowledge that personal, collegial, and communal oversight is embodied and exercised in both our churches in a diversity of forms, in fidelity to the teaching and mission of the apostles. We agree that ordained ministers are called and set apart for the one ministry of Word and Sacrament, and that they do not cease thereby to share in the priesthood of all believers. They fulfill their particular ministries within the community of the faithful and not apart from it. The concept of the priesthood of all believers affirms the need for ordained ministry, while at the same time setting ministry in proper relationship to the laity. The Anglican tradition uses the terms "presbyter" and

"priest" and the Lutheran tradition in America characteristically uses the term "pastor" for the same ordained ministry.

8. In order to give witness to the faith we share (see paragraphs 4 and 5 above), we agree that the one ordained ministry will be shared between the two churches in a common pattern for the sake of common mission. In the past, each church has sought and found ways to exercise the ordained ministry in faithfulness to the apostolic message and mission. Each has developed structures of oversight that serve the continuity of this ministry under God's Word. Within the future common pattern, the ministry of pastors/priests will be shared from the outset (see paragraph 16 below). Some functions of ordained deacons in The Episcopal Church and consecrated diaconal ministers and deaconesses in the Evangelical Lutheran Church in America can be shared insofar as they are called to be agents of the church in meeting needs, hopes, and concerns within church and society. The churches will over time come to share in the ministry of bishops in an evangelical, historic succession (see paragraph 19 below). This succession also is manifest in the churches' use of the apostolic scriptures, the confession of the ancient creeds, and the celebration of the sacraments instituted by our Lord. As our churches live in full communion, our ordained ministries will still be regulated by the constitutional framework of each church.

9. Important expectations of each church for a shared ordained ministry will be realized at the beginning of our new relation: an immediate recognition by The Episcopal Church of presently existing ordained ministers within the Evangelical Lutheran Church in America and a commitment by the Evangelical Lutheran Church in America to receive and adapt an episcopate that will be shared. Both churches acknowledge that the diaconate, including its place within the threefold ministerial office and its relationship with all other ministries, is in need of continuing exploration, renewal, and reform, which they pledge themselves to undertake in consultation with one another. The ordination of deacons, deaconesses, or diaconal ministers by the Evangelical Lutheran Church in America is not required by this Concordat.

10. The New Testament describes a laying-on of hands to set persons apart for a variety of ministries. In the history of the church, many and various terms have been used to describe the rite by which a person becomes a bishop. In the English language these terms include: confecting, consecrating, constituting, installing, making, ordaining, ordering. Both our traditions have used the term "consecration of bishops" for this same rite at some

times. Today the Evangelical Lutheran Church in America uses the term "installation," while The Episcopal Church uses the word "ordination" for the rite by which a person becomes a bishop. What is involved in each case is the setting apart within the one ministry of Word and Sacrament of a person elected and called for the exercise of oversight (*episkope*) wider than the local congregation in the service of the gospel.

11. "Historic succession" refers to a tradition which goes back to the ancient church, in which bishops already in the succession install newly elected bishops with prayer and the laying-on of hands. At present The Episcopal Church has bishops in this historic succession, as do all the churches of the Anglican Communion, and the Evangelical Lutheran Church in America at present does not, although some member churches of the Lutheran World Federation do. The Chicago-Lambeth Quadrilateral of 1886/1888, the ecumenical policy of The Episcopal Church, refers to this tradition as "the historic episcopate." In the Lutheran Confessions, Article 14 of the Apology refers to this episcopal pattern by the phrase, "the ecclesiastical and canonical polity" which it is "our deep desire to maintain."

12. *Commitment and Definition.* As a result of their agreement in faith and in testimony of their full communion with one another, both churches now make the following commitment to share an episcopal succession that is both evangelical and historic. They promise to include regularly one or more bishops of the other church to participate in the laying-on of hands at the ordinations/installations of their own bishops as a sign, though not a guarantee, of the unity and apostolic continuity of the whole church. With the laying-on of hands by other bishops, such ordinations/installations will involve prayer for the gift of the Holy Spirit. Both churches value and maintain a ministry of *episkope* as one of the ways, in the context of ordained ministries and of the whole people of God, in which the apostolic succession of the church is visibly expressed and personally symbolized in fidelity to the gospel through the ages. By such a liturgical statement the churches recognize that the bishop serves the diocese or synod through ties of collegiality and consultation that strengthen its links with the universal church. It is also a liturgical expression of the full communion initiated by this Concordat, calling for mutual planning and common mission in each place. We agree that when persons duly called and elected are ordained/installed in this way, they are understood to join bishops already in this succession and thus to enter the historic episcopate.

13. While our two churches will come to share in the historic institution of the episcopate in the church (as defined in paragraph 12 above),

each remains free to explore its particular interpretations of the ministry of bishops in evangelical and historic succession. Whenever possible, this should be done in consultation with one another. The Episcopal Church is free to maintain that sharing in the historic catholic episcopate, while not necessary for salvation or for recognition of another church as a church, is nonetheless necessary when Anglicans enter the relationship of full communion in order to link the local churches for mutual responsibility in the communion of the larger church. The Evangelical Lutheran Church in America is free to maintain that this same episcopate, although pastorally desirable when exercised in personal, collegial, and communal ways, is nonetheless not necessary for the relationship of full communion. Such freedom is evidenced by its communion with such non-episcopal churches as the Reformed churches of *A Formula of Agreement* and most churches within the Lutheran World Federation.

14. The two churches will acknowledge immediately the full authenticity of each other's ordained ministries (bishops, priests, and deacons in The Episcopal Church and pastors in the Evangelical Lutheran Church in America). The creation of a common and fully interchangeable ministry of bishops in full communion will occur with the incorporation of all active bishops in the historic episcopal succession and the continuing process of collegial consultation in matters of Christian faith and life. For both churches, the relationship of full communion begins when both churches adopt this Concordat. For the Evangelical Lutheran Church in America, the characteristics of the goal of full communion—defined in its 1991 policy statement *Ecumenism: The Vision of the Evangelical Lutheran Church in America*—will be realized at this time. For The Episcopal Church, full communion, although begun at the same time, will not be fully realized until both churches determine that in the context of a common life and mission there is a shared ministry of bishops in the historic episcopate. For both churches, life in full communion entails more than legislative decisions and shared ministries. The people of both churches have to receive and share this relationship as they grow together in full communion.

B. Actions of The Episcopal Church

15. The Episcopal Church by this Concordat recognizes the ministers ordained in the Evangelical Lutheran Church in America or its predecessor bodies as fully authentic. The Episcopal Church acknowledges that the pastors and bishops of the Evangelical Lutheran Church in America

minister as pastors/priests within the Evangelical Lutheran Church in America and that the bishops of the Evangelical Lutheran Church in America are pastors/priests exercising a ministry of oversight (*episkope*) within its synods. Further, The Episcopal Church agrees that all bishops of the Evangelical Lutheran Church in America who are chosen after both churches pass this Concordat and installed within the ministry of the historic episcopate will be understood by The Episcopal Church as having been ordained into this ministry (see paragraph 18 below).

16. To enable the full communion that is coming into being by means of this Concordat, The Episcopal Church pledges to continue the process for enacting a temporary suspension, in this case only, of the seventeenth-century restriction that "no persons are allowed to exercise the offices of bishop, priest, or deacon in this Church unless they are so ordained, or have already received such ordination with the laying-on-of-hands by bishops who are themselves duly qualified to confer Holy Orders" ("Preface to the Ordination Rites," *Book of Common Prayer*, 510). The purpose of this action, to declare this restriction inapplicable to the Evangelical Lutheran Church in America, will be to permit the full interchangeability and reciprocity of all its pastors as priests or presbyters within The Episcopal Church, without any further ordination or re-ordination or supplemental ordination whatsoever, subject always to canonically or constitutionally approved invitation. The purpose of temporarily suspending this restriction, which has been a constant requirement in Anglican polity since the Ordinal of 1662, is precisely in order to secure the future implementation of the ordinals' same principle in the sharing of ordained ministries. It is for this reason that The Episcopal Church can feel confident in taking this unprecedented step with regard to the Evangelical Lutheran Church in America.

17. The Episcopal Church acknowledges and seeks to receive the gifts of the Lutheran tradition which has consistently emphasized the primacy of the Word. The Episcopal Church therefore endorses the Lutheran affirmation that the historic catholic episcopate under the Word of God must always serve the gospel, and that the ultimate authority under which bishops preach and teach is the gospel itself (see AC 28.21-23). In testimony and implementation thereof, The Episcopal Church agrees to establish and welcome, either by itself or jointly with the Evangelical Lutheran Church in America, structures for collegial and periodic review of the ministry exercised by bishops with a view to evaluation, adaptation, improvement, and continual reform in the service of the gospel.

C. Actions of the Evangelical Lutheran Church in America

18. The Evangelical Lutheran Church in America agrees that all its bishops chosen after both churches pass this Concordat will be installed for pastoral service of the gospel with this church's intention to enter the ministry of the historic episcopate. They will be understood by The Episcopal Church as having been ordained into this ministry, even though tenure in office of the Presiding Bishop and synodical bishops may be terminated by retirement, resignation, disciplinary action, or conclusion of term. Any subsequent installation of a bishop so installed includes a prayer for the gift of the Holy Spirit without the laying-on of hands. The Evangelical Lutheran Church in America further agrees to revise its rite for the "installation of a Bishop" to reflect this understanding. A distinction between episcopal and pastoral ministries within the one office of Word and Sacrament is neither commanded nor forbidden by divine law (see *Apology of the AC*, 14.1 and the *Treatise on the Power and Primacy of the Pope*, 63). By thus freely accepting the historic episcopate, the Evangelical Lutheran Church in America does not thereby affirm that it is necessary for the unity of the church (AC, 7.3).

19. In order to receive the historic episcopate, the Evangelical Lutheran Church in America pledges that, following the adoption of this Concordat and in keeping with the collegiality and continuity of ordained ministry attested as early as canon 4 of the First Ecumenical Council (Nicea I, AD 325), at least three bishops already sharing in the sign of the episcopal succession will be invited to participate in the installation of its next Presiding Bishop through prayer for the gift of the Holy Spirit and with the laying-on of hands. These participating bishops will be invited from churches of the Lutheran communion which share in the historic episcopate. In addition, a bishop or bishops will be invited from The Episcopal Church to participate in the same way as a symbol of the full communion now shared. Synodical bishops elected and awaiting installation may be similarly installed at the same service, if they wish. Further, all other installations of bishops in the Evangelical Lutheran Church in America will be through prayer for the gift of the Holy Spirit and with the laying-on of hands by other bishops, at least three of whom are to be in the historic succession (see paragraph 12 above). Its liturgical rites will reflect these provisions.

20. In accord with the historic practice whereby the bishop is representative of the wider church, the Evangelical Lutheran Church in America agrees to make constitutional and liturgical provision that a bishops shall regularly preside and participate in the laying-on of hands at the ordination

of all clergy. Pastors shall continue to participate with the bishop in the laying-on of hands at all ordinations of pastors. Such offices are to be exercised as servant ministry, and not for domination or arbitrary control. All the people of God have a true equality, dignity, and authority for building up the body of Christ.

21. The Evangelical Lutheran Church in America by this Concordat recognizes the bishops, priests, and deacons ordained in The Episcopal Church as fully authentic ministers in their respective orders within The Episcopal Church and the bishops of The Episcopal Church as chief pastors in the historic succession exercising a ministry of oversight (*episkope*) within its dioceses.

D. Actions of Both Churches

Interchangeability of Clergy: Occasional Ministry, Extended Service, Transfer

22. In this Concordat, the two churches declare that each believes the other to hold all the essentials of the Christian faith, although this does not require from either church acceptance of all doctrinal formulations of the other. Ordained ministers serving occasionally or for an extended period in the ministry of the other church will be expected to undergo the appropriate acceptance procedures of that church respecting always the internal discipline of each church. For the Evangelical Lutheran Church in America, such ministers will be expected to preach, teach, and administer the sacraments in a manner that is consistent with its "Confession of Faith" as written in chapter two of the *Constitution, Bylaws, and Continuing Resolutions of the Evangelical Lutheran Church in America*. For The Episcopal Church, such ministers will be expected to teach and act in a manner that is consistent with the doctrine, discipline, and worship of The Episcopal Church. Ordained ministers from either church seeking long-term ministry with primary responsibility in the other will be expected to apply for clergy transfer and to agree to the installation vow or declaration of conformity in the church to which she or he is applying to minister permanently.

Joint Commission

23. To assist in joint planning for mission, both churches authorize the establishment of a joint commission, fully accountable to the decision-making bodies of the two churches. Its purpose will be consultative, to facilitate mutual support and advice as well as common decision making

through appropriate channels in fundamental matters that the churches may face together in the future. The joint commission will work with the appropriate boards, committees, commissions, and staff of the two churches concerning such ecumenical, doctrinal, pastoral, and liturgical matters as may rise, always subject to approval by the appropriate decision-making bodies of the two churches.

Wider Context

24. In thus moving to establish, in geographically overlapping episcopates in collegial consultation, one ordained ministry open to women as well as to men, to married persons as well as to single persons, both churches agree that the historic catholic episcopate can be locally adapted and reformed in the service of the gospel. In this spirit they offer this Concordat and growth toward full communion for serious consideration among the churches of the Reformation as well as among the Orthodox and Roman Catholic churches. They pledge widespread consultation during the process at all stages. Each church promises to issue no official commentary on this text that has not been accepted by the joint commission as a legitimate interpretation thereof.

Existing Relationships

25. Each church agrees that the other church will continue to live in communion with all the churches with whom the latter is now in communion. The Evangelical Lutheran Church in America continues to be in full communion (pulpit and altar fellowship) with all member churches of the Lutheran World Federation and with three of the Reformed family of churches (Presbyterian Church [USA], Reformed Church in America, and United Church of Christ). This Concordat does not imply or inaugurate any automatic communion between The Episcopal Church and those churches with whom the Evangelical Lutheran Church in America is in full communion. The Episcopal Church continues to be in full communion with all the Provinces of the Anglican Communion, with the Old Catholic Churches of Europe, with the united churches of the Indian subcontinent, with the Mar Thoma Church, and with the Philippine Independent Church. This Concordat does not imply or inaugurate any automatic communion between the Evangelical Lutheran Church in America and those churches with whom The Episcopal Church is in full communion.

Other Dialogues

26. Both churches agree that each will continue to engage in dialogue with other churches and traditions. Both churches agree to take each other and this Concordat into account at every stage in their dialogues with other churches and traditions. Where appropriate, both churches will seek to engage in joint dialogues. On the basis of this Concordat, both churches pledge that they will not enter into formal agreements with other churches and traditions without prior consultation with each other. At the same time both churches pledge that they will not impede the development of relationships and agreements with other churches and traditions with whom they have been in dialogue.

E. Conclusion

27. Recognizing each other as churches in which the gospel is truly preached and the holy sacraments duly administered, we receive with thanksgiving the gift of unity which is already given in Christ.

> He is the image of the invisible God, the firstborn of all creation; for in him all things in heaven and on earth were created, things visible and invisible, whether thrones or dominions or rulers or powers—all things have been created through him and for him. He himself is before all things, and in him all things hold together. He is the head of the body, the church; he is the beginning, the firstborn from the dead, so that he might come to have first place in everything. For in him all the fullness of God was pleased to dwell, and through him God was pleased to reconcile to himself all things, whether on earth or in heaven, by making peace through the blood of his cross. (Col 1:15-20)

28. Repeatedly Christians have echoed the scriptural confession that the unity of the church is both Christ's own work and his call to us. It is therefore our task as well as his gift. We must "make every effort to maintain the unity of the Spirit in the bond of peace" (Ep 4:3). We pray that we may rely upon, and willingly receive from one another, the gifts Christ gives through his Spirit "for building up the body of Christ" in love (Ep 4:16).

29. We do not know to what new, recovered, or continuing tasks of mission this Concordat will lead our churches, but we give thanks to God for leading us to this point. We entrust ourselves to that leading in the future, confident that our full communion will be a witness to the gift and goal

already present in Christ, "so that God may be all in all" (1 Cor 15:28). Entering full communion and thus removing limitations through mutual recognition of faith, sacraments, and ministries will bring new opportunities and levels of shared evangelism, witness, and service. It is the gift of Christ that we are sent as he has been sent (Jn 17:17-26), that our unity will be received and perceived as we participate together in the mission of the Son in obedience to the Father through the power and presence of the Holy Spirit.

> Now to him who by the power at work within us is able to accomplish abundantly far more than all we can ask or imagine, to him be glory in the church and in Christ Jesus to all generations, forever and ever. Amen. (Ep 3:20-21)

1—RESOLVED, that the Conference of Bishops affirm the following understandings of "Called to Common Mission":

A. The Conference of Bishops understands that "Called to Common Mission" contains:

1. no requirement that the Evangelical Lutheran Church in America must eventually adopt the threefold order of ministry. Rather, "Called to Common Mission" recognizes that the present understanding of one ordained ministry in the Evangelical Lutheran Church in America, including both pastors and bishops, may continue in effect;
2. no requirement that ELCA bishops be elected to serve as synodical bishops for life. Rather, they will continue to be elected and installed for six-year terms, with eligibility for re-election, subject to term limits, where applicable;
3. no defined role for the presiding bishop or synodical bishops after their tenure in office is completed;
4. no requirement that the Evangelical Lutheran Church in America establish the office of deacon, nor that they be ordained;
5. no requirement that priests of The Episcopal Church will serve congregations of the Evangelical Lutheran Church in America without the congregation's consent;

6. no requirement that the Ordinal (rules) of The Episcopal Church will apply to the Evangelical Lutheran Church in America;
7. no commitment to additional constitutional amendments or liturgical revisions other than those presented to the 1999 ELCA Churchwide Assembly (ELCA constitutional provisions 8.72.10-16; 9.21.02; 9.90-9.91.02; 10.31.a.9; 10.81.01; and parallel provisions in synodical and congregational constitutions); and further

B. The Conference of Bishops has the expectation that

1. ordinations of pastors will continue to be held at synodical worship services and in congregations, as is the present pattern;
2. the Evangelical Lutheran Church in America will continue to receive onto the roster of ordained ministers, without re-ordination, pastors from other traditions, some of whom will not have been ordained by a bishop in the historic episcopate;
3. following the adoption of "Called to Common Mission," if someone who has been received onto the roster of ordained ministers of the Evangelical Lutheran Church in America who was not ordained into the pastoral office in the historic episcopate is elected bishop and installed, he or she will be understood to be a bishop in the historic episcopate;
4. lay persons may continue to be licensed by the synodical bishop in unusual circumstances to administer the Sacraments of Baptism and Holy Communion as is the present practice of the Evangelical Lutheran Church in America;

5. "Definitions and Guidelines for Discipline of Ordained Ministers" will apply to priests of The Episcopal Church and ordained ministers of the Reformed churches serving ELCA congregations [under continuing resolution 8.72.15.b., A . . . to live in a manner consistent with the ministerial policy of this church"];
6. the Evangelical Lutheran Church in America is not in any way changing its confessional stance that "for the true unity of the Church it is enough to agree concerning the teaching of the Gospel and the administration of the sacraments" (AC, Article VII);
7. The Episcopal Church accepts fully, and without reservation, present Lutheran pastors and bishops who are not in the historic episcopal succession;
8. priests of The Episcopal Church and ordained ministers of the Reformed churches will not be asked to subscribe personally to the Confession of Faith of the Lutheran Church as their personal faith. They will be expected to recognize the agreement in faith of the churches and to preach and teach in a manner consistent with the Lutheran Confessions;
9. the Evangelical Lutheran Church in America receives the historic episcopal succession as a sign of and service to the continuity and unity of the Church and in no way as a guarantee of the faithful transmission of the faith;
10. future decisions of the Evangelical Lutheran Church in America on matters of common concern will be made in consultation with churches with whom a relationship of full communion has been declared, but these decisions will not require their concurrence or approval;
11. future Churchwide Assemblies of the Evangelical Lutheran Church in America will be free to make whatever decisions they deem necessary after mutual consultation on matters related to full communion;

12. the joint commission [to which reference is made in "Called to Common Mission"] will have no authority over the appropriate decision-making bodies of the Evangelical Lutheran Church in America or The Episcopal Church; and
13. pastors of the Evangelical Lutheran Church in America will continue to preside at confirmations.

Constitutional Changes Related to "Called to Common Mission"

If the 1999 Churchwide Assembly adopts the proposal "Called to Common Mission" for a relationship of full communion between the Evangelical Lutheran Church in America and The Episcopal Church, the following constitutional changes would be needed. These are the only constitutional and bylaw amendments that would be prompted by the text of "Called to Common Mission," as transmitted in November 1998 to the assembly.

To amend churchwide bylaw 10.31.a.9 by addition of the underlined text:

> 10.31.a.9. As the synod's pastor, the bishop shall: . . . Exercise solely this church's power to ordain (or provide for the ordination by another synodical bishop of) approved candidates . . . [with the remainder of the provision unchanged].

To amend †S8.12.c in the Constitution for Synods by addition of the underlined text:

> †S8.12.c. As the synod's pastor, the bishop shall . . . : . . . Exercise solely this church's power to ordain (or provide for the ordination by another synodical bishop of) approved candidates . . . [with the remainder of the provision unchanged].

To amend churchwide bylaw 10.81.01 by deletion and addition:

> 10.81.01. The presiding bishop of this church, or a member of the Conference of Bishops synodical bishop appointed by the presiding bishop of this church, shall preside for the installation into office, in accord with the policy and approved rite of this church, of each newly elected synodical bishop.

To amend †S8.15 in the Constitution for Synods by addition:

†S8.15. The presiding bishop of this church, or the appointee of the presiding bishop, shall install into office, in accord with the policy and approved rite of this church, each newly elected synodical bishop. Previously adopted continuing resolutions in the *Constitution, Bylaws, and Continuing Resolutions of the Evangelical Lutheran Church in America* provide for certain church-to-church matters, including procedures on the availability and service of ordained ministers, under relationships of full communion, such as the Lutheran-Reformed Formula of Agreement, approved in 1997. These established patterns would not be altered by the Lutheran-Moravian proposal "Following Our Shepherd to Full Communion" or the Lutheran-Episcopal proposal "Called to Common Mission."

Liturgical Changes Related to "Called to Common Mission"

If the 1999 Churchwide Assembly adopts the proposal "Called to Common Mission" for a relationship of full communion between the Evangelical Lutheran Church in America and The Episcopal Church, the following changes in the Rite of Installation of a Bishop would occur. These represent the only liturgical changes that would be prompted by "Called to Common Mission."

The full text of the existing rite, "Installation of a Bishop," is in *Occasional Services—A Companion to Lutheran Book of Worship*, 218-223.

A prayer for the guidance of the Holy Spirit, with the laying-on of hands, would be added to the Rite of Installation of a Bishop after the questions addressed to the one being installed and to the assembled congregation.

P. The Lord be with you.

C. And also with you.

P. Let us pray.

Following silent prayer, the presiding minister lays both hands on the head of the bishop-elect. Other bishops present also shall be invited to lay on hands as well as representatives of churches with which a relationship of full communion has been established with this church.

P. God the Father of our Lord Jesus Christ, it is your Spirit that sustains the Church. By the power of the Spirit you call, gather, enlighten, and sanctify the whole Church. Pour out your Spirit upon N. to empower his/her ministry as a bishop in your Church. Sustain him/her as a shepherd who tends the flock of Christ with love and gentleness, and oversees the ministry of the Church with vision and wisdom. Uphold him/her as a faithful steward of your holy Word and life-giving Sacraments and a strong sign of reconciliation among all people. Give courage and fortitude for this ministry. We ask this through Jesus Christ, your Son, through whom glory and power and honor are yours in your holy Church now and forever.

C. Amen

Inserted in the "Notes on the Service" would be the following:

The laying on of hands and prayer for the Holy Spirit are not repeated for a bishop who has already received installation as a bishop in this church [in accord with paragraph 18 in "Called to Common Mission"]. Three bishops in historic succession join in the laying on of hands in conformity with the canons of the Council of Nicaea. Other bishops and representatives of churches with which a relationship of full communion has been established with this church may participate in the laying-on of hands.

DOCUMENT 5

A FORMULA OF AGREEMENT, 1997

Editors' Note: *In 1997 four historic Protestant churches—the Evangelical Lutheran Church in America, the Presbyterian Church USA, the Reformed Church in America, and the United Church of Christ—affirmed a relationship of full communion with the text* A Formula of Agreement. *The theological consensus reached in this agreement is based on years of previous ecumenical dialogue, including statements in 1966, 1974, and 1983. A noteworthy element of this particular full communion agreement lies in the commitment to the principle of "mutual affirmation and admonition," wherein the churches understand that disagreements are not necessarily church-dividing, but sometimes are complementary perspectives and practices. This principle of "mutual affirmation and admonition" enabled the churches, once having reached fundamental theological consensus on issues formerly perceived to be church-dividing, to move forward even in areas where there remained variation of expression and sometimes difference of opinion.*

The full text of this dialogue can be found in A Common Calling: The Witness of Our Reformation Churches in North America Today, *eds. Keith Nickle and Timothy Lull (Minneapolis: Augsburg, 1993); parts can also be found at the ELCA website,* www.elca.org/ea/relationships/formula.html *(accessed in June 2004). See related texts:* Marburg Revisited, *in GC I, 129-135; and* An Invitation to Action, *in GC I, 141-169.*

Introduction

The Lutheran Reformed Coordinating Committee, on February 3, 1997, called attention to the fact that *A Formula of Agreement* sets forth a fundamental doctrinal consensus that is based on and presumes the theological agreements of earlier Lutheran–Reformed dialogues, including the

1983 statement "our unity in Christ compels us to claim our strong affinities in doctrine and practice":

Both Lutheran and Reformed traditions

a. Affirm themselves a living part of the church catholic.

b. Confess the Nicene and Apostles' Creeds.

c. Affirm the doctrine of justification by faith as fundamental.

d. Affirm the unique and final authority of Holy Scriptures in the church.

e. Affirm the real presence of Christ in the Lord's Supper.

f. Affirm the priesthood of all believers and have interpreted this as our servanthood to God and our service to the world.

g. Affirm the vocation of all the baptized, which is service (ministry) in every aspect of their lives in their care of God's world.

h. Affirm that they are in faithful succession in the apostolic Tradition and that faithful succession in this Tradition is all that is necessary for mutual recognition as part of the church catholic.

i. Share a common definition of a church in the apostolic Tradition: a community where the word is rightly preached and the sacraments rightly administered.

j. Identify a ministry of word and sacrament as instituted by God.

k. Ordain once to a ministry of word and sacrament, and the functions of such persons are identical.

l. Understand that ordination is to the ministry of the church catholic. Such ordinations in both traditions have usually been by presbyters.

m. Have granted the appropriateness under some circumstances of one ordained person exercising *episkop*, oversight (under a variety of titles including that of bishop), but both traditions have ordinarily exercised the function of *episkop* collegially through such structures as presbyteries and synods.

n. Affirm that the church always must be open to further growth and reformation. Both traditions have been willing to be self-critical. Both traditions have become increasingly open to a historical-critical understanding of the history of the church and of their respective traditions within the apostolic Tradition. (*An Invitation to Action*, 2-3)

A FORMULA OF AGREEMENT

***Between the Evangelical Lutheran Church in America, the Presbyterian Church (USA), the Reformed Church in America, and the United Church of Christ on Entering into Full Communion on the Basis of* A Common Calling**

Preface

In 1997 four churches of Reformation heritage will act on an ecumenical proposal of historic importance. The timing reflects a doctrinal consensus which has been developing over the past thirty-two years coupled with an increasing urgency for the church to proclaim a gospel of unity in contemporary society. In light of identified doctrinal consensus, desiring to bear visible witness to the unity of the Church, and hearing the call to engage together in God's mission, it is recommended:

That the Evangelical Lutheran Church in America, the Presbyterian Church (USA), the Reformed Church in America, and the United Church of Christ declare on the basis of *A Common Calling* and their adoption of this *A Formula of Agreement* that they are in full communion with one another. Thus, each church is entering into or affirming full communion with three other churches.

The term "full communion" is understood here to specifically mean that the four churches:

- recognize each other as churches in which the gospel is rightly preached and the sacraments rightly administered according to the Word of God;
- withdraw any historic condemnation by one side or the other as inappropriate for the life and faith of our churches today;
- continue to recognize each other's Baptism and authorize and encourage the sharing of the Lord's Supper among their members;
- recognize each others' various ministries and make provision for the orderly exchange of ordained ministers of Word and Sacrament;
- establish appropriate channels of consultation and decision-making within the existing structures of the churches;
- commit themselves to an ongoing process of theological dialogue in order to clarify further the common understanding of the faith and foster its common expression in evangelism, witness, and service;
- pledge themselves to living together under the Gospel in such a way that the principle of mutual affirmation and admonition becomes the basis of a trusting relationship in which respect and love for the other will have a chance to grow.

This document assumes the doctrinal consensus articulated in *A Common Calling: The Witness of Our Reformation Churches in North American Today* (ACC) and is to be viewed in concert with that document. The purpose of *A Formula of Agreement* is to elucidate the complementarity of affirmation and admonition as the basic principle for entering into full communion and the implications of that action as described in *A Common Calling*.

A Common Calling, the report of the Lutheran-Reformed Committee for Theological Conversations (1988-1992) continued a process begun in 1962.[1] Within that report was the "unanimous recommendation that the Evangelical Lutheran Church in America, the Presbyterian Church (USA), the Reformed Church in America, and the United Church of Christ declare that they are in full communion with one another" (ACC, 66-67).

There followed a series of seven recommendations under which full communion would be implemented as developed within the study from the theological conversations (ACC, 67). As a result, the call for full communion has been presented to the four respective church bodies. The vote on a declaration of full communion will take place at the respective churchwide assemblies in 1997.

Mutual Affirmation and Admonition

A concept identified as early as the first Lutheran-Reformed Dialogue became pivotal for the understanding of the theological conversations. Participants in the Dialogue discovered that "efforts to guard against possible distortions of truth have resulted in varying emphases in related doctrines which are not in themselves contradictory and in fact are complementary . . ." (*Marburg Revisited*, Preface, in GC I). Participants in the theological conversations rediscovered and considered the implications of this insight and saw it as a foundation for the recommendation for full communion among the four churches. This breakthrough concept, a complementarity of mutual affirmation and mutual admonition, points toward new ways of relating traditions of Reformation churches that heretofore have not been able to reconcile their diverse witnesses to the saving grace of God that is bestowed in Jesus Christ, the Lord of the Church.

This concept provides a basis for acknowledging three essential facets of the Lutheran-Reformed relationship: (1) that each of the churches grounds its life in authentic New Testament traditions of Christ; (2) that the core traditions of these churches belong together within the one, holy, catholic, and apostolic Church; and (3) that the historic give-and-take between these churches has resulted in fundamental mutual criticisms that cannot be glossed over, but need to be understood "as diverse witnesses to the one Gospel that we confess in common" (ACC, 66). A working awareness emerged, which cast in a new light contemporary perspectives on the sixteenth century debates.

> The theological diversity within our common confession provides both the complementarity needed for a full and adequate witness to the gospel (mutual affirmation) and the corrective reminder that every theological approach is a partial and incomplete witness to the Gospel (mutual admonition). (ACC, 66)

The working principle of "mutual affirmation and admonition" allows for the affirmation of agreement while at the same time allowing a process of mutual edification and correction in areas where there is not total agreement. Each tradition brings its "corrective witness" to the other while fostering continuing theological reflection and dialogue to further clarify the unity of faith they share and seek. The principle of "mutual affirmation and admonition" views remaining differences as diverse witnesses to the one Gospel confessed in common. Whereas conventional modes of thought have hidden the bases of unity behind statements of differences, the new concept insists that, while remaining differences must be acknowledged, even to the extent of their irreconcilability, it is the inherent unity in Christ that is determinative. Thus, the remaining differences are not church-dividing.

The concept of mutual affirmation and admonition translates into significant outcomes, both of which inform the relationships of these four churches with one another. The principle of complementarity and its accompanying mode of interpretation make it clear that in entering into full church communion, these churches

- do not consider their own traditional confessional and ecclesiological character to be compromised in the least;
- fully recognize the validity and necessity of the confessional and ecclesiological character of the partner churches;
- intend to allow significant differences to be honestly articulated within the relationship of full communion;
- allow for articulated differences to be opportunities for mutual growth of churchly fullness within each of the partner churches and within the relationship of full communion itself.

A Fundamental Doctrinal Consensus

Members of the theological conversations were charged with determining whether the essential conditions for full communion have been met. They borrowed language of the Lutheran confessions: "For the true unity of the church it is enough to agree (*satis est consentire*) concerning the teaching of the Gospel and the administration of the sacraments" (AC, Article 7). The theological consensus that is the basis for the current proposal for full communion includes justification, the sacraments, ministry, and church and world. Continuing areas of diversity, no longer to be seen as "church-dividing," were dealt with by the theological conversations under these headings: The Condemnations, the Presence of Christ, and God's Will to Save.

On Justification, participants in the first dialogue agreed "that each tradition has sought to preserve the wholeness of the Gospel as including forgiveness of sins and renewal of life" (*Marburg Revisited*, 152). Members of the third dialogue, in their Joint Statement on Justification, said, "Both Lutheran and Reformed churches are . . . rooted in, live by, proclaim, and confess the Gospel of the saving act of God in Jesus Christ" (*An Invitation to Action*, 9, in GC I, 141). They went on to say that "both . . . traditions confess this Gospel in the language of justification by grace through faith alone" and concluded that "there are no substantive matters concerning justification that divide us" (*An Invitation to Action*, 9-10).

Lutherans and Reformed agree that in Baptism, Jesus Christ receives human beings, fallen prey to sin and death, into his fellowship of salvation so that they may become new creatures. This is experienced as a call into Christ's community, to a new life of faith, to daily repentance, and to discipleship (cf. *Leuenberg Agreement* [LA], III.2.a). The central doctrine of the presence of Christ in the Lord's Supper received attention in each dialogue and in the theological conversations. The summary statement in *Marburg Revisited*, reflecting agreement, asserts,

> During the Reformation both Reformed and Lutheran Churches exhibited an evangelical intention when they understood the Lord's Supper in the light of the saving act of God in Christ. Despite this common intention, different terms and concepts were employed which . . . led to mutual misunderstanding and misrepresentation. Properly interpreted, the differing terms and concepts were often complementary rather than contradictory. (103-104)

The third dialogue concluded that, while neither Lutheran nor Reformed profess to explain how Christ is present and received in the Supper, both churches affirm that "Christ himself is the host at his table . . . and that Christ himself *is* fully present and received in the Supper" (*An Invitation to Action*, 14; emphasis added). This doctrinal consensus became the foundation for work done by the theological conversations.

The theme of ministry was considered only by the third dialogue. Agreeing that there are no substantive matters which should divide Lutherans and Reformed, the dialogue affirmed that

> Ministry in our heritage derives from and points to Christ who alone is sufficient to save. Centered in the proclamation of the word and the administration of the sacraments, it is built on the affirmation that the benefits of Christ are known only through faith, grace, and Scripture. (*An Invitation to Action*, 24)

The dialogue went on to speak of the responsibility of all the baptized to participate in Christ's servant ministry, pointed to God's use of "the ordained ministers as instruments to mediate grace through the preaching of the Word and the administration of the sacraments," and asserted the need for proper oversight to "ensure that the word is truly preached and sacraments rightly administered" (*An Invitation to Action*, 26, 28, 31).

The first dialogue considered the theme of church and world a very important inquiry. The dialogue examined differences, noted the need of correctives, and pointed to the essentially changed world in which the church lives today. Agreeing that "there is a common evangelical basis for Christian ethics in the theology of the Reformers," (*Marburg Revisited*, 177), the dialogue went on to rehearse the differing "accents" of Calvin and Luther on the relation of church and world, Law and Gospel, the "two kingdoms," and the sovereignty of Christ. The dialogue found that "differing formulations of the relation between Law and Gospel were prompted by a common concern to combat the errors of legalism on the one hand and antinomianism on the other." While differences remain regarding the role of God's Law in the Christian life, the dialogue did "not regard this as a divisive issue" (*Marburg Revisited*, 177). Furthermore, in light of the radically changed world of the twentieth century, it was deemed inappropriate to defend or correct positions and choices taken in the sixteenth century, making them determinative for Lutheran-Reformed witness today. Thus, the theological conversations, in a section on "Declaring God's Justice and Mercy," identified Reformed and Lutheran "emphases" as "complementary and stimulating" differences, posing a challenge to the pastoral service and witness of the churches. "The ongoing debate about 'justification and justice' is fundamentally an occasion for hearing the Word of God and doing it. Our traditions need each other in order to discern God's gracious promises and obey God's commands" (ACC, 61).

Differing Emphases

The Condemnations

The condemnations of the Reformation era were an attempt to preserve and protect the Word of God; therefore, they are to be taken seriously. Because of the contemporary ecclesial situation today, however, it is necessary to question whether such condemnations should continue to divide the churches. The concept of mutual affirmation and mutual admonition of *A Common Calling* offers a way of overcoming condemnation language while allowing for different emphases with a common understanding of the primacy of the Gospel of Jesus Christ and the gift of the sacraments. *A Common Calling* refers with approval to the *Leuenberg Agreement* where, as a consequence of doctrinal agreement, it is stated that the "condemnations expressed in the confessional documents no longer apply to the contemporary doctrinal position of the assenting churches" (LA, IV.32.b). The theological conversations stated,

> We have become convinced that the task today is not to mark the point of separation and exclusion but to find a common language which will allow our partners to be heard in their honest concern for the truth of the Gospel, to be taken seriously, and to be integrated into the identity of our own ecumenical community of faith. (ACC, 40)

A major focus of the condemnations was the issue of the presence of Christ in the Lord's Supper. Lutheran and Reformed Christians need to be assured that in their common understanding of the sacraments, the Word of God is not compromised; therefore, they insist on consensus among their churches on certain aspects of doctrine concerning the Lord's Supper. In that regard Lutheran and Reformed Christians, recalling the issues addressed by the conversations, agree that

> In the Lord's Supper the risen Jesus Christ imparts himself in his body and blood, given for all, through his word of promise with bread and wine. He thus gives himself unreservedly to all who receive the bread and wine; faith receives the Lord's Supper for salvation, unfaith for judgment. (LA, III.1.18)

> We cannot separate communion with Jesus Christ in his body and blood from the act of eating and drinking. To be concerned

> about the manner of Christ's presence in the Lord's Supper in abstraction from this act is to run the risk of obscuring the meaning of the Lord's Supper, (LA, III.1.19)

The Presence of Christ

The third dialogue urged the churches toward a deeper appreciation of the sacramental mystery based on consensus already achieved:

> Appreciating what we Reformed and Lutheran Christians already hold in common concerning the Lord's Supper, we nevertheless affirm that both of our communions need to keep on growing into an ever-deeper realization of the fullness and richness of the eucharistic mystery. (*An Invitation to Action*, 14)

The members of the theological conversations acknowledged that it has not been possible to reconcile the confessional formulations from the sixteenth century with a "common language . . . which could do justice to all the insights, convictions, and concerns of our ancestors in the faith" (ACC, 49). However, the theological conversations recognized these enduring differences as acceptable diversities with regard to the Lord's Supper. Continuing in the tradition of the third dialogue, they respected the different perspectives and convictions from which their ancestors professed their faith, affirming that those differences are not church-dividing but are complementary. Both sides can say together that "the Reformation heritage in the matter of the Lord's Supper draws from the same roots and envisages the same goal: to call the people of God to the table at which Christ himself is present to give himself for us under the word of forgiveness, empowerment, and promise" [LA]. Lutheran and Reformed Christians agree that

> In the Lord's Supper the risen Christ imparts himself in body and blood, given up for all, through his word of promise with bread and wine. He thereby grants us forgiveness of sins and sets us free for a new life of faith. He enables us to experience anew that we are members of his body. He strengthens us for service to all people. (The official text reads, "*Er starkt uns zum Dienst an den Menschen*," which may be translated "to all human beings.") (LA, II.2.15)

> When we celebrate the Lord's Supper we proclaim the death of Christ through which God has reconciled the world with himself. We proclaim the presence of the risen Lord in our midst. Rejoicing that the Lord has come to us, we await his future coming in glory. (LA, II.2.16)

With a complementarity and theological consensus found in the Lord's Supper, it is recognized that there are implications for sacramental practices as well, which represent the heritage of these Reformation churches.

> As churches of the Reformation, we share many important features in our respective practices of Holy Communion. Over the centuries of our separation, however, there have developed characteristic differences in practice, and these still tend to make us uncomfortable at each other's celebration of the Supper. These differences can be discerned in several areas, for example, in liturgical style and liturgical details, in our verbal interpretations of our practices, in the emotional patterns involved in our experience of the Lord's Supper, and in the implications we find in the Lord's Supper for the life and mission of the church and of its individual members. . . . We affirm our conviction, however, that these differences should be recognized as acceptable diversities within one Christian faith. Both of our communions, we maintain, need to grow in appreciation of our diverse eucharistic traditions, finding mutual enrichment in them. At the same time both need to grow toward a further deepening of our common experience and expression of the mystery of our Lord's Supper. (*An Invitation to Action*, 16-17)

God's Will to Save

Lutherans and Reformed claim the saving power of God's grace as the center of their faith and life. They believe that salvation depends on God's grace alone and not on human cooperation. In spite of this common belief, the doctrine of predestination has been one of the issues separating the two traditions. Although Lutherans and Reformed have different emphases in the way they live out their belief in the sovereignty of God's love, they agree that "God's unconditional will to save must be preached against all cultural optimism or pessimism" (ACC, 54). It is noted that "a common language that transcends the polemics of the past and witnesses to the common predestination faith of Lutheran and Reformed Churches has emerged already in theological writings and official or unofficial statements in our churches" (ACC, 55). Rather than insisting on doctrinal uniformity, the two traditions are willing to acknowledge that they have been borne out of controversy, and their present identities, theological and ecclesial, have been shaped by those arguments. To demand more than fundamental doctrinal consensus on those areas that have been church-dividing would be tantamount to denying the faith of those Christians with whom we have shared a common journey toward wholeness in Jesus Christ. An even greater tragedy would occur were we, through our divisiveness, to deprive the world of a common witness to the saving grace of Jesus Christ that has been so freely given to us.

The Binding and Effective Commitment to Full Communion

In the formal adoption at the highest levels of this *A Formula of Agreement*, based on *A Common Calling*, the churches acknowledge that they are undertaking an act of strong mutual commitment. They are making pledges and promises to each other. The churches recognize that full commitment to each other involves serious intention, awareness, and dedication. They are binding themselves to far more than merely a formal action; they are entering into a relationship with gifts and changes for all.

The churches know these stated intentions will challenge their self-understandings, their ways of living and acting, their structures, and even their general ecclesial ethos. The churches commit themselves to keep this legitimate concern of their capacity to enter into full communion at the heart of their new relation.

The churches declare, under the guidance of the triune God, that they are fully committed to *A Formula of Agreement* and are capable of being, and remaining, pledged to the above-described mutual affirmations in faith and doctrine, to joint decision-making, and to exercising and accepting mutual admonition and correction. *A Formula of Agreement* responds to the ecumenical conviction that "there is no turning back, either from the goal of visible unity or from the single ecumenical movement that unites concern for the unity of the Church and concern for engagement in the struggles of the world" (Santiago). And, as St. Paul reminds us all, "The one who calls you is faithful, and he will do this" (1 Th 5:24, NRSV).[2]

NOTES

1. For a summary of the history of Lutheran-Reformed Dialogue in North America, see *A Common Calling* (ACC), 10-11. The results of the first round of dialogue, 1962-1966, were published in *Marburg Revisited* (Minneapolis: Augsburg, 1966). The second round of dialogue took place in 1972-1974. Its brief report was published in *An Invitation to Action* (Philadelphia: Fortress, 1983), 54-60. The third series began in 1981 and concluded in 1983 and was published in the book *An Invitation to Action*. Following this third dialogue, a fourth round of "Theological Conversations" was held from 1988 to 1992, resulting in the report ACC. In addition, the North American participants in Lutheran-Reformed Dialogue have drawn on the theological work found in the *Leuenberg Agreement*, a Statement of Concord between Reformation churches in Europe in 1973, published in *An Invitation to Action* (61-73), as well as the Report of the International Joint Commission of the Lutheran World Federation and the World Alliance of Reformed Churches, 1985-1988, *Toward Church Fellowship* (Geneva: LWF and WARC, 1989) [in GA II].
2. **The Evangelical Lutheran Church in America.** To enter into full communion with these three churches [Presbyterian Church (USA), Reformed Church in America, United Church of Christ], an affirmative two-thirds vote of the 1997 Churchwide Assembly, the highest legislative authority in the ELCA, will be required. Subsequently in the appropriate manner other changes in the constitution and bylaws would be made to conform with this binding decision by an assembly to enter into full communion.

   The constitution and bylaws of the Evangelical Lutheran Church in America (ELCA) do not speak specifically of this church entering into full communion with non-Lutheran churches. The closest analogy, in view of the seriousness of the matter, would appear to be an amendment of the ELCA's constitution or bylaws. The constitution provides a process of such amendment (Chapter 22). In both cases a two-thirds vote of members present and voting is required.

   The Presbyterian Church (USA). Upon an affirmative vote of the General Assembly of the Presbyterian Church (USA), the declaration of full communion will be effected throughout the church in accordance with the Presbyterian *Book of Order* and this *Formula of Agreement*. This means a majority vote of the General Assembly, a majority vote in the presbyteries, and a majority vote of the presbyteries.

   The Presbyterian Church (USA) orders its life as an institution with a constitution, government, officers, finances, and administrative rules. These are instruments of mission, not ends in themselves. Different orders have served the Gospel, and none can claim exclusive validity. A presbyterian polity recognizes the responsibility of all members for ministry and maintains the organic relation of all congregations in the church. It seeks to protect the church from every exploitation by ecclesiastical or secular power and ambition. Every church order must be open to such reformation as may be required to make it a more effective instrument of the mission of reconciliation ("Confession of 1967," *Book of Confessions*, 40).

The Presbyterian Church (USA) shall be governed by representative bodies composed of presbyters, both elders and ministers of the Word and Sacrament. These governing bodies shall be called session, presbytery, synod, and the General Assembly (*Book of Order*, G-9.0100).

All governing bodies of the Church are united by nature of the Church and share with one another responsibilities, rights, and powers as provided in this Constitution. The governing bodies are separate and independent, but have such mutual relations that the act of one of them is the act of the whole Church performed by it through the appropriate governing body. The jurisdiction of each governing body is limited by the express provisions of the Constitution, with the acts of each subject to review by the next higher governing body (G-9.0103).

The Reformed Church in America. Upon an affirmative vote by the General Synod of the Reformed Church in America (RCA), the declaration of full communion will be effected throughout the church, and the Commission on Christian Unity will, in accordance with the responsibilities granted by the *Book of Church Order* (BCO), proceed to initiate and supervise the effecting of the intention of full communion as described in the *Formula of Agreement*.

The Commission on Christian Unity has advised the General Synod and the church of the forthcoming vote for full communion in 1997. The Commission will put before the General Synod the *Formula of Agreement* and any and all correlative recommendations toward effecting the Reformed Church in America declaring itself to be in full communion with the Evangelical Lutheran Church in America, the Presbyterian Church (USA), and the United Church of Christ.

The Constitution of the RCA gives responsibility for ecumenical relations to the General Synod (BCO, Chapter 1, Part IV, Article 2, Section 5). To be faithful to the ecumenical calling, the General Synod empowers its Commission on Christian Unity to initiate and supervise action relating to correspondence and cooperative relationship with the highest judicatories or assemblies of other Christian denominations and the engaging in interchurch conversations "in all matters pertaining to the extension of the Kingdom of God."

The Constitution of the RCA gives responsibility to the Commission on Christian Unity for informing "the church of current ecumenical developments and advising the church concerning its ecumenical participation and relationships" (BCO, Chapter 3, Part I, Article 5, Section 3).

Granted its authority by the General Synod, the Commission on Christian Unity has appointed RCA dialogue and conversation partners since 1962 to the present. It has received all reports and, where action was required, has presented recommendation(s) to the General Synod for vote and implementation in the church.

The United Church of Christ. The United Church of Christ (UCC) will act on the recommendation that it enter into full communion with the Evangelical Lutheran Church in America, the Presbyterian Church (USA), and the Reformed Church in America, by vote of the General Synod in 1997. This vote is binding on the General Synod and is received by local churches, associations, and conferences for implementation in accordance with the covenantal polity outlined in paragraphs 14, 15, and 16 of the Constitution of the United Church of Christ.

The UCC is "composed of Local Churches, Associations, Conferences, and the General Synod." The Constitution and Bylaws of the United Church of Christ lodge responsibility for ecumenical life with the General Synod and with its chief executive officer, the President of the United Church of Christ. Article VII of the Constitution grants to the General Synod certain powers. Included among these are the powers

- to determine the relationship of the UCC with ecumenical organizations, world confessional bodies, and other interdenominational agencies (Article VII, par. 45h)
- to encourage conversation with other communions and when appropriate to authorize and guide negotiations with them looking toward formal union (VII, 45i)

In the polity of the UCC, the powers of the General Synod can never, to use a phrase from the Constitution, "invade the autonomy of Conferences, Associations, or Local Churches." The autonomy of the Local Church is "inherent and modifiable only by its own action" (IV, 15). However, it is important to note that this autonomy is understood in the context of "mutual Christian concern and in dedication to Jesus Christ, the Head of the Church" (IV, 14). This Christological and covenantal understanding of autonomy is clearly expressed in the Constitutional paragraphs which immediately precede and follow the discussion of Local Church autonomy:

The Local Churches of the UCC have, in fellowship, a God-given responsibility for that Church, its labors and its extension, even as the UCC has, in fellowship, a God-given responsibility for the well-being and needs and aspirations of its Local Churches. In mutual Christian concern and in dedication to Jesus Christ, the Head of the Church, the one and the many share in common Christian experience and responsibility (IV, 14).

Actions by, or decisions or advice emanating from, the General Synod, a Conference, or an Association, should be held in the highest regard by every Local Church (IV, 16).

Document 6

FOLLOWING OUR SHEPHERD TO FULL COMMUNION, 1998-1999

Editors' Note: *Since 1992 the Moravian Church and the Evangelical Lutheran Church in America have held regular dialogues. In 1998 the Northern and Southern Provinces of the Moravian Church in America approved this full communion agreement. In 1999 the Evangelical Lutheran Church in America approved it. The following are excerpts from the agreement, reprinted from ELCA, "Following Our Shepherd to Full Communion,"* http://www.elca.org/ea/Relationships/moravian/fostoc.html *(accessed on June 14, 2004).*

Preface

> *"I am the good shepherd. I know my own and my own know me, just as the Father knows me and I know the Father. And I lay down my life for the sheep. I have other sheep who do not belong to this fold. I must bring them also, and they will listen to my voice. So there will be one flock, one shepherd." (John 10:14-16 [NRSV])*

The themes of the Good Shepherd, following Jesus, and fellowship through discipleship were at the forefront from the very start of the Lutheran-Moravian Dialogue. Also present was the realization that this dialogue is unique for both churches.[1] It is unique for the Northern and Southern Provinces of the Moravian Church in America (*Unitas Fratrum*) because it is the first such dialogue in which those provinces have engaged.[2]

It is also unique for the Evangelical Lutheran Church in America (ELCA) because Lutheran churches and Moravian Provinces worldwide have been in virtual full communion, including the interchangeability of ordained clergy and eucharistic hospitality for decades. In this sense, then, the Lutheran-Moravian Dialogue in the United States is catching up with where other Lutherans and Moravians are already. Moravians and Lutherans are regarding themselves as members of one flock who are following their Shepherd in mission and ministry. Participants in the Dialogue realized from the outset that we had much in common, yet our churches were not identical. Over time, we became convinced that this Dialogue, its Report, and its recommendations would take a shape that was both familiar to and different from other dialogue reports and recommendations.

The Recommendations will be familiar to those acquainted with the Concordat of Agreement between The Episcopal Church in the USA and the ELCA.[3] The Report would be unfamiliar on at least four counts. First, the Dialogue papers were not published and distributed to clergy and others prior to this Report, with the exception of a number of Moravian and ELCA congregations which used them in a guided study process. The key reason for that procedure is the severe limits based on funding the Dialogue; neither church could afford the expenses involved in editing, printing and distributing the materials. A grant from the Elfrid L. and Marie F. Hine Fund of Augsburg Lutheran Church, Winston-Salem, North Carolina, made the first four meetings possible. We acknowledge with gratitude the generosity of the congregation in making the funds available.

Second, our respective church leaders and the dialoguers felt that the salient positions which emerged could be covered appropriately in the body of the Report. Persons interested in particular papers may request them through our respective denominational offices.

Third, the Report contains more explanatory and background material than others because American Moravians and Lutherans know less about each other than we know about other Christian bodies. Relative size and geographical distribution in the United States account for some of our mutual non-communication. Other contributing factors are denominational agendas, theological styles, and inertia. The Report, therefore, also serves to introduce Moravians to Lutherans and Lutherans to Moravians.

Fourth, the Report's structure departs from that of others. We present the Recommendations to our churches following the Preface rather than at the conclusion of the whole. Through this arrangement we alert readers to areas, issues, and implications for the future of Moravian-Lutheran relations, to highlight matters which will be presented for decisions at our respective assemblies, and to prompt readers to consider the opportunities for ecumenical developments offered by this dialogue as they join us in attempting to follow our Shepherd.

Geographical and fiscal factors influenced the location and membership of the dialoguers meetings and personnel. Given the size and concentration of the Moravian Church in North America and relevant historical as well as institutional resources of both churches, it was appropriate to hold the sessions in the Allentown-Bethlehem, Pennsylvania, area.[4] We used the facilities of the Moravian Theological Seminary (Bethlehem), Muhlenberg College and Christ Evangelical Lutheran Church (both in Allentown) for our meetings. It was natural for the Moravian dialoguers to be drawn from the Bethlehem and North Carolina areas. The Lutheran members included two from Bethlehem-Allentown and others from beyond. Because of schedules, Dr. Sarah Henrich, a member of the Lutheran team, served as a consultant for the first four meetings before joining personally at the final meeting. Another Lutheran participant, Dr. David Yeago, was not able to attend the first two meetings but was present for the balance of the dialogue. The Moravian dialoguers experienced a change in personnel when Dr. D. Wayne Burkette had to withdraw after three meetings due to other responsibilities. His place was taken by Dr. Robert Helm.

The themes of the Good Shepherd, following Jesus, and fellowship through discipleship grew from the dialoguers' frequent reflections on the Christian life and our dialogue as a journey to communion with God and humanity. We invite our churches and readers to listen with us to the Saviors call and to follow him as we seek to become more faithfully and fully one flock.

NOTES

1. The word "Church" (with the initial letter capitalized) refers to the one, holy, Christian Church except when it is used as part of the title of a particular denomination. The word "church" (with the initial letter in lowercase) refers to a general denominational entity, e.g., the Lutheran church.
2. The formal name of the international Moravian church is the "*Unitas Fratrum* (Moravian Church)." It consists of provinces located in various countries in Africa, Europe, Great Britain, Central America, South America, North America, and the Caribbean, and related organizations in India, China, and Israel. The two Provinces of the Moravian Church in North America (North and South) presently consist of

congregations in the lower forty-eight states of the United States and the Canadian provinces of Alberta and Ontario. The ELCA has congregations in the fifty states of the United States, Puerto Rico, the U.S. Virgin Islands, and the Bahamas. When Moravians refer to the "Ancient Church," they mean that expression of their ecclesial existence which traces its origins to the martyred Bohemian reformer, Jan Hus (c. 1371-1415) and the establishment of the *Unitas Fratrum* at Kunvald, Bohemia, in 1457. The term "Renewed Moravian Church" or "Renewed *Unitas Fratrum*" refers to the eighteenth-century re-emergence of the Unity from persecution and dispersion. That renewal was focused in Saxony at the estate of the Lutheran noble and ordained minister, Nicholas Ludwig, Count von Zinzendorf.

3. See "Toward Full Communion" and "Concordat of Agreement," LED III, in GC I, 253-338.

4. The Moravian Church in North America is concentrated in northeastern Pennsylvania and North Carolina. Clusters of congregations are also in Wisconsin and Minnesota and on the West Coast. The Unity's only seminary and one of its four-year colleges are located in Bethlehem, a city which was settled by Moravians in 1741. The Northern Province's offices and the Moravian Archives are located on the Bethlehem campus. The Winston-Salem, North Carolina, area also is a historical Moravian center and the site of its Salem College. The Southern Province's headquarters and Archives also are in Winston-Salem. Lutheran and Moravian pastors and congregants have long been associated with each other in these areas and cooperated in local discussions and study groups, using materials derived from the Dialogue's papers. The library resources of the Lutheran Theological Seminary at Philadelphia were readily available and utilized in research.

I. The Journey to Full Communion: Recommendations to the Churches

The Northern and Southern Provinces of the Moravian Church in America, hereinafter termed the Moravian Church in America, and the Evangelical Lutheran Church in America hereby agree that in their respective assemblies there shall be one vote to accept or reject, without separate amendment, the resolutions which follow. If adopted by both churches, each church agrees to take these measures to establish full communion:

> WHEREAS Jesus our Shepherd calls us to unity so that the world may believe; and

WHEREAS Moravians and Lutherans share common theological traditions and commitments to mission; and

WHEREAS in North America Lutherans and Moravians have developed distinct church bodies while cooperating in serving our Lord; and

WHEREAS *Following Our Shepherd to Full Communion*, the report of the Lutheran-Moravian dialogue, affirmed that there are no church-dividing differences precluding full communion between the Evangelical Lutheran Church in America and the Moravian Church in America;

therefore be it resolved The Evangelical Lutheran Church in America and the Moravian Church in America hereby recognize in one another the one, holy, catholic and apostolic faith as it is expressed in the Scriptures, confessed in the Church's historic creeds, attested to in the Unaltered Augsburg Confession and Small Catechism, and the Ground of the Unity of the *Unitas Fratrum*;

The Moravian Church in America and the Evangelical Lutheran Church in America hereby recognize the authenticity of each other's baptism and eucharists, and extend sacramental hospitality to one another's members;

The Evangelical Lutheran Church in America and the Moravian Church in America hereby recognize each other's ordinations of persons to the Ministry of Word and Sacrament; and recognize each other's polity and ministries of oversight (including the interpretation of church doctrines, discipline of members, authorization of persons for ordained and lay ministries, and provision for administrative functions);

The Moravian Church in America and the Evangelical Lutheran Church in America hereby recognize the full interchangeability and reciprocity of all ordained ministers of Word and Sacrament, subject to the constitutionally approved invitation for ministry in each other's churches;

The Evangelical Lutheran Church in America and the Moravian Church in America hereby authorize the establishment of a joint commission by June 2000 to coordinate the implementation of these resolutions, to assist joint planning for mission, to facilitate consultation and common decision making through appropriate channels in fundamental matters that the churches may face together in the future, and to report regularly and appropriately to each church;

The Moravian Church in America and the Evangelical Lutheran Church in America through the aforementioned joint commission shall encourage the development of worship materials to celebrate the churches' full communion, encourage ongoing theological discussion, encourage joint formulation of educational materials, and encourage continuing education for church professionals regarding the churches' full communion;

The Moravian Church in America and the Evangelical Lutheran Church in America hereby affirm that neither will issue an official commentary on the text of these resolutions that has not been approved by the joint commission as a legitimate interpretation thereof;

The Evangelical Lutheran Church in America and the Moravian Church in America hereby agree that each will continue to be in communion with all the churches with which each is in communion presently;

The Moravian Church in America and the Evangelical Lutheran Church in America hereby pledge to take each other and these agreements into account at every stage of their dialogues and agreements with other churches and faith traditions, pledge to seek to engage in joint dialogue when appropriate, and pledge not to enter into formal agreements with other churches and faith traditions without prior consultation with the other.

II. The Journey to Full Communion: For the Record

The Lutheran-Moravian Dialogue developed its agenda and character in light of the theological, historical, and sociological realities of the two churches. While we have been close to each other geographically, ethnically, and theologically, our churches in North America proceeded on separate denominational tracks. Our European origins indicate that we have been and still are in mutually enriching relationships. Jan Hus and the Bohemian Brethren who organized themselves as the *Unitas Fratrum* prepared the ground for the German Reformation led by Martin Luther. The latter and his colleagues encouraged and recognized the Brethren as partners in the renewal of the gospel. Persecuted and driven from their Bohemian and Moravian homelands in the seventeenth and eighteenth centuries, some of the *Unitas Fratrum* were given refuge at Herrnhut, the estate of the Lutheran pietist noble, Nicholas Ludwig, Count von Zinzendorf. While at Herrnhut, and ministered to by local Lutheran pastors as well as encouraged by Zinzendorf, the Unity was renewed and re-invigorated. Zinzendorf's theological credentials were recognized on several occasions by Lutheran officials, and he was ordained to the ministry of Word and Sacrament.

Our two churches developed separate ecclesial organizations and identities in North America. The chief reasons for that separate development had much to do with the patterns of immigration from Germany and the religious pluralism which came to characterize English-speaking North America. Although Moravians were indefatigable missionaries to Native Americans in the eighteenth and early nineteenth centuries, they did not attempt, on a consistent basis, to establish Moravian churches on the frontier. The Unity resisted the denominational ecclesial pattern and organizational identity which emerged in the United States. Instead, they often chose to labor cooperatively with Lutheran, Reformed, and Episcopal clergy and laity to advance the mission of the whole Church. The *Unitas Fratrum*, then and now, may provide a valuable precedent for ecumenical experience and attitude. In Asia, Africa, and Europe, Moravians and Lutherans have long enjoyed what is now termed "full communion," including eucharistic hospitality and the full interchangeability of members and clergy.

Our churches have never issued mutual or unilateral condemnations one of the other. As will be shown in the Report, we both use the Scriptures as the source of our faith and life, confess the historic creeds, and consider the Unaltered Augsburg Confession and Small Catechism to be true expressions of the Christian faith. Justification by faith through grace holds the same vital place among Lutherans and Moravians, and we acknowledge the real presence of Christ in the Eucharist. The differences between us have more to do with how we manifest religious devotion (piety), engage in theological reflection, and express ourselves organizationally. These are not unsubstantial differences, but they are well within the circle of full communion. One substantive incident, remembered chiefly by Lutherans, has given Moravian-Lutheran relationships in the United States a negative cast: the 1742 meeting and argument in Philadelphia between Henry Melchior Muhlenberg and Nicholas von Zinzendorf. That encounter and a few subsequent quarrels among our pastors reflect tensions within Lutheran pietism and parish rivalries rather than critical doctrinal or confessional differences which are church-dividing. Indeed, neither the Ancient nor the Renewed Moravian Church experienced anything like the controversies which engaged Lutherans in the latter half of the sixteenth through the eighteenth centuries. In place of a formal emphasis on dogma, Moravians focus on the priority of personal commitment to Jesus as Savior and the relationships among members of the community of believers. Throughout the Dialogue, the participants learned to listen to each other, recognizing that our theological methods have been shaped by our historical experiences. That listening and recognizing shaped the subjects with which we dealt and the ways in which we carried on our discussions.

The Lutheran participants were led to examine their pietist traditions, the influences of their immigrant heritages on their current outlooks, and their need to articulate more clearly their understandings of personal faith, the roles of the Holy Spirit, and the unity of the Church. Moravians, likewise, were moved to express themselves with greater clarity on doctrinal concerns, biblical hermeneutics, their own historical traditions, and church order. Together we searched for the meanings and purposes of ecumenicity, "full communion," and following our Shepherd into God's future.

The Lutheran-Moravian Dialogue began with conversations led by Dr. Arthur Freeman and Dr. Daniel Martensen. Dr. Freeman is a bishop of the Moravian Church and was professor of New Testament and Christian Spirituality at the Moravian Theological Seminary. Dr. Martensen was then the associate director of the Office for Ecumenical Affairs of the ELCA. The formulation of a preliminary set of goals, subsequently endorsed by the respective church bodies and the dialoguers, resulted from the initial conversations.

The goals were:

- to be responsible to the ecumenical vision in harmony with the Bible and the historical Moravian and Lutheran positions on ecumenicity, and to affirm the unity of the Church which already exists in Christ;
- to explore further the historical and international connections of the Lutheran and Moravian churches;
- to explore moving towards full communion with the Lutheran Church, including common recognition of each other's Baptism, Eucharist, and Ministry;
- to test and articulate Moravian and Lutheran theology and theological methodologies;
- and to share with our churches at all levels the ongoing results of the Dialogue and to solicit reactions and counsel. This would also involve the sharing of information on other bilateral dialogues in which we were engaged. The term "full communion" has a technical meaning in the ecumenical discussions in which the ELCA engages with other churches.[1]

The characteristics denoted in that term are a common confessing of the Christian faith; a mutual recognition of Baptism and a sharing of the Lord's Supper, allowing for the exchangeability of members; mutual recognition and availability of ordained ministers to the service of all members of churches in full communion, subject only but always to the disciplinary regulations of the other churches; a common commitment to evangelism, witness, and service; a means of common decision making on critical common issues of faith and life; and a mutual lifting of any condemnations that exist between the churches.

Movement toward full communion, therefore, is broad in scope, penetrating in depth, and far-reaching in its implications. It can involve a gradual process with interim stages of engagement, especially if the churches are significantly different from each other in polity and practice, and if the churches' pasts have been marked by misunderstanding and hostility.

For the background and complete text of this section, visit www.elca.org/ea/Relationships/moravian/fosii.html.

NOTE

1. Ecumenism Statement, ELCA. [William G. Rusch, *The Ecumenical Vision of the ELCA: A Commentary* (Minneapolis: Augsburg Press, 1990).]

III. The Journey to Full Communion: Historical Background from Prague to Philadelphia

For the full text of this section, visit www.elca.org/ea/Relationships/moravian/fosiii.html.

IV. The Journey to Full Communion: Perspectives on Theology, Affirmations, and Complementarities

As Christians listen to the voice of the Shepherd and seek to follow, we will leave some of our traditional securities, yet we will gain deepened identities as God's people in mission. Perhaps we will understand more fully Jesus' prayer, "I ask not only on behalf of these [disciples], but also on behalf of those who will believe in me through their word, that they may all be one" (John 17:20 [NRSV]). The Lutheran-Moravian Dialogue and our churches' movement toward full communion are set in the contexts of dialogues and journeys toward unity in which Christians and their churches encounter each other anew. Today we have concluded that Christian unity need not mean corporate unification, but involves what we have previously called "full communion."

At the same time, the twentieth century, for all its startling scientific and technological advances, has also witnessed the often lethal fragmentation of the human family along racial, ethnic, religious, gender, political, and economic lines. The deconstruction of shared meanings between and within communities, together with rising levels of anxiety and violence, underscore the need and hunger for coherence without coercion and community with continuity. In this time Christians hear and seek to respond to God's summons to recognize the unity which we already have and to manifest our confidence in the Lord who calls all persons to himself.

Part of the response to God and the Church's mission to the world involves new approaches in ecumenical dialogues and actions. One such approach is indicated in *Baptism, Eucharist and Ministry* (BEM) developed by the World Council of Churches Faith and Order Commission.[1] The Commission invited the churches to consider how one church recognizes the apostolic faith in the life and thought of another church. At that level the respective communities are freed from insisting on verbal or conceptual exactitude or uniformity of practice in their formulations and actions. Here BEM foreshadowed what we term shortly "Mutual Affirmations." Next, each church was asked to consider whether it could learn from others so as to gain a fuller understanding of and richer expression for its witness to and praise of God. At this level BEM foreshadowed what we call "Mutual Complementarities."

The Moravian and Lutheran dialoguers recognized that our conversations were roughly analogous to the methods used in BEM and the bilateral dialogues in which Lutherans have engaged in recent decades. We encountered frequently the need to explain our perspectives on theology and theology's roles in the spheres of personal, ecclesial, and social life. In effect, we realized the importance of the fourth goal of our original charge: "to test and articulate Moravian and Lutheran theology and theological methodologies." Our attitudes toward, understandings of theology's functions, and the means we employ to express ourselves emerged as vital to our self-understandings and our understandings of each other. The balance of this Report follows the pattern: Perspectives on Theology, Mutual Affirmations, Mutual Complementarities, and Concluding Statement.

NOTES

1. *Baptism, Eucharist and Ministry*, Faith and Order Paper 114 (Geneva: World Council of Churches, 1982). The way that churches were asked to respond to *Baptism, Eucharist and Ministry* provides a meaningful paradigm for the way churches are called upon to respond to each other. This could be summarized as follows:
    a. the extent to which your church can recognize in these recommendations the faith of the Church through the ages and the church of which you are a member;
    b. the consequences your church may draw from these recommendations and our churches shared and contrasting understandings of the Christian faith; and
    c. the guidance your church can take from these recommendations for its worship, educational ethical and spiritual life and witness.

Several American church bodies of the Reformed tradition have been engaged in dialogue with Lutheran churches since 1962. In the wake of mergers and the formation of new ecclesiastical entities, those churches are now the Presbyterian Church (USA), Reformed Church in America, United Church of Christ, and the ELCA. The Formula of Agreement to establish full communion between the Reformed churches and the ELCA was presented to the respective church conventions/assemblies in 1997 and was accepted by all bodies.

A. Perspectives on Theology

Lutherans and Moravians have different yet complementary attitudes toward and experience with theological discourse and formulations. Lutherans expect their churches to engage in theological discussions, adhere to creedal-confessional formulations, and teach from doctrinal perspectives. The Lutheran movement originated in theological debate and coalesced about a series of confessional documents. Luther, his associates, and their successors in the sixteenth century developed and deepened their understandings of Law and Gospel, biblical interpretation, liturgical renewal, the sacraments, society, pastoral activity, and other major areas of Christian life and witness in the face of and in the heat of theological explorations and disputations with Roman Catholics, with other Reformation movements and leaders, and among themselves. Since the sixteenth century, Lutherans have retained the attitude that theological debate, clarity, and adherence are vital for the integrity and continuity of the Christian faith. They anticipate that theological discourse, personal piety, and intellectual acuity will be balanced and mutually supportive one of the other.

Lutherans are convinced that such theological discourse is more than possible; it is necessary if the Church is to speak and act knowingly as well as feelingly, in seeking to be faithful to the Lord. While Lutherans recognize the importance of social and historical contingencies, they also insist that there are theological consistencies which are to be believed, taught, and confessed as essential for understanding, living, and transmitting the faith. Christian theology involves disciplined reflection on the Triune God, the human condition, the Church, and the world. The roles of such disciplined reflection include the Church's stating to itself and for its own edification as well as correction of what the Christian faith holds true, and how the Church is to be shaped and guided by that faith. Another dimension of theological reflection involves equipping believers for mission and witness in the world. Further, theology has an apologetic function through which

Christians seek to make clear where they stand in relations with other religions and claimants for human devotion and allegiance.

While Lutheran theologians may use different methods to carry on the theological tasks, they do so in reference to a threefold authoritative basis. First, they agree that the basis, criteria, and guide for faith, doctrine, and practice is the Scripture of the Old and New Testaments. In traditional language: "We believe, teach and confess that the prophetic and apostolic writings of the Old and New Testaments are the only rule and norm according to which all doctrines and teachers alike must be appraised and judged."[2] Second, and as a valid witness to the Scriptures, Lutherans receive, use, and pledge themselves to the Apostles', Nicene, and Athanasian Creeds as the "unanimous, catholic, Christian faith and confessions of the orthodox and true church."[3] The place of the third component, a set of specific documents composed in the sixteenth century and compiled as the *Book of Concord*, is more complex.

The documents are the *Augsburg Confession*, *Apology of the Augsburg Confession*, *Smalcald Articles* (with the "Treatise on the Power and Primacy of the Pope" appended), *Large Catechism*, *Small Catechism*, and *Formula of Concord*. These are regarded as consonant with yet subordinate to the Scriptures. Within the circle of confessional literature, the "Unaltered" Augsburg Confession is regarded as having given Lutherans "a clear and unequivocal Christian witness, setting forth the faith and teaching of the Evangelical Christian churches concerning the chief articles, especially those which were in controversy between them and the popes' adherents. [W]e abide by the plain, clear, and pure meaning of its words. We consider this Confession a genuinely Christian symbol which all true Christians ought to accept next to the Word of God, just as in ancient times Christian symbols and confessions were formulated in the church of God."[4] The first twenty-one articles of the Augsburg Confession deal with matters of faith and doctrine, while the remaining six articles concern issues related to human practices. While the other documents are regarded highly among Lutherans, the two Catechisms hold an especially cherished position.[5] We observe that the Formula of Concord and Lutheran practice also give the writings of Martin Luther a significant position as a model for stating the Christian faith.[6]

The constitutions of the ELCA, its synods and congregations contain a section, "Chapter 2: Confession of Faith," which essentially repeats the positions cited from the *Formula of Concord* regarding the roles of the Scriptures, Creeds and the Confessions. It concludes, "This church confesses the Gospel, recorded in the Holy Scriptures and confessed in the ecumenical creeds and Lutheran confessional writings, as the power of God to create and sustain the Church for God's mission in the world" (2.07). At the ordination of a person to the office of the ministry of Word and Sacraments, the bishop states, "The Church into which you are to be ordained confesses that the Holy Scriptures are the Word of God and are the norm of faith and life. We accept, teach, and confess the Apostles', the Nicene, and the Athanasian Creeds. We also acknowledge the Lutheran Confessions as true witnesses and faithful expositions of the Holy Scriptures. Will you therefore preach and teach in accordance with the Holy Scriptures and these creeds and confessions?" The candidate's expected response is, "I will, and I ask God to help me."[7] It is highly unlikely that Lutherans will add to the corpus of their Confessions. They do, however, develop and discuss theological statements and declarations, sometimes adopting them for guidance. Because of their historical conditioning and theological focus, Lutherans look askance at other faith communities which formulate or add confessions to their theological treasuries, especially when some of those confessions appear to contradict or replace or re-interpret the confessions Lutherans cherish.

Explicitly and implicitly, Lutheran methods appear to move from Scripture to Creeds and then to Confessions when Lutherans analyze, assess, express and formulate positions, practices, liturgies, and actions. Actually, within the triad is an inner canon. In the realm of Scripture, Pauline positions on justification (as understood by Lutherans) have priority.[8] The *Augsburg Confession* occupies first place among the Confessions.

Moravians, while influenced deeply and positively by Lutheran individuals and Lutheran theology, have also observed debilitating arguments and confusions created by those who thought they possessed God's truth to the exclusion of other insights. Moravians regard theological polemics as contrary to the Savior's will and love. Having been persecuted and vilified, they decline to use those tactics when dealing with others and when coping with problems within their own communion. A 1979 statement on theology by the Joint Theological Commission of the Northern and Southern Provinces, USA, puts the Moravian understanding of theology's purpose and role clearly: "Theological reflection in the Moravian tradition is not to be understood as an attempt to arrive at final answers but is a way of thinking about God and His relationship to us so that He can, through His Spirit, draw us to Himself, and to His Son, and we can know Him as the Source of our living. Such reflection should lead to sharing of ideas and experiences, articulation of our faith, new levels of trust toward each other as persons through whom God partially discloses Himself in various ways, stimulation of the Christian life and our attentive waiting upon God for His clarification of our understanding."

If "confessional" describes Lutheran theological methods and purposes, "relational and devotional" fit Moravians. Certainly Moravians insist that theological tasks are to be pursued with intellectual rigor and the best means scholarship provides. Certainly Moravians recognize that a person and a community theologize within historical, social, and ecclesiastical contexts. Certainly Moravians are insightful about the degrees that their vibrant connections to Moravia, Saxony, and Pietism still invigorate the Unity. And certainly Moravians have doctrinal, liturgical, and institutional benchmarks to assess positions, proposals, and practices. But these are secondary.

Moravian perspectives on the Christian faith generally, and the Unity's distinctive positions particularly, are formed by the affirmation that at heart Christianity is relational and devotional, not abstract or conceptual. The central goal of theology is to foster the Christian life. Theological inquiry is only partially planned and structured by humans; it is also an openness and discipleship to the Savior. For Moravians, prayer and worship are essential components in undertaking theological study and discourse. *The Ground of the Unity*, a deliberately revisable statement of principles used by the worldwide Moravian Church, opens with the following:[9]

1. The Lord Jesus Christ calls His Church into being so that it may serve Him on earth until He comes. The *Unitas Fratrum* is, therefore, aware of its being called in faith to serve mankind by proclaiming the Gospel of Jesus Christ. It recognizes this call to be the source of its being and the inspiration of its service. As is the source, so is the aim and end of its being based on the will of its Lord.

2. With the whole of Christendom we share faith in God the Father, the Son, and the Holy Spirit. We believe and confess that God has revealed Himself once and for all in His Son Jesus Christ; that our Lord has redeemed us with the whole of mankind by His death and His resurrection; and that there is no salvation apart from Him. We believe that He is present with us in the Word and Sacrament; that He directs and unites us through His Spirit and thus forms us into a Church. We hear Him summoning us to follow Him, and

pray Him to use us in His service. He joins us together mutually, so that knowing ourselves to be members of His body we become willing to serve each other. In the light of divine grace, we recognize ourselves to be a Church of sinners. We require forgiveness daily, and live only through the mercy of God in Christ Jesus our Lord. He redeems us from our isolation and unites us into a living Church of Jesus Christ.

3. The belief of the Church is effected and preserved through the testimony of Jesus Christ and through the work of the Holy Spirit. This testimony calls each individual personally, and leads him to the recognition of sin and to the acceptance of the redemption achieved by Christ. In fellowship with Him the love of Christ becomes more and more the power of the new life, power which penetrates and shapes the entire person. As God's Spirit so effects living belief in the hearts of individuals, He grants them the privilege to share in the fruits of Christ's salvation and membership in His body. To balance what might be perceived as a tilt toward the "internal," or "subjective" or "heart theology," the Ground continues with "external," or "objective," or "mind" factors.

4. The Triune God as revealed in the Holy Scripture of the Old and New Testament is the only source of our life and salvation; and this Scripture is the sole standard of the doctrine and faith of the *Unitas Fratrum* and therefore shapes our life. The *Unitas Fratrum* recognizes the Word of the Cross as the center of Holy Scripture and of all preaching of the Gospel and sees its primary mission, and its reason for being, to consisting in bearing witness to this joyful message. We ask our Lord for power never to stray from this.

   The *Unitas Fratrum* takes part in the continual search for sound doctrine. In interpreting the Scripture and in the communication of doctrine in the Church, we look to two millennia of ecumenical Christian tradition and the wisdom of our Moravian forebears in the faith to guide us as we pray for fuller understanding and ever clearer proclamation of the Gospel of Jesus Christ. But just as the Holy Scripture does not contain any doctrinal system, so the *Unitas Fratrum* also has not developed any of its own, because it knows that the mystery of Jesus Christ which is attested to in the Bible, cannot be comprehended completely by any human mind or expressed completely in any human statement. Also it is true that through the Holy Spirit the recognition of God's will for salvation in the Bible is revealed completely and clearly.

5. The *Unitas Fratrum* recognizes in the creeds of the Church the thankful acclaim of the Body of Christ. These creeds aid the Church in formulating a Scriptural confession, in marking the boundary of heresies, and in exhorting believers to an obedient and fearless testimony in every age. The *Unitas Fratrum* maintains that all creeds formulated by the Christian Church stand in need of constant testing in the light of the Holy Scriptures. It acknowledges as such true professions of faith the early Christian witness: "Jesus Christ is Lord!" and also especially the ancient Christian creeds and the fundamental creeds of the Reformation.*

* In the various provinces of the Renewed *Unitas Fratrum* the following creeds in particular gained special importance, because in them the main doctrines of the Christian faith find clear and simple expression:

The Apostles' Creed

The Athanasian Creed

The Nicene Creed

The Confession of the Unity of the Bohemian Brethren of 1535

The Twenty-One Articles of the Unaltered Augsburg Confession

The Shorter Catechism of Martin Luther

The Synod of Berne of 1532

The Thirty-Nine Articles of the Church of England

The Theological Declaration of Barmen of 1934

The Heidelberg Catechism

Moravians consider truth neither as a quantity to possess nor as able to be finalized in formulas. Truth involves a personal journey in the company of other believers toward the fulfillment God promises in the crucified and risen Lord who is the Way, the Truth and the Life. The

Christian community is part and parcel of the Unity's theological method and purposes. That "company" is a "living Church" which witnesses for Christ to the world.

Again from the *Ground*:

> 52. A church is and remains a living one when it: is attentive to God's Word, confesses its sins and accepts forgiveness for them, seeks and maintains fellowship with its Lord and Redeemer by means of the Sacraments, places its whole life under His rule and daily leading, ministers to its neighbour and seeks brotherhood with all who confess Christ, proclaims to the world the tidings concerning the Saviour, awaits whole-heartedly the coming of its Lord as King.

Moravians, wary of concretizing the Christian faith in humanly developed theological statements, encourage both structure and freedom in theological discourse. Their openness to the personal and devotional dimensions of theological methods is a reminder of the arid arguments of sixteenth- to eighteenth-century successors to the Reformers and places a lively emphasis on the Spirit's activity in theological methods and discussions. Recollection and narration of historical experience, both communal and personal, and worship shape theological method and expression. While worship reflects theology in most communions, the Moravian worship shapes and empowers theology as relational and devotional and recalls significant events in the Unity's history. The Easter Liturgy, for example, is designed to be a confessional service. Citations from the Small Catechism's Explanations to the Apostles' Creed are prominent in the service. Perhaps we may draw a rough analogy between Lutherans and Moravians at this point: what the Confessions are to Lutherans, the Unity's history and worship are to Moravians.

In summary, Lutheran and Moravian theological methods differ from each other, yet we venture to conclude that the differences are mutually supportive and complementary. If Moravians counsel Lutherans about the divisive and self-defeating risks of doctrinal polemics, Lutherans counsel Moravians about the need to develop greater clarity and consistency in stating their interpretations of the faith. Both approaches need each other in order to undertake theological efforts which are carefully formulated and open to the power of God for the Church and the world. We turn now to some key Mutual Affirmations, and Complementarities.

NOTES

2. FC Ep, Part I, 1. Note that all references to the documents contained in the Lutheran Confessions are from *The Book of Concord: The Confessions of the Evangelical Lutheran Church*, trans. and ed. Theodore G. Tappert (Philadelphia: Fortress Press, 1959).
3. FC Ep, Part 1, 2.
4. FC SD, Rule and Norm, 3 and 4. Philip Melanchthon, author/compiler of the Augsburg Confession, re-edited and modified portions after 1530. While the original text and details about the presentation of the original Confession before Emperor Charles V at the Diet of Augsburg are uncertain, Lutherans have settled on a *textus receptus* in Latin and German which is termed the "Unaltered Augsburg Confession."
5. See FC SD, Rule and Norm, 8.
6. See FC SD, Rule and Norm, 6 and 8.
7. *Occasional Services* (Minneapolis: Augsburg-Fortress, 1982), 194, from the rite of ordination.
8. Especially Romans, Galatians, and Ephesians.
9. The most recent text of the *Ground of the Unity* is that revised by the Unity Synod (the international assembly of the Unity), which was held in 1995 in Dar es Salaam, Tanzania. The revision concerned no. 4, "God's Word and Doctrine." The following note accompanied the revision:

> The difficulty experienced with the formulation of 1957 was a wording adopted by the Synod which had never been used by the Moravian Church before. Moravians have always called Scripture "the only rule (norm, standard) of faith and doctrine." In the statement of 1957 it was for the first time also called "the only source" which was interpreted by some Moravians as meaning "the only source of information about everything." Moravians have also always believed that God was the source of their life, not just the book, as important as it is, which bears witness about God. Jesus in John 5:39 says that people search Scriptures because they think to have eternal life in them, but rather do they bear witness to him, the One who is the source of life.

For further information concerning the *Ground* prior to the changes of 1995, see C. Daniel Crews, *Confessing Our Unity in Christ: Historical and Theological Background to "The Ground of the Unity,"* prepared for presentation to the Moravian Clergy Association (January 6, 1994) and published at the request of the Provincial Elders Conference, Southern Province. The changes in no. 4 were proposed by the Northern and Southern Provinces in their 1994 and 1995 meetings prior to the international Synod; further suggestions were proposed by the Theological College in Mbeya, Tanzania, and then Unity Synod modified the text in the process of accepting it. As a source of doctrine we also call attention to the *Church Order of the Unitas Fratrum* (Moravian Church), published by the Moravian Church, *Unitas Fratrum* (Lansdowne, Republic of South Africa, 1988). The present version of this is as revised by the Unity Synod in Dar es Salaam, Tanzania, in 1995. This document, which is foundational for the Church Orders of all the provinces, includes *The Ground of the Unity*, *Essential Features of the Unity*, *Constitution of the Unitas Fratrum*, *Church Life in the Unitas Fratrum*, and *Mission Outreach*. The section on "Church Life" includes subsections on the important areas of sacraments and ministry. Besides these sources of doctrinal reflection and understanding, Moravians would call attention to the *Book of Worship*, especially the Easter Morning Liturgy, which is primarily a confession of the faith of the Church. Moravian Churches around the world may use various catechisms, and there is a history of various catechisms used in the North American Moravian Church, the last revision being *Catechism of the Moravian Church* published by Order of the Provincial Synod of 1956. On the history of Catechisms in the Moravian Church, see "Catechisms in the Moravian Church in America: A Brief Preliminary Report to the Interprovincial Faith and Order Commission" by C. Daniel Crews, November 1994 (unpublished). There is also the *Moravian Covenant for Christian Living* (previously called "the Brotherly Agreement"), which is supposedly signed by members of Moravian congregations and over the years has undergone numerous changes. This has its origin in the manorial rules signed by the congregation in Herrnhut in 1727. Since the 1960s this has had a doctrinal section at the beginning partially based on the *Ground of the Unity*.

B. Mutual Affirmations

The lines between Affirmations and Complementarities may be said to be more porous than they are either sharp or blurred. On the one hand, our backgrounds in the Reformation and Pietism, refracted through our experience in North America, result in significantly large areas of agreement. After all, we affirm the Reformation's principles in virtually identical terms. We seek to apply the Bible to our faith, practice, and mission. Our churches profess and use the three historic creeds of western Christianity, the doctrinal articles of the Augsburg Confession, and the Small Catechism. On the other hand, our backgrounds, experiences and present self-understandings lead us to express ourselves differently in doctrinal and liturgical methods and attitudes. The differences, however, prove to be mutually supportive and enriching—hence the porosity between Affirmations and Complementarities. Put simply, we are not clones one of the other, but sheep from the same fold called to journey more closely with one another as we follow our Shepherd.

Three interpenetrating and important areas fit the description "Mutual Affirmations," and deserve particular comment. Our churches expect to recognize in each other substantial agreement on the nature of the Gospel and on the sacraments. The dialoguers also realized that the Biblical-Reformation principle of justification is essential to that agreement. In presentations and discussions we explored our historical and theological understandings of the Word of God as the traditional framework for the three areas. The dialogue showed that our respective communions have comparable spectrums of diverse attitudes toward and positions on the Word as Law and Gospel and as Scripture. We discerned no significant differences between our churches in content, our attitudes toward, and methods of understanding the Word of God. To aid our churches in the movement toward full communion, the dialoguers concluded that it would be helpful to discuss our mutual affirmations on the Gospel of God in Jesus Christ, Justification By Faith, and the Sacraments.

1. The Gospel

Moravians and Lutherans affirm the centrality, power, and authority of the Gospel in Jesus Christ. God's revelation in and through the Gospel may be expressed in conceptual terms, yet it is far more than doctrines and formulas. Indeed, the Gospel is not an "it;" the Gospel is a person, Jesus of Nazareth. He is the Word made human, alive and present in, with and through our experiences, dilemmas and hopes. He is God in person, that is, really present in every area and situation of life as well as by personally relating God's grace and acceptance to us.

To believe in the Gospel is to trust with our whole beings and to profess in our words and actions that Jesus is our Savior and Shepherd. Through his incarnation, death, resurrection and exaltation, he seals God's promises to be with his people and to raise them to eternal life. The message of God's presence and assurance of everlasting fellowship is proclaimed as saving good news in the Scripture, heard in preaching and words of reconciliation spoken by believers, and made visible in the sacraments. This message is named Jesus; he is the divine Promise in fully human form.

Lutherans and Moravians affirm that all persons need the Gospel because we are sinners unable to merit God's favor. Left to ourselves, we are in bondage to evil and headed toward spiritual death. The good news in Christ, however, bestows forgiveness from and reconciliation with God. Jesus' death and resurrection break the power of sin and evil. Moreover, we agree that God's mercy is inseparable from our being renewed through the

Spirit to serve God and do God's will. To believe the Gospel, that is, to trust in Christ's gift of life through grace produces "good fruits and good works."[10]

At the same time, Moravians and Lutherans agree that believers are far from being perfect. We experience the Word of God as Law as well as Gospel. The Law calls humans to account, accusing us of sin, and driving us to God's mercy in Christ. The Law of God continually sends us to the Gospel and to Jesus, for the Gospel gives us freely what the Law demands of us. Given the dialectic of Law and Gospel, Lutherans and Moravians agree that through the actions of Law and Gospel we are simultaneously sinners and justified. Further, we discuss within our communions the role of the Law in the life and conduct of believers. However we may debate that role of the Law within our churches, we are convinced that the Law is never a means to salvation; we rely fully on the Gospel, the grace of God in Jesus Christ. Concomitantly, our understanding of the persistence of sin leads us to the joint understanding that the realm of political, cultural and organizational structures are to be ruled and judged by God's Law. Neither Moravians nor Lutherans are utopians who expect the Kingdom of God to come through human efforts and arrangements. At the same time, we understand ourselves to be called by God to participate in society as responsible citizens and to seek justice for all persons.

In order to communicate the Gospel faithfully, Lutherans and Moravians proclaim Christ according to the Holy Scriptures. As noted in the *Ground of the Unity* and the *Formula of Concord*, we understand Scripture to be our guide, norm and source for teachings, practices and conduct. Because Moravians and Lutherans understand the Scripture as the normative witness to Jesus Christ for the Church, we affirm scriptural authority without being biblical literalists. We employ historical and other analytical and scholarly means to understand biblical texts and meanings. When we affirm the Reformation principle sola Scriptura, "Scripture alone," we mean, at the very least, that no ecclesiastical authority or pious custom can impose doctrines, actions, and attitudes on persons as conditions for their reconciliation with and salvation by God which are not clearly enjoined in the Scripture.

In summary, Lutherans and Moravians understand the Gospel to be personal and relational, expressed in human form in Jesus. He engages persons and communities, challenges and encouraging them to see, hear and follow him in discipleship. We understand that Gospel to give us freely what the Law demands of us by bringing us into fellowship with Jesus, our Savior-Shepherd. Moravians and Lutherans, then, agree with and affirm each other's understandings of the Gospel, the Scriptures, and the relationship of Law and Gospel.

2. Justification

Lutherans and Moravians share the same emphases and understandings of the biblical and Reformation theme of justification by faith through grace without works of the Law.[11] This doctrine concerns Law and Gospel as well as the role of Jesus. In this area Moravians and Lutherans are in agreement and mutual affirmation on the Reformation principles *sola gratia* (by grace alone) and *sola fide* (by faith alone). There are numerous models which are used biblically and in the Church's history to express the content of justification, yet the point is that God forgives and is reconciled with sinners not by the merits or deeds or worthiness of the sinners but solely by divine free, gracious will and action in and through Jesus Christ. The divine gift is grasped by believers who are called, enlightened, and led to faith through the Holy Spirit.

Once more, our common grounding in the Reformation and the development of the Reformation through Pietism leads Moravians and Lutherans to express themselves clearly about the graciousness of God in justifying sinners and imparting to them the Spirit through Christ. Moravians will speak in terms of the Lamb who was slain and being clothed in his righteousness. One of Zinzendorf's hymns expresses the thought and devotion:

> The Savior's blood and righteousness
> My beauty is, my glorious dress;
> Thus well-arrayed, I need not fear,
> When in his presence I appear.
> The holy, spotless Lamb of God,
> Who freely gave his life and blood
> For all my numerous sins to atone,
> I for my Lord and Saviour own.
> Therefore my Saviour's blood and death
> Are here the substance of my faith;
> And shall remain, when I'm called hence,
> My only hope and confidence.
> Lord Jesus Christ, all praise to thee,
> That thou didst deign a man to be,
> And for each soul which thou hast made

Hast an eternal ransom paid.
Thy incarnation, wounds and death
I will confess while I have breath,
Till I shall see thee face to face
Arrayed with thy righteousness.[12]

Historically Lutherans have tended to use a forensic model of justification in which punishment and condemnation are juxtaposed against justification. A late sixteenth century Lutheran theologian wrote that Romans 8 clearly shows "the proper and true meaning of the word 'justify.' . . . It agrees entirely with the forensic meaning, that we are absolved before the judgment of God, for Christ's sake, from the guilt of sin and from damnation, pronounced just, and received to eternal life. . . . The Law accuses all of being under sin. Every mouth is stopped, and the whole world is made to stand guilty before God, because by the works of the Law no flesh is justified. But we are justified freely by his grace, through the redemption, etc. . . . [The] meaning of the word justify is judicial, namely that the sinner, accused by the Law of God, convicted, and subjected to the sentence of eternal damnation, fleeing in faith to the throne of grace, is absolved for Christ's sake, reckoned and declared righteous, received into grace, and accepted to eternal life."[13]

Both churches teach that sinners are justified by Christ through grace and are called by the Spirit to newness of life. While believers still may sin and need the accusatory use of the Law to humble them, they are nevertheless still justified. Forgiveness and renewal, mercy and transformation are inseparable. That is, forgiveness is not the terminal point of justification. Forgiveness is reception into life with God in the Church, and so leads to discipleship. Justification leads to discipleship (a distinctive Moravian theme) and the new obedience (a Lutheran term rooted in the *Augsburg Confession*, article 8).

To summarize: Lutherans and Moravians agree with and affirm one another's views of justification. This agreement and affirmation also includes our understanding of the Gospel.

3. The Sacraments

Explorations of our respective positions concerning the sacraments are both simple and complex. The simple or uncomplicated aspect is that we agree fully on there being two sacraments, baptism and the Lord's Supper, and our theologies concerning those sacraments are in harmony, perhaps total agreement. This is not surprising since the Small Catechism has not only been used and cherished by Lutherans but has played a significant role historically in the Moravian Church.

Both of us practice infant baptism and maintain the Real Presence of Christ in the Eucharist. Complexity enters through the emphases, explications, and expectations we have in these areas. Again, there is agreement and affirmation, but not uniformity. Again, we learned from one another.

A basic, far-reaching question is why we have sacraments at all? An obvious, profound answer is, "Because Christ commanded his followers to baptize and to share the Supper." Probing the response raises several factors.

First, we are commanded to administer and participate in the sacraments because we are human beings, not disembodied spirits. We need the sacraments. They are physical means through which God addresses us with the divine message of salvation. The sacraments are the Word of God in visible, tangible, even tasteable form. That Word is so intimately conjoined to the earthly elements of water, bread and wine that these elements are bearers of God's revelation of grace to men and women. In, with, and under the physical materials is God's Word—Christ—speaking, cleansing, nourishing, and renewing his people. Because we are bodily creatures, we need the Word in physical as well as spoken form.

Second, we are commanded to administer and participate in the sacraments because we are anxious sinners. The sacraments are God's Word of reconciling assurance, mercy and hope to persons who are in despair, have troubled consciences, and realize their unworthiness. Here the sacraments are active demonstrations of God's justifying grace. While we are yet sinners, helpless to merit divine favor, and alienated from God, God comes to us. The sacraments meet us in our futility and weakness to proclaim purpose and to offer us strength. The sacraments provide us with another means by which we can know of God's faithfulness, and they are an anchor for our faith.

Third, we are commanded to administer and participate in the sacraments because we need the external forms to structure our spiritual responses. The Reformation contained movements which advocated the jettisoning of physical forms in favor of direct or unmediated revelations through persons who claimed special inspirations and insights. The sacraments keep us earthbound, furnish us with a framework which gives us a sense of order in order for the God who created the world to approach us with saving grace in the incarnate Lord.

Fourth, we are commanded to administer and participate in the sacraments because they offer us individual and communal identities. Both baptism and Eucharist name and designate us as members of the Body of Christ and heirs of the Kingdom through Jesus. The Lord who promises to be with us in all conditions knows us by name, by our unique beings, and so incorporates us into the death and resurrection of Jesus, cleanses us from sin, reveals Christ's presence, nourishes us, assures us of forgiveness, and empowers us to new life in the Spirit. While the Word of God in its other forms also testifies of these gifts, the sacraments convey these to us through creaturely means. A corollary of the same point is that the sacraments are means by which the Holy Spirit engages us as individuals and for mission in the world.

Behind the bare commandments to baptize and to share the supper is God's promise of grace. The sacraments are the Gospel in visible form. Through the Gospel, God evokes, sustains, and nourishes the faith by which we are united with Christ and receive his salvation. Another way to express the same idea is to say that through the Gospel, God enters into a personal relationship with us. The sacraments are visible means which form and express that relationship.

Since agreement concerning the sacraments is a major issue in ecumenical discussions, it is appropriate to continue our mutual affirmations further.

a. Sacrament of Baptism

Lutherans and Moravians agree with and affirm one another's positions that through baptism we are initiated into the Church, are united to Christ by the Spirit, and enter into a covenantal relationship with God and our fellow Christians. Through baptism we undertake our life journeys in God's grace and grow in faith through the Spirit. The covenantal dimensions of baptism are stated in our liturgies. At the beginning of the sacramental rite, a Moravian officiant says,

> In grace God called and chose the people of Israel and established with them a covenant: I will be your God and you will be my people. In that relationship they were to be freed from sin and become a blessing to all. Then God came to us in Jesus Christ and fulfilled that covenant for all people. Through Christ's life, death, and resurrection, God made for us a new covenant of grace. . . .

> Our Lord Jesus Christ instituted baptism as the visible means of entry into the new covenant. Baptism is a gift of God. In this sacrament, through grace and the power of the Holy Spirit, we are united with Christ, are cleansed by his saving work, enter into the fellowship of the church, and are called to a life of faith and willing obedience.[14]

The Lutheran officiant begins,

> In Holy Baptism our gracious heavenly Father liberates us from sin and death by joining us to the death and resurrection of our Lord Jesus Christ. We are born children of a fallen humanity: in the waters of Baptism we are reborn children of God and inheritors of eternal life. By water and the Holy Spirit we are made members of the Church which is the Body of Christ. As we live with him and with his people, we grow in faith, love, and obedience to the will of God.[15]

We also share understanding baptism to involve ongoing growth in the Spirit. The Lutheran minister charges the parents of infants and young children who are to be baptized:

> In Christian love you have presented these children for Holy Baptism. You should, therefore, faithfully bring them to the services of God's house, and teach them the Lord's Prayer, the Creed, and the Ten Commandments. As they grow in years, you should place in their hands the Holy Scriptures and provide for their instruction in the Christian faith, that, living in the covenant of their baptism and in communion with the Church, they may lead godly lives until the day of Jesus Christ.[16]

The Moravian minister asks,

> Relying on the power of the Holy Spirit, do you promise to lead your children by prayer, instruction, and example toward that time when they can by grace confirm their faith in the Lord Jesus Christ and commit themselves to the life and work of the church?[17]

Both rites provide for the congregation to welcome the newly baptized into the whole Church through the acclamation of the congregation.[18]

We noted that Moravians and Lutherans consider the rite of confirmation to be an affirmation of baptism. The respective liturgies echo the promises made by parents and sponsors at the baptism of infants and children.[19]

To summarize: Lutherans and Moravians agree with and affirm one another's views of the Sacrament of Baptism.

b. Sacrament of Communion

Moravians and Lutherans agree that Jesus calls the community of believers to be a communion in the Spirit, united in love, and sent to serve. Further, we agree that the Sacrament celebrates this communion, strengthens the bonds of mutual relationships, and promises that God will be with us as we live in the world. Still further, we agree that the Eucharist is "for you and for the forgiveness of sins, life, and salvation are given to us in the sacrament, for where there is forgiveness of sins, there are also life and salvation" (*Small Catechism*, VI).

From the sixteenth to the present century Lutherans have engaged in significant intra-church and ecumenical debates which have centered in the "Real Presence" of Christ in, with, and under the forms of bread and wine. The concerns expressed include whether or not there is a change of substance in the elements, the relation of ordained ministers to the Eucharist, the natures of the Christ who is present, whether the grace of God is diminished by stressing the recipients' faith, and communing with and/or under the auspices of Christians who do not hold the same theological views. Moravians, wary of past polemics and aware of the need for humans to be humble when describing God's ways, appreciate the concerns involved in discussing Christ's presence. Lutherans and Moravians agreed that in the Lord's Supper, Christ gives his body and blood according to his promise to all who partake of the elements. When we eat and drink the bread and the wine of the Supper with expectant faith, we thereby have communion with the body and blood of our Lord and receive the forgiveness of sins, life, and salvation. In this sense, the bread and wine are rightly said to be Christ's body and blood which he gives to his disciples. We are united with Jesus in the Supper and with one another in the fellowship of his body, and we enjoy a foretaste of the great marriage feast of the Lamb. We joyfully confess the mystery of the Lord's Supper in the faith that the love of Christ knows no limits, acknowledging that no human theory can fully or finally account for it.

As anticipated, Moravian liturgies indicate the breadth and depth of their understandings of communion. This may be seen in the Unity's having not one general communion liturgy but four. Each of the four reflects distinct themes correlated to the Church Year.[20] As anticipated, congregational singing and an emphasis on the relationship of the worshipers to one another are prominent. The opening rubric of all the communion services is "The congregation gives the right hand of fellowship, signifying oneness in Christ and the desire to be at peace with one another." The hymn which follows the handshake of peace in the communion liturgies for "Celebration of Christ's Coming" and "Celebration of the Resurrection" illustrates well the twin themes of the unity of believers and the covenantal relationship with God in Christ:

> We covenant with hand and heart to follow Christ our Lord;
> with world, and sin, and self to part, and to obey his word;
> to love each other heartily, in truth and with sincerity,
> and under cross, reproach, and shame, to glorify his name.[21]

The Moravian concern is not for the mode or extent of Christ's presence; they understand that Jesus is fully present with his promises and gifts in manners which God determines and actualizes through the Spirit. A distinctive Moravian contribution is the emphasis on the covenantal unity shared by God, the individual, the local fellowship of believers, and the whole Body of Christ. One hymn in the communion liturgy for atonement expresses it well for both Lutherans and Moravians:[22]

> Own your congregation, gracious Paschal Lamb; we are here assembled in your holy name;
> look upon your people whom you by your blood have in love redeemed and brought nigh to God.
> You have kindly led us through our joys and tears; now accept our praises and remove our fears.
> Grant us all with gladness to obey your voice; let your will and pleasure be our only choice.
> May your church arrayed in the glorious dress of the Lord and Savior's spotless righteousness,
> be both now and forever by your blood kept clean, and in all its members may your grace be seen.

To summarize: Moravians and Lutherans agree with and affirm one another's understandings of the Sacrament of Communion.

The Mutual Affirmations indicate diversity within our agreements, yet the affirmations are extensive, profound, and unforced. Our summary of the summaries at this point is that Lutherans and Moravians agree with and affirm one another's understandings of the Gospel and Sacraments.

NOTES

10. AC, VI. Our liturgies reflect these views with remarkable similarities. *The Moravian Book of Worship* (MBW) (Bethlehem and Winston-Salem: The Moravian Church in America, 1995) reflects phrasings which appear also in the *Lutheran Book of Worship* (LBW) (Minneapolis and Philadelphia: Augsburg Publishing House and Board of Publication, Lutheran Church in America, 1978). Our churches share the following almost verbatim:

    > Most merciful God, we confess that we have sinned against you in thought, word, and deed, by what we have done and by what we have left undone. We have not loved you with our whole heart; we have not loved our neighbors as ourselves. We are truly sorry, and we humbly repent. For the sake of your Son Jesus Christ, have mercy on us and forgive us, that we may delight in your will, and walk in your ways, to the glory of your name. Amen. (MBW, General Liturgy 3, 21)

    See LBW:

    > Most merciful God, we confess that we are in bondage to sin and cannot free ourselves. We have sinned against you in thought, word, and deed, by what we have done and by what we have left undone. We have not loved you with our whole heart; we have not loved our neighbors as ourselves. For the sake of your Son, Jesus Christ, have mercy on us. Forgive us, renew us, and lead us, so that we may delight in your will and walk in your ways, to the glory of your holy name. Amen. (56; repeated on 77, 98)

    The dialoguers recognized that the biblical themes we used varied not in content but proportion. Moravians tend to look first to the life of Jesus as presented in the Gospel of John, and then they move toward the Pauline writings. Lutherans realized they usually began with Paul, especially the epistles to the Galatians, Romans, and Ephesians. Both Lutherans and Moravians rely substantially on the Fourth Gospel for understanding Jesus as the Word of God.

11. A current theological discussion deals with the nuances of stating the principle as "justification by faith through grace" and "justification by grace through faith." The dialoguers did not enter discussions on that issue. For the sake of consistency and

without making a commitment on either side of the question, this report uses "justification by faith through grace."

12. The hymn is no. 327 in the 1969 *Hymnal of the Moravian Church.* A modernized translation is in the new MBW (Hymn 776), and a portion is used in one of the communion rituals (p. 201). The "dress of righteousness" reflects Luther's view of the righteousness of God which is "alien" to humanity; see Luther's sermon on "The Two Kinds of Righteousness" (LW, vol. 31, 293-306). Note also in the *Lutheran Service Book and Hymnal* hymn 376, in which verses two through four are by Zinzendorf and express the same ideas.
13. Martin Chemnitz, *Examination of the Council of Trent*, Part 1, trans. Fred Kramer (St. Louis: Concordia, 1971), 473-474. Melanchthon also used the juridical or forensic model, Apol., Article 4, sections 304-305.
14. MBW, 165.
15. LBW, 121.
16. LBW, 121.
17. MBW, 166.
18. See LBW, 124ff, and MBW, 69. In the Moravian liturgy the acclamation is through a hymn of welcome, which also includes the motif of growth in grace and the congregation's pledge of love.
19. MBW, 170-174, and LBW, 198-201.
20. The four themes are *In Celebration of Christ's Coming*, of *the Atonement*, of *the Resurrection*, and of *the Holy Spirit.* There are seven "General Liturgies" (General, Reconciliation, Adoration, Creation, Grace, Discipleship, and Celebration). A series of other liturgies related to the liturgical calendar and a number of topical liturgies in addition to a cluster of occasional services complete the roster of liturgies. The Lutheran liturgical tradition reflected in the LBW has three different musical settings of what is basically the same service, Holy Communion; a number of formats tied to the times of worship (e.g., morning and evening prayer, compline); other types of services (e.g., Service of the Word, Responsive Prayer, etc.); and some occasional services.
21. The hymn "In Celebration of the Atonement" is "Come, then, come, O flock of Jesus, covenant with him anew; unto him, who conquered for us, pledge we love and service true; let our mutual love be glowing; thus will the world plainly see that we, as on one stem growing, living branches are in thee."

    The hymn "In Celebration of the Holy Spirit" is "I come with joy to meet my Lord, forgiven loved, and free; in awe and wonder to recall his life laid down for me. As Christ breaks bread and bids us share, each proud division ends; the love that made us, makes us one, and strangers now are friends."
22. MBW, 205.

C. Mutual Complementarities

A complement is neither a compliment nor a supplement. The former praises, while the latter appends something related but different to the original. A complement completes an idea or position, moves a discussion or practice toward consummation, expands on what is already present so that the original reaches toward wholeness. Throughout the dialogue, Lutherans and Moravians recognized and discovered complementarities. Sometimes those complementarities were related to our methods and forms of expressing our positions and perspectives. In those instances, one partner discerned that what we said in our separate ways could be enriched by listening to the other's agreement with and expansion of the statement and practice. At other times the position of one illumined a theme which the other had de-emphasized over time, thereby encouraging both to recover and consider cultivating what was present. On still other occasions, we informed one another of problems which our respective traditions had encountered but which could be seen now, with the assistance and prodding of the other to be valued and helpful in our present contexts. Our reciprocal and mutual searching for and finding moved us to appreciate our respective teachings and practices while we deepened our progress toward recommending that our churches establish full communion with each other.

Three areas of complementarities are tightly linked to one another, our methods, and Affirmations. Moreover, each involves the Holy Spirit's involvement with the believer, the Church, and ministry. The three areas are (1) the Holy Spirit, the Believer, and the Christian Life; (2) the Holy Spirit in the Church; and (3) Our Churches' Ministry and Polity. A preliminary comment is in order. While our respective bodies would benefit from thorough examinations and expositions of our understandings about and experiences of the Holy Spirit, this report is limited in scope and purpose. Our joint grounding in the Bible provides us with a wealth of images, ideas, learnings, and perspectives on the interactions of the Spirit within the Godhead, humanity, nature, history, the Church, believers, and the consummation of all existence. Moravians and Lutherans believe, teach, and confess faith in the Triune God in terms which are recognized and confirmed throughout the one, holy, catholic, and apostolic Church. Because both churches have had to respond to significant challenges related to the Spirit, each is cautious, perhaps overly so, when discussing the Spirit's roles in revelation, the lives of individual believers, and the witness of the whole Church. In the present, however, Christians in many communions are overcoming their anxieties related to the Spirit and are recognizing as well as recovering positive and creative emphases about the Spirit.

Among the texts Moravians and Lutherans share is the *Explanation of the Third Article of the Apostles' Creed* in Luther's *Small Catechism*:[23]

> I believe that by my own reason or strength I cannot believe in Jesus Christ, my Lord, or come to him. But the Holy Spirit has called me through the Gospel, enlightened me with his gifts, and sanctified and preserved me in true faith, just as he calls, gathers, enlightens, and sanctifies the whole Christian church on earth and preserves it in union with Jesus Christ in the one true faith. In this Christian church he daily and abundantly forgives all my sins, and the sins of all believers, and on the last day he will raise me and all the dead and will grant eternal life to me and all who believe in Christ. This is most certainly true.

Several articles of another commonly held document, the *Augsburg Confession*, express the same views.[24] The Catechism's statement presupposes the positions and ambiguities developed by the Church over the centuries concerning issues such as the substance, persons, begottenness of the Son, procession of the Spirit, and others related to the Godhead. These matters have never been at issue between Lutherans and Moravians. Likewise, the Explanation does not deal with a number of important areas involving the Spirit, e.g., creation, providence, and wisdom. These may be explored fruitfully in other and subsequent venues.

1. *The Holy Spirit, the Believer and the Christian Life*

The Catechism's Explanations of the first and second articles of the Creed open with the believer's awareness of God's loving care for the person and conclude with the Christian's looking forward in trust and joy to serving the Creator and Redeemer. The central sections of the initial two Explanations present humans as totally helpless to undertake any actions which deserve or merit divine favor, while God is praised for the gifts and assurances which provide for temporal and eternal life.[25] Luther's Third Explanation, however, provides an energy and coherence for the article which can be seen retrospectively as crucial for the other two articles and which extends into the believer's faith, deeds, and relationships. That energy and coherence engage Lutherans and Moravians in agreeing and complementing one another's faith and practice. To illumine our complementarities in this area, we present three points concerning the Spirit's relationship with individual believers which grow out of the following: (a) all persons need the Spirit in order to come to faith in Christ; (b) Christians still need the Spirit to admonish and call them to repentance even though they are justified; and (c) the Spirit is the source and power of sanctification in the life of the believer.

First, although language expressing justification by faith is not used directly, justification, as Moravians and Lutherans affirm it, suffuses and shapes the Explanation's views of humans and Jesus. Parenthetically, that a forensic or other mode of expressing justification is not used here points to the realization that justification is not and cannot be limited to one or another mode. Yet the Catechism takes us deeper. It insists that only through the Spirit can one believe in or come to Jesus as her or his Lord and Savior.

Here as elsewhere, Lutherans underscore justification through grace, whatever the mode or metaphor, deriving their understandings from Pauline, Augustinian, and Reformation sources. These sources stress the sovereignty of God's power to save, and stress that God's will to save through grace is mediated via the Spirit.

Lutherans recognize that there is no other way for us to enter a saving relationship with God except through God's action. The Spirit is that Person of the Trinity through whom we know Christ and the Creator. Moreover, the Spirit generates in us the faith needed to grasp the grace offered so that we may come to Christ and the Maker of all. Lutherans regard justification as "the main doctrine of Christianity. . . . when properly understood, it illumines and magnifies the honor of Christ and brings to pious consciences the abundant consolation that they need."[26] There can be no doubt or compromise, Lutherans claim, about the clarity and certainty that we are justified by faith alone without works of the Law as a gift of God's grace in Christ.[27] Certainly, Lutherans understand justification to be on the basis of Christ's sacrifice, so that through his death and resurrection we have both the promises and the reality of the forgiveness of sins and reconciliation with God. Indeed, the "Gospel is, strictly speaking, the promise of forgiveness of sins and justification because of Christ."[28] And all these "benefits" of Christ are given through the Spirit.

The Lutheran expression of the point that all persons need the Spirit in order to come to faith in Christ has a sonority and passionate logic born of the heat of debates and controversies in the sixteenth and subsequent centuries—and which are still current today. While not losing sight of the incarnate Lord, Lutherans are determined to express their views of the

Spirit, justification, and the Christian life in terms which deny any hint of works of righteousness or human merit which might prompt God's favor. Relying on Pauline terms and their Reformation heritage, Lutherans see and listen to contemporary society, including church life, as prone to both works righteousness and a careless sentimentality about God's love. A Lutheran contribution and complement at this juncture is a staunch insistence on justification as an unmerited gift from God through the Spirit.

The Moravian perspective complements the Lutheran view. Moravians highlight justification as the believer entering a personal relationship with Jesus through the Spirit. The Unity agrees fully that justification is by faith, apart from works of the Law, and recognizes justification as a God-given assurance that the person belongs to and in Jesus. In other words, while recognizing justification as a core doctrine, Moravians express their understanding of it more naturally as God's gracious invitation for a person to walk with the Savior. This fits with the Catechism Explanation's consistent use of the personal pronouns "I, me, and mine." The Spirit is the Person of the Trinity who sheds God's grace abroad in the hearts of men and women so that they come to trust in, depend upon, and live in fellowship with one another as they follow Jesus. *The Ground of the Unity*, in a passage cited earlier, states that each individual is called personally and is led to a recognition of her or his sin, culminating in accepting the redemption achieved by Christ. The Spirit "effects living belief in the hearts of individuals."[29] There is no room here, either, for works righteousness or human pride. Again, a hymn expresses it well:

> Faith is a living power from heaven
> that grasps the promise that God has giv'n,
> a trust that can't be overthrown
> fixed heartily on Christ alone.
> Faith finds in Christ our every need
> to save or strengthen us indeed;
> we now receive that grace sent down,
> which makes us share his cross and crown.
> Faith in the conscience works for peace,
> and bids the mourner's weeping cease,
> by faith the children's place we claim,
> and give all honor to one name.
> We thank you, then, O God of heav'n,
> that you to us this faith have given

In Jesus Christ your Son, who is
our only fount and source of bliss.[30]

The Moravian experience of the Spirit in the life of the believer was not shaped by the polemics of the Reformation but by the Brethren's endurance in the Ancient Church, the "period of the hidden seed," its renewal in Continental Pietism, and its internal struggles to be faithful to the power of the Spirit and the need for witnessing to Christ as individuals and as a community. Especially under the influence of continental Pietism, the *Unitas Fratrum* came to depict the Christian life as a pilgrimage with Jesus as the Leader and Companion through joys and sorrows. The journey's goal, whether called heaven or salvation, was undertaken humbly and gratefully with the Lord in the Spirit.

Zinzendorf's hymn, also used by Lutherans, puts justification through grace in terms of that journey:

Jesus, still lead on till our rest be won;
and although the way be cheerless, we will follow calm
and fearless;
guide us by your hand to the promised land.
If the way be drear, if the foe be near,
let no faithless fears o'ertake us, let not faith and hope
forsake us;
safely past the foe to our home we go.
When we seek relief from a long-felt grief,
when temptations come alluring, make us patient
and enduring;
show us that bright shore where we weep no more.
Jesus, still lead on till our rest be won;
heav'nly leader still direct us, still support, console, protect us,
still we safely stand in the promised land.[31]

Moravians and Lutherans complement each other in agreeing on the point of the need for the Spirit in engendering faith through our central affirmation on justification through grace by means of the Spirit. Lutherans seek to maintain the grace of God bestowed through the Spirit against any shadow of human works and worth. The Unity endeavors to ensure that the believer realizes that clearly we need both dimensions in understanding the wonder and grace of God. The second point is that it is impossible for anyone to claim that a person's faith, devotion, and experiences of God are due to human worthiness or effort in any measure at all. A believer becomes a believer only through the Spirit; and so a person is totally dependent upon God for belief, piety, and good works. The radical nature of human helplessness before God asserts divine sovereignty in salvation, but that sovereignty is recognized and realized through the Spirit who testifies to and applies the grace of Christ in and for humans. In and through the Spirit, a lost and condemned creature's heart and mind are strengthened and enlightened to recognize God's redemptive action in Jesus. Faith is the result of the Spirit's gracious action; without the Spirit, there can be no saving relationship with Jesus. The person who affirms, "This is most certainly true," can make that statement in faith because the Spirit has led and inspired the individual to confess the truth about the Truth, and then to walk on the Way through resurrection, and to abide with God just as Christ and the Father abide together.

Nevertheless, although declared righteous through Christ, the justified person is still a sinner. She or he cannot assume that now good works will earn further care or favor from God. The Spirit's dual function of accuser and comforter applies to the Christian. Through the Spirit, the believer becomes acutely conscious of both the depths of one's sin and the immensity of God's love bestowed through Christ. The Spirit both troubles and calms the believer's conscience. Christians are driven repeatedly to God's mercy in Jesus. They know that they have been redeemed not with silver or gold but with Jesus' innocent sufferings and death. Each day the believer realizes that the Spirit searches the depths of human hearts and each day forgives sins so that the person "may be Christ's and live under him" and "serve him in everlasting righteousness, innocence and blessedness."

The Moravian complement, as anticipated, looks toward Jesus. He is the suffering yet triumphant Lamb, the crucified and forgiving Lord. His sin-healing wounds and blood present the objective reality of God's reconciling love for humanity. Especially through the influence of Pietism as developed by Zinzendorf, the Renewed Unity affirms that centrality of the cross which eliminates any ground for human worthiness or pride. Paradoxically, the Savior's pain and death turn the believer not toward gloom and guilt but to an ever-fuller and more joyful dependence on God's grace and love. One of Christian Renatus Zinzendorf's hymns conveys the follower's heartfelt devotion to and hope in Jesus:

My Redeemer, overwhelmed with anguish, went to Oliviet
for me;
there he kneels, his heart does heave and languish in a
bitter agony;
fear and horror seize his soul and senses,
for the hour of darkness now commences;
ah, how he does weep and groan our rebellion to atone.
Could our hearts and voices then join forces in exalted
songs to raise;
yet, till joined to the celestial chorus, cold would prove our
warmest praise;
Jesus love exceeds all comprehension,
but our love to him we scarce dare mention;
we may weep beneath his cross, but he wept and bled for us.
Lamb of God, you shall remain forever of our songs the
only theme;
for your boundless love, your grace and favor, we will praise
your saving name;
that for our transgressions you were wounded
shall by us in nobler strains be sounded,
when we, perfected in love, once shall join the church above.[32]

The Lutheran complement on the impossibility for humans to claim they are worthy of God's grace at any time may be seen clearly in terms of the Word of God as Law and Gospel. The Law continues to apply to the regenerate because of the persistence of the Old Adam even among those justified by faith. The condemnatory use of the Law drives the Christian away from any security based on human works or worthiness and urges the believer to cling to God's grace in Christ more fervently. Christ is the "mirror of the Father's heart" apart from whom "we see nothing but an angry and terrible Judge." The Law is the mirror "in which the will of God and what is pleasing to him is correctly portrayed." The Spirit employs the Law to teach, admonish, warn, threaten and punish Christians, "egging them on so that they may follow the Spirit of God." Lutherans are acutely aware that while the "perfect obedience of Christ covers" the sins of Christians "so that [those sins] are not reckoned to believers for damnation, and although the Holy Spirit has begun the mortification of the Old Adam and their renewal in the spirit of their minds, nevertheless the Old Adam still clings to their nature and to all its internal and external powers."[33]

This point of complementarity may be summarized from the Moravian perspective as a concentration on Jesus' passion, which binds believers to a personal engagement with the incarnate Word of God who truly suffered and died in giving himself for sinners. In this engagement, the Christian is drawn by the Spirit to follow the Lord humbly and thankfully. The Lutheran complement hews closely to the Law-Gospel construction which Lutherans hold is important in discerning God's will. The Lutheran contribution aids in avoiding a cloying attachment to a helpless Christ while presenting God's gracious action with intensity and clarity. Again, Lutherans and Moravians gain from one another.

The third point of complementarity under consideration deals with the continual presence and activity of the Spirit within the believer; justification is inseparable from sanctification, and sanctification leads the person into fuller awareness of God's justifying sinners by faith through grace, and calling them to live according to their calling to holiness and eternal life. A Christian is called, enlightened, sanctified, and preserved in the true faith. The person who is declared justified, who is dressed in the righteousness of Christ, is nevertheless still a sinner. The sanctifying task of the Spirit is to lead, guide, admonish, strengthen, and, when needed, expose the believer in the believer's growth in grace. Here the Catechism prepares for the Catechism's Explanation to the Lord's Prayer and foreshadows the *Augsburg Confession*'s Article 6:

> [In response to the Prayer's second petition] To be sure, the Kingdom of God comes of itself, without our prayer, but we pray in this petition that it may also come to us. . . . the heavenly Father gives us his Holy Spirit so that by his grace we may believe his holy Word and live a godly life, both here in time and hereafter forever.
>
> [Article 6's traditional title is "The New Obedience."] It is also taught among us that such faith should produce good fruits and good works and that we must do all such good works as God has commanded, but we should do them for God's sake and not place our trust in them as if thereby to merit favor before God. For we receive forgiveness of sin and righteousness through faith.

While faith may be construed as accepting right or orthodox doctrines, the Reformation meaning is far more powerful. In a passage cherished by Moravians and Lutherans alike, Luther wrote,

> Faith, however, is a divine work in us which changes us and makes us to be born anew of God. . . . It kills the old Adam and makes us altogether different men, in heart and spirit and mind and powers; and it brings with it the Holy Spirit. O it is a living, busy, active, mighty thing, this faith. It is impossible for it not to be doing good works incessantly. . . . Faith is a living, daring confidence in God's grace, so sure and certain that the believer would stake his life on it a thousand times. This knowledge of and confidence in God's grace makes men glad and bold and happy in dealing with God and with all creatures. And this is the work which the Holy Spirit performs in faith.[34]

The work of the Spirit may be quiet, steady and gradual. And the Spirit may engender boldness, joy, and confidence. The Spirit's work in the believer's life may be seen in a person's works and words. It may also be felt in the Christian's heart as a warmth, openness, and acceptance generated by trusting that the Spirit seals what Christ has won for our salvation.

Lutherans and Moravians agree fully that the Spirit is active in the life of the believer in ways which lead to the individual's growth in grace. Growth in the Spirit is also growth in the grace which assures us of forgiveness, strengthens us to do God's will, emboldens us to witness to Christ, and draws us ever closer to God and the members of the Body of Christ.

Lutherans, wary of any signs that justification by faith through grace might be compromised, are equally concerned that a legalistic view of human conduct will assert itself. Lutherans are aware that legalism leads to a tyranny over conscience and action, even when advocated for the sake of God's will. The Gospel offers freedom through which the Spirit moves Christians to just and compassionate decisions and deeds. Experience with distortions in pietism and orthodoxy as well as tendencies in North American society legitimate such concerns. In addition, Lutherans are still debating among themselves the role of the Law in the life of the believer. Nonetheless and by whatever means the Spirit may employ, Lutherans agree that we grow in grace through the Spirit. Luther wrote,

> Neither you nor I could ever know anything of Christ, or believe in him and take him as our Lord, unless these were first offered

> to us and bestowed on our hearts through the preaching of the Gospel by the Holy Spirit. The work is finished and completed, Christ has acquired and won the treasure for us by his sufferings, death and resurrection, etc. But if the work remained hidden and no one knew of it, it would have been all in vain, all lost. In order that this treasure might not be buried but put to use and enjoyed, God has caused the Word to be published and proclaimed, in which he has given the Holy Spirit to offer and apply to us this treasure of salvation. Therefore to sanctify is nothing else than to bring us to the Lord Christ to receive this blessing, which we could not obtain by ourselves.[35]

The Lutheran Order for Baptism reflects, "By water and the Holy Spirit we are made members of the Church, which is the body of Christ. As we live with him and with his people, we grow in faith, love, and obedience to the will of God." Parents promise to provide the external means through which children are brought into regular contact with the Christian community and the means of grace, "that, living in the covenant of their baptism and in communion with the Church, they may lead godly lives until the day of Jesus Christ."[36] In the Rite of Confirmation, a person affirms the promises made at baptism, and the whole assembly gives its "amen" to the prayer:

> Gracious Lord, through water and the Spirit you have made these men and women your own. You forgave them all their sins and brought them to newness of life. Continue to strengthen them with the Holy Spirit, and daily increase in them your gifts of grace: the spirit of wisdom and understanding, the spirit of counsel and might, the spirit of knowledge and the fear of the Lord, the spirit of joy in your presence; through Jesus Christ, your Son, our Lord.[37]

Moravians recognize the risks of legalism and crypto-works righteousness. They, too, realize that humans have a knack for binding one another's consciences in subtle as well as blatant ways. While acknowledging the need to be as clear as possible about the differences between Law and Gospel, the Unity construes sanctification in terms of the Holy Spirit's leading the believer to a closer relationship with Jesus. Indeed, the motif of the Christian life as a journey with God in the Spirit is reflected in the Confirmation liturgy. The candidate who affirms her or his baptism is exhorted by the presiding minister, "By affirming your baptismal covenant in public worship today, you have taken another step in your journey with God. You have entered into a new relationship with God and this congregation. We charge you in God's name always to remain faithful to Christ and the church, and to be open to the leading of the Holy Spirit."[38]

The *Unitas Fratrum*'s motto, "Our Lamb has conquered. Let us follow him," is reflected in the Moravian willingness to share with other's ones *Lebenslauf*, that is, story of one's life-faith journey. The *Lebenslauf* is a thoughtful, self-searching examination of events and thoughts, influences, and experiences in which the person humbly seeks to discern in his or her life the presence, guidance, admonition, and blessings of Christ through the Spirit.

The mutual complementarities in the field of sanctification are helpful to Moravians and Lutherans. Lutherans emphasize caution regarding legalism and works righteousness, yet they realize that Christians grow in trusting, understanding, and obeying God through the Spirit. Moravians offer the motif of the journey as a way of expressing that growth in grace and a personal engagement with God which also leads to fellowship with others.

We move now to our complementarities on the Holy Spirit and the believer in the Church.

2. The Holy Spirit and Believers in the Church

The Christian community, extended in space around the globe and throughout time from the New Testament times to the end of the age, is the normal and natural locus for the Spirit's activity. Many biblical images are used to describe that community such as called-out assembly (*ekklesia*), disciples of the Lord, Body of Christ, new Israel, Bride of Christ, and household of faith. The "Followers of the Way" also understood themselves as the branches and Jesus the vine, as sheep who followed the Good Shepherd, friends of Jesus, brothers and sisters in the Lord, and saints—in spite of definitely unsaintly conduct. Often Christians applied to themselves descriptions of ancient Israel, such as royal priesthood, holy nation, faithful remnant, and covenant people. The richness and fluidity of terms indicates a wealth of concepts and self-understandings. Whatever expression or image Christians have used to describe themselves, they have understood themselves as united in Christ through the Holy Spirit, and they also understood that their God-created and -led community was part of God's plan for the salvation of all. We can expect these ideas and images to appear among Lutherans and Moravians. We consider several common and foundational agreements shared by Moravians and Lutherans.

Both agree with the *Augsburg Confession*'s understanding of the Church, Articles VII and VIII:

> VII. It is taught among us that one holy Christian church will be and remain forever. This is the assembly of all believers among whom the Gospel is preached in its purity and the sacraments are administered according to the Gospel. For it is sufficient for the true unity of the Christian church that the Gospel be preached in conformity with a pure understanding of it and that the sacraments be administered in accordance with the Divine Word. It is not necessary for the true unity of the Christian church that ceremonies, instituted by men, should be observed uniformly in all places. . . .
>
> VIII. Again, although the Christian church, properly speaking, is nothing else than the assembly of all believers and saints, yet because in this life many false Christians, hypocrites, and even open sinners remain among the godly, the sacraments are efficacious even if the priests who administer them are wicked men. . . .

When these positions are joined to the Explanation of the Third Article in the Small Catechism, Lutherans and Moravians realize that they have great freedom in structuring rites and church organization and seeking fellowship with other believers whose positions and practices may differ in form. They also realize that it is the substance of the Gospel which is the center of faith, fellowship, and function. Further, the Explanation puts the whole Church and its specific manifestations under the guidance, enlightenment, and judgment of the Spirit. Here freedom is placed in the context of faithfulness to the Triune God. Our ways of expressing the Spirit's presence and action in the Church both complement and encourage us to pursue further conversations and considerations.[39]

Historical experiences move Moravians to consider carefully and boldly the nature of the Church universal and the Unity in particular. At the same time their historic commitments cause them to cultivate close harmony among their members as well as to be willing to engage in mission-oriented and ecumenical ventures. The dialoguers concluded that an exposition of some Moravian perspectives on the complement "The Holy Spirit and Believers in the Church" will be helpful for mutual understanding. *The Ground of the Unity* provides reference markers: (a) the source, aim, and end of the Unity's being; (b) the *Unitas Fratrum* as a unity and the Church as a fellowship; and (c) the Church as a community serving the neighbor and the world.

First and foremost, the opening of the *Ground*:

1. The Lord Jesus Christ calls His church into being so that it may serve Him on earth until He comes. The *Unitas Fratrum* is, therefore, aware of its being called in faith to serve mankind by proclaiming the Gospel of Jesus Christ. It recognizes this call to be the source of its being and the inspiration of its service. As is the source, so is the aim and end of its being based on the will of its Lord.[40]

By situating the Unity within the Church so as to hear Jesus continually call the whole Christian community into existence in order to serve him, Moravians retain the dynamic understanding of member communities sharing with one another a unity which transcends doctrinal and liturgical differences and which empowers those communities to join their distinctive witnesses in serving the Lord who serves all humankind. Given its self-understanding that it is among those ecclesial communities called especially to proclaim the Gospel, Moravians seek to listen to the Spirit's urgings and leadings as to how the *Unitas Fratrum* is to answer the call addressed to it. Other communities may be led and equipped with the Spirit's gifts to other forms of service and witness. Moravians hear the Spirit especially summoning them to present to the Church and the world the Gospel so as to engage children, men, and women in personal relationships with God, a faithful walk with the Savior, and a vibrant community in the Spirit.

Augustus Gottlieb Spangenberg's hymn expresses it well:

> The church of Christ which he has hallowed here to be his house, is scattered far and near, in north, and south, and east, and west abroad; and yet in earth and heav'n, thro' Christ her Lord, the church is one. One member may not know another here, and yet their fellowship is true and near; one is their Savior, and their Father one; one Spirit rules them, and among them none lives to one's self. They live to him who bought them with his blood, baptized them with his Spirit, pure and good; and in true faith and ever-burning love, their hearts and hopes ascend to seek above the'ternal good. O Spirit of the Lord, all life is yours; now on your church your pow'r and strength out-pour, that many

> children may be born to you, and through your knowledge may be brought anew to sing Christ's praise.[41]

For Moravians, the Church certainly has external marks such as the Word rightly preached and the sacraments properly administered. Still, the primary constitutive factor is the relationship which God establishes with the Church and its believers in Christ through the Spirit. As the Triune God is the only source of life and salvation, according to the *Ground*, section 4, so the source of the Church's being and mission is the same Trinity. The Ancient Moravian Church described the relationship between the Church and God in terms of the triad faith, love, and hope.

Emphasis on relationship takes flesh and blood form. The faith-love-hope which exists between God and an individual creates a communal relationship among persons. As the crucified Lord gave his mother and his beloved disciple to each other (Jn 19:25-27), so God brings persons together that they may share life together in Christ's community. The Church, as Moravians describe it, is the fellowship of followers gathered around the cross. And as there can be no Christianity without the cross, there can be no Church without Christ at its center, and no Christianity without the community of believers called the Church. As Spangenberg put it, the Church is scattered but one, a fellowship because of what its members share: the Triune God. The special role of Jesus as Head or Chief Elder of the Church derives from this position, as will be indicated shortly. A distinctive Moravian complementarity in this instance is the Moravian conception of the Church as called into being by God, being given the broad mission to proclaim the Gospel in fellowship with communities within the Church, and linking the Church in its manifold forms in an intimate union with the Triune God so that the Church is a human community sharing Christ's Gospel with the whole of humanity.

The second reference marker develops the Church as a fellowship and the Moravian Church as a unity within that fellowship. Sections 6 and 7 of the *Ground of the Unity* provide the reference mark:

6. We believe in and confess the unity of the church given in the one Lord Jesus Christ as God and Saviour. He died that He might unite the scattered children of God. As the living Lord and Shepherd, He is leading His flock toward such unity. The *Unitas Fratrum* espoused such unity when it took over the name of the Old Bohemian Brethren's Church "*Unitas Fratrum*" (Unity of the Brethren). Nor can we ever forget the

powerful unifying experience granted by the crucified and risen Lord to our fathers in Herrnhut on the occasion of the Holy Communion of August 13, 1727, in Berthelsdorf. It is the Lord's will that Christendom should give evidence of and seek unity in Him with zeal and love. In our own midst we see how such unity has been promised us and laid upon us as a charge. We recognize that through the grace of Christ different churches have received many gifts. It is our desire that we may learn from each other and rejoice together in the riches of the love of Christ and the manifold wisdom of God. We confess our share in the guilt which is manifest in the severed and divided state of Christendom. By means of such divisions we ourselves hinder the message and power of the Gospel. We recognize the danger of self-righteousness and judging others without love. Since we together with all Christians are pilgrims on the way to meet our coming Lord, we welcome every step that brings us nearer the goal of unity in Him. He Himself invites us to communion in His supper. Through it He leads the Church toward that union which he has promised. By means of His presence in the Holy Communion He makes our unity with Him evident and certain even today.

7. The Church of Jesus Christ, despite all the distinctions between male and female, Jew and non-Jew, white and colored, poor and rich, is one in its Lord. The *Unitas Fratrum* recognizes no distinction between those who are one in the Lord Jesus Christ. We are called to testify that God in Jesus Christ brings His people out of "every race, kindred and tongue" into one body, pardons sinners beneath the Cross and brings them together. We oppose any discrimination in our midst because of race or standing, and we regard it as a commandment of the Lord to bear public witness to this and to demonstrate by word and deed that we are brothers and sisters in Christ.

The aim of the Church in proclaiming the Gospel is to unite all persons in Christ and with one another. The Moravian community within the Church is to strive for that unity in a threefold manner: (a) through mission endeavors directed toward those who are not yet believers; (b) through ecumenical partnerships and sharing with other Christian communities; and (c) through providing the world and the Church with a witness of Christian concord and fellowship manifested in the Unity itself. In concept and practice, the Unity's testimony of the reality of oneness in Christ through its congregational and denominational life provides the energy for its ecumenical and missionary ministries. And a vibrant sense of God's presence in Christ through the Spirit is the heart of the Moravian Church's unity. Moravian commitments to the unity of the whole Church, then, are basic to Moravian self-understandings of their Unity and the Church universal.

The Unity knows that oneness in Christ and in their own ranks is neither to be taken for granted nor is it without cost. The *Ground*'s reference to the experience of August 13, 1727, is an admission to the world and subsequent generations in the Renewed Church that they have been tested with divisions and disagreements. In a time of crisis over leadership, direction and the challenge of mission, and after considerable debate and prayer, and in the context of a Lutheran-led Eucharist, the fellowship was deeply moved by what has come to be called the Moravian Pentecost. The members experienced the reality of the Spirit working among them to unite them in spite of different opinions and reasonings. The oneness they shared in the Spirit, members realized, was to be expressed in harmonious love and peace as they lived as a community and as individuals to do God's will. Ever since, August 13 is a cherished day among Moravians. It is a time to recall the events at Berthelsdorf with humility and joy, and to commit themselves anew to their mission to be involved in promoting the unity of the whole Church. A later hymn catches the experience and expresses the Unity's dedication to oneness in Christ, the *Unitas Fratrum*, and the Church:

> They walked with God in peace and love but failed with
> one another;
> while sternly for the faith they strove, they fell out with
> each other.
> But he in whom they put their trust, who knew their frames,
> that they were dust, with pity healed their weakness.
> He found them in his house of prayer with one accord
> assembled,
> and so revealed his presence there, they wept for joy and
> trembled.

One cup they drank, one bread they broke,
    one baptism shared,
one language spoke, forgiving and forgiven.
Then forth they went, with tongues of flame in one blessed
    theme delighting;
the love of Jesus and his name, God's children all uniting.
That love our theme and watch-word still; the law of love may
    we fulfill—
give love as love we're given.[42]

The Moravian "Love Feast" is another means through which congregations enhance and witness to their fellowship. As indicated, poetry, hymnody, and music are used along with history to manifest the Unity's thought, devotion, and practice. The Love Feast has developed into a distinctive form through which a congregation and groups of congregations come together. The forms of the service may differ, but the intent is the same. Although marriages, congregational celebrations, and traditional ways to mark the seasons of the Church Year may be the stipulated occasions, the members gather for singing hymns and listening to special presentations of choral music. The unity afforded through joint listening and common singing is increased through a simple sharing of a bun and a cup of coffee during the musical offering. While the Love Feast is not a sacrament per se, it has the character and climate of a fellowship meal in which the Spirit unites the hearts, minds, and voices of the community.

The third reference marker moves the *Unitas Fratrum* to understand the whole Church and itself as engaged in being a community of service to those near and far. The reference marker is the Ground's sections 8, 9, and 10:

8. Jesus Christ came not to be served but to serve. From this, His Church receives its mission and power for its service, to which each of its members is called. We believe that the Lord has called us particularly to mission service among the peoples of the world. In this, and in all others forms of service both at home and abroad, to which the Lord commits us, He expects us to confess Him and witness to His love in unselfish service.

9. Our Lord Jesus entered this world's misery in order to bear it and overcome it. We seek to follow Him in serving His brethren. Like the love of Jesus, this service knows no

bounds. Therefore we pray the Lord ever anew to point out to us the way to reach our neighbor, opening our heart and hand to him in his need.

10. Jesus Christ maintains in love and faithfulness His commitment to this fallen world. Therefore we must remain concerned for this world. We may not withdraw from it through indifference, pride or fear. Together with the universal Christian Church, the *Unitas Fratrum* challenges mankind with the message of the love of God, striving to promote the peace of the world and seeking to attain what is best for all men. For the sake of this world, the *Unitas Fratrum* hopes for and looks to the day when the victory of Christ will be manifest over sin and death and the new world will appear.

As the Ancient Church was a fellowship of believers who were on the move because of persecution and often were in need, and as continental Pietism provided a missionary impulse to the Renewed Church, the *Unitas Fratrum* today sees itself as a community in mission. The forms of the mission may cover the spectrum from educational programs to preaching for conversion, from assisting poverty-stricken persons to achieve dignity through gaining skills and land to joining with other Christians in the struggle for justice, the Unity is a worldwide mission-service member of the Body of Christ. Perhaps because it never achieved the status of an "established" or national church, Moravians have an awareness of the needs and conditions of the marginalized, the voiceless and the refugees. Mission and service are manifestations of the Moravian response to Christ's call; mission and service are both special assignments and gifts which the members of the Unity feel are given them through the Spirit.

Lutherans are not strangers to the image of Jesus the Shepherd who leads his flock. Luther and the theologians who signed the Smalcald Articles held that the Church is "holy believers and sheep who hear the voice of their shepherd" and so, as do children, pray, "I believe in one holy Christian church." As expected, Lutherans hold that the Church's holiness does not consist in human ceremonies or deeds, but "in the Word of God and true faith."[43] Lutherans provide three dimensions relevant here to complement our common understanding of the Church.

First, the Church has outward marks or signs. God comes to us concretely in the midst of our earthly lives. From the sixteenth to the present century, Lutherans have realized that freedom and order, external and internal elements are required to hold the community together:

> The church is not merely an association of outward ties and rites like other civic governments, however, but it is mainly an association of faith and of the Holy Spirit in men's hearts. To make it recognizable, this association has outward marks, the pure teaching of the Gospel and the administration of the sacraments in harmony with the Gospel of Christ. This church alone is called the body of Christ, which Christ renews, consecrates, and governs by his Spirit. . . . the "communion of saints" seems to have been added [to the Apostles' Creed] to explain what church means, namely the assembly of saints who share the association of the same Gospel or teaching and of the same Holy Spirit, who renews, consecrates and governs their hearts. . . . We are not dreaming about some Platonic republic, as has been slanderously alleged, but we teach that this church actually exists, made up of true believers and righteous men scattered throughout the world. And we add its marks, the pure teaching of the Gospel and the sacraments. . . . Of course, there are also many weak people in it who build on this foundation perishing structures of stubble, that is, unprofitable opinions. . . . In accordance with the Scriptures, therefore, we maintain that the church in the proper sense, is the assembly of saints who truly believe the Gospel of Christ and who have the Holy Spirit.[44]

On the one hand, Lutherans hold that the Spirit uses external means and forms, so that the Spirit's work can be distinguished from human passions and fads, enthusiasms and distortion. There are benchmarks or standards for doctrine and practice which can be used to protect the core interpretations and understandings, validate new insights, and serve as norms for theology and practice. On the other hand, the Lutheran position recognizes that mere conformity to rituals and structures is also dangerous. The Church is not utopia; its members are fallible sinners who need correcting, enlivening, inspiration by the Spirit. The Church has God's promise that it will always have the Spirit which will give the community of believers guidance, forgiveness and hope.

The second dimension relevant at this juncture is the Lutheran view of the relationships of persons within this community to one another and the wider society. In the Large Catechism, the Reformer taught that the sum and substance of "I believe in the holy Christian Church" is

> I believe that there is on earth a little holy flock or community of pure saints under one head, Christ. It is called together by the Holy Spirit in one faith, mind and understanding. It possesses a variety of gifts, yet is united in love without sect or schism. Of this community I also am a part and member, a participant and co-partner in all the blessings it possesses. I was brought into it by the Holy Spirit and incorporated into it through the fact that I have heard and still hear God's Word.[45]

The work of the Spirit in the Church is aimed to proclaim and assure members that they are forgiven by and reconciled to God through Christ, then to enlighten them about God's will, to move them in the process of sanctification, and to preserve them in true faith. All baptized Christians are to engage in mutual prayer and concern, service, and assistance for one another. The vocation or call to be a Christian is expressed through sharing the Word in worship, praise, and speaking mutual consolation and hope to one another. In other words, each Christian is a member of the priesthood of all believers. What was noted earlier about the relationship of the Spirit to the individual believer is lived out in the community of the faithful. Again, the Large Catechism noted that the Spirit "makes me holy . . . through the Christian church." The Church is the Spirit's unique community: "It is the mother that begets and bears every Christian through the Word of God. The Holy Spirit reveals and preaches that Word, and by it he illumines and kindles hearts so that they grasp and accept it, cling to it, and persevere in it. The Spirit can be said to place the believer upon the bosom of the Church."[46]

The Spirit through the Church is also active in the world to bring God's Word—as Law and Gospel—to society and its power structures. As believers go into the world, they go in the power of the Spirit. The Spirit's enlightening role involves guiding and aiding Christians in their daily lives in the world, at work and through their responsibilities as citizens: "All this then is the office and work of the Holy Spirit, to begin and daily increase holiness on earth through these two means, the Christian church and the forgiveness of sins."[47]

The third dimension concerns the ecumenical perspective on the whole Church. The Lutheran position holds that agreement on two factors is sufficient for believers to agree upon the pure teaching of the Gospel and the proper administration of the sacraments in accordance with the Word. This position permits maximum discussion and room for exploration, arenas for the Spirit to lead Christ's followers in discerning the unity they already have in Christ, and then moving toward fuller forms of fellowship. At the same time, agreement in the Gospel and on the sacraments are of such critical importance to Lutherans that they will expend significant time and effort to ask themselves and their partners about the essence of the Gospel and the nature of the sacraments.

Lutherans are willing to learn from others and to share their views, to recognize that forms of worship and expression may differ from one ecclesial communion to another and even within communions. Their fundamental concern runs straight to the heart of justification by faith through grace. From that point outward and inward, Lutherans engage in ecumenical relationships of different intensities and breadth. Lutherans are willing to say both "yes" to ecclesial ecumenical sharing at the deepest levels, and they are also willing to say "no" in love when they feel that such sharing is either not appropriate or not yet appropriate given current understandings.

Discussions of the Spirit in the lives of believers and in the Church lead to Moravian and Lutheran forms and views of the ministry.

3. *Mutual Complementarities About Ministries*

Probably no issue is more vexing and problematic in intra-church and ecumenical discussions than understandings of ministry. This is, however, not the case for Moravian and Lutheran relations. Within our own ranks there may be substantial reflection and debate, yet we have common understandings and positions, even common internal discussions. Lutherans and Moravians share a lively sense of the priesthood of all believers through our own historical developments, Reformation heritages, and backgrounds derived from continental Pietism. We agree that all baptized members of the Body of Christ are called to pray for one another and the world, proclaim through word and deed that Jesus is Lord, share the strengthening hope of forgiveness and reconciliation, and live so that we may bear the fruits of the Spirit.

At the same time, Moravians and Lutherans agree that the ministry of Word and sacraments requires a recognizable and authorized form. Within the community of the baptized and for the sake of due order, we understand the Spirit to lead the Church to authorize men and women publicly to represent within the whole Church and to the world the proclamation of the Word and the administration of the sacraments through what is called traditionally the pastoral office. The office authorizes a person to preach, teach, administer the sacraments, and provide spiritual leadership among us. Normally the rite of ordination authorizes persons who have been called by the Spirit and the Church to fulfill the office of the ministry of Word and sacraments. We do not understand ordination to be God's granting a person spiritual superiority over others. The ministry of the ordained is a public office to which a person is called by the Spirit working within the heart of the believer and within the Christian community. While we recognize a variety of public offices in the Christian community which are filled by persons who are not ordained, and while we may use several titles for those who are ordained, Lutherans and Moravians understand the roles of the ordained in remarkably similar ways.[48]

Ordained ministers have a triple accountability. Chiefly, they are accountable to God for the stewardship of the ministry which has been entrusted to them. At times they may have to address the Word as Law to the believing community and the wider society in spite of opposition and risk which may result from the faithful proclamation of the will of God. Naturally, they are also called upon to test what they say and do by the Scriptures. In the same category, ordained ministers are to be accountable to the Shepherd, faithful to their responsibilities in caring for the flock of Christ, competent communicators of the doctrines of the Church, examples of Christian living, and advocates of God's mercy and justice in society. Above all, they are expected to be devout Christians, sinners who depend on the grace of God and who manifest their relationship to Christ through lives dedicated to his service in and through the Church. Second, they are accountable to the Church and their ecclesial body for exercise of their ministries among the people of God. In other words, they are subject to the discipline and afforded the counsel of the Church in matters of life, doctrine, and other appropriate support. Third, they are accountable to the congregation, agency, or institution of the church which has called them to serve in their midst.

In terms of ordained ministry, Lutherans and Moravians emphasize the roles and responsibilities of congregational pastors. While Lutherans continue to consider the advisability of ordaining persons to an office titled "deacon," Moravians have such an office as the entry point into pastoral ministry. Moravians and Lutherans are recognizing the historic office of the bishop as a pastoral figure who provides advice and guidance for the church and the church's ordained and lay leadership. Both churches expect their ordained ministers normally to be educated in a theological seminary and to have demonstrated academic competence as well as ministerial skills in the context of spiritual commitment to the Gospel. From these common positions, each church complements the other's understanding of the Church and ministry. At this juncture some brief descriptions of the ministry in our respective churches may be helpful in showing that while there are differences of form, there are complements and common grounds which encourage us to recommend full communion between our churches.

A Lutheran understanding of the ministry of the ordained in the context of the ministry of the whole people of God may be seen in terms of some of the Constitution of the ELCA's statements about the Church, the specific Lutheran church, and its leaders. In describing the Nature of the Church:

> 3.01 All power in the Church belongs to our Lord Jesus Christ, its head. All actions of this church are to be carried out under his rule and authority.
>
> 3.02 The Church exists both as a fellowship and as local congregations gathered for worship and Christian service. Congregations find their fulfillment in the universal community of the Church, and the universal Church exists in and through congregations. This church, therefore, derives its character and powers from both the sanction and representation of its congregations and from its inherent nature as an expression of the broader fellowship of the faithful. In length, it acknowledges itself to be in the historic continuity of the communion of saints; in breadth, it expresses the fellowship of believers and congregations in our day.

The ELCA is a member of the World Council of Churches, the National Council of Churches of Christ in the USA, and the Lutheran World Federation. The latter is a body which describes itself as "a communion of Churches" which has no jurisdictional authority over its member Churches. The ELCA's Constitution is the church's statement to itself and the whole Church that the ELCA will understand itself in the universal Church. Indeed, the Constitution makes commitments to seek wider unity among Lutherans and the Church ecumenically understood. The constitution for synods of the ELCA contains the same provisions regarding the unity of the Church and the ELCA's commitments to such endeavors.[50] Seminaries of the ELCA are expected to provide candidates for ordination and other leadership positions as well as those serving in those capacities with educational opportunities to engage them in ecumenical thinking and action.

While the ELCA continues to devote study to the nature of the ordained and other ministries, it does have succinct statements in its Constitutions for the national church, synods, and congregations concerning the responsibilities of ordained ministers. Among these are the following:

> Consistent with the faith and practice of this church, every ordained minister shall preach the Word, administer the sacraments, conduct public worship, provide pastoral care, and, shall speak publicly to the world in solidarity with the poor and oppressed, calling for justice and proclaiming God's love for the world. Each ordained minister with a congregational call shall, within the congregation, offer instruction, confirm, marry, visit the sick and distressed, and bury the dead. . . .[51]

The office of bishop is part of the ministry in the ELCA. Considerations about the balance between pastoral and managerial aspects of a bishop's duties and responsibilities are ongoing in the church. Again, portions from the Model Constitution for Synods:

> S.8.12 As this synod's pastor, the bishop shall:
>
> a. Oversee and administer the work of this synod.
>
> b. Preach, teach, and administer the sacraments in accord with the faith of this church.
>
> c. Provide pastoral care and leadership for this synod, its congregations, its ordained ministers, and its associates in ministry.
>
> d. Advise and counsel its related institutions and organizations.
>
> e. Be its chief ecumenical officer. . . .

The synodical bishop, elected for a term by the synod assembly composed of congregational lay persons and ordained ministers, also ordains candidates for the ministry of Word and sacraments.

The Moravian understanding of ministry also may be seen as rooted in the Lordship of Jesus Christ over the Church. During 1741 the responsibilities of the far-flung enterprises of the Moravian Church weighed heavily on

Leonard Dober, its Chief Elder. In a Synodal Conference held in London in September, he declined to continue to serve in this position, and no other was willing, nor was the use of the lot supportive of selecting another.[52] The question was then put to the Savior by the use of the lot as to whether he desired this office for himself. For the first time the lot provided a positive answer, and so it was recognized that Jesus was Chief Elder of the church in jurisdictional and organizational matters. This was announced to the international Moravian church on November 13, 1741, and since then this stands as the day when Moravians celebrate this insight. Given the historical context of the church-state relations in Germany and the situation among the members of the Unity, the proclamation of Christ's Chief Eldership was a daring step. Zinzendorf's hymn provides us with some insight on the senses of reconciliation and mission which flowed from November 13 and which is still part of Moravian practice:

> Heart with loving heart united, met to know God's holy will,
> Let his love in us ignited more and more our spirits fill.
> He the Head, we are his members; we reflect the light he is.
> He the Master, we disciples, he is ours and we are his.
> May we all so love each other and all selfish claims deny,
> so that each one for the other will not hesitate to die.
> Even so our Lord has loved us; for our lives he gave his life.
> Still he grieves and still he suffers, for our selfishness and strife.
> Since, O Lord, you have demanded that our lives your love
> should show
> so we wait to be commanded forth into your world to go.
> Kindle in us love's compassions so that ev'ry one may see
> in our faith and hope the promise of a new humanity.[53]

The provinces of the *Unitas Fratrum* are members of the World Council of Churches and the national or geographical councils where they exist. Thus, it has an ecumenical and international commitment. However, the *Unitas Fratrum* in itself is an international church, uniquely ecumenical because of the special relationships which it cherishes with various Christian traditions in the countries where it has provinces. In its governmental structure, the Unity Synod is its highest deliberative and legislative body. The provinces, represented usually by three voting members, which make up the Unity Synod meet usually every seven years. It does not have a presiding bishop but an executive board composed of persons drawn from the provinces. The board elects its own chair for a maximum of two consecutive two-year terms. Proposals reflecting doctrine or the Unity's polity are referred to the Unity Synod. Each province may develop its own Book of Order, which is to be in harmony with the *Church Order of the Unity*. The Northern and Southern Provinces of the Moravian Church in America have their respective Provincial Elders Conferences, which serve as administrative bodies for the provinces. These also make the basic approvals for candidates for ordination and provide the calls to pastors to congregations on the basis of congregations' approving such calls with the agreement of the person to be called. Each province may explore what ecumenical relations it deems advisable, yet it is customary for provinces to keep the Unity Board informed and to seek advice from the Board. A province meets in assembly (synods) every two to three years. The synods elect persons to be bishops from among the ordained elders and may elect as many as seems appropriate to the synod.

A Moravian congregation typically has a Board of Elders and a Board of Trustees, and the pastor presides over the former. The Board of Elders is concerned with spiritual and educational life of the congregation, while the Board of Trustees deals with the "temporal" affairs.

The Moravian Church has a threefold ordained ministry: deacons, presbyters (elders), and bishops. There is one ordination (to the office of deacon) and subsequent consecrations to the other offices.[54] The Moravian Church in America began to ordain women in 1975.[55] The *Church Order of the Unity*, as revised at Dar es Salaam in 1995, describes the office of the bishop as follows:

> 687. The Renewed Unity received the episcopacy as an inheritance from the Ancient Unitas Fratrum.
>
> Today we regard the episcopacy in the Renewed Unity in a different way from that of the Ancient *Unitas Fratrum*. Formerly, a Bishop had a Church-governmental and administrative function. In our day, however, this function is not necessarily linked to the episcopal office. We hold to the understanding, common both to the Ancient and Renewed Unity, that only Christ is Head of the Church and pastoral oversight is exercised in responsibility to Him.
>
> A Bishop of the Moravian Church is consecrated to a special priestly pastoral ministry in the name of and for the whole Unity.
>
> The office of Bishop represents the vital unity of the Church and the continuity of the Church's ministry, although the Unity

does not place emphasis on any mechanical transmission of the apostolic succession.

The office and function of a Bishop is valid throughout the Unity as a whole.

Duties of Bishop

688. A Bishop as a Bishop has responsibility primarily for providing pastoral care to pastors and the Church, and assisting the Church in its faithfulness to Christ and the Gospel.

All Provincial and District Boards shall consult a Bishop or Bishops in all matters concerning the work in the Province or District which fall within his/her sphere of responsibility.

A Bishop has a special duty of intercession for the Unity, and also for the Church of Christ as a whole.

Bishops in active service should be enabled to visit congregations for the deepening of their spiritual life.

The opinion of a Bishop (Bishops) shall customarily be sought and given due consideration and weight in matters of doctrine and practice.

A Bishop represents the Church in the act of ordination.

Only bishops have the right to ordain or to consecrate to the various orders of the ministry, but only when they are commissioned to do so by a Provincial Board or Synod.

A Bishop, however, has the right to decline a commission to ordain, should he/she wish to do so.

In exceptional cases the ordination of a Deacon may be performed by a Presbyter in the name of and by commission of a Bishop.

A Bishop (Bishops) should share in the decisions regarding the training of candidates for the ministry and should maintain a special pastoral relationship with such candidates throughout their training.

The Synod of the Bishop's Province may also add administrative responsibility by electing him/her a member of the Provincial Board.

A Bishop may be assigned by his/her Province to represent the Province in ecumenical gatherings and before governmental agencies.

Clearly, there are variations of practices and polity regarding the nature of the ministry, but there are no factors which raise theological issues or which might impede progress toward achieving full communion between our churches.

The Mutual Complementarities indicate diversity within the context of unity. Yet the nature of that diversity is seen as completing and enhancing what we already have. Our summary at this point is that Moravians and Lutherans agree with and complement each other's understandings of the Holy Spirit in the life of the Believer and in the Church, and we agree with and complement each other's positions on the Church's ministry.

NOTES

23. As noted previously, the Explanation of the Third Article is included in the Moravian liturgy for Easter morning and has the character of a statement of faith. The Explanations to the articles are widely known and cherished by Lutherans.
24. See the AC, Articles 2, 3, 5, 18, and 20.
25. The Explanation to the First Article reads,

    I believe that God has created me and all that exists; that he has given me and still sustains my body and soul, all my limbs and senses, my reason and all the faculties of my mind, together with food and clothing, house and home, family and property; that he provides me daily and abundantly with all the necessities of life, protects me from all danger, and preserves me from all evil. All this he does out of his pure, fatherly and divine goodness and mercy, without any merit or worthiness on my part. For all of this I am bound to thank, praise, serve, and obey him. This is most certainly true.

    The Explanation to the Second Article is:

    I believe that Jesus Christ, true God, begotten of the Father from eternity, and also true man, born of the virgin Mary, is my Lord, who has redeemed me, a lost and condemned creature, delivered me and freed me from all sins, from death, and from the power of the devil, not with silver and gold but with his own holy and precious blood and with his innocent sufferings and death, in order that I may be his, live under him in his kingdom, and serve him in everlasting righteousness, innocence, and blessedness, even as he is risen from the dead and lives and reigns to all eternity. This is most certainly true.

26. Apol., article IV, 2 [in BC].
27. See Smalcald Article I, 1-5 [in BC].
28. Apol., article IV, 43.
29. *Ground of the Unity*, 3.
30. MBW, 700; words and tune date from 1556.
31. MBW, 799; The hymn also is in the LBW, 341.
32. MBW, 346.
33. For the quotations and paraphrases see FC SD, Article VI, 7-9 and 21.
34. LW, vol. 35, 370ff., Preface to Romans.
35. Large Catechism, Part II, 38 [in BC].
36. Order for Baptism, LBW, 121.
37. Affirmation of Baptism, LBW, 201. The title "Affirmation of Baptism" is given to the rite traditionally called "Confirmation."
38. The Rite of Confirmation, MBW, 173.
39. This is particularly the case with Zinzendorf's expression that the Spirit is the Mother of the Church and believers. He did not intend this to ascribe gender to the Spirit, but depicted in this way the Spirit's care for the family of God and its members. Moravians today are largely unaware of Zinzendorf's thinking on the matter. It may be a way for Lutherans and Moravians to engage in discussions about the relationship of the Spirit to the Church, believer, and Christ.
40. *Ground of the Unity*, no. 1.
41. MBW, 516.
42. MBW, 396.
43. Smalcald Article XII, 2-3.
44. Apol., Articles VII-VIII, 5, 8, 20, and 28.
45. *Large Catechism*, II, 51.
46. *Large Catechism*, II, 41, 37.
47. *Large Catechism*, II, 59. We note that one of the areas which we have discussed but not included references about in this report is social-political attitudes. These were not seen as issues of disagreement or complementarities, but of general affirmation. Again, further explorations will be fruitful for our respective churches.
48. In the ELCA there are official yet unordained offices such as deaconess, deacons, and associates in ministry. There are a variety of functions which persons may fulfill,

e.g., nurses, directors of religious education, musicians, parish workers, etc. There are requirements in these instances which involve theological study, requisite skills for the position, and certification by an appropriate body in the church. Included are requirements concerning continuing education. In order for a person to remain on the official roster of the church, the person is to have served under appointment or be designated as on leave from appointment for a designated period of time.

49. See the ELCA Constitution, 4.02 f and 4.03 d and f. Please note *Ecumenism: Vision of the ELCA* [see earlier citation] is the official policy statement of the ELCA (1991 Assembly).
50. See the *Model Constitution for Synods*, chapters 5 and 6.
51. *Model Constitution for Synods*, excerpted from 14.02.
52. The use of the lot and similar methods were popular within Pietism to discern a right decision when sufficient information was not available otherwise to make a decision. Moravians used Scripture verses, one indicating a positive answer, another indicating a negative answer, and a third slip was blank. The slip drawn was used to indicate the Savior's guidance.
53. MBW, 401.
54. Usually a Moravian deacon is consecrated as an elder after serving several years in a congregation. The process involves recommendation of the consecration and the commissioning of a bishop to do the consecration by the executive board of the Province, the Provincial Elders' Conference. There are no functional differences between a Moravian deacon and elder; both may preach, administer both sacraments, officiate at weddings, etc. Those deacons consecrated as Presbyters must be considered spiritually prepared for the office. Deacons who do not elect to proceed to consecration as Presbyters are not considered less mature spiritually than those who do take that step. Bishops are elected from the ranks of Presbyters.
55. The ELCA was formed in 1987. It continued the practice of its earliest predecessor bodies, the American Lutheran Church and the Lutheran Church in America. Those churches began to ordain women in 1970.

V. Concluding Statement: The Journey Continues

The members of the Lutheran-Moravian Bilateral Dialogue recommend to their respective churches that our churches move forward as expeditiously as possible to approve our churches entering full communion with each other, as indicated in the recommendations at the beginning of this report. We thank our churches for the opportunity to engage in this endeavor, and we thank God for helping us to grow in faith as we undertook this journey with our Savior.

We conclude by continuing the journey with our Shepherd:

> *I am the good shepherd. I know my own and my own know me, just as the Father knows me and I know the Father. And I lay down my life for the sheep. I have other sheep who do not belong to this fold. I must bring them also, and they will listen to my voice. So there will be one flock, one shepherd. [Jn 10:14-16]*

Full Communion Proposal: Churches Uniting in Christ

DOCUMENT 7

"MARKS" OF CHURCHES UNITING IN CHRIST

Churches Uniting in Christ, January 2002

Editors' Note: *In January 1999, the Eighteenth Plenary of the Consultation on Church Union gathered in St. Louis, Missouri, to determine the future of the relationship between the nine member communions: the African Methodist Episcopal Church, the African Methodist Episcopal Zion Church, the Christian Church (Disciples of Christ), the Christian Methodist Episcopal Church, the Episcopal Church USA, the International Council of Community Churches, the Presbyterian Church (USA), the United Church of Christ, and the United Methodist Church. For background on the Consultation, see Growing Consensus I (9-95). At the conclusion of the Plenary it was agreed that the communions would move forward in a new relationship, no longer "consulting" but now committed to a relationship of full reconciliation called "Churches Uniting in Christ."*

Emerging from the work of that Plenary were the "Marks of Commitment" on which the member communions agreed to base their life together. The "Marks of Commitment," the text of which appears below, was formally adopted by all nine member communions in January 2002 in Memphis, Tennessee, at the Inaugural Plenary for Churches Uniting in Christ. It is clear from the text that reconciliation in this setting requires work not only in the arena of ordained ministries, but in the area of racial justice as well.

Entering into Churches Uniting in Christ means that the participating churches will express their relationship with one another through the following visible marks:

1. *Mutual recognition of each other as authentic expressions of the one church of Jesus Christ*—Specifically, this means that the participating churches will publicly recognize the following in one another:

- Faith in one God who through Word and in the Spirit creates, redeems, and sanctifies
- Commitment to Jesus Christ as Savior and as the incarnate and risen Lord
- Faithfulness to the Holy Scripture, which testifies to Tradition and to which Tradition testifies, as containing all things necessary for our salvation as well as being the rule and ultimate standard of faith
- Commitment to faithful participation in the two sacraments ordained by Jesus Christ, Baptism and the Lord's Supper
- Commitment to the evangelical and prophetic mission of God and to God's reign of justice and peace
- Grateful acceptance of the ministry the Holy Spirit has manifestly given to the churches

2. *Mutual recognition of members in one Baptism*—This also implies recognition of the ministry all believers share in the common priesthood and from which God calls those members who will be ordained.

3. *Mutual recognition that each affirms the apostolic faith of Scripture and Tradition* expressed in the Apostles' and Nicene Creeds, and that each seeks to give witness to the apostolic faith in its life and mission.

4. *Provision for celebration of the Eucharist together with intentional regularity*—This recognizes that the sacrament is at the heart of the church's life. Shared celebration of the Lord's Supper is a sign of unity in Christ. As Christians gather in all their diversity at one Table of the Lord, they give evidence that their communion is with Christ and that they are in

communion with one another in Christ. When Christians are unable or unwilling to partake together of the one Eucharist, they witness against themselves and give a visible demonstration of the brokenness of Christ's body and the human community.

5. *Engagement together in Christ's mission on a regular and intentional basis, especially a shared mission to combat racism*—The church engages in Christ's mission through worship, proclamation of the gospel, evangelism, education, and action that embodies God's justice, peace, and love. The commitment made by the members of Churches Uniting in Christ includes all of these, so that hearts and minds may be changed. The participating churches will also recognize, however, a particular and emphatic call to "erase racism" by challenging the system of white privilege that has so distorted life in this society and in the churches themselves. Indeed, this call is a hallmark of the new relationship.

6. *Intentional commitment to promote unity with wholeness and to oppose all marginalization and exclusion* in church and society based on such things as race, age, gender, forms of disability, sexual orientation, and class.

7. *Appropriate structures of accountability and appropriate means for consultation and decision making*—While some provision must be made for effecting the marks of the new relationship and for holding the churches mutually accountable to the commitments they have made, the structures developed for these purposes should be flexible and adapted to local circumstances. Apart from ongoing structures, the members of Churches Uniting in Christ may want to assemble from time to time in order to consider pressing issues and to bear witness together on matters of common concern.

8. *An ongoing process of theological dialogue*—Such dialogue will specifically attempt to

- Clarify theological issues identified by the members of Churches Uniting in Christ in order to strengthen their shared witness to the apostolic faith
- Deepen the participating churches' understanding of racism in order to make an even more compelling case against it
- Provide a foundation for the mutual recognition and reconciliation of ordained ministry by the members of Churches Uniting in Christ by the year 2007

DOCUMENT 8

CALL TO CHRISTIAN COMMITMENT AND ACTION TO COMBAT RACISM

Churches Uniting in Christ, January 2001

Editors' Note: *When the nine member-communions of the Consultation on Church Union gathered in the Eighteenth Plenary in St. Louis, Missouri, in January 1999, a key component of deliberation centered on the way in which the participating communions would commit to overcoming racism both within and among themselves, not as a programmatic initiative but as an integral component of what it means to be in full communion. In 2001 in Memphis, Tennessee, the following text was adopted by all nine member communions at the Inaugural Plenary of Churches Uniting in Christ and was signed by the head of communion of each participating church at that time.*

These nine commitments are articulated in greater detail in "Erasing Racism: A Strategy in Quest of Racially Just Unity," a basic resource document for the Eighteenth Plenary of the Consultation on Church Union, published in Mid-Stream *37:3-4 (July/October 1998). The Executive Committee of COCU commended the paper to the member communions for study and implementation.*

Appeal to the Churches

To Seek God's Beloved Community

This letter was signed at the inaugural ceremonies in Memphis, Tennessee, on January 21, 2002. Pastors and other church leaders are encouraged to share it with their congregations.

Call to Christian Commitment and Action to Combat Racism

The following is a call to action from delegates to the Eighteenth Plenary of the Consultation on Church Union (COCU) to the nine member-churches. Common witness and service are two marks of an ecumenical body. The COCU member-churches have chosen to live this commitment especially by focusing attention on the need to combat racism within and among the member-churches, in all churches, and in society.

The experience of the Consultation on Church Union makes clear that the unity of the Church is God's gift expressed in creation and redemption. This unity is given not only for the church but also for the whole human community and all creation. It is the gift of God's own life offered to all humanity. For this reason the church is called to be a sign and instrument of the communion and justice God intends for all people.

This truth informs COCU's search for visible church unity in particular ways. It implies that there is an irrefutable link between the churches' search for unity in faith, sacraments, and ministry and the struggle to overcome racism in the churches and the human community. It implies that authentic unity is inclusive and requires racial justice within the life of the churches and of society. It implies that our prophetic witness against racism and all the powers of oppression is a primary test of the faithfulness of these churches.

In combating racism, the Eighteenth Plenary Session of the Consultation on Church Union calls upon the nine member-churches to commit themselves to a unity that is liberating and reconciling, a unity offered in the Gospels yet not fully expressed in the life and structures of these churches. It is in this context that the COCU churches, seeking to become Churches Uniting in Christ, are making commitments to change ourselves and our society.

Something is seriously wrong with race relations in the United States. One of the most prominent and pervasive evils in our national heritage and cultural routines is racism—that is, biased assumption about the genetic or cultural inferiority of certain racial-ethnic groups, and/or subordinating practices that exclude persons or deprive them of their full humanity because of their racial-ethnic identity.

Racism so permeates our customs and institutions that none can fully escape participation in it. Indeed, no member of a dominant group can fully avoid benefiting from it, and no member of a subordinate group can avoid the intention of oppression. Racism is finally about power—the abuses of power by a dominant group intent upon preserving its economic, social, political, or ecclesiastical privileges and the resulting deprivations of opportunity imposed on a subordinate group. Unless significant initiatives are taken to counter current conditions and trends, racism—especially white racism—will continue to corrupt our national and ecclesiastical aspirations for a society that truly incarnates "liberty and justice for all."

We, therefore, appeal to the peoples of our nation and our churches for a renewed commitment to combat the sin of racism and white privilege. The moral integrity and credibility of both our nation and our churches are at stake in this struggle. For the churches in COCU particularly, our quest for visible unity is irrelevant—in fact, fraudulent—unless that unity embodies racial solidarity and produces a vital public witness for racial equality and fairness.

The churches seek to embody this commitment together, through the Church of Christ Uniting envisioned by the COCU member churches. From the perspective of the Christian gospel whose mandate is reconciliation of all God's children, racism is demonic and sinful. It denies the image of God given each person in creation, and in the new creation each person enters by baptism.

How then shall the member-churches of the Consultation on Church Union, yearning to become Churches Uniting In Christ, combat racism? How shall we make our vision of church truly catholic, truly evangelical, and truly reformed, visible through our struggle against racism?

In view of what we discern that God is calling all the churches to be and to do, and in view of the present impediments to effective responses to that call, this Eighteenth Plenary appeals to our member-churches to make the following nine strategic commitments and to implement these commitments together:

1. Continue to make a compelling theological case against racism. Racism must find no refuge in and no solace from the church. It is a denial of the truth known in Christ, who breaks down the humanly constructed walls that partition us into alienated communities of faith (Eph. 2:13-14). The church cannot be "truly catholic" unless it is fully open to all people on an equal basis. The church we seek to become, therefore, must be a model, a prophetic sign of the unity in diversity of God's creation. Christians must hear this affirmation regularly and convincingly.

2. Identify, name, and share information with each other regarding those concrete programs and initiatives in combating racism that are already taking place within our member churches. A consultative conference should be explored to bring together this information and to take

further action in light of these learnings as a good faith first step anticipating the inaugural liturgical celebration of Churches Uniting in Christ in 2002.

3. Claim Martin Luther King Jr. Day observances and similar appropriate occasions for dialogue leading to systemic change. Encourage and enable interracial dialogue within and among churches, as well as among members of the whole community. When properly designed, such dialogue can be an indispensable instrument of justice and reconciliation—reducing fears, suspicions, and resentments, and enhancing mutual respect and understanding. The connection between the date of Martin Luther King Jr. Day observance and the Week of Prayer for Christian Unity has important potential in forging the concerns of addressing racism and pursuing our unity in Christ.

4. Take the discipline of social ethics seriously, because the careful arguments and nuanced distinctions demanded by that discipline can save us from the simplistic exhortations that hinder effective advocacy. An adequate defense of some preferential forms of affirmative action, for example, depends in part on sound and subtle interpretations of distributive and compensatory justice. Social ethics can bring a necessary depth to a strategy against racism.

5. Ensure that worship is an intentional witness against racism and therefore reflects the fullness of the Gospel. Worship is sometimes an instrument of racial separation and oppression. Not only is the eucharistic table divided by theological barriers, but also by the racial separation within and among the churches. As the member-churches of COCU seek a common table, they must evaluate all liturgical resources and practices and ensure their racial sensitivity and inclusiveness.

6. Maintain a strong program of Christian education on the dynamics of racism and the demands of racial justice. Educational resources, like liturgical ones, need to be evaluated to ensure that they are consistent witnesses against racism and for racial equality, especially in relation to family education.

7. Engage in rigorous institutional self-examinations, searching for racism embedded in the structures, politics, and programs of churches, and set goals for measuring our progress. This self-auditing is imperative to overcome racial offenses and advance racial reconciliation, while providing targets for change. It is most effectively accomplished in a context of mutual accountability, admonition, and affirmation among the churches.

8. Renew the churches' commitment to the struggle for equal human rights through advocacy. In continuing the civil rights agenda, four instruments of justice seem especially relevant for our time:

1. the preservation and enhancement of federal civil rights laws
2. the continuation of key affirmative action initiatives to address imbalances and deprivations caused by racism
3. the defense of economic rights, such as adequate housing, health care, nutrition, employment, and other essential material conditions
4. reform of the criminal justice system

9. Develop resources to address the issues related to racism in the member churches' capacity and responsiveness to new immigrant and cultural groups. As a first step in this "Call to Commitment and Action To Combat Racism," the delegates to the Eighteenth Plenary Session have covenanted together to actively pursue the commitment of our communions to combating racism in our churches and in our nation as an essential component in our pursuit to become Churches Uniting in Christ.

Combating racism is a formidable task—and eradicating it will appear to many as beyond realistic possibilities. It demands both the conversion of individuals and the transformation of churches. Yet we have good reasons for hope and persistence in struggle—primarily because God is ever creating new possibilities for racial solidarity.

The commitment by the COCU churches to overcome racism and live more intentionally the unity and catholicity of Christ's Church is a promise and a prayer. It will lead us into deeper understandings of the triune God, the redemption offered in Jesus Christ, the nature of the Church, and the world as created by God. In this commitment these nine churches, seeking to become the Church of Christ Uniting, will be a sign and foretaste of the unity of the whole people of God.

Adopted by unanimous vote of the delegates of the nine member communions to the Eighteenth Plenary of the Consultation on Church Union, January 24, 1999, in St. Louis, Missouri.

PART TWO

Bilateral Documents

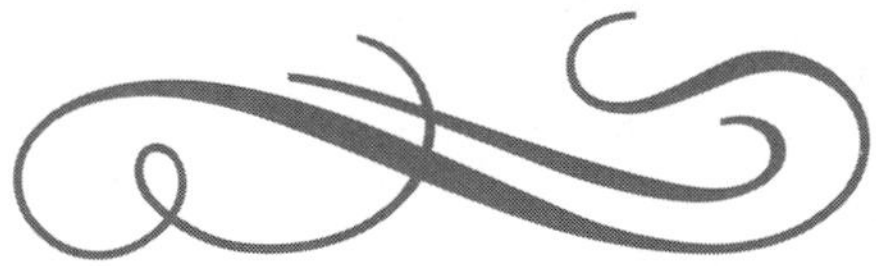

LUTHERAN-CATHOLIC

Editors' Note: *Earlier volumes in this series (see BU, 85-87; GC I, 374) give the background and context of the relationship between the Lutheran and Catholic churches.*

The full text of Document 9, Scripture and Tradition, *Round IX of the Lutheran-Catholic dialogue in the United States, consists of five parts, three of which are reproduced here. The original text begins with parts on the Word of God (I) and an overview of the evolution of the problem (II); the excerpt in this volume begins with part III, "Theological Considerations." Notes and paragraph numbers included here correspond to the original text and have not been renumbered. (For the full text, see* Scripture and Tradition, *eds. Harold C. Skillrud, J. Francis Stafford, and Daniel F. Martensen [Minneapolis, Augsburg, 1995].)*

Between 1993 and Round X, efforts were given to providing a summary of the dialogues, contributing to the drafting of the Joint Declaration on the Doctrine of Justification *and making clear, public recommitment of the two churches to full communion. For a summary of the dialogues, see* The Lutheran-Catholic Quest for Visible Unity: Harvesting Thirty Years of Dialogue *(Chicago: Evangelical Lutheran Church in America; Washington, DC: United States Catholic Conference, 1998).*

Finally, the second text published here, Round X's The Church as Koinonia of Salvation, *continues the work on the Church, now in the context of the agreement on justification and developments on ministry and structures. (For background essays on this text, see Randall Lee and Jeffrey Gros,* eds., The Church as Koinonia of Salvation: Its Structures and Ministries *[Washington, DC: United States Conference of Catholic Bishops; Chicago: Augsburg Fortress, 2004].)*

Document 9

SCRIPTURE AND TRADITION

Round IX of the Lutheran-Catholic Dialogue in the United States, 1995

III. Theological Considerations

32. In the wake of Vatican II the question between Lutherans and Catholics amounts to this: Is the permanent interconnection between Scripture, tradition, and Magisterium that is envisaged in Catholic thought compatible with the historic Lutheran principle that Scripture alone provides the norm by which tradition and Magisterium are to be judged? Because the standard formulations that are commonly used by Lutherans and by Catholics are obviously different, the theological question may also be framed this way: Are there conditions under which the two positions may be reconciled? What follows is a delineation of Lutheran and Catholic views on Scripture and tradition so that points of convergence can be discerned.

33. Because Lutherans ascribe prime importance to the oral proclamation of the Word of God, the *sola scriptura* principle not only does not rule out but demands continuing interpretation and application of Scripture. In addition, the Lutheran Confessions recognize the authority of the patristic tradition and early councils. Summing up the doctrines it has presented, for example, the Augsburg Confession argues that its position is in continuity with the writings of the ancient church: "Since this teaching is grounded clearly on the Holy Scripture and is not contrary or opposed to that of the universal Christian church, or even of the Roman church (insofar as the latter's teaching is reflected in the writings of the Fathers), we think that our opponents cannot disagree with us in the articles set forth above."[46] Similarly, in the Apology the Confessors responded to the charge that they

had undermined the authority of bishops by attesting to their "deep desire to maintain church polity and various ranks of the ecclesiastical hierarchy, although they were created by human authority," because "the Fathers had good and useful reasons for instituting ecclesiastical discipline in the manner described by the ancient canons."[47] Stressing the conviction that "our confession is true, godly, and catholic," the Apology declares the importance of right governance and affirms the office of those who teach the Word of God and administer the sacraments: "We want at this time to declare our willingness to keep the ecclesiastical and canonical polity."[48] There is one condition: that bishops cease condemning the sort of doctrine that Lutherans confess and allow the preaching of the gospel that is right and true. Thus it is characteristic of the Lutheran position to affirm the function of the episcopal teaching office if it exercises its basic responsibility to promote trustworthy preaching of the abundant mercy of God poured out in Jesus Christ apart from any merits of sinners.

34. Both the Lutheran Confessions and the Council of Trent spoke only of traditions in the plural. Now, however, the distinction between tradition and traditions is widely used in theology and can be described in this way. Tradition involves a process in a community; in this case, it refers to the Word of God precisely as it is handed on in the church: *verbum Dei traditum*. Tradition also denotes the content of what is handed on, namely, the totality of the gracious presence of Christ passed on in history through the power of the Spirit in the life, teaching, and worship of the church. Insofar as the community is the locus of Christ's redeeming presence in the world, tradition connotes that the church hands on in a living way all that it is, all that it believes.[49] Traditions (*traditiones*) are particular ideas, forumulations, and practices handed down in this process. To some of these the church commits itself as true expressions of the gospel, for example, *homoousios* and infant baptism. Others become customary in the course of the church's life, many of them not essential to the preaching of the gospel but valuable for Christian life. It is also possible for unsound customs or superstitious beliefs to creep into common use, so that discernment is needed to judge which traditions do not compromise the gospel and which are distortions.

35. In examining the question of what status may be given to human traditions in the church, the Apology of the Augsburg Confession teaches "that we receive forgiveness of sins freely for Christ's sake by faith"[50] and that this must be kept paramount in the church. Hence one should resist traditions that compromise the gospel: that is, traditions that are promoted

as if they merit the forgiveness of sin, or are acts of worship that please God as righteousness, or are performed of necessity because their omission is judged to be a sin. Yet even the apostles ordained many things, legitimate traditions that preserved order for the sake of peace, "and they did not set them down as though they could not be changed."[51] Hence, "this is the simple way to interpret traditions. We should know that they are not necessary acts of worship, and yet we should observe them in their place and without superstition, in order to avoid offenses."[52] Thus it is characteristic of the Lutheran position to allow for traditions that do not compromise the gospel and to cherish those that effectively promote it, even though these are not mentioned in Scripture.

36. In this perspective the *sola* of *sola scriptura*, as it is intended in the Lutheran Confessions, is not a term that would rule out the usefulness of everything that is not stated in the Scriptures. Like the other instances of *sola*, it expresses all that is necessary for the proper reception of divine saving grace, fundamentally pointing to Christ alone. The bright and shining light that is Scripture is the norm or rule that ensures adherence to the gospel in the historical proliferation of human traditions in the church. As the written testimony of all that Christ is and does for the sake of our salvation, it needs no supplement. Rather, Scripture alone is the arbiter in matters of faith and life.

37. The affirmation that *sola scriptura* as source and norm does not exclude the function of a teaching office or the value of many traditions in the church is, at first glance, a negative statement. However, there is a positive Lutheran investment in the formula, particularly with regard to the clarity (*claritas*) and self-interpretation (*sui ipsius interpres*) of Scripture, and its material sufficiency Scripture in itself, as the clear, written Word of God, gives the assurance that we are saved by grace through faith in Christ alone rather than through any works or merits of our own.

38. In the sixteenth century these considerations were a key area of polemic. Lutherans, on the one hand, held that the written word of God witnesses to all that needs to be known about the salvation of sinners and testifies to this so brilliantly that the general reader, the ordinary baptized person, can grasp the good news. The certainty of faith is based on the word of the gospel proclaimed according to Scripture alone. Catholics, on the other hand, asserted at that time that Scripture on its own is neither sufficient nor clear, thus making necessary the writings of the fathers and interpretation by the community.[53] This position was nuanced insofar as the Council of Trent retained as binding only apostolic traditions, written and

unwritten, with even these having no permanent value unless they dealt with matters of faith and morals. Although this approach converged with statements of the Lutheran Confessions on apostolic tradition, it differed from the *sola scriptura* understood by Lutherans.

39. Furthermore, Catholics at that time argued that *sola scriptura* was largely responsible for the theoretical and practical excesses of various sectarian groups labeled enthusiasts (*Schwärmer*) by Luther. These enthusiasts affirmed the right of all believers to private interpretations of the Bible, rejected the value of all traditions, denied the existence of any authority able to speak for the church, and consequently destroyed the received ecclesial structure. While this radical critique was aimed at Lutherans and Catholics alike, it seemed to Catholics to be a consequence of disconnecting Scripture from traditions and the teaching office, and thus Luther's *sola scriptura* was blamed for the spread of such ideas.

40. Today the issue assumes a somewhat different shape. For Lutherans *solus Christus* radically entails *sola gratia*, *sola fides*, and *sola scriptura*, all of which must be taken together as part of an integrated whole that proclaims how persons come to the salvation that God has appointed for them: only Scripture can make clear that it is Christ alone, by grace, through faith, who saves sinners. There is a lively suspicion on the Lutheran side that the Catholic appeal to tradition and the teaching office erodes and subverts this teaching of justification by grace and faith alone. If Scripture must be supplemented by something else, if its word of truth is so ambiguous that it needs interpretation by a normative authority, then its nature as the clear and bright written Word of God is compromised, with devastating effects on the power of the gospel to assure people of Christ's effective saving action.

41. Convergence, however, is opened up by Vatican II's position on Scripture, tradition, and the teaching office, a position not won without keen struggle and lively debate. The first schema on the topic, which was rejected, had urged recognition that tradition had material content to offer over and above what was contained in Scripture. (This is the neo-scholastic two-source theory.) The final teaching sees them more as a functioning unity, with Scripture having a nourishing and ruling function, while tradition interprets and hands on the whole living experience of Christ testified to by Scripture. Underlying this shift are two basic ideas, namely, that tradition is a Spirit-inspired process in the church rather than a set of materials, and that it is concerned with the life of the community in all of its dimensions, including personal example, prayer and worship, and structures, rather than with teachings only.

42. The standard Catholic teaching now holds that both Scripture and tradition derive from the same wellspring who is Christ, the source of grace and truth. Christ is witnessed to by his followers, who through their oral preaching, example, and institutions handed on what they had received. They committed the message of salvation to writing, giving us the Word of God in Scripture. Whether written in Scripture or preached and lived, the saving power and presence of Christ continues in the living voice of the gospel heard in the church through the ages.

43. Both the vigor of the conciliar debate and subsequent developments show that the Catholic community is in a process of rethinking that is not yet finished. It has clearly moved to reaffirm the irreplaceable centrality of Scripture for the preaching, teaching, and life of the church. It has moved away from the two-source theory of revelation which ascribed independent validity to tradition as a separate source of faith. At the same time it has not explicitly affirmed *sola scriptura* in at least two important Lutheran senses.

44. *Clarity*. The standard Catholic position is not that Scripture is unclear. To the contrary, it is lucidly articulate about God's saving will and, in the New Testament, about how this becomes living and effective in Christ for those who believe. It has the power so to interpret itself to the receptive reader. But for Catholics Scripture is the book of the church, its new writings written and received by the apostolic church which also interpreted the Scriptures of Israel in the light of Christ. Hence Scripture would be less than perfectly clear if it were read in isolation from the community, its tradition, and its interpretation. For Catholics to say this is not to compromise the certainty of faith but to broaden the base from which it is derived.[54]

45. *Norm or rule of faith*. In the Catholic view, Scripture, tradition, and teaching office are so linked and joined together that one cannot stand without the others.[55] However, the criterion or critical principle to be used to judge distortions that historically creep in has not been clearly articulated. Scripture is affirmed as a rule that governs preaching and the whole of religion, but it is not affirmed as the only rule.[56] During the conciliar debate this lack of a clear criterion was noted, along with the fact that there are distorting as well as legitimate traditions. As a result, while saying that the church hands on all that she is, all that she believes, the Council deleted the phrase "*omne quod habet*," all that she has, realizing that not all the church has is always and everywhere in accord with the gospel.[57] Nevertheless, the Council did not endorse Scripture as the sole rule of faith, thus leaving unresolved questions about the necessity of criticism of

tradition and the teaching office, and about the critical principle to be followed in conflict.[58]

46. Is there a possibility of convergence between Lutheran and Catholic theological positions on Scripture and tradition? A measure of agreement already exists. Lutherans adhere to apostolic and patristic tradition in the form of creeds, christological and trinitarian doctrines, church order, and the like, insofar as these are normed by Scripture, and they allow for developments in history such as the Lutheran Confessions according to the same rule. They attach great importance to oral proclamation and affirm the legitimacy of episcopal authority and the permissibility of human traditions. Catholics, by contrast, affirm the centrality of Scripture as the word of God for the life of the church. They have a growing appreciation of its normative character as it nourishes and rules preaching and the whole of religion. They no longer speak of tradition as a separate source of revelation. While affirming that there is growth in the understanding of the realities and the words which have been handed down, they see tradition as fundamentally this handing on and thus as a process of transmitting something already given.

47. There is obviously convergence here, although not complete unity. Both communities wholeheartedly affirm *solus Christus*: we are saved through faith in Jesus Christ alone. On the question of *sola scriptura*, basic theological affirmations can be made in common while there are still differences regarding Scripture's relation to tradition in the life of the church.

IV. The Living Word in the Community of Faith

48. The church in every age and in every part of the world continues to preach and receive the Word of God in faith and to respond actively in word and deed. Through its proclamation and response the church echoes the Word of God communicated through Scripture and earlier tradition, and makes it possible for believers everywhere to have access to the Word of God, no matter how far removed they may be in time, place, and culture from the original events of revelation. Through the power of the Holy Spirit the Word of God lives on in the memory of the church and is differently interpreted in different contexts.

49. Lutherans and Catholics are at one in their conviction that the Bible has a preeminent and irreplaceable role as the inspired Word of God committed to writing once for all. The Bible sustains and strengthens the

faith of its readers and becomes for them an abiding source and guide for life in Christ.[59] The Word of God as permanently given in Scripture is to be proclaimed in and by the church, the community of faith.

50. When the church assembles for worship, as it regularly does on Sundays, the Word of God is transmitted through proclamation and sacrament. A qualified minister is appointed to preside at the service. The readings at the liturgy and many of the prayers are taken from Holy Scripture, which accordingly plays a paramount role in the worship of the church.[60] The sermon commonly takes the form of proclamation based on biblical texts or that of exposition of a Scripture lesson, especially the Gospel for the day, and these are the forms of preaching most strongly encouraged by both our churches.[61] Not only preaching, but all forms of catechesis and religious instruction, not to say theology itself, are based primarily upon the Word of God in Scripture.[62]

51. The Word of God is not to be understood as an inert collection of words to be extracted from Scripture as stones from a quarry. It is living and active, the demanding voice of the law and the promising voice of the gospel (Jer 23:29; Heb 4:12). God is present in the Word, accomplishing the divine purpose (Is 55:11), ending the old and bringing in the new, exposing sin and working salvation in those who believe (Rom 1:16). This view of the relationship between Scripture and the proclaimed Word is deeply rooted in the Lutheran confessional tradition and is consonant with Catholic teaching.[63]

52. The role of liturgy in the shaping and testing of doctrine deserves fuller exploration than has yet been given to it by Lutherans and Catholics in dialogue. A convergence on the subject is noted in an earlier volume.[64] Because faith is continually renewed by personal confrontation with the realities of faith in communal prayer and sacramental worship, the church has from ancient times recognized the intimate connection between liturgy and belief, between the *lex orandi* and the *lex credendi*.[65] In both our traditions the axiom *lex orandi, lex credendi* is cited, but there are different views regarding the relative priorities. Expressing a more recent Catholic view, Pius XII pointed out that liturgical prayer offers testimonies and assists in the determination of doctrine, but he added that, "if one desires to differentiate and describe the relationship between faith and the sacred liturgy in absolute and general terms," the rule of belief should determine the rule of prayer.[66] From a Lutheran point of view, there is an interaction of prayer, testimony, and doctrine in the life of the church.[67] Recognizing the power of the liturgy to shape belief, Luther, like the other Reformers of his age, set out to revise the ceremonies to bring them into conformity with the Word of God.[68]

Notwithstanding their different emphases, Lutherans and Catholics agree in principle that sometimes the liturgy must be revised in order to make it a more faithful instrument for communicating the Word of God, while at other times the explicit teaching of the church may be enriched and improved by reflection on the implications of the forms of prayer and worship.

53. The Word of God is transmitted also by means of the confession of faith in word and deed. Scripture reports how the Israelites, in a pagan environment, and sometimes in the face of persecution, confessed their faith in the one true God who had saved them from slavery. The New Testament tells the story of how the apostles and their companions spread the good news of Christ through their courageous witness, extending at times to martyrdom. Embedded in the New Testament are brief confessional formulas in which Christians articulated their distinctive identity, proclaiming their faith in the one God and in Jesus as sole Lord, against opposing views, often polytheistic (1 Cor 8:5-6; Eph 4:5; cf. Rom 10:9). These confessional statements have inspired modern "confessions of faith," especially in situations of crisis.[69] Recently the Lutheran World Federation, considering that such a crisis had arisen in southern Africa, issued a statement that suspended membership of churches that tolerated apartheid.[70] Vatican Council II, in its *Decree on Ecumenism*, exhorted all Christians to "confess together before the whole world their faith in the triune God and in the incarnate Son of God, our Redeemer and Lord."[71] This decree expressed appreciation for "those Christians who openly confess Jesus Christ as God and Lord and as the sole Mediator between God and man" and who feel compelled to "bear witness to their faith among all the peoples of the earth."[72]

54. Although confessions of faith grounded in our common Scriptures can serve as a bond between our traditions, we still have to deal with a heritage of mutually opposing confessional statements. The Augsburg Confession of 1530 expressed ecumenical reform proposals on the part of the Lutheran party, but it has never been formally accepted by Catholic ecclesiastical authorities. Nevertheless, Pope John Paul II in 1980 recognized that this confession reflects "a full accord on fundamental and central truths."[73] Some later Lutheran confessional writings, such as the Smalcald Articles, were directed in part against what were perceived as Roman Catholic errors. Similarly from the Catholic side, the Profession of Faith of Pius IV (1564) was intended as a warning against what were perceived as false doctrines of the Protestant Reformers. A major concern of twentieth-century ecumenical dialogues has been to bridge the gap that is evident in these polemical confessions.[74]

55. Together with Scripture, a resource for overcoming the divisions has been, and still is, the adherence of our respective churches to three early Christian creeds, the Apostles' Creed, the Nicene-Constantinopolitan Creed, and the Athanasian Creed.[75] We agree that the Nicene dogma of the *homoousios* successfully "gathered up the sense of the Scriptures," to borrow the expression of Athanasius,[76] and to that extent expresses the Word of God. Catholics may speak of these creeds, as do the Lutheran authors of the Formula of Concord, as being "catholic and general creeds possessed of the highest authority" (*illa catholica et generalia summa auctoritatis symbola*).[77]

56. Like the creeds, the solemn definitions and anathemas of early councils, such as Nicea, Constantinople, Ephesus, and Chalcedon, are accepted in our respective churches as authoritative statements of the apostolic faith. Some differences, however, remain. Lutherans avoid speaking of infallible decisions, but they can agree with Catholics that the dogma of Nicea about God the Son, for example, is a "definitive reply to an ever-recurring question."[78] Catholics, while holding that such determinations of the faith are irreversible, can agree with Lutherans that the language and conceptuality of the early councils must not be absolutized.[79] The formulations of dogma are subject to human and historical limitations;[80] they demand new interpretations as new questions arise and as older cultural limitations are overcome. In the interpretation and reformulation of dogma the testimony of the Scriptures must always be fundamental,[81] but there can be normative doctrinal developments beyond the express statement of Scripture.

57. An example in both our traditions may be found in the endorsement of the title *Theotokos*, "God-bearer" or "Mother of God," for Mary.[82] While the title had apparently been coined earlier, the Council of Ephesus (431) adopted it as a corollary of the affirmation that Jesus Christ, while being both human and divine, was a single, undivided being. The christological synthesis of Jesus as God and man fostered the conviction that it was possible, and indeed necessary, to give Mary the title of *Theotokos* inasmuch as she gave birth to the divine Son according to his human nature. This development of ancient theology, formulated in terms of Greek culture, found general acceptance in most churches of the East as well as in the West. They all agreed that the dogmatic statement needed to be made authoritatively for the purpose of explicating and safeguarding a basic point of faith found in Scripture.

58. An example of development of Marian doctrine not shared by both our traditions is the Assumption of the Blessed Virgin Mary. On November 1, 1950, Pope Pius XII solemnly declared the bodily Assumption of Mary into heaven to be a dogma of Catholic faith. The first written

evidence of a belief in the Assumption goes back to the apocryphal literature on the "Dormition of the Virgin," which appeared in the late fourth century. While the Assumption was widely accepted in the West from the Middle Ages on, it is a doctrine found neither in the New Testament nor in the early fathers. The papal bull *Munificentissimus Deus* itself admitted that "theologians and preachers have [often] . . . been rather free in their use of events and expressions taken from Sacred Scripture to explain their belief in the Assumption" (no. 26).[83] Such scriptural usage, indeed, was often no more than an accommodation of unrelated texts by allegory or spiritual intuition. The document also invoked the liturgy but pointed out that liturgy "does not engender Catholic faith but springs from it" (no. 20). Liturgy, in this case, is a witness, not a source. Thus the decisive element in the definition of the dogma appears to be the universal assent of the episcopate supported by, and perhaps based on, the faith of the people. These elements are combined with the view that such a belief, having long been accepted and being universally held by Catholics as divinely revealed, is capable of being declared a dogma by the supreme teaching authority of the church (no. 41).

59. Although Lutherans have insisted that necessary articles of faith must be grounded in Scripture, they have not rejected all postbiblical formulations. A few spoke of a "patristic consensus" (*consensus patrum*) or a "consensus of the first five centuries" (*consensus quinquesaecularis*)[84] in order to express their sense of solidarity with the church catholic and their concern for the proper expression of biblical truth. When Socinians threatened the trinitarian basis of the church's confession on the ground that the doctrine of the Trinity was not literally in Scripture, Lutheran theologians rejected the notion that all true doctrine had to be simply and literally present in the Bible.[85] Nevertheless, Lutherans are critical of other postbiblical formulations. While they agree that as a matter of historical fact Marian devotion in the fourth century contributed to the definition of the *Theotokos* title, they cannot see how such devotion provides a legitimate basis for the dogma of Mary's Assumption into heaven. Here the earlier move from biblical text to postbiblical formulation to designate Mary as *Theotokos*, which extols Christ, has not been simply replicated; rather, interpretation has been stretched beyond what Lutherans consider to be a legitimate use of Scripture. For them, therefore, a dogmatic declaration such as that of 1950 cannot be justified.[86]

60. In both the Lutheran and the Catholic traditions, great importance is attached to the process of ensuring sound doctrine. The structures

for authenticating doctrine, however, are not the same.[87] According to Catholic doctrine the college of bishops, together with the pope as its head, succeeding respectively to the college of the apostles and to Peter, received from Christ the duty of teaching the faith with divine authority. Assisted by the Holy Spirit, these officeholders can on occasion make irrevocable determinations of the faith, binding on the whole church.[88] Such decisions, while they embody or protect the Word of God, are not regarded as being themselves the Word of God. They depend upon God's Word given in Scripture and tradition.

61. According to the *Augsburg Confession* the bishop is a pastor exercising the function of oversight and thus possesses the "power of the keys" to teach and preach the Word of God and to condemn doctrine that is contrary to the gospel.[89] In the Lutheran churches represented in this dialogue, the highest teaching authority is exercised by the churchwide assembly. The differing attitudes of Lutherans and Catholics toward episcopacy, papacy, and infallible teaching authority have been explored in volumes 4, 5, and 6 of this dialogue.

62. The Word of God is efficacious when it is received and welcomed by the faithful. Lutherans and Catholics alike hold that in accepting the faith as set forth in Scripture, creeds, and confessions members of the church submit their minds and hearts to the Word of God, and this reception, they add, is a vital, personal response empowered by the Holy Spirit who testifies within the hearts of the faithful.[90] Catholics understand that the teaching of popes and bishops, while it is authenticated by the Word of God and the authority of these teachers, is differently nuanced and sometimes takes on a richer significance in proportion to the spiritual gifts and talents of those who receive it.[91] When consensus is achieved between the authoritative teachers and the faithful, this unanimity is considered by Catholics to be a sign of the working of the Holy Spirit, who leads the whole church into the truth of revelation.[92]

63. Vatican II spoke in this connection of the "sense of the faith" (*sensus fidei*), and many theologians, especially in the Catholic tradition, have referred to the concordant sense (or consent) of the faithful (*sensus fidelium*) as a criterion of true doctrine. These terms, infrequently used in Lutheranism, can have a positive meaning in both our traditions, but must be cautiously applied. Catholic theologians, like Lutheran theologians, are generally aware of the danger of confusing the "sense of the faithful" with public opinion. Public opinion, even in the church, is not a norm of doctrine; it is ambiguous to the extent that it is influenced by sinful or

merely worldly considerations and lacks solid grounding in Scripture and apostolic tradition. The "sense of the faithful," as an authentic response to the Word of God, cannot be verified in a merely statistical way, but must be identified as a discernment issuing from a genuine obedience of faith.[93]

V. Conclusion

64. Our discussions have shown a large measure of agreement and some remaining differences of doctrine or emphasis. We note these significant points of agreement:

- Holy Scripture has preeminent status as the Word of God, committed to writing in an unalterable manner.
- Before the Old and New Testaments existed in written form, the Word of God was carried by tradition.
- Under the guidance of the Holy Spirit Scripture gives rise to the oral proclamation of law and gospel.
- The preeminent status of Scripture does not exclude the function of a teaching office or the legitimacy of doctrinal traditions that protect and promote the reliance of the faithful on the gospel message of Christ and grace alone (*solus Christus* and *sola gratia*).
- There are no historically verifiable apostolic traditions that are not attested in some way by Scripture.
- Not all true doctrine needs to be simply and literally present in the Bible, but may be deduced from it.
- The teaching of doctrine in the church is never above the Word of God, but must serve that Word and be in conformity with it.

65. We note these principal differences:

- Lutherans hold that Scripture alone is the ultimate norm by which traditions must be judged. Catholics hold that the decisive norm by which doctrines or traditions are judged is Scripture together with living apostolic tradition, which is perpetuated in the church through the influence of the Holy Spirit.

- Lutherans "question the appropriateness of speaking of the church's teaching office as infallible."[94] They consequently hold that all magisterial decisions are in principle subject to revision and correction in the light of a better reading of Scripture. Catholics hold that under certain conditions the bishop of Rome or the college of bishops with him, thanks to the assistance of the Holy Spirit, speak with infallibility. The gift of infallibility does not preclude further refinement in the teaching but gives assurance that the teaching will not have to be reversed.
- As a consequence of the two differences just noted, Lutherans and Catholics differ in their understandings of the development of doctrine. Lutherans recognize some developments, notably those declared by the early ecumenical councils, as expressing the true meaning of Scripture, but they do not accept developments that lack what Lutherans perceive as a clear basis in Scripture. For Catholics the supreme teaching authority of the church, with the assistance of the Holy Spirit, can proclaim doctrines expressing the faith of the whole church that go beyond the explicit statements of Scripture and beyond what can be strictly deduced from these statements.

66. In the present round of dialogue we have found that the Lutheran *sola scriptura*, when taken in conjunction with other Reformation principles, such as *sola fide*, *sola gratia*, and *solus Christus*, gives rise to a dynamic understanding of the Word of God that approximates what Catholics often understand as tradition in the active sense: the Spirit-assisted "handing on" of God's revelation in Christ. We also found that Catholics no longer speak of tradition as a separate source but see it, together with Scripture, as the Word of God for the life of the church. Scripture is seen as central to the preaching of the church and as the very soul of theology. For Lutherans and Catholics alike, the gospel is God's free and undeserved gift in Christ, the only Mediator, presented in the Scriptures that were inspired by the Spirit, proposed and explained by the preaching of the apostles and of the church's ministers, witnessed to in the church's creeds and confessions, formulated in many ways in the church's tradition, offered to believers in the celebration of Word and sacrament, received in faith with love and gratitude, and attested in the lives and a utterances of the saints. Thus, the present statement ties together the previous work of this dialogue in a joint affirmation

of the one faith in Christ alone that is communicated fundamentally and abidingly in Holy Scripture, the written form of the Word of God.

NOTES

46. CA, end of Part I; BC, 47; BS, 83 c-d.
47. Rev 14; BC, 214-215; BS, 296-297.
48. Rev 14:5; BC, 214; BS, 296.
49. DV, no. 8; see Joseph Ratzinger, "The Transmission of Divine Revelation," *Commentary on the Documents of Vatican II*, 5 vols., ed. Herbert Vorgrimler (New York: Herder and Herder, 1969), 3:183-184.
50. Rev 28:7; BC, 282; BS, 398.
51. Rev 28:16; BC, 283; BS, 401.
52. Rev 28:17; BC, 283-284; BS, 401.
53. In his *Quodlibetum* 17, printed in 1523, Konrad Köllin ascribes to his nephew Ulrich the conclusion that "the Sacred Letters teach nothing," adding, however, "This I would not say myself" (quoted in George Tavard, *Holy Writ or Holy Church: The Crisis of the Protestant Reformation* [London: Burns & Oates, 1959], 135); for other expressions that seem to devalue the Scriptures, see *Holy Writ*, 116 (Prierias), 132 (Henry VIII), 133 (Eustache of Zichen), 134 (Cornelius Snecanus).
54. The issue of "certainty of faith," including the Lutheran emphasis on *claritas* and on the contrast of *certitudo* and *securitas* (L/RC 8, 127) and involving the Catholic emphasis on the church community, calls for further future discussion.
55. DV, no. 10.
56. DV, no. 21.
57. DV, no. 8.
58. See Ratzinger, "The Transmission," 185-186, 191-192.
59. FC SD Rule and Norm 1; BC, 503; BS, 834; DV, no. 21.
60. LC, 1:84-86; BC, 376; BS, 581-582; SC, 24.
61. Rev 15:42; BC, 221; BS, 305:42; SC, no. 52; DV, no. 21.
62. LC Preface; BC, 361:17; BS, 552; DV, no. 24.
63. LC, 1:100-101; BC, 379; BS, 585-586; cf. SC, no. 7; DV, no. 21.
64. L/RC 8, 61.
65. The approved ritual of the church has often been seen as evidence for the beliefs reflected in that ritual. For example, Augustine in his debate with Julian of Eclanum used the practice of infant baptism to establish his doctrine of original sin. Many other examples from the early centuries are given by Geoffrey Wainwright, *Doxology: The Praise of God in Worship, Doctrine, and Life* (New York: Oxford, 1980),

218-235. He shows how Ignatius of Antioch, Irenaeus, Tertullian, Cyprian, Optatus of Milevis, Ambrose, and Prosper of Aquitaine, among others, used the practice of the church in prayer as a basis for holding the truth of doctrines that are reflected in that practice. The maxim "*Legem credendi lex statuat supplicandi*" in chapter 8 of the *Indiculus gratiae* (DS 246) is generally attributed to Prosper of Aquitaine.

66. *Mediator Dei* (1947), no. 48: text in *The Papal Encyclicals*, 5 vols., ed. Claudia Carlen (Wilmington, NC: McGrath Publishing Company, 1981), 4:119-154, at 128.

67. Edmund Schlink points out that creeds partake of the structure of doxology and that dogma is a second-order language having its basis in worship and witness: *The Coming Christ and the Coming Church* (Philadelphia: Fortress, 1968), 16-84.

68. See Luther's *Forma missae et communionis* of 1523 and his *Deutsche Messe* of 1526 for the removal of sacrificial language from the Mass. See Wainwright, *Doxology*, 268-269.

69. For example, faithful Protestants protested against the Nazi-inspired "German Christian" movement in the Barmen Declaration of 1934. Confessional language is likewise present in the encyclical of Pius XI, *Mit brennender Sorge* (1937: AAS [1937] 145-167), with its prophetic warnings against the idolatrous cult of race and state.

70. See LWF Report 19/20 (1985): 179-180. In taking this action in 1984, the Seventh Assembly of the LWF reaffirmed the statement against apartheid of the sixth assembly (Dar es Salaam, 1977).

71. UR, no. 12.

72. UR, no. 20.

73. The pope, addressing representatives of the Council of the German Evangelical Church at Mainz on November 17, 1980, is here quoting with approval a pastoral letter of the German bishops issued on January 20, 1980, in connection with the 450th anniversary of the Augsburg Confession. The text of the pope's address in German may be found in AAS 73 (1981) 71-75, at 73. For the English translation see LWF Report 10 (1980), Document 9, 62-66, at 64; also *Information Service* of the Secretariat for Promoting Christian Unity, 45 (1981): 5-7, at 6. The pastoral letter of the German bishops is printed in LWF Report 10, Document 6, 55.

74. For some proposed steps toward reconciliation see *The Condemnations of the Reformation Era: Do They Still Divide?*, ed. Karl Lehmann and Wolfhart Pannenberg (Minneapolis: Fortress, 1990). Dealing primarily with the condemnations of the Council of Trent and those of the Formula of Concord, this report, issued by a joint Ecumenical Commission in Germany, concludes, "A whole series of sixteenth-century condemnatory pronouncements rested on misunderstandings about the opposite position. Others were directed at extreme positions that were not binding on the church. Again, others do not apply to today's partner" (27). But the report acknowledges also that in some disputed matters, possibly not church-dividing, the dialogue group was unable to establish a sufficient consensus. It declared, "There is

as yet no explicit consensus about the critical function of Scripture over against the formation of the church's tradition" (27).

75. These "ecumenical" creeds are printed at the beginning of the Lutheran Book of Concord and appear in standard collections of Catholic official teaching, such as Denzinger-Schonmetzer. The "Athanasian" creed (*Quicumque*), at least today, does not enjoy as high a doctrinal and liturgical status in the practice of our churches as do the other two.
76. Letter *De Decretis nicaenae synodi*, PG 25:451; cf. John Courtney Murray in L/RC 1, 17.
77. FC SD, Rule and Norm 2; BC, 504; BS, 834.
78. "Summary Statement," L/RC 1, 32, §6a. The statement acknowledged in §6c: "The way in which doctrine is certified as dogma is not identical in the two communities, for there is a difference in the way in which mutually acknowledged doctrine receives ecclesiastical sanction."
79. In the words of George Lindbeck, quoted by Warren A. Quanbeck, "The church is obligated to a continuous search (in reliance on the Holy Spirit and with the help of reason) for fuller understanding of what faithfulness to the scriptural witness involves"; see "The Second Theological Consultation between Lutherans and Catholics" in L/RC 2, 76.
80. UR, no. 6; Congregation for the Doctrine of the Faith, *Mysterium Ecclesiae*: AAS 65 (1973): 396-408, esp. no. 5, at pages 402-404.
81. Cf. International Theological Commission, "On the Interpretation of Dogmas," *Origins* 20 (May 17, 1990): 1-14, at 10.
82. See L/RC 8, 88, "Common Statement," no. 164, with note 149, on page 352.
83. The numbers in parentheses refer to the English translation, *The Dogma of the Assumption* (New York: Paulist, 1951). The official text is found in AAS 42 (1950) no. 26, p. 762; no. 20, p. 760; no. 41, p. 769. Around the time of the definition, a considerable amount of literature was published on the theme of the progress of dogma. See, e.g., Clement Dillenschneider, *Le sens de la foi et le progres dogmatique du mystere marial* (Rome: Academia Mariana Internationalis, 1954). See also Avery Dulles, "The Dogma of the Assumption," L/RC 8, 279-294.
84. The term is attributed to Georg Calixt (d. 1656). See J. Wallmann in TRE 7 (1981): 554. An early translation of the *Book of Concord*, vol. 2: *Historical Introduction, Appendices and Indexes* (ed. Henry E. Jacobs [Philadelphia: General Council Publication Board, 1883]), included Calovius, as quoted in "Catalogue of Testimonies," 272-293.
85. Heinrich Schmid, *The Doctrinal Theology of the Evangelical Lutheran Church*, 3rd rev. ed., translated from German and Latin (Minneapolis: Augsburg, 1899, reprinted 1961), 95.
86. L/RC 8, 55.
87. See "Catholic and Lutheran Reflections" in L/RC 6, 38-68.

88. LG, no. 25.
89. CA 28:5-8, 21-22; BC, 81-82, 84; BS, 121-122, 123-124.
90. Rev 7–8:5; BC, 169; BS, 234-235; *Small Catechism* 3:6; BC, 345; BS, 511-512; DV, nos. 5 and 8.
91. UR, nos. 14, 17; AG, no. 22.
92. DV, no. 8; LG, no. 12; cf. LG, no. 25; also Jn 14:25-26, 16:22-23.
93. The Catholic understanding of *sensus fidei*, in contrast to mere public opinion, is explained in the Congregation for the Doctrine of the Faith's *Instruction on the Ecclesial Vocation of the Theologian*, no. 35, in *Origins* 20 (July 5, 1990): 117-126, at 124. See also John Paul II, apostolic exhortation *Familiaris consortio*, no. 5, in *Origins* 11 (December 24, 1981): 437-468, at 440.
94. L/RC 6, 67.

Document 10

THE CHURCH AS *KOINONIA* OF SALVATION: ITS STRUCTURES AND MINISTRIES

Round X of the Lutheran Catholic Dialogue in the United States, 2004

Part One: Deepening Communion in Structures and Ministries

Introduction

1. From 1965 to 1993, the continuing dialogue between Lutherans and Roman Catholics in the United States addressed doctrines and issues that have united or separated our churches since the sixteenth century. Considerable convergences and even consensus at times have been expressed in nine rounds of discussion on the Nicene Creed (round I); baptism (round II); the eucharist (round III); the ministry of the eucharist (round IV); papal primacy (round V); teaching authority and infallibility (round VI); justification (round VII); the one mediator, the saints, and Mary (round VIII); and Scripture and tradition (round IX).[1] The summaries and joint or common statements in these volumes of findings and supporting studies have been important for relations between our churches and for wider ecumenical discussion.

2. A coordinating committee[2] was appointed by the United States Conference of Catholic Bishops' Committee for Ecumenical and Interreligious Affairs and by the presiding bishop of the Evangelical Lutheran Church in America (ELCA) after the completion of round IX in 1993. It met from 1994 to 1996 to plan for a new round of dialogue and to take part in the development and reception process for a statement on justification by

faith and the reassessment of the condemnations connected with justification in the sixteenth century. The Coordinating Committee made a common Lutheran-Catholic response to a draft of the *Joint Declaration on the Doctrine of Justification* in 1995. It also developed the topic proposal dealt with in this volume, *The Church as Koinonia of Salvation: Its Structures and Ministries*, and in the guidelines[3] accepted by our sponsoring church authorities for a new dialogue team.

3. This tenth round of Lutherans and Catholics in Dialogue, begun in 1998, carried out its study of ecclesiology and ministries with a new basis in the important results from earlier discussions affirmed in a *Joint Declaration on the Doctrine of Justification* (JDDJ). An Official Common Statement confirming the *Joint Declaration*, accompanied by an Annex to the Official Common Statement, was signed by representatives of the LWF and the Roman Catholic Church[4] in Augsburg, Germany, on October 31, 1999.

4. The seventh volume of the U.S. dialogue, Justification by Faith, which was completed in 1983, was among the resources[5] that contributed to this worldwide agreement, especially with its own Declaration that set forth the gospel we encounter in Scripture and church life:

> Thus we can make together, in fidelity to the gospel we share, the following declaration:
>
> We believe that God's creative graciousness is offered to us and to everyone for healing and reconciliation so that through the Word made flesh, Jesus Christ, "who was put to death for our transgressions and raised for our justification" (Rom. 4:25), we are all called to pass from the alienation and oppression of sin to freedom and fellowship with God in the Holy Spirit. It is not through our own initiative that we respond to this call, but only through an undeserved gift which is granted and made known in faith, and which comes to fruition in our love of God and neighbor, as we are led by the Spirit in faith to bear witness to the divine gift in all aspects of our lives. This faith gives us hope for ourselves and for all humanity and gives us confidence that salvation in Christ will always be proclaimed as the gospel, the good news for which the world is searching.[6]

5. The Joint Declaration was a harvest from such statements in the U.S. and international dialogues. In Germany between 1981 and 1985, the Joint Ecumenical Commission and Ecumenical Study Group of Protestant

and Catholic Theologians dealt with the condemnations by Catholics and Lutherans in the sixteenth century on justification and related topics.[7] The Joint Declaration sets forth a common understanding of justification (§§14-18), in light of the biblical message (§§8-12), with explication in seven problem areas of what Lutherans and Catholics can confess together ecumenically, as well as the distinctive accents of each, now acceptable to the other (§§19-39). In light of the "consensus in basic truths of the doctrine of justification" (§40), the Joint Declaration states that "it becomes clear that the mutual condemnations of former times do not apply to the Catholic and Lutheran doctrines of justification as they are presented in the Joint Declaration" (Annex, §1; cf. JDDJ, §41; Official Common Statement, §1). But it is also recognized that this consensus "must prove itself" in "further clarification" of topics that include "ecclesiology, ecclesial authority, church unity, ministry, the sacraments, and the relation between justification and social ethics" (§43).

6. The *Joint Declaration* has great implications and holds much promise for life in our parishes, in reshaping preaching, teaching, worship, and daily life. It has found expression in agreements and covenants between local congregations, synods, and dioceses, and in national celebrations in the United States, even among Christians neither Catholic nor Lutheran, not to mention reflections in other parts of the world. For our dialogue, it has given fresh impulse and encouragement to our work together.

7. As we have dealt with structures and ministries, we have been mindful of how the dialogue's rounds IV and V (1968-1980) took up the topic of ministry in connection with the eucharist and then papal ministry (also in the sixth volume, *Teaching Authority and Infallibility*). Our review of much of the work done in rounds IV and V made us aware of how helpful and significant these contributions were. Round IV dealt only with local ministry in the local congregation where the eucharist is celebrated and the word is preached. Round V dealt with a universal ministry and the possibility of a renewed papacy. The present round considers the interrelation among local, regional, national, and worldwide ministries and church structures, in the context of an understanding of the church as *koinonia* of salvation.[8] Thus, in continuity with past dialogues and the *Joint Declaration*, our analysis moves from Christ and the gospel of salvation to *koinonia*. We understand this gospel particularly as the message of justification by grace through faith, and we treat *koinonia* as a lens through which to view ecclesiology and ministries of those ordained, within the whole people of God.

8. This report will proceed from a general consideration of *koinonia* ecclesiology (section I) and the specific concept of the "local church" (section II) to a consideration of the particular structures of *koinonia* in our two churches (section III) and the ordained ministries that serve them (section IV). A brief discussion of the ecumenically significant question of apostolic succession and its relation to ministry follows (section V). All of this analysis and description then forms the background for an argument for a fresh vision of how structures and ministry can be understood, including recommendations (sections VI, VII, and VIII).

9. This new vision confronts us with the wounds to mission and ministry that are the result of our continuing division and calls us to repentance and greater fidelity to the gospel. It invites us to partial mutual recognition of ordained ministry. It opens new paths in the exploration of a universal ministry of unity. The analysis offers a basis for a deeper recognition of each other's churchly reality and of our local, regional, and universal ministries and structures. This recognition will involve stronger acknowledgment of the churchly reality of the parish for Catholics, and of the theological significance of synods for Lutherans.

I. Koinonia Ecclesiology

10. There are good reasons why viewing the church as *koinonia* came into prominence ecumenically in the latter decades of the twentieth century (see §§15-20 below). The basic word *koinōnia* in Greek, is ancient, occurring twenty-two times in the Bible,[9] but it was not a term or concept prominent in Catholic or Lutheran documents of the sixteenth century. Thus it has been spared some of the partisan usage that often has made other concepts divisive. *Koinonia* has never been a church-dividing issue for Lutherans and Catholics. It is a useful lens through which this present dialogue reconsiders our differences concerning ministry and church structures. We speak together about this lens in three propositions: the church shares in salvation; the church shares salvation with others; and the church is a community shaped by salvation. All three are expressed in Scripture through words related to *koinonia*.

A. The Church Shares in Salvation

11. We, the justified, share in salvation from God in Christ in a number of ways. We are called by God into the fellowship of his Son (see 1 Cor. 1:9).[10]

We share in the gospel (see Phil. 1:5). We share in Christ's body and blood in the bread we break and the cup we share as presentation for us of Jesus' death on the cross and of its benefits for us (see 1 Cor. 10:16). We participate in the Spirit (see 2 Cor. 13:13; Phil. 2:1) and share in faith in all the good that is ours in Christ (see Phlm. 6). We also share in Christ's and each other's affliction and sufferings (see Phil. 3:10; 4:14), amid which there is consolation (see 2 Cor. 1:7) and the promise of participation in joy and future glory (see 1 Pet. 4:13; 5:1; 2 Pet. 1:4, on future sharing in God's own nature). Witnesses share the kingdom as well as experience persecution and patient endurance (see Rev. 1:9). The sharing in the Spirit that characterizes Christians is also part of the basis for the love and agreement with one another that we, the church, are called to have (see Phil. 2:1). The fellowship that 1 John 1:3-7 depicts is with God the Father and his Son, as well as with one another.[11] In God's plan of salvation, Gentile Christians too came to share, as branches, the riches of the olive tree, Israel (see Rom. 11:17).

B. The Church Shares Salvation

12. *Koinonia* characterizes not only the way we receive salvation but also the way it is offered to others through the church. Through evangelization we share the gospel with others (see Phil. 1:5, 7) as part of its advance (see Phil. 1:12, 25; 4:14-15) in mission (see Mt. 28:19-20). This sharing transforms the church itself as well as the world. The agreement between Paul and other church leaders to evangelize both Jews and Gentiles cuts across boundaries of racial and ethnic divisions of the day; it was a mutual pledge for mission, unity, and support for the poor (see Gal. 2:9-10). We support the proclamation of the gospel through our financial gifts (see Phil. 4:15); we share our resources with the poor and those in need throughout the world. In Paul's time, that meant a collection from his Gentile churches for "the saints," impoverished Jewish Christians in Jerusalem (see 2 Cor. 8:4; 9:13; Rom. 15:26-27); this economic aid showed concern for the unity of the church (see Gal. 2:9-10).[12] Acts depicts Christians in Jerusalem as sharing not only the gospel message but also their temporal resources (see Acts 2:42, 45; 4:32). In subsequent centuries, such active sharing, *koinonia*, has become the norm for Christian life and has been manifested in sharing food, time, and the results of all sorts of human abilities, as well as money.

C. The Church Is a Community Shaped by Salvation

13. The *koinonia* of salvation has called forth a type of community, the church, appropriate to the grace and calling we have received. We are a *koinonia* called in Christ by and for the gospel (see 1 Cor. 1:9; Phil. 1:5), a community that comes from the Holy Spirit (see 2 Cor. 13:13). The vertical and horizontal fellowship with God and fellow believers (see 1 Jn. 1:2-7) results in a people conformed to Christ's death on the cross (see Phil. 3:10, on the cross and resurrection of Jesus; 1 Pet. 4:13, on suffering and rejoicing). That means for the justified an existence determined by God's love and faithfulness, a life lived with love, in faith and trust, marked by hope. This vertical and horizontal fellowship exists in and with the world and its institutions. It is shaped internally by its relationship with God through Christ and the Spirit and by the participation in Christ and salvation of all members of Christ's body. Externally the church relates to the world not merely as a social institution amid the other public structures (*ta koina*) of the Greco-Roman world,[13] but more important, as a sign of God's will that all share in salvation. Divisions in fellowship blunt the impact of our witness to salvation.

D. Summary

14. In sum, therefore, *koinonia* in the New Testament especially concerns the relationship of justified believers with God and Christ (1 Cor. 1:9; 1 Jn. 1:2-7) and the Spirit (2 Cor. 13:13), thus with the Trinity. (The word "*koinonia*" does not refer in the New Testament to fellowship within the Godhead, as it does in patristic writers who spoke of *koinonia* between the Father and the Son[14]). *Koinonia* also has ecclesiological (Gal. 2:9; 2 Cor. 13:13) and eucharistic connotations (1 Cor. 10:16). The concept appears as a basis for ethical admonitions (Phil. 2:1) and can also itself be an admonition to share, both in the church and with the poor (Rom. 15:26-27). The New Testament references speak of sharing in sufferings (Phil. 3:10) and of sharing in consolation for people who share in suffering (2 Cor. 1:7). *Koinonia* connects with themes like mission, life together (Acts 2:42), stewardship, and future hope.

E. Recent Developments in *Koinonia* Ecclesiology

15. From New Testament usage, *koinonia* came to be employed over the centuries as "communion" (*communio*) and in many other renderings, particularly with reference to the church. While the terminology did not

play a role of any importance in sixteenth-century Reformation or Catholic theology, it became more prominent in the twentieth century.[15]

In Eastern Orthodoxy, *koinonia* ecclesiology has recently centered on eucharistic communion with Christ.[16]

16. Ecclesiology can be called "a chapter of Christology"[17] as long as it also is pneumatological. The terminology also came into the World Council of Churches (WCC), especially through the work of the Faith and Order Commission: "fuller *koinonia*" is the goal of life together in Christ.[18] Bilateral dialogues have found the theme helpful,[19] as have theologians from a variety of traditions.[20]

17. Among Catholics, "communion" was used to speak in a non-juridical way of "a network of sacramentally focused local churches bound together ultimately by the mutual openness of their eucharistic celebrations," with the bishop of Rome "as the focal point of the network of churches linked together in the catholic, or universal, *communio*."[21] Communion as "the permanent form of the unity of the church" was articulated on the eve of the Second Vatican Council.[22] J. M. R. Tillard explored communion ecclesiology as conforming "best to the biblical notion and to the intuitions of the great ecclesiological traditions."[23] The 1985 Synod of Bishops recognized communion ecclesiology as "the central and fundamental idea" of the documents of the Second Vatican Council.[24] The concept of communion came to be applied in a wide range of contexts. The 1992 statement from the Congregation for the Doctrine of the Faith "Some Aspects of the Church as Communion" explained that "ecclesial communion is at the same time visible and invisible" and this link "makes the church 'sacrament of salvation.'"[25] The 1993 Directory for Ecumenism stressed the presence and activity of the universal church in the particular churches.[26] Pope John Paul II said in 1995 that the "elements of sanctification and truth" shared by "the other Christian communities" show that "the one Church of Christ is effectively present in them." This is the reason for the communion that persists between the Catholic Church and "the other Churches and Ecclesial Communities," in spite of their divisions.[27]

18. For Lutherans, the term *koinonia* was used in German discussions on Protestant church fellowship in the 1950s.[28] In the latter part of the twentieth century, the LWF increasingly employed *koinonia/communio* themes.[29] In 1990 it defined itself as "a communion of churches which confess the triune God, agree in the proclamation of the Word of God and are united in pulpit and altar fellowship."[30] Lutherans and Catholics in dialogue have related *koinonia* to the doctrine of the Trinity and ecclesiology.[31]

19. *Koinonia* encompasses all Christians and the salvation of all who share in the gospel. *Koinonia* ecclesiology has many aspects but no uniform definition. The New Testament references to "*koinonia*" do not directly relate the term to "church," let alone to "ministries," but repeatedly deal with all the faithful. In presenting the church as *koinonia*, the Lutheran–Roman Catholic International Commission placed the church within a series of biblical images, beginning with "people of God," and added that, in both our traditions, "we rightly speak of the 'priesthood of all the baptized' or the 'priesthood of all believers.'"[32] All structures and ministries, as instruments of *koinonia*, serve God's people. Whatever is said, then, of "*koinonia* ecclesiology" and "ministry in service of community" is to be embedded in this context: the people of God, all Christian believers.

20. This dialogue now wishes to contribute further to these varied understandings of the church as *koinonia*. The following sections will focus on *koinonia* ecclesiology in the context of historical and current Lutheran-Catholic relationships. Our ecclesiologies and our ordained ministries of presbyters and bishops are viewed afresh through the lens of *koinonia*. Our dialogue is intended to foster reconciliation between our churches and is offered to the wider ecumenical community for study and reflection.

II. The Local Church Within the *Koinonia* of Salvation

21. An important element in much recent *koinonia* ecclesiology of particular significance for this report's analysis is the concept of the "local church," understood in similar but different ways by our two traditions. On the one hand, both Lutherans and Catholics agree that there is a local body which is not merely a part of the church, but is wholly church, even if not the whole church and not in isolation from the rest of the church. Our traditions agree: "The local church is truly church. It has everything it needs to be church in its own situation. . . . The local church is the place where the church of God becomes concretely realized."[33] To say that the local church is "church" in an integral sense is to say that the essential elements of the community—which participates in, shares, and is shaped by salvation—are present in a complete and integral way.

22. On the other hand, Lutherans and Catholics differ over what "local church" designates. For Lutherans, the local church is the congregation; for Catholics, it is most often the diocese.[34] This difference is closely related to a parallel set of differences over the status of the ordained minis-

ters who minister to these two communities: the minister of the congregation or parish (the pastor, priest, or presbyter) and the minister of the regional grouping of these communities (the bishop). This difference is rooted in the complex history of the development of local and regional church bodies (see §§159-195).

23. This complex history begins with the variety of community structures and ministries within first-century Christianity. By the second and third centuries, the pattern was established of local communities gathered for worship around the bishop, who was surrounded by a council of presbyters and was assisted by deacons.[35] During the profound changes of the late patristic and early medieval periods, the role of the bishop and the nature and size of the communities he headed changed. The primary Christian community for most Christians in the West came to be the parish under the care of a presbyter or priest. The diocese headed by the bishop came to include many such parishes. These shifts contributed to the medieval uncertainties about the relation between priest and bishop and lie at the root of the Lutheran-Catholic difference about what is to be designated "local church" (see §§172-175).

A. The Local Church in Catholic Ecclesiology

24. In continuity with one aspect of the early church, Roman Catholics define the local church (or, more often, the particular church or diocese) as "a portion of the people of God whose pastoral care is entrusted to a bishop in conjunction with his priests. Thus, in conjunction with their pastor and gathered by him into one flock in the Holy Spirit through the gospel and the eucharist, they constitute a particular church."[36] The basic unit of the church is therefore defined both eucharistically and ministerially. The ministry of the bishop is a constitutive element of the most basic ecclesiastical unit, the diocese, which includes all that is necessary to be a church. The link between the parish eucharist and the bishop is not obvious to most Roman Catholics, however, since they only occasionally experience a eucharistic assembly in which their bishop presides, even though they mention the bishop by name in every eucharistic liturgy the parish celebrates.

25. The descriptions of the local or particular church in the documents of the Second Vatican Council emphasize both elements. On the one hand, it is said that "the faithful are gathered together through the preaching of the gospel" and the eucharist.[37] On the other hand, it also is said, "the principal manifestation of the church consists in the full, active

participation . . . at one altar, at which the bishop presides."[38] Since the bishop cannot always or everywhere preside over the whole flock, he establishes multiple assemblies of believers. "Parishes, organized locally under a parish priest who acts in the bishop's place, are the most important of these, because in some way they exhibit the visible church set up throughout the nations of the world."[39]

B. The Local Church in Lutheran Ecclesiology

26. Lutherans, in continuity with a different aspect of the early church, have generally held that the congregation is church in the full sense. As the international Roman Catholic–Lutheran Joint Commission expressed this view in Church and Justification:

> Lutherans understand the *una sancta ecclesia* to find outward and visible expression wherever people assemble around the gospel proclaimed in sermon and sacrament. Assembled for worship the local congregation therefore is to be seen, according to the Lutheran view, as the visible church, *communio sanctorum*, in the full sense. Nothing is missing which makes a human assembly church: the preached word and the sacramental gifts through which the faithful participate in Christ through the Holy Spirit, but also the ministers who preach the word and administer the sacraments in obedience to Christ and on his behalf, thus leading the congregation.[40]

This understanding can be seen as a return to the pattern of the early church in which the basic ecclesial unit was a face-to-face assembly. Nevertheless, such a return involves a break with the pattern, both patristic and medieval, in which the bishop heads the local church. The office of ministry is included as an essential element of the local church in the Lutheran understanding, but this office is seen as exercised by the pastor/presbyter.

C. Catholic-Lutheran Similarities on the Local Church

27. This difference between what Lutherans and Catholics designate as the local church masks a deep structural similarity: Lutherans and Catholics each experience the church in a geographically local, face-to-face assembly where the word is preached and sacraments are celebrated: the parish or congregation. In addition, for both of our churches, this local

assembly is not freestanding, but rather exists within a regional community of such assemblies, namely, a diocese or synod. These groupings reach to the national and international level, but the diocese or synod, as the primary regional community, forms the immediate institutional context of the life of the congregation or parish. Lutherans and Catholics differ as to whether the face-to-face assembly or the primary regional community is the local church in the theological sense, but the institutional life of both traditions is shaped by this pairing.

28. This pairing of face-to-face assembly and regional community developed over an extended period without a conscious intent to create this pattern. How is this development to be understood theologically? Is it completely fortuitous, or does it express an institutional truth about how the *koinonia* of salvation is rightly realized, namely, the need both for the immediate experience of *koinonia* in the physical presence of one to another and for the embodiment of the catholicity and diversity of *koinonia* in a community of such face-to-face communities? It may be a theological mistake to insist that one or the other is "local church" in an exclusive sense without also saying that there is something about this pairing of face-to-face assembly and primary regional community that is ecclesiologically normative. If this pairing is normative, we must inquire what significance this structure has for our understanding of the ministries of those who preside over these communities, the pastor and the bishop.

29. Already in the New Testament, the worshiping community did not live in isolation, but rather joined in *koinonia* with other communities. Paul took up a collection (*koinonia*) among his predominantly Gentile churches of Greece and Asia Minor for the church in Jerusalem (see Acts 11:29; Rom. 15:25-27; 1 Cor. 16:3-5). This action extended that initial sharing of common life in Jerusalem by which "distribution was made to each as any had need" (see Acts 4:35).[41] Typically, in the closing of the various letters of the New Testament, churches sent greetings to other churches (see 1 Cor. 16:19; Phil. 4:22; 2 Tim. 4:21; Titus 3:15; Heb. 13:24; 1 Pet. 5:13; 2 Jn. 13; 3 Jn. 15).

30. In the post-biblical period, various ecclesial practices emphasized the communion among local churches. The practice of regional synods and the development of creedal expressions of the faith and of the common canon of Scripture are exercises of *koinonia*. Individuals presented letters of communion to be admitted to the eucharist of another bishop, indicating that the two sees were in communion with each other. The participation of three bishops in the ordination of a brother bishop signified that he was

being admitted into the episcopal college, and bishops frequently visited and corresponded with each other to maintain communion (see §§159-162).[42]

31. Christian communities experience *koinonia* across both space and time. Across space they experience the catholicity of the church in its extension throughout the world as one church consisting of many particular churches in communion with one another. Across time they experience continuity with the apostolic faith of the originating Christian community, the eschatological community founded on the apostles (see Rev. 21:14), and with all communities before and after it that have pursued and will pursue the apostolic mission. The local church is church only within this comprehensive *koinonia*.

III. Realizations of Ecclesial Koinonia

32. As the concept of local church indicates, the *koinonia* of salvation is realized in concrete communities with specific structures. The structures and ministries of the church embody and serve the *koinonia* of salvation. It has been a fruitful ecumenical strategy to work from a renewed theology of communion toward a renewed consideration of longstanding, difficult issues in relation to structure and ministries. In this document, we attempt on the basis of a reflection on concrete structures of *koinonia* in our churches to look anew at controversies in relation to structure and ministry that have divided our churches in the past.

33. Lutherans and Catholics affirm together a variety of interdependent realizations of ecclesial *koinonia*: the congregation or parish (i.e., a face-to-face worshiping assembly gathered by word and sacrament), a regional community or grouping of congregations or parishes (the synod in the ELCA; the diocese in the Catholic Church), a multiplicity of national structures, and a worldwide organization.

34. These realizations and our theological understanding of them, however, are not symmetrical in our two churches. As already noted, Lutheran and Catholic ecclesiologies differ on which realizations may actually be called a "church." In addition, Lutherans, unlike Catholics, have no worldwide body that is itself a church. Roman Catholics do not have national churches in the same sense as Anglicans, Lutherans, or Orthodox do. These differences in ecclesiology involve parallel differences in evaluations of ministry. For example, Catholics consider the bishop to possess the "fullness of the sacrament of order,"[43] while Lutherans follow the teaching of

Jerome that there is no difference other than jurisdiction between a presbyter and a bishop.[44] In Catholicism, the ministry of worldwide communion is exercised by the college of bishops, inclusive of the bishop of Rome as member and head, who also can act on the college's behalf. While various ministries occur among Lutherans on a global level, there is no formally recognized minister of worldwide communion.

35. In each of our traditions, the ecclesiological understanding of these various realizations of *koinonia* requires deeper reflection. Larger Lutheran churches around the world are typified by a structure including face-to-face assemblies or congregations, regional groupings of such congregations (called "synods" in the ELCA), and a national or supraregional body with extensive authority to make doctrinal and ecumenical decisions.[45] This structural pattern has rarely, however, been theologically explicated[46] and does not include the universal church. In Catholicism, more recent general councils have primarily focused upon theologies of ministry, which then have shaped the understanding of the structures of ecclesial *koinonia*. For example, the First Vatican Council addressed the theology of the papacy, and the Second Vatican Council developed a theology of the episcopacy from which emerged a theology of the local church. A theology of the presbyterate remained comparatively undeveloped in Lumen Gentium (LG), the Dogmatic Constitution on the Church, since only one section discusses the priesthood within the chapter on the hierarchy.[47] It is not surprising, then, that the parish has not been the subject of much theological reflection within Catholicism.[48] An ecumenical reflection on the structures and ministries of *koinonia* thus promises not only new possibilities for the relation between our churches, but also an occasion for consideration of our own ecclesiological blind spots.

A. The Congregation or Parish

36. Lutherans and Roman Catholics affirm together that Christians share in the *koinonia* of salvation most immediately in the worshiping assembly gathered around the baptismal font, the pulpit, and the eucharistic table. Within these communities, the gospel is preached and the faith is professed, the catechumens are evangelized and are formed, the community receives the baptized, and all are nurtured. There the faithful partake of one bread and become one body (see 1 Cor. 10:16). Mission is carried out there, to and for the world.[49] For both Catholics and Lutherans, this face-to-face

community is of ecclesiological significance; it is a *koinonia* of salvation, whether or not it is labeled "local church" in the sense discussed above.

1. Lutherans on the Congregation

37. The interdependence of congregation and the wider community finds expression in the definition of a congregation in the ELCA: "a community of baptized persons whose existence depends on the proclamation of the gospel and the administration of the sacraments and whose purpose is to worship God, to nurture its members, and to reach out in witness and service to the world. To this end it assembles regularly for worship and nurture, organizes and carries out ministry to its people and neighborhood, and cooperates and supports the wider church to strive for the fulfillment of God's mission in the world."[50]

38. Each congregation participates with the wider church in God's mission to the world. The sense of relationship, partnership, and commitment to the wider community of faith is reflected in the basic criteria for recognition of ELCA congregations for they must agree to support the life and work of this church (meaning the whole Evangelical Lutheran Church in America).[51] Furthermore, they must pledge to foster and participate in interdependent relationship with other congregations, the synod, and the churchwide organization.[52]

2. Catholics on the Parish

39. For Catholics also, the parish, especially as a place of Sunday eucharistic worship and as the place of Christian initiation, is where the people of God experience the church most immediately. The universal church is actualized in specific places and circumstances, in specific cultures and within particular communities, or not at all. The parish is both gathered together by the preaching of the gospel of Christ[53] and joined together through the flesh and blood of the Lord's body in its celebration of the Lord's Supper.[54]

40. The theology of the parish has been strengthened by the implementation of the Rite of Christian Initiation of Adults, which presumes a local community that helps the candidates and catechumens throughout the whole process of initiation and in their further formation in faith and witness. Within a theology of baptism, the parish is the context and specific place of formation in Christian living. The tie to the diocesan church also finds expression within the Rite of Christian Initiation of Adults, in the "rite of election," when candidates are presented to the bishop by name in the cathedral church.[55]

B. The Synod or Diocese

41. Catholics and Lutherans affirm together that congregations and parishes cannot exist in isolation, but rather must be in communion with one another within larger regional communities in order to realize *koinonia* and to carry out mission. In both our churches, essential ecclesial functions are carried out within the regional community of the diocese or synod, such as ordaining pastors and priests, pastoral care of clergy and congregations, and important aspects of ecclesial discipline. In both churches, the diocese/synod is understood to be church in the full sense. Most importantly, this community is the primary location of the congregation's or parish's connection with the wider church.

1. Lutherans on Synodical Realizations

42. The ELCA seeks "to function as people of God through congregations, synods, and the churchwide organization, all of which shall be interdependent. Each part, while fully church, recognizes that it is not the whole church and therefore lives in a partnership relationship with the others."[56] Furthermore, "congregations find their fulfillment in the universal community of the Church, and the universal Church exists in and through congregations."[57]

43. The interdependence of congregations, synods, and churchwide organization reflects the earliest Lutheran self-understanding. As early as 1523, "Luther does not speak of the local congregation as being . . . self-sufficient. The practical expression of his conviction is seen in the fact that visitations were carried out. In particular, the observance of the 'evangelical doctrine' (doctrina evangelica) is not the concern of the individual congregation [alone]; it is the concern of all those who profess this doctrine."[58]

44. In the ELCA, synods are composed of congregations. Congregations in a synod function together both through the synodical assembly and through the ongoing cooperation that is led by the synodical bishop and is guided by the elected Synod Council. The ELCA's churchwide constitution mandates: "Each synod, in partnership with the churchwide organization, shall bear primary responsibility for the oversight of the life and mission of this church in its territory."[59] In the ELCA, synods are the primary locus for the oversight of ordained ministry. All ordinations are regularly performed by synodical bishops. Synods carry out the full range of ecclesial activities and are themselves realizations of the *koinonia* of salvation.[60]

2. *Catholics on Diocesan Realizations*

45. For Catholics, the particular church, most often a diocese, already embraces a number of parishes—the face-to-face congregations, in which the word is preached, the eucharist is celebrated, and new members are initiated. Every particular church must be in communion with other particular churches and in continuity with its apostolic foundations. Each particular church shows solicitude for the entire church, which includes proclaiming the gospel to the entire world, collaborating with one another, keeping unity with the church in Rome, helping the missions, and extending assistance to other churches.[61]

46. A particular church is not a subdivision of the universal church, although there is an interdependence between the particular and universal church. "In and from these particular churches there exists the one unique catholic church. For this reason individual bishops represent their own church, while all of them together with the pope represent the whole church in the bond of peace, love and unity."[62] Within the episcopal college, bishops represent their particular church in the communion of churches, the collegiality of bishops paralleling the communion of churches.

C. National Realizations of *Koinonia*

47. Lutherans and Catholics affirm together the significance of national elements in the life of the church. Conferences of bishops for the Latin Catholic Church most often serve national groupings. From the time of the Reformation, Lutheran churches have been organized along the lines of national or other political units.[63]

1. *Lutherans on National Realizations*

48. For historical reasons, such as language and the close relationship between church and state, Lutherans have tended to be organized into national churches for mission, among other purposes.[64] For example, the ELCA is "church" in the theological sense and is not a federation or association of congregations or synods. As church, the ELCA has a pastor, its presiding bishop, who carries out a range of pastoral activities in service of this church.[65] The churchwide organization has extensive authority. Only this churchwide expression can enter into relations of full communion with other churches.[66] Lutherans have rarely sought to provide a theological rationale for the importance that such national churches have played in their life.[67]

2. *Catholics on National Realizations*

49. In the history of the church, various structures have existed at a level more geographically extensive than the diocese, but less extensive than the church as a whole: e.g., provinces or patriarchates. These structures have varied widely in their powers and responsibilities. The Eastern Catholic Churches have retained synodal structures. Since the Second Vatican Council, national conferences of bishops have come to play an important role in the life of the Latin Catholic Church. They gather bishops of a given nation or territory and foster a closer *koinonia* among the churches and collegiality among the bishops for the people of that area.[68] The exact theological status of these conferences is not entirely determined.[69] The *motu propio* of Pope John Paul II *Apostolos Suos* describes the extent of the conferences' authority:

> The Conference of Bishops can issue general decrees only in those cases in which the common law prescribes it, or a special mandate of the Apostolic See, given either motu proprio or at the request of the Conference, determines it. In other cases the competence of individual diocesan Bishops remains intact; and neither the Conference nor its president may act in the name of all the Bishops unless each and every Bishop has given his consent.[70]

50. The authority of the episcopal conference is limited by the individual responsibility of each bishop as pastor of his particular diocese and by the supreme authority of the church.[71] Episcopal conferences do not have the ecclesial status of the diocese, the patriarchate, or the worldwide church. They are headed by a president who does not have pastoral authority over the churches represented in the conference. The national bishops' conferences do not play the role in the Catholic Church that the autonomous national churches play within Lutheranism.

D. Worldwide Realization

51. Lutherans and Catholics affirm together that the worldwide expression of ecclesial life is a communion of churches, embodying the apostolicity and catholicity of the church. Each understands the universal church to be realized in local or particular churches, and these are not parts of the church, but rather realizations of the one church. They are in communion with one another and with their apostolic origins. The universal church as the comprehensive *koinonia* of salvation forms the

context within which all churches are church. Both Lutherans and Catholics have structures of worldwide decision-making and action, no matter how these structures and their authority may differ.

1. *Lutherans on Worldwide Realization*

52. For most of its history, Lutheranism had no worldwide structural realization. A growing sense of a need for international Lutheran solidarity led first to the gathering of individual Lutherans in the Lutheran World Convention (1923), and later to the organization of Lutheran churches in the LWF (1947). As noted earlier, the LWF does not define itself as a church, but rather as "a communion of churches which confess the triune God, agree in the proclamation of the Word of God and are united in pulpit and altar fellowship."[72] As a communion of churches, the LWF acts on behalf of its member churches in areas of common interest such as ecumenical relations, theology, humanitarian assistance, human rights, communication, and various aspects of mission and development.[73] But it does not perform the full range of ecclesial actions, does not have the authority of a church, and is not structured as a church. The LWF is headed by a president and a general secretary who are not understood as pastors of world Lutheranism. However, the LWF has exercised what amounts to discipline in relation to its German-language churches in Southern Africa during the apartheid era, and it was the organ by which a consensus of its member churches was formed around the *Joint Declaration on the Doctrine of Justification*. The LWF is a realization of the *koinonia* of salvation, even if it is not in itself church.

2. *Catholics on Worldwide Realization*

53. The Roman Catholic Church understands itself as one church, which finds concrete, historical objectification in a plurality of particular churches: "The Catholic Church herself subsists in each particular church, which can be complete only through effective communion in faith, sacraments and unity with the whole body of Christ."[74] Thus the universal church does not result from an addition or a federation of particular churches. The particular church embodies the universal church in the sense that it is the specific place where the universal church is found, yet it manifests this universality in communion with other particular churches. The bishops in communion with one another and with the bishop of Rome assure the continuity of the particular churches with the apostolic church and repre-

sent their churches in communion with other particular churches. LG refers to the mystical body of Christ also as a "body of churches."[75]

IV. Ministry in Service of Communion

54. Lutheran-Catholic differences in the understanding of the structure of the church at the local, regional or national, and worldwide realizations are paralleled by differences in the understanding of ministry. Distinct ministries serve the *koinonia* of salvation in every ecclesial realization. Lutheran pastors and Catholic priests serve face-to-face assemblies. Bishops serve regional communities of such assemblies. In the Roman Catholic Church, the bishop of Rome has a special role in serving the communion of the universal church. Asymmetry between the two traditions occurs because Catholics locate the basic unit of the church in the particular church or diocese, while for Lutherans the basic unit of the church is the congregation. This asymmetry is paralleled by where they locate the fullness of ministerial office. Catholics locate the fullness of ministry in the bishop, while Lutherans find the office of word and sacrament fully realized in the pastor.

A. A History of the Present Differences Between Lutherans and Roman Catholics

55. As shown in the accompanying Explanation (New Testament and history sections), the theological understanding of ordained ministry has varied significantly over the history of the church. The New Testament churches knew offices that were present only at the church's origin (e.g., apostle), but also used terms such as *presbyteros* and *episkopos* which became standard titles of offices in later church history. The exact nature and function of these ministries varied in the New Testament. The threefold ordering of bishop, presbyter, and deacon became widespread in the patristic church, but the function of these ministries changed over time, especially with the rise of the parish presided over by the priest as the most widespread form of face-to-face Christian community. As discussed below (§§168-170), the nature of the distinction between priest or presbyter and bishop was an unsettled matter even in medieval theology. The Lutheran and Catholic understandings of ordained ministry in the sixteenth century were worked out against the background of this medieval uncertainty.

56. Peter Lombard, Thomas Aquinas, and many medieval theologians taught that bishop and priest belonged to the same order (*sacerdotium*). The

Lutheran Reformers went further and held that the distinction in dignity and power between bishop and presbyter was not established by divine law (*iure divino*), but instead by human authority (*iure humano*) (see §§176-182 below). Whatever "power" (*potestas*) is needed to "preside over the churches" belongs "by divine right to all who preside over the churches, whether they are called pastor, presbyters, or bishops."[76] Since the congregation is the community gathered by word and sacrament which mediate salvation, the congregation must be church. In a situation of emergency, a church can provide for the needed ministry of word and sacrament by its own pastors' ordaining clergy since in principle a presbyter can do what a bishop can do, regardless of how matters may be ordered in non-emergency situations.[77] On this basis, when the Catholic bishops would not ordain evangelical clergy, Lutheran churches within the Holy Roman Empire proceeded in the 1530s to ordain clergy with pastors acting as the presiding ministers.[78] The Lutheran argument was complex, appealing both to ecclesiological claims about the powers of the church and to claims about the essential equality of presbyter and bishop. This argument reflects the idea that the presbyter could in a situation of necessity exercise all essential functions of the office of ordained ministry.

57. Consistent with this confessional Lutheran understanding, the ELCA is characterized throughout its structures by the interdependence between the assembly and the ordained ministry. The congregation is served by a pastor; the synod is served by a bishop; the ELCA as a whole is served by a presiding bishop. This structure is typical of Lutheran churches, and some Lutheran theologians have seen in this structure a normative expression of the Lutheran understanding of the church.[79]

58. At the Council of Trent, the Catholic Church spoke of "a hierarchy in the church, instituted by divine appointment, consisting of bishops, priests, and ministers," but it stopped short of stating that the office of bishop exists in the church *iure divino* or that the episcopate is an order distinct from the presbyterate.[80] It did affirm, however, that bishops in particular belong to this hierarchical order (*gradus*), that they have been made by the Holy Spirit rulers of the church of God, that they are higher than priests, and that they are able to confer the sacrament of confirmation and to ordain the ministers of the church.[81] Those who "have neither been duly ordained nor [been] commissioned by ecclesiastical and canonical authority" are not "legitimate" (*legitimos*) ministers of word and sacraments.[82]

59. The Second Vatican Council, in continuity with the implications of the apostolic constitution of Pope Pius XII *Sacramentum Ordinis*,[83] affirmed

that episcopal ordination alone confers the fullness of the sacrament of Order.[84] The priest or presbyter participates in the sacrament of Order in a less complete manner.[85] That the bishops as a body are successors to the apostles is by divine institution.[86] However, the Second Vatican Council left open whether the distinction between bishop and presbyter is of divine institution.[87] Only a bishop confers the sacrament of Order. If the local or particular church possesses all that is needed to be truly church, then it must include within itself all ministries essential to the church. If the bishop alone exercises the fullness of the ministerial priesthood, then only that church which includes a bishop can be such a local or particular church.[88]

B. Ordained Ministry Serving the Congregation or Parish

60. Catholics and Lutherans affirm together that the ministry of an ordained pastor or priest is a constitutive element of the *koinonia* of salvation gathered around font, pulpit, and altar. Central to this ministry is preaching the gospel, presiding in the sacramental life of the community, and leading as pastor the community in its life and mission. The activities of this minister are instruments of the life of the congregation as a *koinonia* of salvation.

1. Catholics

61. The pastor, a member of the presbyterate,[89] is the proper shepherd of the parish. He exercises the duties of teaching, sanctifying, and pastoral care in the community entrusted to him under the authority of the diocesan bishop in whose ministry of Christ he has been called to share.[90] In a certain sense, presbyters make the bishop present in the individual local congregation.[91] Together with the bishop, presbyters constitute one presbyterium,[92] evidence of the collegial character of the order. A presbyter carries out the duties of teaching, sanctifying, and governing with the cooperation of other presbyters or deacons and the assistance of other members of the Christian faithful. In their own locality, priests also make visible the universal church.[93] The pastor of a parish works with the bishop and with the presbyterate of the diocese to ensure that "the faithful be concerned for parochial communion and that they realize that they are members both of the diocese and of the universal church and participate in and support efforts to promote such communion."[94]

2. Lutherans

62. Lutherans have historically emphasized the single office of word and sacrament exercised by all ordained ministers. The vast majority of such

ministers are congregational pastors. In preaching the word and celebrating the sacraments, their ministry is essential to the congregation as church and intimately related to the character of the congregation as a *koinonia* of salvation. They "stand both within the congregation and over against it. They stand with the whole people of God because all share in the one ministry of the church. They stand over against the congregation because in God's name they proclaim the saving gospel to God's people, and therefore bear the authority of God's word, but only insofar as their proclamation is faithful to the gospel."[95]

C. Ordained Ministry Serving Regional Communities

63. Lutherans and Catholics affirm together that the realization of *koinonia* in the primary regional community is presided over by an ordained minister, called a bishop. Lutherans and Catholics agree that the bishop exercises a priesthood or ministry of word and sacrament also shared in by the priest or pastor. Episcopal ministry finds its center in word, sacrament, and pastoral leadership. This ministry serves the unity of the church, both within the regional community and in the relation of this regional community with the church of all times and places.[96]

1. Catholics

64. In the Catholic Church, a bishop is a priest who has the "fullness of the sacrament of order."[97] Ordination to the episcopacy confers the offices of sanctifying, teaching, and governing.[98] By virtue of his ordination, the bishop's authority in his diocese is "proper, ordinary, and immediate,"[99] which means that it is not delegated by higher ecclesiastical authority. He is able to exercise this authority, however, only in communion with the college of bishops and the bishop of Rome. Among his duties, "the preaching of the gospel occupies the pre-eminent place."[100] He is the pastor of a particular church, which includes multiple parishes.

65. In the Catholic Church, bishops function within the college of bishops to which they are admitted by virtue of their episcopal ordination and hierarchical communion with the bishop of Rome.[101] A bishop represents his own church within this college, and all the bishops together with the bishop of Rome represent the whole church[102] and share responsibility for preaching the gospel to the whole world.[103] The college of bishops does not constitute a legislative body apart from the bishop of Rome, but instead includes the pope as member and head of the college.

66. The Second Vatican Council did not specify what constitutes the fullness of the sacrament of Order given in ordination as a bishop. This "fullness of the sacrament of order" can refer (among other things) to the regional bishop's representing his particular church in the communion of churches. The very nature of the episcopacy requires that a bishop exercise his office, even within his own particular church, only in communion with the college of bishops into which he is "incorporated" by his sacramental ordination. The college of bishops symbolizes the unity among the particular churches that each bishop represents in his office. The episcopacy is a relational office, connecting eucharistic communities with one another across space and time as well as fostering the ministry of the local church in faith and love. The collegiality of the episcopacy represents the catholicity of the churches. The episcopacy also connects eucharistic communities with the college of the apostles, and thus represents the apostolicity of the churches.[104]

2. Lutherans

67. At the time of the Reformation, Lutherans in the Holy Roman Empire organized ministries of oversight in their territorial churches to replace those of the bishops who, they judged, had abandoned the gospel and who would not ordain evangelical clergy. While these ministers of oversight had various titles, their ministry was understood to be episcopal.[105] Various Lutheran church orders spoke of this office of oversight as necessary to the life of the church[106] because it was oriented to the church's faithfulness in those ministries that served its life as a *koinonia* of salvation. Following 1918 and the end of the state-church system within which the princes played a quasi-episcopal role, the German Lutheran churches reintroduced the title "bishop."[107] The Nordic Lutheran churches, in lands where the entire nation became Lutheran, preserved the pre-Reformation episcopal order, with varying degrees of continuity with their predecessors in office (see §§189-195 below). The predecessor bodies of the ELCA introduced the title "bishop" in the second half of the twentieth century (see §232 below).

68. In the ELCA, a bishop is called to be a "synod's pastor" and as such "shall be an ordained minister of Word and Sacrament."[108] Like all pastors, the bishop shall "preach, teach, and administer the sacraments." In addition, the bishop has "primary responsibility for the ministry of Word and Sacrament in the synod and its congregations, providing pastoral care and leadership."[109] The ministry and oversight of the bishop thus relate directly to that which makes the synod a realization of the *koinonia* of salvation.

69. Lutherans also affirm the role of the episcopacy in linking regional churches to the universal church. The ELCA constitution stipulates that the synodical bishop shall provide "leadership in strengthening the unity of the Church."[110] This responsibility is affirmed by the ELCA–Episcopal Church agreement "Called to Common Mission:" "By such a liturgical statement [entrance into the episcopate through the laying on of hands by other bishops] the churches recognize that the bishop serves the diocese or synod through ties of collegiality and consultation that strengthen its links with the universal church."[111] Similarly, in the Northern European *Porvoo Common Statement*, the participating Lutheran and Anglican churches "acknowledge that the episcopal office is valued and maintained in all our churches as a visible sign expressing and serving the Church's unity and continuity in apostolic life, mission and ministry."[112]

D. Ordained Ministry Serving the Universal Church

70. Catholics and Lutherans affirm together that all ministry, to the degree that it serves the *koinonia* of salvation, also serves the unity of the worldwide church. A specific ministry that serves universal unity is affirmed by Catholics and not excluded by Lutherans. Lutherans and Catholics together need to discuss how such a ministry can be formed and reformed so that it can be received by a greater range of the world's churches and thus better fulfill its own service to unity.

1. Catholics

71. As bishop of the particular church of Rome, the bishop of Rome, successor of Peter, has a unique responsibility as pastor and teacher to the universal church. He is, in his Petrine ministry, the visible "principle of the unity both of faith and of communion."[113] The common statement *Papal Primacy and the Universal Church* spoke of a "Petrine function" to describe "a particular form of Ministry exercised by a person, officeholder, or local church with reference to the church as a whole," a function that "serves to promote or preserve the oneness of the church by symbolizing unity, and by facilitating communication, mutual assistance or correction, and collaboration in the church's mission."[114] Since the pope must ensure and serve the communion of the particular churches, he is the first servant of unity.[115] While the pope does not take the place of the diocesan bishop, his pastoral authority and responsibility extends throughout the church around the world. He must assure that the local churches keep and transmit the apostolic faith with integrity. He promotes and coordinates the activities of the

churches in their missionary task. He speaks in the name of all the bishops and all their local churches when necessary and has the authority to declare officially and solemnly the revealed truth in the name of the whole church. The bishop of Rome always fulfills his office in communion with the college of bishops as a member and its head.[116] His office is not separate from the mission entrusted to the whole body of bishops.

72. In *Ut Unum Sint*, Pope John Paul II's concern for the unity of the churches is not limited to the Catholic communion, but extends to all Christian communities. He acknowledges that the exercise of the papacy at times has been an obstacle to Christian unity. Therefore, he seeks "a way of exercising the primacy which, while in no way renouncing what is essential to its mission, is nonetheless open to a new situation."[117] To this end, he has called upon church leaders and theologians to engage with him in a patient and fraternal dialogue on this subject.[118]

2. Lutherans

73. Openness to a rightly exercised primacy is part of the Lutheran theological legacy. The Lutheran Reformers' rejection of the papacy focused on "the concrete historical papacy as it confronted them in their day" rather than on the very idea of a universal ministry of unity.[119] In Luther's *Against the Papacy in Rome, Instituted by the Devil* (1545), perhaps his sharpest writing against the papacy, Luther nevertheless affirms that the pope might have a primacy of "honor and superiority" and "of oversight over teaching and heresy in the church."[120] This "conditional openness" to papal primacy is dependent upon a reformed papacy, subject to the gospel, that would not arbitrarily restrict Christian freedom.[121]

74. The Lutheran argument did not merely contest abuses, however; it also challenged the alleged *iure divino* character of the papacy. Philip Melanchthon added to his subscription to the Smalcald Articles that, if the pope "would allow the gospel," the papacy's "superiority over the bishops" could be granted *iure humano*.[122] Historical criticism has significantly altered understandings of divine and human law and criteria for distinguishing them.[123] Especially in relation to the papacy, but also in relation to other traditionally controversial questions relating to ministry, the categories of divine and human law need to be re-examined and placed in the context of ministry as service to the *koinonia* of salvation.

V. Ministry and the Continuity with the Apostolic Church

A. Succession in Apostolic Mission, Ministry, and Message

75. Both Lutherans and Catholics have a strong commitment to maintaining apostolicity in the Christian faith.[124] The *koinonia* of salvation requires continuity in the mission, ministry, and message of the apostles. The discussion of ordained ministry between Lutherans and Catholics, however, often has been dominated by the issue of apostolic succession understood as a succession of episcopal consecrations. As a result, the question of apostolicity has been discussed in a narrowly canonical and mechanistic manner. The renewed ecclesiology of *koinonia* instead has sought first to understand ministry as a bond of *koinonia* within the church and then to recover the rich patristic sense of the bonds of the church to the apostles' mission, ministry, and message across space and time. Lutherans and Catholics agree that the continuity of the apostolic church and the continuity of its mission, ministry, and message are promised to it by its Lord.[125] In the mission given by Jesus to the apostles, the Lord has promised to be present until the end of the age (see Mt. 28:19-20). There is one household of God, founded on the apostles and prophets, with Christ as the cornerstone (see Eph. 2:20). The gates of Hell shall never prevail against this church (see Mt. 16:18).

76. Lutherans and Catholics agree that "apostolic succession" in this comprehensive sense is essential to the church's being. Such succession is continuity with both the past and the future, both with the apostles as witnesses of the resurrection two thousand years ago and with the apostles whose names will be on the twelve foundations of the New Jerusalem (see Rev. 21:14). Such continuity is an element of "the Church's communion which spans time and space, linking the present to past and future generations of Christians."[126]

77. Continuity in apostolic mission, ministry, and message is not a human achievement, but rather a gift of the Spirit. God is faithful to his promise, despite our failings. Our confidence in this continuity is not based upon our fidelity, but upon God's promise. God maintains the church in the apostolic mission, ministry, and message through concrete means: the apostolic scriptures, faithful teachers, the creeds, and the continuity of ordained ministry. Through these various means, the community as a whole remains apostolic.[127]

B. The Bishop as Sign and Instrument of Apostolic Succession

78. As a regional minister of oversight, the bishop is called to foster the *koinonia* that extends beyond any one local community. The bishop maintains *koinonia* with the church's apostolic foundations through proclamation of the gospel and apostolic faith. A truly evangelical oversight will focus on the church's faithfulness to the gospel and thus seek to safeguard and further its true apostolicity. The episcopal task is thus inherently bound up with a concern for apostolic continuity. As the ELCA–Episcopal Church agreement stated, a ministry of *episcopé*, conferred through the laying on of hands by other bishops and prayer for the gift of the Holy Spirit, is one of the ways "in the context of ordained ministries and of the whole people of God, in which the apostolic succession of the church is visibly expressed and personally symbolized in fidelity to the Gospel through the ages."[128]

79. While a focus on a continuity in ordinations or consecrations can make the concept of succession appear simply human, such a focus should bring to the fore the divine initiative in preserving the church. The laying on of hands is a classical form of intensive prayer. In both of our churches, the laying on of hands for the episcopal office is accompanied by a prayer for the pouring out of the Spirit upon the new bishops to empower their ministry. The church thus celebrates the continuity of apostolic ministry, a continuity that lies ultimately in the hands of God. The church must pray for that ministry to continue, and it prays confidently in the knowledge that God will be faithful to the promise that goes with the command to "go out into all the world" (see Mt. 28:19-20; Mk. 16:14).

80. Prior to the late 1530s, the theme of succession played little role in Reformation debates on the role and authority of the bishop. The authority and ministry of the bishop, not any particular concept of succession, were the subject of debate. The Lutheran Confessions explicitly regret the loss of the "order of the church"[129] that resulted from the presbyteral ordinations the Lutherans judged to be necessary for the life of their churches, but neither Article 28 of the *Augsburg Confession* on the power of bishops nor the response by the imperial Catholic theologians to it in the *Confutation* refers explicitly to succession.[130] Thus, when the Lutheran churches felt compelled to ordain pastors apart from the Catholic hierarchy, they were not consciously rejecting any concept of episcopal succession, for such a concept was not current in theological discussions of the period. Only with the renewed attention to patristic sources in the subsequent debates was such a concept reasserted.[131] Unfortunately, when the writings

of such figures as Irenaeus were taken up in the debate, they were used within a canonical argument over validity which the Lutherans could only reject.[132] More recent ecumenical discussions of succession as a sign of the continuity of the church (e.g., the Anglican-Lutheran *Niagara Report*, 1987) have found much greater (though not universal) acceptance in Lutheran circles.[133] In 2001, the ELCA entered a new relation with The Episcopal Church, committing both to "share an episcopal succession that is both evangelical and historic."[134] Similar Lutheran-Anglican agreements in Canada and Northern Europe in which Lutherans have affirmed episcopal succession put Lutheran-Catholic relations in a new context.

81. The Roman Catholic Church has preserved the succession of episcopal consecrations; this succession was broken in continental Lutheranism, maintained in parts of Nordic Lutheranism, and has been reclaimed by the ELCA. What is the significance of either preserving or breaking this succession? That question must not be isolated and made to bear the entire weight of a judgment on a church's ministry. Whether a particular minister or church serves the church's apostolic mission does not depend only upon the presence of such a succession of episcopal consecrations, as if its absence would negate the apostolicity of the church's teaching and mission.[135] Recent ecumenical discussions of episcopacy and succession do not remove our former disagreements, but they do place them in a richer and more complex context in which judgments made exclusively on the basis of the presence or absence of a succession of consecrations are less possible.

VI. Local and Regional Structures and Ministries of Communion

A. The Relationship Between Local and Regional Churches

82. The interdependent polarity between "face-to-face eucharistic assembly" and "primary regional community of such assemblies" elaborated above (see §§27-29, 33) forms the background for a reconsideration of the relation between bishop and presbyter. Bishop and pastor are the presiding ministers, respectively, of the synod or diocese and of the congregation or parish gathered around word and sacrament.[136] Church unity rests in *koinonia* or sharing in word and sacrament. Because ordained ministry of word and sacrament is essential to the church's sharing in and sharing of salvation, such ministry is intrinsically related to the church's unity and *koinonia*.

83. The relation between bishop and pastor parallels in important ways the relation between synod or diocese, on the one hand, and parish or congregation, on the other. Within this parallelism, the differing understandings of the structure of church held by Lutherans and Catholics have each grasped an essential dimension of the church: the primacy of the face-to-face community gathered around font, pulpit, and altar, on the one hand, and the essential character of *koinonia* with other such communities for the life of any eucharistic assembly, on the other. In seeking to determine which is "local church" in the theological sense noted above, however, false choices have been forced upon theological reflection. As a result, both Lutherans and Catholics suffer from an imbalance in their theological account of the church.

84. With respect to Roman Catholics, the international Roman Catholic–Lutheran Joint Commission has noted that, despite the definition of the local church as the diocese, "in actual fact it is the parish, even more than the diocese, which is familiar to Christians as the place where the church is to be experienced."[137] The Second Vatican Council recognized this role of the parish when it stated that "parishes set up locally under a pastor who takes the place of the bishop . . . in a certain way represent the visible Church as it is established throughout the world."[138] For Catholic doctrine, however, the church is identified by the minister who presides over it. The presence of the bishop signals the continuity of the local church in the apostolic faith as well as the communion of that church with other churches, essential components in the definition of a local church in the Roman Catholic tradition. But Catholics do not often perceive their eucharistic community as headed by the bishop. Although the bishop directs and is named in every celebration of the eucharist in the diocese,[139] and there is an understanding that the priest in some sense makes present the bishop,[140] in the experience of most Roman Catholics, the diocese is not the primary eucharistic expression of the church.

85. With respect to Lutherans, the local/presbyteral realization of the church in the congregation has priority. A theological understanding of the need to realize regional *koinonia* with ongoing structures remains underdeveloped. The church is identified as "the assembly of saints in which the gospel is taught purely and the sacraments are administered rightly."[141] But the church is not limited to the congregation, for Luther says, "The church is the number or gathering of the baptized and the believers under one pastor, whether this is in one city or in one province or in the whole world."[142] Herein lies the difficulty. While a community gathered by word and sacrament suggests a local congregation, the Reformers and most of later

Lutheranism[143] have stressed the need for regional structures and discipline. In the same text to the Bohemians in which Luther urges them to ordain their own ministers, he also suggests that if a number of communities do this, then "these bishops may wish to come together and elect one or more from their number to be their superiors, who would serve them and hold visitations among them, as Peter visited the churches, according to the account in the Book of Acts. Then Bohemia would return again to its rightful and evangelical archbishopric, which would be rich, not in large income and much authority, but in many ministers and visitations of the churches."[144]

86. Here Luther clearly urges a regional structure. The term "particular church" was applied by later Lutheran theology equally to the congregation and to the regional or national body.[145] What Lutheranism lacks is a clear and convincing theological rationale for its actual practice of embedding the congregation in a regional body, which is also called "church." The temptations of congregationalism and the understanding of regional structures as merely sociological necessity have recurred within Lutheran history.[146] The theological basis for the realization of the essential catholicity of the face-to-face assembly in lived *koinonia* with other such assemblies is theologically underexpressed.

87. Lutherans and Catholics agree that neither the local congregation or parish nor the regional community of these congregations or parishes is sufficient in itself without the other. Due weight must be given both to the assembly of word and sacrament and to the regional community of such assemblies. Catholics are challenged to develop more fully a doctrine of the parish and to address the contemporary implausibility of its depiction of the diocese as "local church" or eucharistic assembly. The Lutheran viewpoint suffers from an incompleteness in its theological account of the significance of the regional church. Each viewpoint tends to treat ministry in the same way that it treats ecclesiology. Lutheran ecclesiology emphasizes the congregation and the pastor, while Catholic ecclesiology emphasizes the bishop and the regional structure.

88. A way forward beyond this contrast between the two traditions is to regard the regional/episcopal and the local/presbyteral difference as a normative complementarity, both in relation to ecclesiology and in relation to the doctrine of ministry. The exclusive prioritizing of either the regional or the geographically local is a false alternative. An initial agreement on this point already has been reached in relation to ministry by the international Roman Catholic–Lutheran Joint Commission: "*If* both churches acknowledge that for faith this historical development of the one apostolic ministry

into a more local and a more regional ministry has taken place with the help of the Holy Spirit and to this degree constitutes something essential for the church, then a *high degree of agreement* has been reached."[147] If the difference between a local and a regional ministry, paralleling a difference between the face-to-face assembly and the regional community of such assemblies, is a development helped by the Holy Spirit, then an ecclesiology that devalues this difference by reducing one side of it to theological insignificance fails to follow where the Spirit has led.

89. If the church as the *koinonia* of salvation is born from and borne by the gospel proclaimed in word and sacrament, and if the eucharist, including the proclamation of the word and the celebration of the Supper, is the event from which and toward which the church lives,[148] then the face-to-face eucharistic assembly must be a basic unit of the church. It is a place where "church" is essentially realized.[149] Indeed, there can be no church without such face-to-face eucharistic assemblies. In that sense, they are fundamental.[150] That which is realized in this face-to-face eucharistic assembly is truly "church," the body of Christ, the assembly of all the saints across time and space. This relation is manifest in the Supper, where the congregation praises God "with the church on earth and the hosts of heaven."

90. Each eucharistic assembly lives out its constitutive relation with the wider church by its concrete relations with other assemblies in a network of *koinonia*. The JWG affirmed the importance of this *koinonia* for the local church. "The local church is not a free-standing, self-sufficient reality. As part of a network of communion, the local church maintains its reality as church by relating to other local churches."[151] This relationship with other local churches is essential to the catholicity that every church must embody. "Communion with other local churches is essential to the integrity of the self-understanding of each local church, precisely because of its catholicity. Life in self-sufficient isolation . . . is the denial of its very being."[152] The same must be said about the relation of the eucharistic assembly to the wider church. For Catholic theology, the communion of the local face-to-face eucharistic assemblies with their bishop is essential for their ecclesiality, and they cannot be considered "churches" apart from that communion. For these communities, catholicity requires not only communion with other local churches, but also communion with the ministry of the bishop. It was stated forcefully in the context of an LWF study on church unity that "the already existing spiritual unity of the Church of Jesus Christ demands the realization of concrete, historical,

tangible church fellowship."[153] Thus, "all local *ecclesiae* in the whole world should stand in a concrete, actually lived, legally effective *koinonia*."[154]

91. The most immediate and concrete way this network of relations among face-to-face eucharistic assemblies is realized is in some primary regional community: a Catholic diocese, a Lutheran synod. These primary regional communities embody in an explicit way the essential interconnection of every eucharistic assembly within the one *koinonia* of salvation. Such a regional community is itself church, not just a collection of churches, for it is the assembly (even if only representative) of assemblies, each of which relates to the others internally, not merely externally,[155] for *koinonia* with other communities is essential to the catholicity and thus the ecclesiality of each. The assemblies come together as one church. If the ecclesial reality of any larger grouping is inseparable from that of face-to-face eucharistic assemblies, the converse is also true: the ecclesial reality and catholicity of face-to-face eucharistic assemblies requires their existence within regional communities. The complementarity of face-to-face eucharistic assembly and primary regional community is thus theologically normative.

B. The Relation Between Priest/Presbyter/Pastor and Bishop

92. The preceding analysis leads to the conclusion that the complementarity of local and regional ministry is normative within the ordained ministry of the church, paralleling the normative complementarity of the face-to-face eucharistic assembly and the primary regional community. It would be a mistake to insist that either the parish/congregation or the diocese/synod is exclusively *the* local church. Likewise, the doctrine of ministry would be distorted by insisting that either the presbyter or the bishop is the only theologically necessary ordained minister, thereby dismissing the other, bishop or presbyter, as practically necessary but theologically insignificant. Lutherans often have insisted that the bishop is a pastor with a larger sphere of ministry, without seeing the distinctiveness of the role of a pastor to a communion of communities, each led by its own ordained minister. Recent Catholic theology often fails adequately to explain why priests are theologically necessary, in addition to bishops, rather than merely practically necessary to the church.

93. If we think of the ordained ministry as structured by this complementarity, the specific emphases of each tradition might come to be seen in a new light. Because the regional grouping served by the bishop manifests in a fuller way the unity of the church by manifesting the unity of

the communities within it more fully than any one of these communities can do alone, one can say that the ministry of the bishop *is in this sense* fuller than that of any single presbyter. As the minister of the actual face-to-face eucharistic assembly, however, the presbyter might be said *in this sense* to have a richer, more fundamental ministry. Each ministry depends upon the other.

94. At the same time that we strive to show what is distinctive and complementary between the office of bishop and that of pastor/priest/presbyter with respect to their service to different levels of ecclesiality, it is also important that we keep in mind the profound similarities in these two offices. In many ways, they are distinct but inseparable offices. Both bishops and presbyters are ordained to serve word, sacrament, and the pastoral life of the church. For Lutherans, both bishops and pastors exercise the one office of word and sacrament. In Roman Catholic theology, the sacrament of Order is one; both bishops and presbyters are priests; priests are associated with their bishop in one presbyterium. What these ministries share is much greater than that which distinguishes them.

VII. Recommendations for an Ecumenical Way Forward

A. Toward a Recognition of the Reality and Woundedness of Our Ministries and Churches

95. What follows for the relations between our churches from the analysis above, supported by the biblical and historical explanations below? Building upon the earlier Lutheran–Roman Catholic dialogue texts, *Eucharist and Ministry* and *Facing Unity*,[156] we propose steps toward a full, mutual recognition and reconciliation of our ministries and the ultimate goal of full communion. We are aware of common challenges to overcome. Nevertheless, the mutual recognition of ministries need not be an all-or-nothing matter and should not be reduced to a simple judgment about validity or invalidity. In order to assess the degree of our *koinonia* in ordained ministry, a more nuanced discernment is needed to reflect the way that an ordained ministry serves the proclamation of the gospel and the administration of the sacraments, stands in continuity with the apostolic tradition, and serves communion among churches.

96. **We recommend that our churches recognize our common understanding of the interdependent structures of church life and ministry, namely, the diocese/synod with its bishop and the parish/congregation with its pastor or priest. This common understanding is**

reflected in a shared sense of the single sacrament of Order (*sacramentum Ordinis*) or the one office of ministry (*Amt*). The differences between us in emphasis and terminology need not be church-dividing even though they challenge each church to overcome imbalances in its own tradition.

97. Our affirmations about ordained ministry go together with our affirmations about our communities (see §§85–89), for ministry parallels the ordering of the church. If real but imperfect recognition exists between our ministers and our communities, neither community can lack churchly reality. Movement toward deeper mutual recognition of our ministries is both rooted in and contributes to our growing sense of the ecclesial reality of each of our communities. In particular, the Catholic non-recognition of Lutheran ministries has hindered Catholic affirmation of the Lutheran churches as churches. If our proposal for deeper mutual recognition of ministries is accepted, then new possibilities should open for reconsideration of mutual recognition as churches. Mutual recognition of our churches and ministries need not be an all-or-nothing matter.[157]

98. **We recommend that each church recognize that the other realizes, even if perhaps imperfectly, the one church of Jesus Christ and shares in the apostolic tradition.**

99. **We recommend that each church recognize that the ordained ministry of the other effectively carries on, even if perhaps imperfectly, the apostolic ministry instituted by God in the church.**

100. To say that each church understands itself and the other as exercising the apostolic ministry is not to say that either church escapes the damage done to our ministries by the ongoing scandal of our division. To the extent that the ordained ministry of one church is not in communion with the ordained ministry of other churches, it is unable to carry out its witness to the unity of the church as it should. Such a ministry inevitably bears a wound or defect. Ministry carries this wound whenever the *koinonia* among eucharistic communities and different realizations of the church are broken. Because our relationships are broken, our ministry is wounded and in need of healing by God's grace.

101. This need affects both of our churches. The Roman Catholic Church acknowledges that it is wounded by a lack of communion. As the *Decree on Ecumenism* stated, "The divisions among Christians prevent the church from realizing in practice the fullness of catholicity proper to her."[158] The 1992 letter from the Congregation for the Doctrine of the Faith "Some Aspects of the Church as Communion," after noting the wound that lack of

communion inflicts on the Orthodox and Reformation churches, concluded that this division:

> in turn also wounds (*vulnus iniungitur*) the Catholic Church, called by the Lord to become for all "one flock" with "one shepherd," in that it hinders the complete fulfillment of her universality in history.[159]

The entire Catholic priesthood, including the bishop of Rome, is wounded in an important dimension of its ministry insofar as unity and communion are lacking with other churches and their ministries.

102. The same must be said of the Lutheran churches and their ministries. Lutherans understand their ministries to be realizations of the one ministry of the one church, yet they cannot manifest communion in this one ministry with many other churches. This woundedness provides a helpful basis for a new understanding of the Catholic assertion of *defectus* in the sacrament of Order in Lutheran churches (§§108-109).

103. **We recommend a mutual recognition that (1) our ordained ministries are wounded because the absence of full communion between our ecclesial traditions makes it impossible for them to adequately represent and foster the unity and catholicity of the church, and that (2) our communities are wounded by their lack of the full catholicity to which they are called and by their inability to provide a common witness to the gospel.**

104. Addressing these wounds in our churches will require repentance and conversion. Each church must examine its theology and practice of ministry and ask whether they truly serve the mission and unity of the church. Division offers occasions for sin, to which our churches have sometimes succumbed.[160] The Second Vatican Council teaches that "there can be no ecumenism worthy of the name without a change of heart."[161] Pope John Paul II concluded on this basis that "the Council calls for personal conversion as well as for communal conversion."[162]

105. **We recommend that our churches pray together for the grace of repentance and conversion needed for healing the wounds of our division.**

1. Catholic Discernment

106. Repentance and conversion call for steps toward healing the wounds of our division. For Catholics, a necessary step will be a reassessment of Lutheran presbyteral ordinations at the time of the Reformation. This reassessment on the part of proper church authorities now can take

into account the nature of the presbyteral ministry and its relation to episcopal ministry, the nature of apostolic succession, the sort of community that decided to carry out such ordinations, the intent behind these ordinations, and the historical situation that led to such a decision. The argument presented above about the normative complementarity between presbyter and bishop holds significance for the evaluation of the ministries in continuity with these Reformation actions. The historical findings (see §§171-182 below) show that the theology that supported the Lutheran action was not a conscious rejection of all earlier tradition, but instead bore significant continuities with New Testament, patristic, and medieval understandings. The recent commitment of the ELCA to enter into episcopal succession for the sake of ecclesial *koinonia*[163] is a new and significant factor in this regard.

107. Catholic judgment on the authenticity of Lutheran ministry need not be of an all-or-nothing nature. The *Decree on Ecumenism* of the Second Vatican Council distinguished between relationships of full ecclesiastical communion and those of imperfect communion to reflect the varying degrees of differences with the Catholic Church.[164] The communion of these separated communities with the Catholic Church is real, even though it is imperfect. Furthermore, the decree positively affirmed the following:

> Our separated brothers and sisters also celebrate many sacred actions of the Christian religion. These most certainly can truly engender a life of grace in ways that vary according to the condition of each church or community, and must be held capable of giving access to that communion in which is salvation.[165]

Commenting on this point, Cardinal Joseph Ratzinger, prefect of the Congregation on the Doctrine of the Faith, wrote the following in 1993 to Bavarian Lutheran bishop Johannes Hanselmann:

> I count among the most important results of the ecumenical dialogues the insight that the issue of the eucharist cannot be narrowed to the problem of 'validity.' Even a theology oriented to the concept of succession, such as that which holds in the Catholic and in the Orthodox church, need not in any way deny the salvation-granting presence of the Lord [*Heilschaffende Gegenwart des Herrn*] in a Lutheran [*evangelische*] Lord's Supper.[166]

If the actions of Lutheran pastors can be described by Catholics as "sacred actions" that "can truly engender a life of grace," if communities served by such ministers give "access to that communion in which is salvation," and if "the salvation-granting presence of the Lord" is to be found at a eucharist at which a Lutheran pastor presides, then Lutheran churches cannot be said simply to lack the ministry given to the church by Christ and the Spirit. In acknowledging the imperfect *koinonia* between our communities and the access to grace through the ministries of these communities, we also acknowledge a real although imperfect *koinonia* between our ministries.

108. Ecumenical understanding would be furthered if, in official Roman Catholic documents, the Second Vatican Council's reference to *defectus* in the sacrament of Order among "ecclesial communities" were translated using such words as "defect" or "deficiency."[167] As Cardinal Walter Kasper has stated, "On material grounds [*aus der Sachlogik*], and not merely on the basis of the word usage of the Council, it becomes clear that *defectus ordinis* does not signify a complete absence, but rather a deficiency [*Mangel*] in the full form of the office."[168] Translations of *defectus* as "lack" misleadingly imply the simple absence of the reality of ordination. Translations of the word as "defect" or "deficiency" would be consistent with the sort of real but imperfect recognition of ministries proposed above. While short of full recognition, such partial recognition would provide the basis for first steps toward a reconciliation of ministries as envisioned, e.g., in the international Roman Catholic–Lutheran statement *Facing Unity*.[169]

109. **We recommend that Roman Catholic criteria for assessing authentic ministry include attention to a ministry's faithfulness to the gospel and its service to the communion of the church, and that the term *defectus ordinis* as applied to Lutheran ministries be translated as "deficiency" rather than "lack."**

2. Lutheran Discernment

110. In ecumenical discussions, Lutherans have shown little hesitancy in recognizing the ordained ministries of the Catholic Church. During the Reformation era, the Lutheran churches did not re-ordain Catholic priests who joined the evangelical movement.[170] At times in the past, Lutherans doubted that the Catholic priesthood was in fact the one evangelical ministry of word and sacrament of the one church, because Lutherans thought the Catholic priesthood was oriented toward an unevangelical understanding of the Mass.[171] These doubts have been removed by convergence and agreement on the gospel[172] and by such affirmations as that of the Second Vatican Council that "among the principal tasks of bishops the preaching of the gospel is pre-eminent."[173]

111. Lutherans also need repentance and conversion to take steps toward healing the wounds of our division. They must constantly reassess some of their own traditions of ordained ministry. Regarding "the order of the church and the various ranks in the church" including bishops, the *Apology of the Augsburg Confession* testifies that the "greatest desire" of the Reformers was to retain this ministerial structure.[174] This desire stated in the Lutheran Confessions still is normative for present-day Lutheranism. The office of bishop as regional pastor is the normal polity of the church, "a gift of the Holy Spirit,"[175] and it implies bishops in communion with other ministers exercising *episcopé*. A church may be compelled to abandon such a shared episcopal office for a time, but it should return to it whenever possible. Recent actions by the ELCA and some other Lutheran churches to reclaim shared episcopal ordering, both among themselves and as an aspect of communion with Anglican churches, are signs of a willingness to engage in such a reassessment.[176]

3. *Common Challenges*

112. Asymmetry exists between our churches in relation to our mutual recognition of ordained ministry. Lutheran churches are able fully to recognize Catholic ordained ministries on the basis of ecumenical developments, but the Catholic Church has not fully recognized the ordained ministries of a church such as the ELCA.[177] This asymmetry makes life together more difficult. Any reconciliation of ministries needs to find ways of addressing this asymmetry that accord with the self-understanding of each church.

113. The ordination or non-ordination of women is a significant difference between our two traditions. The decision to ordain both women and men to the ministry of word and sacrament involves questions about the church's authority. The ELCA, continuing the practice of its predecessor bodies, holds itself free under the gospel to ordain women.[178] The Catholic Church does not hold itself authorized to make such a decision.[179] The reconciliation or full mutual recognition of ministries will need to address this sensitive difference.

B. Universal Church and Universal Ministry

114. In relation to a universal ministry at the service of the unity of the universal church, this dialogue is far less ready to propose any official actions. The bishop of Rome, the only historically plausible candidate for such a universal ministry, remains a sign of unity and a sign of division among us. Pope John Paul II has called for an ecumenical dialogue on the

papacy and its exercise as a pastoral office in service of the unity of Christians.[180] We are hopeful that this invitation for "a patient and fraternal dialogue"[181] on the papacy and its exercise might be taken up with a renewed commitment to overcoming the divisions of the past and present.

1. Catholic Reflections on Universal Ministry

115. Pope John Paul II in *Ut Unum Sint* (1995) emphasized the bishop of Rome's responsibility to serve the unity and communion of the church: "The mission of the Bishop of Rome within the College of all the Pastors [Bishops] consists precisely in 'keeping watch' (*episkopein*). . . . With the power and authority without which such an office would be illusory, the Bishop of Rome must ensure the communion of all the Churches. For this reason, he is the first servant of unity."[182] In this encyclical, Pope John Paul II invited a consideration of reform and change in the papal office in order that this office would not be a stumbling block to Christian unity.

116. Catholics see the papal office as part of the mission entrusted to the whole people of God. A renewed exercise of the papacy will need to witness to its communal dimension by reconciling a number of tensions within the exercise of authority: the bishop of Rome's primacy and the collegiality he shares within the college of bishops; the authority reserved to clerics and the participation of the laity in governance; the relationship between the proper, ordinary, and immediate authority of a bishop in his diocese and the universal jurisdiction of the pope; the communion within a universal church and a decentralization which respects the particularity of a local church; and finally, a common Catholic identity and increased openness to diversity.[183] The Second Vatican Council's *Decree on Ecumenism (Unitatis Redintegratio)* provides a guiding principle for this task:

> While preserving unity in essentials, let all members of the Church, according to the office entrusted to each, preserve a proper freedom in the various forms of spiritual life and discipline, in the variety of liturgical rites, even in the theological elaborations of revealed truth. In all things let charity be exercised. If the faithful are true to this course of action, they will be giving even richer expression to the authentic catholicity of the Church, and, at the same time, to her apostolicity.[184]

117. **We recommend that Catholics explore how the universal ministry of the bishop of Rome can be reformed to manifest more visibly its subjection to the gospel in service to the *koinonia* of salvation.**

2. Lutheran Reflections on Universal Ministry

118. In light of *Ut Unum Sint* and other Catholic and ecumenical statements on papacy, Lutherans have been involved in considerable discussion of universal ministry. If, as the Nordic and Baltic Lutheran churches affirmed in the *Porvoo Common Statement*, "the personal, collegial, and communal dimensions of oversight find expression at the local, regional, and universal levels of the Church's life,"[185] then the question cannot be avoided of who might exercise such a personal ministry of oversight at the universal level and of how it might be exercised in subservience to the gospel. Again, if the interdependence of assembly and ordained ministry is typical of the structure of the church at the local, regional, and national level, then why should such an interdependence not also be found at the universal level?[186]

119. Lutherans have been concerned with whether the papal office is necessary for salvation. Today, when the pastoral nature of the papacy and its reform have been taken seriously by the Catholic Church itself, the question of the papacy may be perceived in a different way, in terms of the ecclesial necessity of the papal office. To what extent may such an office of universal ministry be needed for the unity of the church in a *koinonia* of salvation?[187] Exploring these questions might clarify what Lutherans mean when they insist that any universal ministry of unity must be "under the gospel." What would be the characteristics of a universal ministry "under the gospel?"

120. **We recommend that Lutherans explore whether the worldwide *koinonia* of the church calls for a worldwide minister of unity and what form such a ministry might take to be truly evangelical.**

VIII. Toward Deeper Communion

121. *Ut Unum Sint*, Pope John Paul II's encyclical on ecumenism, echoes the Second Vatican Council's *Decree on Ecumenism* in affirming a certain but imperfect communion between the Roman Catholic Church and other churches and ecclesial communities.[188] Roman Catholics and churches of the LWF agree on the good news of justification.[189] If the ELCA and the Roman Catholic Church are in imperfect communion, it follows that the ministers within these communities are also in imperfect communion with one another, for ministry serves the communion of the church. Too often in our past, the judgment of the "wound" or the "defect" in another's orders based on juridical categories of validity prevented our recognition of the ministry that is truly shared. We share a common ministry

of baptism, proclamation of the word, and pastoral care, and we recognize that each other's eucharist gives "access to that communion in which is salvation."[190] This present study of the structures and ministries of the church through the lens of *koinonia* asks our churches to seek ways of implementing the imperfect ministerial communion that we already experience.[191] Truly living out our communion, albeit imperfect, may provide a foundation for living toward the full communion we seek.

122. **We recommend that our churches recognize the real but imperfect communion among our ministers and encourage appropriate forms of pastoral collaboration between our ministries. Specifically, we propose (1) that common activities among Lutheran and Roman Catholic bishops be promoted in order to signify the level of communion that exists between them, such as regular joint retreats, co-authored pastoral letters on topics of mutual concern, and joint efforts on matters of public good; (2) that mutual activities be intensified among ordained ministers, such as regular retreats, homily or sermon preparation study, participation in non-eucharistic prayer services and weddings, and common sponsorship of events or services in the life of the church, including as appropriate other leadership ministries; (3) that the faithful, in light of their common baptism into the people of God, engage together in catechesis, evangelization, peace and justice ventures, social ministry, and attendance at each other's diocesan and synodical assemblies; and (4) that social ministry organizations, educational institutions, chaplaincies, and other church agencies engage together in activities that further the gospel and the common good.**

123. On our journey toward full communion, including mutual recognition of ministry and churchly reality, this round of dialogue has sought to help Lutherans and Catholics move toward that goal

- by accepting *koinonia* of salvation as an interpretive lens for this study;
- by proposing an analysis of the varying local, regional, national, and worldwide realizations of the *koinonia* of salvation as a framework within which to consider mutual recognition of ministries;
- by recalling the issues of recognition of ministries as discussed in round IV in *Eucharist and Ministry* and of reconciliation of ministries stressed in *Facing Unity*;

- by relating ministerial communion to ecclesial communion, with recognition of imperfect ecclesial communion leading to recognition of imperfect ministerial communion;
- by clarifying ministerial identity in relation to service to various levels of ecclesial communion;
- by demonstrating the normative complementarity of congregational and regional structures and ministries; and
- by examining in a preliminary way the role of national and worldwide structures and urging a "patient and fraternal dialogue" on the possibility of a worldwide minister of unity.

124. A fuller mutual recognition of ministries cannot be separated from a fuller common life in Christ and the Spirit. Lutherans and Catholics together have found a greater common basis in the gospel as can be seen in the *Joint Declaration on the Doctrine of Justification*. Mutual recognition of doctrine, ministries, and ecclesial realities, rooted in a common existence in the one body of Christ, can bear fruit by the grace of God in life shared together.

125. Ministry and structures of communion are at the service of the *koinonia* of salvation realized in the life of the church. Mutual recognition of ministry and of ecclesial reality are important conditions for our full and uninhibited common participation in the salvation given us in Christ and the Spirit. We offer our work to our respective churches with the prayer that it may foster the *koinonia* in salvation we are convinced is the will of our Risen Lord.

Part Two: Further Biblical and Historical Support for Deepening Communion in Structures and Ministries

I. Biblical Foundations for the Church as *Koinonia* of Salvation in Jesus and the Christ Event

126. "Salvation," "church," and "ministries" will be treated chronologically below in various segments of the New Testament. *Koinonia* as a biblical term has been introduced above (§§11-13). A term with a range of meanings,[192] *koinonia* and its related verbs and adjectives occur thirty-eight times in the New Testament. The background for this terminology lies entirely in the Greek world, as there is no counterpart term in Hebrew and little significant use of *koinonia* in the Greek translations of the Hebrew Scriptures.[193]

No recorded usage by Jesus of the term exists, and the Gospels contain little about it (see Lk. 5:10; "partners" in the fishing business). *Koinōnia* is preeminently a Pauline term.

127. One possible starting point in the Greek world is the adjective *koinos*,[194] "common" or "communal," as at Acts 2:44, believers "had all things in common (*koina*)," or Titus 1:4, our "common faith" (NRSV: "the faith we share"). Thus, *to koinon* could refer to the state, the public treasury, the commonwealth, or (with *agathon*) the common good. A "public" and financial side may cling to the terminology in Christian usage. The Greek adage "Friends have all things in common," is reflected in Acts 4:32, "No one claimed private ownership of any possessions, but everything they owned was held in common (*koina*)."

128. A second approach is through the verb *koinōnein*, which can mean (1) "have a share" of something (Heb. 2:14; human beings all share in flesh and blood) or (2) "give a share" of something (the Philippian church shared funds with Paul; Phil. 4:15).[195] Language of participation also can be used, "having a part" in something or being a partner.

129. Pioneering studies, mainly by Protestants, emphasized "participation" or "fellowship."[196] Later commentators, often Catholic, stressed "association," "community," and "(church) fellowship," sometimes with a sacramental emphasis, cf. Latin *communio*.[197] Increasingly it was concluded that no single clear-cut meaning is possible; *koinōnia* is a multivalent term.[198] One may speak of church fellowship, grounded in participation in Christ.[199] New Testament studies sometimes have an eye toward ecumenical implications.[200]

130. How much of the structured church as *koinōnia* of salvation can be traced back to Jesus of Nazareth himself? As a general principle, one must take care "not to read in evidence from later sources or theories."[201] "The church" is known from the earliest Pauline writings, which antedate the written Gospels (e.g., 1 Thess. 1:1; 2:14; Gal. 1:2, 22; 1 Cor. 1:2; 4:17; 7:17; 2 Cor. 8:1). *Hē ekklēsia* often denotes in such passages a particular or local church in a certain area, but it eventually comes to mean "the church" in a sense that transcends local or geographical boundaries (see below). Significantly, however, *ekklēsia*, in either a local or a transcendent sense, is not mentioned in the Gospels of Mark, Luke, or John—or in other New Testament writings such as Titus, 2 Timothy, 1-2 Peter, and 1-2 John. *Ekklēsia* (church) is used in Matthew 16:18: "You are Peter (*Petros*), and on this rock (*petra*) I will build my church" (cf. 18:17, of the local assembly). This church-founding statement is paralleled in John 21:15-17 in a post-resurrection setting, without the word *ekklesia*; Peter's role is to feed

the "flock" of Christ.[202] There is little more that one can cull from the Gospels about the structure of Jesus' church to be built.[203]

131. Jesus had followers (see Mk. 1:18; 2:15; Mt. 4:20; Lk. 5:11, 28; Jn. 1:37, 40), eventually called "disciples,"[204] i.e., those taught by Jesus (see Mk. 2:16; Mt. 5:1; Lk. 6:13; Jn. 2:2), and even "apostles," i.e., those sent forth by him to carry on his mission (Mk. 6:30; Mt. 10:2; Lk. 6:13). One can speak of a "Jesus-movement," but such disciples or apostles are not portrayed in the Gospels as aware of themselves as "church" during Jesus' earthly ministry. The charge to "make disciples of all nations" (Mt. 28:19-20; differently formulated in Lk. 24:47) comes from the risen Christ.

132. It is as an effect of the Christ-event that the New Testament speaks of salvation (*sōtēria* and the verb *sōzein*), e.g., Matthew 1:21 ("he will save his people from their sins"); John 3:17 ("that the world might be saved through him"); and John 12:47 ("I came not to judge the world, but to save the world"). He is said to "save" individuals as he heals them (Mt. 9:21-22; Mk. 5:34; 10:52), and in Luke, Jesus is announced as *sōter*, "savior," (Lk. 2:11; cf. 19:9-10).

133. Jesus lays hands on individuals during healings or cures (Mk. 6:5; 8:23, 25; Mt. 19:13, 15; Lk. 4:40; 13:13), but never for commissioning or ordaining, as occurs in the Old Testament (e.g., Moses commissioning Joshua, in Num. 27:18-19; Deut. 34:9).[205] Church structures develop as the Jesus-movement evolves after the resurrection.[206]

II. The Shape of Early Christian Communities

134. In the Acts of the Apostles, "the fellowship" (*hē kōinonia*) is the first term that occurs for Jesus' followers as they share their faith and life in common (2:42). Another early name for them is "the Way" (*hē hodos*; 9:2; 19:9, 23; 22:4; 24:14, 22).[207] *Ekklēsia* becomes in later chapters of Acts the standard and enduring designation of Christians as a group (8:1, 3),[208] in Jerusalem (11:22; 15:4) and elsewhere (11:26; 13:1; 14:23, 27; 15:3, 41). In time, there also appears an awareness of *ekklēsia* that transcends local boundaries (9:31 ["the church throughout all Judea, Galilee, and Samaria"]; 12:5; 15:22; 20:28 ["the church of God"]).

135. The Twelve and the apostles function in the early chapters of Acts. The Twelve initially guide the early Jerusalem church, with Peter as its spokesman (Acts 1:15; 2:14). Later, the Seven are chosen "to serve tables" (Acts 6:2-5; cf. 21:8): "These men they presented to the apostles, who

prayed and laid their hands on them" (6:6),[209] which is the last time the Twelve are mentioned. The apostle James, the brother of John, is not replaced at his death (12:1-2), as was the case after the death of Judas Iscariot (1:16-17). "Apostles" still are mentioned as having a part in the Jerusalem "Council" (Acts 15:2, 4, 6, 22, 23), where they are always linked with *hoi presbyteroi* in the Jerusalem church. After 16:4, the apostles disappear from the Lucan story. In the subsequent Christian tradition, there is no office called either the "apostolate" or "the Twelve."[210]

136. Pauline use of *ekklēsia* for a local or particular church often involves "house churches" (1 Cor. 16:19; Rom. 16:5; Phlm. 2; Col. 4:15).[211] Such groupings of Christians were usual in the pre-Constantinian period for various functions, but nothing in the Pauline letters links the house church with the eucharistic celebration.[212] In some Pauline letters, the phrase "the church(es) of God" (1 Thess. 2:14; Gal. 1:13; 1 Cor. 11:16; 15:9) seems to refer to the mother-communities of Jerusalem or Judea; but it eventually is extended to the Corinthian community (1 Cor. 1:2; 2 Cor. 1:1), as the idea of the church regional and universal begins to emerge (1 Cor. 6:4; 10:32; 11:22). The latter idea becomes even clearer in the Deutero-Paulines (Col. 1:18, 24; Eph. 1:22; 3:10, 21), even if it is never said to be *mia ekklēsia*, despite the emphasis in Ephesians on the unity of the church.

137. *Ekklēsia* occurs in 3 John 6, 9, 10 for a local congregation, but there is otherwise no awareness in the Johannine Gospel or Epistles of *ekklēsia* in either a local or a universal sense. Commentators speak either of a "Johannine community," "Johannine circle," or "a community of the Beloved Disciple," characterized by their contrast with those they opposed: "the Jews" (e.g., 2:6, 13; 5:1, 16; 6:4; 8:48, 52; 19:40); crypto-Christians (9:22, 30-38); disciples of John the Baptist (4:1).[213]

138. Many Pauline and Johannine verses using *koinōnia* terms have been cited above (§§11-13). No New Testament passage using *koinōnia* is directly related to *ekklēsia*, but "the fellowship of his Son, Jesus Christ our Lord" (1 Cor. 1:9) is the underlying reality expressing the union of Christ and Christians in the "one body" of Christ, which is the church. Passages using *koinōnia* or *koinōnein* tell us little about the structure of such fellowship or the ministries exercised by Christians in it. Paul's description of Titus as "my partner (*koinōnos*)" in 2 Corinthians 8:23 says nothing about Titus's specific ministry. Galatians 6:6, in a reference to oral instruction, possibly a baptismal catechesis, says, "Let the one who is taught the word share (*koinōneitō*) all good things with the one who teaches."[214]

139. Salvation, as an effect of the Christ-event, is an important element in Pauline theology. In light of Old Testament imagery of Yahweh delivering his people Israel (Isa. 45:15; Zec. 8:7), Paul sees that deliverance now coming through Christ: Christians "are being saved" by the cross of Christ (1 Cor. 1:18, 21). First Corinthians 15:2 speaks of "the gospel . . . by which you are saved" (cf. 2 Cor. 2:15). Paul identifies "the gospel" as "the power of God for the salvation of everyone who believes" (Rom. 1:16). Only in Philippians 3:20 does Paul call Jesus *sōtēr*, and as such he is still awaited. The end result is still something of the future, having an eschatological aspect (see 1 Thess. 2:16; 5:8-9; 1 Cor. 3:15; 5:5; Rom. 5:9-10; 8:24 ["In hope we have been saved!"]; 10:9-10, 13). He urges the Philippians, "Work out your own salvation in fear and trembling" (2:12), adding immediately, however, "for God is at work in you, both to will and to work for his good pleasure" (2:13), lest anyone think that salvation is achieved without God's grace.[215] In the passages cited, Paul addresses Christians in the plural; a corporate sense of salvation is thereby expressed. Hebrews 2:3 cautions Christians, "how shall we escape if we neglect such great salvation, which was initially announced by the Lord and attested to us by those who heard him?"

140. In the New Testament, explicit indications of the early church's ministries are diverse and lack uniformity.[216] In his earliest letter, Paul counsels Thessalonians to "respect those who labor among you and who are over you (*proïstamenous*) in the Lord and admonish you" (1 Thess. 5:12),[217] but with no details about their specific titles or functions. The three participles (laboring, standing over, admonishing) refer to one group, either a group of leaders or all members of the community together.[218]

141. In Philippians, Paul greets the saints at Philippi, along with *episkopoi kai diakonoi*, often rendered "overseers and ministers,"[219] possibly meaning two ministries not otherwise defined. Some see "overseers and ministers" as referring to the same reality (a *hendiadys*), and thus to one ministry, "overseers who serve."[220] The two titles, however, more likely arose in Philippi out of the Greco-Roman distinct usage of *episkopos* and *diakonos* in government, guilds, and societies.[221] Possibly episkopoi designates leaders of Philippian house churches. *Diakonoi* may imply agents of the overseers, perhaps in financial matters.[222]

142. In 1 Corinthians the conception of the church as "the body of Christ" first emerges in 12:27-28 and becomes an important notion in the Deutero-Paulines (Col. 2:17; Eph. 4:12; cf. Col. 1:18; Eph. 1:22-23; 4:15-16). In that body, where all members have some function, Paul lists, among the various gifts (*charismata*) coming from the Spirit and endowing the

members, those whom "God has appointed in the church": apostles, prophets, teachers, miracle-workers, healers, helpers, administrators, and speakers in tongues (12:28). Romans 12:6-8 lists them in abstract form: prophecy, ministry, teaching, exhorting, contributing, leading, and acts of mercy. Note also the gifts to the church from the ascended Christ in Ephesians 4:11: apostles, prophets, evangelists, pastors, and teachers. Apropos of such passages, an earlier round of this dialogue commented that "some of these categories belong in the special Ministry of the church (e.g., apostles, prophets, teachers) and that others reflect the ministry of the people of God (acts of mercy, aid, and helping), and that some are hard to categorize (healing, teaching)."[223]

143. In Acts 14, it is said of Paul and Barnabas, "In each church they installed presbyters (*presbyterous kat' ekklēsian*) and with prayer and fasting commended them to the Lord" (v. 23).[224] In Paul's own uncontested letters, "presbyters" are never mentioned. At Acts 20:17, the Apostle addresses the Ephesian *presbyterous tēs ekklēsias*, counseling them to keep watch over themselves and "over the whole flock, of which the Holy Spirit has appointed you overseers (*episkopous*), to shepherd the church of God" (Acts 20:28).[225] Here the "church of God" is clearly under the supervision of "presbyters," who are called "overseers" appointed by the Holy Spirit. So the question arises, What is the difference in the New Testament between presbyteros and *episkopos*? Moreover, it is noteworthy that *episkopoi* in this passage are understood to be "appointed" by "the Holy Spirit," not by apostles; so even if they carry on a ministry begun by apostles, there is no indication that their authority to do so is transmitted to them by apostles.[226]

144. The Pastoral Epistles stress structured ministry and orthodox teaching, especially Titus and 1 Timothy. But *ekklēsia* appears only three times: in 1 Timothy 5:16 (probably meaning the local congregation in Ephesus); 3:5 (*ekklēsia tou theou*, "God's church," with a more universal connotation); and 3:15 ("the household of God . . . , the church of the living God, the pillar and bulwark of the truth," probably meant in a universal sense). The concept of the body of Christ is absent from the Pastoral Epistles, as is the term *koinōnia*. The church is the collectivity of Christians that must be properly managed and governed in the interest of sound doctrine.

145. In the Pastoral Epistles, ministry is described, first, apropos of Titus and Timothy, and second, of other members of the church. In the first case, Titus and Timothy function as emissaries of the author, but they are called neither *episkopos* nor *presbyteros*.[227] The author seeks to make sure that the apostolic gospel will continue to be preached without contamination or

perversion. Timothy is instructed to administer the church of Ephesus, above all to "teach" (1 Tim. 4:11, 16; 6:2; cf. 2 Tim. 2:2, 24), and "not be hasty in the laying on of hands" (1 Tim. 5:22).[228] Titus too is to exercise his "authority" (*epitagē*, in Titus 2:15), to amend what is defective in the church of Crete, and appoint presbyters (1:5); he is also to "teach what befits sound doctrine" (2:1). In the second case, among the tasks that others are to carry out in Ephesus and Crete are teaching (1 Tim. 4:13, 16; 5:17; Titus 1:9); "the work of an evangelist" (2 Tim 4:5); preaching the word (2 Tim. 4:2; cf. 1 Tim. 5:17); exhorting (1 Tim. 4:13); guarding the deposit (1 Tim. 6:20); caring for the "public reading of Scripture" (1 Tim. 4:13); and common prayer (1 Tim. 2:8). There is, however, no reference to eucharistic ministry in the Pastoral Epistles, nor any indication about who would preside over it.

146. The titles for Paul,[229] "herald," "apostle," and "teacher of the Gentiles" (1 Tim. 2:7), are given to no one else in these letters. Timothy is to be *kalos diakonos*, "a good minister," of Christ Jesus (1 Tim. 4:6),[230] but here *diakonos* is used generically and hardly means that he was a "deacon." Timothy has been commissioned[231] by the laying on of hands by the presbyteral college (*presbyterion*, 1 Tim. 4:14), and by the laying on of hands by the writer (2 Tim. 1:6); i.e., a grace (*charisma*) has been conferred on Timothy, which was not simply the "authority" (*epitagē*) of an office bestowed. Nothing similar is said of Titus, who is directed "to appoint presbyters in every town" (Titus 1:5).

147. The Pastoral Epistles list qualities to be sought in individuals who are called *episkopos*, "overseer" (in the singular),[232] *presbyteroi*, "presbyters" (in the plural),[233] *diakonoi*, "ministers" or "intermediary agents,"[234] and *chērai*, "widows."

148. The qualifications of the *episkopos* are set forth in 1 Timothy 3: 1-7:[235] eight positive, five negative, with the most important being "skillful in teaching" (*didaktikos*, 3:2), but he is also to "provide for (*epimelēsetai*) God's church" (3:5), implying an administrative role.[236]

149. The term *presbyteros* is used in Pastoral Epistles in two senses: (1) as an adjective denoting dignity of age, "older" (1 Tim. 5:1, "older man"; 5:2, "older woman");[237] and (2) as a substantive, a title for a Christian community official, "presbyter" (Titus 1:5; 1 Tim. 5:17, 19). In Titus 1:5-9, the author lists many of the same qualifications, required for the *episkopos* in 1 Timothy 3:1-7, as requirements for the *presbyteroi*, and Titus 1:5-9, which begins with qualifications of "presbyters," suddenly shifts in verse 7 to *episkopos*, "an overseer," where the qualifications are ten positives and seven negatives. The most important difference from 1 Timothy is that the *episkopos* is now called *theou*

oikonomos, "God's steward" (1:7), and an exhorter with sound doctrine (1:9). Moreover, in 1 Timothy 5:17, the author speaks of "presbyters who preside well" and "those who labor in preaching and teaching," which may denote two different kinds of presbyters.[238]

150. In the Pastoral Epistles, *diakonos* and *diakonia* are used in a generic sense—"minister" and "ministry" (1 Tim. 4:6; 2 Tim. 4:5)—and also in the specific sense of a group often called "deacons." The qualifications for the latter are given in 1 Timothy 3:8-13, five positive, three negative; some of them echo the qualifications for the presbyters and overseers. This institution in the early church may be a development of the action taken in Acts 6:1-6, resulting in the appointment of the Seven (Acts 21:8); but they are never called *diakonoi* in Acts, even though their function is said to be *diakonein trapezais*, "to serve tables."[239] Scholars debate whether *gynaikas* (1 Tim. 3:11) refers to women deacons (somewhat like Phoebe of Rom. 16:1) or to the wives of deacons.[240]

151. Finally, mention must be made of the enrolled *chērai*, "widows," of 1 Timothy 5:3-16, where the qualifications are set forth for those who may be considered such. What their function would be in the structured church is not explained.[241]

152. Of the four groups, the most important seems to be *episkopos*, called *theou oikonomos*, "God's steward" (Titus 1:7; 1 Tim. 1:4; cf. 1 Tim. 3:15).

153. The problem is how to distinguish *presbyteroi* from *episkopos* in the Pastoral Epistles, to say what is the difference in the function or role that they are thought to play.[242] Interpreters debate whether in the Pastoral Epistles the church-structure involves two or three offices: either deacons and bishop/presbyters; or deacons, presbyters, and bishop, each clearly distinct.[243]

154. In other New Testament writings, presbyters (*presbyteros/-oi*) appear widely for Christians serving as community leaders (Acts 11:30; 20:17; Heb. 11:2; Jas. 5:15; 1 Pet. 5:1, 5; 2 Jn. 1; 3 Jn. 1), with no hint of accompanying *episkopos* or *diakonos*. The author of 1 Peter even speaks of himself as "fellow elder" (*sympresbyteros*) as he exhorts other *presbyteroi*.[244] Whatever its origin, "presbyter" was a frequent designation of office in the New Testament, even if the term tells us little about the nature of this office.

155. Churches in the New Testament period were related to each other in terms of concern and sharing. For instance, in Acts 15, Paul and Barnabas are sent by the Antiochene church to the apostles and presbyters of Jerusalem to consult them about whether Gentiles have to be circumcised and observe the Mosaic law in order to "be saved" (Acts 15:1-2; the so-called Jerusalem Council; cf. Gal 2:1-10). Concern for other churches is

found in the decision of James and other Jerusalem leaders to send a letter to the particular churches of Antioch, Syria, and Cilicia about *porneia* ("fornication" [NRSV] or "unlawful marriage" [NABRNT]) and dietary matters (Acts 15:13-29).[245] Here one sees the mother-church of Jerusalem guiding the activity of daughter-churches.

156. Paul manifests concern for *koinōnia* in his appeals to his churches for a contribution for "the saints" in Jerusalem (1 Cor. 16:1; 2 Cor. 8:1-5; Gal. 2:9-10).[246] Often the churches of one area send greetings to other churches (1 Cor. 16:19 [Aquila and Prisca and their house church]; Rom. 16:23; cf. Col. 4:13, 15-16). Such a sharing of concern for other ecclesial communities of a certain region is a form of *koinōnia*, even if the term itself is not used.

157. To summarize, the New Testament evidence reveals that after the resurrection of Jesus his followers became aware of themselves as *ekklēsia*, a community united by faith in him and sharing a destiny of salvation. They spoke of the *koinōnia* in which they shared. Leadership always existed in the earliest Christian churches, some of it Spirit-appointed, some of it established by apostles or others; but no one pattern of leadership emerged. Jesus' words to Simon Peter imply a Petrine function among his followers in his church to be built or flock to be fed, but they supply no specific form of that function. According to Acts, the Twelve impose hands on the Seven, who are to "serve tables," but some of whom act as preachers and teachers. Others appoint presbyters in local churches, and Paul greets *episkopoi kai diakonoi* as distinct from the rest of the Christians of Philippi. Yet the specific function of these ministers is never fully stated. Even when desired qualities of *episkopos*, *presbyteroi*, or *diakonoi* are spelled out in the Pastoral Letters, the precise function of such ministers of the Christian community remains unclear.

III. Historical Development After the New Testament

158. The ministry and structures which serve the church as a *koinōnia* of salvation have changed in various ways over two thousand years. In what follows, we attempt to present the phases of that development that are most relevant to this dialogue. There will be a single narrative for developments up to the Reformation (see §§159-170); distinctive Catholic and Lutheran developments starting with the Reformation will receive separate treatments (see §§171-242).

A. Developments in Service to *Koinonia*

1. Church Structures and Leadership

159. After, or even in some cases contemporary with, the developments exhibited in the New Testament, a certain variety in the structure of the churches[247] began to yield to the pattern that became normal after Constantine. It became customary for each church to have a single principal leader, who was often assisted by counselors and one or more deputies; the terminology used by Ignatius of Antioch has become standard for these roles: bishop, presbytery or group of elders, and deacons.[248] Together these leaders were responsible for the activity and especially the cohesion of the church they served.[249] Cohesion between churches was part of their task, and it was carried out by letter,[250] personal travel,[251] and meetings (synods), even in the second and third centuries.

160. A special role in this maintenance of *koinonia* was played by the consecrated eucharistic bread itself, whether taken to those who were unable to attend the common liturgy,[252] offered as a sign of *koinonia* from one bishop to another,[253] or shared from the bishop's liturgy to the altars of other eucharistic celebrations in the neighborhood of his city, the so-called *fermentum*.[254] The exclusion of a Christian from the eucharistic assembly was intended to bring about conversion, serving as a grave warning to repent, and even in serious cases of apostasy in persecution, this *koinonia* could be restored as death approached.[255] Likewise the refusal to be "in communion" was the most solemn declaration that *koinonia* did not exist.[256]

161. *Koinonia* was exhibited through the participation by other neighboring bishops in the ordination of a new colleague.[257] Letters of communion established the same kind of link with bishops farther away, attesting both to the orthodoxy of a new bishop's belief and the integrity of his election, thus certifying his place as a successor to the apostles. Among the criteria which made communion with other bishops possible, we should note the use of orthodox scriptures,[258] the common celebration of the principal Christian festivals,[259] and the exclusion of those denounced by other churches as heretics.[260]

162. The oldest and largest churches played a leading role in maintaining these bonds.[261] Sometimes prominence was determined by Roman imperial organization, e.g., the early importance of the see of Caesarea Maritima in Palestine, the Roman provincial capital, whose prerogatives are preserved even at the Council of Nicaea (325); and the sudden rise to prominence of Byzantium, renamed Constantinople, as the eastern capital

of the Roman Empire, recognized at the Council of Constantinople (381) and even more emphatically in the twenty-eighth canon of Chalcedon (451), which was not accepted by the church of Rome. Another sort of prominence derived from Christian history: Thus in the fourth century, Jerusalem, which had an insignificant place in the Roman scheme, came to take precedence of honor over Caesarea Maritima in Palestine, the capital city of the province, and was deemed a fifth patriarchate at the Council of Chalcedon (451).

163. Until the third century, there seems not to have been a clear distinction between the titles "bishop" and "presbyter": the former could be seen as a presbyter with the main responsibility for a church and the authority and powers necessary for carrying out that responsibility.[262] At first, churches could be designated by a pair of terms, *ekklesia* and *paroikia*, as in "the church of God which sojourns (*paroikousa*) at. . . ."[263] Even if quite small, churches would normally be led by someone who could be called a "bishop"; village and rural churches were headed by country bishops (chorbishops) until the fourth century.[264] The collegial presbyterate was concerned mainly with decision-making and doctrine and cannot be shown to have priestly liturgical duties until the mid-third century.[265] Apart from that, we are poorly informed about the ways in which pastoral leadership and care were exercised in different settings.

2. The Special Nature of Metropolitan Churches

164. In very large city churches such as the one in Rome, there might have been a number of different Christian communities or "schools," existing side by side, serving different populations, sometimes complementing each other, sometimes competing with each other. The several congregations faced the rest of the Christian world with a single voice, which we call that of the "bishop," but the internal arrangements of the church in Rome and in other large centers of Christian population are unclear to us. In Rome a unified structure can be seen by the third century.[266] At the beginning of the 250s, Cornelius lists the membership of his community as, in addition to the bishop, "forty-six presbyters, seven deacons, seven sub-deacons, forty-two acolytes, fifty-two exorcists, readers and door-keepers, above fifteen hundred widows and persons in distress, all of whom are supported by the grace and loving-kindness of the Master."[267] Such large numbers could hardly have met in a single place, but Cornelius does not inform us about the various congregations which must have existed in Rome or how they were related to each other.

165. The church of Rome and its bishop claimed a certain precedence[268] and broad responsibility in the church as a whole, founded upon its connection with the apostles Peter and Paul, who preached in Rome and were martyred there,[269] and this claim was generally accepted by other churches, though they did not hesitate to speak up for their own rights and traditions.[270] Irenaeus of Lyon made a case for the continuous orthodoxy of the church of Rome and its presiding bishops, one after another,[271] and though he insisted that a similar case could be made for the other ancient churches, such as that of Ephesus, the church in Rome's role as a benchmark of orthodoxy only grew with the passage of time.

B. Communion and Ministry in the Patristic and Medieval Church

166. With the legalization of Christianity in the Roman Empire,[272] the number of Christians rose rapidly, and structure and ministry in the church developed to meet the task of assuring continuity of doctrine among those newly added to the church, consistency of discipline in the many new eucharistic communities, and communion in the apostolic faith in the church as a whole. The boundary between laity and clergy became more distinct, and certain tasks (e.g., catechesis) were absorbed by the clergy, especially the presbyters.[273] Larger churches, instead of subdividing into smaller ones headed by their own bishops, developed in the opposite direction, with the suppression of the institution of chorbishop[274] and the delegation of pastoral responsibility to presbyters under the bishop's authority.[275] Cities in the western church seem not to have been divided into parishes before the ninth century.[276] In rural areas, the rising number of proprietary churches erected by newly converted feudal lords[277] and the many local congregations cared for by monasteries[278] were gradually integrated into this episcopal structure as well. Bishops tried to foster the unity of the congregations under their care by gathering their clergy regularly[279] and by encouraging the urban clergy to live in community.[280]

167. The emperor Constantine and his successors encouraged the bishops to continue the practice of meeting in councils or synods, and canon 5 of the Council of Nicaea, which Constantine convened, legislated that provincial and regional councils should be held regularly. This legislation, which was reiterated by later directives, was observed to a varying degree in different times and regions.[281] Greater councils, including those technically known as "ecumenical" councils,[282] were of great importance for the main-

tenance of communion, though they were not always successful in achieving church unity.[283] In addition, communion among churches coexisted with and even benefitted from a hierarchical grouping, under the metropolitan (bishop of the metropolis of the civil diocese)[284] and the patriarch, through whom each congregation was in communion with the rest of the church.[285] A high level of leadership, both doctrinal and disciplinary, was offered by the patriarchs: the bishops of Rome, Alexandria, and Antioch, a group to which were later added Constantinople, as the "new Rome" and seat of the emperor, and Jerusalem, as the church of origin of Christianity and a focus of pilgrimage.[286] Although as a practical matter, "the organization of the church in five patriarchates did not last long,"[287] the ideal has continued to be a powerful symbol of the compatibility of distinction between churches and effective communion.[288]

168. While these developments made it difficult to envisage every local parish as embodying everything which is required in order to be "church," the ancient equivalence of presbyter and bishop was not forgotten. Jerome insists upon that equivalence when he is making the argument that it is normal for bishops to be chosen from among the presbyters of the church, rather than from the deacons.[289] He argued, "For also at Alexandria, from Mark the evangelist down to bishops Heraclas and Dionysius, the presbyters always chose one of themselves and, having elevated him in grade, named him bishop—just as if an army might make an emperor by acclamation, or deacons choose one of themselves, whom they know to be hard-working, and call him archdeacon. For what, apart from ordaining, does a bishop do which a presbyter does not?" "Ambrosiaster" (thought to be Pelagius), in his comments on the Pauline epistles, makes the same point regarding New Testament usage.[290]

Both Jerome and Ambrosiaster are reflected in the *De Ecclesiasticis Officiis* of Isidore of Seville (c. 560-636). He tells us that "'Bishop,' as one of the prudent says, is the name of a work, not of an honor. . . . Therefore we can say in Latin that the bishop *superintends*, so that someone who would love to preside but not to assist may understand that he is not a bishop."[291] For Isidore, presbyters correspond to Old Testament priests as bishops do to the high priest. Presbyters and bishops are alike in regard to the Eucharist, teaching the people, and preaching. He adds,

> and only on account of authority is ordination and consecration reserved to the high priest, lest if the discipline of the

> church were arrogated by many it might dissolve concord and generate scandals.[292]

Isidore, like Jerome and Ambrosiaster, cites 1 Timothy 3:8, Titus 1:5; Philippians 1:1, and Acts 20:28, and his other sources are as follows: the line about bishops as superintendents is from Augustine;[293] the statement about the common duties of bishops and presbyters, with a purely disciplinary restriction of certain powers to the former, comes from an anonymous treatise "On the Seven Orders of the Church";[294] and the comments on Scripture are from Pelagius's commentary on 1 Timothy. All Isidore's observations about the bishop/presbyter relationship are taken up by later canonical and theological authors, particularly Peter Lombard,[295] and became part of the standard repertory of authorities with which western Christian theologians had to deal.[296]

169. How undefined the distinction between presbyters and bishops was can also be seen occasionally on the practical level, where there were some striking instances of presbyters exercising powers typical of bishops when the occasion called for it. For example, two eighth-century missionaries, Willehad and Liudger,[297] whom Charlemagne had sent to convert the Saxons on his eastern border, ordained clergy for the churches they founded, long before they themselves received consecration as bishops. In the fifteenth century, three different popes delegated the power to ordain to abbots who had not been ordained to the episcopate; in two of those cases, the privilege included ordination to the priesthood.[298] For many medieval theologians, the limiting of ordination to bishops was associated with the episcopal dignity, but not with orders as such. After the introduction of pseudo-Dionysius's *De Ecclesiastica Hierarchia* into Latin theology in the early thirteenth century, Dionysius's pervasive arrangement of everything in patterns of three seems to have deepened the sense of a distinction among the orders of deacon, presbyter, and bishop.[299]

170. While the communion among local congregations was primarily the charge of the bishop, there were various attempts to assure unity in the church on a wider scale during the Middle Ages. In the East, the rise of Islam, the Russian adoption of Christianity, and the growth of autocephalous churches led to the type of structure characteristic of the Orthodox communion. In the West, the church of Rome maintained and developed an ascendancy which was often advanced by the desire of other particular churches to free themselves from domination from lay feudal lords. The bishops of Rome claimed that anyone in the church might appeal

to them[300] and that they inherited the power of St. Peter.[301] The Symmachan Forgeries of the sixth century,[302] the "Donation of Constantine" of the eighth century,[303] and the False Decretals brought in from France in the ninth century[304] all tended to support and promote the papal primacy. Bernard of Clairvaux hailed that primacy as universal,[305] and despite challenges from figures like Marsilius of Padua and scandals like the Great Schism of the West, papal primacy persisted into Reformation times. The struggle against feudal control of the church was not an unmixed success, however: in the process, bishops, abbots, and the popes themselves became feudal lords and consequently, a part of that system;[306] and the pope's success in divesting kings of responsibility for the *ecclesia universalis* laid the groundwork for the rise of the autonomous state and the dichotomy between sacred and secular.

IV. The Lutheran Reformation

171. The traditional, though varied and often unsettled, medieval structures of church and ministry provided the background for the Lutheran reformers of the sixteenth century and "the impact of the gospel"[307] that they brought to the fore. They sought removal of unacceptable aspects and renewal of the existing church, not wholesale restructuring, as part of their conservative reformation. But, with some exceptions outside the Holy Roman Empire,[308] the bishops of the day, many of whom had feudal positions to protect, refused to endorse the aims of the Wittenberg reformers and would not ordain candidates committed to the Reformation gospel. In spite of this opposition, the reformers continued the principle of one ordained ministry, employing a variety of approaches to structure, on the basis of biblical and patristic sources and medieval precedents. Self-appointment to the ministry was not even considered, nor was direct appointment by the Spirit. The steps Lutherans took in this emergency situation were not all intended to be permanently normative. New situations in later times stimulated further development and often variety in Lutheran praxis for church and ministry within the framework of the confessional commitments of the sixteenth century.

A. The Nature of the Church as Communion and Its Ministry

1. *Communion and Local Church*

172. "Communion" as a term applied specifically to the church is not found in the writings of the Reformers or their opponents. But Luther does apply the closely related notions of the communion of saints and eucharistic communion. His sermon on *The Blessed Sacrament of the Holy and True Body of Christ and the Brotherhoods*[309] seeks to provide a basis for Christian life in both church and city. The transforming power of love, the bonds of unity, and participation in the body of Christ (comprehending both Christ and fellow Christians) are all centered in the Lord's Supper:

> The blessing of this sacrament is fellowship and love. . . . This fellowship is twofold: on the one hand we partake of Christ and all saints; on the other hand we permit all Christians to be partakers of us, in whatever way they and we are able. Thus by means of this sacrament, all self-seeking love is rooted out and gives place to that which seeks the common good of all; and through the change wrought by love there is one bread, one drink, one body, one community. This is the true unity of Christian brethren.[310]

The faithful truly participate in Christ and Christ in them.[311] In this relationship, they share the goods or gifts that are the fruits of that communion. These goods include a sharing not only in each other's joys, but also in each other's sufferings.[312] Such mutual participation is communicated through the means of grace, a sacramental reality that presumes ministers of the word.[313] The existence of ministers, in turn, presumes an ecclesiastical ordering or structure, in short, a church as communion.[314]

173. According to the *Augsburg Confession*, "The church is the assembly of saints in which the gospel is taught purely and the sacraments are administered rightly" (CA 7), and "no one should teach publicly in the church or administer the sacraments unless properly called" (CA 14). Because the local congregation has the word proclaimed and the sacramental gifts of God, it is "church," in that place, in the full sense. In lands that embraced the teaching of Luther, the local church continued to be geographically and often physically the same as that which had existed previously, in village, town, or city. Lutheran immigrants in the United States and Canada formed local congregations where they settled.[315] In such assemblies, Lutherans participate in Christ and live out their faith.[316]

174. For Luther and the Lutheran tradition, the local church, to use biblical language (as in Ezek. 34, Jn. 10, 1 Pet. 5:1-4), consists of a shepherd and the flock. The term "shepherd" refers to the pastor with tasks of word and sacraments, "the flock," to the people of God in a particular place. The pastor as minister of word and sacrament also has oversight responsibilities in the congregation. Luther could describe the pastor/bishop as a supervisor or watchman, i.e., one who carefully observes his flock to see to it that among them the word is taught and proclaimed in its purity, that the sacraments are used rightly, and that the community strives to live according to the word and command of God.[317] Such a function is common to all ordained ministers whether they preside over a congregation or a diocese, and it takes the form of personal oversight.[318]

175. It can further be argued, as of critical importance, that all visible means and structures, all the institutional realities of the church, must reflect and embody the gospel in as clear and as unmistakable a manner as possible. Therefore *koinonia* can neither be forced, nor can it exist apart from *faith*. A true faith (i.e., one that is a participation in *Christ*) will foster a communion that is authentic (i.e., one that is a real *participation* in Christ).

2. The One Office of Pastor/Bishop

176. That the office of presbyter and bishop was one and the same was a teaching widespread in the Middle Ages inherited ultimately from Jerome and the New Testament. Luther asserted the position from 1519 on.[319] He wrote in 1520:

> according to the institution of Christ and the apostles, every city should have a priest or bishop, as St. Paul clearly says in Titus 1[:5]. . . . According to St. Paul, and also St. Jerome, a bishop and a priest are one and the same thing. But of bishops as they now are the Scriptures know nothing. Bishops have been appointed by ordinance of the Christian church, so that one of them may have authority over several priests.[320]

Luther's point was "that originally the *episcopus* was the leader of the congregation in one city, i.e., the pastor, and not the leader of a diocese with many such congregations."[321]

177. In the Lutheran Confessions, this position is forcefully expressed in the *Treatise on the Power and Primacy of the Pope*:

> It is universally acknowledged, even by our opponents, that this power is shared by divine right by all who preside in the churches, whether they are called pastors, presbyters, or bishops. For that reason Jerome plainly teaches that in the apostolic letters all who preside over churches are both bishops and presbyters. . . . What, after all, does a bishop do, with the exception of ordaining, that a presbyter does not?"[322]

178. The Reformers, while denying any *iure divino* difference between presbyter (pastor) and bishop, also allowed, however, for the later, historical development of the episcopal office beyond the individual congregation and even for "distinctions of degree" between bishops and pastors. But this is by human authority, not by divine right.[323]

179. This understanding of the relation between bishop and presbyter not only opened possibilities for needed reform of the episcopate, but also justified the establishment of new (though recognizable) forms through which the ministry of oversight could be exercised alternatively, if necessary and as circumstances required. Melanchthon applied this reasoning and developed it to meet the urgent practical problem of providing for the orderly succession of ministers in areas that embraced the movement for reform. He maintained that, inasmuch as in the ancient church presbyters had been permitted to ordain, presbyters may once again assume this function in the absence of responsible bishops, as the current crisis clearly demanded, for the sake of the gospel. When bishops become heretics or refuse ordination, Melanchthon said, then "the churches are by divine right compelled to ordain pastors and ministers for themselves."[324] Luther also had claimed that the church should not be deprived of ministers on account of neglectful, cruel, or renegade bishops. "Therefore, as the ancient examples of the church and the Fathers teach us, we should and will ordain suitable persons to this office ourselves."[325] Such action should not be regarded as a deliberately provocative or independent attempt to forge a new ecclesiastical structure. One index of their firm hope to avoid schism is that, while one Lutheran ordination may have taken place in Wittenberg in 1525, there were no more until 1535.[326] The Lutherans believed they were proposing the *more* ancient, and thus original, ministerial structure more conducive to authentic *koinonia*.

180. The Reformers, as indicated above, embraced the view that the office of bishop developed historically, after the New Testament period, as that of a presbyter with special oversight in an area larger than a single

congregation or town. While established by human authority, this structure "was instituted by the Fathers for a good and useful purpose."[327] As early as 1522, Luther sketched what an Evangelical bishop would be like, oriented to the gospel of justification and the church as a *communio* for salvation. His tract *Against the Falsely Named Spiritual Estate of the Pope and Bishops* was an appeal for support from, and reform by, the then-reigning bishops.[328] It has been argued that, "Had this attempt been successful, the German Lutheran churches—and most of the United ones [Lutheran and Reformed]—would today have a similar appearance to those of Scandinavia."[329] But none of the bishops within the Holy Roman Empire supported the Reformation. Therefore the Lutheran charges against them increasingly became that they were not true bishops, but rather princes, and that they ultimately opposed the gospel.

181. Fundamental was the problem of the *power* of bishops. The *locus classicus* of the Lutheran argument regarding this power is found in *Augsburg Confession* Article 28, "In former times there were serious controversies about the power of bishops, in which some people improperly mixed the power of the church and the power of the sword." The reformers requested that bishops restrict themselves to doing what is according to the gospel: "the power of the keys or the power of the bishops is the power of God's mandate to preach the gospel, to forgive and retain sins, and to administer the sacraments. . . . If bishops possess any power of the sword, they possess it not through the command of the gospel but by human right, granted by kings and emperors." The reformers' indictment of the bishops was that they were using the power of the sword to impose and enforce religious practices contrary to the gospel.[330]

182. While *Augsburg Confession* Article 28 was immediately concerned with the practical need to distinguish temporal from spiritual power, it also contained a positive proposal to reform and reorient the church's episcopal structure by returning it to its evangelical, spiritual, and pastoral foundations.

> Consequently, according to the gospel, or, as they say, by divine right, this jurisdiction belongs to the bishops as bishops (that is, to those to whom the ministry of the Word and sacraments has been committed): to forgive sins, to reject teaching that opposes the gospel, and to exclude from the communion of the church the ungodly whose ungodliness is known—doing all this not with human power but by the Word. In this regard, churches are

bound by divine right to be obedient to the bishops according to the saying [Lk. 10:16], "Whoever listens to you listens to me."[331]

B. Structures for Regional Oversight

1. The German Lands

183. It soon became apparent in Reformation territories that, if the aims of the reformers were to be carried through in the life of the churches, the oversight that they believed was a special task of the bishops continued to be necessary to congregations embracing the Evangelical faith. A number of steps were taken to carry this out in an Evangelical way.

184. (a) The traditional system of episcopal *visitation* of congregations had collapsed, and the reigning bishops would scarcely carry out visits with encouragement and admonishment along the lines of Reformation theology. Therefore Melanchthon provided an "Instruction" for visitation of the churches and schools of Electoral Saxony, to which Luther wrote a preface (1528). This *episkopē* was to be conducted by centrally appointed visitors from outside the individual parish, to measure what was being done by the standards of the word of God.[332] Catholicity and accountability to the gospel criterion were involved.[333]

185. (b) In some exceptional instances, Catholic bishops in German lands joined the Reformation.[334] Luther watched such developments with interest but was disappointed that no similar cases of a bishop's and region's becoming Lutheran occurred within the Empire.[335] Thus, outside of Prussia (and Sweden and Finland), existing bishops did not come into the Lutheran orbit with their regional churches.

186. (c) In three instances, pastors holding to the Reformation were appointed bishops of existing dioceses in Saxony.[336] In one case, an attempt to involve an existing bishop in the consecration came to nothing.[337] Luther and superintendents and pastors from nearby cities conducted the laying on of hands in the ordination/installation service for two of these bishops; neighboring superintendents laid hands on the third. An episcopate without political power and finance proved unworkable within the structure of the Holy Roman Empire.[338] With the Smalcald War and eventually the Peace of Augsburg, such experiments with Evangelical bishops came to an end. The Protestant princes took over as governors of the episcopal sees, an inheritance of the prince-bishop of the Middle Ages. It was not until 1918, after World War I and the collapse of the Empire and creation of a republic in Germany, that the role of the prince as *summus episcopus* finally was abolished.[339]

187. (d) There emerged, nonetheless, an office of oversight for the German Lutheran churches, called *Superintendent*[340] (etymologically a Latin-derivative equivalent of *episkopos*, one who oversees), *Dekan*, or *Propst*. In so doing, the reformers "held fast to the episcopal office itself."[341]

188. The domination of the church by the princes, especially after the Peace of Augsburg, and the appropriation by the princes of the authority of the former bishops meant that the church in Germany tended to be organized along the political lines of the principalities (not nationally, as in Sweden and England, which were more unified politically). The problem that *Augsburg Confession* Article 28 originally addressed, namely, the confusion of temporal and spiritual authority that had existed with the medieval episcopate, continued to require solution.

2. *Nordic Countries*

189. The political and ecclesiastical situation in the Nordic lands was different from that of the Holy Roman Empire. In both Nordic kingdoms (Sweden-Finland and Denmark-Norway-Iceland), civil wars, which were more political than religious in their motivation, opened the way for the introduction of the Reformation. Since the ruling authorities in both kingdoms came to support the Reformation, the political realities that forced the creation of new church structures in continental Europe did not exist in the North. Thus, the Lutheran intention to preserve the episcopal structure was realized in the Nordic countries.[342]

190. In Sweden and Finland (under Swedish rule until 1809), the medieval episcopal structure was preserved relatively intact. In the Swedish Lutheran *Church Ordinance* of 1571, the importance of episcopacy was stressed as "an irreplaceable order of the church."[343] This document maintains that, while "the distinction which now exists between bishops and simple priests was not known at first in Christendom, but bishop and priest were all one office," the "agreement that one bishop among them [the pastors] should be chosen, who should have superintendence over all the rest . . . was very useful and without doubt proceeded from God the Holy Ghost . . . so it was generally approved and accepted over the whole of Christendom," a ministerial function that has remained in the church "and must remain in the future, so long as the world lasts, although the abuse, which has been very great in this as in all other useful and necessary things, must be set aside."[344] This text has been reaffirmed in modern Swedish church statements.[345]

191. While a succession of episcopal consecrations was threatened during the sometimes tumultuous sixteenth century, it was not broken and has been continued in Sweden to the present.[346] In 1884, all three Finnish bishops died within a short period of time. As a result, no bishop was available to consecrate a new bishop. After some debate, focusing on the question of inviting a Swedish bishop to consecrate a bishop in Russian-ruled Finland, a new archbishop was consecrated by a professor of theology at the University of Helsinki.[347] After independence from Russia in 1917, Swedish bishops were invited to participate in Finnish episcopal consecrations and a succession of consecrations was re-established.

192. In 1536, the Reformation was carried through in Denmark, which at that time ruled Norway and Iceland.[348] The previous bishops were replaced in 1537 by "superintendents"[349] for the Danish and Norwegian dioceses, consecrated by Johannes Bugenhagen, city pastor of Wittenberg. While a succession of consecrations was thus broken, the medieval diocesan and cathedral structures were preserved and bishops continued to exercise a ministry of oversight.[350] A significant episcopal continuity or *sucessio sedis* or *localis* was preserved.

193. The ecclesial structures of the Baltic lands went through complex changes as political power shifted among the Teutonic Knights, Poland, Sweden, and Russia.[351] Episcopal structures remained in place for the most part in Estonia until Russian rule arrived in the early eighteenth century. Lutheran churches in Latvia and Lithuania tended to follow patterns more like those in Germany, with consistories and superintendents. In the early twentieth century, following the independence of all three of the Baltic republics, the Estonian and Latvian churches turned to episcopal structures. Swedish and Finnish bishops were invited to participate in their episcopal consecrations, and thus these churches deliberately entered episcopal succession. World War II and the Soviet annexation led to a severe disruption of church life, including the interruption of succession, but in both countries such succession was re-established when it again became possible to invite foreign bishops to participate in episcopal consecrations. The Lithuanian church gave the chair of the consistory the title "bishop" in 1976, and the first bishop was consecrated by the Estonian archbishop.

194. In the Porvoo declaration (see §§69, 111, 118, 241), all the Nordic and Baltic Lutheran churches (with the exception of the churches in Denmark and Latvia) have committed themselves theologically to "the episcopal office . . . as a visible sign expressing and serving the Church's unity and continuity in apostolic life, mission and ministry" and procedurally "to

invite one another's bishops normally to participate in the laying on of hands at the ordination of bishops as a sign of the unity and continuity of the Church."[352] As a result, all the Nordic and Baltic churches are episcopally structured, and all but Denmark's have taken on succession as a sign of unity and continuity.

195. In other nearby countries, the Swedish episcopal succession was reintroduced into Finland early in the twentieth century;[353] into Latvia after World War I (but later interrupted);[354] and into Estonia in the 1960s.[355] The *Porvoo Common Statement* envisions the process extending to the churches in Norway and Iceland (to the church in Denmark otherwise).[356]

C. Beyond the Local and Regional: The Universal Church

196. Reformation critiques of the papacy were shaped by the contrast developed during the Middle Ages between that which was *iure divino* and that which was *iure humano*. For the Lutheran Reformers, this distinction was exhaustive and exclusive: every practice in the church was either *iure divino* or *iure humano*. No practice could be both; no practice could be neither. For the most part, the Lutherans held that only practices mandated by God within Scripture or practices directly implied by the gospel could be *iure divino*. That which was *iure divino* could not be changed by human design; that which was *iure humano* was open to human alteration. Because the Lutherans could not find an unambiguous institution of the papacy in Scripture, they denied its *iure divino* character.

197. Luther subscribed to the universal ministry of the bishop of Rome, but especially in view of what he saw as a long history of abuses, he could not accept the claim that papal primacy existed by divine right (*iure divino*). The bishop of Rome could claim such primacy (even given the history of abuse), he acknowledged, but only by human right (*iure humano*). As Luther became convinced that the pope was deliberately obstructing the preaching of the gospel, he did not hesitate to draw on the traditional popular apocalyptic imagery and call the pope "Antichrist."[357] Luther saw the pope's intransigence as a sure indication that the last days were at hand. Such a strong reaction need not be read as a simple rejection of his earlier acknowledgment of a possible universal ministry, but rather as an expression of despair regarding the apparently irreformable nature of the papacy. The pope appeared unlikely to do what all ministry was established to do, namely proclaim the word of God, administer the sacraments, and guard the truth of the gospel.[358]

198. This negative assessment of the papacy did not rule out the possibility that Lutherans might accept a universal ministry involving the bishop of Rome, provided its authority was based clearly in the gospel and spoke for it.[359] As Luther states in his commentary on Galatians (1531-1535),

> All we aim for is that the glory of God be preserved and that the righteousness of faith remain pure and sound. Once this has been established, namely that God alone justifies us solely by his grace through Christ, we are willing not only to bear the pope aloft on our hands but also to kiss his feet."[360]

V. The Sixteenth-Century Catholic Reformation

199. Even before the Council of Trent, priestly ministry had begun to develop in new ways in the Catholic Church. The need for renewal, which was already widely recognized, was answered by the creation of specially trained priests not restricted to particular parishes or dioceses in their work. More than a dozen new religious orders of priests were founded in the sixteenth and early seventeenth centuries, e.g., Jesuits and Theatines, to preach the gospel both in Europe and in newly discovered lands, to promote deeper piety among the clergy and the faithful, and to work in education and care for the sick. Reform of the older orders and of the diocesan clergy took place in many countries and was reinforced by the Council's insistence that bishops reside in their dioceses and visit parishes regularly. While the religious priests were ordained for the work of their orders, not as pastors of local churches, they brought a more vigorous and consistent preaching of the gospel and a revival of congregational life to Catholic parishes, and their example stimulated the diocesan clergy to greater zeal.[361]

A. The Council of Trent

200. In the face of the controversy and restructuring of the church involving the Lutherans, the Council of Trent attempted to sort out what it understood to be Catholic teaching regarding ordination. It undertook this task cautiously and conservatively, with a view toward addressing the most pressing of the contemporary challenges enumerated above. During the debates at the Council of Trent, many of the issues with which this dialogue is concerned made their appearance.[362] Long discussion was devoted to questions about the ministry of bishops, including whether bishops' ministry

was *de iure divino*: how could one avoid eroding papal primacy or dismissing the respectable tradition which saw *sacerdotium* as adequately exemplified in the simple priest?[363] Regarding the latter issue "it became clearer and clearer that the gradations of Order, the steps of the *sacramentum ordinis*, lead not to the simple priest but to the bishop,"[364] but the issue of the relation between bishop and pope remained intractable.[365] In the end, lest there be no decree on the sacrament of Order at all, the Council fathers produced simplified canons which left untouched several matters in dispute.[366] While the debate about the sacrament of Order was longer and more complex than any other besides the debate over justification, the decree itself with its canons was brief, owing mainly to the variety of theological and canonical approaches which existed to the understanding of priesthood. Both the Lutheran attempts at reforming the presbyterate and episcopate described earlier and Trent's extended and sometimes contentious debates on the sacrament of Order should be considered in light of this variety.

201. Trent's doctrine on the sacrament of Order was formulated in a decree of session XXIII (July 15, 1563).[367] Priesthood (*sacerdotium*) itself is linked to sacrifice in the Old Testament; the new visible priesthood to which Jesus Christ entrusted "the power to consecrate, offer, and administer his body and blood," along with the power of forgiving sin, is linked to the eucharist, the sacrifice of the New Testament. The New Testament prescribes only how priests and deacons are to be ordained, but other orders of ministers, ascending by degrees to the priesthood, go back to the beginning of the church. Scripture, the apostolic tradition, and patristic tradition all say that grace is conferred by ordination, which must therefore be accounted a sacrament of the church. Because ordination, like baptism and confirmation, "imprints a character that cannot be destroyed or removed," the Council insists that the priesthood that ordination confers is permanent and not to be confused with the spiritual power received by all the baptized. Regarding the difference between priests and bishops, the Council says that bishops, who succeed the apostles and receive from the Spirit the task of "ruling the church of God," are superior to the priests and can confer confirmation, ordain, and "do many other functions for which the lower order has no power." As for the laity, whether congregations or civil magistrates, the Council denies that they have a necessary, much less a sufficient, role in ordination. It is important to note, however, that while the council fathers maintained that the hierarchy was instituted by divine ordinance, they took no position on whether the declared superiority of bishops over priests was instituted *iure divino*.[368]

202. Eight canons condemning views opposed to the Council's doctrine were attached to the doctrinal decree. It can be said of them that they "are purely 'defensive.' They simply defend the legitimacy and validity of Catholic ordinations but say nothing whatever about the ministries of the Protestant churches."[369] While canon 3 boldly says that ordination is "a sacrament . . . instituted by Christ the Lord" (*a Christo domino institutum*), canon 6 says that the hierarchy of bishops, presbyters, and other ministers was "instituted by divine ordinance" (*divina ordinatione institutam*), a slightly less lofty claim which still distinguishes hierarchy from mere human invention.[370] Canon 7 insists upon the power of bishops, in particular that power which they do not have in common with presbyters and which makes them higher than the latter,[371] namely the power to confirm and ordain.

203. The eighteen canons of the reform decrees of session XXIII reinforced the connection between the power of Order and the power of jurisdiction, located above all in the bishop. Between the first canon, on the requirement of residency for all who have the care of souls, and the eighteenth, which prescribed the formation of seminaries, come canons concerned with fitness for ministry and the proper procedure for advancing people though the degrees of ordination. The central role of the bishop was underlined again and again, and privileges granted earlier to other prelates or church bodies were rescinded.[372] This reorientation of the sacrament of Order in the direction of the bishop could not be carried through completely at Trent because the Council was unable to clarify the relation of episcopacy and papal primacy, but it did succeed in articulating the difference between bishop and priest in sacramental, and not merely jurisdictional, terms.[373]

204. Modern ecumenical dialogue has included a re-examination of the decrees of the Council of Trent and the debates which led up to them. One of the fullest studies of the eight canons on the sacrament of Order has been produced by the *Ökumenische Arbeitskreis* (Ecumenical Working Group)[374] as part of their study of the Tridentine anathemas on the sacraments. It noted a difference of emphasis between the Reformers, who stressed the primacy of the task of proclamation of the gospel including the administration of the sacraments, and the bishops at Trent, who "still held fast to the concept of *sacerdos*, or priest, and the relationship of this to the sacrifice of the mass."[375] It is not apparent whether the decree describes or refutes the positions of the Lutheran reformers, and with what accuracy; canons 2, 6, and 8 rejected opinions of radical Reformers such as the Anabaptists, opinions which were not shared by Luther. The group's study concluded that canons 1, 3, 4, 5, and 6 are not applicable to Lutherans

today; canon 7 is still applicable in part, since in Catholic teaching and practice priests are ordained by bishops only.[376]

B. The Roman Catechism (1566)

205. While the Council of Trent itself was quite guarded in many of its statements about the sacrament of Order, the *Roman Catechism* issued at the Council's behest attempts some simple explanations. It distinguishes between the internal priesthood by which "all the faithful are said to be priests" and the external priesthood which pertains "only to certain men who have been ordained and consecrated to God by the lawful imposition of hands and by the solemn ceremonies of holy Church, and who are thereby devoted to a particular sacred ministry."[377] In regard to the external priesthood, whose office "is to offer Sacrifice to God and to administer the Sacraments of the Church," the *Catechism* says,

> Now although (the sacerdotal order) is one alone, yet it has various degrees of dignity and power. The first degree is that of those who are simply called priests. . . . The second is that of Bishops, who are placed over the various dioceses to govern not only the other ministers of the Church, but the faithful also, and to promote their salvation with supreme vigilance and care.[378]

Three higher degrees follow: archbishops, patriarchs, supreme pontiff.[379] The bishop is declared to be the exclusive administrator of the sacrament of Order, although "it is true that permission has been granted to some abbots occasionally to administer those orders that are minor and not sacred."[380] One can observe in these texts the absence of the sharp polemic or analytical intensity that appear in other genres and later Catholic authors..

VI. Subsequent Catholic Developments Regarding Structures and Ministry

206. The Council of Trent itself, as we have just noted, defended Catholic doctrine about the sacrament of Order without dealing specifically with the Reformers' arguments. After the Council of Trent, Catholic theologians like Robert Bellarmine (1542-1621) responded more directly to the Protestant Reformers' views on church structure and ministry. In his *Disputations on the Controversies of the Christian Faith*,[381] Bellarmine defended the traditional medieval doctrine that bishops and presbyters share one

priesthood, but he argued for bishops' superior power of both order and jurisdiction.[382] He dealt at length with the New Testament texts in which bishops and presbyters seem to be one and the same (Phil. 1, 1 Tim. 3-4, Titus 1, Acts 20), and especially with arguments drawn from Jerome's interpretation of those passages in his Letter to Evangelus. In an apparent rebuttal to Reformers like Melanchthon, Bellarmine questions the inference from the letter that every presbyter is a bishop. If at the start all presbyters were true bishops, then the distinction which was already known to Jerome must have arisen when some accepted ordination of a lower degree. This, says Bellarmine, would not help Jerome to prove his argument that presbyters had more claim than deacons to be promoted to bishop; therefore it is more likely that bishops arose as a higher degree of Order than the presbyterate.[383]

207. Bellarmine was influential, but his solution to this question of the origin of the hierarchy was not the only one proposed by Catholic scholars. At the end of the nineteenth century, Pierre Batiffol proposed a more complicated evolution. First, the successors of the missionary leadership in the primitive church were overseers (i.e., *episcopoi*) in each community, perhaps several of them working in partnership at first but eventually just one. Presbyter, thought Batiffol, was the name applied in each place to the first converts, benefactors, and owners of house-churches.

> Thus one could be a presbyter without priesthood, and that must have been the case with many of the first presbyters. But it was from among these presbyters without priesthood that they chose—if not by necessity, at least in fact—the members of the community who were raised to the function of *episkopé*. . . . This primitive presbyterate was the original envelope of the hierarchy; as a simply preparatory form, it disappeared. Just the word was preserved to designate the priests, that is, the bishops subordinated to the chief bishop.[384]

Thus, unlike Bellarmine, Batiffol theorized that later presbyters did come into being as bishops of inferior rank: the role of bishop began as

> a liturgical, social and preaching function, the episcopate—an episcopate of several persons, like the diaconate; the plural episcopate disappears when the apostles disappear, and separates to give rise to the chief episcopacy of the bishop and the subordinated priesthood of the priests.[385]

That meant that later priests were really descendants of the bishops, not of the early presbyters.[386] While this might seem to favor the Reformers' view, Batiffol's theory was diametrically opposed to an ecclesiology which saw bishops as a human invention, necessary only for practical reasons; such a description would apply more properly to presbyters.

208. For two centuries after Trent, Catholic theology took the form of treatises (often polemical) on particular topics; but eventually the demand for comprehensive theological education called forth new-style scholastic textbooks known as "manuals." One of the first of the sets of manuals included a volume on the sacrament of Order by Thomas Holtzclau, SJ (1716-1783).[387] He set himself against many of the Reformers' ideas. He denounced any claim that civil rulers have a God-given right to authorize ordinations[388] and argued that Jerome's Letter to Evangelus "attributes to bishops a different degree of Order, by apostolic tradition or *iure divino*, a greater dignity in the Church as Aaron excelled the Levites."[389] He was aware of disagreements among Catholics concerning the extraordinary minister of Order, including whether a simple priest could ordain by papal delegation.[390] He rejected the idea that a simple priest could confer the presbyteral order under any circumstances, even with papal delegation, and he could find neither actual instances nor plausible arguments, though he cited alleged instances.[391] Later manuals continued to report the view of some other Catholic theologians that all the powers of bishops are radically contained in the sacrament of Order conferred in the ordination of presbyters, though these powers are incapable of being exercised until enabled by the granting of appropriate jurisdiction.[392] Already in Holtzclau, we can observe a trait of the manuals which contributes to the incomplete way in which more recent Catholic tradition has treated the issues of the present dialogue: the theology of the church appears early in the manuals, as an argument for the authority and credibility of the church's teaching[393]; the theology of the sacrament of Order, on the other hand, resides in the final section of the manuals, usually between anointing of the sick and marriage.[394] In this arrangement of the material, there is no occasion to ask how the relation of bishop and presbyter might be paralleled by the relation between diocese and parish.[395]

A. Vatican I and Subsequent Developments

209. The First Vatican Council (1869-1870) approved two dogmatic constitutions: *Dei Filius*, the *Dogmatic Constitution on the Catholic Faith*, on

the relationship between faith and reason, and *Pastor Aeternus*, the *Dogmatic Constitution on the Church of Christ*, on the primacy of the papacy and the infallibility of papal pronouncements *ex cathedra*. Three positions were represented at the Council: a group of ultramontane infallibilists led by Manning and Senestrey, who upheld the infallibility of all papal teaching, including the Syllabus of Errors, and who advocated papal infallibility as the source of the Catholic Church's infallibility; the majority of the bishops who wanted to strengthen papal authority, and who were thus open to defining papal infallibility; and a third group, comprising about one fifth of the Council, who vehemently opposed defining papal infallibility. Because more than sixty members of this third group deliberately left Rome before the final vote, the *Dogmatic Constitution on the Church* (*Pastor Aeternus*) was passed on July 18, 1870, with only two negative votes. Because of the outbreak of the Franco-Prussian War, the council adjourned prematurely on October 20, 1870.

210. *Pastor Aeternus* teaches that "a primacy of jurisdiction over the whole church of God was immediately and directly promised to the blessed apostle Peter and conferred on him by Christ the Lord."[396] Furthermore, "whoever succeeds to the chair of Peter obtains, by the institution of Christ himself, the primacy of Peter of the whole church."[397] It also teaches that the Roman pontiff is the successor of Peter, vicar of Christ, head of the whole church, and father and teacher of all Christian people. He has been given full power to rule and govern the universal church. Consequently, "the Roman church possesses a pre-eminence of ordinary power over every other church. And that this jurisdictional power of the Roman pontiff is both episcopal and immediate."[398] The Council added that this power of the supreme pontiff does not detract from that ordinary and immediate power of episcopal jurisdiction by which individual bishops govern their particular churches. Nevertheless, because of the premature adjournment of the Council, the theology of the papacy was not inserted into a larger theology of the episcopacy.

211. The Council defined papal infallibility as a divinely revealed dogma, but it specified strictly limited conditions under which infallibility is given by God:

> that when the Roman pontiff speaks *ex cathedra*, that is, when in the exercise of his office as shepherd and teacher of all Christians, in virtue of his supreme apostolic authority, he defines a doctrine concerning faith or morals to be held by the whole church, he possesses, by the divine assistance promised to him in blessed

> Peter, that infallibility which the divine Redeemer willed his church to enjoy in defining doctrine concerning faith or morals. Therefore, such definitions of the Roman pontiff are of themselves, and not by the consent of the church, irreformable.[399]

The Council's definition of papal infallibility limited its scope far more than what the Ultramontanes had advocated. Infallibility is assistance given by God first and foremost to the church. Like a council, the pope teaches infallibly on the church's behalf under certain conditions. Infallibility protects the pope from error only when he speaks in his official capacity as "the shepherd and teacher of all Christians," not as an individual theologian. The content of the teaching must be directly related to revelation. The pope does not teach infallibly out of his own abilities, but by virtue of "divine assistance." His definitions are not subject to the juridical ratification of the church.

212. The treatment in the 1917 *Code of Canon Law* does not explicitly lay out the relationships between bishop and pastor, diocese and parish. Some slight attention to dioceses and parishes is prefaced to the treatment of clerics, i.e., canons 215-216 of the 1917 Code. Canon 215 names the major territories, including dioceses, of which it is the prerogative of supreme ecclesiastical authority, i.e., the pope, "to erect, reconfigure, divide, merge, suppress." Canon 216 lists lesser territories, which include parishes. Thereafter the nature of those forms of church must be inferred from what the Code says about bishops and pastors, as if they were functions of their ordained ministers, not realities in their own right. What is clear is the sense that smaller realizations of church are formed by subdivision of larger ones, not larger ones by the accumulation of smaller. As a canonist's study of pastors says, parishes arose relatively late: but, in the fourth century,

> there appeared among the chapels and oratories that dotted the Gallic and Spanish countryside a more permanent pastoral institution called the "*ecclesia baptismalis*" or "*ecclesia major.*" Here for the first time there was established a stable, juridic relationship between the faithful in a definite locality and one individual church that was presided over by a priest.[400]

Until the ninth century, cities were not divided into parishes, but instead were served from the cathedral church.[401]

213. In the 1947 apostolic constitution *Sacramentum Ordinis*, Pope Pius XII revised the ritual of ordination to the diaconate, presbyterate, and epis-

copate, spelling out what is essential for the validity of each rite.[402] Pope Pius XII brought the Latin rite back into conformity with Eastern tradition by insisting upon the laying on of hands and prayer, rather than the presentation of the liturgical vessels, as the essential rites of ordination. This also was the practice of the Reformers. For purposes of this dialogue, it is important to note the pope's insistence on the "unity and identity" of the sacrament of Order, "which no Catholic has ever been able to call in question," despite the fact that there are slightly different rites for ordaining deacons, presbyters and bishops,[403] and that the pope refers to the three "orders" in the plural when discussing the rites. The new prayer for the ordination of the bishop asks God to "complete in your priest the fullness of your ministry."[404]

B. The Second Vatican Council

1. The Papacy

214. The Second Vatican Council (1962-1965) confirmed the teaching of the First Vatican Council regarding the institution, the permanence, and the nature and import of the sacred primacy of the Roman pontiff and his infallible teaching office.[405] The Roman pontiff is a visible source and foundation of the unity of the Catholic Church both in faith and in communion.[406] The council situates this teaching, however, within a theology of the episcopacy that balances and complements the teaching on the papacy of the Second Vatican Council with an emphasis on collegiality. Thus the teaching on the episcopacy provides a context for the teaching on the papacy and yet is itself interpreted within a teaching on papal authority.

2. Episcopacy

215. Bishops represent an historical continuation of the apostolic office and therefore are essential to the Roman Catholic understanding of the apostolicity of the church.[407] LG speaks of a succession that goes back to the beginning by which the bishops are the "transmitters of the apostolic line."[408] They thus serve the church's communion in apostolic faith. Among the principal tasks of bishops, preaching of the gospel is preeminent.[409]

216. By virtue of their episcopal consecration and hierarchical communion with the bishop of Rome and other bishops, bishops constitute a college or permanent assembly whose head is the bishop of Rome.[410] A bishop represents his own church within this college, and all the bishops, together with the pope, represent the whole church.[411] The bishop is responsible for the unity and communion of his church with the other churches.

The college of bishops does not constitute a legislative body apart from the pope, but rather includes the pope as member and head of the college. The episcopal college exercises its collegiality in a preeminent way in an ecumenical council. Bishops chosen from different parts of the world may also serve in a council called the Synod of Bishops where they act on behalf of the whole episcopate in an advisory role to the bishop of Rome.[412] Episcopal conferences, "a kind of assembly in which the bishops of some nation or region discharge their pastoral office in collaboration,"[413] are another form of collegial activity. Collegiality is also exercised by the solicitude of the bishops for all the churches, by contributing financial resources, training lay and religious ministers for the missions, and contributing the services of diocesan priests to regions lacking clergy.[414]

217. Although the Roman pontiff can always freely exercise full, supreme, and universal power over the church, the order of bishops is also the subject of supreme and full power over the universal church, provided it remains united with the head of the college, the pope.[415]

218. The Second Vatican Council documents teach that the fullness of the sacrament of Order is conferred by episcopal consecration.[416] The priesthood of the bishop is a sharing in the office of Christ, the one mediator.[417] By virtue of his ordination, a bishop's authority is proper, ordinary, and immediate.[418] This means that a bishop possesses authority by virtue of his ordination that is not juridically delegated by the bishop of Rome. The exercise of this authority, however, is ultimately controlled by the supreme authority of the Church.

3. *Presbyterate*

219. The Second Vatican Council documents define the nature and function of the presbyterate in relation to the episcopacy. The *Constitution on the Liturgy* (*Sacrosanctum Concilium*) subordinates both the local parish to the diocese and a priest to the bishops: "since the bishop himself in his church cannot always or everywhere preside over the whole flock, he must of necessity set up assemblies of believers. Parishes, organized locally under a parish priest who acts in the bishop's place, are the most important of these, because in some way they exhibit the visible church set up throughout the nations of the world."[419] Priests depend on bishops for the exercise of their power and are united with them by virtue of the sacrament of Order.[420] In a certain sense, presbyters make the bishop present. The "unity of their consecration and mission requires their hierarchical

communion with the order of bishops."[421] As the fellow-workers of bishops, priests "have as their first charge to announce the gospel of God to all."[422]

220. Through the sacrament of Order, priests are "patterned to the priesthood of Christ so that they may be able to act in the person of Christ the head of the body."[423] Priests exercise their sacred function above all in the eucharistic worship. They also exercise the office of Christ, the shepherd and head, according to their share of authority in their pastoral work.[424] In addition to their care of individuals, priests are exhorted to form real Christian community, embracing not only the local but also the universal church.[425] In their own locality, priests make visible the universal church.[426] Priests are to "take pains that their work contributes to the pastoral work of the whole diocese, and indeed of the whole church."[427]

221. Along with their bishop, priests constitute one presbyterium.[428] By virtue of their common ordination and shared mission, all priests are bound together in a close fraternity. This is symbolized by their laying on of hands with the ordaining bishop in the ordination rite. No priest can adequately fulfill his charge by himself or in isolation. Thus "priestly ministry can only be fulfilled in the hierarchical communion of the whole body."[429]

222. The Second Vatican Council balanced a theology of the papacy and the universal church with a renewed emphasis on the episcopacy and the local church, with the help of resources that had been recovered from the biblical and patristic heritage. The understanding of church as communion shaped its teaching on collegiality. These Catholic developments have been driven by the desire to be faithful to its tradition, and at the same time to be open to renewing its structures of ministry.

223. Throughout Roman Catholic history, the emphasis on the unitary nature of the office of ordained ministry has remained constant. There is but one sacrament of Order conferred in discrete ordinations of bishops, presbyters, and deacons. The unitary nature of the sacrament mitigates differences between Lutherans and Roman Catholics on the distinctions between presbyter/pastor and bishop.

VII. Subsequent Lutheran Developments

A. The Reformation Heritage Continued

224. The impact of Luther and the Confessions (IV.A. above) continued over the centuries through "one order of ordained Ministers, usually called pastors, which combines features of the episcopate and the

presbyterate,"[430] in local congregations and in structures for regional oversight, including episcopacy (IV.B. above). In contrast to the Middle Ages, there was emphasis on preaching of the word and administration of the sacraments in concrete relationship with a congregation; church office was seen "over against" (*gegenüber*) congregation, an office grounded in the priority of the word of God which constitutes the church (cf. §62).[431]

225. For all the adherence to "one office of ministry," there were varieties of structural patterns among Lutherans in church organization and different emphases in the periods of Lutheran Orthodoxy and Pietism (in its emphasis on the priesthood of all baptized believers), the Confessional Revival in the nineteenth century, and later, under the influence of the ecumenical movement.[432] As Lutherans emigrated from Europe to other parts of the world and mission work produced new churches, especially in Africa and Asia, the Lutheran confessional tradition adapted to new needs and possibilities.[433]

226. A significant step in Germany was the introduction of the office of bishop as spiritual leader in the decade after World War I, when princes ceased to exercise the role of "bishops *pro tempore*" or *Summepiskopat* in Protestant territorial churches (see §190 above). "[L]egislative features were entrusted to the synod, but the administrative functions more or less to single individuals," standing vis-à-vis or *gegenüber* the synod, just as the office of ministry stands "over against" the local congregation.[434] Luther's ideas were recovered to become part of a picture of what an Evangelical bishop would be, in distinction from the usually congregational *Pfarramt* (pastoral office), a distinction only by human law. During the Nazi period (1933-1945) and *Kirchenkampf* (Church Struggle), "'spiritual leadership' became in an unexpected way concrete";[435] a dubious *Führerprinzip* (leader principle) was introduced into the church, even while some bishops opposed the Nazi take-over of the Protestant churches. After 1945 the term "bishop" came to be used in additional *Landeskirchen*. The concept of "synodical episcopate" (*synodales Bischofsamt*) developed, with emphasis on the bishop as preacher and "pastor of the church" (speaking for the church, ecumenical contacts) as well as *pastor pastorum* (e.g., in ordination and visitation).[436] The United Evangelical Lutheran Church in Germany (VELKD) developed a conference of bishops (from member churches), with a presiding bishop; the Evangelical Church in Germany (EKD) did not.

B. Specific Developments in North America

227. The ELCA reflects the backgrounds of many immigrant streams from Lutheran lands in central, northern, and eastern Europe. Their coming, settling in, and amalgamation stretch from the seventeenth century (Dutch and Swedish colonies in New Amsterdam [New York] and the Delaware Valley) until the present, when immigrants are more likely to come from Africa or Asia. The ELCA is "the child of *many* mergers, not just the one that occurred in 1987-1988."[437]

228. The pioneer pietist mission pastor Henry Melchior Muhlenberg (1711-1787) illustrates the situation in colonial America and the beginnings of the United States. His experiences are reflected by many later clergy serving Lutheran immigrants. Muhlenberg was sent by Gotthilf August Francke, of Halle, to serve three "United Congregations" (Philadelphia, New Hannover, and Providence [Trappe]), "the Lutheran people in the province of Pennsylvania."[438] He traveled there via London in order to meet with the Court Preacher to the Hannoverian king of England. Muhlenberg, in the face of self-appointed itinerants and congregations sometimes beguiled by them, demonstrated his authority in America by exhibiting his letters of call and instruction from "the Rev. Court Preacher," whom he regarded—along with the revered fathers in Halle, Germany, to whom he sent regular reports—as his ecclesiastical superiors.

229. In many ways, Muhlenberg was more a unifier of congregations, to be served by trained and properly called pastors, than a planter of new congregations. His efforts led to the formation of the first Lutheran synod in North America, the Ministerium[439] of Pennsylvania and Adjacent States, in 1748. The history of "the three dozen or so church organizations and church bodies that finally were united in the Evangelical Lutheran Church in America" often parallels aspects of Muhlenberg's ministry and the founding of the Ministerium of Pennsylvania. The sheer number of synods formed over the years[440] suggests how strong the desire of individual congregations was to work with other congregations for larger purposes beyond the local community of word and sacrament. The concern to have pastors ordained by other Lutheran pastors, often across lines of language, ethnicity, and even views on ministry, can be seen in the histories of these groups.[441]

230. Lutherans in North America inherited from Europe, and took part in, debates over the ministry in the nineteenth century, and the outcomes were sometimes reflected in the positions and practices of synods in America. At one extreme was the "transference theory" (*Übertra-*

gungslehre) that authority is transferred from the local priesthood of believers to one of its members to serve as minister.[442] This position found reflection in The Lutheran Church–Missouri Synod,[443] e.g., C. F. W. Walther (1811-1887): "The holy ministry is the authority conferred by God through the congregation, as holder of the priesthood and of all church power, to administer in public office the common rights of the spiritual priesthood in behalf of all."[444] But a statement for the Missouri Synod in 1981 moves away from the transference theory: "The office of public ministry . . . is not derived" from "the universal priesthood of believers."[445]

231. At the opposite extreme, opposing any transference theory, were views that stressed ministerial office and its authority as divine institution, apart from or at least prior to the local congregation or universal priesthood. In a time of change in society, there was a revival of emphasis on the Lutheran Confessions. F. J. Stahl (1802-1861) saw the contemporary preaching office as identical with the New Testament office of apostle. He favored episcopacy because "it alone can guarantee authority of administration and spiritual care," authority in contrast to majority or mob rule.[446] A. F. C. Vilmar (1800-1868) emphasized that only pastors can ordain, determine doctrine, and decide who is qualified for ordained ministry.[447] J. K. Wilhelm Loehe (1808-1872), pastor in Neuendettelsau, Bavaria, emphasized presbyter-bishops closely connected with the divine order of salvation.[448] His vision of the church remained rooted in the local congregation.[449] The institutions he created in Neuendettelsau had great influence in America through support of pastors for Lutheran immigrants who became part of the Missouri Synod and, more importantly, the Iowa Synod.[450] In between what have been called "low"and "high church" extremes were a variety of views on ministry, though differences on ministry were not the chief obstacle to American Lutheran unity.

232. Because the ministry is a matter on which Lutherans, while having certain confessional and theological commitments, possess degrees of flexibility to meet changing situations and needs in church, society, and culture, there have periodically been studies and action on the topic by Lutheran bodies. In the course of the 1970s, the predecessor bodies of the ELCA all adopted the term "bishop," which was carried over into the ELCA.[451]

233. The ELCA mandated in 1988-1994 "an intensive study of the nature of ministry" with "special attention" to the following: "(1) the tradition of the Lutheran Church; (2) the possibility of articulating a Lutheran understanding and adaptation of the threefold ministerial office of bishop, pastor, and deacon and its ecumenical implication; and (3) the appropriate

forms of lay ministries to be officially recognized and certified by this church, including criteria for certification, relations to synods, and discipline." The study presented recommendations in four areas, of which two are of particular relevance to this dialogue.[452]

234. First, the reaffirmation of the universal priesthood and of all baptized Christians in their various callings in the world and in the church was received with probably the greatest enthusiasm of all proposals.[453]

235. Second, the final report found that "threefold ministry" (or other "folds") "is not the way in which most of the people of this church approach the issues either of unity or mission."[454] Recommendations followed the heritage of, as an LWF study put it (see §237 below), "basically one ministry, centered in the proclamation of the Word of God and the administration of the Holy Sacraments," by pastors "within and for a local congregation" and by bishops "with and for a communion of local churches."[455]

236. Specifically, the ELCA Churchwide Assembly voted as follows:

> To reaffirm this church's understanding that ordination commits the person being ordained to present and represent in public ministry, on behalf of this church, its understanding of the Word of God, proclamation of the Gospel, confessional commitment, and teachings. Ordination requires knowledge of such teachings and commitment to them. Ordained persons are entrusted with special responsibility for the application and spread of the Gospel and this church's teachings.[456]

And with regard to bishops, they decided the following:

> (1) To retain the use of the title "bishop" for those ordained pastoral ministers who exercise the ministry of oversight in the synodical and churchwide expressions of this church; and
>
> (2) To declare that the ministry of bishops be understood as an expression of the pastoral ministry. Each bishop shall give leadership for ordained and other ministries; shall give leadership to the mission of this church; shall give leadership in strengthening the unity of the Church; and shall provide administrative oversight.[457]

C. Aspects of Ministry in the Evangelical Lutheran Church in America in Light of World Lutheranism and Ecumenism

237. American Lutheran churches, in dealing with ministry issues in the second half of the twentieth century, did not do so in isolation, but rather often cooperatively and with international Lutheran and ecumenical resources. The Lutheran Council in the U.S.A. (1966-1987), involving The Lutheran Church–Missouri Synod and the bodies that merged into the ELCA, produced studies on the Ministry and on Episcopacy.[458] Its study on women's ordination is noted in §235 above, note 455. The LWF provided studies on the ministry, episcopacy, the ordination of women, and laity.[459] LWF leadership at times was active in advocating bishops in episcopal succession. There was also Lutheran involvement in producing and responding to the Faith and Order Commission report *Baptism, Eucharist and Ministry*.[460] In such ways, the ELCA received and participated in world-wide treatments and understandings on ministry and structure, while being able to act appropriately for its own particular situation.

238. Ordaining women to the ministry of word and sacrament occurred in German, Scandinavian, and other European Lutheran churches prior to the decision to do so in the United States. The significant debate in Sweden and its decision to ordain women as priests in 1958 was a turning point for many.[461] A Lutheran Council study, carried out in 1968-1969, centered especially on scriptural questions. The Lutheran Church in America and American Lutheran Church voted at conventions in 1970 to ordain women.[462] The practice, found also in the Association of Evangelical Lutheran Churches, was readily carried into the ELCA. Since Lutherans have one office of ministry, no theological obstacle existed to female pastors' becoming bishops.[463]

239. The ELCA, in addition to sharing in the *Joint Declaration on the Doctrine of Justification* with the Roman Catholic Church, has entered into full communion[464] with Reformed, Episcopal, and Moravian churches in the United States.[465] Although Reformed polity and ordering of elders and deacons differ from Lutheran practices, the ministry did not emerge as an issue in *A Formula of Agreement*.[466] The ELCA entered into full communion with two Moravian provinces in North America in 1999; ministry was treated in the section "Mutual Complementarities."[467] Thus the ELCA has entered into full communion with churches holding varying views of ministry.

240. Anglican emphasis on episcopacy made Lutheran-Episcopal dialogue toward full communion a more complicated matter. After narrowly

failing to achieve the necessary two-thirds majority at the 1997 Churchwide Assembly of the ELCA, a proposal for full communion between the ELCA and The Episcopal Church, entitled "Called to Common Mission,"[468] was approved by the ELCA Churchwide Assembly in 1999[469] and subsequently affirmed in 2000 by The Episcopal Church. In this agreement, the two churches commit themselves "to share an episcopal succession that is both evangelical and historic" (see §12). Lutherans and Episcopalians promised "to include regularly one or more bishops of the other church to participate in the laying-on of hands at the ordinations/installations of their own bishops, as a sign, though not a guarantee, of the unity and apostolic continuity of the whole church"; *episcopé* is valued as "one of the ways, in the context of ordained ministries and of the whole people of God, in which the apostolic succession of the church is visibly expressed and personally symbolized in fidelity to the gospel through the ages" (see §12). Each church "remains free to explore its particular interpretations of the ministry of bishops in episcopal and historic succession," whenever possible in consultation with one another (see §13).

241. "Called to Common Mission" was able to refer to the 1993 full communion agreement between British and Irish Anglican Churches, on the one hand, and Nordic and Baltic Lutheran Churches, on the other, the *Porvoo Common Statement*.[470] The Meissen Agreement between the Church of England and the Evangelical Church in Germany[471] represents the stage of "interim eucharistic hospitality," not full communion. The Waterloo Declaration[472] between the Evangelical Lutheran Church in Canada and the Anglican Church of Canada, adopted in 2001, provides for full communion. "Called to Common Mission" and these other Lutheran-Anglican agreements represent variations on a common vision of apostolicity and episcopacy in the church.

242. The ELCA and other Lutheran churches, in varied relations of communion with other churches, have reflected their Lutheran commitments, demonstrated ecumenical openness, and honored the heritages of their partners in dialogue. These agreements, with their differences, all reflect a firm belief in the church as *koinonia* of salvation.

NOTES

1. Lutherans and Catholics in Dialogue, nine volumes: (1) *The Status of the Nicene Creed as Dogma of the Church* (1965) (L/RC-1); (2) *One Baptism for the Remission of Sins* (1966) (L/RC-2); (3) *The Eucharist as Sacrifice* (1967) (L/RC-3); (4) *Eucharist and Ministry* (1970) (L/RC-4); (5) *Papal Primacy and the Universal Church* (1974) (L/RC-5); (6) *Teaching Authority and Infallibility in the Church* (1980) (L/RC-6); (7) *Justification by Faith* (1985) (L/RC-7); (8) *The One Mediator, the Saints, and Mary* (1992) (L/RC-8); (9) *Scripture and Tradition* (1995) (L/RC-9). Volumes 1-4 were originally published by the Bishops' Committee for Ecumenical and Interreligious Affairs, Washington, D.C., and the U.S.A. National Committee of the Lutheran World Federation, New York, New York. Volumes 5-9 were published by Augsburg Fortress, Minneapolis. Volumes 1-3 have been reprinted together in one volume by Augsburg Fortress (n. d.), as has volume 4 (1979).
2. Its Catholic members included the Rev. Avery Dulles, SJ, Bronx, New York; the Most Rev. Raphael M. Fliss, Bishop of Superior, Wisconsin; the Rev. Patrick Granfield, OSB, Washington, D.C.; Brother Jeffrey Gros, FSC, Washington, D.C.; the Rev. John F. Hotchkin, Washington, D.C.; Dr. Margaret O'Gara, Toronto; the Most Rev. J. Francis Stafford, Archbishop of Denver (chair); the Rev. Georges Tavard, Milwaukee, Wisconsin; and Dr. Susan K. Wood, SCL, Collegeville, Minnesota. Its Lutheran members included the Rev. H. George Anderson, Decorah, Iowa (elected presiding bishop of the ELCA in 1995); the Rev. Sherman G. Hicks, Chicago; Dr. David Lotz, New York, New York; Dr. Daniel F. Martensen, Chicago; the Rev. Joan A. Mau, Washington Island, Wisconsin; Dr. John H. P. Reumann, Philadelphia; Dr. Michael J. Root, Strasbourg, France; Dr. William G. Rusch, Chicago (until 1995); and Bishop Harold C. Skillrud, Atlanta (chair). A consultation involving U.S. and European Lutherans and Catholics, held February 18-21, 1993, at Lake Worth, Florida, had assessed the dialogues to date and examined future possibilities.
3. The Objectives were described thus: "The ultimate goal is to establish full communion between our churches. This round of dialogue should focus on church-dividing issues and communion-hindering differences. There may result mutual instruction of our churches, learning from each other, and convergences that contribute to deeper *koinonia* between Lutherans and Catholics." "Structures" and "Ministries as Servants and Bonds of *Koinonia*" were to include the local, regional, national, and international, with "the themes of authority and freedom (collegiality, conciliarity)" running "through the entire document."
4. *Joint Declaration on the Doctrine of Justification: The Lutheran World Federation and the Roman Catholic Church* (Grand Rapids, MI: Eerdmans, 2000). *Gemeinsame Erklärung zur Rechtfertigungslehre* (Frankfurt am Main: Verlag Otto Lembeck/Paderborn,

Bonifatius-Verlag, 1999; Lutherischer Weltbund, Päpstlicher Rat zur Förderung der Einheit des Christen).

5. Others, listed in the *Joint Declaration*, 27-28, include *The Condemnations of the Reformation Era: Do They Still Divide?* ed. K. Lehmann and W. Pannenberg (Minneapolis: Fortress, 1990), from the work by the Joint Ecumenical Commission of the Roman Catholic Church and churches of the Reformation (Lutheran, Reformed, United), published as *Lehrverurteilungen—kirchentrennend?* I. *Rechtfertigung, Sakramente und Amt im Zeitalter der Reformation und heute*, Dialog der Kirchen 4 (Freiburg im Breisgau: Herder/Göttingen: Vandenhoeck & Ruprecht, 1986); II. *Materialien zu den Lehrverurteilungen und zur Theologie der Rechtfertigung*, Dialog der Kirchen 5 (1988); III. *Materialien zur Lehre von den Sakramenten und vom kirchlichen Amt*, Dialog der Kirchen 6 (1990). (LV) The study in Germany dealt especially with the condemnations (anathemas) attached by the Council of Trent to its decree on Justification (1547) and statements of condemnation in the Lutheran Confessions.

6. The reading continues: "This gospel frees us in God's sight from slavery to sin and self (Rom. 6:6). We are willing to be judged by it in all our thoughts and actions, our philosophies and projects, our theologies and our religious practices. Since there is no aspect of the Christian community or of its life in the world that is not challenged by this gospel, there is none that cannot be renewed or reformed in its light or by its power.

   "We have encountered this gospel in our churches' sacraments and liturgies, in their preaching and teaching, in their doctrines and exhortations. Yet we also recognize that in both our churches the gospel has not always been proclaimed, that it has been blunted by reinterpretation, that it has been transformed by various means into self-satisfying systems of commands and prohibitions.

   "We are grateful at this time to be able to confess together what our Catholic and Lutheran ancestors tried to affirm as they responded in different ways to the biblical message of justification. A fundamental consensus on the gospel is necessary to give credence to our previously agreed statements on baptism, on the Eucharist, and on forms of church authority. We believe that we have reached such a consensus." L/RC-7, §§161-164. 73-74.

7. See LV, n. 5, esp. Vol. III, and *The Condemnations of the Reformation Era*, where 147-159 deal with the ministry.

8. In the international dialogue, attention was given to *Church and Justification: Understanding the Church in the Light of the Doctrine of Justification* Lutheran-Roman Catholic Joint Commission (LWF/RC-9) in *Growth in Agreement II* (GA II), ed. J. Gros, H. Meyer, and W. G. Rusch, Faith and Order Paper No. 187 (Geneva: WCC/Grand Rapids, MI: Eerdmans, 2000), 485-565. Apostolicity is the theme of the new round of international dialogue, begun in 1994.

9. Nineteen of them in the New Testament, three in the Septuagint Old Testament; see further §§126-129.

10. This calling depends on God's faithfulness and involves election (1 Cor. 1:2, "called [to be] saints"; 1 Thess. 1:4; Rom. 8:33). Paul regularly assumes a response in faith to the message of the gospel (as in 1 Thess. 1:5), followed by baptism (1 Cor. 6:11, "washed, sanctified, justified"), with a resulting *koinonia* (1 Cor. 1:9, with Christ). No passage in Paul, however, connects koinon-terms with baptism. But note 1 John 1:6-9, *koinonia* with God, the blood of Jesus cleanses us from sin; "if we confess our sins, God who is faithful and just will forgive us our sins and cleanse us from all unrighteousness"; cf. R. Brown, *The Epistles of John, Anchor Bible* 30 (Garden City, NY: Doubleday, 1982), 242-245.
11. Both aspects are stressed by J. Hainz, *Koinonia: "Kirche" als Gemeinschaft bei Paulus* (Biblische Untersuchungen 16; Regensburg: Pustet, 1982). A. Weiser, "Basis und Führung in kirchlicher Communio," *Bibel und Kirche* 45 (1990), 66-71, speaks of "spiritual" dimensions (with God) and "societal."
12. Cf. O. Cullmann, *Katholiken und Protestanten. Ein Vorschlag zur Verwirklichung christlicher Solidarität* (Basel, Reinhardt, 1958); trans. J. Burgess, *Message to Catholics and Protestants* (Grand Rapids, MI: Eerdmans, 1958). Cullmann, later a Protestant observer at the Second Vatican Council, suggested, as early as 1957, "a yearly offering by both sides for one another; by Protestants for needy Catholics, and by Catholics for needy Protestants" (9-10) as a step toward Christian solidarity. The collection and *koinonia* in the New Testament are mentioned, 33-39. It could today take the form of parish and diocesan gathering of gifts.
13. Thus, e.g., "diocese" (Latin *dioecesis*) reflects terminology from Roman provincial administration, likewise "synod" and "council." Cf. A. Brent, *The Imperial Cult and the Development of Church Order: Concepts and Images of Authority in Paganism and Early Christianity before the Age of Cyprian*, Supplements to Vigiliae Christianae 45 (Leiden: Brill, 1999), who claims (77), "The Order of the Christian community, constituted by an apostolate whose *koinonia* continued the teaching and healing ministry of Jesus along with the breaking of bread (Acts 2,42), was the true means of producing the *pax dei*, in contrast to Augustus's *pax deorum*," (cf. Lk. 2:14; 19:38), thus "a refashioned Christian version of the Augustan *saeculum aureum*."
14. A *Patristic Greek Lexicon*, ed. G. W. H. Lampe (Oxford: Clarendon, 1964), "*koinōnia*" B.3.b., "*community* of essence," of Father and Son, citing Athenagoras (2nd cent.), Dionysius Alexandrinus (3rd cent.), Basil and Gregory of Nyssa (fourth century), of the Trinity, and Chrysostom (fourth-fifth century).
15. Christoph Schwöbel, "Koinonia," *Religion in Geschichte und Gegenwart*—vierte Auflage, 4 (2001), 1477-1479; Rolf Schäfer, "Communio," *Religion in Geschichte und Gegenwart*—vierte Auflage, 2 (1999), 435-438.
16. Nicolai Afanasev, *L'Eglise du Saint-Esprit* (Paris: Le Cerf, 1975). John D. Zizioulas, *Being as Communion. Studies in Personhood and the Church* (Crestwood, NY: St. Vladimir Seminary Press, 1985) interpreted *koinonia* in light of the anti-Arian trinitarianism of St. Athanasius. It is an ontological reality founded on the identity of

Jesus Christ with the eternal Word of God. Because, by virtue of the Incarnation, substance is seen to possess "almost by definition a relational character," the faithful who are united with Christ by faith and the Spirit are necessarily in the mutual relationships of a Communion that is at the same time spiritual and sacramental. John D. Zizioulas, *Eucharist, Bishop, Church*, trans. Elizabeth Theokritoff (Brookline, MA: Holy Cross Orthodox Press, 2001).

17. G. Florovsky, "Le corps du Christ vivant," in Florovsky et al, *La sainte Eglise universelle. Confrontation oecuménique* (Paris: Delachaux et Niestlé, 1948), 12, quoted in Zizioulas, *Being as Communion* (n. 16 above), 124. Thus a synthesis of Christology and Pneumatology is manifest in the Communion of the Church and the Churches. Since pneumatology implies eschatology and communion, which coincide in the Holy Liturgy, one may say that "*eschatology* and *communion* have determined Orthodox ecclesiology" (131).
18. See Thomas Best, Gunther Gassmann, eds., *On the Way to Fuller Koinonia* (Geneva: WCC, 1993) (Santiago) and the earlier working document and discussion paper "Towards Koinonia in Faith, Life, and Witness," 263-295. "The unity of the Church to which we are called is a *koinonia* given and expressed in a common confession of the apostolic faith; a common sacramental life entered by the one baptism and celebrated together in one eucharistic fellowship; a common life . . . ; and a common mission" (Canberra 1991, 2.1, 269), thus a gift, as well as a calling.
19. The *Final Report* of ARCIC-I (1993), in *Growth in Agreement*, Ecumenical Documents II, ed. H. Meyer and L. Vischer (New York/Ramsey: Paulist/Geneva: WCC, 1984) (GA I), 62-67; ARCIC-II, *The Church as Communion*, in GA II, 328-343; ARC-USA, "Agreed Report on the Local/Universal Church" (1999) summed the matter up thus, "'Communion' has emerged . . . as the concept that best expresses the reality of the Church as diverse yet one on faith, as both local and universal," *Origins* 30:6 (2000): 85-95; Pentecostal-Roman Catholic, "Perspective on *Koinonia*" (1989), in *Pneuma* 12 (1990): 117-142, in GA II, 735-752; Christian Church/Disciples of Christ-Roman Catholic, "The Church as a Communion in Christ" (1992), GA II, 386-398; Anglican/World Methodist Council, "Sharing in Apostolic Communion" (1996), GA II, 55-76; Catholic/World Methodist Council, "The Church as Koinonia of Salvation" (2001). Cf. S. Wood, "Ecclesial Koinonia in Ecumenical Dialogues," *One in Christ* 30 (1994): 124-145.
20. Miroslav Volf, *After Our Likeness: The Church as Image of the Trinity* (Grand Rapids, MI: Eerdmans, 1998) and "Kirche als Gemeinschaft: Ekklesiologische Überlegungen aus freikirchlicher Perspektive," *Evangelische Theologie* 49 (1989): 52-76. Veli-Matti Kärkkäinen, *An Introduction to Ecclesiology: Ecumenical, Historical and Global Perspectives*, Downers Grove, IL: InterVarsity Press (2002).
21. Ludwig Hertling, *Communio: Church and Papacy in Early Christianity*, trans. with introduction by Jared Wicks (Chicago: Loyola University Press, 1972), 4-5 and 2; German, in *Xenia Piana*: *Miscellanea historiae pontificiae* 7 (1943): 1-48; cf. "Communio und

Primat," *Una Sancta* 17 (1962). [J. Reumann, "Toward U.S. Lutheran/Roman Catholic Dialogue on Koinonia," paper for L/RC Coordinating Committee, April 1996]. For a survey of theologians on this, see Dennis M. Doyle, *Communion Ecclesiology: Vision and Versions* (Maryknoll, NY: Orbis, 2000).

22. See Jérôme Hamer, *L'église est une communion*. Paris: Cerf, 1962. English trans. Ronald Matthews, New York: Sheed and Ward, 1965. Jan Jacobs, "Beyond Polarity: On the Relation between Locality and Universality in the Catholic Church," in *Of All Times and Places: Protestants and Catholics on the Church Local and Universal*, ed. Leo J. Koffeman and Henk Witte (Zoetemeer: Meinema, 2001), 49-68, at 55-58.

23. *Church of Churches. The Ecclesiology of Communion* (Collegeville, MN: Liturgical Press, 1992), xii. This very defective translation of *Eglise d'Eglises: L'ecclésiologie de communion* (Paris: les Editions du Cerf, 1987), 9 ("au donné biblique") should not be used without checking the French text. Cf. also Walter Kasper, *Theology and Church* (New York: Crossroad, 1989, German 1987), "The Church as a Universal Sacrament of Salvation," 111-128, and "The Church as Communion: Reflections on the Guiding Ecclesiological Idea of the Second Vatican Council," 148-165 (literature in n. 5). Avery Dulles, *Models of the Church* (Garden City, NY: Doubleday, 1974), 56 treated *koinonia* as "a network of friendly interpersonal relationships" and as "a mystical communion of grace" under "The Church as Mystical Communion" (43-57), rev. ed. (1987), 60-61 and 47-62.

24. The Second Extraordinary General Assembly of the Synod of Bishops (1985), *Ecclesia sub Verbo Dei Mysteria Christi Celebrans pro Salute Mundi. Relatio Finalis*, II. C. 1. Available in English in *Origins* 15: 27 (December 19, 1985): 448. Pope John Paul II reaffirmed this in his post-synodal apostolic exhortation, *Christifideles Laici* (December 30, 1988), §19.

25. *Communionis Notio* (CN), in *Origins* 22:7 (June 25, 1992): 108-112. This text (1) equates "the Church of Christ" with "the worldwide community of the disciples of the Lord" (§7), which is more than "a communion of Churches"; (2) while there is a close connection between the eucharist and the Church, the eucharist is not sufficient by itself to ensure the being of a church; and (3) the communion is also served by institutions, like religious communities, that are not confined to one particular church; unity in diversity is one aspect of the communion. Cf. also Jörg Haustein, "Entmythologiseirung einer Zauberformel: Schreiben der Glaubenskongregation über die Kirche als Communio," *MD: Materialdienst der Konfessionskundlichen Instituts Bensheim* 43 (1992): 61-62.

26. *Directory*, §§13-15; Pontifical Council for Promoting Christian Unity, "Directory for the Application of Principles and Norms on Ecumenism" (Directory), in *Origins* (June 29, 1993): 129, 131-160.

27. *Ut Unum Sint* (UUS), 11, in *Origins* 49 (June 8, 1995): 51-72, §§11-14.

28. *Koinonia: Arbeiten des Oekumenischen Ausschusses der Vereinigten Evangelisch-Lutherischen Kirche Deutschlands zur Frage der Kirchen und Abendmahlgemeinschaft*

(Berlin: Lutherisches Verlagshaus, 1957). The essay by Werner Elert, "Abendmahl und Kirchengemeinschaft in der alten Kirche," 57-78, was expanded as a book translated by Norman Nagel as *Eucharist and Church Fellowship in the First Four Centuries* (St. Louis: Concordia, 1966).

29. Harding Meyer, "Zur Entstehung und Bedeutung des Konzepts 'Kirchengemeinschaft.' Eine historische Skizze aus evangelischer Sicht," in *Communio Sanctorum: Einheit der Christen–Einheit der Kirche, Festschrift für Bischof Paul-Werner Scheele*, ed. Josef Schreiner and Klaus Wittstadt (Würzburg: Echter Verlag, 1988) 204-230; Eugene L. Brand, *Toward a Lutheran Communion: Pulpit and Altar Fellowship*, LWF Report 26 (Geneva: LWF, 1988); *Communio/Koinonia: A New Testament-Early Christian Concept and its Contemporary Appropriation and Significance*, A Study by the Institute for Ecumenical Research, Strasbourg, 1990, repr. in A Commentary on *Ecumenism: The Vision of the ELCA*, ed. W. G. Rusch (Minneapolis: Augsburg, 1990), 119-141; *The Church as Communion: Lutheran Contributions to Ecclesiology*, ed. Heinrich Holtze, LWF Documentation 47 (Geneva: LWF, 1997), including "Toward a Lutheran Understanding of Communion," 13-29. [Reumann, April 1999, "'Koinonia' in Lutheran Use"].
30. LWF Constitution, Art. 3; text in *From Federation to Communion: The History of the Lutheran World Federation*, ed. J. H. Schjørring, P. Kumari, N. A. Hjelm; V. Mortensen, coordinator (Minneapolis: Fortress, 1997), 530; the 1947 Constitution said simply "a free association of Lutheran churches" (527).
31. LWF/RC-9.
32. Ibid. (§§51-62).
33. Joint Working Group of the World Council of Churches and the Roman Catholic Church (JWG), *The Notion of "Hierarchy of Truths" and The Church: Local and Universal*. Faith and Order Paper No. 150 (Geneva: WCC Publications, 1990), §13ff.
34. Within Roman Catholicism, the terms "particular church" and "local church" are often used interchangeably. Most often the Second Vatican Council documents use the term "particular church" to refer to the diocese, but this term can also refer to churches in the same rite, region, or culture. There is no standard practice governing the use of this terminology. In spite of the Second Vatican Council's use of the term "particular church," this term has not enjoyed widespread acceptance. Whether or not it refers to a diocese or a larger region has to be discerned from its context. The present document explores the asymmetry between Lutheran and Roman Catholic understandings of what constitutes the basic unit of ecclesiality implied by the term "local" or "particular" church.
35. A forthright expression of this pattern is found in Ignatius (Smyr. 8.1), but the bishop as head of a local community came to be the common pattern.
36. CD, 11.

37. LG, 26, states that "the faithful are gathered together through the preaching of the Gospel of Christ, and the mystery of the Lord's Supper is celebrated 'so that, by means of the flesh and blood of the Lord the whole brotherhood of the Body may be welded together.'"
38. *Sacrosanctum Concilium*, 41, states, "The principal manifestation of the church consists in the full, active participation of all God's holy people in the same liturgical celebrations, especially in the same eucharist, in one prayer, at one altar, at which the bishop presides, surrounded by the college of priests and by his ministers."
39. SC, 42.
40. LWF/RC-9, 85.
41. Nicholas Sagovsky, *Ecumenism, Christian Origins and the Practice of Communion* (Cambridge: Cambridge University Press, 2000), 128.
42. Council of Nicaea, canon 4.
43. LG, 26. The Latin text speaks of a "sacrament of order" (singular) rather than "of orders" (plural); "Episcopus, plenitudine *sacramenti ordinis* insignitus, est 'oeconomus gratiae supremi sacerdotii'" (emphasis added).
44. *Treatise on the Power and Primacy of the Pope* (TPPP), §63. *The Book of Concord* (BC), ed. Robert Kolb and Timothy J. Wengert (Minneapolis: Fortress Press, 2000), 340.
45. On Lutheran church structures around the world, see E. Theodore Bachmann and Mercia Brenne Bachmann, *Lutheran Churches in the World: A Handbook* (Minneapolis: Augsburg, 1989). The German Lutheran churches are organized regionally within the nation rather than nationally, but they still have this threefold structure. Lutheran churches of course recognize the one, holy, catholic, and apostolic Church.
46. An exception is Wolfgang Huber, *Kirche*, 2nd ed. (Munich: Chr. Kaiser, 1988).
47. LG, 28. Cf. PO, 4-6.
48. For some exceptions, see James A. Coriden, *The Parish in Catholic Tradition: History, Theology and Canon Law* (Paulist Press, 1997); U.S. Bishops' Committee on the Parish, "The Parish: A People, A Mission, A Structure," in *Origins* 10 (§41; March 26, 1982): 641, 633-646; Philip J. Murnion, "Parish: Covenant Community," *Church* 12:1 (Spring 1996): 5-10.
49. AG, 37; Provision 9.11, in the *Constitution, Bylaws, and Continuing Resolutions of the Evangelical Lutheran Church in America* (CBCR), 2001 ed. (Chicago: ELCA), 58.
50. Provision 9.11 in CBCR, 58.
51. See Provision 9.21 in CBCR, 58.
52. Provision 9.41 in CBCR, 60. The same text is found in required provision *C4.03. in the *Model Constitution for Congregations* as contained in the ELCA churchwide constitution, 221-222.
53. LG, 26.

54. LG, 26. Even though the document does not actually say that these groups are parishes, it does refer to them as local congregations. The text affirms that Christ, by whose power the one, holy, catholic, and apostolic church is gathered together, is present in these communities.
55. *Rite of Christian Initiation of Adults*, 9.
56. Provision 8.11 of CBCR, 50.
57. Provision 3.02 of CBCR, 20.
58. Werner Elert, *The Structure of Lutheranism*, translated by Walter A. Hansen (St. Louis: Concordia, 1962), 369.
59. Provision 10.21 in CBCR, 75.
60. Provisions †S6.03 and †S8.12 in the *Constitution for Synods* as printed in CBCR, 187-189 and 193-195.
61. LG, 23.
62. LG, 23.
63. The Church of Sweden and the German Landeskirchen are examples.
64. The ELCA is only a slight exception to this pattern of national organization; it includes a Caribbean Synod in Puerto Rico and the U.S. Virgin Islands.
65. Provision 13.21 in CBCR, 90.
66. Provision 8.71 in CBCR, 54.
67. This lack was noted in an important address by E. Clifford Nelson to the 1963 Assembly of the Lutheran World Federation, "The One Church and the Lutheran Churches," in *Proceedings of the Fourth Assembly of the Lutheran World Federation*, Helsinki, July 30–August 11, 1963 (Berlin: Lutherisches Verlagshaus, 1965).
68. CD, 38. "Pope Paul VI, in his 1966 *motu proprio Ecclesiae Sanctae* called for Episcopal Conferences to be established wherever they did not yet exist; those already existing were to draw up proper statutes; and in cases where it was not possible to establish a Conference, the Bishops in question were to join already existing Episcopal Conferences; Episcopal Conferences comprising several nations or even international Episcopal Conferences could be established. Several years later, in 1973, the Pastoral Directory for Bishops stated once again that 'the Episcopal Conference is established as a contemporary means of contributing in a varied and fruitful way to the practice of collegiality.' These Conferences admirably help to foster a spirit of communion with the Universal Church and among the different local Churches." Pope John Paul II, *Motu proprio On the Theological and Juridical Nature of Episcopal Conferences [Apostolos Suos]* May 21, 1998, §5; *Ecclesiae Sanctae* and the *Pastoral Directory of Bishops*, in *Origins* 28:9 (July 30, 1998): 153, §5.
69. Ibid.
70. Ibid.

71. LG, 23, stipulates that "individual bishops, in so far as they are set over particular churches exercise their pastoral office over the portion of the people of God assigned to them, not over other churches nor over the church universal. But as members of the Episcopal college and legitimate successors of the apostles, by Christ's arrangement and decree, each is bound to be solicitous for the entire church; such solicitude, even though it is not exercised by an act of jurisdiction, is very much to the advantage of the universal church."
72. LWF Constitution, Article III: Nature and Function.
73. Ibid.
74. Pope John Paul II, Address on September 12, 1987, in *Origins* 17:16 (October 1, 1987): 258. Here Pope John Paul II extends the assertion in LG, 8, that the Church of Christ subsists in the Roman Catholic Church to the relationship between the universal church and particular churches.
75. LG, 23.
76. TPPP, 60f.
77. TPPP, 72.
78. See §§187-188 regarding ordinations in continental Lutheranism by pastors with responsibilities as superintendent; regarding bishops' continuing to ordain in Nordic countries, see §§189-195.
79. See the discussions in Kurt Schmidt-Claussen, "The Development of Offices of Leadership in the German Lutheran Church: 1918-Present, "in *Episcopacy in the Lutheran Church? Studies in the Development and Definition of the Office of Church Leadership*, ed. Ivar Asheim and Victor R. Gold (Philadelphia: Fortress Press, 1970), 72-115; Wilhelm Maurer, *Das synodale evangelische Bischofsamt seit 1918, Fuldaer Hefte* 10 (Berlin: Lutherisches Verlagshaus, 1955).
80. Council of Trent, Session 23, Canons on the sacrament of Order, 6.
81. Council of Trent, Session 23, chap. 4.
82. Council of Trent, Session 23, Canons on the sacrament of Order, 7.
83. DHn 3860. Pope Pius XII, *Sacramentum Ordinis*, in *Acta Apostolicae Sedis* (AAS) 40 (1948): 5-7.
84. LG, 21.
85. LG, 28; PO, 2.
86. LG, 20.
87. Avery Dulles, "*Ius Divinum* as an Ecumenical Problem," *Theological Studies* 38 (1977): 689.
88. The Second Vatican Council defines the diocese as "a portion of the people of God whose pastoral care is entrusted to a bishop in cooperation with his priests" (CD, 11).
89. *Code of Canon Law* (CIC), canon 521 º1.
90. CIC, canon 519.

91. LG, 28.
92. LG, 28. PO, 8.
93. LG, 28.
94. CIC, canon 529 º2.
95. LWF, *The Lutheran Understanding of Ministry* (1983), reprinted in *Ministry: Women, Bishops*, LWF Studies (1993), §21.
96. Presbyterian polities stress the interrelation of the face-to-face assembly and the regional community of such assemblies. Ministry at the regional level, however, is exercised by the presbytery as a college rather than by a single ordained minister such as a bishop. The possibility of such a polity has not been a part of the discussions of this dialogue. While Lutheran churches have generally included a regional ordained minister of oversight, a presbyterian polity has not been seen as unacceptable, and the ELCA is in full communion with the Presbyterian Church (U.S.A.). Catholic theology requires the presence of a bishop.
97. LG, 26.
98. LG, 21.
99. LG, 27.
100. LG, 25.
101. LG, 19.
102. LG, 22.
103. LG, 24.
104. LG, 20.
105. See especially Luther's Preface to the 1528 Saxon Visitation Articles (*Luther's Works* 40, 271) and, more comprehensively, Werner Elert, "Der bischöfliche Charakter der Superintendentur-Verfassung." *Luthertum* 46 (1935): 353-367.
106. See orders cited in Werner Elert, "Der bischöfliche Charakter der Superintendentur-Verfassung." *Luthertum* 46 (1935): 355f.
107. Kurt Schmidt-Clausen, "The Development of Offices of Leadership in the German Lutheran Church: 1918-Present," *in Episcopacy in the Lutheran Church? Studies in the Development and Definition of the Office of Church Leadership*, edited by Ivar Asheim and Victor R. Gold (Philadelphia: Fortress Press, 1970), 72-115.
108. Provision †S8.11 of CBCR, 193.
109. Provision †S8.12 of CBCR, 193.
110. Provision †S8.12.h of CBCR, 194.
111. "Called to Common Mission: A Lutheran Proposal for a Revision of the Concordat of Agreement" (CCM) (Chicago: ELCA, November 1998), 12.
112. *Porvoo Common Statement*, in *Together in Mission and Ministry: The Porvoo Common Statement* (Porvoo) (London: Church House Publishing, 1993), §58a vi.

113. LG, 18; cf. 22-23.

114. *Papal Primacy and the Universal Church.* Lutherans and Catholics in Dialogue V (L/RC-5), ed. P. C. Empie and T. A. Murphy (Minneapolis: Augsburg, 1974), II, 34, 30. As early as 1972, the "Malta Report" stated, "But in the various dialogues, the possibility begins to emerge that the Petrine office of the Bishop of Rome also need not be excluded by Lutherans as a visible sign of the unity of the church as a whole 'insofar as [this office] is subordinated to the primacy of the gospel by theological reinterpretation and practical restructuring'" (66).

115. UUS, 94.

116. Ibid., 95.

117. Ibid.

118. Ibid., 96.

119. L/RC-5, §30.

120. WA, 54, 231; Luther's Works 41, 294; cf. Harding Meyer, "Suprema auctoritas ideo ab omni errore immunis: The Lutheran Approach to Primacy" in *Petrine Ministry and the Unity of the Church*, ed. James Puglisi (Collegeville: The Liturgical Press, 1999), 16-18.

121. On the shape of such reforms, see *Papal Primacy and the Universal Church*, §§23-25.

122. BC, 326.

123. This ambiguity with regard to the precise nature of the *ius divinum/ius humanum* distinction was pointed out in the international Roman Catholic–Lutheran dialogue on "The Gospel and the Church" ("Malta Report," 1972) (LWF/RC-1), §31: "Greater awareness of the historicity of the church in conjunction with a new understanding of its ecclesiological nature, requires that in our day the concepts of the *ius divinum* and *ius humanum* be thought through anew. . . . *Ius divinum* can never be adequately distinguished from *ius humanum*. We have *ius divinum* always only as mediated through particular historical forms." The problem was addressed by George Lindbeck in his article, "Papacy and *Ius Divinum*: A Lutheran View" in L/RC-5.

124. The issue of "apostolic succession" was taken up by L/RC-4, 138-188, in articles by McCue, Burghardt, and Quanbeck. Note the Common Statement, §44. It expands the notion of apostolic succession beyond that of a succession in episcopal office to include transmission of the apostolic gospel and grants that Lutherans have preserved a "form of doctrinal apostolicity," leading to the tentative conclusion of the Catholic participants that they "see no persuasive reason to deny the possibility of the Roman Catholic Church recognizing the validity of this Ministry" (54). See more recently the Lutheran-Roman Catholic Joint Study Commission, *The Ministry in the Church* (1981), (LWF/RC-5), 62: "The apostolic succession in the episcopal office does not consist primarily in an unbroken chain of those ordaining to those ordained, but in a succession in the presiding ministry of a church, which stands in the continuity of apostolic faith and which is overseen by a bishop in order to keep

it in communion with the Catholic and Apostolic church" (quoted also in *The Niagara Report. Report of the Anglican-Lutheran Consultation on Episcope*, 1987, 53). See also *Baptism, Eucharist and Ministry*. Report of the Faith and Order Paper No. 111 (BEM) (Geneva: WCC, 1982), 35: "The primary manifestation of apostolic succession is to be found in the apostolic tradition of the church as a whole." Cf. CCM, 12.

It should be noted that the dogmatic constitution of the Second Vatican Council on the church stated that "among those various ministries which, as tradition witnesses, were exercised in the Church from the earliest times, the chief place belongs to the office of those who, appointed to the episcopate in a sequence running back to the beginning (*per successionem ab initio decurrentem*), are the ones who pass on the apostolic seed." (LG, 20 [trans. W. M. Abbott (ed.), 39]). Other translations of the cited Latin phrase wrongly use the word "unbroken." Thus A. P. Flannery (ed.), *Documents of Vatican II* (Grand Rapids, MI: Eerdmans, 1975), 371: "in virtue consequently of the unbroken succession, going back to the beginning." Similarly, S. Garofalo (ed.), *Sacro Concilio Ecumenico Vaticano II: Constituzioni, Decreti, Dichiarazioni* (Milan: Editrice Ancora, 1966), 189: "per successione che decorre ininterrotta dall'origine." See also *Ecclesia de Eucharistia*, in *Origins* 32:46 (May 1, 2003): 753-768, 28, 29.

125. AC VII.1; LG, 20.

126. ARCIC, *The Church as Communion*, §31.

127. Anglican-Lutheran International Continuation Committee, *The Niagara Report*, §§28-30; in GA II, 17f.

128. CCM, 12.

129. Apol XIV.1.

130. BC, 90-103; Robert Kolb and James A. Nestingen, *Sources and Contexts of the Book of Concord* (Minneapolis: Fortress Press, 2001), 137-139.

131. Georg Kretschmar, "Die Wiederentdeckung des Konzeptes der 'Apostolischen Sukzession' im Umkreis der Reformation," in *Das bischöfliche Amt: Kirchengeschichtliche und ökumenische Studien zur Frage des kirchlichen Amtes*, edited by Dorothea Wendebourg (Göttingen: Vandenhoeck and Ruprecht, 1999), 300-344.

132. For an example of a vehement rejection by the Reformers of the argument that episcopal succession is essential to a valid ministry, see Philip Melanchthon, "The Church and the Authority of the Word," in *Melanchthon: Selected Writings*, translated by Charles Leander Hill (Minneapolis: Augsburg, 1962), 130-186. Latin original in *Melanchthons Werke im Auswahl*, vol. 1, 323-386.

133. See also BEM, M38.; Warren A. Quanbeck, "A Contemporary View of Apostolic Succession," in L/RC-4, 187; The Lutheran responses to BEM on ministry and succession are analyzed in Michael Seils, *Lutheran Convergence? An Analysis of the Lutheran Responses to the Convergence Document "Baptism, Eucharist and Ministry" of*

the World Council of Churches Faith and Order Commission, LWF Report 25 (Geneva: Lutheran World Federation, 1988), 126-131. A more positive reading of Lutheran responses is in Michael Root, "Do Not Grow Weary in Well-Doing: Lutheran Responses to the BEM Ministry Document" *dialog* 27 (1988): 23-30.

134. CCM, 12.

135. Cf. *Niagara Report*, §§54-55.

136. This analysis presumes that bishops and pastors working within congregational, parochial, and diocesan structures are paradigmatic for ecclesiology.

137. Roman Catholic–Lutheran Joint Commission, 1994 (LWF\RC-8), §93.

138. SC, 42.

139. CD, 15.

140. LG, 28.

141. AC, 7.

142. WA 30II: 421 quoted in Althaus 1966, 288, n. 10.

143. The major exception here might be The Lutheran Church–Missouri Synod. For a significant Missouri discussion of these issues, see Pieper 1950-1957, vol. 3, 419-435.

144. "Concerning the Ministry," *Luther's Works* 40.41.

145. See Quenstedt, cited in Heinrich Schmid, *Doctrinal Theology of the Evangelical Lutheran Church* (1899; rpt. Minneapolis: Augsburg, 1961), 591.

146. See Conrad Bergendoff, *The Doctrine of the Church in American Lutheranism*, The Knubel-Miller Lecture, 1956 (Philadelphia: Board of Publication of the United Lutheran Church in America, 1956).

147. LWF/RC-6, 49 (emphasis in original text).

148. See SC, 10.

149. See SC, 41. Karl Rahner makes this point in "Theology of the Parish," in *The Parish: From Theology to Practice*, ed. Hugo Rahner (Westminster, MD: The Newman Press, 1958), 23-35. He identifies the parish as "the representative actuality of the Church; the Church appears and manifests itself in the event of the central life of the parish" (25). Rahner argues that the church is necessarily a local and localized community. It achieves its highest degree of actuality where it acts, that is, where it teaches, prays, offers the Sacrifice of Christ, etc. For Rahner the parish is not a division of a larger segment of the church, but "the concentration of the Church into its own event-fullness" (30). The parish is "the highest degree of actuality of the total church" (30). See also Jerry T. Farmer, *Ministry in Community: Rahner's Vision of Ministry*, Louvain Theological and Pastoral Monographs, §13 (Leuven: Peeters Press; and Grand Rapids, MI: Eerdmans, 1993), 134-136.

150. In the reference just cited, Rahner also makes the point that the parish and the pastor are *iure divino* in the same way that the Church, papacy, and episcopate are, even though a canonist would not easily concede this point. Ibid., 25.

151. JWG, §13.

152. ARCIC, 1991, §39.

153. Peter Brunner, "The Realization of Church Fellowship," in *The Unity of the Church: A Symposium*, papers presented to the Commission on Theology and Liturgy of the Lutheran World Federation (Rock Island, IL: Augustana Press, 1957): 22.

154. Ibid., 18f.

155. CN, 7.

156. L/RC-4, proposed, "As Lutherans, we joyfully witness that in theological dialogue with our Roman Catholic partners we have again seen clearly a fidelity to the proclamation of the gospel and the administration of the sacraments which confirms our historic conviction that the Roman Catholic church is an authentic church of our Lord Jesus Christ. For this reason we recommend to those who have appointed us that through appropriate channels the participating Lutheran churches be urged to declare formally their judgment that the ordained Ministers of the Roman Catholic church are engaged in valid ministry of the gospel, announcing the gospel of Christ and administering the sacraments of faith as their chief responsibilities, and that the body and blood of our Lord Jesus Christ are truly present in their celebrations of the sacrament of the altar" (§35); and "As Roman Catholic theologians, we acknowledge in the spirit of the Second Vatican Council that the Lutheran communities with which we have been in dialogue are truly Christian churches, possessing the elements of holiness and truth that mark them as organs of grace and salvation. Furthermore, in our study we have found serious defects in the arguments customarily used against the validity of the eucharistic Ministry of the Lutheran churches. In fact, we see no persuasive reason to deny the possibility of the Roman Catholic church recognizing the validity of this Ministry. Accordingly we ask the authorities of the Roman Catholic church whether the ecumenical urgency flowing from Christ's will for unity may not dictate that the Roman Catholic church recognize the validity of the Lutheran Ministry, and, correspondingly, the presence of the body and blood of Christ in the eucharistic celebrations of the Lutheran churches" (§54). The International Lutheran-Roman Catholic Commission text, *Facing Unity*, which built on earlier agreements, outlines a proposal for Lutheran-Catholic unity by stages including mutual teaching of the apostolic faith, mutual engagement in apostolic mission, and recognition and reconciliation of apostolic ministries by mutual installation/ordination of bishops. Unlike "Called to Common Mission," it does not propose immediate, full mutual recognition of ministry, but rather a phased recognition and reconciliation.

157. UR, 3. Lutherans long had a complex view of the ecclesial status of the Roman church, stressing both its character as church and its perceived failings that were asserted to undercut its faithfulness in a fundamental way. On Rome as church despite its failings, see *Luther's Works* 26.24; for an apparently contrary assertion, see *Luther's Works* 41.144.

158. UR, 4.

159. CN, §17.

160. Cf. LWF/RC-9, 153-156.

161. UR, 7.

162. UUS, 15.2.

163. "Called to Common Mission" describes the ELCA's relationship of full communion with the Episcopal Church.

164. UR, 3.

165. UR, 3.

166. "Briefwechsel von Landesbischof Johannes Hanselmann und Joseph Kardinal Ratzinger über das Communio-Schreiben der Römischen Glaubenskongregation," *Una Sancta* 48 (1993): 348.

167. LWF/RC-8, §§75-77. *Defectus* is translated as "lack" in the English edition of UR on the Vatican website (§22c), in UUS, §67, and in the official English translation of the *Catechism of the Catholic Church*, §1400. See also *Ecclesia de Eucharistia*, in *Origins* 32:46 (May 1, 2003): 753-768. 30.

168. Walter Kasper, "Die apostolische Sukzession als ökumenisches Problem," LV, III, 345.

169. *Growth in Agreement II*, 443-484.

170. See Arthur Carl Piepkorn, "A Lutheran View of the Validity of Lutheran Orders." In L/RC-4, 215; Wolfgang Stein, *Das kirchliche Amt bei Luther* (Wiesbaden: Franz Steiner Verlag, 1972), 192f.

171. For example: "It is a definite conclusion that no one confers holy orders and makes priests less than those under the papal dominion. A semblance, indeed, of ordination and of making priests is magnificently present but it behooves the king of semblance to grant nothing but semblance so as to guarantee his abominations" (*Luther's Works* 40.15; WA 12, 176). See further Helmut Lieberg, *Amt und Ordination bei Luther und Melanchthon* (Göttingen: Vandenhoeck & Ruprecht, 1962), 168-171.

172. JDDJ, 40.

173. LG, 25.

174. BC, Apol, 14, 222-223.

175. Church of Sweden Church Ordinance of 1571, in John Wordsworth, *The National Church of Sweden* (London: Mowbray, 1911), 232; on this Ordinance and its importance for later Swedish theology, see Sven-Erik Brodd, "The Swedish Church Ordinance of 1571 and the Office of Bishop in an Ecumenical Context," in *The Office of Bishop: Swedish Lutheran-Roman Catholic Dialogue* LWF Studies (Geneva: LWF, 1993), 147-157.

176. CCM, esp. §§15-21; Porvoo, esp. §§34-57 of the Common Statement; *Called to Full Communion: The Waterloo Declaration* (http://generalsynod.anglican.ca/ministries/departments/doc.php?id=71 &dept=primate) (May 1, 2004), esp. §§A 3, 5.

177. Although there is no general Catholic ruling on Lutheran orders, consistent Catholic practice has been to re-ordain Lutheran ministers entering the Catholic priesthood.

178. John Reumann, "The Ordination of Women: Exegesis, Experience, and Ecumenical Concern," in *Ministries Examined* (Minneapolis: Augsburg Fortress, 1987).

179. *Ordinatio Sacerdotalis*, 4 (cf. Origins 24 [June 9, 1994]: 51). Cf. Congregation for the Doctrine of the Faith, *From "Inter Insigniores" to "Ordinatio Sacerdotalis,"* (Washington: United States Catholic Conference, 1996).

180. UUS, §79.1.4.

181. UUS, §96.

182. UUS, 94.

183. Recent discussion on the reform of the papacy in the light of UUS includes Carl Braaten and Robert Jenson, eds., *Church Unity and the Papal Office: An Ecumenical Dialogue on John Paul II's Encyclical UUS* (Grand Rapids, MI: Eerdmans, 2001); Michael J. Buckley, *Papal Primacy and the Episcopate: Towards a Relational Understanding* Ut unum sint: *Studies on Papal Primacy* (New York: Crossroad, 1998); William Henn, *The Honor of my Brothers: A Short History of the Relation between the Pope and the Bishops* Ut unum sint: *Studies on Papal Primacy* (New York: Crossroad, 2000); Hermann J. Pottmeyer, *Towards a Papacy in Communion: Perspectives from Vatican Councils I & II* Ut Unum Sint: *Studies on Papal Primacy* (New York: Crossroad, 1998); John R. Quinn, *The Reform of the Papacy: The Costly Call to Christian Unity* (New York: Crossroad, 1999); James Puglisi, *Petrine Ministry*.

184. UR, 4.

185. Porvoo, §45.

186. "Therefore we ask the Lutheran Churches: (1) if they are prepared to affirm with us that papal primacy renewed in the light of the gospel, need not be a barrier to reconciliation; (2) if they are able to acknowledge not only the legitimacy of the papal Ministry in the service of the Roman Catholic communion but even the possibility and the desirability of the papal Ministry, renewed under the gospel and committed to Christian freedom, in a larger communion which would include the Lutheran churches; (3) if they are willing to open discussion regarding the concrete implications of such a primacy to them," from "Toward the Renewal of Papal Structures" Part C, "Lutheran Perspectives," §32, 22-23.

187. Cf. L/RC-5, its use of the "Petrine principle" and questions to Lutheran churches, including "that papal primacy, renewed in light of the gospel, need not be a barrier to reconciliation" (§32), and including to the Roman Catholic Church, "if it is prepared to envisage the possibility of a reconciliation that would recognize the self-government of Lutheran churches within a communion" (§33); LWF/RC-6,

§§67-73, in *Growth in Agreement*, 269-271; Harding Meyer, "Suprema Auctoritas" in *Petrine Ministry and the Unity of the Church*, 15-34, esp. 29.

188. UUS, 11. Cf. UR, 3.

189. JDDJ, 15.

190. UR, 3.

191. LWF/RC-8, §§92-93; §§120-122.

192. *A Greek-English Lexicon of the New Testament and other Early Christian Literature*, 3rd ed. (hereafter BDAG), rev. and ed. F. W. Danker (Chicago: University of Chicago Press, 2000), 552-553, offers four basic definitions (in boldface type, meanings, functional use; English equivalents in italics):

[1] "close association involving mutual interests and sharing, *association, communion, fellowship, close relationship*," as in marriage or friendship or the bond of life that unites Pythagoreans; Phil. 1:5 a close relation with the gospel, or with the poor (Rom. 15:26);

[2] "attitude of good will that manifests an interest in a close relationship, *generosity, fellow-feeling, altruism*," 2 Cor. 9:13, generosity in sharing;

[3] abstract term for the concrete "*sign of fellowship, proof of brotherly unity;* even *gift, contribution*"; Rom.15:26 might fit here, so might 1 Cor 10:16ab, "a means for attaining a close relationship with the blood and body of Christ";

[4] *participation, sharing* in something, Christ's sufferings (Phil. 3:10), the body and blood of Christ (1 Cor. 10:16), the Holy Spirit (2 Cor. 13:13), faith (Phlm. 6).

Cf. further F. Hauck, "*koinos, . . . koinonia, etc.*," (German 1938), *Theological Dictionary of the New Testament* 3 (Grand Rapids, MI: Eerdmans, 1965), 789-809, supplement in *Theologisches Wörterbuch zum Neuen Testament* 10:2 (Stuttgart: Kohlhammer, 1979), 1145-1146; J. Hainz, "*koinonia* etc.," (German 1981), *Exegetical Dictionary of the New Testament* 2 (Grand Rapids, MI: Eerdmans, 1991), 303-305.

193. In the Old Testament, the noun, verb, and adjective occur twenty-five times. There are seven more New Testament examples if compounds (*synkoinōnos, synkoinōnein*) are counted, for a New Testament total of forty-five instances. There are a maximum 119 occurrences in the entire Greek Bible if *koinos*, "common" or "impure," is included. Examples that do occur are mainly in later (deuterocanonical) books under Hellenistic influence; *koinōnia* occurs only at Wisdom of Solomon 6:23 and 8:18, for associating with wisdom and her words. Charts on *koinon*-terms in J. Reumann, "*Koinonia* in Scripture: Survey of Biblical Texts," in *On the Way to Fuller Koinonia*, ed. T. F. Best and G. Gassmann, Faith and Order Paper No. 166 (Geneva: WCC, 1994), 39, where all New Testament passages are treated, and bibliography provided, some of which cannot be included here.

194. BDAG, 551-552.

195. BDAG, 552. The verb *metechō*, "have a share in, partake of something," is sometimes associated with *koinōnein*, as at 1 Cor. 10:17 (cf. 16) and 10:21, 30; and Heb. 2:14. Cf. N. Baumert, *KOINONEIN und METECHEIN—synonym? Eine umfassende semantische Untersuchung*, SBB, 51 (Stuttgart: Katholisches Bibelwerk, 2003) distinguishes them and gives a variety of meanings to *koinonein*, not a single sense that some like Hainz (n. 11 above) sought.

196. J. Y. Campbell, "*KOINŌNIA* and Its Cognates in the New Testament," *Journal of Biblical Literature* 51 (1932): 352-382; H. Seesemann, *Der Begriff KOINŌNIA im Neuen Testament, Beihefte zur Zeitschrift für die neutestamentliche Wissenschaft* 14 (Giessen: Töpelmann, 1933); Hauck (n. above). A. R. George, *Communion with God in the New Testament* (London: Epworth, 1953), took communion as "have a share, give a share," and sharing, partly in reaction to those who made "the Fellowship" a name for the church, as was argued by C. A. Anderson Scott, *Christianity According to St. Paul* (Cambridge: Cambridge Univ. Press, 1927, reprinted 1961), 158-169.

197. K. Kertelge, "Abendmahlsgemeinschaft und Kirchengemeinschaft im Neuen Testament und in der Alten Kirche," in *Interkommunion–Konziliarität. Zwei Studien im Auftrag des Deutschen ökumenischen Studienausschusses, Beiheft zur Ökumenischen Rundschau* 25 (1974), 2-51, reprinted in *Einheit der Kirche: Grundlegung im Neuen Testament*, ed. F. Hahn, K. Kertelge, and R. Schnackenburg, *Quaestiones Disputatae* 84 (Freiburg: Herder, 1979), 94-132, and "Kerygma und Koinonia: Zur theologischen Bestimmung der Kirche des Urchristentums," in *Kontinuität und Einheit*, Festschrift for F. Mussner, ed. P. G. Müller and W. Stenger (Freiburg: Herder, 1981), 317-339. R. Schnackenburg, "Die Einheit der Kirche unter dem Koinonia-Gedanken," in *Einheit der Kirche* (1979), 52-93. J. Hainz, *Koinonia* (1982) (n. 11 above).

198. See J. M. McDermott, "The Biblical Doctrine of KOINŌNIA," *Biblische Zeitschrift* N. F. 19 (1975), 64-77 and 219-233. J. Hainz, *Koinonia* (see n. 11 above), was critical of earlier studies for failing to find an underlying unity or for reading in traditional dogmatic theology (178, 185, 188); history of research and results, 162-204.

199. F. Hahn, "Einheit der Kirche und Kirchengemeinschaft in neutestamentlicher Sicht," in *Einheit der Kirche* (n. 197 above), 9-51. Hahn (13-14) suggested that the Greek *koinōnia* is like the Latin *participatio* and partly like *communio*, while the German *Gemeinschaft* is like Latin *societas*.

200. J. G. Davies, *Members One of Another: Aspects of Koinonia* (London: Mowbray, 1958), originally presented to the WCC's Division of Interchurch Aid and Service to Refugees; G. Panikulam, *Koinōnia in the New Testament: A Dynamic Expression of Christian Life, Analecta Biblica* 85 (Rome: Biblical Institute Press, 1979); J. Hainz, *Ekklesia: Strukturen paulinischer Gemeinde-Theologie und Gemeinde-Ordnung, Biblische Untersuchungen* 9 (Regensburg: Pustet, 1972); Hainz's *Koinonia* (n. 11 above) includes sections on Roman Catholic, Reformation, and Orthodox views on the concept (206-272). Reumann's tradition-history approach (n. 193 above) was

presented at the Fifth World Conference on Faith and Order in 1993. Further, S. Brown, "Koinonia as a Basis of New Testament Ecclesiology?" *One in Christ* 12 (1976), 157-167; J. D. G. Dunn, "'Instruments of Koinonia' in the Early Church," *One in Christ* 25 (1989), 204-216; K. Kertelge, "Koinonia und Einheit der Kirche nach dem Neuen Testament," in *Communio Sanctorum: Einheit der Christen–Einheit der Kirche, Festschrift für Bischof Paul-Werner Scheele*, ed. Josef Schreiner and Klaus Wittstadt (Würzburg: Echter Verlag, 1988), 53-67.

201. J. Reumann, "Church Office in Paul, Especially in Philippians," *Origins and Method: Toward a New Understanding of Judaism and Christianity: Essays in Honour of John C. Hurd* (*Journal for the Study of the New Testament*: Supplement Series 86; ed. B. H. McLean; Sheffield: Sheffield Academic Press, 1993), 82-91, esp. 83. See J. P. Meier, "Are There Historical Links between the Historical Jesus and the Christian Ministry?" *Theology Digest* 47/4 (2000): 303-315; E. Schweizer, *Church Order in the New Testament* (SBT 32; London: SCM, 1961), 20-33 (2 a-m).

202. Today it is widely recognized among New Testament interpreters that the added assertions in Matthew 16:16b-19 may be a retrojected account of an episode in the gospel tradition rooted in a post-resurrection appearance of the risen Christ, such as that preserved in John 21:15-17. In other words, Matthew 16:16b-19 may be a Matthean version of the "feed my lambs/sheep" conversation of John 21. See, e.g., R. E. Brown et al. (eds.), *Peter in the New Testament: A Collaborative Assessment by Protestant and Roman Catholic Scholars* (Minneapolis: Augsburg; New York: Paulist, 1973), 83-101. Cf. J. Roloff's estimate: "Vielmehr tritt Petrus an dieser Stelle lediglich als Garant der Jesusüberlieferung in Erscheinung, die die Grundlage von Verkündigung und Leben der Gemeinde darstellt" *Exegetische Verantwortung in der Kirche: Aufsätze* (ed. M. Karrer; Göttingen: Vandenhoeck & Ruprecht, 1990), 339. Cf. P. Perkins, *Peter: Apostle for the Whole Church* (Minneapolis: Fortress, 2000), 86. Such an interpretation of the Caesarea Philippi scene would not deny that Jesus founded a "church," but it would reveal rather an awareness that his early followers had of themselves as the "flock" or "church," which developed during the course of the decades between AD 30 and 90, when the Matthean and Johannine Gospels were eventually composed. In other words, Matthew would have interpreted with hindsight the meaning of Peter's acknowledgment and the implications of Jesus' reaction to it in thus formulating the church-building statement, which appears on Jesus' lips.

203. In Luke 22:31-32, Jesus prays for the repentant Simon that he might "strengthen" his "brethren." This supportive Petrine function, however, is set out in a context making no mention of *ekklesia*.

204. This title seems to be derived by the evangelists from the Hellenistic world, because *talmîd* is almost wholly absent from the Old Testament (save in 1 Chr. 25:8, used of pupils in the Temple choir!). *Mathētēs* occurs in the Septuagint of Jer. 13:21; 20:11; 46:9, but always with a variant reading that makes the deriving of the New Testament usage from it problematic. See further J. A. Fitzmyer, "The Designations

of Christians in Acts and Their Significance," in Commission Biblique Pontificale, *Unité et diversité dans l'Eglise* (Vatican City: Libreria Editrice Vaticana, 1989), 223-236, esp. 227-229.

205. See further E. Lohse, *Die Ordination im Spätjudentum und im Neuen Testament* (Göttingen: Vandenhoeck & Ruprecht, 1951), 19-21. Cf. J. Newman, *Semikhah (Ordination): A Study of Its Origin, History and Function in Rabbinic Literature* (Manchester: Manchester University, 1950), 1-3. From Old Testament passages, rabbinic tradition developed its practice of ordination, a practice attested only several centuries later in the Tannaitic Midrashim (Sifre Num. 27:18 §140; Sifre Deut. 34:9 §357); cf. Str-B, 2. 647-648.

206. J. Roloff has summed up the matter: "Jesus, to be sure, neither founded the Church nor installed office-holders, but even so by his *calling of followers*, by *establishing a community of disciples*, and by his *summons to service* he supplied the momentum, without which the post-Easter development of the Church would not be explicable" ("Amt / Ämter / Amtsverständnis IV," *Theologische Realenzyklopädie* 2 [1978], 510). Similarly, H. von Lips, "Amt, IV. Neues Testament," *Religion in Geschichte und Gegenwart*—vierte Auflage 1 (1998), 424-426.

207. See further J. A. Fitzmyer, "The Designations of Christians in Acts" (n. 204 above), 227, 229-232.

208. The first occurrence (Acts 5:11) is a comment of the author himself about the effect of Ananias's deception as he uses a term current in his own day to report how "fear fell upon the whole church," i.e., the whole Jerusalem church.

209. J. Fitzmyer, "The Acts of the Apostles," *Anchor Bible* 31 (New York: Doubleday, 1998), 343. Although the Seven are chosen *diakonein trapezais*, "to serve tables," they are not called *diakonoi* by Luke. The later ecclesiastical tradition often considered them to be the first "deacons." See 1 Clement 42:4. Luke hardly intended his readers "to see the origin of the diaconate in this episode."

210. Bishops in the Catholic tradition are regarded as successors of the apostles (Second Vatican Council, LG, §20); cf. F. A. Sullivan, *From Apostles to Bishops: The Development of the Episcopacy in the Early Church* (New York: Newman, 2001). Does that mean successors of the "Twelve Apostles" (Mt. 10:2; Rev. 21:14)? In the New Testament, others beyond the Twelve bear the title *apostolos*: Matthias, Acts 1:26; Barnabas and Paul, Acts 14:4, 14; unnamed "apostles," 2 Corinthians 8:23; and possibly Andronicus and Junia, Romans 16:7. See further J. Hainz, *Kirche im Werden: Studien zum Thema Amt und Gemeinde im Neuen Testament* (ed. J. Hainz; Munich/Paderborn: Schöningh, 1976), 109-122.

211. Although the phrase *hē kat' oikon ekklēsia* does not occur in Acts, the idea may be found in Acts 2:46; 5:42; 12:12 and may be derived from the conversion of individuals and their "households" (Lydia, Acts 16:15; the jailer, 16:34; Crispus, 18:8; possibly also "the house of Jason," 17:5). On the house church, see R. Banks, *Paul's Idea of Community: The Early House Churches in Their Historical Setting* (Grand

Rapids, MI: Eerdmans, 1980); F. V. Filson, "The Significance of the Early House Churches," *Journal of Biblical Literature* 58 (1939) 105-112; H. J. Klauck, *Hausgemeinde und Hauskirche im frühen Christentum* (*Stuttgarter Bibelstudien* 103; Stuttgart: Katholisches Bibelwerk, 1981); A. J. Malherbe, "House Churches and Their Problems," *Social Aspects of Early Christianity* (Baton Rouge, LA: Louisiana State University, 1977), 60-91; W. Rordorf, "Was wissen wir über die christlichen Gottesdiensträume der vorkonstantinischen Zeit?" *Zeitschrift für die neutestamentliche Wissenschaft und die Kunde der älteren Kirche* 32 (1986): 476-480.

212. In such gatherings the *paterfamilias* or *prostatis*, "patroness" (Rom. 16:2), presumably provided the leadership in the house church, which eventually came to be called *episkopē* (1 Tim. 3:1).

213. See further P. Benoit, "L'Unité de la communion ecclésiale dans l'Esprit selon la quatrième Evangile," *Unité et diversité dans l'Eglise* (see n. 204 above), 265-283; R. E. Brown, *The Community of the Beloved Disciple* (New York: Paulist, 1979); F.-M. Braun, "Le cercle johannique et l'origine du quatrième évangile," *Revue d'histoire et de philosophie religieuses* 56 (1976): 203-214; R. Fernández Ramos, "La comunidad joánica," *Ciencia Tomista* 106 (1979): 541-586; H.-J. Klauck, "Gemeinde ohne Amt? Erfahrungen mit der Kirche in den johanneischen Schriften," *Biblische Zeitschrift* 29 (1985): 193-220.

214. See further J. Hainz, *Koinonia: "Kirche" als Gemeinschaft*, 62-89 (n. 11 above); idem, "*Koinōnia,*" *Exegetical Dictionary of the New Testament* 2: 303-305, esp. 304. Cf. J. Reumann, "Koinonia in Scripture" (n. 193 above), 48-49.

215. See further N. Brox, "*Sōtēria* und Salus: Heilsvorstellungen in der Alten Kirche," EvT 33 (1973), 253-279; K. H. Schelkle, "*Sōter*" and "*Sōtēria,*" *Exegetical Dictionary of the New Testament*, 3, 325-329.

216. In 1 Corinthians 3:5-15, Paul hints at the role that all ministers in the church are to play for its upbuilding; they are there as "God's fellow workers," as he comments on his own and Apollos' role.

217. As translated by the RSV, similarly in NABRNT; the NRSV has "those who labor among you, and have charge of you in the Lord and admonish you." So too J. Roloff, "Amt," Theologische Realenzyklopädie 2 (1978), 521: "Vorsteher"; F. Neugebauer, *In Christus: En Christō: Eine Untersuchung zum paulinischen Glaubensverständnis* (Göttingen: Vandenhoeck and Ruprecht, 1961) 139-140; C. Masson, *Les deux épîtres de saint Paul aux Thessaloniciens* (*Commentaire du Nouveau Testamant* 11a; Neuchâtel/Paris: Delachaux et Niestlé, 1957), 71-72.

In Romans 12:8, the same participle appears, *ho proistamenos en spoudē*, which the RSV there renders, "he who gives aid, with zeal," but the NRSV has, "the leader, in diligence"; and the NAB, "if one is over others, with diligence." Compare 1 Tim. 5:17, where the perfect participle of the same verb is used, *proestōtes presbyteroi*, "elders who rule" (RSV, NRSV), "presbyters who preside" (NAB). Cf. 1 Tim 3:4, 5, 12; Josephus, *Jewish Antiquities* 8.12.3 §300 ("govern"); 12.2.13 §108 ("chief officers").

Some commentators, however, would rather translate the three verbs thus: "who labor, give care, and admonish." Thus J. Reumann, "Church Office" (n. 201 above), 89; A. J. Malherbe, *First Thessalonians* (*Anchor Bible* 32B; New York: Doubleday, 2000), 310-314; R. F. Collins, "The First Letter to the Thessalonians," NJBC, art. 46, §37; E. J. Richard, *First and Second Thessalonians* (*Sacra Pagina* 11; Collegeville, MN: Liturgical Press, 1995), 267-268.

218. See J. Hainz, *Ekklēsia: Strukturen paulinischer Gemeinde-Theologie und Gemeinde-Ordnung* (Regensburg: Pustet, 1972), 37-42; also idem, "Die Anfänge des Bischofes- und Diakonenamtes," and "Amt und Amtsvermittlung bei Paulus," in *Kirche im Werden* (n. 210 above) 91-108, 109-122.

219. The NRSV has "bishops and deacons," but with a marginal note, "overseers and helpers." The same twosome occurs later in *1 Clement* 42,4-5 (supposedly based on the LXX of Isa. 60:17); *Didache* 15:1.

220. See G. F. Hawthorne, *Philippians* (*Word Biblical Commentary*, 43; Waco, TX: Word, 1983), 9-10; A. Lemaire, *Les ministères aux origines de l'église: Naissance de la triple hiérarchie: évêques, presbytres, diacres* (LD 68; Paris: Cerf, 1971) 27-31, 96-103, 186; "The Ministries in the New Testament," *Biblical Theology Bulletin* 3 (1973), 133-166, esp. 144-148.

221. The origin of the office of "overseer" is debated. See H. Lietzmann, "Zur urchristlichen Verfassungsgeschichte," ZWT 55 (1914) 97-153, repr. in *Das kirchliche Amt im Neuen Testament* (Wege der Forschung 189; ed. K. Kertelge; Darmstadt: Wissenschaftliche Buchgesellschaft, 1977) 93-143; J. M. Balcer, "The Athenian Episkopos and the Achaemenid 'King's Eye,'" *American Journal of Philology* 98 (1977) 252-263; H. W. Beyer, "*Episkopos*," *Theological Dictionary of the New Testament*, 2. 618-620; L. Porter, "The Word *episkopos* in Pre-Christian Usage," *ATR* 21 (1939) 103-112; A. Adam, "Die Entstehung des Bischofsamtes," *Wort und Dienst* 5 (1957) 104-113; W. Nauck, "Probleme des frühchristlichen Amtsverständnisses (I Ptr 5,2f.)," *Zeitschrift für die neutestamentliche Wissenschaft und die Kunde der älteren Kirche* 48 (1957) 200-220, esp. 202-207; H. Braun, *Qumran und das Neue Testament* (2 vols.; Tübingen: Mohr [Siebeck], 1966), 2. 329-332; W. Eiss, "Das Amt des Gemeindeleiters bei den Essenern und der Christliche Episkopat," *Die Welt des Orients* 2 (1959) 514-519; J. A. Fitzmyer, "Jewish Christianity in Acts in Light of the Qumran Scrolls," *Studies in Luke-Acts: Essays Presented in Honor of Paul Schubert* (ed. L. E. Keck and J. L. Martyn; Nashville: Abingdon, 1966) 233-257, esp. 245-248; J. Hainz, "Die Anfänge des Bischofs- und Diakonenamtes," *Kirche im Werden* (n. 210 above), 91-107; R. E. Brown, "*Episkopē* and *Episkopos*: The New Testament Evidence," TS 41 (1980): 322-338. On house churches and episcopacy, see E. Dassmann, "Zur Entstehung des Monepiskopats," *Jahrbuch für Antike und Christentum* 17 (1974), 74-90; "Haus-gemeinde und Bischofsamt," in *Vivarium: Festschrift Theodor Klausner* (*Jahrbuch für Antike und Christentum* Ergänzungsband 11; Münster in W.: Aschendorff, 1984), 82-97; *Ämter und Dienst in den*

frühchristlichen Gemeinden (Hereditas 8; Bonn: Borengässer, 1994); G. Schöllgen, "Hausgemeinden, *Oikos*-Ekklesiologie, und monarchischer Episkopat," *Jahrbuch für Antike und Christentum* 31 (1988), 72-90; "Bischof, I. Neues Testament," *Religion in Geschichte und Gegenwart*—vierte Auflage, 1. 1614-1615; J. Reumann, "Church Office" (n. 201 above), 87-89; "One Lord, One Faith, One God, but Many House Churches," *Common Life in the Early Church: Essays Honoring Graydon F. Snyder* (ed. J. V. Hills et al.; Harrisburg, PA: Trinity Press International, 1998), 106-117. Cf. B. L. Merkle, *The Elder and Overseer: One Office in the Early Church*, Studies in Biblical Literature 57 (New York: Peter Lang, 2003).

222. See J. N. Collins, *Diakonia: Re-interpreting the Ancient Sources* (New York: Oxford University Press, 1990) 235-237; cf. BDAG, 230: "agent, intermediary, courier." J. Roloff suggest that it was "aus der Funktion beim Gemeindemahl entwickelt" ("Amt," *Theologische Realenzyklopädie* 2 [1978], 522).

223. L/RC-4, 10, n. 6.

224. J. Fitzmyer, "Acts" (n. 209 above), 534-535. Roloff considers this as unhistorical ("ganz sicher ungeschichtlich"), "Amt," *Theologische Realenzyklopädie* 2 (1978), 521.

225. J. Fitsmyer, "Acts" (n. 209 above), 673.

226. See F. A. Sullivan, *From Apostles to Bishops*, 65 ("such authority was seen as coming directly from the Holy Spirit or the risen Christ").

227. "The anachronistic comparisons of these figures with 'apostolic delegates' or 'metropolitans' or 'monarchical heads' or 'coadjutors' are seductively charming, but the text of the Pastoral Epistles employs the father-child model for expressing the way in which the apostolic task was shared and transmitted" (J. D. Quinn, *The Letter to Titus* (*Anchor Bible* 35; New York: Doubleday, 1990), 71.

228. Our translation. This might refer to the commissioning or ordaining of an *episkopos* or *presbyteroi*, but its meaning is debated. Some commentators have even understood it as a penitential rite because of the following clause about participation in the sins of another. See N. Adler, "Die Handauflegung im NT bereits ein Bussritus? Zur Auslegung von 1 Tim. 5,22," *Neutestamentliche Aufsätze: Festschrift für Prof. Josef Schmid* (ed. J. Blinzler; Regensburg: Pustet, 1963), 1-6; J. P. Meier, "*Presbyteros* in the Pastoral Epistles," *Catholic Biblical Quarterly* 35 (1973): 323-345, esp. 325-337.

229. The Pastoral Epistles are widely regarded as Deutero-Pauline, perhaps by a disciple or disciples in the Pauline School. Cf. Raymond E. Brown, *An Introduction to the New Testament* (New York: Doubleday, 1997), 662-668: "about 80 to 90 percent of modern scholars would agree that the Pastorals were written after Paul's lifetime," having "some continuity with Paul's own ministry and thought, but not so close as manifested in Col. and Eph. and even 2 Thess." (668). On various hypotheses, see J. D. Quinn, "Timothy and Titus, Epistles to," *Anchor Bible Dictionary* 6 (New York: Doubleday, 1992), 568-569.

230. In 2 Timothy 4:5, the author charges: "Do the work of an evangelist (*ergon euangelistou*), fulfill your ministry (*diakonian*)."

231. Or "ordained," since it is not easy to say precisely what is implied by this "laying on of hands." Acts 8:18 associates it with the gift of the Spirit. Note also *lectio varia* in some MSS of 1 Timothy 4:14: *presbyterou*. Cf. Hebrews 6:2.

232. Often translated later "bishop."

233. This term often is rendered "elders." That translation is acceptable for members of local councils in various towns in pre-Christian Judaism: e.g., among Jews in Jerusalem (Acts 4:5; 6:12), or in the Old Testament (Josh. 20:4; Ruth 4:2). As a designation for those with a special function among Christians, "presbyters" is preferred (as in Acts 11:30; 15:2, 4, 6, 22; 21:18).

234. Later called "deacons."

235. The abstract noun *episkopē* means "the act of watching over" or "visitation," as in Luke 19:44 and 1 Peter 2:12; in Acts 1:20 it denotes a "position" or "assignment"; but in 1 Timothy 3:1 it is used in the sense of "engagement in oversight, supervision," of leaders in Christian communities, i.e., the office of overseer (BDAG, 379).

236. The term is used in a generic sense in 1 Peter 2:25 of Christ, who is called *episkopos tōn psychōn hymōn*, "guardian of your souls."

237. Corresponding substantives *presbytēs* and *presbytis* occur in Titus 2:2-3.

238. See R. E. Brown, *Priest and Bishop: Biblical Reflections* (New York: Paulist, 1970), 34-40.

239. It is debatable whether one should understand "tables" in a dining sense or in a banking sense (i.e., "to look after financial tables"). See W. Brandt, *Dienst und Dienen im Neuen Testament* (*Neutestamentliche Forschungen* 2/5; Gütersloh: Bertelsmann, 1931; repr. Münster: Antiquariat Th. Stenderhoff, 1983); E. Schweizer, *Church Order* (n. 201 above), 49 (3 o), 70 (5 i).

240. See Ambrosiaster, *Ad Tim. prima* 3.11 (*Corpus scriptorum ecclesiasticorum latinorum*, 31/3. 268); J. N. D. Kelly, *Commentary on the Pastoral Epistles* (*Harper's New Testament Commentaries*; New York: Harper & Row, 1963) 83-84; R. M. Lewis, "The 'Women' of 1 Timothy 3:11," *Bibliotheca Sacra* 136 (1979), 167-175.

241. See B. B. Thurston, *The Widows: A Women's Ministry in the Early Church* (Minneapolis: Fortress, 1989), 36-55.

242. Even though one might argue from Titus 1:5-9 that *episkopos* and *presbyteroi* stand for one administrative office in the Cretan church, one cannot predicate that one office so easily of the Ephesian church, because the qualifications of the *episkopos* are treated in 1 Timothy 3, quite distinctly and independently of what is said about *presbyteroi* in 1 Timothy 5, so that the church in Ephesus might have been structured with these administrators separately considered. This might affect one's consideration of regional churches and the way they received each other in hospitality or eucharistic sharing more so than in structural uniformity. See J. Reumann, "Koinonia in Scripture" (n. 193 above), 63 (§52); R. Schnackenburg, "Ephesus:

Entwicklung einer Gemeinde von Paulus zu Johannes," *Biblische Zeitschrift* 35 (1991), 41-64; W. Thiessen, *Christen in Ephesus: Die historische und theologische Situation in vorpaulinischer und paulinischer Zeit und zur Zeit der Apostelgeschichte und der Pastoralbriefe* (Texte und Arbeiten zum neutestamentlichen Zeitalter 12; Tübingen/Basel: Francke, 1995).

243. See G. W. Knight, "Two Offices (Elders/Bishops and Deacons) and Two Orders of Elders (Preaching/Teaching and Ruling Elders): A New Testament Study," *Presbyterion* 12 (1986): 105-114; F. M. Young, "On *episkopos* and *presbyteros*," *Journal of Theological Studies* 45 (1994), 142-148 (on the origin of the presbyterate as distinct from that of the episcopate and the diaconate); R. A. Campbell, *The Elders: Seniority Within Earliest Christianity* (Edinburgh: Clark, 1994); J. D. Quinn, "Ministry in the New Testament," *Eucharist and Ministry* (see n. 183 above), 69-100, esp. 97.

244. For *presbyteroi* as derived from the "elders" of the Jewish synagogue, see J. T. Burtchaell, *From Synagogue to Church: Public Services and Offices in Earliest Christian Communities* (New York: Cambridge University Press, 1992); and "Amt, III. Antikes Judentum," *Religion in Geschichte und Gegenwart*—vierte Auflage 1 (1998), 424. For backgrounds in the Greco-Roman world, see in contrast R. A. Campbell, *The Elders* (n. above), 67-96, 246, 258-259.

245. Note that Paul is informed about this decision in Acts 21:25, on his return to Jerusalem at the end of his third missionary journey. Nothing is said about it in Galatians 2. See further J. A. Fitzmyer, *The Acts of the Apostles* (*Anchor Bible* 31; New York: Doubleday, 1998), 538-567, 691-694; on porneia as "illicit marital union," rather than the traditional "unchastity" or "prostitution," 557-558; i.e., *BDAG porneia* 2, rather than 1.

246. In Romans 15:26, *koinōnia* is the word for "contribution," which in this case comes from Achaia and Macedonia.

247. In the New Testament, Apostolic Fathers, and apologists we encounter apostles, prophets and teachers, then bishops and deacons, presbyters (*Didache* 11,3-12; 13,1-7; 15,1-2; *1 Clement* 42,4; 44,1-6; Polycarp, *Ep. Phil.* praef.; 5,1-6,3), teachers and leaders (Justin speaks of the "president," *1 Apol.* 61, 65 and 67; he himself was a teacher [*Mart. Iust.* recension C, 3,3]), and various others in service to their communities.

248. For the three titles in conjunction with each other, see Ignatius, *Magn.* 2; 6; 13,1; *Trall.* 2,3; *Philad.* praef. and 7,1; *Polyc.* 6,1. For the presbytery as a group, see *Eph.* 2,2; 4,1; 20,2; *Magn.* 6,1; 7,1; 13,1; *Trall.* 2,2; *Philad.* 7,1. The bishop is to be respected as the grace of God, in the place of God, as Jesus Christ or the Father or the commandment, or followed as Jesus Christ follows the Father. The presbytery is to be respected as the law of Jesus Christ, God's council or the apostles. The deacon is to be respected as the one who serves Jesus Christ or his mysteries, or as Jesus Christ himself, or as God's commandment.

249. In the bishop Ignatius says he meets the bishop's church (*Ephes.* 1,3 and *Magn.* 6,1; in *Magn.* 2 he meets their church in all three ranks). He asks for messengers to be

sent to his own people to give them encouragement, and for his church to be remembered in prayer.

250. See the section "*Communio* through Letters" in Hertling, *Communio* (n. 21 above), 28-36; Werner Elert, *Eucharist and Church Fellowship in the First Four Centuries*, trans. N. E. Nagel (St. Louis: Concordia, 1966), 125-160; and also the papyrus letters of recommendation studied by Hans Reinhard Seeliger, "Das Netzwerk der *communio*: Überlegungen zur historischen Soziologie des antiken Christentums und ihrer Bedeutung für die Ekklesiologie," in *Communio—Ideal oder Zerrbild von Kommunikation?*, edited by Bernd Jochen Hilberath (Freiburg: Herder, 1999), 19-38.

251. *1 Clement*, e.g., 51,1-4 (Rome even sends official emissaries: 65,1).

252. Justin, 1 *Apol.* 65,5 and 67,5. The absent are not only the sick: Otto Nussbaum, *Die Aufbewahrung der Eucharistie* (Bonn: Hanstein, 1979) 177.

253. The practice of sending *eulogia*, portions of consecrated bread from one bishop—especially a metropolitan—to bishops of nearby or dependent churches was condemned by a Synod of Laodicea in the late fourth century (Synod of Laodicea, canon 14 [Mansi 2.566E]), which implies that the practice existed earlier. See Robert F. Taft, "One Bread, One Body: Ritual Symbols of Ecclesial Communion in the Patristic Period," in *Nova Doctrina Vetusque: Essays on Early Christianity in Honor of Fredric W. Schlatter*, ed. Douglas Kries and Catherine Brown Tkacz (New York: Peter Lang, 1999), 30-31.

254. In Rome in the fifth century, the bishop sent a particle of his eucharist to presbyters conducting services at *tituli* within the walls (but not beyond), according to a letter of Innocent I to Decentius of Gubbio, March 19, 416; see Taft, art.cit. 32-34.

255. Tertullian, *Apol.* 39,4; on readmission to communion in the end, Cyprian, *ep.* 18,1; 55,13 (but repentance is required, 55,23).

256. Hertling, *Communio* (n. 21 above), 36-42, e.g., "In some circumstances, a layman or the people could break off communion with their own bishop. . . . In these ruptures of fellowship, the essential issue is sharing in eucharistic communion (37). . . . From our point of view, it is striking that nowhere in antiquity do we find a precise statement as to who had the right to excommunicate someone. Instead, it appears that everyone had this right—which, however, corresponds exactly with the early Christian conception of *communio*" (41).

257. Council of Nicaea I (325), canon 4, says that all the bishops of a province should take part, but in any case at least three.

258. The growth of agreement concerning authoritative texts, what is called the "formation of the canon" of scripture, involved the inclusion of some texts and the exclusion of others. The condemnation of Marcion in the 140s solidified the Christian commitment to their Jewish biblical heritage, and through exchange and copying the churches came to possess and use quite similar collections of their own basic texts.

259. Easter is a good example. See the controversy described in Eusebius, *H.E.* 5,23-25, and the resolution of the date at the Council of Nicaea (325), mentioned in its synodal letter, §3, Socrates, *H.E.* 1,9.

260. Warnings about heretics, e.g., Eusebius, *H.E.* 4,7,6; 5,13,1-4; 5,18,1; 5,19,1-4; 6,43,3; 7,30; Socrates, *H.E.* 1,6 and Theodoret, *H.E.* 1,4 (regarding Arius).

261. On the importance of the principal churches in maintaining and documenting *koinonia* via letters and lists of the orthodox, see Hertling, *Communio*, (n. 21 above), 30-35.

262. New Testament texts cited by the Fathers in this connection include especially Acts 20:17-28; Phil. 1:1; Titus 1:5-10; 1 Tim. 3:1-7 and 4:14. Ignatius of Antioch addresses Polycarp of Smyrna as "bishop" (*ep. ad Polyc.* praef.), but Polycarp's own letter to the Philippians never mentions the term, suggesting that titles were fluid in the mid-second century.

263. Numerous examples include *1 Clement*, Polycarp *To the Philippians*, the Letter of the martyrs at Lyons and Vienne (Eusebius, *H.E.* 5,1-3). When the term "dioecesis" was taken into Christian use later, it bore no resemblance to the imperial (civil) diocese.

264. See the *Dictionnaire de droit canonique*, ed. R. Naz, s.v. "Chorévèque" (Jacques Leclef). In the East, the institution survived into the eightth century, although canon 57 of the Synod of Laodicea (Mansi 2.574B) in the fourth century calls for the replacement of such village or country bishops by pastors who travel amongst these small communities (*periodeutas*). The Synods of Ancyra, Neocaesarea, and Nicaea's "regulations consistently emphasize the full dependence of the *chorepiscopus* on the real head of the community, who alone defined the sphere of his functions," says Karl Baus in *The Imperial Church from Constantine to the Middle Ages*, volume two of *History of the Church*, edited by Hubert Jedin and John Dolan (New York: Seabury Press, 1980), 233.

265. Alexandre Faivre, *Ordonner la fraternité: Pouvoir d'innover et retour à l'ordre dans l'Église ancienne* (Paris: Cerf, 1992), 33 and 80-82.

266. Peter Lampe, *Die stadtrömischen Christen in den ersten beiden Jahrhunderten*, 2nd ed. (Tübingen: J. C. B. Mohr [Paul Siebeck], 1989), 334-342, suggests as early as the late second century; Allen Brent, *Hippolytus and the Roman Church in the Third Century* (Leiden: Brill, 1995), 417-432, would put the date of a monarchical bishop in Rome later.

267. Eusebius, *H.E.* 6,43,11.

268. One of the best treatments of the development of Rome's preeminence, up till the sixth century, is Robert B. Eno, *The Rise of the Papacy* (Wilmington: Michael Glazier, 1990). Eno participated in many earlier rounds of the U.S. Lutheran-Catholic Dialogue. See also James F. McCue and Arthur Carl Piepkorn, "The Roman Primacy in the Patristic Era," in L/RC-4, 43-97.

269. Irenaeus, *haer.* 3,1,1 (cf. Eusebius, *H.E.* 5,8,2-4) and 3,3,2. Willy Rordorf, "Was heisst: Petrus und Paulus haben die Kirche in Rom 'gegründet'? Zu Irenäus, Adv. haer. III,1,1; 3,2.3," in *Unterwegs zur Einheit*, FS Heinrich Stirnimann, ed. Johannes Brantschen and Pietro Salvatico (Freiburg/Schweiz: Universitätsverlag, 1980), says that they "founded" it by their oral preaching, constituted it by the installation of bishops.

270. See the examples of Victor and Irenaeus in the Easter controversy (Eusebius, *H.E.* 5,23-25); Stephen, Firmilian, Dionysius of Alexandria and Cyprian in the dispute about rebaptizing heretics (Cyprian, *ep.* 69-75 and Eusebius, *H.E.* 7,9,1-5).

271. Irenaeus, *haer.* 3,3,3. In the huge literature on this passage, which has been rather tendentiously summarized by Domenic Unger in "St. Irenaeus and the Roman Primacy," *Theological Studies* 13 (1952): 359-418, and "St. Irenaeus on the Roman Primacy," *Laurentianum* 16 (1975): 431-445, one can discern the desire of scholars to maximize or to minimize the basis of the Roman church's importance. Walter Ullmann, "The Significance of the *Epistola Clementis* in the Pseudo-Clementines," *Journal of Theological Studies* n.s. 11 (1960): 310-311, contends that Linus and Cletus may have been Roman bishops, but the first proper successor or "heir" of Peter, succeeding to his powers, was Clement, and that the language in Irenaeus supports this. Enrico Cattaneo, "*Ab his qui sunt undique*: una nuova proposta su Ireneo, *Adv. haer.* 3,3,2b," *Augustinianum* 40 (2000): 399-405, thinks that Irenaeus is referring to the succession of presbyters, and emends *undique* to *presbyteri*.

272. Edict of Galerius, 311, Eusebius, *H.E.* 8,17,3-10; Licinius and Constantine's declaration of toleration ("Edict" of Milan), 313, Eusebius, *H.E.*10,5,2-14. In 380, Christianity was given almost exclusive legal status in the Roman Empire (*Codex Theodosianus* XVI 1,2; see *Creeds, Councils and Controversies*, edited by J. Stevenson [New York: Seabury, 1966], 160-161). We are less well informed about the legal circumstances in other parts of the Christian world.

273. Faivre, *Ordonner la Fraternité*, 77-84, 93-96. Faivre calls the process "sacerdotalization."

274. In the West, these first appear early in the eighth century in Germany, especially Bavaria and Frankish lands, but have virtually disappeared by the eleventh and twelfth centuries. From the first they are assistants to the bishop, and teach, oversee, confirm, consecrate altars and churches, ordain clergy (even major orders), take part in synods. *Dictionnaire de Droit Canonique*, (DDC) s.v. "Chorévèque," 691-693. Archpriests were an earlier phenomenon (Merovingian times): as the number of country converts grew, they needed more service than a deacon could give, and the priest in charge of them came to live with them. He did not have authority over several churches, nor could he ordain (A. Amanieu, "Archiprêtre," DDC 1, 1007-1009). See also n. 264 above.

275. The late ninth century saw the replacement of earlier archpriests and chorbishops by rural deans and archdeacons, who supervised all types of parishes. Ewig, in Friedrich Kempf, Hans-Georg Beck, Eugen Ewig and Josef Andreas Jungmann, *The*

Church in the Age of Feudalism, "History of the Church 3," ed. Hubert Jedin and John Dolan (New York: Herder and Herder, 1969), 165-166.

276. Bernard M. Kelly, *The Functions Reserved to Pastors*, The Catholic University of America Canon Law Studies 250 (Washington: Catholic University of America Press, 1947), 4; he adds (8), "This parochial unity of the city (*civitas*) was one of the most characteristic marks of the ancient diocese. The cathedral was the only parish church in the city. Around the ninth century, however, other parishes appeared in the city, administered by collegiate chapters."

277. See the article by R. Schieffer, "Eigenkirche," *Lexikon des Mittelalters* III (München: Artemis-Verlag, 1986): 1705-1708.

278. Pierre Riché, in *Évêques, moines et Empereurs* (610-1054), ed. Gilbert Dagron et al. (Paris: Desclée, 1993), 768-769, writing about the late ninth and early tenth century, says that some bishops sold off churches to lay patrons, and rural churches were fortunate if they belonged to monasteries. On 697, he gives as a rough estimate that during the ninth century, the proportion of monks who were priests and deacons rose from 20 percent to 60 percent.

279. See Riché (n. 278 above), 695: "Every year the bishop gathered the urban and rural clergy at his palace. At that time, the diocesan statutes would be formulated." He is speaking of the ninth century.

280. One focus in the Carolingian reform of the clergy under Louis the Pious (814-840) was to bring urban priests together in a canonical life and to draw rural priests closer together. Kempf, in Kempf et al., 307-311; cf. 330-332.

281. Ewig points out, in Baus *et al.*, 532, that while church synods were separate in the sixth century, later "the boundaries begin to become blurred" with royal councils. Y. M.-J. Congar, *L'Ecclésiologie du haut Moyen Age* (Paris: Cerf, 1968), 133, n. 11 speaks of a great number of councils in the sixth through eighth centuries, declining in the ninth and especially the tenth.

282. For example, the first reference to Nicaea I (325) as "ecumenical" came in 338, borrowing a term used by the worldwide associations of professional athletes and Dionysiac artists, according to Henry Chadwick, "The Origin of the Title, 'Oecumenical Council,'" *Journal of Theological Studies*, n.s. 23 (1972): 132-135. Constantinople I (381) was called "ecumenical" soon after the fact, in 382. The ecumenical status of Ephesus II (449) never was achieved, despite the fact that it seems to have complied with the proposed conditions for that designation as well as the acknowledged ecumenical councils; see Wilhelm De Vries, "Das Konzil von Ephesus 449, eine 'Räubersynode'?" *Orientalia Christiana Periodica* 41 (1975): 357-398.

283. The conciliar attempts to hold the churches of the East together in the face of disagreements over the theology of the Incarnation, from Ephesus I (431) through Constantinople III (680-681), ended in church division. For the painful story, see W. H. C. Frend, *The Rise of the Monophysite Movement: Chapters in the History of the*

Church in the Fifth and Sixth Centuries (Cambridge: Cambridge University Press, 1972), or *Les Églises d'Orient et Occident*, ed. Luce Pietri (Paris: Desclée, 1998), 387-481: "Justinien et la vaine recherche de l'unité."

284. Wilhelm de Vries, "Die Patriarchate des Ostens: Bestimmende Faktoren bei ihrer Entstehung," in *I Patriarcati orientali nel primo millennio*, "Orientalia Christiana Analecta 181" (Roma: Pontificium Institutum Studiorum Orientalium, 1968): 20-21, says, "The bishops were fundamentally equal, but their cities were not." The leader of the Christian churches of each province was the bishop of its metropolis; he oversaw the election and ordination of bishops, presided at synods and served as a court of appeal from the local bishops.

285. These groupings were reflected in an important liturgical affirmation of communion, where in the eucharistic prayer itself, the presider prayed explicitly for the bishop of the place and for the patriarch or patriarchs through whom the congregation was in communion with the rest of the church. This practice is well attested from at least the sixth century in both the East (the "diptychs") and the West (the prayer "Memento" in the Roman rite); see Joseph A. Jungmann, *The Mass of the Roman Rite*, trans. Francis A. Brunner (New York: Benziger Brothers, 1955), II, 154-156.

286. Constantinople's importance was recognized at the Council of Constantinople (381); Jerusalem was first under the metropolitan of Caesarea in Palestine and overseen by the church of Antioch, but its unique place in Christian history and piety was recognized when it was named a fifth patriarchate at the Council of Chalcedon (451). Bernard Flusin, in *Les Églises d'Orient et d'Occident*, ed. Luce Pietri (Paris: Desclée, 1998) 510-511, says that "if the system of five patriarchs ever existed, it was not yet fully developed"; at the time of Chalcedon, "patriarch" was not yet a technical term.

287. Vittorio Parlato, *L'ufficio patriarcale nelle chiese orientali dal IV al X secolo: Contributo allo studio della 'communio'*, (Padova: Edizioni Cedam, 1969), 26-27, assigns several causes: "heresies, schisms, political factors, persecutions, occupation of Christian territories by the Muslims, and not least the revival of nationalism in the Greek-speaking parts of the empire." By 543, Antioch had a Monophysite hierarchy, and its Melkite (imperial or Chalcedonian) bishop preferred to live in Constantinople from 609-742, so a third patriarch of Antioch was chosen by the North Syrians; from 566 there were competing Monophysite and Melkite patriarchs in Alexandria.

288. See H. Marot, "Notes sur la Pentarchie," *Irénikon* 32 (1959): 436-442; Ferdinand R. Gahbauer, *Die Pentarchie-Theorie. Ein Modell der Kirchenleitung von den Anfängen bis zur Gegenwart* (Frankfurt: Josef Knecht, 1993).

289. Hieronymus, *ep.* 146 1,6, ed. I. Hilberg, *Corpus scriptorum ecclesiasticorum latinorum* 66 (Vienna: F. Tempsky, 1918), 310: "nam et Alexandriae a Marco euangelista usque ad Heraclam et Dionysium episcopos presbyteri semper unum de se electum et in excelsiori gradu conlocatum episcopum nominabant, quomodo si exercitus impera-

torem faciat aut diaconi eligant de se, quem industrium nouerint, et archdiaconum uocent. quid enim facit excepta ordinatione episcopus, quod presbyter non facit?"

290. Pelagius, Commentarii in Ep. 1 ad Tim. 3, 8, ed. A. Souter (three volumes), Texts and Studies 9: 1-3 (Cambridge: University Press, 1922-1931), reprinted in *Patrologiae Latinae Supplementum* 1.1110-1374; the treatment of 1 Timothy 3.8 is at PLS 1.1351.

291. "Episcopatus autem, ut quidam prudentium ait, nomen est operis non honoris. . . . Ergo episcopum Latine superintendere possumus dicere; ut intelligat non se esse episcopum qui non prodesse sed praeesse dilexerit." Isidorus Hispaliensis, *De ecclesiasticis officiis* II 5,8, ed. Christopher M. Lawson, *Corpus Christianorum Series Latina* 113 (Turnholti: Brepols, 1989), 59 (PL 83.782).

292. II 7,2 (ed. Lawson [n. 291 above], 65): "Praesunt enim ecclesiae Christi, et in confectione diuini corporis et sanguinis consortes cum episcopis sunt, similiter et in doctrina populorum et in officio praedicandi; ac sola propter auctoritatem summo sacerdoti clericorum ordinatio et consecratio reseruata est, ne a disciplina ecclesiae uindicata concordiam solueret, scandala generaret."

293. Augustine, *Civ.Dei* 19,19.

294. The treatise, *De VII ordinibus Ecclesiae*, appears among the *spuria* of Jerome in PL 30.148-162; the cited text from chapter 6 is in columns 155-156. J. Lécuyer, "Aux origines de la théologie thomiste de l'Épiscopat," *Gregorianum* 35 (1954): 65, n. 24, says that PL gives a faulty text; see the critical edition by A. Kalff (Würzburg, 1935). Lest we assume that the unknown author of "De VII ordinibus Ecclesiae" thought of bishops as simply presbyters with special duties, we should note that the quoted words come from section six of that little treatise; the seventh section exalts the *ordo episcopalis* remarkably (PL 30.158-159A). In contrast to later lists of the seven orders, this treatise lists diggers (*fossarii*), porters, readers, subdeacons, levites or deacons, priests, bishops.

295. *IV Sent.* dist. 24, c. 11 and 12.

296. Thomas Aquinas, for example, in his lectures on Philippians 1:1, 1 Timothy 3:1, 4:14, and Titus 1:6 accepts the New Testament equivalence; *Super Epistolas S. Pauli lectura*, ed. Raphael Cai, 8. ed. revisa (Torino: Marietti, 1953) II, 91, 231, 245, 305.

297. *Vita s. Willehadi* 5-8, in Monumenta Germaniae Historiae, Scriptorum t. II, 380-383; *Vita s. Liudgeri* 19-20, same volume, 410-411. These presbyters were mentioned already in a paper by the late A. C. Piepkorn, a member of an earlier round of the present dialogue, L/RC-4, 221-222.

298. The popes were Boniface IX (Bull "Sacrae Religionis," February 1, 1400), Martin V (Bull "Gerentes ad Vos," November 16, 1427), Innocent VIII (Bull "Exposcit Tuae Devotionis," April 9, 1489). See Ludwig Ott, *Das Weihesacrament*, Handbuch der Dogmengeschichte IV 5 (Freiburg: Herder, 1969), 106-107, and his *Fundamentals of Catholic Dogma*, 6th ed. (St. Louis: B. Herder, 1964), 459, and other Catholic manuals since the discovery of Martin V's bull in 1943, such as H. Lennerz, *De*

Sacramento Ordinis (2 vols.; Rome: Gregorian University, 1953), 145-153 (Appendix I). A. C. Piepkorn cited these instances in *Eucharist and Ministry*, 222-223. For a full discussion, see John de Reeper, "Relation of Priesthood to Episcopate," *Jurist* 16 (1956): 350-358.

299. Dionysius was thought to have been Paul's convert, so his testimony conflicted with the equivalence of bishop and presbyter in the New Testament. Medieval theologians like Thomas Aquinas tried to resolve the conflict by postulating a very rapid development from Paul to Dionysius. Not until the sixteenth century did theologians recognize that Dionysius wrote much later than the first century. In two of the passages of Thomas Aquinas cited above, he notes that Dionysius gives the triple order; Thomas explains the difference by saying it was not that way at the very beginning.

300. Baus, 38-39 and 260, n. 58, describes the origins of this claim, which was strongly resented by the Eastern churches. Hamilton Hess, *The Canons of the Council of Serdica* a.d. 343 (Oxford: Clarendon Press, 1958), 52, says, "None of the early references to the canons which were made by the Roman church ascribe them to the Council of Serdica. Their attributed source, when given, is invariably the Council of Nicaea."

301. According to Walter Ullmann, "Leo I and the Theme of Papal Primacy," *Journal of Theological Studies* n.s. 11 (1960), 25-51, Leo's innovation was a legal theory of the pope's inheritance of Peter's fullness of power, which Peter in turn had received from Christ. The notion of heir turned up first in a letter written by Siricius (384-399): "We carry the burdens of all who are heavy laden—or rather, the blessed apostle Peter in us bears them, he who protects us and keeps us safe as his heir in all points of his ministry, as we believe" (30-31). As Ullmann observes, the heir in Roman law acts in all things with the full rights of the testator, and if he were not of the same moral stature as the testator, he would be unworthy (*indignus*), but heir nonetheless—in this case, of Peter's office and fullness of power. Ullmann insists on several points: that it is Peter's office which is inherited, not his apostolic commission; "that no pope succeeds another pope, but succeeds St. Peter immediately"; that this is not a matter of orders, so a layman can become pope; and that "bishops received their (jurisdictional) *office* (not their sacramental *ordo*) from the pope" (33-35; 43; 50; 44-45). No unbroken line of succession is needed in this theory.

302. Their "aim . . . was to prove by the example of alleged cases from the history of the papacy the principle that the first episcopal see cannot be subjected to any court—*Prima sedes a nemine iudicatur*" (Baus, in Baus et al., 621). The Latin axiom has been retained in the Roman Catholic *Code of Canon Law* (1917 Code: canon 1556; 1983 Code: canon 1404; 1990 *Codex Canonum Ecclesiarum Orientalium*: canon 1058).

303. Itself based on fifth-century forged acts of Pope Silvester (Baus, in Baus et al., 247), the *Constitutio Constantini* or "Donation of Constantine" appeared in Rome under mysterious circumstances "not later than the early fifties of the eighth century,"

writes Walter Ullmann, *The Growth of Papal Government in the Middle Ages*, 3rd ed. (London: Methuen, 1970), 74-86.

304. Ewig, in Kempf et al., 168. On 169, he adds that the effect of these texts was not fully felt until they were incorporated into canon law collections in the 11th century. For the decretals themselves, see PL 130 or the edition by P. Hinschius, *Decretales Pseudo-Isidorianae et Capitula Angilramni* (Leipzig, 1863).

305. Colin Morris, *The Papal Monarchy: The Western Church from 1050 to 1250* (Oxford: Clarendon Press, 1989), 206, says that *plenitudo potestatis*, fullness of power, "had a long history beginning with the letter of Leo I [ep. 14,1], but up to the time of Gratian it had attracted little notice. Its use was confined to Leo's letters and two pseudo-Isidorian texts based on it, and it simply contrasted the authority of the apostolic see with those (such as legates or metropolitans) who had been authorized to perform a subordinate function. It was Bernard's *De consideratione* [*consid.* II 8,16; *Opera* III 424] which introduced a new interpretation. . . . Bernard understood it as referring to the universal power of the Roman pontiff to intervene in all parts of the church."

306. Morris, *Papal Monarchy*, 388, observes, "The prince-bishop was not (or not only) produced by original sin, but by the structure of ecclesiastical property."

307. The phrase "der evangelische Ansatz" is from Werner Elert, *Morphologie des Luthertums*, Bd. 1: *Theologie und Weltanschaung des Luthertums hauptsächlich in 16. und 17. Jahrhundert* (Munich: C. H. Beck, 1931, 3rd ed. 1965); Bd. 2, *Soziallehren und Sozialwirkung des Luthertums* (1932), as trans. by Walter A. Hansen, *The Structure of Lutheranism, Vol. 1, The Theology and Philosophy of Life of Lutheranism in the Sixteenth and Seventeenth Centuries* (St. Louis: Concordia, 1962), xix, for discussion on the rendering; on this impact and "The Office of the Ministry," 1:297-307 = Eng. trans. 339-351.

308. For example, Georg von Polentz, Bishop of Samland, and Erhard of Queiss, Bishop of Pomerania.

309. Preached in 1519; *Luther's Works* 35.49-73.

310. *Luther's Works* 35.67. The "Brotherhoods" (*Brüderschaften*) were societies of laymen who practiced devotional exercises and good works (BC, 54, n. 103). They are here regarded by Luther as a distortion of true *communio*.

311. While Luther and his colleagues emphasized Christ the word, they did not exclude the Trinitarian tradition; see, e.g., Luther's explanation of the Third Article of the Creed in his *Large Catechism*. Cf. *Luther und die trinitarische Tradition: Ökumenische und philosophische Perspektiven*, Veröffentlichen der Luther-Akademie Ratzeburg, 23, ed. Robert W. Jenson (Erlangen: Martin-Luther-Verlag, 1994).

312. From the New Testament understanding of *koinonia* and this Sermon by Luther on "The Blessed Sacrament," Paul Lehmann has, more recently, understood the church as a place where God's acts become concrete in the world, a place or field

of relationships for ethical reflection; see his *Ethics in a Christian Context* (New York: Harper & Row, 1963); Nancy J. Duff, *Humanization and the Politics of God: The* Koinonia *Ethics of Paul Lehmann* (Grand Rapids, MI: Eerdmans, 1992).

313. CA 5; 28.8-9.

314. See several articles in *The Church as Communion*, ed. Heinrich Holze, LWF Documentation No. 42/1997 (Geneva: LWF, 1997), especially Alejandro Zorzin, "Luther's Understanding of the Church as Communion in his Early Pamphlets," 81-92; Simo Peura, "The Church as Spiritual Communion in Luther," 93-131. David Yeago, "The Church as Polity? The Lutheran Context of Robert W. Jenson's Ecclesiology" in *Trinity, Time, and Church: A Response to the Theology of Robert W. Jenson*, ed. C. Gunton (Grand Rapids, MI; Cambridge, U.K, 2000), 236, states, "[T]he goal of Luther and the early Lutheran movement was not to isolate the eschatological from the outward and bodily church but to ask how the communion of the church could and should 'take up space in the world' in a manner appropriate to its eschatological character as the body of Christ. On this reading, therefore, the Lutheran tradition already contains elements of something like a 'communion-ecclesiology' in its normative sources."

315. E. Clifford Nelson, ed., *The Lutherans in North America* (Philadelphia: Fortress Press, 1980), 52-56.

316. Cf. Gerd Haendler, *Luther on Ministerial Office and Congregational Function* (Philadelphia: Fortress, 1981); Dorothea Wendebourg, "The Ministry and Ministries," *Lutheran Quarterly* 15/2 (Summer 2001) 159-194, esp. "The Local Ministry of the Pastor as the Primary Form of the Ordained Ministry," 163-166.

317. *Luther's Works* 28.283; *Luther's Works* 39.154-155. Cf. *Luther's Works* 37.367: "The bishops or priests are not heads [of the church] or lords or bridegrooms, but servants, friends, and—as the word 'bishop' implies—superintendents, guardians, or stewards." Such tasks are so important that subsequently in local congregations the elected leadership of lay people, usually the congregational council, is assigned also a part in the task of oversight, shared with the pastor(s); ELCA *Model Constitution for Congregations*, C12.04., "The Congregational Council shall have general oversight of the life and activities of this congregation, and in particular its worship life, to the end that everything be done in accordance with the Word of God and the faith and practice of the Evangelical Lutheran Church in America." Cf. *C9.03. for what ordained ministers are to do, including (besides preaching) sacraments, conduct of public worship, and pastoral care, "and supervise all schools and organizations of this congregation."

318. See Dorothea Wendebourg, "The Reformation in Germany and the Episcopal Office" in *Visible Unity and the Ministry of Oversight* (London, 1997), 54: "the Wittenberg theologians generally envisage [*episcope*] as taking place in personal rather than synodical form" (this is in the context of visitation in parishes, on which see §184 of this text).

319. Martin Brecht, "Die exegetische Begründung des Bischofsamt," 10-14, and Heinz-Meinolf Stamm, "Luthers Berufung auf die Vorstellungen des Hieronymus vom Bischofsamt," 15-26, esp. 15-17, in *Martin Luther und das Bischofsamt*, ed. M. Brecht (Stuttgart: Calwer, 1990).

320. *Luther's Works* 44.175 "An Open Letter to the Christian Nobility," *The Christian in Society I* (ed. J. J. Pelikan, H. C. Oswald, and H. T. Lehmann) =WA 6:440.21-29.

321. Wendebourg, "The Ministry and Ministries," 184, n. 32, but she goes on, "Luther does recognize a difference between bishops and presbyters at a time as early as that of the Pastoral Epistles, but it is a difference—and this is his point—within a single congregation led by one pastor-bishop: Here the bishop had presbyters and deacons as his assistants." Cf. WA 6:440, 33-35; *Luther's Works* 44.175, the pastor or bishop should "have several priests and deacons by his side. . . , who help him rule the flock and the congregation through preaching and sacraments."

322. BC, 340. On Jerome, see §§163, 168 above.

323. As Melanchthon put it in the TPPP: "Jerome, then, teaches that the distinctions of degree between bishop and presbyter or pastor are established by human authority [*humana auctoritate*]. That is clear from the way it works, for, as I stated above, the power is the same. One thing subsequently created a distinction between bishops and pastors, and that was ordination, for it was arranged that one bishop would ordain the ministers in a number of churches. However, since the distinction in rank between bishop and pastor is not by divine right [*iure divino*], it is clear that an ordination performed by a pastor in his own church is valid by divine right." BC, 340. In this connection, Wendebourg speaks of "the office of diocesan bishop" as "a secondary phenomenon, owing its existence to historical circumstance"; the tasks of pastor and bishop remain the same, though their areas of jurisdiction differ; in principle, even the right to ordain is still embodied in the office of the local pastor. "The Ministry," 165.

324. TPPP, 72. On the historical and political context of the early Lutheran situation concerning the problem of episcopacy, see especially Wendebourg, "The Reformation in Germany," 49-55.

325. *Smalcald Articles*, Part 3, Art. 10.3, Kolb and Wengert, 324; Cf. Formula of Concord Solid Declaration 10.19.

326. Archdeacon Georg Rörer was ordained to some office in the *Stadtkirche* at Wittenberg, on May 14, 1525; see Wendebourg, "The Ministry," 191, n. 91; at least this was Rörer's claim, Schwiebert, *Luther and His Times*, 621; cf. WA 16:226; 17, xvii, xxxviii, 243; 38, 403. BC, 324, n. 159 (on Smalcald Articles III.10,3) says, "The first ordination by the Wittenberg reformers in Wittenberg took place on 20 October 1535." See the more detailed note in *Die Bekenntnissschriften der lutherischen Kirche* (1930 ed., 458, n. 2); involved is Luther's understanding that call (by a congregation) was the decisive matter (WA 38, 238, 7f.; 41, 240-242 and 457f.).

327. Apol 14.2, BC, 222.

328. WA 10:2, 105-158; cf. Gottfried Krodel, "Luther und das Bischofsamt nach seinem Buch 'Wider den falsch genannten geistlichen Stand des Papstes und der Bischöfe,'" in Martin Luther und das Bischofsamt, 27-65.

329. Wendebourg (n. 318 above), "Reformation," 55. The pre-Reformation dioceses would have had bishops "who could look back to a chain of predecessors into the Middle Ages and in some cases even into antiquity" but after acceptance of Reformation teaching "committed to proclaiming the Gospel according to the teaching of the Wittenberg Reformation and to undertaking their specific duties in accordance with it."

330. CA 28.1, 5, 19. BC, 91-93.

331. CA 28.20-22. BC, 95.

332. In the sense of Luke 19:44, oversight visitation; *Besuchdienst*.

333. WA 26:195-240; *Luther's Works* 40.269-320; Wendebourg, "The Ministry" 169-170.

334. Cf. J. Höß, "The Lutheran Church of the Reformation. Problems of its formation and organization in the middle and north German territories," in *The Social History of the Reformation. Festschrift H. J. Grimm*, ed. L. P. Buck, J. W. Zophy (Columbus, 1972), 317-339; "Episcopus Evangelicus. Versuche mit dem Bischofsamt im deutschen Luthertum des 16. Jahrhunderts," in *Confessio Augustana und Confutatio*, ed. E. Iserloh (Münster, 1980), 499-516. See also Merlyn E. Satrom, "Bishops and Ordination in the Lutheran Reformation of Sixteenth-Century Germany," *Lutheran Forum* 33:2, Summer 1999, 12-15; Gerhard Tröger, *Das Bischofsamt in der evangelisch-lutherischen Kirche* (1965) and "Das evangelische Bischofsamt," *Theologische Realenzyklopädie* 6. Two of these were in Prussia, which was not part of the Holy Roman Empire, namely, Georg von Polentz, bishop since 1519 of the Samland (his see in Königsberg) and Erhard von Queiß, elected bishop of Pomesania in 1523 but not yet confirmed by the pope or consecrated.

335. Wendebourg, "Reformation," 56-57. In the 1540s, Hermann von Wied, Archbishop and Elector of Cologne, was forced to abdicate when he sought to reform his diocese along Evangelical lines (and died under excommunication in 1552), and Franz von Waldeck, in Osnabrück, had to renounce his turn to Protestantism in order to remain bishop. The one exception was the Bishop of Brandenburg, Matthias von Jagow (bishop 1516-1544), who continued to serve as a Lutheran bishop, for the territory under his secular control was not under the Emperor. Literature in Wendebourg, "Reformation," nn. 63-66.

336. Nikolaus von Amsdorff (1483-1565) in Naumberg (1542), Georg von Anhalt (1507-1553) in Merseburg (1544), and Bartholomäus Suave in Pomeranian Kammin (1545).

337. Hermann von Wied of Cologne, Matthias von Jagow, or one of those in Prussia.

338. See Wendebourg, "Reformation," 58-62.

339. A. F. von Campenhausen, "The Episcopal Office of Oversight," 175.

340. A *Superintendent* was usually a prominent pastor from one of the cities who frequently worked with a consistory, to supervise, coordinate and provide for the area's pastoral needs. Pastors of principal congregations in the territorial capitals, as was the case, e.g., in Electoral Saxony, were sometimes called *Generalsuperintendenten*. Whatever the drawbacks might have been, such arrangements preserved a personal (rather than collective) form of oversight, involving the authority (delegated by the prince) to make visitations.

341. A. F. von Campenhausen, "The Episcopal Office of Oversight in the German Churches, its Public Status and its Involvement in Church Decision in History and the Present," in *Visible Unity and the Ministry of Oversight. Second Theological Conference held under the Meissen Agreement between the Church of England and the Evangelical Church in Germany* (London: Church House Publishing, 1977), 171-183, who gives the other terms sometimes used, like *Landessuperintendent*, *Kreisdekan*, or *Prälat*; quotations from 173 and 181, n. 10 (P. Brunner, who thought that "superintendent" matched well the office of bishop in the early church). See further, D. Wendebourg, "The Office of Superintendent as a Distinct Type of Episcopate," in "Reformation," 63-66, noting the "flexibility in the practical exercise of *episkope*" that "characterizes the form which the episcopal office takes in protestant churches to the present day."

342. Dorothea Wendebourg, "The Reformation," 55f.

343. So Sven-Erik Brodd, in an excursus, "The Swedish *Church Ordinance* 1571 and the Office of Bishop in an Ecumenical Context," attached to *The Office of Bishop*. Report of the Official Working Group for Dialogue between the Church of Sweden and the Roman Catholic Diocese of Stockholm (Geneva: LWF, 1993), 148; compare 45-47 and 82 in the dialogue report itself. Brodd notes that in Petri's other writings both the monarchy and the episcopacy are divinely ordained institutions.

344. The translation is that of John Wordsworth, *The National Church of Sweden* (London: A. R. Mowbray, 1911), 232-233.

345. See Bishops' Conference [Church of Sweden], *Bishop, Priest and Deacon in the Church of Sweden: A Letter from the Bishops Concerning the Ministry of the Church* (Uppsala: Bishops' Conference, 1990), 23-24.

346. On the history of episcopacy in Sweden, see Sven-Erik Brodd, "Episcopacy in Our Churches: Sweden," in Porvoo, 59-69.

347. On these events, see "The Church of England and the Church of Finland: A Summary of the Proceedings at the Conferences Held at Lambeth Palace, London, on October 5th and 6th, 1933, and at Brandö, Helsingfors, on July 17th and 18th, 1934," in *Lambeth Occasional Reports* 1931-1938 (London: SPCK, 1948), 154-155, and Fredric Cleve, "Episcopacy in Our Churches: Finland," in Porvoo, 77-78.

348. On these events in Denmark, see Lars Österlin, *Churches of Northern Europe in Profile: A Thousand Years of Anglo-Nordic Relations* (Norwich: Canterbury Press, 1995), 83-87, and Svend Borregaard, "The Post-Reformation Developments of the Episcopacy in Denmark, Norway, and Iceland," in *Episcopacy in the Lutheran Church? Studies in the Development and Definition of the Office of Church Leadership*, Episcopacy in Lutheran Church (Philadelphia: Fortress Press, 1970), 116-124.

349. The use of the term "superintendent" alongside that of bishop is not seen as indicative of a significant break with earlier understandings of the role of the bishop; see Österlin, *Churches of Northern Europe*, 85, and Gerhard Pedersen, "Episcopacy in Our Churches: Denmark," in Porvoo, 87. The term "bishop" was made standard again in 1685.

350. On the episcopate in Denmark, Iceland, and Norway, see the essays in Porvoo, 85-108.

351. Information in this paragraph is all taken from Porvoo, 109-123.

352. Porvoo, §§58a(vi) and 58b(vi); in Porvoo, 30-31.

353. Martii Parvio, "Post Reformation Developments of the Episcopacy in Sweden, Finland, and the Baltic States," in *Episcopacy in the Lutheran Church? Studies in the Development and Definition of the Office of Church Leadership*, edited by Ivar Asheim & Victor Gold (Philadelphia: Fortress Press, 1970), 132-135; Frederic Cleve, "Episcopacy in Our Churches: Finland," in Porvoo, 77f.

354. Ringolds Muziks, "Latvia," in Porvoo, 117-120.

355. Tiit Pädam, "Estonia," in Porvoo, 109-115.

356. Porvoo (n. 352 above), 31; Gunnar Lislerud, "Norway," and Hjalti Hugason, "Iceland," in Porvoo, 93-99 and 101-108.

357. Cf. Scott Hendrix, *Luther and the Papacy: Stages in a Reformation Conflict* (Philadelphia, 1981), who, on the basis of Luther' s later reflections on his early career, labels Luther's attitude toward the papacy even prior to 1517 as essentially "ambivalent" (7). Melanchthon, in TPPP, 38, expressed himself similarly: "Even if the Bishop of Rome did possess the primacy by divine right, he should not be obeyed inasmuch as he defends impious forms of worship and doctrines which are in conflict with the gospel. On the contrary, it is necessary to resist him as Antichrist." Bernard McGinn, *AntiChrist: Two Thousand Years of the Human Fascination with Evil* (San Francisco: Harper San Francisco, 1994). Luther's usage is consistent with venerable predecessors of the period, such as St. Birgitta of Sweden.

358. See e.g., Hendrix, 42-43, 69-70, 84, 156-159. Cf. Luther's *Babylonian Captivity of the Church* (*Luther's Works* 36.113). See also *Luther's Works* 36.115.

359. L/RC-4, 23-32, Raymond Brown et al., *Peter in the New Testament* (New York: Paulist Press, 1973).

360. *Luther's Works* 26.99.

361. For a brief overview of the new orders, particularly the Society of Jesus (Jesuits), see Karl Bihlmeyer and Hermann Tüchle, *Church History* (Westminster: Newman Press, 1966), III, 83-98.

362. A summary can be found in Josef Freitag, "Church Offices: Roman Catholic Offices," in *The Oxford Encyclopedia of the Reformation*, ed. Hans J. Hillerbrand (New York: Oxford University Press, 1996) I, 342-346, and in A. Duval, "The Council of Trent and Holy Orders," in [Centre de Pastorale Liturgique], *The Sacrament of Holy Orders* (London: Aquin Press, 1962), 219-258. Fuller particulars are in Josef Freitag, "Schwierigkeiten und Erfahrungen mit dem 'Sacramentum ordinis' auf dem Konzil von Trient," *Zeitschrift für katholische Theologie* 113 (1991): 39-51, and Josef Freitag, *"Sacramentum ordinis" auf dem Konzil von Trient*, Innsbrucker theologische Studien 32 (Innsbruck: Tyrolia, 1991).

363. Freitag, ibid., 41-42.

364. Ibid., 44.

365. The question of papal authority was discussed at Trent in this context. "To prevent the cumulation of benefices with the cure of souls, the Spaniards and the French requested the council to declare that the obligation of residence is *iure divino* and both of these national groups supported the thesis that episcopal jurisdiction comes directly from God and not from the pope. The Italians vigourously opposed this opinion. Thus the old controversy regarding *episcopal jurisdiction* and *papal primacy* was revived. Finally . . . it was agreed to dismiss this question without a decision." Bihlmeyer and Tüchle, *Church History* III, 110.

366. Duval, "Council of Trent" 244-245; Freitag, "Schwierigkeiten," 48-50. Freitag goes so far as to say that "Trent did not make any decision about a determinate approach to understanding the sacrament of Order" (50).

367. Thus almost at the end of the Council, which closed December 4, 1563, and after the deaths of Luther and Melanchthon. The decree and canons can be found in *Conciliorum Oecumenicorum Decreta*, ed. G. Alberigo et al. (Bologna: Instituto per le Scienze Religiose, 1973), 742-744, and translations of that text such as *Decrees of the Ecumenical Councils*, ed. Norman P. Tanner (London: Sheed & Ward, Washington, DC: Georgetown University Press, 1990), and in Henrich Denzinger, *Enchiridion symbolorum definitionum et declarationum de rebus fidei et morum*, 37th. ed., ed. Peter Hünermann (Freiburg-im-Breisgau, Herder, 1991) (DHn), 1763-1778.

368. Session 23, chap. 4, canon 7. Ibid., 1768, 1776-1777. Cf. L/RC-4, "Reflections of the Roman Catholic Participants," §40: "When the episcopate and presbyterate had become a general pattern in the church, the historical picture still presents uncertainties. . . . For instance, is the difference between a bishop and a priest of divine ordination? St. Jerome maintained that it was not; and the Council of Trent, wishing to respect Jerome's opinion, did not undertake to define that the preeminence of the bishop over presbyters was by divine law. If the difference is not of divine ordination, the reservation to the bishop of the power of ordaining Ministers

of the eucharist would be a church decision. In fact, in the history of the church there are instances of priests (i.e., presbyters) ordaining other priests, and there is evidence that the church accepted and recognized the Ministry of priests so ordained." See also §169 above.

369. Harry J. McSorley, "Trent and the Question: Can Protestant Ministers Consecrate the Eucharist," in L/RC-4, 295.

370. Freitag, "*Sacramentum ordinis*," 374, says that canon 6 goes beyond the rejection of any Lutheran claim that there was no fundamental difference of priesthood between priest and lay person: "[n]ow the sacerdotium is seen as a hierarchy of Order and as such is oriented on the bishop, not on the priest," priest being a concept embracing both presbyter and bishop.

371. Karl J. Becker, "Der Unterschied von Bischof und Priester im Weihedekret des Konzils von Trient und in der Kirchenkonstitution des II Vatikanischen Konzils," in *Zum Problem Unfehlbarkeit*, ed. Karl Rahner (Freiburg-im-Breisgau: Herder, 1971), 289-327.

372. The privileges granted to abbots to give tonsure and minor orders to members of their religious orders, were not abrogated (canon 10), but even religious order candidates for subdiaconate, diaconate, and presbyterate had to be examined and approved by the bishop (canon 12).

373. Freitag, "*Sacramentum ordinis*," 388.

374. This group of Evangelical and Catholic theologians began working just after World War II; its work formed an important part of the background to the JDDJ. For its history, see Barbara Schwahn, *Der oekumenische Arbeitskreis evangelischer und katholischer Theologen von 1946 bis 1975* (Göttingen: Vandenhoeck & Ruprecht, 1996).

375. Lehmann, Pannenberg, *The Condemnations of the Reformation Era*, 149. The original, LV I, was published in 1985.

376. Ibid., 157.

377. *The Catechism of the Council of Trent for Parish Priests*, trans. with notes by John A. McHugh and Charles J. Callan, 2nd rev. ed. (New York: Joseph F. Wagner, 1934), 330-331.

378. Ibid., 332.

379. "Above all these, the Catholic Church has always placed the Supreme Pontiff of Rome, whom Cyril of Alexandria, in the Council of Ephesus, named the Chief Bishop, Father and Patriarch of the whole world. He sits in that chair of Peter in which beyond every shadow of doubt the Prince of the Apostles sat to the end of his days, and hence it is that in him the Church recognizes the highest degree of dignity, and a universality of jurisdiction derived, not from the decree of men or Councils, but from God himself. Wherefore he is the Father and guide of all the faithful, of all the Bishops, and of all the prelates, no matter how high their power and office; and as successor of St. Peter, as true and legitimate vicar of Christ our

Lord, he governs the Universal Church" (ibid., 333). This is one of only two passages in the *Roman Catechism* that discuss the place of the Pope; the other, in the discussion of the unity of the church in Part I on the Creed, refers to him simply as (after the Church's "one ruler and governor, the invisible one, Christ") "the visible one, the Pope, who, as legitimate successor of Peter, the Prince of the Apostles, fills the Apostolic chair. It is the unanimous teaching of the Fathers that this visible head is necessary to establish and preserve unity in the Church." (ibid., 102).

380. Ibid., 334.

381. *Disputationes de Controversiis Christianae Fidei* (Ingolstadt, 1586-1593), cited here from Roberto Bellarmino, *Opera Omnia* (Naples: C. Pedone Lauriel, 1872). In the sections on ministry and the sacrament of Order, he argues with writings by Chemnitz, Calvin, and Melanchthon, as well as Luther himself.

382. *Secunda Controversia* I, 14 (*Opera Omnia* II, 167-169). Chief among the bishops' special powers of order is the power to ordain; among the Fathers, Bellarmine cites Jerome in his Letter to Evangelus ("What does a bishop do beyond what a presbyter does, except ordain?") not only in this section on order but on 170 against Chemnitz, 171 against the Franciscan Miguel de Medina, and in his book *De Sacramento Ordinis* I, 11 (Opera Omnia III, 773).

383. II Controv. I, 15 (II, 170-171).

384. Pierre Batiffol, *Études d'histoire et de théologie positive*, 2nd ed. (Paris: Victor Lecoffre, 1902), 265. Batiffol's essay, "La hiérarchie primitive," occupies 223-275 of this second edition; it appeared first in *Revue biblique* in 1895.

385. Ibid., 266.

386. Ibid., 264.

387. Known generally as the "Theologia Wirceburgensis," it represents Jesuit instruction at the University of Würzburg, and Francis Schüssler Fiorenza, "Systematic Theology: Task and Methods," *Systematic Theology: Roman Catholic Perspectives* (Minneapolis: Fortress, 1991) I, 30, calls it the first text to present church teaching in the form of theses, followed by arguments. The first edition in fourteen volumes appeared in that city between 1766-1771; citations are from Holtzclau's "Tractatus de Ordine et Matrimonio," in *Theologia dogmatica, polemica, scholastica et moralis*, 2nd ed., vol. 5, 2 (Paris: Julien, Lanier, 1854), 295-584.

388. Diss. 1, c. 1, art. 3, §30-33, ibid., 325-327.

389. Diss. 1, c. 2, art. 7, §97, ibid., 367; cp. §105, ibid., 374.

390. Diss. 1, c. 2, art.9, §129, ibid., 394.

391. Diss. 1, c. 2, art. 9, §129-142, ibid., 394-401. One is the passage from John Cassian about Paphnutius and Daniel, which was cited also by Arthur Carl Piepkorn, L/RC-4, 221. Holtzclau thought that a priest probably could not even be empowered to ordain a deacon, despite the faculty conceded by Innocent VIII to Cistercian abbots

in 1489; one key reason was that the Bull of concession had not been found (§§143-144, ibid., 401-402).

392. Cf., e.g., the manuals of H. Lennerz (see above note); E. Hugon, *De Sacramentis in Communi et in Speciali*, 5th ed. (Paris: P. Lethielleux, 1927), 729-730; Francisco a P. Sola, "De Sacramentis Initiationis Christianae," *Sacrae Theologiae Summa* IV, 3rd ed. (Madrid: B.A.C., 1956), 215.

393. See Francis Schüssler Fiorenza, *Foundational Theology: Jesus and the Church* (New York: Crossroad, 1984), 67-71. Besides the "Theologia Wirceburgensis," many other manuals follow this pattern, such as the often-revised *Manuale Theologiae Dogmaticae* of J. M. Hervé (Paris: Berche et Pagis, 1924-1926 and into the 1950s), where "De ecclesia" is in v. 1, "De ordine" in v. 4.

394. The latter placement may be due to the order in which the sacraments are named in the canons of the Council of Trent, Session 7, canon 1 (D 844 = DS 1601); see page 1 of the volume containing Holtzclau's treatise on order.

395. Some twentieth-century manuals placed the treatise on the church among the means of sanctification, after the Incarnation and before the sacraments, but the disjunction of church and ministry remained and neither parish nor diocese received explicit attention. E.g., Franz Diekamp, *Theologiae dogmaticae manuale*, trans. Adolphus M. Hoffmann from the sixth German edition (Paris: Desclée, 1933-1934), listed "De Ecclesia" for vol. 3, part 1, between Incarnation and Grace; Ludwig Ott, *Fundamentals of Catholic Dogma*, trans. Patrick Lynch (Cork: Mercier Press, 1963), has "The Church" between "The Doctrine of Grace" and "The Sacraments."

396. *Pastor Aeternus*, chap. 1.

397. Ibid., chap. 2.

398. Ibid., chap. 3.

399. Ibid., chap. 4.

400. Bernard M. Kelly, *The Functions Reserved to Pastors*, Catholic University of America Canon Law Studies 250 (Washington: Catholic University of America Press, 1947), 4.

401. Kelly, *Functions* 8: "This parochial unity of the city (civitas) was one of the most characteristic marks of the ancient diocese. The cathedral was the only parish church in the city. Around the ninth century, however, other parishes appeared in the city, administered by collegiate chapters." *DHn* 3857-3861.

402. Pope Pius XII, "Sacramentum Ordinis," AAS 40 (1948): 5-7. The Constitution was dated November 30, 1947.

403. *Sacramentum Ordinis*, 2. This paragraph is not quoted in Denzinger-Schönmetzer or the more recent edition by Peter Hünermann.

404. Ibid., 5. Jean Beyer, "Nature et position du sacerdoce," *Nouvelle revue théologique* 76 (1954): 358, points out that while the 1917 *Code of Canon Law*, canon 949, called the sub-diaconate, diaconate, and the presbyterate "sacred orders," Pope Pius XII in this constitution applies the term to the diaconate, presbyterate, and episcopate.

405. LG, 18.
406. LG, 18.
407. LG, 20.
408. LG, 20.
409. LG, 25, CD, 12.
410. LG, 19, 22.
411. LG, 22.
412. CD, 5.
413. CD, 38.1
414. CD, 6.
415. LG, 22.
416. LG, 21, 26 ; CD, 15.
417. See 1 Tim. 2:5; LG, 28.
418. LG, 27.
419. SC, 42.
420. LG, 28.
421. PO, 7.
422. PO, 4.
423. PO, 2.
424. LG, 28, PO, 6.
425. PO, 6.
426. LG, 28.
427. LG, 28.
428. LG, 28.
429. PO, 7, 15.
430. L/RC-4, "Common Observations" §21, 14.
431. Thomas Kaufmann, "Amt," *Religion in Geschichte und Gegenwart*—vierte Auflage, 1 (1998), 428-429.
432. Cf. J. Reumann, "Ordained Minister and Layman in Lutheranism," in Eucharist and Ministry §§38-48, reprinted in J. Reumann, *Ministries Examined: Laity, Clergy, Women, and Bishops in a Time of Change* (Minneapolis: Augsburg, 1987), 36-41.
433. Gottfried Brakemeier, "Amt. 3. Außereuropäisch," *Religion in Geschichte und Gegenwart*—vierte Auflage, 1, 429-430, where parallels in Roman Catholicism are noted (e.g., base communities in Latin America, with their "Ortsgebundenheit," in light of the Second Vatican Council's "people of God" theology; cf. Faustino Teixeira, "Basisgemeinden in Lateinamerika," 1:1156-1157.

434. Hans Martin Mueller, "Bishop," *Encyclopedia of the Lutheran Church* 1:311; Heinrich de Wall, "Bischof, 3. Evangelisch," *Religion in Geschichte und Gegenwart*—vierte Auflage, 1, 1622-1623, with specific functions that include ordination and in some Landeskirchen even veto power over synodical decisions (Bayern, Württemberg). See for details Schmidt-Clausen, cited above §66, n. 107, who (110-115) treats a VELKD Declaration in 1957 on apostolic succession, of which the bishop is not a guarantee, but it is "an essential dimension" of "the Church in its entirety and all its members" (115). In Schmidt-Clausen, n. 112, Gregory Dix is quoted on "that unhappy phrase 'the historic episcopate,'" as one particular theory under which so many "variant manifestations of the episcopate" have been put, when the "apostolate" is the real question (Dix, "The Ministry in the Early Church," in *The Apostolic Ministry: Essays on the History and Doctrine of Episcopacy*, ed. K. E. Kirk [London: Hodder & Stoughton, 1946]), 296-298.

435. Schmidt-Clausen (n. 107 above), 97.

436. Martin Hein and Hans-Gernot Jung, "Bishop, Episcopate," *The Encyclopedia of Christianity* (Grand Rapids, MI: Eerdmans/Leiden: Brill) 1 (1999), 263-264; Gerhard Tröger, "Bischof, IV, Das synodale Bischofsamt," *Theologische Realenzyklopädie* 6 (1980), 694-696.

437. Lowell G. Almen, "Law and Koinonia: An Overview of the Structures and Ministries of the Evangelical Lutheran Church in America" (paper, December 2, 1999), 1. See further *The Lutherans in North America*, ed. E. Clifford Nelson (Philadelphia: Fortress, 1975), where in the section on the years 1650-1790, T. G. Tappert takes up clergy on 43-49, and for 1790-1840, H. George Anderson, 102-105 and 125; see also "Theological Education," 104-108, 129, 204-206, 284-292, 432-434, and 520.

438. *The Journals of Henry Melchior Muhlenberg in Three Volumes*, trans. T. G. Tappert and J. W. Doberstein (Philadelphia: the Evangelical Lutheran Ministerium of Pennsylvania and Adjacent States and Muhlenberg Press, 1942, 1945, 1958), 1:7. Harvey L. Nelson, "A Critical Study of Henry Melchior Muhlenberg's Means of Maintaining his Lutheranism" (dissertation; Drew University, Madison, NJ, 1980): 373-374, observes how German settlers, "despite the voluntaristic, pluralistic, congregationally oriented religious climate of the Middle Colonies . . . clung to their German views of the pastor and his office."

439. Muhlenberg envisioned especially a gathering of those ordained as pastors and serving as teachers, but even at the first meeting there was an effort to have every congregation represented by members, often elders or deacons. The name "Ministerium," found also in New York and elsewhere, was retained in eastern Pennsylvania until 1962.

440. Between 1840 and 1875, some fifty-nine, listed in *The Lutherans in North America*, 175.

441. Cf. Charles P. Lutz, *Church Roots: Stories of Nine Immigrant Groups That Became the American Lutheran Church* (Minneapolis: Augsburg, 1985); J. Reumann, *Ministries Examined*, 71, "presbyterial succession."

442. So Justus Henning Böhmer (1674-1749) and J. W. F. Höfling (1802-1853). Cf. Reumann, "Ordained Minister" §44, repr. 39, with encyclopedia references, and Edmund Schlink, *Theology of the Lutheran Confessions*, trans. P. F. Koehneke and H. J. A. Bouman (Philadelphia: Fortress, 1961), 244, n. 13. In Böhmer's work in church law, the influence of Pietism is to be seen; Detlef Döring, *Religion in Geschichte und Gegenwart*—vierte Auflage, 1 (1998), 1671; Höfling's Erlangen theology distinguished the ordering of salvation (*Heilsgeschichte*) from church orders; the ministerial office rests on the universal priesthood, which is "the only office that exists by divine right"; Hanns Kerner, *Religion in Geschichte und Gegenwart*—vierte Auflage, 3 (2000), 1830.

443. *The Lutherans in North America*, 155-157, 168-169, 178.

444. "On the Ministry," Thesis VII, in, among other places, D. H. Steffens, "The Doctrine of the Church and the Ministry," in *Ebenezer*, ed. W. H. T. Dau (St. Louis: Concordia, 1922), 152-153; Reumann, "Ordained Minister," §§59-60 = repr. 45-46. Cf. So James H. Pragman, *Traditions of Ministry: A History of the Doctrine of the Ministry in Lutheran Theology* (St. Louis: Concordia, 1983), 140-146; cf. *Ministries Examined*, 66-67.

445. *The Ministry: Office, Procedures, and Nomenclature* (St. Louis: Commission on Theology and Church Relations), Thesis 1, 25.

446. "Ordained Minister," §45 = repr. 40; Pragman, 129-131, where Stahl's *Kirchenverfassung* is cited.

447. "Ordained Minister," §45 = repr. 39-40; Pragman, 136-137. K. Scholder, *Religion in Geschichte und Gegenwart*, 3rd ed., 6 (1962), 1401-1403, notes Vilmar's stance against a Kurhessen-Waldeck "Summepiskopat" that introduced the Church of the Prussian Union in some regions and his stand for separation of church and state. Such views led to the "Renitent" or resistence movement in 1873, some of whose members emigrated to America. Vilmar regarded statements in the "Treatise on the Power and Primacy of the Pope" (69-70, 72) about congregations in emergencies electing and ordaining ministers as "superfluous remarks" for an "inconceivable" situation, the absence of all pastors called by pastors (Schlink, *Theology of the Lutheran Confessions*, [n. 442 above] 244, n. 12). At Treatise 72, the Kolb and Wengert edition has not added the phrase to which A. C. Piepkorn called attention in L/RC-4, 110-111, n. 14, *adhibitis suis pastoribus*, "the church retains the right to choose and ordain ministers *using their own pastors*."

448. "Ordained Minister" §58 = repr. 44-45, stressing Loehe's distrust of democracy and support for episcopacy as found in Scripture, i.e., identical with the presbytery; Pragman, 132-136. See Loehe's *Three Books About the Church* (1845; trans. 1908; Philadelphia: Fortess, 1969); *Aphorismen über die neutestamentichen Ämter: Zur*

Verfassungsfrage der Kirche (1849), rev. ed. *Kirche und Amt: Neue Aphorismen* (1851); S. Hebert, *Wilhelm Löhes Lehre von der Kirche, ihrem Amt und Regiment: Ein Beitrag zur Geschichte der Theologie im 19. Jahrhundert* (Neuendettelsau; Friemund-Verlag, 1939); J. L. Schaaf, "Loehe's Relation to the American Church," diss. Heidelberg 1962.

449. Gerhard Schoenauer, *Religion in Geschichte und Gegenwart*—vierte Auflage, 5 (2002), 502, "eine apostolisch-episkopale Brüderskirche . . . innerhalb deren an der Bedeutung der Ortsgemeinde als primäre Gestalt der Kirche festgehalten wird."

450. *The Lutherans in North America*, 158-159, 180-183, quotation from 181; 228, Missouri alleged "hierarchical tendencies" on church and ministry in the Iowa Synod.

451. *Ministries Examined*, 200-219; Edgar R. Trexler, *Anatomy of a Merger: People, Dynamics, and Decisions That Shaped the ELCA* (Minneapolis: Augsburg, 1991), 63-66, 85-86, 97-100, 112, 116-121, 141-143, 182-183, and passim. Points of debate over ministry lay elsewhere, especially involving parochial school teachers and a wide variety of "deacons" and rostered ministers. There had been a long history of discussion in The Lutheran Church-Missouri Synod on the ministerial status of teachers; cf. "Ordained Minister" §§65-66 = repr. 47-48 plus 67-68; Pragman, 171-176. A particular problem here were women day-school teachers; if considered "ordained," the LCMS would immediately have had the largest number of women clergy of any U.S. church.

452. *Together for Ministry*, §§152-163, 23-24. The other two recommendations of the task force related thirdly to the ELCA's officially recognized lay ministries, which include deaconesses, deacons, certified lay professionals, and commissioned teachers, from predecessor bodies; ELCA Associates in Ministry; and the creation of a new category of Diaconal Ministers. Fourth was a recommendation on "Flexibility for Mission" allowing, among other items, for non-stipendiary ("tent-making") ministers and licensed ministers.

453. *Together for Ministry*, §108, 16. Pragman, 154-156, observed that the universal priesthood "was not a significant issue for 20th-century Lutheran theologians." Similarly, J. Reumann, "The Priesthood of Baptized Believers and the Office of Ministry in Eastern Lutheranism, from Muhlenberg's Day to Ours," Lutheran Historical Conference 1999 (forthcoming).

454. *Together for Ministry* §§77, 79, 11.

455. *The Lutheran Understanding of Ministry: Statement on the Basis of an LWF Study Project*, LWF Studies, Reports and Texts from the Department of Studies (Geneva: LWF, 1983), cited in *Together for Ministry*, §123. Recommendations on bishops were purposely limited because of agreement that major discussion should come on proposals from the Lutheran-Episcopal dialogue III (1983-1991) in the *Concordat of Agreement* (1991).

456. *1993 Reports and Records: Vol. 2, Minutes* (Chicago: ELCA, 1995), 691. Lowell G. Almen, "Review of Governing Documents of the Evangelical Lutheran Church in

America on the Role and Responsibility of Bishops as an Indication of the Underlying Theology of that Office" (paper, December 1, 2000), 6.

457. Lowell G. Almen, "Review of Governing Documents," 6-7, *Minutes* 692; the term of office of bishops was changed from four to six years, with reelection possible; "constitutional provision †S8.12. was revised 'to reflect more clearly the pastoral and oversight functions of the bishop' in synods,'" Almen, 7, *Minutes* 692, for the resolution; 424-427, for the amended text of the provision. Almen, 7-9, added a statement adopted by the ELCA Conference of Bishops in 1999 for their collegial guidance, "Relational Agreement Among Synodical Bishops of the Evangelical Lutheran Church in America."

458. *The Ministry of the Church: A Lutheran Understanding*, Studies series, Division of Theological Studies (New York: Lutheran Council in the USA, 1974), where ordination and installation were seen as *kairoi* in "the continuum of ordained ministry"; *The Historic Episcopate* (1984), including definition of *ius divinium* as "divine law" according to God's word, by Christ's institution, with American Lutherans "free to create under the guidance of the Spirit forms of leadership that embody *episcopé* and hold ecumenical promise"; see *Ministries Examined*, 75 and 163.

459. See n. 455 above for the 1983 report on Ministry. *Episcopacy in the Lutheran Church?* (1970) has been cited above in n. 79. *Lutheran Understanding of the Episcopal Office*, Reports and Texts series (Geneva: LWF Department of Studies, 1983). *Women in the Ministries of the Church* appeared under the same auspices, also in 1983. *The Ministry of All Baptized Believers: Resource Materials for the Churches' Study in the Area of Ministry* (Geneva: LWF, Department of Studies, 1980) reprints the 1974 LCUSA study (n. 458 above) and other Lutheran and ecumenical documents.

460. BEM. Michael Seils, *Lutheran Convergence? An Analysis of Lutheran Responses to the Convergence Document "Baptism, Eucharist and Ministry" of the World Council of Churches Faith and Order Commission* (Geneva: LWF, 1988) found less agreement on ministry than on other areas. Cf. also Daniel Martensen, "Ministry," and J. Reumann, "Eucharist and Ministry," in *Lutherans in Ecumenical Dialogues: A Reappraisal*, ed. Joseph A. Burgess (Minneapolis: Augsburg, 1990), 123-135, 136-147.

461. In the extensive literature on the topic, see Krister Stendahl, *The Bible and the Role of Women: A Case Study in Hermeneutics*, trans. Emilie T. Sander, Facet Books Biblical Series 15 (Philadelphia: Fortress, 1966); Brita Stendahl, *The Force of Tradition: A Case Study of Women Priests in Sweden* (Philadelphia: Fortress, 1985).

462. See *Ministries Examined*, 78-100, for the section "What in Scripture Speaks to the Ordination of Women?" originally published in *Concordia Theological Monthly* 44 (1973): 5-30; 120-125, for "The Lutheran Experience," and 131-139, for subsequent discussions, including discussions among Roman Catholics. The LCMS in 1969 acted to allow women to vote in congregational or synodical assemblies and to serve on boards or agencies, provided there is no violation of the orders of creation or women exercising authority over men (1 Tim. 2:11). Cf. Pragman, 158-177.

463. As of September 15, 2002, the ELCA counted 2,738 pastors who were women, out of a total of 17,725 ordained ministers. In 2003 there have been seven bishops in the ELCA who are women.

464. *Ecumenism: The Vision of the Evangelical Lutheran Church in America* (adopted 1991), 14. "Preliminary recognition" can involve eucharistic sharing but "without exchangeability of ministers." Under "full communion" there is not only mutual recognition of ordained ministers but also their "availability . . . to the service of all members of churches in full communion, subject only but always to the disciplinary regulations of the other churches."

465. The Lutheran-Episcopal *Concordat of Agreement*, Lutheran-Reformed *Formula of Agreement*, and *Joint Declaration* (as then framed) were presented together as *Ecumenical Proposals, Documents for Action by the 1997 Churchwide Assembly* of the ELCA.

466. The issues of the presence of Christ in the Lord's Supper and God's will to save (predestination) were treated in terms of "complementarity." Affirmed together were "a ministry of word and sacrament as instituted by God," to which one is ordained once, "usually by presbyters," with recognition of *episcopé* carried out by one ordained person or collegially (presbyteries and synods).

467. *Following Our Shepherd to Full Communion: Report of the Lutheran-Moravian Dialogue with Recommendations for Full Communion in Worship, Fellowship and Mission* (ELCA, 1997), 38-42, with quotation from 41. The Moravian Church has "a threefold ordained ministry: deacons, presbyters (elders) and bishops," with one ordination (to deacon, "subsequent consecrations to other offices"), and "historic episcopacy." The "historic episcopacy" was retained from the Ancient Moravian Church but with bishops as non-diocesan, so as to avoid competition in Germany with "the established church and their offices" (13), a feature continued in North America; cf. Piepkorn, *Profiles in Belief* 2: 344-348.

468. CCM.

469. *1999 Reports and Records: Assembly Minutes* (Chicago, 2000), 378, revised text as voted 378-387.

470. Porvoo (n. 352 above).

471. *The Meissen Agreement: Texts* (Council for Christian Unity Occasional Paper No. 2, 1992) London.

472. *Called to Full Communion (The Waterloo Declaration)*, available online at *www.elcic.ca*, ELCIC Documents (May 1, 2004). It was preceded by Canadian Lutheran Anglican Dialogue 1983-1986 (CLAD I, with Report and Recommendations) and CLAD II, 1989, Interim Sharing of the Eucharist, with agreement in 1995 to take steps toward full communion by 2001.

ANGLICAN-CATHOLIC

Editors' Note: *The Anglican Roman Catholic International Commission produced one of the most dramatic and earliest results of dialogues between the Catholic Church and a Reformation Church in the period after the Second Vatican Council: the 1982 Final Report. The responses to this report entailed totally new processes in the two communions. (See Christopher Hill and Edward Yarnold, SJ,* Anglicans and Roman Catholics: The Search for Unity: The ARCIC Documents and Their Reception *[London: SPCK/CTS, 1994].) Documents 12 and 13 contribute to clarifying this process.*

ARCIC has been challenged by new developments such as the ordination of women and differences on ethical issues. Documents 11 and 14 attend to these challenges. (For further reading, see Rozanne Elder, Ellen Wondra, and Jeffrey Gros, eds., Common Witness to the Gospel: Anglican Roman Catholic Documents 1983-1995 *[Washington, DC: United States Catholic Conference, 1997].)*

The structure of the Church and its authority were among the issues treated in the Final Report, but they were not fully resolved there. Documents 15 and 16 contribute to this discussion, the latter by commenting on ARCIC II's The Gift of Authority *(New York: Church Publishing Incorporated, 1999), which can also be found at* www.prounione.urbe.it/dia-int/arcic/doc/e_arcicII_05.html *(accessed in June 2004).*

DOCUMENT 11

A RECOMMITMENT TO FULL COMMUNION

Anglican–Roman Catholic Dialogue in the United States, 1992

The members of the Anglican–Roman Catholic Consultation, meeting in Baltimore on June 14-17, 1992, as representatives of our two Churches recommit ourselves to the restoration of visible unity to and full ecclesial communion between our two Churches.

In 1965 the first Anglican–Roman Catholic International Commission (ARCIC I) came into being under the auspices of Pope Paul VI and the Archbishop of Canterbury, Michael Ramsey. At the same time, the ARC dialogue began to meet in this country. ARCIC I ended its work in 1981 with the publication of its *Final Report*, in which delegates of both of our Churches affirmed that they had reached "substantial agreement" on such formerly divisive issues as the eucharist and the nature of the ordained ministry, and also a degree of convergence on authority in the Church. This *Report* was then submitted to the authorities of both Churches for evaluation.

The Lambeth Conference of bishops of the Anglican Communion in 1988 judged the ARCIC statements on eucharist and ministry to be "consonant in substance with the faith of Anglicans" and welcomed the authority statement as "a firm basis for the direction and agenda of the continuing dialogue."

The Vatican *Response* published in December 1991 gave a warm welcome to the *Final Report* and commended its achievements, but it was not able to endorse the affirmation that substantial agreement on the eucharist and ordained ministry had been reached.

We here acknowledge that there has been a widespread disappointment with the official Roman Catholic *Response* to the *Final Report*, and we note the concern of some theologians about the language and methodology of the *Response*. And yet we also note and underline that in its *Response* the Vatican acknowledges that "notable progress" has been achieved in the *Final Report* in respect to eucharistic doctrine and that "significant consensus" has been achieved on the understanding of ordained ministry. And above all we rejoice that the *Response* reaffirms the ecumenical goal of our two Churches as "the restoration of visible unity and full ecclesial communion."

We ourselves take up this mission in the United States once again in full knowledge of the discouragement with which many view the slow progress of Christian reconciliation. We do so because, in the words of the 1989 Common Declaration of the pope and the archbishop of Canterbury, "to seek anything less would be to betray Our Lord's intention for the unity of his people." We do so because the united witness of Christians makes an important contribution to the development of peace and justice at this time of heightened tension and conflict in our society. We pledge to the members of our two Churches that we will continue to explore the problems that divide us and the opportunities that lie before us. During the next few years we intend to offer to our Churches pastoral, liturgical, and theological initiatives through which we all may move to new levels of common life. In recording this determination we recall the words of Holy Scripture used by Pope Paul VI and Archbishop Michael Ramsey in their original mandate instituting the first Anglican–Roman Catholic Conversation: "forgetting those things which are behind, and reaching forth unto those things which are before, I press towards the mark for the prize of the high calling of God in Christ Jesus" (Phil 3:13-14).

Document 12

HOW CAN WE RECOGNIZE "SUBSTANTIAL AGREEMENT"?

Anglican–Roman Catholic Dialogue in the United States, 1993

Introduction

1. With the issuance of the Anglican–Roman Catholic International Commission's *Final Report* in 1982, a new context was established for Anglican–Roman Catholic dialogue, a context shaped in large measure by the invitation for response and reception that accompanied the *Final Report*. Now that responses have been given by both Churches, the context has changed again. We of the Anglican–Roman Catholic Consultation–USA understand this context to be one of continuing study and reception, which we look forward to with hope that further clarifications of the issues addressed by this dialogue at every level will deepen the unity that we already share and bring us closer to that full unity that the Lord intends for his people.

2. In this country, our two Churches have been in productive dialogue since 1965. During that time, ARC-USA has issued eight major documents and four texts that were reactions to three agreed statements of ARCIC.[1] It is from this experience that we face the new context. While looking forward in hope, we also recognize among ourselves a range of assessments concerning the import and implications of the two Churches' responses to the *Final Report*. Nevertheless, we find ourselves both encouraged and challenged by this new context, and we hope to stir up in the members of our Churches the same sense of encouragement and challenge.

3. Therefore, in this document we will indicate a number of points in the responses that we find both significant and of concern, and we will set forth our own understanding of the path forward in this new context.

Status of the Responses

4. On March 24, 1966, Pope Paul VI and Archbishop of Canterbury Michael Ramsey met in Rome and signed a common agreement declaring their intention "to inaugurate between the Roman Catholic Church and the Anglican Communion a serious dialogue which, founded on the Gospels and on the ancient common traditions, may lead to that unity in truth for which Christ prayed."[2] Following the 1968 Malta Report of the joint preparatory commission, the Anglican–Roman Catholic International Commission (ARCIC I) met for the first time in 1970. In 1982, ARCIC I issued its *Final Report*, which includes three agreed statements, two elucidations, a further statement on authority in the Church, and an introduction to the Church as *koinonia.*

5. In issuing the *Final Report*, ARCIC I hoped to help "begin a process of extensive prayer, reflection and study that will represent a marked advance toward the goal of organic union between the Roman Catholic Church and the Anglican Communion."[3]

6. Even as ARCIC I began its work on salvation and the nature of the Church, the Anglican Communion and Roman Catholic Church each began their own process of study and response to the *Final Report* of ARCIC I.

7. In the Anglican Communion, in preparation for the Lambeth Conference of 1988, the Anglican Consultative Council[4] asked each province to consider "whether the agreed statements on eucharistic doctrine, ministry and ordination, and authority in the Church (I and II), together with elucidations, are consonant in substance with the faith of Anglicans and whether *The Final Report* offers a sufficient basis for taking the next concrete step toward the reconciliation of our Churches grounded in agreement in faith."[5] The formal synodical responses of nineteen out of twenty-nine provinces were summarized and discussed in the *Emmaus Report* issued in 1987. The Lambeth Conference, meeting the next year, responded to the *Final Report* by a resolution in which the conference "recognizes the agreed statements of ARCIC I on eucharistic doctrine, ministry and ordination, and their elucidations, as consonant in substance with the faith of

Anglicans and believes that this agreement offers a sufficient basis for the direction and agenda of the continuing dialogue on authority."[6]

8. We note here that the authority of the Lambeth response for Anglicans is not entirely clear. This point arises out of a statement printed in the 1988 Lambeth Conference proceeding (9, n. 1). This statement, which is similar to statements found in Lambeth proceedings since 1888, says that "resolutions passed by a Lambeth conference do not have legislative authority in any province until they have been approved by the provincial synod of the province." At the same time, however, the *Emmaus Report* emphasizes that "though there can be no question of a legislative or juridical decision, there are moments when the Lambeth conferences have discerned, articulated, and formed the common mind of the Anglican Communion on important matters of faith and morals. . . . In the end the bishops have a special responsibility for guarding and promoting the apostolic faith, a responsibility which is theirs by ordination and office."[7] The Lambeth Conference of 1988 did recognize "the agreed statements of ARCIC I on eucharistic doctrine, ministry and ordination, and their elucidations, as consonant in substance with the faith of Anglican and believes that this agreement offers a sufficient basis for taking the next step forward toward the reconciliation of our Churches grounded in agreement in faith."[8]

9. The December 1991 document from the Vatican is the official response of the Roman Catholic Church to the *Final Report*. It is described as "the fruit of close collaboration between the Congregation for the Doctrine of the Faith and the Pontifical Council for Promoting Christian Unity."[9] Since the apostolic constitution of 1988 *Pastor Bonus*, the Congregation for the Doctrine of the Faith has had final responsibility in matters of faith and doctrine.

10. When the *Final Report* was issued in 1982, Cardinal Willebrands, then president of the Secretariat for Promoting Christian Unity, also asked Roman Catholic episcopal conferences to evaluate *The Final Report*. He asked for careful study and considered judgment and requested that the replies of the conferences address the question of "whether it [the *Final Report*] is consonant in substance with the faith of the Catholic Church concerning matters discussed."[10]

11. Since a number of these evaluations were never published and none is cited in the Vatican response, it is hard to determine how much influence these evaluations had on the December 1991 text. The Vatican response, however, would still be the official position of the Roman Catholic

Church concerning the *Final Report*,[11] even in the unlikely case that the conference evaluations were not used at all.

12. Where the Lambeth response found "consonance in substance on the eucharist and ministry and ordination," the Vatican response judged "that it is not yet possible to state that substantial agreement has been reached on all the questions studied" by ARCIC I, although the Vatican response considers the *Final Report* a "significant milestone not only in relations between the Catholic Church and the Anglican Communion but in the ecumenical movement as a whole."[12]

13. ARCIC I itself claimed only "a high degree of agreement" on authority. With this, both the Lambeth response and the Vatican response seem to concur. Lambeth found ARCIC I's *Authority in the Church I* and *II*, together with the elucidation, "a firm basis for the direction and continuing dialogue on authority,"[13] while the Vatican said that "the most that has been achieved is a certain convergence, which is but a first step along the path that seeks consensus as a prelude to unity."[14]

14. The Vatican response does not close off discussion of the issues in the *Final Report*. On the contrary, it encourages further study and clarification (cf. no. 30). Its authors hope that the response itself will contribute to the dialogue that is leading to "the restoration of visible unity and full ecclesial communion" (no. 34).

15. Accordingly, the *Final Report* constitutes both resource and agenda in the Anglican–Roman Catholic relationship. Together with the responses to it, the *Final Report* clarifies certain questions and poses certain challenges that seem to mark where the next steps must be taken in our journey together.

The Search for a Common Language

16. ARCIC I's method was to engage in serious dialogue on "persisting historical differences" in order to contribute to the "growing together" of the two Churches.[15] Therefore, ARCIC I was "concerned not to evade the difficulties, but rather to avoid the controversial language in which they have often been discussed. We have taken seriously the issues that have divided us and have sought solutions by re-examining our common inheritance, particularly the Scriptures."[16] This method was approvingly summarized by John Paul II in his address to the Commission:

> Your method has been to go behind the habit of thought and expression born and nourished in enmity and controversy to

> scrutinize together the great common treasure, to clothe it in a language at once traditional and expressive of the insights of an age which no longer glories in strife but seeks to come together in listening to the quiet voice of the Spirit.[17]

17. The Vatican response, however, does not allude to ARCIC I's method. It perceives ambiguities in the language of the *Final Report*. Thus, it calls for certain clarifications to ensure that "affirmations are understood in a way that conforms to Catholic doctrine [of the eucharist]" (no. 6). Likewise, it calls for clarification of statements on ordained ministry in the *Final Report*. The Vatican response seems to urge that clarification be given through the use of language that is closer to and even identical with traditional Roman Catholic theological formulations. (For example, the response identifies a number of points it would like to have "explicitly affirmed." One of these is "the propitiatory character of the Mass as the sacrifice of Christ." The *Response* also asks that clarification be given on a number of matters and cites "the fact that the ARCIC document does not refer to the character of priestly ordination, which implies a configuration to the priesthood of Christ."[18])

18. If an agreed statement does not employ the traditional language of one or both Churches, does it thereby fail to express adequately the faith of those Churches? Some commentators have pointed to the obstacle to ecumenical progress created by one Church's demanding adherence to its own formulation. It seems to us that the Vatican response calls us to more painstaking study of the criteria by which each Church should evaluate the language of agreed statements.

The Issue of Substantial Agreement

19. The use of phrases such as "substantial agreement," "substantial identity," and "consonant in substance" in the *Final Report* and in the Vatican *Response* to it has been widely criticized as ambiguous. *Substantial* and *in substance* can mean either "in very large part" or "fundamental, basic." In addition, the term "substantial" carries overtones from various historical theological controversies and from its use in scholastic theology.

20. The resolution that makes up the brief Lambeth response to ARCIC I "recognizes the agreed statements of ARCIC I on eucharistic doctrine, ministry and ordination, and their elucidations, as consonant in substance with the faith of Anglicans."[19] In formulating this reply, the Lambeth response seems to have taken *consonance in substance* in a broader

sense as meaning something like "compatibility." Thus, while the overall evaluation of the Lambeth Conference was positive, it also reported "continuing anxieties" regarding eucharistic sacrifice and presence as well as on "Ministry and Ordination," requests "for a clarification of 'priesthood.'" As E. J. Yarnold has remarked: "The point seems to be that a statement is consonant with Anglican faith if it can be said to fall within the legitimate range of Anglican comprehensiveness, though individual Anglicans would be under no obligation to subscribe to it themselves."[20]

21. The Vatican response, on the other hand, seems to have taken *consonance in substance* as meaning full and complete identity: "What was asked for was not a simple evaluation of an ecumenical study, but an official response as to the identity of the various statements with the faith of the Church" (no. 33). From this perspective, the Vatican response must be understood, then, as claiming that ARCIC I failed to reach agreement on basic issues.

22. The main criterion for judgment used by the Churches "consonance in substance with the faith" was identically stated. But, as we have noted here, the meaning of this phrase varies between the two Churches. We suggest, then, that beyond the ambiguity in the term *substantial* there exists a much larger issue which lies in the assumption that everyone knows what substantial (in the sense of "fundamental") agreement would look like and how it might be expressed.

The Issue of Doctrinal Language

23. The intrinsic problem is the complex question of doctrinal language. How does one express the faith of the Church? This is, of course, a question with a long history of controversy.

24. What is meant by "the faith of the Church"? For members of the Anglican and Roman Catholic communities, the tendency may be to assume, without very much hesitation, that the faith of the Church is identical with the official pronouncements of the community, however these pronouncements may be framed. But the fact is that the faith of the women and men who make up our communities is never simply the same as the words of our doctrinal formulas, liturgical forms, and catechetical statements. In Roman Catholic theology, a distinction has long been made between the *fide implicita* of the members of the Church and magisterial doctrinal statements. What must always be kept in mind is that the saving

faith of the Church is the concrete faith of the people of God, which the official formulations of the faith are intended to support.

25. Yet two further questions arise: First, how does one know what the faith of any person or any group is, save through that faith's expression in word and deed? Second, by what processes and on what grounds have the words of councils, popes, bishops, and theologians come to be accepted as more authoritative than the word of any other believer or group of believers?

26. The first of these questions cannot be answered by appealing to the words of doctrine, for at least as many differences exist in the devotional styles and practices of various believers as in their verbal expressions of faith. The *lex orandi* does not circumvent the question of adequacy of expression that confronts the *lex credendi.*

27. The second question is not simply another way of raising the issue of magisterial authority. The problem to which it points is that the words of official doctrinal and liturgical formulas, as well as the faith statements of any individual or community, all fall short of the mysteries that they seek to express. At best, when Christians seek to articulate the faith of the Church, we deal with degrees of inadequacy.

28. Certainly in our communities we live and pray together in the assumption that there is an agreement which, despite the differences in the ways we express our faith both in word and in practices, is substantial. But how do we know that? We pray the creed together Sunday after Sunday, and as we recite the words of the creed, we assume that the persons surrounding us intend substantially the same as we do. But on what grounds do we make this assumption?

29. The Vatican *Response*'s use of the language of official Roman Catholic formulas to test whether agreement has been reached on the substance of faith seems at odds with the practice employed in other ecumenical conversations. For example, few would argue against the statement that the doctrines of the Trinity and the Incarnation are the central articles of the Christian creed and that those articles have received normative expression in the formulas of the first four ecumenical councils.

30. Nevertheless, the Roman Catholic Church has been willing to join in a common declaration of faith which deliberately avoids conciliar language that has proven controversial. One such declaration was deemed sufficient to permit some sacramental sharing between the Roman Catholic and the Syrian Orthodox Churches. In their 1984 declaration, Pope John Paul II and Patriarch Zakka I appeal to the Council of Nicaea and then affirm:

> The confusion and schisms that occurred between their Churches in the later centuries, [the pope and the patriarch] realize today in no way affect or touch the substance of their faith, since these arose only because of differences in terminology and culture and in the various formulas adopted by different theological schools to express the same matter.[21]

Here the substance of faith is distinguished from culturally determined terminology and formulas of theological schools, including terminology and formulas worked out and adopted by one of the first four ecumenical councils.

31. From this example, it is apparent that the Roman Catholic Church has found it possible to affirm "substantial agreement" without agreement on specific doctrinal formulas, even when those formulas are as hallowed as the Chalcedonian formula. This common declaration does not indicate how the "substance" of faith is to be discerned when even the formula of Chalcedon is judged a matter of "terminology and culture."

32. This question raises the issue of doctrinal language. If, indeed, thought is dependent upon language and experience is dependent upon thought, then it is highly problematic to claim that one can distinguish the substance of faith from the culturally determined language of its expression.[22] How does one discern the substance beneath the words save through the words? It is a mistake to assume that when one speaks of the mysteries of faith, one can refer beyond the various attempts to speak about those mysteries to the mysteries themselves as if they are simply "there" and available for inspection.

33. One way of dealing with this puzzle of doctrinal language is to accept orthopraxies as the test of orthodoxy: that is, to recognize that doctrines are expressions of the communal life of the Church and that shared life may make differing doctrinal formulas intelligible and reveal them to be compatible and even identical in intent. But such an interpretation means that attempts to share life must precede or at least accompany attempts to compare doctrinal statements. It might even suggest that shared sacramental life must precede or at least accompany attempts to compare doctrines on sacraments.

34. In any case, the very different understanding of "substantial agreement" in the Lambeth and Vatican responses to the *Final Report* raise important questions on the understanding of doctrine and the hermeneutics of doctrinal language at work in the dialogues. These questions lie beneath any assumptions that the substance of faith is readily available for consultation

as the criterion of doctrinal language. These questions must be addressed in the future by our two Churches.

The Challenge of Reception in the New Context

35. We understand that the importance of the process of reception was not fully realized in 1966 when Archbishop Ramsey and Pope Paul VI established the Anglican–Roman Catholic dialogue. How were the commission's agreements to be fully accepted or rejected by each Church? As has been noted above, the Anglican Communion has produced a response of its bishops gathered at the Lambeth Conference of 1988, but while the bishops have "a special responsibility for guarding and promoting the apostolic faith, their response is not a legislative or juridical decision."[23] The dependence of the Roman Catholic Church's response on prior consultations of bishops' conferences remains unclear. We ask whether texts such as the *Final Report* require new procedures of reception that more adequately reflect our affirmation of the real but imperfect communion in which we already live.

36. The sparse documentation style of the Vatican and Lambeth responses has also complicated the process of receiving them. While the Vatican response is longer and more detailed, neither response contains adequate reference to the materials upon which the responses build. With further documentation, the bases for the judgments expressed would be easier to discern. To this extent, the contribution of the responses to the dialogue could be made more effective than it currently is. We hope that future responses from our two Churches will provide the material needed to facilitate understanding, appreciation, and acceptance of their judgments.

37. ARCIC I said:

> We are convinced that if there are any remaining points of disagreement they can be resolved on the principles here established. We acknowledge a variety of theological approaches within both our communions. But we have seen it as our task to find a way of advancing together beyond the doctrinal disagreements of the past.[24]

We take this to indicate that ARCIC I claims "substantial agreement" in the sense that, whatever differences may remain on the issues explored in the *Final Report*, they would not today provoke division between our two Churches. Hence, they cannot warrant our continuing division.

38. Thus, we take our two Churches' different judgments on whether "substantial agreement" has been reached as both encouragement and challenge: encouragement, in that both responses rejoice in the notable progress that has been achieved; challenge, in that we are confronted with our willingness to stay divided over matters that would not initiate a division. This reality places in front of us our need for continuous repentance of our willingness to be divided and continuous conversion toward the unity Christ offers us with one another, which is a mirror of his own unity with the Father.

NOTES

1. George Tavard, "The Work of ARCUSA: A Reflection Postfactum," *One in Christ* 29:3: 247-259.
2. The common declaration by Pope Paul VI and the archbishop of Canterbury, March 24, 1966, in *Called to Full Unity: Documents on Anglican–Roman Catholic Relations 1966-1983*, ed. Joseph W. Witmer and J. Robert Wright (Washington, DC: United States Conference of Catholic Bishops, 1986), 3.
3. Herbert J. Ryan, "Foreword to the American Edition," Anglican–Roman Catholic International Commission, *The Final Report* (FR) (Cincinnati: Foreward Movement Press; Washington, DC: United States Catholic Conference, 1982), vi.
4. The Anglican Consultative Council was created after the 1968 Lambeth Conference to provide communion-wide continuity of consultation and guidance on policy; it has neither legislative nor jurisdictional powers.
5. *The Emmaus Report: A Report of the Anglican Ecumenical Consultation* (ER) (Cincinnati: Forward Movement, 1987), 44.
6. Resolution 8, Lambeth Conference 1988, published in *The Truth Shall Make You Free*, 210-212.
7. ER, 73; cf. Lambeth Conference 1988, Resolution 13.
8. Lambeth 1988, Resolution 8.
9. "Vatican Response to ARCIC *Final Report*," *Origins* 21:28 (December 19, 1991): 443.
10. National Conference of Catholic Bishops, "Evaluation of the ARCIC Final Report," *Origins* 14:25 (1984): 409.
11. Report of the Catholic Theological Society of America Committee on the Profession of Faith and the Oath of Fidelity (April 15, 1990), 51-52.
12. "Vatican Response," 441.
13. See note 6.
14. "Vatican Response," 443.
15. FR, 1.

16. FR, 5.
17. John Paul II address found in *One in Christ* 16: 341.
18. "Vatican Response," 445.
19. See note 5.
20. In *The Tablet*, December 7, 1991, 1525.
21. Pope John Paul II and Patriarch Zakka I of Antioch, common declaration "Toward a Fully Unanimous Gospel Witness" (June 23, 1984), *Catholic International* 2:14 (July 15-31,1991): 662-663, in GA II, 691-693.
22. This problem is foreshadowed in John XXIII's opening speech to the Second Vatican Council: "The substance of the ancient doctrine of the deposit of faith is one thing, and the way in which it is represented is another." Quoted in Francis A. Sullivan, "The Vatican Response to ARCIC I," *Bulletin*/Centro Pro Unione, 39.
23. ER, 73.
24. FR, 16.

Document 13

FIVE AFFIRMATIONS ON THE EUCHARIST AS SACRIFICE

Anglican–Roman Catholic Dialogue in the United States, 1994

At the forty-first meeting of the Anglican–Roman Catholic Dialogue of the United States of America (ARC-USA), on January 6, 1994, having in mind the significant agreement on the Eucharist represented by the *Final Report* of the Anglican Roman Catholic International Commission and responding to the request in the *Vatican Response to the ARCIC I Final Report* for clarification, we wish as the official representatives of our two Churches in the United States to make together the following affirmations:

1. *We affirm* that in the Eucharist the Church, doing what Christ commanded his apostles to do at the Last Supper, makes present the sacrifice of Calvary. We understand this to mean that when the Church is gathered in worship, it is empowered by the Holy Spirit to make Christ present and to receive all the benefits of his sacrifice.

2. *We affirm* that God has given the eucharist to the Church as a means through which all the atoning work of Christ on the Cross is proclaimed and made present with all its effects in the life of the Church. His work includes "that perfect redemption, propitiation, and satisfaction, for all the sins of the whole world" (cf. *Book of Common Prayer* [USA] [BCP], art. 31, p. 874). Thus the propitiatory effect of Christ's one sacrifice applies in the eucharistic celebration to both the living and the dead, including a particular dead person.

3. *We affirm* that Christ in the eucharist makes himself present sacramentally and truly when under the species of bread and wine these earthly realities are changed into the reality of his body and blood. In English the

terms "substance," "substantial," and "substantially" have such physical and material overtones that we, adhering to the *Final Report*, have substituted the word "truly" for the word "substantially" in the clarification requested by the Vatican *Response*. However, we affirm the reality of the change by consecration as being independent of the subjective disposition of the worshipers.

4. *Both our Churches affirm* that after the eucharistic celebration the body and blood of Christ may be reserved for the communion of the sick, "or of others who for weighty cause could not be present at the celebration" (BCP, 408-409). Although the American *Book of Common Prayer* directs that any consecrated bread and wine not reserved for this purpose should be consumed at the end of the service, American Episcopalians recognize that many of their own Church members practice the adoration of Christ in the reserved sacrament. We acknowledge this practice as an extension of the worship of Jesus Christ present at the eucharistic celebration.

5. *We affirm* that only a validly ordained priest can be the minister who, in the person of Christ, brings into being the sacrament of the eucharist and offers sacramentally the redemptive sacrifice of Christ which God offers us.

As the Vatican *Response* had already recorded the notable progress toward consensus represented by *The Final Report* in respect of eucharistic doctrine, in the light of these five affirmations ARC/USA records its conclusions that the eucharistic as sacrifice is not an issue that divides our two Churches.

DOCUMENT 14

CHRISTIAN ETHICS IN THE ECUMENICAL DIALOGUE: ANGLICAN–ROMAN CATHOLIC INTERNATIONAL COMMISSION II AND RECENT PAPAL TEACHING

Anglican–Roman Catholic Dialogue in the United States, 1995

1. Our Churches have long recognized the need for serious engagement with Christian ethics as an important component of our endeavor to restore full ecclesial communion. The Second Vatican Council had suggested that "on the common basis of the Gospel, dialogue can lead to a more profound understanding on both sides" (UR, no. 23). Although ecclesiological and other doctrinal issues took priority in the various bilateral dialogues initiated after the Council, including the international and national Anglican–Roman Catholic dialogues, it became increasingly clear that ecumenical dialogue on ethics could not be long postponed.

In 1979, addressing an ecumenical assembly of church leaders toward the close of his first U.S. visit as pope, John Paul II spoke of "deep division which still exists over moral and ethical matters," and declared, "The moral life and the life of faith are so deeply united that it is impossible to divide them" (October 7, 1979, Trinity College, Washington, D.C.). During the next decade, the perception grew that progress toward Christian unity might now be hampered by differences over current moral issues even more than by the doctrinal differences inherited from the Reformation era.

2. That discouraging perception has now been challenged in an agreed statement on morals published by the Second Anglican–Roman Catholic International Commission (ARCIC II), entitled *Life in Christ: Morals,*

Communion and the Church (LinC) (1994). Drawing upon the Commission's previous agreed statement, *Church as Communion* (1994), the present statement on morals emphasizes that the communion to which we are all called involves responsibilities to God, to society, and to the world we inhabit. From the outset, *Life in Christ* affirms that Anglicans and Roman Catholics "share the same fundamental moral values" (no. 1). The opening chapters set forth the shared vision and common heritage of our two Churches as regards the meaning of Christian life (nos. 4-35). Differences between us in the articulation of this moral vision—"for example, concerning the respective roles of personal conscience, ecclesial tradition, and magisterial teaching in Christian moral formation"—are seen and presented as a matter of varying emphasis rather than substantive disagreement (nos. 43-53).

In addressing certain specific moral issues where some measure of real disagreement is evident, *Life in Christ* endeavors to situate these differences within the context of broader areas of basic agreement between the Anglican and Roman Catholic Churches. Regarding divorce and remarriage, and also contraception, the divergent official positions of our two Churches are seen as differences over detailed moral conclusions which should not obscure our fundamental agreement on the nature of marriage as a permanent covenant open to procreation (nos. 64-80). Our differing approaches to abortion in certain difficult cases are seen as expressing diverse understandings of the status of absolute moral prohibitions in ethical discourse, a diversity which leaves intact our common reverence for the sacredness of all human life (nos. 85-86). As regards to homosexuality, *Life in Christ* acknowledges differences between Anglican and Roman Catholic pastoral practice but does not view these differences as compromising a shared appreciation of the marriage covenant as "the normative context for a fully sexual relationship" (no. 87).

According to *Life in Christ*, therefore, it would appear that our differences concerning morals amount to relatively narrow disagreements over secondary issues, or to variations of emphasis which involve no real disagreement at all, or to matters of practice which are not seen to present a significant challenge to moral teaching. *Life in Christ* claims that the importance of all such differences has been exaggerated by the very fact of our broken communion, which tempts us to exalt our differences into church-dividing issues (nos. 53, 89). In the perspective of *Life in Christ*, none of our differences regarding morals is a valid warrant for our Churches to remain separated. On the contrary, strengthening our communion offers the best hope for resolving our outstanding moral differences and bearing more effective common witness to our shared Gospel values (no. 88).

3. The optimistic thesis of *Life in Christ* appears to be significantly challenged, in its turn, by the papal encyclical *Veritatis Splendor* (VS), which was published only months earlier (October 5, 1993). We note with regret that these two documents were prepared independently of each other, and we find our Churches challenged to be more collaborative in the future. Still, now we must take account of important contrasts in outlook between the two documents and the likely implication of these contrasts for the eventual assessment of *Life in Christ* by the papal magisterium.

Whereas *Life in Christ* sees the fundamental moral question as "What kind of persons are we called to become?", rather than "What ought we to do?" (no. 6), *Veritatis Splendor* is mainly concerned with "What must we do?" This divergence on the primary ground of ethics "in character or in behavior" has long standing in the Christian tradition overall, and indeed it remains currently a focus of much lively discussion. Furthermore, other differences in approach between *Life in Christ* and *Veritatis Splendor* are also significant.

Veritatis Splendor is intended as a magisterial directive specifically for Roman Catholics, rather than as a contribution to ecumenical dialogue (which is the intent of *Life in Christ*). *Veritatis Splendor* bases its moral vision primarily on the concept of divine law, rather than the relationship-responsibility concept which governs *Life in Christ*. By contrast with ARCIC's acceptance of a degree of ethical diversity as compatible with healthy ecclesial communion, it is a major objective of the papal encyclical to reprove the growth of such diversity among Roman Catholics as inimical to authentic communion (VS, no. 113). Finally, while *Life in Christ* advocates closer ecumenical dialogue as the preferred remedy for moral confusion, in *Veritatis Splendor* the major remedy indicated is the firmer exercise of papal and episcopal authority (VS, nos. 114-116).

Some of the above contrasts between *Life in Christ* and *Veritatis Splendor* may very well be seen as matters of divergent emphases dictated by different specific objectives. For example, the concentration in *Veritatis Splendor* on the question "What must we do?" can be understood in terms of the Pope's special concern to address current internal Roman Catholic controversies about how to determine moral rectitude in human actions; and this need not be taken as negating ARCIC's attribution of fundamental primacy to the question "What kind of persons are we called to become?" Likewise, the encyclical's preference for the "divine law" model in articulating its moral vision could well be based on the special aptitude of that particular model for asserting absolute principles governing specific human actions. This preference need not imply a devaluing of other moral models highlighted in *Life in Christ*.

Other points of contrast are more formidable, however. As indicated above, the two documents appear to take incompatible positions concerning the impact of ethical diversity on ecclesial communion and concerning the appropriate role of ecclesiastical authority in dealing with such diversity. More specifically, ARCIC's suggestion that differing Anglican and Roman Catholic views on "absolute moral prohibitions" are not of central importance seems hardly reconcilable with the major concern of *Veritatis Splendor* "reiterated, in part, in the subsequent encyclical *Evangelium Vitae* (EV) (25 March 1995)" to underline the importance of such absolute prohibitions particularly as regards issues involving human life, sexuality, and marriage (VS, nos. 80-83; EV, no. 62). Nor does ARCIC's suggestion appear congruent with the intense debate among Roman Catholics themselves about the status of absolute prohibitions and about the authoritative force of various papal statements.

4. It is the view of ARC-USA that, in light of the difficulties noted above, certain conclusions of ARCIC-II as presented or suggested in *Life in Christ* stand in need of further study and refinement, so as to secure the possibility of fruitful ecumenical dialogue in relation to current authoritative Roman Catholic teaching. More attention must be given particularly to (1) the significance of divergent Anglican and Roman Catholic positions on absolute moral prohibitions regarding specific categories of human action; (2) the contemporary influence of theological, geographical, and cultural diversity on the formulation of Anglican doctrines concerning moral questions, by contrast with the universal teaching that characterizes the Roman Catholic magisterium in such matters; and (3) the role of ecclesiastical authority in shaping the formation of moral judgments by individual Christians and by the whole Church.

The experience of our two Churches in the United States indicates further that the specific moral issues highlighted in *Life in Christ* are considerably more conflictual "both within each of our Churches and between us" than ARCIC appears to have recognized. Even if basic areas of agreement exist as regards the sacredness of human life, the nature of marriage, and the meaning of human sexuality, our very diverse specifications and practical applications of these general principles cannot be regarded as non-essential in moral discourse and indeed profoundly affect the extent and quality of communion. The sometimes sharply divergent specific teachings and practices of our Churches regarding divorce, contraception, abortion, and homosexuality are actually a frequently given reason why Roman Catholic and Episcopalian Christians leave one Church and enter the other.

ARC-USA welcomes and commends *Life in Christ* as a groundbreaking exploration of the ethical dimension of Christian communion. We affirm, with *Life in Christ*, that the best way to deal constructively with the differences that divide us lies in closer consultation and collaboration. At the same time, this collaborative process requires that our conflicting positions on vital issues be acknowledged openly in all their seriousness, and engaged resolutely and wisely.

Document 15

AGREED REPORT ON THE LOCAL/UNIVERSAL CHURCH

Anglican–Roman Catholic Consultation in the United States of America, 1999

Introduction

The Anglican Communion and the Roman Catholic Church have been in high-level, official dialogue with each other for more than thirty years.[1] Again and again during that time we have discovered that we already share a "real though as yet imperfect communion" (CC, 2) rooted in a common faith and shared inheritance (MR, 3 and 4), and that we are often involved together in the life of service and mission to which the Gospel calls us. Again and again, we have discovered convergences in thought and practice and have found ways in which our differences are complementary, to the benefit of each of our churches and the increase of Christian unity. We have also been able to recognize a significant and hopeful extent of agreement on matters which have in the past been divisive and even church-dividing, such as the mode of Christ's presence in the Eucharist, the ordained ministry, and the role of the Bishop of Rome in the apostolic mission of the church. These were treated in the 1981 *Final Report* of ARCIC I, the responses made by our churches to it, the clarifications offered by ARCIC II, and the acceptance of these clarifications by the Pontifical Council for Promoting Christian Unity.

Within our real communion, however, imperfections remain. Often these take the form of important differences and disagreements. Of great significance at the present time is the fact that Anglicans and Roman

Catholics have different understandings and structures of authority. These have engendered different experiences and expectations, indeed different cultures, of authority within each church. Our differing traditions of authority set us apart and are in that sense divisive. But are they "church-dividing?" Do they stem from fundamentally different understandings of the Gospel so that they must continue to stand in the way of full communion between our churches?

In their *Common Declaration* (October 1989), Archbishop of Canterbury Robert Runcie and Pope John Paul II maintained, "The ecumenical journey is not only about the removal of obstacles but also about the sharing of gifts." Voices within our churches suggest that our Anglican and Roman Catholic traditions of authority contain precisely such gifts to be shared.

Voices in each Church recognize and express a need for the gifts of the other. Anglican statements[2] have called for a primatial counterweight to the centrifugal forces of provincial and diocesan autonomy (e.g., by giving more authority to the Anglican Consultative Council or the Lambeth Conference of Bishops or the Archbishop of Canterbury or the Primates of the Provinces of the Communion), in recognition that "the unity in truth of the Christian community demands visible expression" (FR, Elucidation [1981], 8). Roman Catholic statements[3] have called for the implementation of collegial and local structures to complement the exercise of primacy and better to safeguard the legitimate and necessary autonomy of local churches.

We welcome the publication of *The Gift of Authority*, an agreed statement of the Second Anglican–Roman Catholic International Commission, in May 1999, and we hope that it proves to be a significant step forward in our coming to a common mind on these issues. Since it appeared just as this report was being completed, together with other Anglicans and Roman Catholics, we shall be reflecting on this rich text in the months ahead.[4]

In the realm of authority, therefore, it is necessary once again to assess areas where we differ in order to discern in what ways we may be divided, and in what ways we each may possess gifts in which the other may benefit by sharing.

In 1991 the Second Anglican–Roman Catholic International Commission (ARCIC II) released its agreed statement *Church as Communion*. Not only did this statement explicate the ecclesiology underlying the *Final Report* of ARCIC I and *Salvation and the Church* of ARCIC II, but it also substantiated the claim that "Anglicans and Roman Catholics are already in a real though as yet imperfect communion . . ." (CC, 2; see also 47, 50, and the *Common Declaration* of October 1989).

Although the Anglican Communion and the Roman Catholic Church have not issued official evaluations of *Church as Communion*, in the first part of our report we intend to explore the implications of this communion ecclesiology because "within the perspective of communion the outstanding difficulties that remain between us will be more clearly understood and are more likely to be resolved" (CC, 2). The ARCIC consensus that our communion is "real though as yet imperfect" provides the context for investigating the issues of authority. These issues cannot be addressed adequately without collaborative discernment and implementation.

We intend this agreed report of ARC-USA to be a contribution to the healing of wounds and the sharing of gifts. In the context of our relationship, each of our churches needs to reach a more profound understanding of authority and to embody it more faithfully. Each church needs to learn better how to learn from the other. As we strive together to cooperate more fully with the Holy Spirit, we hasten "progress towards that goal which is Christ's will—the restoration of complete communion in faith and sacramental life" (Common Declaration of Paul VI and Archbishop Donald Coggin, April 29, 1977).

Concepts

In general, discussions of "communion," "local church," "particular church," and "universal church" have been hobbled by problems of definition; these are not univocal terms in theology. We Anglicans and Roman Catholics, however, share a common theology of "communion," "local church," "particular church," and "universal church" which is grounded in a common profession of faith in the Triune God who is the "divine life-giving source" of the Church. "We are thus directed to the life of God, Father, Son, and Holy Spirit, the life God wills to share with all people. There is held before us the vision of God's reign over the whole creation and of the Church as the first fruits of humankind which is drawn into that divine life through acceptance of the redemption given in Jesus Christ" (CC, 3). We rejoice in the extent to which this common theology is contributing to an emerging ecumenical consensus through such groups as the Joint Working Group (JWG) between the Roman Catholic Church and the World Council of Churches.[5] Anglicans and Roman Catholics enjoy a remarkable range of agreement that must remain the context for exploring our differences.

I. Communion

"Communion" has emerged in the ecumenical movement as the concept that best expresses the reality of the Church as diverse yet one in faith, as both local and universal (JWG, 5). An ecclesiology of communion may be found in the *Final Report* (FR, Introduction, 4), as well as the documents of the Second Vatican Council[6] and of the decennial Lambeth Conferences of bishops of the Anglican Communion.[7] We recall here, therefore, just one of the many articulations of our Anglican–Roman Catholic understanding of communion:

> For a Christian the life of *communion* means sharing in the divine life, being united with the Father, through the Son, in the Holy Spirit, and consequently to be in fellowship with all those who share in the same gift of eternal life. This is a spiritual communion in which the reality of the life of the world to come is already present. But it is inadequate to speak only of an invisible spiritual reality as the fulfilment of Christ's will for the Church; the profound communion fashioned by the Spirit requires visible expression. The purpose of the visible ecclesial community is to embody and promote this spiritual communion with God (cf. nos. 16-24). (CC, 43; see also the biblical and theological bases for this understanding in 6-11)

II. The Local Church

The church is local because:

> it is a gathering of the baptised brought together by the apostolic preaching, confessing the one faith, celebrating the one eucharist, and led by an apostolic ministry. This implies that this local church is in communion with all Christian communities in which the essential constructive elements of ecclesial life are present. (CC, 43)

In this we agree with the Joint Working Group between the Roman Catholic Church and the World Council of Churches who describe a local church as "a community of baptized believers in which the Word of God is preached, the apostolic faith confessed, the sacraments are celebrated, the redemptive work of Christ for the world is witnessed to, and a ministry of episkope exercised by bishops or other ministers is serving the community" (JWG, 15).

The Anglican Communion and the Roman Catholic Church most often use the term "diocese" to refer to the local church, and that is the usage we have followed in this report. The Eucharist actualizes and expresses the local church as the several parishes gather around the bishop and celebrate the Eucharist in obedience to Jesus' command to "do this in memory of me" (Luke 22:19; cf. 1 Cor. 11:24-25).

We agree, then, that the whole church is present in the local church in that "each local church is rooted in the witness of the apostles and entrusted with the apostolic mission" (FR, *Authority in the Church*, I, 8). We recognize that in a "particular church . . . the one, holy, catholic, and apostolic church is truly present and operative" (CD, no. 11; see also LG, no. 23).

"For churches of the 'Catholic' tradition the bishop is essential for the understanding and structure of a local church" (JWG, 15-16). In the tradition that we share, a parochial congregation sees in its bishop a personal sign and expression of its continuance in the apostolic tradition and a personal link to all the other local churches which confess and live by the apostolic faith. As successor to the apostles, the bishop is the primary liturgical presider, the primary preacher, and the primary teacher. Each parish depends on its being in communion with the bishop as the unitive sign of its life of witness to the Gospel.

III. The Universal Church

The Church is universal because it is sent by the risen Christ in the power of the Holy Spirit to proclaim the Good News throughout the world to *every* person and "to unite in one eucharistic fellowship men and women of *every* race, culture, and social condition in *every* generation" (CC, 34; italics added). The Eucharist actualizes and expresses the Church's unity across time and space since those who share in it have "one Lord, one faith, one baptism, one God and Father of all" (Eph. 4:5-6a).

> For all the local churches to be *together in communion*, the one visible communion which God wills, it is required that all the essential constitutive elements of ecclesial communion are present and mutually recognized in each of them. Thus the visible communion between these Churches is complete and

their ministers are in communion with each other. This does not necessitate precisely the same canonical ordering; diversity of canonical structures is part of the acceptable diversity which enriches the one communion of all the Churches. (CC, 43; cf. CC, 45, quoted in footnote 15)

The church is universal, therefore, not simply as the aggregate of all the local churches. Rather, the Church is universal in virtue of the one Christian faith, realized in various ways. Again, our Anglican–Roman Catholic consensus converges with that of the Joint Working Group: "The universal church is the communion of all the local churches united in faith and worship around the world" (JWG, 19). Because the church is situated across the world within cultures which transcend merely diocesan boundaries, both the Anglican Communion and the Roman Catholic Church have developed wider, regional structures that are intermediate between the local church and the universal church. We will examine the import of this development in a future report.

Our Anglican–Roman Catholic Consensus

From these considerations, the main elements of our remarkable consensus can be discerned. We agree that the unity of faith and the communion of the faithful must be visible, for "it is inadequate to speak only of an invisible spiritual unity as the fulfilment of Christ's will for the Church; the profound communion fashioned by the Spirit requires visible expression" (CC, 43). That is, "the gift of communion from God is not an amorphous reality but an organic unity that requires a canonical form of expression" (JWG, 42).

I. The Local and Universal Church

We also agree that the church local and the church universal are co-constitutive and co-inherent, since in a "particular church . . . the one, holy, catholic, and apostolic church is truly present and operative" (CD, 11) and the church universal is the communion of the local churches.

Thus, the *Catechism of the Catholic Church* can speak for Anglicans, too, in saying:

In Christian usage, the word "church" designates the liturgical assembly, but also the local community or the whole universal

> community of believers. These three meanings are inseparable. "The Church" is the People that God gathers in the whole world. She exists in local communities and is made real as a liturgical, above all a Eucharistic, assembly. She draws her life from the word and the Body of Christ and so herself becomes Christ's body (no. 752).[8]

The Church is, therefore, *both* local and universal. The church local is not merely a subdivision of the church universal, nor is the church universal merely an aggregate of the local churches. Each is fully interdependent with the other. When the balance between local and universal is upset, there is danger for the church's institutional embodiment. The Church of Christ may appear to be a simple aggregate of local communities, or it may appear as a totality that diminishes legitimate and necessary diversities. When, however, the proper balance is kept, the Church's real catholicity is more easily seen, because the Church appears as a communion of communities whose very diversity manifests the riches of the one faith in the one God known through the one Christ.

II. The Eucharist

We also agree that the celebration of the Eucharist in communion with the bishop as the primary presider is essential, effectual, and indispensable to the life of the Church. The Eucharist, celebrated in obedience to Jesus' command "Do this in memory of me," actualizes the Church's unity and vitality in the power of the Holy Spirit. In the Eucharist the Church as local and universal is manifested and celebrated: "At every eucharistic celebration of Christian communities dispersed throughout the world, in their variety of cultures, languages, social and political contexts, it is the same one and indivisible body of Christ reconciling divided humanity that is offered to believers. In this way the Eucharist is the sacrament of the Church's catholicity in which God is glorified" (CC, 36).

III. Episcopacy

We also agree on the roles of the bishop in service of the unity of the church local and the church universal. In interdependence with the whole people of God (laity and clergy), the bishop is to symbolize, preserve, and promote the unity and mission of the local church, to foster its communion with all the local churches, and to share in leading the church into that full unity for which Christ prayed. These responsibilities are specifically enjoined on the bishops in our rites of the ordination.[9] These rites also provide that at least three bishops, themselves ordained in apostolic succession, ordain the new bishop. In this way, these rites give the Church's affirmation that the local church and its bishop belong to the communion of the whole church that is constituted and sustained by the apostolic faith. The new bishop is a sign of continuity, a personal symbol of the historic succession of the apostolic church. The new bishop now shares in the corporate responsibility of all the bishops for the unity and fidelity of the church universal. In the Episcopal Church, this responsibility is most obviously exercised in synodical, conciliar and collegial forms, such as diocesan and national councils and committees and the General Convention (including the House of Bishops) of the Episcopal Church and Lambeth Conferences of the Anglican Communion. In the Roman Catholic Church, this responsibility is most obviously exercised in diocesan synods, episcopal conferences (like the National Conference of Catholic Bishops) and ecumenical councils and synods of the Catholic Church (CC, 33; see also BEM, 29, JWG 16).

IV. Primacy

The Episcopal Church and the Roman Catholic Church share a high degree of agreement that primacy at the universal level ought to complement the collegiality of all the bishops: "If God's will for the unity in love and truth of the whole Christian community is to be fulfilled, this general pattern of the complementary primatial and conciliar aspects of *episcope* serving the *koinonia* of the churches needs to be realized at the universal level" (FR, *Authority in the Church* I, 12, 23). We further agree that universal primacy must be exercised in a manner that fosters genuine *koinonia* (FR, *Authority in the Church* I, 21): "In the context of the communion of all the Churches the episcopal ministry of a universal primate finds its role as the visible focus of unity" (CC, 45). We recognize that ARCIC I has deemed it appropriate that in any future union the universal primacy be held by the see of Rome (FR, *Authority in the Church* I, 12 and 23).[10] At the same time, we also recognize that the primacy has been and is one of the major barriers to unity—a recognition made by Pope Paul VI in his address to the members of the Secretariat for Christian Unity on April 28, 1967.[11]

V. Authentic Catholicity

In sum, we agree that the Church's authentic catholicity requires visible manifestation of the unity of faith in a communion in which the local and the universal church are interdependent and co-constitutive. The unity of the communion is effected by the Eucharist and preserved by its bishops, whose unity with each other is manifested in conciliar practice and primatial service. We are agreed that the Church's catholicity does not require ecclesial uniformity. Indeed, it is antithetical to it: "Amid all the diversity that the catholicity intended by God implies, the Church's unity and coherence are maintained by the common confession of the one apostolic faith, a shared sacramental life, a common ministry of oversight, and joint ways of reaching decisions and giving authoritative teaching" (CC, 39). Catholicity is realized in each local church's recognition of the other local churches as embracing the same Gospel, celebrating the same Eucharist, living in the same communion, and pursuing the same mission. Their mutual recognition and communion show that their diversity is compatible with the unity of faith.

Divisive Issues

While we share a significant degree of agreement on important matters of faith and order, major differences remain between us. Many—but by no means all—Anglicans and Roman Catholics will regard some or all of them as "church-dividing"; that is, differences requiring that we remain visibly separated until these differences are resolved. We hope and urge that members of both our churches approach these differences with prayer and with repentance for our churches' share in these divisions. Both churches have found that the work of ARCIC I has been a positive step toward unity, and that it has pointed the direction for further dialogue between Anglicans and Roman Catholics (SA, 8, 14).[12] In other words, at the highest levels, our two Churches remain committed to the goal of full communion and the restoration of visible unity. Even so, serious differences remain between us.

Some of these have been identified by ARCIC I: the Roman Catholic doctrine of infallibility and the Roman Catholic attribution to the pope of universal immediate jurisdiction.[13] Others have been identified by our churches in their responses to the work of ARCIC I, as in the official responses to *Final Report* which have raised questions about the degree of agreement actually reached.[14] Questions have emerged through events and developments during the time of our official dialogue, such as the ordination of women, which, among other issues, raises the question as to the authority of the church regarding the discipline and administration of the sacraments and the discernment of the signs of the times.[15] We are convinced that, no matter how serious the differences between Anglicans and Catholics on the exercise of authority in the church may appear, with the help of the Holy Spirit they can become differences which enrich, gifts to be shared with one another and with the whole Church of Christ. In fact, they *must* become so because our churches' commitment to full visible unity means that we cannot rest until contentious differences are changed into gifts.

Certain issues of authority which remain are variously refracted when they are put into the context of the Church as local and universal. We single out five areas: requirements for full communion; primacy; the balance between local and universal church; episcopacy and apostolicity; and the relations between ecumenical experience and ecumenical theology.

I. Requirements for "Full Communion"

In the same *Common Declaration* quoted near the beginning of this Report, Archbishop Runcie and Pope John Paul II reiterated that our goal is full communion, that is, confessing the one faith, embracing one baptism, celebrating the same Eucharist, living in the same communion, and pursuing the same mission of concern for others (CC, 45). In pursuit of that goal, they urged "our clergy and faithful not to neglect or undervalue that certain yet imperfect communion we already share," an echo of UR, no. 3, and FR's Introduction. The recognition that we already share a degree of communion is based upon a renewed understanding of baptism as incorporation into Christ and upon an ecclesiology of communion, according to which essential elements of the Church of Christ are shared in different degrees and ways between our churches. We have a remarkable range of agreement on the constitutive elements of "ecclesial communion," which are outlined in *Church as Communion*, 45.[16] Yet we still disagree (within each of our churches and between our two churches) on the requirements for *full* communion with each other.

Anglicans and Roman Catholics take the Second Vatican Council's dictum as a given: "in order to restore communion and unity or preserve them, one must 'impose no burden beyond what is indispensable' (Acts 15:28)" (UR, no. 18). We do not agree, however, on what is indispensable. No wonder, then, that, after recording the elements of ecclesial communion on which our churches agree (CC, 45) and reaffirming "a significant degree of doctrinal agreement" (CC, 49), ARCIC II could still say only that we are able "to recognize in each other's Church a true affinity" (CC, 49).

The Roman Catholic Church

On the one hand, the Roman Catholic Church sees itself as having a particular reality not shared by other churches, including those of the Anglican Communion. It states that the Church of Christ "subsists in the Catholic Church" (LG, no. 8) and so "it is through Christ's Catholic Church alone, which is the universal help towards salvation [*generale auxilium salutis*], that the fullness of the means of salvation can be obtained" (UR, no. 3). The *Catechism of the Catholic Church* specifies the "fullness of the means of salvation" as "correct and complete confession of faith, full sacramental life, and ordained ministry in apostolic succession" (no. 830). Baptism indeed "constitutes a sacramental bond of unity linking all who have been reborn by means of it" (UR, no. 22), but it is "oriented toward a complete profession of faith, a complete incorporation into the system of salvation such as Christ himself willed it to be, and finally, toward a complete participation in Eucharistic communion" (UR, no. 22). Thus, in his recent encyclical on ecumenism, Pope John Paul II deemed it important to say that "the Catholic Church, both in her praxis and in her solemn documents, holds that the communion of the particular churches with the church of Rome, and of their bishops with the bishop of Rome, is—in God's plan—an essential requisite of full and visible communion . . . of which the eucharist is the highest sacramental manifestation . . ." (UUS, no. 97).

On the other hand, Vatican II also teaches that reality of the Church admits of different means and degrees of participation in its fullness (LG, no. 13). As a requirement of full communion with the Catholic Church, then, must another church "accept her entire system and all the means of salvation given to her" (LG, no. 14), *as the Catholic Church understands these?* If so, what role does the "hierarchy of truths" (UR, no. 11) play here, with its notion that "neither in the life nor the teaching of the whole Church is everything presented on the same level"?[17]

There are no *a priori* answers to these questions. Instead, possible directions to take might be discerned in the common declarations between the pope and the heads of certain eastern churches, for example the Armenian Orthodox Church, the Syrian Orthodox Church, the Coptic Orthodox Church, and the Assyrian Church of the East. Two critical factors entered into the recognition of these other churches as being in very close but still imperfect communion with the Roman Catholic Church: apostolic succession in the episcopacy and the sacrament of orders. The first is a means for safeguarding the faith that comes to us from the apostles, and the second is necessary for the valid celebration of the Eucharist, the chief sign and means of the Church's unity (UR, no. 2). We reiterate here our earlier observation that "the Roman Catholic Church has been willing to join in a common declaration of faith which deliberately avoids conciliar language that has proven controversial. One such declaration was deemed sufficient to permit some sacramental sharing . . ." (SA, 30).

The Episcopal Church

In July 1997 the Episcopal Church formally accepted the *Concordat of Agreement* with the Evangelical Lutheran Church of America. This approval was based upon the Episcopal Church's recognition of "the essentials of the one catholic and apostolic faith" in the ELCA, despite their considerable canonical, liturgical, and theological differences, and upon both churches' strong commitment to the goal of full communion. Such recognition was based on the lengthy and detailed official Lutheran-Episcopal Dialogue series, and the reception of that dialogue by the Episcopal Church, culminating in resolutions of the 1982 General Convention in which the churches constituting the ELCA were "recognize[d] . . . as Churches in which the Gospel is preached and taught" (TFC, 1). Thus the way was cleared to move toward full communion: "By full communion we here understand a relationship between two distinct churches or communions. Each maintains its own autonomy and recognizes the catholicity and apostolicity of the other, and each believes the other to hold the essentials of the Christian faith" (TFC, 107, n. 2).[18]

Thus, the Episcopal Church has made clear its ecumenical "bottom line." The Chicago-Lambeth Quadrilateral (1886/1888) sets out four elements as the basis for unity: the Holy Scriptures as the rule and standard of faith; the Apostles' and Nicene Creeds as authoritative statements of faith; Baptism and Eucharist using Christ's own words of institution and elements; and the historic episcopate, locally adapted. The Episcopal Church, acting both through official resolutions and official dialogues with other churches, has acted in consistency with this Quadrilateral. In doing so, the Episcopal Church has specified precisely what it must retain to be faithful to the Gospel and what it can—and perhaps even should—forego for the sake of the unity that Christ desires for the Church.

II. Primacy and the Bishop of Rome

ARCIC I has sketched the benefits that Anglicans and Roman Catholics would gain from a common recognition of the primacy of the bishop of Rome (FR, Preface to *Authority in the Church* I). To reap these benefits, however, we must face and overcome the challenges to both churches that are linked to the role of the Bishop of Rome, whose office, as Pope John Paul II has recognized, "constitutes a difficulty for most other Christians, whose memory is marked by certain painful recollections" (UUS, no. 88).

Authority in the Church I and II, as well as the *Elucidation* of 1981, detail consensus on the basic principles of primacy reached by ARCIC I. "The *episcope* of the ordained ministry" is recognized as one of the "gifts of the Spirit for the edification of the Church" (FR *Authority in the Church I*, 5). "This pastoral authority belongs primarily to the bishop," who does not, however, act alone (FR *Authority in the Church I*, 5). Rather it is the whole community which shares in "the perception of God's will for his Church"; and so it is the whole community which "must respond to and assess the insights and teaching of the ordained ministers." Thus there is a "continuing process of discernment and response" (FR *Authority in the Church I*, 6) under the leadership and guidance of bishops who are in communion with each other. This pattern is one of synodality, collegiality, and conciliarity: a "communion of these communities with one another" (FR *Authority in the Church I*, 8). But in addition, ARCIC I states, "If God's will for the unity in love and truth of the whole Christian community is to be fulfilled, this general pattern of the complementary primatial and conciliar aspects of *episcope* serving the *koinonia* of the churches needs to be realized at the universal level" (FR *Authority in the Church I*, 23). This universal primacy is one of service:

> Primacy fulfils its purpose by helping the churches to listen to one another, to grow in love and unity, and to strive together towards the fullness of Christian life and witness; it respects and promotes Christian freedom and spontaneity; it does not seek uniformity where diversity is legitimate, or centralize administration to the detriment of local churches. A primate exercises his ministry not in isolation but in collegial association with his brother bishops. (FR *Authority in the Church I*, 21)

Further, ARCIC concludes, in light of both historical and current considerations, it is *appropriate* that in any future union a universal primacy be held by the Roman see (FR *Authority in the Church I*, 23; cf. *Authority in the Church* II, 9). Thus, ARCIC I's work on authority has provided principles for agreement on these topics. Yet problems and disagreements about the role of the Bishop of Rome in a united and universal Church remain.

One of the areas of disagreement is posed by the Roman Catholic Church's understanding of full communion that identifies communion with the Bishop of Rome as "an *essential* requisite of full and visible communion" (UUS, no. 97; italics added). "The Roman Pontiff, as the successor of Peter, is the perpetual and visible principle and foundation of the unity of the bishops and of the multitude of the faithful" (LG, no. 23; "*Romanus Pontifex, ut successor Petri, est unitatis . . . perpetuum ac visibile principium et fundamentum.*"). This understanding is reflected in the teaching of the *Catechism of the Catholic Church* that particular churches are fully catholic through their communion with the Church of Rome (no. 834).

ARCIC I accurately noted the remaining obstacle: "if it were . . . implied that as long as a church is not in communion with the bishop of Rome, it is regarded by the Roman Catholic Church as less than fully a church, a difficulty would remain" (FR *Authority in the Church* I, 24b). The Anglican Communion understands itself to be already part of the Catholic Church.[19] Further, Anglicans hold that the divisions between churches mean that full catholicity is not a characteristic of any one church.[20]

Thus, many in both churches have called for a renewed understanding of primacy in the Roman Catholic Church. Not least among these voices has been that of John Paul II himself in *Ut Unum Sint*, no. 96, in his important invitation to "church leaders and their theologians to engage with me in a patient and fraternal dialogue" on "the ways in which the papal ministry might become a service of love recognized by all Christians."

III. The Balance Between the Local and the Universal Church

Because we profess one Body and One Spirit, one hope in God's call to us, one Lord, one Faith and one Baptism, one God and Father of all (Eph. 4:4-6), our churches agree that the Church is necessarily both local and universal. A completely autonomous local church is a contradiction in terms, according to our shared understanding. We differ between and among ourselves, however, on how to best maintain and invigorate the indispensable communion of local churches.

Anglicans hold that the Church Universal is the Body of which Jesus Christ is the Head and all baptized persons are members. Within the Anglican Communion, local churches are organized into provinces, each of which is an independent church with its own primate. All the primates are in communion with the Archbishop of Canterbury. The communion of local churches in each province is symbolized by the communion of bishops with each other.

The Roman Catholic Church holds that the Church of Christ "subsists in the [Roman] Catholic Church which is governed by the successor of Peter and by the bishops in communion with him" (LG, no. 8). Hence, the Petrine office is an indispensable element of the mutual coinherence of the universal church and the local church. Communion with the bishop of Rome symbolizes and actualizes the unity of the church.

Thus, in the theology and practice of the Church, Anglicans tend to emphasize conciliarity, while Roman Catholics tend to emphasize primacy. Each of these emphases brings with it certain gifts. But each also presents certain challenges. As ARCIC I noted, "although primacy and conciliarity are complementary elements of *episcope* it has often happened that one has been emphasized at the expense of the other, even to the point of serious imbalance. When churches have been separated from one another, this danger has been increased. The *koinonia* of the churches requires that a proper balance be preserved between the two with the responsible participation of the whole people of God" (FR *Authority in the Church* I, 22).

Many Anglicans have called for a renewed understanding and a reformed exercise of conciliarity in the Anglican Communion. The Lambeth Conferences have repeatedly stated that "resolutions passed by a Lambeth conference do not have legislative authority in any province until they have been approved by the provincial synod of the province" (as quoted in SA, 7). How then, Anglicans ask, can the Church be truly one and catholic if each province of the Communion may determine matters of faith without the assent of the other provinces and the Archbishop of Canterbury—and sometimes even in the face of their disapproval? A common liturgy, a common heritage, and bonds of affection with the See of Canterbury may not be sufficient to sustain authentic communion and to render it visible. And the various international structures of the Anglican Communion which function as instruments of communion—the office of the Archbishop of Canterbury, the Primates' Meeting, the Anglican Consultative Council, and the Lambeth Conference—individually and together lack formal authority to speak definitively to and for the Communion.

For instance, neither the Porvoo Agreement among the Anglican and Lutheran Churches of Northern Europe, nor the proposed Concordat between the Episcopal Church in the USA and the Evangelical Lutheran Church in America, require the prior or the subsequent approval of the whole Anglican Communion to become operative and binding. While these agreements are significant and hopeful ecumenical breakthroughs, Roman Catholics may wonder how well they reflect and safeguard the communion of the Anglican Church. In this light, we greet with hope the Virginia Report of the Inter-Anglican Theological and Doctrinal Commission, in which many of the issues mentioned here are addressed, and the increasing significance of the Anglican Consultative Council, with its synodal relationship of bishops, other clergy, and laity. We also look forward to the studies urged by the 1998 Lambeth Conference, which are expected to clarify how the structures of the Anglican Communion may more effectively express the balance between local and universal church.

On the other hand, the Roman Catholic Church faces continuing concerns about the exercise of primacy by the Bishop of Rome, as that may restrict the legitimate autonomy of local churches. The Roman Catholic position that the pope possesses supreme, ordinary, universal, and immediate jurisdiction over the whole church is not acceptable to Anglicans as long as the limits to that jurisdiction remain unclear (*Authority in the Church*, in FR I, 24d; cf. *Authority in the Church*, in FR II, 18-22).[21] Anglicans see the need for "further discussion of the relation between primacy and episcopal collegiality" (ER, 66) in order to be assured that primacy not "be exercised heteronomously, to the detriment, rather than to the welfare of the Body of Christ" (ER, 66).[22] Such discussions could be devoted to issues such as the norms and procedures for selecting bishops, relations between a diocesan bishop and officials of the Holy See, and the theological nature and authority of episcopal conferences in relation to the Roman See and to local bishops. Pope John Paul II's invitation to "church leaders and their theologians to engage" with him in dialogue on the universal primacy exercised in service to the unity of the Church in *Ut Unum Sint* (no. 96) may help to stimulate such discussion.

The Church's mission and witness are effective to the extent that its local and universal actualizations work to nourish and complete each other. Ecclesial structures, policies, and practices can diminish or obscure the unity of the Church, making faith in Christ seem to be a divisive, not a reconciling, power. On the other hand, ecclesial structures, policies, and practices can inhibit local churches from exercising their proper autonomy in living the Gospel in their particular circumstances. Then the authentic fullness of the Church's faith is obscured. So the challenge that faces both our churches is to renew our structures, policies, and practices so that the proper balance between the church local and the church universal can be realized.

IV. Episcopacy and Apostolicity

Anglicans and Roman Catholics share the catholic understanding of the role of the bishop in the local church (see above; cf. JWG, 16). While "differences between World Communions are connected with the role and place of the bishop in relation to the local church" (JWG, 15), these differences do not divide our two churches.

Furthermore, as part of the worldwide Anglican Communion, the Episcopal Church believes that episcopacy is one element among many which together preserve the church's apostolicity. These elements include "Scripture, Tradition, Creeds, the Ministry of the Word and Sacraments, the witness of saints, and the *consensus fidelium*, which is the continuing experience of the Holy Spirit through His faithful people in the Church."[23] The Roman Catholic Church believes that "what was handed on by the apostles comprises everything that serves to make the people of God live their lives in holiness and increase their faith. In this way, the church, in its doctrine, life, and worship, perpetuates and transmits to every generation all that it itself is, all that it believes" (DV, no. 8). Thus, for both churches, not the bishops alone, but the entire church hands on the apostolic tradition. However, each church gives different weight to the role of the episcopate in the transmission of the apostolic heritage.

The Roman Catholic Church holds that there is an essential role for bishops: episcopacy is not the sole carrier of apostolicity, but it is the primary carrier. DV, no. 7, reflects this conviction in teaching that "in order to keep the gospel forever whole and alive . . . the apostles left bishops as their successors, 'handing over their own teaching role to them [*suum locum magisterii*].'" DV, no. 10, states, "the task of giving an authoritative interpretation of the Word of God, whether in its written form or in the form of Tradition, has been entrusted to the living teaching office of the Church alone. Its authority in this matter is exercised in the name of Jesus Christ." In Roman Catholic understanding, this teaching office is vested in the episcopate. In line with this, the Roman Catholic Church's official response to the *Final Report* noted its reservation: "the unbroken lines of episcopal succession and apostolic teaching stand in causal relationship to each other" (RFR, 27).

As noted above, Anglicans hold that episcopacy is one element among many that together ensure the church's fidelity to the apostolic inheritance. While the Chicago Quadrilateral (1886) states that episcopacy is "essential to the restoration of unity among the divided branches" of the

Church, and though the Lambeth Quadrilateral (1888) does not identify episcopacy as essential, still Lambeth 1888 terms episcopacy as "a *basis* on which approach may be with God's blessing made towards" unity among divided churches.[24]

For Anglicans, the episcopate is not necessarily the primary carrier of apostolicity. The Episcopal Church holds that apostolic ministry resides with all Christians by virtue of their baptism. Ordained ministries exist "to serve, lead and enable this ministry" (PU, 4). Among the ordained, bishops are to be "the focus and personal symbols of this inheritance as they preach and teach the Gospel and summon the people of God to their mission of worship and service" (PU, 4). Both the teaching office and the governance of the church are conciliar. Thus, it is the General Convention of the Episcopal Church, not the House of Bishops alone, that states the teachings and canon law of the church, including canons specifying how bishops, priests, and deacons are to be disciplined.

Where the historic episcopate is absent, other ecclesial qualities may be recognized as indicating apostolicity. Thus, in the case of the Evangelical Lutheran Church in America, the Episcopal Church found that the basic teaching of the ELCA is "consonant with the Gospel and is sufficiently compatible with the teaching of [the Episcopal] Church" (TFC, 1) to warrant movement toward full communion with the ELCA. Because such full communion would eventually include the historic episcopate, the Episcopal Church was able to envision temporarily suspending its long-standing restriction of ministry in this case only.[25] This suspension was envisioned as preserving, not impairing, apostolicity. In light of the Roman Catholic Church's understanding of episcopacy, however, it is unlikely that the Roman Catholic Church would find itself authorized to enact a similar suspension.[26]

In sum, we are in significant agreement that bishops are successors to the apostles and hold the teaching office and the governance of the church. However, our two churches differ significantly in that the Roman Catholic Church sees bishops in apostolic succession as essential to apostolicity, while the Episcopal Church sees bishops as one important element of apostolicity. Further, the Roman Catholic church reserves the authoritative teaching office and governance of the church to its bishops, while the Episcopal Church holds that both functions reside with its bishops in council with other clergy and the laity. While these differences are significant, it is not yet clear whether or not they are church-dividing. Therefore, the relation of episcopacy and apostolicity is an area that requires further theological reflection within the context of the significant agreement we already share.

V. Ecumenical Experience and Ecumenical Theology

This Report has highlighted the scope of the "real though as yet imperfect communion" between Catholics and Episcopalians in the United States. The long and continuous work of Anglican–Roman Catholic Consultation in the United States reflects our two churches' eagerness for unity. Some members of ARC-USA have also been members of ARCIC. Over the course of more than three decades, the "real though as yet imperfect communion" our churches share has grown more extensive and deep in our local churches through shared Bible study and prayer, collaboration in service to society, interchurch marriages, covenants between Roman Catholic and Episcopal parishes, and covenants between Roman Catholic and Episcopal dioceses. Through such ecumenical experience, Episcopalians and Roman Catholics have come to recognize in each other a shared faith which issues in shared mission and service and which shapes their daily lives and their hopes for themselves, their families, their communities, and the world in which they live. Such experience not only points toward the future unity of the Church. It already manifests it. And the limitations and imperfections of the communion which we already share—so wrenchingly evident in the inability of people who work, study, and pray together to share the Eucharist together regularly—further fuel the desire for fuller communion—with each other and with the one God and the one Lord.

These experiences of unity, of communion, are not accidents. We hold that the work of the Holy Spirit can be discerned in them. It is, therefore, incumbent upon Church leaders to attend to what the Spirit may be saying and calling us to by means of these experiences. It is incumbent on us to reflect more deeply on these experiences in our dialogue on matters of faith and order. Clarification of doctrinal matters is not an end in itself, but a means to the larger end of recovering and receiving the communion which is God's will for the Church. Official dialogue and the lived experience of the members of our churches must enrich and inform each other.

Since the communion that we already share in the United States may not yet be reflected on the universal level, the leaders of our churches must ask how they can nurture communion in local churches without diminishing communion with the universal church as our churches understand this. What further ways are there for members of our churches to express their common faith in worship, in study of Scripture, in service, in common life? In certain areas of the United States, Eucharistic sharing is a strongly felt need, and its lack, a frustration. Under what conditions might some regular sharing of the Eucharist be authorized? In both our churches, church leaders at all levels have vivid and direct experience of the great degree of convergence our churches have reached. How might these persons more effectively convey their own experience of catholicity and of communion which is real though imperfect?

Conclusion

In this Report, we have highlighted some of the many ways in which the Anglican Communion and the Roman Catholic Church have recognized and understood the "real though as yet imperfect communion" that we already share. We have given some of the ecclesiology and theology that underlie this communion, showing that our remarkable consensus is not merely an accident, but a manifestation of our faith as it is expressed in both churches by the grace of God and the work of the Holy Spirit. We rejoice that our two churches share a converging theology of the local and universal church, the Eucharist, episcopacy, primacy, and authentic catholicity.

We also recognize that there continue to be serious theological issues that divide us. Even so, our two Churches remain committed to the goal of full communion and the restoration of visible unity. For this goal to be attained, each of our two churches, and our two churches together, must carefully and prayerfully come to deeper understanding of the requirements for full communion, primacy, the balance between local and universal church, episcopacy and apostolicity, and the relation between ecumenical experience and ecumenical theology. While recognizing the complexity of these problems and the pain that our continued division causes, we also live in that hope that, by the work of the Holy Spirit, differences that divide will be transformed into differences that enrich our common faith and life.

Future Prospects

In order to address some of the theological issues that contribute to our continued division, ARC-USA has undertaken a long-term project of study and dialogue on ecclesiology and authority. We have begun by studying how the relation of the local and the universal church is understood; this Report is one result of that study. We are currently engaged in examining the national experience of our churches as hierarchical catholic churches in a democratic secular environment, and in studying the consensus Anglicans and Roman Catholics already share on the Eucharist. We expect this work to aid us in developing new ecclesial and theological perspectives on authority which, we hope and pray, will contribute to greater convergence between our churches on these important matters.

Our collaborative study is part of a multifaceted discussion of ecclesiology and authority that may lead to significant shifts in the understanding and practice of both churches. Among the more significant contributions to this conversation are the responses to Pope John Paul II's invitation to conversation on the papacy in service to Christian unity, and, in particular, the response of the House of Bishops of the Church of England; the symposia on the papacy held in Rome in December 1996 and December 1997; Pope John Paul II's *Apostolos Suos* (1998) on the theology and authority of episcopal conferences; the Virginia Report of the Inter-Anglican Doctrinal Commission; the Resolutions of the 1998 Lambeth Conference which commend this report to the Anglican Communion for study; and ARCII's May 1999 statement *The Gift of Authority*.

Some of the issues that face us are theological. Clearly, the divine gift of communion is most fully realized in the celebration of the Eucharist. The limitations of our "real though as yet imperfect" communion are experienced most widely and painfully in our inability to celebrate the Eucharist fully and completely together. For this reason, ARC-USA is currently examining the agreements we have already reached. With many others engaged in this conversation, we urge shared prayer on more and more occasions.

Some of the issues that face us are practical. Within our respective traditions, communion among members of our churches may be obscured and diminished when the Eucharist is celebrated with less than the full and active participation of all, according to their distinctive roles. For example, the existence of very large dioceses may diminish communion when the bishop is more an administrator than a primary presider or shepherd (CD, 22-23). Communion may also be obscured and diminished in situations where the closing or clustering of parishes damages communicants' recognition of the reality of the church in a particular place. Likewise, communities that are deprived of the celebration of the Eucharist for lack of a priest will have more difficulty in perceiving and living out their full ecclesial reality. We will explore the consequences of such phenomena and their implications for our movement toward full communion at a later stage in our ongoing study of authority in the church. We hope to profit from the contribution of others who seek to clarify these issues.

Communion may also be obscured and diminished when individuals enter into unauthorized sharing of the Eucharist. Our two churches currently have distinct policies on who may receive the Eucharist and under what circumstances. At the same time, members of our churches are experiencing such a high degree of communion of faith, service, and life that sharing the Eucharist seems to many not only desirable but warranted. But "it is no service to the unity of Christ's Church when one group contributes to the weakening of loyalty and undermining of discipline of another. Dealing honestly with the problems raised . . . is a pastoral responsibility of the church" (SES). It is incumbent upon church leaders at every level to address this situation with the utmost pastoral skill and with the greatest respect for the teachings of both churches. Pastoral skill and respect are both elements of our movement into full communion, a movement in which we must follow the guidance of the Spirit, as difficult as that may be at some points to discern.

Our proximity offers us many opportunities for growth in communion which even now is real yet imperfect. Among the salient practical issues posed is the question of joint decision making. If our communion is real, our churches must continually examine their consciences according to the famous question posed by Faith and Order's third world conference at Lund, Sweden, in 1952: "Should not our Churches ask themselves . . . whether they should not act together *in all matters* except those in which deep differences of conviction *compel* them to act separately?" (emphases added). This imperative has been echoed by John Paul II in *Ut Unum Sint*, no. 96, and, earlier, in the Roman Catholic Church's 1993 Ecumenical Directory. It has also been reaffirmed in reports and resolutions of various Lambeth Conferences,[27] as well as in the policies and practices of local churches within the Anglican Communion.

Yet for each church the task remains of making decisions now in ways that render our communion as visible as possible, at the local, national, and international levels. Both churches continue to seek effective ways of structuring our diversity. Our churches must consider what we can do if we find that our decision-making processes are irreconcilable. What *should* we do? Finally, only our deepened communion and collaboration will enable us to answer these questions and find the way to the full unity to which we are called. Yet we are convinced that even now exploration of how we currently answer these questions may help us recognize new ways toward full unity.

It is undeniable that "the precise shape the united church of the future should take and the forms of diversity it could embrace is an important but still unresolved question for all Christian communities" (JWG, 49). We ourselves do not yet see that shape, but we are confident that the Holy

Spirit will lead the Church into all truth. We already rejoice in the Spirit's having brought us to the remarkable degree of communion and agreement that we have highlighted in the first parts of this Report. We hope and pray that our work, present and future, may contribute to the resolution of this question and hasten the unity for which Christ our Lord prayed—in order that the world may believe.

NOTES

1. The Anglican–Roman Catholic Consultation in the USA (ARC-USA) was planned jointly in 1965 and first met in 1966. The Most Rev. Michael Ramsey, Archbishop of Canterbury, and Pope Paul VI established the official international dialogue in 1966. Subsequent to the work of a joint preparatory commission, the Anglican–Roman Catholic International Commission (ARCIC) first met officially in 1970.
2. ER, 66; VR.
3. CD, 36-38; *Code of Canon Law* (1983), cc. 439-446, 447-459.
4. GofA.
5. See JWG, Sixth Report, in GA II, 862-875.
6. See LG, no. 8, UR, no. 3, and CD as well as the more recent UUS, no. 49, and Directory, 9-17.
7. "An Appeal to All Christian People," Resolution 9, Lambeth Conference 1920; "The Anglican Communion: Its Meaning, Organization, and Future Policy," Lambeth Conference 1948; "Full Communion and Intercommunion," Resolution 14, Lambeth 1958; "Anglican–Roman Catholic International Commission," Resolution 8, Lambeth 1988; The Agros Report of the Ecumenical Advisory Group of the Anglican Communion in preparation for Lambeth 1998.
8. See also the sections on *The Church and the Ministry* in "An Outline of the Faith," commonly called "the Catechism" in BCP: "The Church is one, because it is one Body, under one Head, our Lord Jesus Christ. . . . The mission of the Church is to restore all people to unity with God and each other in Christ. . . . The Church pursues its mission as it prays and worships, proclaims the Gospel, and promotes justice, peace, and love. . . . The Church carries out its mission through the ministry of all its members. . . . The ministers of the Church are lay persons, bishops, priests, and deacons. . . ."
9. See, e.g., "The Examination" in *The Ordination of a Bishop*, in The Roman Pontifical, vol. 2, trans. International Commission on English in the Liturgy (Rome: Vatican Polyglot Press, 1978).
10. See also Elucidation (1981), 8.

11. AAS 59 (1967) 497-498.
12. See RFR, nos. 1, 5, 30, 31, and Resolution 8, Lambeth 1988.
13. FR *Authority in the Church* I, 24; *Authority in the Church* II, 9 and 15.
14. ER of 1987 and "The Official Roman Catholic Response to the Final Report of ARCIC I (1991)" in *Common Witness to the Gospel. Documents on Anglican–Roman Catholic Relations 1983-1995,* ed. Jeffrey Gros, E. Rozanne Elder, and Ellen K. Wondra (Washington, DC: United States Conference of Catholic Bishops, 1997), 69-77. See also the report of the National Ecumenical Consultation of the Episcopal Church (November 5-9, 1978) (The Detroit Report) and the National Conference of Catholic Bishops' "Evaluation of the ARCIC Final Report" in *Origins* 14:25 (December 6, 1984): 409-412.
15. ARCIC *Elucidation* 1979, 5: "This question [about conferring priestly ordination on women] puts into clear relief the need to reach an understanding of how the Church authoritatively discerns the teaching and practice which constitute the apostolic faith entrusted to us." Homily of Pope John Paul II during the Solemn Vespers service celebrated with the Archbishop of Canterbury at St. Gregory's Church on the Caelian Hill, Rome, December 5, 1996. See also "Dogmatic and Pastoral Concerns," Lambeth 1988, 136-146; and "Report of the Archbishop of Canterbury's Commission on Communion and Women in the Episcopate," 1989 (The Eames Report).
16. CC, 45, states that ecclesial communion is "rooted in the confession of the one apostolic faith, revealed in the Scriptures, and set forth in the Creeds. It is founded upon one baptism. The one celebration of the eucharist is its pre-eminent expression and focus. It necessarily finds expression in shared commitment to the mission entrusted by Christ to his Church. It is a life of shared concern for one another in mutual forbearance, gentleness, and love; in the placing of the interests of the others above the interests of self; in solidarity with the poor and the powerless; and in the sharing of gifts both material and spiritual (cf. Acts 2:44). Also constitutive of life in communion is acceptance of the same basic moral values, the sharing of the same vision of humanity created in the image of God and recreated in Christ, and the common confession of the one hope in the final consummation of the Kingdom of God."
17. SPCU, "Reflections and Suggestions Concerning Ecumenical Dialogue (1970)," IV, 4b; quoted in JWG, Appendix I.
18. This recognition is in accord with the Chicago-Lambeth Quadrilateral (1886/1888) and subsequent statements by the Lambeth Conferences of 1958 and 1988, the latter of which commended to churches in the Communion the 1983 Cold Ash statement, in GA II, 2-10.
19. LC 20; LC 78.
20. LC 20; "Report on Ecumenical Relations," Lambeth Conference 1988, esp. 29-35.

21. ARCIC II's GofA (May 1999) pursues these questions and is now under study in both churches.
22. Resolution III.8, h and i, Lambeth Conference 1998.
23. 1948 Lambeth Conference Committee Report on "The Anglican Communion," 84-86.
24. BCP, 876-877; italics added.
25. The BCP's Preface to the Ordination Rites states, "No persons are allowed to exercise the offices of bishop, priest, or deacon in the Church unless they are so ordained [by solemn prayer and the laying on of episcopal hands], or have already received such ordination with the laying on of hands by bishops who are themselves duly qualified to confer Holy Orders" (BCP, 510). It is this clause which is to be suspended temporarily, and in the case of the ELCA only.
26. See, for example, LG, no. 22.
27. See, e.g., Resolution 50 of the Lambeth Conference of 1948, Resolution 44 of the Lambeth Conference of 1968, "What Is the Church For?" (Document 20 of the Lambeth Conference of 1978), "Ecumenical Relations" (Document 24 of the Lambeth Conference of 1988), and Resolution 13 of the Lambeth Conference of 1988.

DOCUMENT 16

RESPONSE TO THE ANGLICAN–ROMAN CATHOLIC INTERNATIONAL COMMISSION'S *THE GIFT OF AUTHORITY*

Anglican–Roman Catholic Consultation in the United States of America, 2003

The Gift of Authority at This Moment of History

1. The world situation has changed radically since the publication of *The Gift of Authority* in 1999. This change has affected the context in which we now read the agreed statement of ARCIC. We nevertheless believe that the commitment to ecumenical relations among Christians has a positive contribution to make in times of conflict and vulnerability. In this context the bishops of our two churches have expressed their concern for peace in our country and in the community of nations.

2. The members of ARC-USA, representing our two churches, have met for their regular semi-annual meeting, March 27-30, 2003, to formulate their assessment of *The Gift of Authority* and to suggest ways in which our Churches ought to move ahead, theologically and practically, toward the goal of full communion. In this endeavor we hope to further one of the purposes of ecumenism: to ensure on earth what St. Augustine called *tranquillitas ordinis,* the tranquility of order (cf. John Paul II, *Message for the Celebration of the World Day of Peace 2003*, 6).

Strengths of *The Gift of Authority*

3. *The Gift of Authority* founds its reflections on authority upon the Christological substance of the Gospel: the Good News of Jesus Christ who is God's "Yes" to humanity and humanity's "Amen" to God's Truth. Though the confession of Jesus Christ is certainly present in other ARCIC statements, it is nowhere underscored in such a deep and creative way. We find this confession especially important at a time when the ecumenical movement itself risks shipwreck because of what the late Jean-Marie Tillard characterizes as "an erosion of the basis of koinonia by a fragmentation of faith in Christ" ("Ecumenism: The Church's Costly Hope," *One in Christ* 35 [1999], 224).

4. Thus *The Gift of Authority* insightfully reconfigures the consideration of scripture and tradition by presenting them as joint witness to Jesus Christ who is the fulfillment of all God's promises. Hence Christianity stands forth clearly as a religion not of the book, but of the person of Jesus Christ. From this acknowledgement the statement's welcome doxological and mystagogical tone proceeds.

5. All authority in the Church, whether the *sensus fidei* of the whole people of God or the *episcope* of the bishops, is in service to this witness of faith to Jesus Christ who alone is the Light of the nations—*lumen gentium*. He is the Truth of God which the whole Church receives and which it proclaims.

6. *The Gift of Authority* recognizes that this witness of faith needs visible vehicles of synodical discernment and articulation: conciliar, collegial, and primatial (cf. no. 45). It rightly calls for the active participation of the whole body of the faithful in this discernment, drawing upon that *sensus fidei* which is itself a gift of the Holy Spirit. But the statement, faithful to our common episcopal tradition, accords a special role and responsibility to the bishops, who exercise *episcope*, the "ministry of memory" (no. 30) and of witness within the community. The collegiality of their ministry is rightly emphasized.

7. Since the whole Church is in service to the witness of Jesus Christ, the promise of Christ that the Spirit will maintain the Church in truth grounds the possibility for authoritative judgments regarding the content of the faith that are preserved from error (no. 42). Here, *The Gift of Authority's* Christological perspective adds further depth to its consideration of this issue.

8. *The Gift of Authority* sketches a rich ecclesiology of communion, in which the many and varied gifts of the community are integrated into the Gift who is Jesus Christ himself to the honor and glory of God.

Concerns Regarding *The Gift of Authority*

9. The idealism and optimism of the document, though praiseworthy, do not take sufficiently into account the concrete difficulties on the path to full agreement regarding the matters under discussion or the historical instances of authority's abuse.

10. We find that the prominent role and theological understanding of the office of bishop in *The Gift of Authority* are at a remove from our actual experience, though for different reasons for Roman Catholics and Anglicans. On the side of Anglicans the document appears to exaggerate the independent role of the bishops and downplay the role of priests and laity. On the Roman Catholic side, the document seems not to take into account the exercise of Roman supervision that on occasion tends to limit the ability of bishops to serve in the role as the vicars of Christ in their own local churches.

11. Furthermore, the role and participation of the laity, while affirmed, is not probed in depth, and what is affirmed does not fully reflect the experience of either of our churches. For example, *The Gift of Authority*, no. 39, says that the decisions of an Anglican diocesan synod can stand only with the diocesan bishop's consent; this is not the case with regard to diocesan conventions and councils of the Episcopal Church. On the Roman Catholic side the document understates the relative lack of structures that would enable effective lay participation in decision making (cf. nos. 54, 57).

12. The document affirms the importance of "synodality" in our two traditions (no. 34) but does not sufficiently explore the difference in the two churches' history and present experience. In both traditions the full potential of synods has not been adequately realized. For example, in the Roman Catholic Church the present code of canon law limits the decision-making authority in diocesan synods to the bishop. In the Anglican Communion the unilateral actions of individual bishops, dioceses, and provinces undermine the reality of synodality. Such differences require further examination.

13. The restoration of communion with the bishop of Rome as universal primate is an ecclesiological goal that many Anglicans would welcome, but its present implementation would be premature since Anglicans and Roman Catholics are still looking for the reformed understanding and practice of primacy that Pope John Paul II both acknowledges as needful and encourages (*Ut Unum Sint*, nos. 95-96).

14. Paragraph 42 in *The Gift of Authority* explains what is meant "when it is affirmed that the church may teach infallibly." It adds that "such

infallible teaching is at the service of the Church's indefectibility." However, the theological understanding and ecclesial implications of the doctrine of infallibility and its relationship to indefectibility need to be further clarified. Anglicans have serious reservations about the doctrine of infallibility.

15. Paragraphs 60 to 62 call attention to Universal Primacy as a gift that the Roman Catholic Church can share with others churches. The document does not place commensurate emphasis on the rich Anglican tradition of lay participation in the deliberations of the church, which is also an important gift to be shared.

Ecclesiological Issues Requiring Joint Investigation

16. In seeking to take further steps toward full communion, we need to continue the exploration that was begun in *Church as Communion* (ARCIC II, 1991) of how our churches understand full communion. What would be the essential elements of "full communion" between the Anglican Communion and the Roman Catholic Church?

17. What would full communion between the Anglican Churches and the Bishop of Rome necessarily involve? How would a papal primacy be exercised fully according to the principles of communion, collegiality, and subsidiarity?

18. Could a restored communion be patterned on the communion that existed between the Eastern Churches and the Church of Rome during the first millennium? Could the restoration of communion between the Anglican Communion and the Bishop of Rome be accomplished in such a way that the traditions of the Anglican Churches would be maintained and the Anglican Churches would enjoy a relative autonomy in relationship to Roman jurisdiction?

19. Ecclesial reception has played a role in the recognition that certain doctrinal decisions have been preserved from error. Could further ecumenical study of that role contribute to convergence on the notion of infallible teaching in the service of the church's indefectibility?

Concrete Steps for Participating Together in Interim Structures of Authority

20. *The Gift of Authority* proposes that, even before full communion, our two Churches "make more visible the *koinonia* we already have." ARCUSA agrees that sharing in interim structures of authority at the international and the national level would be positive in the current situation

and in the future. As representatives of our two Churches in the United States, we suggest an expansion of the "specific practical aspects of sharing *episcope*" proposed in nos. 58-59.

21. Ad Limina *Visits*

Among the concrete steps suggested in the document is that Anglican bishops now join their Roman Catholic colleagues on *ad limina* visits to the Holy See. We agree that such joint visits would now testify to three things:

1. The relationship of our Churches has moved to a deeper, more positive level in the "real, but imperfect communion that we already share."
2. Ecumenical solidarity at this time of vulnerability is real and visible.
3. The bishops of both of our Churches need opportunities for deeper acquaintance with one another at this moment of rapid transition in the world situation.

22. *Synods of Bishops*

We recommend the regular participation of some Anglican bishops in the Synods of Bishops of the Roman Catholic Church.

23. *The Lambeth Conference*

At the Lambeth Conference, Roman Catholic visitors are currently designated as "Ecumenical Participants." We propose that, until full communion is achieved, Roman Catholic bishops be designated as "Roman Catholic Bishop-Delegates" with voice and participation in all Conference activities, but with no vote.

24. *The Anglican Consultative Council*

We propose that Roman Catholic clergy and laity, as well as bishops, be invited to the meetings of the Anglican Consultative Council.

25. *Episcopal Church House of Bishops*

We propose that Roman Catholic bishops be invited to attend the meetings of the House of Bishops of the Episcopal Church as "Roman Catholic Bishop-Delegates," with voice and participation in all House of Bishops activities, but no vote.

26. *United States Conference of Catholic Bishops*

We propose that Episcopal bishops be invited to attend the meetings of the United States Conference of Catholic Bishops as "Episcopal Bishop-Delegates," with voice and participation in all conference activities, but no vote.

27. *Episcopal Church House of Deputies*

We propose that Roman Catholic clergy and laity be invited to the meetings of the House of Deputies of the General Convention of the Episcopal Church as "Roman Catholic-Delegates," with voice and participation in all House of Deputies activities, but no vote.

28. *Plenary Councils and Diocesan Synods*

We propose that Episcopal clergy and laity be invited to participate in Roman Catholic plenary councils and diocesan synods as "Episcopal Church-Delegates," with voice and participation in all activities, but no vote.

Conclusion

29. We recognize that some of the thorny theological issues raised by *The Gift of Authority* have not been addressed in our response. We are convinced, however, that the most productive context for dealing with outstanding divisive issues is a relationship of mutual understanding, trust, and affection. Friends will always take each other's statements in the most positive light. Therefore, we are grateful for *The Gift of Authority's* invitation to deepen our relationship. We remain strongly committed to this effort.

BAPTIST-CATHOLIC

Editors' Note: *The Conversation between these two largest U.S. Christian communities ended in 2001 after thirty years. The relationships continue on local, congregational level. Earlier conversations had also produced reports (see BU, 45-51, and GC I, 557-566).*

Document 17

REPORT ON SACRED SCRIPTURE

Southern Baptist–Roman Catholic Conversation, 1999

Sixteen scholars and church leaders appointed by the Interfaith Evangelism of the North American Mission Board of the Southern Baptist Convention and the Bishops' Committee on Ecumenical and Interreligious Affairs of the National Conference of Catholic Bishops have been meeting in conversation for five years. The purpose of our conversation has been to understand one another better through honest mutual exchange and to clarify our mutual understandings of the nature and authority of the Holy Bible.

This first report of our conversation is directed to Interfaith Evangelism of the North American Mission Board of the Southern Baptist Convention and the Bishops' Committee on Ecumenical and Interreligious Affairs of the National Conference of Catholic Bishops. While we share a great deal in our Christian faith concerning the authority and truth of the Bible, this report is not intended as a confessional statement either for our churches or from the participants in the conversation. It is an account of the topics we have discussed, the processes we have followed and the clarification of terms at which we have arrived. While fully cognizant of our serious differences, our goal has been truth and clarity in charity. Our common and ongoing quest for the truth of Christ has deepened our appreciation for one another and strengthened our love for the Holy Scriptures.

Southern Baptists and Roman Catholics believe in the Triune God, the Father, the Son, and the Holy Spirit, and we confess the full deity and perfect humanity of Jesus Christ. We find these truths of faith in God's written Word, the Sacred Scriptures. While our two traditions differ with regard to the extent of the biblical canon, we cherish the Sacred Scriptures, use them regularly in our worship and devotion, and seek by God's grace to understand them more clearly. On the basis of these core convictions, we addressed important issues on which Roman Catholics and Southern Baptists have differed historically, including the inspiration and authority of the Bible, its inerrancy and infallibility, the role of the Church in the interpretation of the Scriptures, and the nature and significance of historical-critical approaches to the study of the Bible.

We have met at both Roman Catholic and Southern Baptist institutions, and at each gathering we have shared together in the reading of Scripture and in common prayer. In the context of patient listening and candid sharing with one another, we have each read and reported on documents in the two traditions that illustrate our points of agreement and disagreement. Among the documents we have studied are the *Dogmatic Constitution on Divine Revelation* of the Second Vatican Council (DV; 1965), *Baptist Faith and Message* (1963), the instruction of the Pontifical Biblical Commission *The Interpretation of the Bible in the Church* (1993), the Chicago Statements on Biblical Inerrancy (1978, 1982), the *Dogmatic Constitution on the Catholic Faith* of the First Vatican Council (1870), and the Report of the Presidential Theological Study Committee (1993).

Our sessions also included study and exegesis of selected biblical texts. Included in this document is a list of key terms that we formulated with a view toward clear articulation of our points of agreement, our points of disagreement, and issues still to be considered.

We have learned a great deal from each other. We will continue this conversation on other themes that concern our Christian faith. We hope that this report will be useful to teachers and students of our Christian faith, and thus contribute to better mutual understanding and deeper devotion to the Bible.

The List of Terms

The Bible

Revelation. God's free self-communication to the world. Both Catholics and Southern Baptists agree that God is manifested in nature (Ps 19:1-4) and in the human heart (Rom 2:14-15) and reveals Himself in the books of the Old and New Testaments (2 Pt 1:20-21). For Catholics, Jesus, the incarnate Word, is the revelation of God; Scripture contains revelation, while both Scripture and Tradition witness to revelation. Southern Baptists prefer to speak simply of Scripture as the revealed, written Word of God, which is inerrant.

Word of God. The expression "Word of God" is used in at least three senses. First, Jesus, the Word made flesh, is the Word of God incarnate. Second, God's message of salvation, made known in the story of Israel and reaching its fullness in the life, death, and resurrection of Jesus, is the Word of God proclaimed. Finally, the Holy Scripture, both Old and New Testaments, is recognized as the Word of God inspired and written.

Inspiration. The belief that the biblical books were fully inspired by the Holy Spirit, so that God may be said to be the primary and ultimate author (cf. 2 Tm 3:16-17).

Inerrancy. The conviction that the Bible is "without error" in what it affirms. But there are different interpretations of what this actually means. For Southern Baptists, inerrancy means that the original biblical text was composed precisely as God inspired it and intended it to be because of God's superintendence: not just the thought comes from God, but every word with every inflection, every verse and line, and every tense of the verb, every number of the noun, and every little particle are regarded as coming from God. Scripture is "God-breathed," and God does not breathe falsehood, so the text is faithful and true in all it affirms, including the miracle accounts, the attributed authors, and the historical narratives. The 1978 and 1982 Chicago statements on biblical inerrancy are representative of this doctrine. For Roman Catholics, inerrancy is understood as a consequence of biblical inspiration; it has to do more with the truth of the Bible as a whole than with any theory of verbal inerrancy. Vatican II says that "the books of Scripture must be acknowledged as teaching firmly, faithfully, and without error that truth which God wanted put into the sacred writings for the sake of our salvation" (DV, no. 11). What is important is the qualification of "that truth" with "for the sake of our salvation."

Infallibility. For Catholics, infallibility is a charism or gift of the Spirit which belongs to the Church for faithfully expounding the deposit of faith. Vatican I (1870) taught that the Church's infallibility can be exercised when the pope speaks *ex cathedra* in defining a doctrine regarding faith or morals (DS 3074). Developing this, Vatican II (1964) said that the bishops united among themselves and with the pope can also proclaim doctrine infallibly. To such definitions the assent of the Church can never be wanting because of the activity of the Holy Spirit preserving the whole flock of Christ in unity of faith (LG, no. 25). Traditionally, Southern Baptists have understood "infallibility" to be equivalent to "inerrancy." That is to say, the Bible alone never fails to be God's perfect word. More recently, "infallibility" has been construed in a weaker and inadequate sense to mean only that the Bible accomplishes the purpose which God intended.

Canon. Refers to those books and writings recognized by the religious community or Church as being divinely inspired and thus uniquely authoritative for faith and practice. While Roman Catholics and Protestants recognize the same New Testament canon, the Catholic Old Testament canon contains seven Jewish books (1 and 2 Maccabees, Tobit, Judith, Sirach, Wisdom of Solomon, and Baruch, plus some additional parts of Daniel and Esther) found in the Greek translation of the Hebrew Scriptures used by the early church. The Reformers rejected them in the sixteenth century since they were not included in the Palestinian Jewish canon drawn up after the fall of Jerusalem. Most Protestants call them "the Apocrypha"; Catholics refer to them as the "Deuterocanonical books."

Biblical Interpretation

Historical/Historicity. Relating to or having the character of having actually happened in space and time, as distinct from myth, fable, story, or legend. Both Catholics and Southern Baptists hold that God's revelation takes place in history and develops through the biblical tradition. For example, both affirm the historicity of the gospel tradition, but they differ about the extent to which each gospel story can be affirmed as historical. Southern Baptists interpret as historical all biblical events which are clearly intended by the sacred authors to be taken as such. Catholics believe that not all biblical narratives should be understood as historical, since the sacred writers also use narratives in a symbolic way to teach religious truths.

Historical-Critical Method. A method of interpreting biblical texts which seeks to discover the "literal sense" or historical meaning of a text, using historical and literary methods of investigation, e.g., form criticism (identifying various biblical literary forms such as sayings, parables, miracle stories, pronouncements, psalms, genealogies), source criticism, redaction criticism, textual criticism, etc. Southern Baptists prefer to speak of the Grammatical-Historical Method in which these tools are employed with a commitment to biblical inerrancy.

Literal Sense. That which the inspired author intends to convey; the literal sense may be expressed poetically, prosaically, or figuratively.

Literalism. An interpretative approach which focuses only on the surface meaning of the text, without reference to authorial intent.

Fundamentalism. An early twentieth-century movement among Protestants in response to liberal Protestant theology, first marked by subscription to such doctrinal "fundamentals" as biblical inerrancy, the virgin birth, substitutionary atonement, bodily resurrection, and the second coming of Christ. In the mid-twentieth century, fundamentalism came to identify itself as strongly separationist. Outsiders came to identify fundamentalism with an anti-intellectual literalism and to extend the term to conservative non-Christian groups, such as "Islamic fundamentalists." Because of the pejorative connotations, the *Associated Press Stylebook* appropriately suggests, "In general, do not use 'fundamentalist' unless a group applies the word to itself."

ORTHODOX-CATHOLIC

Editors' Note: *After the 1989 fall of Soviet regimes in many Eastern European countries, tensions between Catholics and Orthodox resurfaced in Eastern Europe. The international theological dialogue, begun in 1980, has not been able to produce a text since 1993, making the U.S. dialogue's contribution particularly important.*

After 1989, tension over the role of Eastern Catholic Churches was central to the dialogue agenda, as the Orthodox saw it. Documents 18 and 19 deal with that issue. Because of the aforementioned international difficulties, it has been important for the U.S. dialogue to reinforce the commitments to visible unity, as shown in Documents 22 and 23. Theological issues around mutual recognition of baptism and the procession of the Holy Spirit remain unresolved between these two churches worldwide. Documents 21 and 24 contribute to these discussions. Document 20 responds to a proposal for a common Easter date for East and West.

These seven documents continue series recorded in previous volumes of this series (see BU, 223-258, and GC I, 485-504). For the original texts and those of international dialogues, please see John Borelli and John Erickson, eds., The Quest for Unity *(Washington, DC: United States Catholic Conference, 1996).*

Document 18

JOINT STATEMENT OF THE UNITED STATES ORTHODOX/ROMAN CATHOLIC CONSULTATION ON TENSIONS IN EASTERN EUROPE RELATED TO "UNIATISM," 1992

The most recent (forty-third) meeting of the U.S. Orthodox/Roman Catholic Consultation at the Holy Cross Greek Orthodox School of Theology, Brookline, Massachusetts, during May 26-28, 1992, focused upon the question of "Uniatism" and reviewed a number of recent statements regarding religious conflicts in Eastern Europe. Included among these texts were the joint text of the Roman Catholic Church and Russian Orthodox Church (January 17, 1990), the "Freising Statement of the Joint International Commission for Theological Dialogue Between the Roman Catholics Church and the Orthodox Church" (June 15, 1990), our Consultation's previous joint communique on "Current Tensions between Our Churches in Eastern Europe" (October 20, 1990), the Ariccia draft statement of its Coordinating Committee on "Uniatism as a Method of Union in the Past and the Prevent Search for Full Communion" (June 15, 1991), the statement of the U.S. Orthodox and Roman Catholic Bishops Commission (September 19, 1991), and the "Message of the Primates of the Most Holy Orthodox Churches" from the fourteen primates of patriarchates and autocephalous and autonomous churches (March 15, 1992). We, the members of this Consultation, formulate this joint statement of concern.

1. Our own experience of cooperation and dialogue in North America has generally been a harmonious and fruitful one. This experience convinces us that resolution of the present difficulties will be possible only through prayer and a deepened dialogue in truth and love.

2. We recognize that it is not always possible for us to judge the accuracy of reports on abuses of justice or proselytism in distant parts of the world. We decry publication of unverified alleged events or incidents that only fan the feelings of fear and prejudice as well as inflammatory reactions to verified incidents. We also decry one-sided or prejudicial reporting on religious developments in Eastern Europe and elsewhere, which, through emotionalism or sensationalism, would tend to undercut efforts toward genuine cooperation and reconciliation. We therefore appeal to worldwide human rights' agencies and the media to lend their service for a balanced presentation of events, and we commit ourselves to the task of sharing and attempting to verify such information as we receive.

3. We recognize that, because of the burden of past history and the painful actions of governments and churches, there exist among Christians in many parts of the world, especially Eastern Europe, a high degree of resentment, antipathy, suspicion, and even fear of other Christian communities. If such attitudes are to be overcome, it is essential that our churches together formulate and implement practical recommendations, such as those prevented in the Ariccia working draft, the January 1990 agreement between the Roman Catholic Church and the Russian Orthodox Church, and elsewhere, effectively addressing the specific issues that divide us.

4. Therefore, we encourage mutual consultation at all levels, particularly before any activities are undertaken which might even inadvertently give offense to others. Such consultation would help all parties to avoid needless misunderstandings.

5. In reviewing the various documents which have dealt with recent tensions between our churches, we find that expressions like "Uniatism" have been used and understood in diverse ways. We believe that such expressions require more careful analysis. Among other things, a distinction should be made between "Uniatism" understood as an inappropriate, indeed unacceptable, model or method for church union, and "Uniatism" understood as the existence of convinced Eastern Christians who have accepted full communion with the See of Rome as part of their self-understanding as a church. "Uniatism" in the former sense is no longer accepted by either of our churches.

6. We are convinced that in countries previously under Communist oppression, as well as elsewhere, a healthy interaction between the Orthodox Church and the Roman Catholic Church or even between the Orthodox Church and the Eastern Catholic Churches could lead to important

developments in theological renewal, liturgical reform, and useful formulation of Christian social and political doctrine.

7. We recognize the importance of participating jointly in and sharing the results of theological, ecclesiastical, and historical research among clergy, seminarians, and laity, especially in countries where freedom of the press and easy access to international scholarship have been systematically hindered.

8. The present difficulties offer theologians opportunities to explore, from a new perspective, certain theological themes which have been discussed repeatedly in recent ecumenical dialogues. We are challenged, to give only two examples, to explain what "mutual recognition as sister churches" means in practice, and to explore structures needed for achieving communion among the worldwide community of local churches.

Document 19

UNIATISM, METHOD OF UNION OF THE PAST, AND THE PRESENT SEARCH FOR FULL COMMUNION, 1994

A Response of the Orthodox/Roman Catholic Consultation in the United States to the Joint International Commission for Theological Dialogue Between the Orthodox Church and the Roman Catholic Church Regarding the Balamand Document (June 23, 1993)

1. Since the early 1980s, the Orthodox/Roman Catholic Consultation in the United States, established by the Standing Conference of Canonical Orthodox Bishops in the Americas (SCOBA) and the National Conference of Catholic Bishops (NCCB), has closely followed the work of the Joint International Commission for Theological Dialogue between the Orthodox Church and the Roman Catholic Church. The U.S. Consultation has responded to documents published by the International Commission as part of its original plan for theological dialogue set down at Rhodes in 1980: "The Mystery of the Church and of the Eucharist in the Light of the Mystery of the Holy Trinity" (Munich, 1982), "Faith, Sacraments and the Unity of the Church" (Bari, 1987), and "The Sacrament of Order in the Sacramental Structure of the Church" (Valamo, 1988) [in GA II].

2. More recently, as the International Commission has interrupted its original plan in order to give immediate attention to the question of "Uniatism," the U.S. Consultation has also studied this question, reflecting not only on the preliminary document released by the International Commission

in Freising (1990), the draft prepared for the Commission in Ariccia (1991) and widely diffused, and related texts, but also on our own North American experience. Three brief statements already have been issued: "A Joint Communiqué of the Orthodox/Roman Catholic Consultation in the United States on Current Tensions between our Churches in Eastern Europe" (Brighton, Massachusetts, 1990), "Joint Statement of the United States Orthodox/Roman Catholic Consultation on Tensions in Eastern Europe Related to `Uniatism'" (Brookline, Massachusetts, 1992), and "A Statement of the Catholic Members of the U.S. Orthodox/Roman Catholic Consultation" (Douglaston, New York, 1992).

3. Now that the final expression of the International Commission's work has appeared in the document "Uniatism, Method of Union of the Past, and the Present Search for Full Communion" (Balamand, 1993 [in GA II]), we in the U.S. Consultation have analyzed the document and taken note of reactions to it by various Catholics and Orthodox, some of which have been positive but others negative and even abusive. We now wish to submit our common response and reflections to the Joint International Commission and to others of the wider community of faith.

4. Our Consultation rejoices that the International Commission has been able to complete the work it set out for itself on the difficult question of "Uniatism." With the Commission, we hope that "by excluding for the future all proselytism and all desire for expansion by Catholics at the expense of the Orthodox Church" ([Balamand,] no. 35), enough has been achieved in re-establishing trust between Orthodox and Roman Catholics after the events which led to the interruption of the theological work of the Commission in 1990, so that all members of the Commission can now return to that work. The theological dialogue itself must be deepened if it is to progress, and further issues relating to the ecclesial status of the Eastern Catholic churches, only touched upon at Balamand, need to be relocated within this deepening of the properly theological task facing the Joint International Commission.

5. We applaud the Commission's efforts in the second part of the document to formulate various practical rules and guidelines intended "to lead to a just and definitive solution to the difficulties which the Oriental Catholic Churches present to the Orthodox Church" (no. 17). These rules and guidelines call for

- reciprocal exchanges of information about various pastoral projects (no. 22)

- avoidance of those forms of philanthropic activity that might be construed as attempts to buy new adherents to the detriment of the other church (no. 24)
- open dialogue at the local level (no. 26)
- avoidance of all forms of violence (no. 27)
- mutual respect for each other's places of worship and even sharing of facilities when circumstances require (no. 28)
- respect for the spiritual life and sacramental discipline of the other church (no. 29a)
- consultation before the establishment of new pastoral projects which might unnecessarily parallel or even undermine those of the other church in the same territory (no. 29b)
- dissipation of inherited prejudicial readings of the historical record, especially in the preparation of future priests (no. 30)
- resolving differences through fraternal dialogue, thus avoiding recourse to the civil authorities or to merely legal principles when seeking solutions to property disputes or other pressing practical problems (no. 31)
- objectivity in the presentation of events and issues in the mass media (no. 32)

6. In our estimation, however, most important of the practical rules and guidelines is the document's emphasis on the need for "a will to pardon" (no. 20). We are all aware that the history of relations between our two churches often has been a tragic one, filled with persecutions and sufferings, but we must not remain prisoners of this past. At the present critical moment in the life of our churches, particularly in those parts of the world which only now are emerging from many decades of insidious pressures and overt persecution at the hands of atheistic forces, the energies of our churches must be directed toward ensuring that "the present and the future conform better to the will of Christ for his own." As for "whatever may have been the past, it must be left to the mercy of God" (no. 23). But how can our churches and our faithful truly acquire this will to pardon? The Balamand Document offers a very helpful proposal: "It is necessary that the churches come together in order to express gratitude and respect towards all, known and unknown . . . who suffered, confessed their faith, witnessed

their fidelity to the Church, and in general, towards all Christians, without discrimination, who underwent persecutions" (no. 33).

7. The Balamand Document very appropriately seeks to present certain historical events such as the genesis of the Eastern Catholic churches and their impact on relations between Catholics and Orthodox (nos. 6-11) in an even-handed way, without rendering specific judgments. However, its presentation is rather schematic and contains some incomplete formulations. Future theological and historical statements on these and related items will call for more nuanced presentations.

8. The document's historical account does not highlight the important role which the Protestant Reformation played in the West and its impact on Roman Catholic ecclesiology. Mention of this would help to explain how attitudes of exclusivism, justly criticized in the document, developed among Roman Catholics not primarily in response to the Orthodox but to other crises and controversies.

9. While the document's rejection of re-baptism is clear (nos. 10, 13), the question of re-baptism will need further articulation in subsequent studies. In the text the juxtaposition of re-baptism and "the religious freedom of persons" (no. 10) is somewhat confusing. Such an important issue as re-baptism demands deeper historical and theological investigations. The groundwork for this has been laid in the International Commission's Bari Document (1987), which was devoted to the intimate connection between "Faith, Sacraments and the Unity of the Church." If, as that agreed statement suggests (cf. 20, 21), mutual recognition of sacraments is inseparable from mutual recognition of faith, do our churches in fact find the same essential content of the faith present in each other, notwithstanding inevitable differences in verbal formulation?

10. The Balamand Document's goal is preeminently practical: to create a "serene atmosphere" for renewed progress in dialogue "toward the reestablishment of full communion" (no. 34) by rejecting the proselytism and expansionist practices and policies (no. 35) associated with "Uniatism." In our judgment, its greatest strength lies in the rules and guidelines presented in its second part. With the International Commission, we would strongly recommend "that these practical rules be put into practice by our churches, including the Oriental Catholic churches who are called to take part in this dialogue" (no. 34). We also appreciate the effort made in its first part to set forth the ecclesiological principles which serve as a basis for these practical rules. We would hope that our churches will also take them seriously. It is likewise our hope that the International Commission will be able

to return to consideration of these ecclesiological principles in the near future in the context of its theological study.

11. We are aware that the International Commission did not intend the Balamand Document to be a complete presentation of ecclesiology. Nevertheless, the document does draw our attention to several promising avenues for discussion. For example, it presupposes the "communion ecclesiology" which many theologians have found to be the most promising way of conceiving the complexity of the Church. This approach, in our estimation, changes the context of past disputes and creates new possibilities for fresh examination of the issues which historically have divided us, even though more work in this area obviously is needed before full agreement is reached.

12. We also note the document's use of the concept of "sister churches" (no. 14). The use of this venerable term in modern Orthodox/Catholic dialogue has helped to place relations between our churches on a new footing. We hope that, when the International Commission resumes work on ecclesiology, it will be able more fully to explore its precise significance and manifold implications. The concept of sister churches includes the notion of mutual respect for each other's pastoral ministry. As the Balamand Document states, "bishops and priests have the duty before God to respect the authority which the Holy Spirit has given to the bishops and priests of the other church and for that reason to avoid interfering in the spiritual life of the faithful of that church" (no. 29). The concept also includes the notion of the co-responsibility of our churches for "maintaining the Church of God in fidelity to the divine purpose, most especially in what concerns unity" (no. 14). This, we believe, is a point which should be developed further. The Document's forceful treatment of proselytization needs to be balanced by a proper understanding of mission. Bishops are responsible not simply for the pastoral care of their own faithful but also for the good estate and upbuilding of the whole Church and for the evangelization of the world.

13. In ecumenical efforts there often is a tension between the views and actions of "higher authorities" (no. 26) and ecumenists on the one hand, and those of many Christians at the grassroots level on the other. The Balamand Document as a whole expects higher authorities to act vigorously in enforcing policies it deems advisable even while emphasizing the importance of the activities of the local church (no. 26). In particular, it points to the necessity of a "a will to pardon" at every level of church life. In a balanced and even-handed way, it seeks to put an end to the present tensions occasioned by the existence of the Eastern Catholic churches. On

the one hand, as the Document points out repeatedly: "'uniatism' can no longer be accepted either as a method to be followed or as a model of the unity our churches are seeking" (no. 12), "because it is opposed to the common tradition of our churches" (no. 2). At the same time, as the document also states, "concerning the Oriental Catholic churches, it is clear that they, as part of the Catholic Communion, have the right to exist and to act in answer to the spiritual needs of their faithful" (no. 3).

14. The Balamand Document speaks frequently of the "religious freedom of persons" (no. 10) and "the religious liberty of the faithful" (no. 24), of "freedom of conscience" (no. 27) and "respect for consciences" (no. 25), acknowledging "the inviolable freedom of persons and their obligation to follow the requirements of the consciences" (no. 15). The language employed in modern presentations of this theme is familiar enough in the Western world in its concern for human rights and is certainly not alien to either of our churches. In developing this theme, however, our churches have called attention to the need for a coherent understanding of community and therefore to the need to locate individual rights and responsibilities within the common good. When the Document speaks of "the faithful" and of their religious liberty "to express their opinion and to decide without pressure from outside if they wish to be in communion either with the Orthodox Church or with the Catholic church" (no. 24), this distinction becomes crucial. Neither the Orthodox nor the Catholic understanding sees the "faithful" only as referring to an individual Christian apart from community. Rather, we both urge that personhood can only ultimately be grasped in relation to the "Body" and, through the Body, to the tri-personal life of God. Where concern for the solidarity and spiritual health of the community as a whole is absent, the exercise of "freedom" and "liberty" can lead all too easily to the fragmentation of society and to the alienation of persons from each other and from God.

15. Important in this connection is the Balamand Document's rejection of the premise that only one of our churches is the unique possessor of the means of grace in such a way that conversion to that church from the other is necessary for salvation. The Document asserts that "on each side it is recognized that what Christ has entrusted to his Church . . . cannot be considered the exclusive property of one of our churches" (no. 13). To be sure, there may be cases in which conscience leads an Orthodox or a Catholic Christian to enter the other church (cf. no. 14). This, however, does not mean that our churches should set out to "win converts" by cultivating inappropriate fears and anxieties.

16. At the same time, the assertion that "what Christ has entrusted to his Church . . . cannot be considered the exclusive property of one of our churches" (no. 13) does not necessarily imply that the fullness of the faith resides indifferently in each of our churches, as some critics of the Balamand Document have incorrectly charged. There are still a number of serious issues that divide us. Yet the assertion does imply that the deficiencies and errors which we may see in one another's understanding of doctrine and church structures are not failures that would altogether exclude the other from the mystery of the Church.

17. The Document speaks of itself as "a necessary stage" (no. 15) in the current theological dialogue. We may hope and expect that it will be superseded as the International Commission continues its work, beginning with "Ecclesiological and Canonical Consequences of the Sacramental Structure of the Church: Conciliarity and Authority in the Church." Even the practical rules and guidelines are described as "leading to" rather than constituting a definitive solution to the problems raised up by "Uniatism" (no. 17). As the document stresses, a "climate for deepening our dialogue" (no. 20) must be created, beginning with a "will to pardon." Our best energies must be put into the task of creating that climate. While pointing out some shortcomings of the Balamand Document, we nevertheless regard it to be a strong and positive contribution to the theological dialogue between our churches.

Brighton, Massachusetts
October 15, 1994
Forty-Eighth Meeting

DOCUMENT 20

COMMON RESPONSE TO THE ALEPPO STATEMENT ON THE DATE OF EASTER/PASCHA

North American Orthodox-Catholic Theological Consultation, 1998

In March 1997, a consultation jointly sponsored by the World Council of Churches and the Middle East Council of Churches, meeting in Aleppo, Syria, issued a statement "Towards a Common Date for Easter." The North American Orthodox-Catholic Theological Consultation, meeting in Washington, D.C., from October 29-31, 1998, studied this Aleppo Statement [AS] and reviewed reactions to it thus far. Our Consultation strongly endorses the Aleppo Statement. The Aleppo Statement rightly calls attention to the centrality of Christ's resurrection as the basis of our common faith. As "the ultimate expression of the Father's gift of reconciliation and unity in Christ through the Spirit," the resurrection "is a sign of the unity and reconciliation which God wills for the entire creation" (AS, no. 5).

Yet by celebrating the feast of Christ's resurrection, the Holy Pascha, or Easter, on different Sundays in the same year, "the churches give a divided witness" to this mystery, "compromising their credibility and effectiveness in bringing the Gospel to the world" (no. 1). The question of the date of Easter/Pascha, therefore, is not simply an academic issue, void of pastoral implications. It is a matter of concern in our own North American context. It has become an even more urgent issue in some parts of the world such as the Middle East, where Christians constitute a divided minority in a larger non-Christian society. After reviewing twentieth-century discussion of the question of a common date for Easter/Pascha and historical background to present differences of calculation among Christians, the Aleppo

Statement recommends maintaining the norms established by the First Ecumenical Council in Nicaea (AD 325), according to which Easter/Pascha should fall on the Sunday following the first full moon of spring, and calculating the necessary astronomical data (spring equinox and full moon) by "the most accurate possible scientific means," using the Jerusalem meridian as the basis for reckoning.

Noting that in the year 2001 the Paschal calculations now in use in our churches will coincide, the Aleppo Statement also recommends that, in the interval between now and then, the churches study and consider means to implement these recommendations. Our Catholic-Orthodox Consultation welcomes the Aleppo Statement's recommendations for the following reasons:

The Aleppo Statement does well to call attention to the continuing relevance of the Council of Nicaea—a fundamental point of reference for the traditions of both our churches—and in so doing to reject proposals to establish a fixed date for Easter/Pascha. As the Aleppo Statement points out, the Council of Nicaea was willing to make use of contemporary science to calculate the date of Easter/Pascha. We believe that this principle still holds valid today. Scientific observations about the cosmos reveal the goodness and wonder of God's creation, which he embraced in the incarnation of his Son. Moreover, to deny an observable truth about the world is to reject God's gift to us. As they witness to God's love for the world, our churches need to use the findings of contemporary science as did the Fathers of Nicaea.

The Aleppo Statement accurately presents historical circumstances relating to such matters as the Council of Nicaea's treatment of the relationship between the Christian Pascha and the Jewish Passover. The practice of continuing to celebrate Pascha according to the ancient Julian calendar has often been defended, by some Eastern Christians, as resting on a decision associated with that council prohibiting the churches from celebrating the Paschal feast "with the Jews." As scholars of both our traditions have very clearly demonstrated, this prohibition was directed against making the calculation of the date of Easter depend upon contemporary Jewish reckoning, not against a coincidence of date between the two festivals. In fact, a coincidence of Passover and Easter dates continued to occur from time to time as late as the eighth century. Only later, when the increasing "lag" of the Julian Calendar made any coincidence impossible, did the prohibition come to be misinterpreted as meaning that the Jewish Passover must necessarily precede the Christian Passover each year. In short, we consider that the implementation of the recommendations of the Aleppo Statement would allow our churches to adhere more exactly to the mode of calculation mandated by the First Council of Nicaea.

As the Aleppo Statement indicates, its recommendations will have different implications for our churches "as they seek a renewed faithfulness to Nicaea." For the Eastern churches, "changes in the actual dating of Easter/Pascha will be more perceptible than for the Western churches" (no. 13). The fact that the recommendations of the Aleppo Statement substantially repeat proposals already developed by the Orthodox themselves in connection with their preparations for a Great and Holy Council of the Orthodox Church should significantly enhance the Aleppo recommendations' prospects for success. At the same time, as the Aleppo Statement notes, in many of the Eastern churches adherence to their present method of calculation often has been a symbol of the Church's integrity and freedom from the hostile forces of this world. Implementation of the Aleppo recommendations in these circumstances must proceed carefully and with great pastoral sensitivity.

The material presented in the Aleppo Statement can be of great help to these churches should they attempt to carry out this effort to be faithful to the great tradition of the Church. The Aleppo Statement is faithful to the decisions of the First Ecumenical Council regarding the date of Easter/Pascha. At the same time, it takes into account the contemporary situation, which calls for a common witness to the resurrection of our Lord Jesus Christ, the central mystery of the Christian faith. Our consultation therefore urges our churches to give serious consideration to its recommendations.

DOCUMENT 21

BAPTISM AND "SACRAMENTAL ECONOMY"

An Agreed Statement of the North American

Orthodox-Catholic Theological Consultation, 1999

I. Introduction

For the past three years the North American Orthodox-Catholic Theological Consultation has directed its attention to the concluding section of the Nicene-Constantinopolitan Creed: in particular to the confession of "one baptism" and to the faith in one Holy Spirit and in "one holy, catholic, and apostolic Church," to which this single baptism is so closely related, and with which it constitutes an indivisible unity. We have chosen to consider this topic, first of all, as part of a larger and continuing reflection on baptism's constitutive role in establishing and revealing the fundamental character of the Church as a communion.

Secondly, we wish to respond to the criticisms made by various groups of the statement issued by the Joint International Commission for Theological Dialogue between the Catholic and Orthodox Churches at Balamand, Lebanon, in 1993, "Uniatism, Method of Union of the Past, and the Present Search for Full Communion," especially to protests against that statement's call for an end to the practice of rebaptism of converts (no. 13) and its reference to the Catholic and Orthodox communions as "sister churches" (no. 14).

Finally, we recognize that our consideration of these protests directs us back to earlier statements which our own Consultation has issued: "The Principle of Economy" (1976); "On the Agenda of the Great and Holy Council" (1977); "On the Lima Document" (1984); "Apostolicity as God's

Gift to the Church" (1986); our "Response" (1988) to the Bari Document issued by the International Commission in 1987; and finally our "Response" (1994) to the Balamand Document itself. In drafting this present statement, we have elected to take our own advice and to offer a "deeper historical and theological investigation" of whether "our churches do in fact find the same essential content of faith present in each other" ("Response to the Balamand Statement," no. 9).

In the following sections we shall endeavor (a) to summarize our findings regarding our common understanding of baptism, as well as its unity with the life of the Church and the action of the Holy Spirit; (b) to elucidate the problems which, in relatively recent times, have arisen with respect to the mutual recognition of each other's baptism; and (c) to present our conclusions, together with certain recommendations which we feel are necessary, in order that on various levels our dialogue be established on a solid and unambiguous foundation. Only if we have reached clarity on our common understanding of baptism, we believe, can our churches proceed to discuss, charitably and truthfully, those issues which at present appear to constitute genuine impediments to our unity in the one Bread and Cup of Christ.

II. On Baptism

A. On Baptism a Matter of Faith: Baptism rests upon and derives its reality from the faith of Christ himself, the faith of the Church, and the faith of the believer.

1. *The faith of Christ:* With this Pauline expression we refer to the fact that baptism, like all the sacraments, is given to us first of all as the result of Christ's loving fidelity to his Father, and as a sign of his faithfulness in the Holy Spirit to fallen humanity, "so that we are justified not by the works of the law but through the faith of Christ Jesus" (Gal 2:16; cf. Rom 3:22, 26; Phil 3:9). Baptism is not a human work, but the rebirth from above, effected through "water and the Spirit," that introduces us into the life of the Church. It is that gift by which God grounds and establishes the Church as the community of the New Covenant, the "Israel of God" (Gal 6:16), by engrafting us into the body of the crucified and risen Messiah (Rom 6:3-11; 11:17-24), into the one sacrament (*mysterion*) which is Christ himself (Eph 1:3, 3:3; Col 1:27, 2:2).

2. *The faith of the Church:* In the Church of the Apostles and Fathers, baptism was never understood as a private ceremony but was a corporate

event. This is indicated by the development of the Lenten fast in the fourth century, when catechumens attended their final instructions before baptism at the paschal vigil: their baptism was the occasion for the whole community's repentance and renewal. Likewise, the definitive statement of the whole Church's faith, the "We believe" of the Creed, was derived from the solemn questions addressed by the sacramental minister to the candidate in the baptismal font. Whoever, then, is baptized, is baptized into the unique community of the Messiah, and it is that community's common faith in the Savior's person and promises that the candidate is obliged to make his or her own. As the Church, we acknowledge the trustworthiness of him who said, "Whoever believes in me, though he die, yet shall he live" (Jn 11:25). This is the faith of the Apostles and Fathers, of the martyrs and ascetics, and of "all the saints who in every generation have been well-pleasing to God" (Liturgy of St. John Chrysostom). In the words of the renewal of baptismal promises in the Easter liturgy of the Roman Rite, "this is our faith. This is the faith of the Church. We are proud to profess it in Christ Jesus our Lord."

3. *The faith of the Christian:* As just noted, every Christian is obliged to make his or her own the faith of the Church. The "We believe" of the whole Church must become the individual Christian's "I believe," whether spoken by the adult candidate for baptism on his or her own behalf, or on behalf of a child by its sponsor and the assembled community, in the full expectation that, when it has grown, the child will make the common faith its own as well. By baptism, every Christian becomes a "new creation" (2 Co 5:17) and is called to believe and to grow "into the unity of the faith and of the knowledge of the Son of God . . . to the measure of the stature and fullness of Christ" (Eph 4:13). Baptism is the beginning of each believer's life in the Spirit, the implanting within each of the seed of the fullness of Christ "who fills all in all" (Eph 1:23): a life on earth which is at once the present reality and the continuing vocation of each Christian, as the "temple of the Holy Spirit" (1 Co 6:19) and the dwelling place of divine glory (Jn 17:22-24). Christian initiation is the ground of our transfiguration "from glory to glory" (2 Co 3:18). It calls each of us to spiritual warfare as Christ's soldiers (Eph 6:10-17) and anoints us each with the oil of the Holy Spirit as priests who, in imitation of Christ, are to offer up ourselves as "a living sacrifice pleasing to God" (Rom 12:1; cf. Phil 4:18) and as prophets who are to call down upon ourselves and upon our world the fire from heaven which transforms (cf. 1 Kg 18:36-39; Mt 3:11; Lk 12:49). Also in baptism, we believe that we recover the royalty of Adam in Paradise, and that, as "having been clothed

with Christ" (Rom 13:14), we are called to become ourselves the "christs"—the "anointed ones"—of God.

B. Baptism Within the Rites of Initiation

1. *One Moment in a Single Action:* In ancient times, initiation into the Church was understood as a single action with different "moments." Thus in Acts 2:38-42, we find baptism with water directly followed by the reception of the Holy Spirit and "the breaking of bread" (Eucharist) by the community; other texts in Acts present the gift of the Spirit as preceding baptism (Acts 10:44-48, 11:15-17). This continuity between the various stages of initiation is consistently reproduced in the oldest liturgical texts and in early patristic witnesses: baptism with water in the name of the Trinity, a post- (or pre-) baptismal anointing and/or laying-on of hands invoking the Spirit, and participation in the Eucharist. The present-day ordering of the Eastern Christian rites of initiation and the Rite of Christian Initiation of Adults in the Roman liturgy preserve this unity. In the case of infant baptism, medieval Latin practice separated this unity of action, deferring confirmation by the bishop and Eucharistic communion to a later date. Indeed, the distinction which is customarily made today in both churches between baptism and chrismation, or confirmation, was never intended to separate the reception of the Spirit from incorporation into the body of Christ, whose quickening principle is the same Spirit (see, e.g., Rom 8:9-11, as well part III, B5 below).

2. *The Method of Baptism:* In ancient times, and in the contemporary Orthodox Church, baptism is administered as a threefold immersion in water hallowed by prayer and oil, while the baptizing minister invokes the Holy Trinity. In the Roman rite of the Catholic Church since the later Middle Ages, baptism has usually been administered by the infusion or pouring of water sanctified by prayer and the sign of the Cross, accompanied by the Trinitarian invocation. In past centuries and even today, some Orthodox have protested against infusion as being an invalid form of baptism, basing their protest on the mandate of baptismal immersion implied in such Biblical passages as Rom 6:4 ("We were buried with [Christ] by baptism into death, so that as Christ was raised from the dead, we too might walk in newness of life").

This criticism, however, should be measured against the following considerations: (a) "immersion" in the ancient church did not always mean total submersion—archaeological research indicates that many ancient baptismal pools were far too shallow for total submersion; (b) the Orthodox

Church itself can and does recognize baptism by infusion as valid in cases of emergency; (c) for most of the past millennium, the Orthodox Church has in fact recognized Catholic baptism as valid (see our discussion in Part II below).

3. *The Symbolism of Baptism:* Baptism is at once a death and a new birth, a washing-away of sin and the gift of the living water promised by Christ, the grace of forgiveness and regeneration in the Spirit, a stripping-off of our mortality and a clothing with the robe of incorruption. The baptismal font is the "tomb" from which the newborn Christian rises, and, as the place of our incorporation into the life of the Church, the "womb" and "mother" of the Christian, the pool of the divine light of the Spirit, the well-spring of immortality, the gate of heaven, entry into the kingdom of God, cleansing, seal, bath of regeneration, and bridal chamber. All these are meanings the Fathers saw in this sacrament, and all of them we continue to affirm.

4. *The Non-Repeatability of Baptism:* It is our common teaching that baptism in water in the name of the Holy Trinity, as the Christian's new birth, is given once and once only. In the language of fourth-century Fathers of East and West, it confers the indelible seal (*sphragis*, character) of the King. As the definitive entry of an individual believer into the Church, it cannot be repeated. To be sure, the grace of baptism may be betrayed by serious sin, but in such cases the modes prescribed for the recovery of grace are repentance, confession, and—in the Orthodox usage for apostasy—anointing with the sacred chrism; reconciliation with the Church is never accomplished by baptism, whose repetition we have always recognized as a sacrilege.

C. The Results of Our Investigation: "We Confess One Baptism"

The Orthodox and Catholic members of our Consultation acknowledge, in both of our traditions, a common teaching and a common faith in one baptism, despite some variations in practice which, we believe, do not affect the substance of the mystery. We are therefore moved to declare that we also recognize each other's baptism as one and the same. This recognition has obvious ecclesiological consequences. The Church is itself both the milieu and the effect of baptism, and is not of our making. This recognition requires each side of our dialogue to acknowledge an ecclesial reality in the other, however much we may regard their way of living the Church's reality as flawed or incomplete. In our common reality of baptism, we discover the foundation of our dialogue, as well as the force and urgency of the Lord Jesus' prayer "that all may be one." Here, finally, is the certain basis for the modern use of the phrase "sister churches." At the same time, since some are unwilling to accept this mutual recognition of baptism with all its consequences, the following investigation and explanation seems necessary.

II. Problems in the Mutual Recognition of Baptism

A. Inconsistencies in the Reception of Adults into Ecclesial Communion

1. The centralized administration of the modern Catholic Church, and the absence of any office resembling the papacy in the modern Orthodox Church, helps to explain the contrast between the diversity in modes of reception of Catholics practiced by local Orthodox churches and the (relatively) unitary practice of the Catholic Church over the past five hundred years in receiving Orthodox. From the fifth-century writings of St. Augustine on the Donatist Schism, the Latin tradition has been able to draw on a clearly articulated rationale for recognizing the validity, though not necessarily the fruitfulness, of trinitarian baptism outside the bounds of the visible church.

This does not mean, however, that the rebaptism of Orthodox has never occurred in the Catholic Church; it appears, in fact, to have occurred rather frequently in the Middle Ages. Pope Alexander VI affirmed the validity of Orthodox baptism just after the turn of the sixteenth century, and Rome has periodically confirmed this ruling since then. Nevertheless, re-baptism continued to be practiced on the eastern frontiers of Catholic Europe in Poland and the Balkans—contrary to Roman policy—well into the seventeenth century. In addition, the practice of "conditional baptism," a pastoral option officially intended for cases of genuine doubt about the validity of a person's earlier baptism, was also widely—and erroneously—used in the reception of "dissident" Eastern Christians up to the era of Vatican II itself, and afterwards was practiced occasionally in parts of Eastern Europe. Vatican II, however, was explicit in recognizing both the validity and the efficacy of Orthodox sacraments (UR, no. 15; cf. *Ecumenical Directory* [1993], 99a).

2. In the Orthodox Church, a consistent position on the reception of those baptized in other communions is much more difficult, though not impossible, to discern. On the one hand, since the Council in Trullo (AD 692), the canonical collections authoritative in Orthodoxy have included the enactments of third-century North African councils presided over by Cyprian of Carthage, as well as the important late-fourth-century Eastern

collection, the Apostolic Canons. Cyprian's position, supported by his contemporary bishop Firmilian of Caesaraea in Cappadocia, was that salvation and grace are not mediated by schismatic communities, so that baptism administered outside the universal apostolic communion is simply invalid as an act of Christian initiation, deprived of the life-giving Spirit (see Cyprian, Epp. 69.7; 71.1; 73.2; 75.17, 22-25). Influential as it was to be, Cyprian and Firmilian both acknowledge that their position on baptism is a relatively new one, forged probably in the 230s to deal with the extraordinary new challenges presented by Christian sectarianism in an age of persecution, but following logically from a clear sense of the Church's boundaries. The Apostolic Canons, included in the larger apostolic constitutions and probably representative of Church discipline in Syria during the 380s, identifies sacraments celebrated by "heretics" as illegitimate (c. 45 [46]), although it is not clear in what sense the word "heretic" is being used; the following canon brands it as equally sacrilegious for a bishop or presbyter to re-baptize someone who is already truly baptized and to recognize the baptism of "someone who has been polluted by the ungodly." Both Cyprian and the Apostolic Canons, in any case, draw a sharp line between the authentic visible Church and every other group which exists outside its boundaries, and accords no value whatever to the rites of those "outside."

On the other hand, continuing Eastern practice from at least the fourth century has followed a more nuanced position. This position is reflected in Basil of Caesarea's First Canonical Epistle (Ep. 188, dated 374), addressed to Amphilochius of Iconium, which—claiming to follow the practice of "the ancients"—distinguishes between three types of groups "outside" the Church: heretics, "who differ with regard to faith in God"; schismatics, who are separated from the body of the Church "for some ecclesiastical reasons and [who] differ from other [Christians] on questions that can be resolved"; and "parasynagogues," or dissidents who have formed rival communities simply in opposition to legitimate authority (Ep. 188.1). Only in the case of heretics in the strict sense—those with a different understanding of God, among whom Basil includes Manichaeans, Gnostics, and Marcionites—is baptism required for entry into communion with the Church. Concerning the second and third groups, Basil declares that they are still "of the Church," and as such are to be admitted into full communion without baptism. This policy is also reflected in Canon 95 of the Council in Trullo, which distinguishes between "Severians" (i.e., non-Chalcedonians) and Nestorians, who are to be received by confession of faith; schismatics, who are to be received by chrismation; and heretics, who alone require baptism. Thus, in spite of the solemn rulings of the Fifth and Sixth Ecumenical Councils against their christological positions, "Severians" and Nestorians are clearly reckoned as still "of the Church" and seem to be understood in Basil's category of "parasynagogues"; their baptisms are thus understood—to use scholastic language—as valid, if perhaps illicit.

3. The schism between Catholics and Orthodox, unlike the schisms of the Non-Chalcedonian and East Syrian Churches, came into being much later, and only very slowly. Relations between Catholics and Orthodox through the centuries have been, in consequence, highly varied, ranging from full communion, on occasion, well into the late Middle Ages (and, in certain areas, until later still), to a rejection so absolute that it seemed to demand the rebaptism of new communicants.

There are, however, in the Orthodox tradition two important synodical rulings which represent the continuation of the policy articulated by Basil, and affirmed by the Synod in Trullo and later Byzantine canonists, rulings which we believe are to be accorded primary importance: those of the Synod of Constantinople in 1484, and of Moscow in 1667. The first ruling, part of a document marking the Constantinopolitan Patriarchate's formal repudiation of the Union of Ferrara-Florence (1439) with the Catholic Church, prescribed that Catholics be received into Orthodox communion by the use of chrism. In the service for the reception of Catholic converts which the Synod published, this anointing is not accompanied by the prayers which characterize the rite of initiation; we find instead formulas of a penitential character. The rite therefore appears to have been understood as part of a process of reconciliation, rather than as a reiteration of post-baptismal chrismation. It is this provision of Constantinople in 1484, together with Canon 95 of the Synod in Trullo, which the Council of Moscow in 1667 invokes in its decree forbidding the rebaptism of Catholics, a decree that has remained authoritative in the East Slavic Orthodox churches to the present day.

B. Constantinople 1755, the Pedalion of Nicodemus of the Holy Mountain, and "Sacramental Economy"

1. *Constantinople 1755:* In an atmosphere of heightened tension between Orthodoxy and Catholicism following the Melkite Union of 1724 and of intensified proselytism pursued by Catholic missionaries in the Near East and in Hapsburg-ruled Transylvania, the Ecumenical Patriarch Cyril V issued a decree in 1755 requiring the baptism of Roman Catholics, Armenians, and all others presently outside the visible bounds of the Orthodox Church, when they seek full communion with it. This decree has never been formally rescinded, but

subsequent rulings by the Patriarchate of Constantinople (e.g., in 1875, 1880, and 1888) did allow for the reception of new communicants by chrismation rather than baptism. Nevertheless, these rulings left re-baptism as an option subject to "pastoral discretion." In any case, by the late nineteenth century a comprehensive new sacramental theology had appeared in Greek-speaking Orthodoxy which provided a precise rationale for such pastoral discretion; for the source of this new rationale, we must examine the influential figure of St. Nicodemus of the Holy Mountain (1748-1809).

2. *Nicodemus and the* Pedalion: The Orthodox world owes an immense debt to this Athonite monk, who edited and published the *Philokalia* (1783), as well as numerous other works of a patristic, pastoral, and liturgical nature. In the *Pedalion* (1800), his enormously influential edition of—and commentary on—canonical texts, Nicodemus gave form and substance to the requirement of rebaptism decreed by Cyril V. Thoroughly in sympathy with the decree of 1755, and moved by his attachment to a perceived golden age in the patristic past, he underscored the antiquity and hence priority of the African Councils and Apostolic Canons and argued strenuously, in fact, for the first-century provenance of the latter. Nicodemus held up these documents, with their essentially exclusivist ecclesiology, as the universal voice of the ancient Church. In so doing, he systematically reversed what had been the normative practice of the eastern church since at least the fourth century, while recognizing the authority of both Cyprian's conciliar legislation on baptism and the Apostolic Canons. Earlier Byzantine canonists had understood Cyprian's procedure as superseded by later practice and had interpreted the Apostolic Canons in the light of the rulings of Basil the Great, the Synod in Trullo, and other ancient authoritative texts.

3. *"Sacramental Economy" According to Nicodemus of the Holy Mountain:* Nicodemus was clearly obliged, however, to reckon with the approach of Basil the Great and the ecumenically ranked Synod in Trullo to baptism "outside" the visible Church, different though it was from that of Cyprian. His attempt to reconcile his sources with each other drew on a very ancient term, *oikonomia*, used in the New Testament and patristic literature to denote both God's salvific plan and the prudent "management" of the Church's affairs, and employed in later canonical literature as roughly the equivalent of "pastoral discretion" or stewardship. In adapting this term to differentiate between what he understood as the "strict" policy (*akriveia*) of the ancient Church and the apparently more flexible practice (*oikonomia*) of the Byzantine era, Nicodemus inadvertently bestowed a new meaning on the term *oikonomia*. By means of this new understanding, Nicodemus was

able to harmonize the earlier, stricter practice of Cyprian with that of Basil and other ancient canonical sources; so he could read the fathers of the fourth century as having exercised "economy" with regard to baptism by Arians in order to facilitate their reentry into the Church, just as the Synod in Trullo had done with respect to the "Severians" and Nestorians, and could interpret the treatment of Latin baptism by Constantinople at the Synod of 1484 and later Orthodox rulings as acts of "economy" designed to shield the Orthodox from the wrath of a more powerful Catholic Europe. In his own day, he argued, the Orthodox were protected by the might of the Turkish Sultan and so were again free to follow the perennial "exactness" of the Church. Latins were therefore now to be rebaptized.

4. *Varying Understandings of the Phrase "Pastoral Discretion"*: After the publication of the *Pedalion* in 1800, backed by Nicodemus's formidable personal authority, the opposed principles of *akriveia* and *oikonomia* came to be accepted by much of Greek-speaking Orthodoxy as governing the application of canon law in such a way as to allow for either the re-baptism of Western Christians (*kat'akriveian*), or for their reception by chrismation or profession of faith (*kat'oikonomian*), without in either case attributing to their baptism any reality in its own right. This is the understanding that underlies the "pastoral discretion" enjoined by the Synod of Constantinople of 1875, as well as by numerous directives and statements of the Ecumenical Patriarchate since then.

In the work of some modern canonists, *oikonomia* is understood as the use of an authority by the Church's hierarchy, in cases of pastoral need, to bestow a kind of retroactive reality on sacramental rites exercised "outside" the Orthodox Church—rites which in and of themselves remain invalid and devoid of grace. The hierarchy is endowed, in this interpretation, with a virtually infinite power, capable, as it were, of creating "validity" and bestowing grace where they were absent before. This new understanding of "economy" does not, however, enjoy universal recognition in the Orthodox Church. We have already noted that the East Slavic Orthodox churches remain committed to the earlier understanding and practice of the Byzantine era, which does not imply the possibility of making valid what is invalid, or invalid what is valid. Even within Greek-speaking Orthodoxy, "sacramental economy" in the full Nicodemean sense does not command universal acceptance. As a result, within world Orthodoxy, the issue of "sacramental economy" remains the subject of intense debate, but the Nicodemean interpretation is still promoted in important theological and monastic circles. Although these voices in the Orthodox world are significant ones, we do not believe that they represent the tradition and perennial teaching of the Orthodox Church on the subject of baptism.

III. Conclusions and Recommendations

A. Conclusions

The "inconsistencies" to which we referred at the beginning of our second section turn out, on closer inspection, to be less significant than they might appear to be. Granted, a vocal minority in the Orthodox Church refuses to accord any validity to Catholic baptism and thus continues to justify in theory (if less frequently in fact) the (re)baptism of converts from Catholicism. Against this one fact, however, we present the following considerations:

1. The Orthodox and Catholic churches both teach the same understanding of baptism. This identical teaching draws on the same sources in Scripture and Tradition, and it has not varied in any significant way from the very earliest witnesses to the faith up to the present day.

2. A central element in this single teaching is the conviction that baptism comes to us as God's gift in Christ, through the Holy Spirit. It is therefore not "of us," but from above. The Church does not simply require the practice of baptism; rather, baptism is the Church's foundation. It establishes the Church, which is also not "of us" but, as the body of Christ quickened by the Spirit, is the presence in this world of the world to come.

3. The fact that our churches share and practice this same faith and teaching requires that we recognize in each other the same baptism and thus also recognize in each other, however "imperfectly," the present reality of the same Church. By God's gift we are each, in St. Basil's words, "of the Church."

4. We find that this mutual recognition of the ecclesial reality of baptism, in spite of our divisions, is fully consistent with the perennial teaching of both churches. This teaching has been reaffirmed on many occasions. The formal expression of the recognition of Orthodox baptism has been constant in the teaching of the popes since the beginning of the sixteenth century and was emphasized again at the Second Vatican Council. The Synods of Constantinople in 1484 and Moscow in 1667 testify to the implicit recognition of Catholic baptism by the Orthodox churches, and do so in a way fully in accord with the earlier teaching and practice of antiquity and the Byzantine era.

5. The influential theory of "sacramental economy" propounded in the *Pedalion* commentaries does not represent the tradition and perennial

teaching of the Orthodox Church; it is rather an eighteenth-century innovation motivated by the particular historical circumstances operative in those times. It is not the teaching of scripture, of most of the Fathers, or of later Byzantine canonists, nor is it the majority position of the Orthodox churches today.

6. Catholics in the present day who tax the Orthodox with sins against charity, and even with sacrilege, because of the practice of re-baptism should bear in mind that, while the re-baptism of Orthodox Christians was officially repudiated by Rome five hundred years ago, it nonetheless continued in some places well into the following century and occasionally was done, under the guise of "conditional baptism," up to our own times.

B. Recommendations

On the basis of these conclusions we would like to offer to our churches the following suggestions:

1. That the International Commission begin anew where the Bari statement of 1987, "Faith, Sacraments, and the Unity of the Church," came to an abrupt conclusion, simply recognizing similarities and differences in our practice of Christian initiation; and that it proceed to reaffirm explicitly and clearly, with full explanation, the theological grounds for mutual recognition by both churches of each other's baptism.

2. That our churches address openly the danger that some modern theories of "sacramental economy" pose, both for the continuation of ecumenical dialogue and for the perennial teaching of the Orthodox Church.

3. That the Patriarchate of Constantinople formally withdraw its decree on re-baptism of 1755.

4. That the Orthodox churches declare that the Orthodox reception of Catholics by chrismation does not constitute a repetition of any part of their sacramental initiation.

5. That our churches make clear that the mutual recognition of baptism does not of itself resolve the issues that divide us, or reestablish full ecclesial communion between the Orthodox and Catholic Churches, but that it does remove a fundamental obstacle on our path towards full communion.

DOCUMENT 22

SHARING THE MINISTRY OF RECONCILIATION: STATEMENT ON THE ORTHODOX-CATHOLIC DIALOGUE AND THE ECUMENICAL MOVEMENT

North American Orthodox-Catholic Theological Consultation, 2000

The Ministry of Reconciliation

Christ our Lord has called us to be his disciples through the life of his Church and for the sake of his world. By our baptism, we are united with Christ and with all those who are in Christ. By this mystery which unites our life with him, we receive the gift of the Holy Spirit and come to know the Father. In gathering for the Eucharist, we celebrate the presence of the Lord among us as we recall the mighty actions of God through which he seeks the salvation of all and draws us all towards unity. In communion with the Lord, we are called to proclaim in both word and deed, here and now, the divine love which heals and reconciles and saves. As the Apostle Paul says, "all this is from God who reconciled us to himself through Christ, and has given us the ministry of reconciliation" (2 Cor. 5:18).

As we commemorate thirty-five years of dialogue between Orthodox and Catholic theologians in North America, we give thanks to God for the opportunity to share in this ministry of reconciliation.

The Orthodox-Catholic Theological Consultation was established in 1965 by the Standing Conference of Canonical Orthodox Bishops in America and the National Conference of Catholic Bishops. Since 1997, the Canadian Conference of Catholic Bishops has also been a co-sponsor. The establishment of this consultation reflected the decisions of the Second Vatican Council (1962-1965) and the decisions of the Pan-Orthodox Conferences (1961-1968). This Consultation was the first official dialogue between theologians of the Orthodox and Catholic churches to be established in modern times. It marked a new phase in the relationship between our churches. Since its beginnings, this Consultation has sought to contribute to the ultimate goal of restoration of full communion between our churches, through theological dialogue nurtured by prayer and characterized by mutual respect.

We believe that, through God's grace, our Consultation has already contributed to the growing rapprochement between our two churches. Our discussions and our twenty agreed statements have examined both issues which have divided our churches and teaching and practices which have expressed an essential unity of faith. The Consultation has also made recommendations for addressing a variety of challenges that we face together in modern society. We have addressed concerns in the areas of mixed marriages, the spiritual formation of children in Orthodox-Catholic families, and the common commitment to uphold the dignity of human life. Our studies have contributed to our churches' pastoral care of God's people, as well as to the progress of other ecumenical dialogues and to scholarly work on the topic of church unity. Through God's love and mercy, the results of this Consultation have been very positive.

The experience of our Consultation also has provided a valuable background for a number of other forums which bring together representatives of the Orthodox and Catholic churches. We are especially grateful for the important witness and work of the Joint International Commission for Theological Dialogue between the Roman Catholic Church and the Orthodox Church since 1979, as well as the Joint Committee of Orthodox and Catholic Bishops in the United States since 1981. We appreciate the opportunities we have had to assist in their work, through our responses to the statements of the International Commission and through providing theological advice to the Joint Committee of Bishops.

Moreover, during these thirty-five years we have noticed, in many places, a growth in positive relationships between Orthodox and Catholic clergy and laity. Our churches' various encounters for prayer, study, and common witness have done much to eliminate age-old misunderstandings and to deepen mutual respect. We take special note of the pilgrimage of Orthodox and Catholic bishops to Rome and Constantinople in 1995. Similar pilgrimages were made by groups of Orthodox and Catholics from the Boston and Chicago areas. These journeys bear witness to the spirit of reconciliation and the desire for unity that seems, in increasing measure, to characterize the People of God.

The encounter of representatives from both churches for theological conversation and common worship of God expresses, as Patriarch Bartholomew has said, "the firm decision of the two sister churches to remain estranged no longer from one another but to make an effort to prepare by sincere, honest and appropriate means, the way towards the restoration of unity and communion in Christ, for the glory of the all-powerful God and the salvation of his people everywhere" (1993).

Reaffirming Our Common Commitment to Restoring Full Communion

As our dialogue completes its thirty-fifth year, the members of the Orthodox-Catholic Consultation in North America take this opportunity to reaffirm the importance of the ecumenical commitment and witness of our churches. We especially reaffirm the significance of theological dialogue between the Orthodox and Catholic churches, which seeks the restoration of full communion based upon the profession of the apostolic faith, and expressed in eucharistic sharing and concelebration. We are convinced that a unique relationship exists between our churches in spite of our division. This relationship is rooted in the fact that we continue to proclaim and to share the essential elements of the apostolic faith. Over the years, our own discussions in North America and our agreed statements on such critical topics as the Eucharist, the Church, the Pastoral Office, and Baptism bear witness to this affirmation. It is for this very reason that in recent times the Catholic and Orthodox churches have been described as "sister churches."

The bonds that continue to unite our sister churches are powerfully expressed when—together or separately—we worship the Father through Christ in the Spirit and honor those who are close to God. While we have become separated as churches, our union with Christ and his saints has remained an unbreakable bond of faith, hope, and love. Through the life of both our churches, we share a special bond with Mary, the Virgin Mother of

God, and with the other saints who surround us as a "cloud of witnesses" (Heb. 12:1). Among them, both Orthodox and Catholics are especially mindful of the countless martyrs of the twentieth century who have shed their blood in common witness to Christ, the Savior.

Supported by the examples and prayers of these faithful witnesses, we cannot overlook the difficult issues which continue to divide us and prevent the restoration of full communion between the Orthodox Church and the Catholic Church. The disputed points dividing our churches are serious and demand our continuing attention. Among these, we feel especially that issues related to conciliarity, primacy, and the exercise of authority require much deeper theological reflection both within our churches and in our bilateral dialogues. Pope John Paul II himself has recognized the difficulties which the papacy presents to many and has repeatedly invited theological reflection from all Christian traditions on this critical topic (e.g., UUS, nos. 95-96).

The relationships between our churches today are very different from even thirty-five years ago, when our Consultation began. Many of the issues that divide Orthodox and Catholics date back centuries. They often reflected significantly different perspectives on scripture and tradition and were frequently compounded by tragic historical events and bitter memories. Yet, as we examine these issues today, it is clear that our context is very different. We are no longer strangers to one another. Isolation has given way to regular contacts, especially here in North America. The prayer of Our Lord for the unity of his followers (John 17:21) rings urgently in our ears. The prayers of faithful people for the unity of the churches are bearing fruits in our meetings and in the way we approach the difficult issues that still divide us.

We believe that, with the guidance of the Spirit, the issues which continue to divide us are not beyond resolution. We are convinced that the Lord is calling us not only to speak honestly about our differences, but also to find resolutions to them which are loving, truthful, and salutary. With this in mind, we echo the words of Pope John Paul II and the late Patriarch Dimitrios: "Seeking only the glory of God through the accomplishment of his will, we state anew our resolute determination to do everything possible to hasten the day when full communion will be reestablished between the Catholic Church and the Orthodox Church, and when we will be at last able to concelebrate the divine Eucharist" (1979).

The Importance of Dialogue

We are aware that the ecumenical enterprise is considered highly suspect in some circles within both our churches. Indeed, a professed anti-ecumenism is the hallmark of some uncanonical Orthodox bodies, and similar ways of thinking have a significant following within the canonical Orthodox churches as well. Within the Catholic Church, despite the affirmation of the central importance of ecumenical dialogue expressed by the Second Vatican Council as well as by hierarchical and theological leadership on both world and regional levels, there are still groups which remain apathetic towards or even directly opposed to the spirit of ecumenism.

Even though on the surface these Catholic and Orthodox groups which oppose ecumenical dialogue appear to have diametrically opposed theological beliefs, there are certain underlying characteristics that they hold in common. They tend, first of all, to be convinced that theirs is the only true Church, and that outside its visible boundaries there can be nothing but error and confusion. Thus there is the tendency to see the world in black and white: there is either the Church in its fullness, or there is utter darkness. This is usually coupled with the conviction that "the world," along with other Christian churches and world religions, is unrelentingly hostile to the one Church, which stands in radical contradiction to it. In this way of thinking, to enter into dialogue with other Christian bodies is to run the risk of exposing the Church to the possibility of compromise or syncretism, and even to the loss of the Christian faith itself. According to this view, the only acceptable form of Christian dialogue is to proclaim the truth one possesses, in the hope that the others will recognize their errors and return to the one Church.

We recognize that some concerns of these adversaries of ecumenism have a certain merit. The Christian faith is indeed a precious gift from God and cannot in any way be negotiated or compromised. Moreover, both the Catholic and Orthodox Churches have a strong sense of possessing, as ecclesial bodies, the fullness of truth and the means of salvation. And yet we do not believe that this implies for either church that other Christian communions necessarily are devoid of truth and grace.

One of the basic principles of ecumenical dialogue is to make a distinction between the content of faith and the words in which that faith is expressed. Since human words can never exhaust the divine mystery, our effort in dialogue is to look beyond what appear to be contradictory verbal formulas to the faith that underlies them, to determine whether or not those formulas are witnessing to the same faith in different ways. Thus ecumenical dialogue, far from compromising the faith of either party, is an effort to rediscover and rearticulate the common faith that unites us in the same Jesus Christ, our Lord and Savior. Our conviction is that dialogue is not the abandonment of the truth of the Christian faith but rather an attempt to deepen together our understanding of that truth, free from the polemics of the past, by listening to the witness of the one truth that is given by our two traditions. Far from encouraging relativism, genuine dialogue begins with an immersion in one's own tradition and a desire to share its richness with others for the sake of the salvation of the world.

The Challenge Before Us

Recent statements by Pope John Paul II and Ecumenical Patriarch Bartholomew have forcefully reaffirmed this commitment to ecumenical dialogue on behalf of their churches. The recent visit of Pope John Paul II to Romania and his meeting with Patriarch Teoctist was a memorable occasion which further strengthened the commitment of our churches to reconciliation and visible unity. Both the Catholic Church and the Orthodox Church are committed to the process of Christian reconciliation and the visible unity of the churches, for the sake of the world and for the glory of God.

At the same time, we also recognize that in recent years the relationship between our churches has been severely strained in many places. The positive accomplishments of recent decades have been, on some occasions, set aside, and old animosities have resurfaced. Within parts of Eastern Europe, the reestablishment of religious freedom after a period of intense repression by various Communist regimes has led to disputes between Catholics and Orthodox involving not only church teachings but also property and social rights. Accusations of proselytism and misunderstandings regarding episcopal appointments have rekindled old hostilities. Sadly, these events have been compounded at times by insufficient communication between our hierarchies. In addition, those who oppose the dialogue between our churches have, in some cases, intentionally distorted the truth about what those churches believe and how they live.

Mindful of these facts, this Consultation wishes to express the following convictions, not only for the sake of our own churches but also for all those involved in the ecumenical movement:

- We believe that the quest for the unity of Christians and the restoration of the visible unity of the churches is rooted in the very actions of God who "desires everyone to be saved and to come to the knowledge of the truth" (1 Tim. 2:4). As Catholics and Orthodox, we profess our faith in the Triune God who loves, heals, forgives, and reconciles. Christ has come to break down the barriers caused by sin and to restore us to fellowship with the Father through the Holy Spirit. As Catholics and Orthodox who seek to follow Christ through the preaching and sacraments of his Church, we are called to live a life which bears witness to the healing actions of our God. We are called to be "ambassadors of Christ" (2 Cor 5:20) proclaiming the Gospel of reconciliation in our words and through our deeds, within our churches, our families, and our society.
- The historic divisions within Christianity have genuinely and seriously wounded the life of our churches over the centuries. Our appreciation of the apostolic faith in all its richness and fullness has been distorted by our divisions. Our understanding of the Church and its scripture, sacraments, ministry, witness, and mission has been narrowed and tainted by the divisive theological debates of the past. The historic divisions of the churches have led in many cases to diverse emphases and perspectives in doctrine and ethics, which have not always been complementary.
- Church divisions reflecting divergent teachings do not honor God or help to proclaim the Gospel to all nations (Matt. 28:19). How can we proclaim a God of reconciliation and be disunited among ourselves? How can we speak to the nations of the earth of the need for peace and unity and be disunited as churches? The division among the churches is a scandal that impedes the proclamation of the Gospel in the world today. Sadly, the divisions of the churches often contribute to bitter divisions within families and national cultures.
- The process of reconciliation of the churches, however, is not merely a matter of good will; it requires solid and consistent theological reflection. In order for this theological reflection to bear good fruit, it must be rooted in scripture and tradition

> and nurtured by prayer. It must be oriented toward the needs of God's people today. Our reconciliation requires a theology which is truly life-giving and which serves the Author of life.

In this Consultation, our common study has enabled us to view difficult issues from a variety of perspectives. In so doing, we have sought together to make a distinction between the faith of the Church and the historical explications of that faith. We have also been guided by the experience of the Church of the first millennium where a diversity of theological expression and liturgical practice was generally able to enrich Christian faith throughout the world.

As Catholics and Orthodox, we honor those before us who boldly and creatively taught the apostolic faith, often in the face of heresies. They sought to maintain the unity of the churches and, where necessary, to heal the divisions between the churches; their desire to teach the apostolic faith free from error was complemented by their desire to maintain the unity of the churches. They were ready, when necessary, to find new terminology which expressed the faith more precisely and which could reconcile divisions.

The process of reconciliation requires from us, as well, that our churches be engaged in genuine renewal, which aims at bearing witness more clearly to the presence of the Risen Lord in our midst. Trusting in the guidance of the Holy Spirit, both our churches are called to examine our worship, our teaching and preaching, and our exercise of authority, so that the message of the Gospel may be proclaimed clearly in all we say and in all we do.

We recognize that theological discussion between the Orthodox and Catholic churches and our gradual growth towards reconciliation take place within the broader context of the ecumenical movement. Both churches view the ecumenical movement primarily as a means through which all the churches of the divided Christian family are seeking to restore their visible unity in accordance with the apostolic faith. From our perspective, we are convinced that the ecumenical movement must always be centered upon Christ and his Gospel, as that Gospel has been proclaimed through twenty centuries. It must serve the churches in their quest for the restoration of visible unity in accordance with the apostolic faith. We acknowledge the important work of various other bilateral and multilateral dialogues and other expressions of the ecumenical movement. Many of these dialogues have contributed to our own work, particularly through their renewed attention to the doctrine of the Holy Trinity and its relationship to an ecclesiology of communion. Several of these other dialogues have reached agreement on significant topics. Now, in some cases, their conclusions and recommendations are being implemented and incorporated into church life. Our own Consultation has been inspired by their example, and enriched by their theological contributions. We are challenged to make our own theological work equally meaningful to the faithful of all Christians.

Conclusion

The ultimate goal of dialogue between the Catholic Church and the Orthodox Church is restoration of full communion. We recognize that this is a gradual process. Just as our alienation took place over the course of time, so also our reconciliation, under the guidance of the Holy Spirit, is taking place gradually. In order to be faithful to Our Lord, this process must be rooted in the Gospel and nurtured by prayer for unity. It must be fostered by theological dialogue and expressed in acts of love and mutual forgiveness. As members of sister churches which are responsible for upholding the apostolic faith, we cannot seek the victory of one tradition over another. Rather, we seek the victory of Christ over our divisions, for the sake of the salvation of all. To him be glory together with his eternal Father and his all-holy, good, and life-giving Spirit, now and forever and unto ages of ages. Amen.

Document 23

AT THE DAWN OF A NEW MILLENNIUM

North American Joint Committee of Orthodox and Catholic Bishops, 2000

Our Joint Committee of Orthodox and Catholic bishops was founded in 1981 as a forum where Orthodox and Catholic hierarchs from the United States and Canada could discuss pastoral matters of concern to both our churches. Gathered together now at our seventeenth meeting, we wish to take stock of our Joint Committee's work and to affirm the importance of continued and intensified dialogue between our two communions.

We look back with joy on the dramatic events of the 1960s that brought an end to the many centuries of hostility that kept us apart from one another. The meeting between Ecumenical Patriarch Athenagoras and Pope Paul VI in Jerusalem in 1964 was followed by the formal lifting of the 1054 anathemas on December 7, 1965. Those excommunications were reversed, to be replaced by relationships of love—they were "erased from the memory of the Church" and "consigned to oblivion." The growing dialogue of charity between Catholics and Orthodox led finally to the establishment of an official International Joint Commission for Theological Dialogue between the Catholic Church and the Orthodox Church by Ecumenical Patriarch Dimitrios I and Pope John Paul II when the pope visited Istanbul in November 1979. This renewed relationship has been symbolized by the semiannual exchange of delegations between the sister churches of Rome and Constantinople on their respective feast days, and a rejection among our faithful of "every form of proselytism, every attitude which would or could be perceived as a lack of respect" (Common Declaration of Pope John Paul II and Ecumenical Patriarch Dimitrios I, December 7, 1987).

With gratitude we note that this theological dialogue was anticipated by almost fifteen years in the United States. Prior to the establishment of our

Joint Committee of Orthodox and Catholic Bishops in 1981, an official Orthodox-Catholic Theological Consultation had been meeting since September 9, 1965, even before the excommunications were lifted. In North America, where Catholics and Orthodox live side by side in a place that is to a large extent free of the political and religious tension that has often been present in our countries of origin, our theological dialogue has been able to make much progress and to address various theological and pastoral questions touching upon our relationship. At its June 2000 meeting, our North American Theological Consultation issued a document entitled "Sharing the Ministry of Reconciliation: Statement on the Orthodox-Catholic Dialogue and the Ecumenical Movement." We wish to express our satisfaction with this important text, and we recommend it warmly to our faithful. We make our own its evaluation of the Catholic-Orthodox dialogue and the broader ecumenical movement as rooted in the very actions of God who "desires everyone to be saved and to come to the knowledge of the truth" (1 Tim. 2:4).

The fall of communism in Eastern and Central Europe and the establishment of religious freedom in those countries ten years ago now is a source of deep joy for all people of faith. But these profound changes also unleashed hostilities between our communities there that had remained under the surface, unaddressed during the long years of persecution, isolation, and silence. These problems focused on the status of the Eastern Catholic Churches and questions of property. At the same time, strident currents emerged in both our churches in those areas, fueled in part by the suspicion that ecumenism was a betrayal of the true faith and that it had been manipulated by the communist authorities for their own ends in an attempt to weaken authentic Christian witness. This points to the urgent need to present the true nature of ecumenical dialogue, not as a betrayal of anyone's faith, but as an effort to understand what we truly have in common at a level deeper than our divisions and theological formulae.

All this has had a negative impact on the international dialogue which for the past ten years has been struggling to deal in a satisfactory way with the question of the status of the Eastern Catholic Churches. We regret that the Eighth Plenary Session of the international dialogue, held in July 2000 at Emmitsburg, Maryland, was unable to make progress on this and other significant issues. The difficulties that have recently beset the international dialogue do not alter our conviction that continued dialogue in love is the only way that our churches can be faithful to Our Lord's command to love one another and to be reconciled. Indeed, when difficulties arise the need for dialogue becomes even greater.

As we look back on our experience of dialoguing with one another as bishops of the Orthodox and Catholic churches, we realize that through an honest and well informed exchange of views a solution to even the most persistent disagreements can be perceived. Our Joint Committee of bishops has issued statements dealing with ordination, mixed marriages, and the recent tensions in Eastern and Central Europe, and we are confident that much more progress can be made on these and other issues. We encourage our Orthodox and Catholic faithful everywhere to engage one another in an exchange of views in a spirit of openness and humility so that the Spirit's work of reconciliation might continue, for the glory of God.

Our Joint Committee is meeting on the island of Crete, whose soil has been fed by the blood of a host of martyrs and whose history has not been unaffected by our sad divisions. We take this opportunity to give thanks to God for the great strides that have been made to overcome what divides us. As the new millennium dawns, we join our prayer to those of Orthodox and Catholic faithful around the world that our churches may continue to set aside the animosities of the past and look forward in hope to that blessed day when we shall once again be united around the common table of our Lord.

DOCUMENT 24

THE *FILIOQUE*: A CHURCH-DIVIDING ISSUE?

An Agreed Statement of the North American Orthodox-Catholic Theological Consultation, 2003

From 1999 until 2003, the North American Orthodox-Catholic Consultation has focused its discussions on an issue that has been identified, for more than twelve centuries, as one of the root causes of division between our Churches: our divergent ways of conceiving and speaking about the origin of the Holy Spirit within the inner life of the triune God. Although both of our traditions profess "the faith of Nicaea" as the normative expression of our understanding of God and God's involvement in his creation and take as the classical statement of that faith the revised version of the Nicene Creed associated with the First Council of Constantinople of 381, most Catholics and other Western Christians have used, since at least the late sixth century, a Latin version of that Creed, which adds to its confession that the Holy Spirit "proceeds from the Father" the word *Filioque*: "and from the Son." For most Western Christians, this term continues to be a part of the central formulation of their faith, a formulation proclaimed in the liturgy and used as the basis of catechesis and theological reflection. It is, for Catholics and most Protestants, simply a part of the ordinary teaching of the Church and, as such, integral to their understanding of the dogma of the Holy Trinity. Yet since at least the late eighth century, the presence of this term in the Western version of the Creed has been a source of scandal for Eastern Christians, both because of the Trinitarian theology it expresses, and because it had been adopted by a growing number of Churches in the West into the canonical formulation of a received ecumenical council without corresponding ecumenical agreement. As the medieval rift between Eastern and Western Christians grew more serious, the theology associated with the term *Filioque* and the issues of Church structure and authority raised by its adoption grew into a symbol of difference, a classic token of what each side of divided Christendom has found lacking or distorted in the other.

Our common study of this question has involved our Consultation in much shared research, prayerful reflection, and intense discussion. It is our hope that many of the papers produced by our members during this process will be published together as the scholarly context for our common statement. A subject as complicated as this, from both the historical and the theological point of view, calls for detailed explanation if the real issues are to be clearly seen. Our discussions and our common statement will not, by themselves, put an end to centuries of disagreement among our Churches. We do hope, however, that they will contribute to the growth of mutual understanding and respect, and that in God's time our Churches will no longer find a cause for separation in the way we think and speak about the origin of that Spirit whose fruit is love and peace (see Gal 5:22).

I. The Holy Spirit in the Scriptures

In the Old Testament "the spirit of God" or "the spirit of the Lord" is presented less as a divine person than as a manifestation of God's creative power—God's "breath" (*ruach YHWH*)—forming the world as an ordered and habitable place for his people and raising up individuals to lead his people in the way of holiness. In the opening verses of Genesis, the spirit of God "moves over the face of the waters" to bring order out of chaos (Gen 1:2). In the historical narratives of Israel, it is the same spirit that "stirs" in the leaders of the people (Jud 13:25—Samson), makes kings and military chieftains into prophets (1 Sam 10:9-12, 19:18-24—Saul and David), and enables prophets to "bring good news to the afflicted" (Is 61:1; cf. 42:1; 2 Kg 2:9). The Lord tells Moses he has "filled" Bezalel the craftsman "with the spirit of God" to enable him to fashion all the furnishings of the tabernacle according to God's design (Ex 31:3). In some passages, the "holy spirit" (Ps 51:13) or "good spirit" (Ps 143:10) of the Lord seems to signify his guiding presence within individuals and the whole nation, cleansing their own spirits (Ps 51:12-14) and helping them to keep his commandments, but "grieved" by their sin (Is 63:10). In the prophet Ezekiel's mighty vision of the restoration of Israel from the death of defeat and exile, the "breath" returning to the people's desiccated corpses becomes an image of the action of God's own breath creating the nation anew: "I will put my spirit within you, and you shall live . . ." (Ezek 37:14).

In the New Testament writings, the Holy Spirit of God (*pneuma Theou*) is usually spoken of in a more personal way and is inextricably connected with the person and mission of Jesus. Matthew and Luke make it clear that Mary conceives Jesus in her womb by the power of the Holy Spirit, who "overshadows" her (Mt 1:18, 20; Lk 1:35). All four Gospels testify that John the Baptist—who himself was "filled with the Holy Spirit from his mother's womb" (Lk 1:15)—witnessed the descent of the same Spirit on Jesus, in a visible manifestation of God's power and election, when Jesus was baptized (Mt 3:16; Mk 1:10; Lk 3:22; Jn 1:33). The Holy Spirit leads Jesus into the desert to struggle with the devil (Mt 4:1; Lk 4:1), fills him with prophetic power at the start of his mission (Lk 4:18-21), and manifests himself in Jesus' exorcisms (Mt 12:28, 32). John the Baptist identified the mission of Jesus as "baptizing" his disciples "with the Holy Spirit and with fire" (Mt 3:11; Lk 3:16; cf. Jn 1:33), a prophecy fulfilled in the great events of Pentecost (Acts 1:5), when the disciples were "clothed with power from on high" (Lk 24:49; Acts 1:8). In the narrative of Acts, it is the Holy Spirit who continues to unify the community (4:31-32), who enables Stephen to bear witness to Jesus with his life (8:55), and whose charismatic presence among believing pagans makes it clear that they, too, are called to baptism in Christ (10:47).

In his farewell discourse in the Gospel of John, Jesus speaks of the Holy Spirit as one who will continue his own work in the world, after he has returned to the Father. He is "the Spirit of truth," who will act as "another advocate (*parakletos*)" to teach and guide his disciples (14:16-17), reminding them of all Jesus himself has taught (14:26). In this section of the Gospel, Jesus gives us a clearer sense of the relationship between this "advocate," himself, and his Father. Jesus promises to send him "from the Father" as "the Spirit of truth who proceeds from the Father" (15:26); and the truth that he teaches will be the truth Jesus has revealed in his own person (see 1:14; 14:6): "He will glorify me, for he will take what is mine and declare it to you. All that the Father has is mine; therefore I said that he will take what is mine and declare it to you" (16:14-15).

The Epistle to the Hebrews represents the Spirit simply as speaking in the Scriptures, with his own voice (Heb 3:7; 9:8). In Paul's letters, the Holy Spirit of God is identified as the one who has finally "defined" Jesus as "Son of God in power" by acting as the agent of his resurrection (Rom 1:4; 8:11). It is this same Spirit, communicated now to us, who conforms us to the risen

Lord, giving us hope for resurrection and life (Rom 8:11), making us also children and heirs of God (Rom 8:14-17), and forming our words and even our inarticulate groaning into a prayer that expresses hope (Rom 8:23-27). "And hope does not disappoint us because God's love has been poured into our hearts through the Holy Spirit which has been given to us" (Rom 5:5).

II. Historical Considerations

Throughout the early centuries of the Church, the Latin and Greek traditions witnessed to the same apostolic faith but differed in their ways of describing the relationship among the persons of the Trinity. The difference generally reflected the various pastoral challenges facing the Church in the West and in the East. The Nicene Creed (325) bore witness to the faith of the Church as it was articulated in the face of the Arian heresy, which denied the full divinity of Christ. In the years following the Council of Nicaea, the Church continued to be challenged by views questioning both the full divinity and the full humanity of Christ, as well as the divinity of the Holy Spirit. Against these challenges, the fathers at the Council of Constantinople (381) affirmed the faith of Nicaea and produced an expanded Creed, based on the Nicene but also adding significantly to it.

The acts of the Council of Constantinople were lost, but the text of its Creed was quoted and formally acknowledged as binding, along with the Creed of Nicaea, in the dogmatic statement of the Council of Chalcedon (451). Within less than a century, this Creed of 381 had come to play a normative role in the definition of faith, and by the early sixth century was even proclaimed in the Eucharist in Antioch, Constantinople, and other regions in the East. In regions of the Western churches, the Creed was also introduced into the Eucharist, perhaps beginning with the third Council of Toledo in 589. It was not formally introduced into the Eucharistic liturgy at Rome, however, until the eleventh century—a point of some importance for the process of official Western acceptance of the *Filioque*.

No clear record exists of the process by which the word *Filioque* was inserted into the Creed of 381 in the Christian West before the sixth century. The idea that the Spirit came forth "from the Father through the Son" is asserted by a number of earlier Latin theologians, as part of their insistence on the ordered unity of all three persons within the single divine Mystery (e.g., Tertullian, *Adversus Praxean*, 4 and 5). Tertullian, writing at the beginning of the third century, emphasizes that Father, Son, and Holy

Spirit all share a single divine substance, quality, and power (ibid., 2), which he conceives of as flowing forth from the Father and being transmitted by the Son to the Spirit (ibid., 8). Hilary of Poitiers, in the mid-fourth century, in the same work speaks of the Spirit both as simply being "from the Father" (*De Trinitate*, 12.56) and as "having the Father and the Son as his source" (ibid., 2.29); in another passage, Hilary points to John 16:15 (where Jesus says, "All things that the Father has are mine; therefore I said that [the Spirit] shall take from what is mine and declare it to you"), and wonders aloud whether "to receive from the Son is the same thing as to proceed from the Father" (ibid., 8.20). Ambrose of Milan, writing in the 380s, openly asserts that the Spirit "proceeds from (*procedit a*) the Father and the Son," without ever being separated from either (*On the Holy Spirit*, 1.11.20). None of these writers, however, makes the Spirit's mode of origin the object of special reflection; all are concerned, rather, to emphasize the equality of status of all three divine persons as God, and all acknowledge that the Father alone is the source of God's eternal being.

The earliest use of *Filioque* language in a credal context is in the profession of faith formulated for the Visigoth King Reccared at the local Council of Toledo in 589. This regional council anathematized those who did not accept the decrees of the first four Ecumenical Councils (c. 11), as well as those who did not profess that the Holy Spirit proceeds from the Father and the Son (c. 3). It appears that the Spanish bishops and King Reccared believed at that time that the Greek equivalent of *Filioque* was part of the original creed of Constantinople and apparently understood that its purpose was to oppose Arianism by affirming the intimate relationship of the Father and Son. On Reccared's orders, the Creed began to be recited during the Eucharist, in imitation of the Eastern practice. From Spain, the use of the Creed with the *Filioque* spread throughout Gaul.

Nearly a century later, a council of English bishops was held at Hatfield in 680 under the presidency of Archbishop Theodore of Canterbury, a Byzantine asked to serve in England by Pope Vitalian. According to the Venerable Bede (*Hist. Eccl. Gent. Angl.*, 4.15 [17]), this Council explicitly affirmed its faith as conforming to the five Ecumenical Councils and also declared that the Holy Spirit proceeds "in an ineffable way (*inenarrabiliter*)" from the Father and the Son.

By the seventh century, three related factors may have contributed to a growing tendency to include the *Filioque* in the Creed of 381 in the West and to the belief of some Westerners that it was, in fact, part of the original creed. First, a strong current in the patristic tradition of the West, summed up in the works of Augustine (354-430), spoke of the Spirit's proceeding from the Father and the Son (e.g., *On the Trinity*, 4.29; 15.10, 12, 29, 37; the significance of this tradition and its terminology will be discussed below). Second, throughout the fourth and fifth centuries a number of credal statements circulated in the Churches, often associated with baptism and catechesis. The formula of 381 was not considered the only binding expression of apostolic faith. Within the West, the most widespread of these was the Apostles' Creed, an early baptismal creed, which contained a simple affirmation of belief in the Holy Spirit without elaboration. Third, however, and of particular significance for later Western theology, was the so-called Athanasian Creed (*Quicumque*). Thought by Westerners to be composed by Athanasius of Alexandria, this Creed probably originated in Gaul about 500 and is cited by Caesarius of Arles (d. 542). This text was unknown in the East but had great influence in the West until modern times. Relying heavily on Augustine's treatment of the Trinity, it clearly affirmed that the Spirit proceeds from the Father and the Son. A central emphasis of this Creed was its strong anti-Arian Christology: speaking of the Spirit as proceeding from the Father *and* the Son implied that the Son was not inferior to the Father in substance, as the Arians held. The influence of this Creed undoubtedly supported the use of the *Filioque* in the Latin version of the Creed of Constantinople in Western Europe, at least from the sixth century onwards.

The use of the Creed of 381 with the addition of the *Filioque* became a matter of controversy towards the end of the eighth century, both in discussions between the Frankish theologians and the see of Rome and in the growing rivalry between the Carolingian and Byzantine courts, which both now claimed to be the legitimate successors of the Roman Empire. In the wake of the iconoclastic struggle in Byzantium, the Carolingians took this opportunity to challenge the Orthodoxy of Constantinople and put particular emphasis upon the significance of the term *Filioque*, which they now began to identify as a touchstone of right Trinitarian faith. An intense political and cultural rivalry between the Franks and the Byzantines provided the background for the *Filioque* debates throughout the eighth and ninth centuries.

Charlemagne received a translation of the decisions of the Second Council of Nicaea (787). The Council had given definitive approval to the ancient practice of venerating icons. The translation proved to be defective. On the basis of this defective translation, Charlemagne sent a delegation to Pope Hadrian I (772-795) to present his concerns. Among the points of objection, Charlemagne's legates claimed that Patriarch Tarasius of

Constantinople, at his installation, did not follow the Nicene faith and profess that the Spirit proceeds from the Father and the Son, but confessed rather his procession from the Father *through the Son* (Mansi [Giovan Domenico Mansi, *Sacrorum conciliorum nova et amplissima collectio*, Florence: Expensis Antonii Zatta Veneti], 13.760). The pope strongly rejected Charlemagne's protest, showing at length that Tarasius and the Council, on this and other points, maintained the faith of the Fathers (ibid., 759-810). Following this exchange of letters, Charlemagne commissioned the so-called *Libri Carolini* (791-794), a work written to challenge the positions both of the iconoclast council of 754 and of the Council of Nicaea of 787 on the veneration of icons. Again because of poor translations, the Carolingians misunderstood the actual decision of the latter Council. Within this text, the Carolingian view of the *Filioque* also was emphasized again. Arguing that the word *Filioque* was part of the Creed of 381, the *Libri Carolini* reaffirmed the Latin tradition that the Spirit proceeds from the Father and the Son and rejected as inadequate the teaching that the Spirit proceeds from the Father through the Son.

While the acts of the local synod of Frankfurt in 794 are not extant, other records indicate that it was called mainly to counter a form of the heresy of "Adoptionism" then thought to be on the rise in Spain. The emphasis of a number of Spanish theologians on the integral humanity of Christ seemed, to the court theologian Alcuin and others, to imply that the man Jesus was "adopted" by the Father at his baptism. In the presence of Charlemagne, this council—which Charlemagne seems to have promoted as "ecumenical" (see Mansi, 13.899-906)—approved the *Libri Carolini*, affirming, in the context of maintaining the full divinity of the person of Christ, that the Spirit proceeds from the Father and the Son. As in the late sixth century, the Latin formulation of the Creed, stating that the Spirit proceeds from the Father and the Son, was enlisted to combat a perceived Christological heresy.

Within a few years, another local council, also directed against "Spanish Adoptionism," was held in Fréjus (Friuli) (796 or 797). At this meeting, Paulinus of Aquileia (d. 802), an associate of Alcuin in Charlemagne's court, defended the use of the Creed with the *Filioque* as a way of opposing Adoptionism. Paulinus, in fact, recognized that the *Filioque* was an addition to the Creed of 381 but defended the interpolation, claiming that it contradicted neither the meaning of the creed nor the intention of the Fathers. The authority in the West of the Council of Fréjus, together with that of Frankfurt, ensured that the Creed of 381 with the

Filioque would be used in teaching and in the celebration of the Eucharist in churches throughout much of Europe.

The different liturgical traditions with regard to the Creed came into contact with each other in early ninth-century Jerusalem. Western monks, using the Latin Creed with the added *Filioque*, were denounced by their Eastern brethren. Writing to Pope Leo III for guidance, in 808, the Western monks referred to the practice in Charlemagne's chapel in Aachen as their model. Pope Leo responded with a letter to "all the churches of the East" in which he declared his personal belief that the Holy Spirit proceeds eternally from the Father and the Son. In that response, the pope did not distinguish between his personal understanding and the issue of the legitimacy of the addition to the Creed, although he would later resist the addition in liturgies celebrated at Rome.

Taking up the issue of the Jerusalem controversy, Charlemagne asked Theodulf of Orleans, the principal author of the *Libri Carolini*, to write a defense of the use of the word *Filioque*. Appearing in 809, *De Spiritu Sancto* of Theodulf was essentially a compilation of patristic citations supporting the theology of the *Filioque*. With this text in hand, Charlemagne convened a council in Aachen in 809-810 to affirm the doctrine of the Spirit's proceeding from the Father and the Son, which had been questioned by Greek theologians. Following this council, Charlemagne sought Pope Leo's approval of the use of the creed with the *Filioque* (Mansi, 14.23-76). A meeting between the pope and a delegation from Charlemagne's council took place in Rome in 810. While Leo III affirmed the orthodoxy of the term *Filioque* and approved its use in catechesis and personal professions of faith, he explicitly disapproved its inclusion in the text of the Creed of 381, since the Fathers of that Council—who were, he observes, no less inspired by the Holy Spirit than the bishops who had gathered at Aachen—had chosen not to include it. Pope Leo stipulated that the use of the Creed in the celebration of the Eucharist was permissible, but not required, and urged that in the interest of preventing scandal it would be better if the Carolingian court refrained from including it in the liturgy. Around this time, according to the *Liber Pontificalis*, the pope had two heavy silver shields made and displayed in St. Peter's, containing the original text of the Creed of 381 in both Greek and Latin. Despite his directives and this symbolic action, however, the Carolingians continued to use the Creed with the *Filioque* during the Eucharist in their own dioceses.

The Byzantines had little appreciation of the various developments regarding the *Filioque* in the West between the sixth and ninth centuries.

Communication grew steadily worse, and their own struggles with monothelitism, iconoclasm, and the rise of Islam left little time to follow closely theological developments in the West. However, their interest in the *Filioque* became more pronounced in the middle of the ninth century, when it came to be combined with jurisdictional disputes between Rome and Constantinople, as well as with the activities of Frankish missionaries in Bulgaria. When Byzantine missionaries were expelled from Bulgaria by King Boris, under Western influence, they returned to Constantinople and reported on Western practices, including the use of the Creed with the *Filioque*. Patriarch Photios of Constantinople, in 867, addressed a strongly worded encyclical to the other Eastern patriarchs, commenting on the political and ecclesiastical crisis in Bulgaria as well as on the tensions between Constantinople and Rome. In this letter, Photios denounced the Western missionaries in Bulgaria and criticized Western liturgical practices.

Most significantly, Patriarch Photios called the addition of the *Filioque* in the West a blasphemy and presented a substantial theological argument against the view of the Trinity which he believed it depicted. Photios's opposition to the *Filioque* was based upon his view that it signifies two causes in the Trinity and diminishes the monarchy of the Father. Thus, the *Filioque* seemed to him to detract from the distinctive character of each person of the Trinity and to confuse their relationships, paradoxically bearing in itself the seeds of both pagan polytheism and Sabellian modalism (*Mystagogy*, 9, 11). In his letter of 867, Photios does not, however, demonstrate any knowledge of the Latin patristic tradition behind the use of the *Filioque* in the West. His opposition to the *Filioque* would subsequently receive further elaboration in his Letter to the Patriarch of Aquileia in 883 or 884, as well as in his famous *Mystagogy of the Holy Spirit*, written about 886.

In concluding his letter of 867, Photios called for an ecumenical council that would resolve the issue of the interpolation of the *Filioque*, as well as illuminate its theological foundation. A local council was held in Constantinople in 867, which deposed Pope Nicholas I—an action which increased tensions between the two sees. In 863, Nicholas himself had refused to recognize Photios as Patriarch because of his allegedly uncanonical appointment. With changes in the imperial government, Photios was forced to resign in 867 and was replaced by Patriarch Ignatius, whom he himself had replaced in 858. A new council was convened in Constantinople later in 869. With papal representatives present and with imperial support, this Council excommunicated Photios and was subsequently recognized in the Medieval West, for reasons unrelated to the *Filioque* or Photios, as the Eighth Ecumenical Council, although it was never recognized as such in the East.

The relationship between Rome and Constantinople changed when Photios again became patriarch in 877, following the death of Ignatius. In Rome, Pope Nicholas had died in 867 and was succeeded by Pope Hadrian II (867-872), who himself anathematized Photios in 869. His successor, Pope John VIII (872-882), was willing to recognize Photios as the legitimate patriarch in Constantinople under certain conditions, thus clearing the way for a restoration of better relations. A Council was held in Constantinople in 879-880, in the presence of representatives from Rome and the other Eastern Patriarchates. This Council, considered by some modern Orthodox theologians to be ecumenical, suppressed the decisions of the earlier Council of 869-870 and recognized the status of Photios as patriarch. It affirmed the ecumenical character of the Council of 787 and its decisions against iconoclasm. There was no extensive discussion of the *Filioque*, which was not yet a part of the Creed professed in Rome itself, and no statement was made by the Council about its theological justification; yet this Council formally reaffirmed the original text of the Creed of 381, without the *Filioque*, and anathematized anyone who would compose another confession of faith. The Council also spoke of the Roman See in terms of great respect and allowed the papal legates the traditional prerogatives of presidency, recognizing their right to begin and to close discussions and to sign documents first. Nevertheless, the documents give no indication that the bishops present formally recognized any priority of jurisdiction for the see of Rome, outside of the framework of the patristic understanding of the communion of Churches and the sixth-century canonical theory of the Pentarchy. The difficult question of the competing claims of the pope and the patriarch of Constantinople to jurisdiction in Bulgaria was left to be decided by the emperor. After the Council, the *Filioque* continued to be used in the Creed in parts of Western Europe, despite the intentions of Pope John VIII, who, like his predecessors, maintained the text sanctioned by the Council of 381.

A new stage in the history of the controversy was reached in the early eleventh century. During the synod following the coronation of King Henry II as Holy Roman Emperor at Rome in 1014, the Creed, including the *Filioque,* was sung for the first time at a papal Mass. Because of this action, the liturgical use of the Creed, with the *Filioque*, now was generally assumed in the Latin Church to have the sanction of the papacy. Its inclusion in the Eucharist, after two centuries of papal resistance of the practice, reflected a new dominance of the German emperors over the papacy as well as the papacy's growing sense of its own authority, under imperial protection, within the entire Church, both western and eastern.

The *Filioque* figured prominently in the tumultuous events of 1054, when excommunications were exchanged by representatives of the Eastern and Western Churches meeting in Constantinople. Within the context of his anathemas against Patriarch Michael I Cerularios of Constantinople and certain of his advisors, Cardinal Humbert of Silva Candida, the legate of Pope Leo IX, accused the Byzantines of improperly deleting the *Filioque* from the Creed and criticized other Eastern liturgical practices. In responding to these accusations, Patriarch Michael recognized that the anathemas of Humbert did not originate with Leo IX and cast his own anathemas simply upon the papal delegation. Leo, in fact, was already dead, and his successor had not been elected. At the same time, Michael condemned the Western use of the *Filioque* in the Creed, as well as other Western liturgical practices. This exchange of limited excommunications did not lead, by itself, to a formal schism between Rome and Constantinople, despite the views of later historians; it did, however, deepen the growing estrangement between Constantinople and Rome.

The relationship between the Church of Rome and the Churches of Constantinople, Alexandria, Antioch, and Jerusalem were seriously damaged during the period of the crusades, and especially in the wake of the infamous Fourth Crusade. In 1204, Western Crusaders sacked the city of Constantinople, long the commercial and political rival of Venice, and Western politicians and clergy dominated the life of the city until it was reclaimed by Emperor Michael VIII Palaiologos in 1261. The installation of Western bishops in the territories of Constantinople, Antioch, and Jerusalem, who were loyal to Rome and to the political powers of Western Europe, became a tragically visible new expression of schism. Even after 1261, Rome supported Latin patriarchs in these three ancient Eastern sees. For most Eastern Christians, this was a clear sign that the papacy and its political supporters had little regard for the legitimacy of their ancient churches.

Despite this growing estrangement, a number of notable attempts were made to address the issue of the *Filioque* between the early twelfth and mid-thirteenth century. The German Emperor Lothair III sent Bishop Anselm of Havelberg to Constantinople in 1136 to negotiate a military alliance with Emperor John II Comnenos. While he was there, Anselm and Metropolitan Nicetas of Nicomedia held a series of public discussions about subjects dividing the Churches, including the *Filioque*, and concluded that the differences between the two traditions were not as great as they had thought (PL,

188.1206B-1210B). A letter from Orthodox Patriarch Germanos II (1222-1240) to Pope Gregory IX (1227-1241) led to further discussions between Eastern and Western theologians on the *Filioque* at Nicaea in 1234. Subsequent discussions were held in 1253-1254 at the initiative of Emperor John III Vatatzes (1222-1254) and Pope Innocent IV (1243-1254). In spite of these efforts, the continuing effects of the Fourth Crusade and the threat of the Turks, along with the jurisdictional claims of the papacy in the East, meant that these well-intentioned efforts came to no conclusion.

Against this background, a Western council was held in Lyons in 1274 (Lyons II), after the restoration of Constantinople to Eastern imperial control. Despite the consequences of the crusades, many Byzantines sought to heal the wounds of division and looked to the West for support against the growing advances of the Turks, and Pope Gregory X (1271-1276) enthusiastically hoped for reunion. Among the topics agreed upon for discussion at the council was the *Filioque*. Yet the two Byzantine bishops who were sent as delegates had no real opportunity to present the Eastern perspective at the Council. The *Filioque* was formally approved by the delegates in the final session on July 17, 1274, in a brief constitution which also explicitly condemned those holding other views on the origin of the Holy Spirit. Already on July 6, in accord with an agreement previously reached between papal delegates and the Emperor in Constantinople, the reunion of the Eastern and Western Churches was proclaimed, but it was never received by the Eastern clergy and faithful or vigorously promoted by the popes in the West. In this context it should be noted that in his letter commemorating the seven-hundredth anniversary of this council (1974), Pope Paul VI recognised this and added that "the Latins chose texts and formulae expressing an ecclesiology which had been conceived and developed in the West. It is understandable . . . that a unity achieved in this way could not be accepted completely by the Eastern Christian mind." A little further on, the pope, speaking of the future Catholic-Orthodox dialogue, observed, "it will take up again other controverted points which Gregory X and the Fathers of Lyons thought were resolved."

At the Eastern Council of Blachernae (Constantinople) in 1285, in fact, the decisions of the Council of Lyons and the pro-Latin theology of former Patriarch John XI Bekkos (1275-1282) were soundly rejected, under the leadership of Patriarch Gregory II, also known as Gregory of Cyprus (1282-1289). At the same time, this council produced a significant statement addressing the theological issue of the *Filioque*. While firmly rejecting the "double procession" of the Spirit from the Father and the Son, the statement spoke of an "eternal manifestation" of the Spirit *through* the Son. Patriarch Gregory's language opened the way, at least, towards a deeper, more complex understanding of the relationship between Father, Son, and Holy Spirit in both the East and the West (see below). This approach was developed further by Gregory Palamas (1296-1359) in the context of his distinction between the essence and the energies of the divine persons. Unfortunately, these openings had little effect on later medieval discussions of the origin of the Spirit, in either the Eastern or the Western Church. Despite the concern shown by Byzantine theologians, from the time of Photios, to oppose both the idea of the *Filioque* and its addition to the Latin creed, there is no reference to it in the *Synodikon of Orthodoxy*, a collection containing more than sixty anathemas representing the doctrinal decisions of Eastern councils through the fourteenth century.

One more attempt was made, however, to deal with the subject authoritatively on an ecumenical scale. The Council of Ferrara-Florence (1438-1445) again brought together representatives from the Church of Rome and the Churches of Constantinople, Alexandria, Antioch, and Jerusalem to discuss a wide range of controversial issues, including papal authority and the *Filioque*. This Council took place at a time when the Byzantine Empire was gravely threatened by the Ottomans and when many in the Greek world regarded military aid from the West as Constantinople's only hope. Following extensive discussions by experts from both sides, often centered on the interpretation of patristic texts, the union of the Churches was declared on July 6, 1439. The Council's decree of reunion, *Laetentur caeli*, recognized the legitimacy of the Western view of the Spirit's eternal procession from the Father and the Son, as from a single principle and in a single spiration. The *Filioque* was presented here as having the same meaning as the position of some early Eastern Fathers that the Spirit exists or proceeds "through the Son." The Council also approved a text which spoke of the Pope as having "primacy over the whole world," as "head of the whole church and father and teacher of all Christians." Despite Orthodox participation in these discussions, the decisions of Florence—like the union decree of Lyons II—were never received by a representative body of bishops or faithful in the East and were formally rejected in Constantinople in 1484.

The fall of Constantinople in 1453 and the fracturing effect of the Protestant Reformation in the West, as well as subsequent Latin missions in the former Byzantine world and the establishment of Eastern Churches in communion with Rome, led to a deepening of the schism, accompanied by much polemical literature on each side. For more than five hundred years, few opportunities were offered to the Catholic and Orthodox sides for serious discussion of the *Filioque* and of the related issue of the primacy and teaching authority of the bishop of Rome. Orthodoxy and Roman Catholicism entered into a period of formal isolation from each other, in which each developed a sense of being the only ecclesiastical body authentically representing the apostolic faith. For example, this is expressed in Pius IX's encyclical *In Suprema Petri Sede* of January 6, 1848, and in Leo XIII's encyclical *Praeclara Gratulationis Publicae* of June 20, 1894, as well as the encyclical of the Orthodox patriarchs in 1848 and the encyclical of the Patriarchate of Constantinople of 1895, each reacting to the prior papal documents. Ecumenical discussions of the *Filioque* between the Orthodox Churches and representatives of the Old Catholics and Anglicans were held in Germany in 1874-1875 and were occasionally revived during the century that followed, but in general little substantial progress was made in moving beyond the hardened opposition of traditional Eastern and Western views.

A new phase in the relationship between the Catholic Church and the Orthodox Church began formally with the Second Vatican Council (1962-1965) and the Pan-Orthodox Conferences (1961-1968), which renewed contacts and dialogue. From that time, a number of theological issues and historical events contributing to the schism between the churches have begun to receive new attention. In this context, our own North American Orthodox-Catholic Consultation was established in 1965, and the Joint International Commission for Theological Dialogue between the Orthodox and Catholic Churches was established in 1979. Although a committee of theologians from many different Churches, sponsored by the Faith and Order Commission of the World Council of Churches, studied the *Filioque* question in depth in 1978 and 1979 and concluded by issuing the "Klingenthal Memorandum" (1979), no thorough new joint discussion of the issue has been undertaken by representatives of our two Churches until our own study. The first statement of the Joint International Commission (1982), entitled "The Mystery of the Church and of the Eucharist in the Light of the Mystery of the Trinity," does briefly address the issue of the *Filioque* within the context of an extensive discussion of the relationship of the persons of the Holy Trinity. The statement says,

> Without wishing to resolve yet the difficulties which have arisen between the East and the West concerning the relationship between the Son and the Spirit, we can already say together that this Spirit, which proceeds from the Father (Jn. 15:26) as the

> sole source of the Trinity, and which has become the Spirit of our sonship (Rom. 8:15) since he is already the Spirit of the Son (Gal.4:6), is communicated to us, particularly in the Eucharist, by this Son upon whom he reposes in time and eternity (Jn. 1:32). (no. 6)

Several other events in recent decades point to a greater willingness on the part of Rome to recognize the normative character of the original creed of Constantinople. When Patriarch Dimitrios I visited Rome on December 7, 1987, and again during the visit of Patriarch Bartholomew I to Rome in June 1995, both patriarchs attended a Eucharist celebrated by Pope John Paul II in St. Peter's Basilica. On both occasions the pope and patriarch proclaimed the Creed in Greek (i.e., without the *Filioque*). Pope John Paul II and Romanian Patriarch Teoctist did the same in Romanian at a papal Mass in Rome on October 13, 2002. The document *Dominus Iesus (On the Unicity and Salvific Universality of Jesus Christ and the Church)*, issued by the Congregation for the Doctrine of the Faith on August 6, 2000, begins its theological considerations on the Church's central teaching with the text of the Creed of 381, again without the addition of the *Filioque*. While no interpretation of these uses of the Creed was offered, these developments suggest a new awareness on the Catholic side of the unique character of the original Greek text of the Creed as the most authentic formulation of the faith that unifies Eastern and Western Christianity.

Not long after the meeting in Rome between Pope John Paul II and Ecumenical Patriarch Bartholomew I, the Vatican published the document "The Greek and Latin Traditions Regarding the Procession of the Holy Spirit" (September 13, 1995). This text was intended to be a new contribution to the dialogue between our churches on this controversial issue. Among the many observations it makes, the text says, "The Catholic Church acknowledges the conciliar, ecumenical, normative and irrevocable value, as the expression of one common faith of the Church and of all Christians, of the Symbol professed in Greek at Constantinople in 381 by the Second Ecumenical Council. No confession of faith peculiar to a particular liturgical tradition can contradict this expression of faith taught and professed by the undivided Church" [in *Information Service* (of the PCPCU) 89 (1995/II-III): 88]. Although the Catholic Church obviously does not consider the *Filioque* to be a contradiction of the creed of 381, the significance of this passage in the 1995 Vatican statement should not be minimized. It is in response to this important document that our own study of the *Filioque* began in 1999, and we hope that this present statement will serve to carry further the positive discussions between our communions that we have experienced ourselves.

III. Theological Reflections

In all discussions about the origin of the Holy Spirit within the Mystery of God and about the relationships of Father, Son, and Holy Spirit with each other, the first habit of mind to be cultivated is doubtless a reverent modesty. Concerning the divine Mystery itself, we can say very little, and our speculations always risk claiming a degree of clarity and certainty that is more than their due. As Pseudo-Dionysius reminds us, "No unity or trinity or number or oneness or fruitfulness, or any other thing that either is a creature or can be known to any creature, is able to express the Mystery, beyond all mind and reason, of that transcendent Godhead which in a super-essential way surpasses all things" (*On the Divine Names*, 13.3). That we do, as Christians, profess our God, who is radically and indivisibly one, to be the Father and the Son and the Holy Spirit—three "persons" who can never be confused with or reduced to one another, and who are all fully and literally God, singly and in the harmonious whole of their relationships with each other—is simply a summation of what we have learned from God's self-revelation in human history, a revelation that has reached its climax in our being able, in the power of the Holy Spirit, to confess Jesus as the Eternal Father's Word and Son. Surely our Christian language about God must always be regulated by the Holy Scriptures and by the dogmatic tradition of the Church, which interprets the content of Scripture in a normative way. Yet there always remains the difficult hermeneutical problem of applying particular Scriptural terms and texts to the inner life of God, and of knowing when a passage refers simply to God's action within the "economy" of saving history or when it should be understood as referring absolutely to God's being in itself. The division between our Churches on the *Filioque* question would probably be less acute if both sides, through the centuries, had remained more conscious of the limitations of our knowledge of God.

Secondly, discussion of this difficult subject has often been hampered by polemical distortions, in which each side has caricatured the position of the other for the purposes of argument. It is not true, for instance, that mainstream Orthodox theology conceives of the procession of the Spirit, within God's eternal being, as simply unaffected by the relationship of the Son to the Father, or thinks of the Spirit as not "belonging" properly to the Son when the Spirit is sent forth in history. It is also not true that mainstream Latin theology has traditionally begun its Trinitarian reflections from an abstract, unscriptural consideration of the divine substance, affirms two causes of the Spirit's hypostatic existence, or means to assign the Holy Spirit a role subordinate to the Son, either within the Mystery of God or in God's saving action in history.

We are convinced from our own study that the Eastern and Western theological traditions have been in substantial agreement, since the patristic period, on a number of fundamental affirmations about the Holy Trinity that bear on the *Filioque* debate:

- Both traditions clearly affirm that *the Holy Spirit is a distinct hypostasis* or person within the divine Mystery, equal in status to the Father and the Son, and is not simply a creature or a way of talking about God's action in creatures.
- Although the Creed of 381 does not state it explicitly, both traditions confess the Holy Spirit to be God, *of the same divine substance (homoousios)* as Father and Son.
- Both traditions also clearly affirm that *the Father is the primordial source (arch') and ultimate cause (aitia) of the divine being*, and thus of all God's operations: the "spring" from which both Son and Spirit flow, the "root" of their being and fruitfulness, the "sun" from which their existence and their activity radiates.
- Both traditions affirm that *the three hypostases or persons in God are constituted* in their hypostatic existence and distinguished from one another solely *by their relationships of origin*, and not by any other characteristics or activities.
- Accordingly, both traditions affirm that *all the operations of God*—the activities by which God summons created reality into being and forms that reality, for its well-being, into a unified and ordered cosmos centered on the human creature, who is made in God's image—are *the common work of Father, Son, and Holy Spirit*, even though each of them plays a distinctive role within those operations that is determined by their relationships to one another.

Nevertheless, the Eastern and Western traditions of reflection on the Mystery of God have clearly developed categories and conceptions that differ in substantial ways from one another. These differences cannot simply be explained away or be made to seem equivalent by facile argument. We might summarize our differences as follows:

1. Terminology

The *Filioque* controversy is first of all a controversy over words. As a number of recent authors have pointed out, part of the theological disagreement between our communions seems to be rooted in subtle but significant differences in the way key terms have been used to refer to the Spirit's divine origin. The original text of the Creed of 381, in speaking of the Holy Spirit, characterizes him in terms of John 15:26, as the one "who proceeds (*ekporeuetai*) from the Father": probably influenced by the usage of Gregory the Theologian (Or., 31.8), the Council chose to restrict itself to the Johannine language, slightly altering the Gospel text (changing "*to pneuma . . . ho para tou Patros ekporeuetai*" to "*to pneuma to hagion . . . to ek tou Patros ekporeuomenon*") in order to emphasize that the "coming forth" of the Spirit begins "within" the Father's own eternal hypostatic role as source of the divine Being and so is best spoken of as a kind of "movement out of (*ek*)" him. The underlying connotation of *ekporeuesthai* ("proceed," "issue forth") and its related noun, *ekporeusis* ("procession"), seems to have been that of a "passage outwards" from within some point of origin. Since the time of the Cappadocian Fathers, at least, Greek theology almost always restricts the theological use of this term to the coming-forth of the Spirit from the Father, giving it the status of a technical term for the relationship of those two divine persons. In contrast, other Greek words, such as *proienai*, "go forward," are frequently used by the Eastern Fathers to refer to the Spirit's saving "mission" in history from the Father and the risen Lord.

The Latin word *procedere*, on the other hand, with its related noun *processio*, suggests simply "movement forwards," without the added implication of the starting-point of that movement; thus it is used to translate a number of other Greek theological terms, including *proienai*, and is explicitly taken by Thomas Aquinas to be a general term denoting "origin of any kind" (*Summa Theologiae* I, q. 36, a.2), including—in a Trinitarian context—the Son's generation as well as the breathing-forth of the Spirit and his mission in time. As a result, both the primordial origin of the Spirit in the eternal Father and his "coming forth" from the risen Lord tend to be designated, in Latin, by the same word, *procedere*, while Greek theology normally uses two different terms. Although the difference between the Greek and the Latin traditions of understanding the eternal origin of the Spirit is more than simply a verbal one, much of the original concern in the Greek Church over the insertion of the word *Filioque* into the Latin translation of the Creed of 381 may well have been due—as Maximus the Confessor explained (*Letter to Marinus*: PG, 91.133-136)—to a misunderstanding on both sides of the different ranges of meaning implied in the Greek and Latin terms for "procession."

2. The Substantive Issues

Clearly two main issues separate the Eastern and Western Churches in their history of debating the *Filioque*: one theological, in the strict sense, and one ecclesiological.

a. Theological

If "theology" is understood in its patristic sense as reflection on God as Trinity, the theological issue behind this dispute is whether the Son is to be thought of as playing any role in the origin of the Spirit, as a hypostasis or divine "person," from the Father, who is the sole ultimate source of the divine Mystery. The Greek tradition, as we have seen, has generally relied on John 15:26 and the formulation of the Creed of 381 to assert that all we know of the Spirit's hypostatic origin is that he "proceeds from the Father," in a way distinct from, but parallel to, the Son's "generation" from the Father (e.g., John of Damascus, *On the Orthodox Faith*, 1.8). However, this same tradition acknowledges that the "mission" of the Spirit in the world also involves the Son, who receives the Spirit into his own humanity at his baptism, breathes the Spirit forth onto the Twelve on the evening of the resurrection, and sends the Spirit in power into the world, through the charismatic preaching of the Apostles, at Pentecost. On the other hand, the Latin tradition since Tertullian has tended to assume that since the order in which the Church normally names the persons in the Trinity places the Spirit after the Son, he is to be thought of as coming forth "from" the Father "through" the Son. Augustine, who in several passages himself insists that the Holy Spirit "proceeds from the Father," because as God he is not inferior to the Son (*De Fide et Symbolo*, 9.19; *Enchiridion*, 9.3), develops, in other texts, his classic understanding that the Spirit also "proceeds" from the Son because he is, in the course of sacred history, the Spirit and the "gift" of both Father and Son (e.g., *On the Trinity*, 4.20.29; *Tractate on Gospel of John*, 99.6-

7), the gift that begins in their own eternal exchange of love (*On the Trinity*, 15.17.29). In Augustine's view, this involvement of the Son in the Spirit's procession is not understood to contradict the Father's role as the single ultimate source of both Son and Spirit, but is itself given by the Father in generating the Son: "the Holy Spirit, in turn, has this from the Father himself, that he should also proceed from the Son, just as he proceeds from the Father" (*Tractate on Gospel of John*, 99.8).

Much of the difference between the early Latin and Greek traditions on this point is clearly due to the subtle difference of the Latin *procedere* from the Greek *ekporeuesthai*: as we have observed, the Spirit's "coming forth" is designated in a more general sense by the Latin term without the connotation of ultimate origin hinted at by the Greek. The Spirit's "procession" from the Son, however, is conceived of in Latin theology as a somewhat different relationship from his "procession" from the Father, even when—as in the explanations of Anselm and Thomas Aquinas—the relationship of Father and Son to the Holy Spirit is spoken of as constituting "a single principle" of the Spirit's origin: even in breathing forth the Spirit together, according to these later Latin theologians, the Father retains priority, giving the Son all that he has and making possible all that he does.

Greek theologians, too, have often struggled to find ways of expressing a sense that the Son, who sends forth the Spirit in time, also plays a mediating role of some kind in the Spirit's eternal being and activity. Gregory of Nyssa, for instance, explains that we can only distinguish the hypostases within the Mystery of God by "believing that one is the cause, the other is from the cause; and in that which is from the cause, we recognize yet another distinction: one is immediately from the first one, the other is through him who is immediately from the first one." It is characteristic of the "mediation" (*mesiteia*) of the Son in the origin of the Spirit, he adds, that it both preserves his own unique role as Son and allows the Spirit to have a "natural relationship" to the Father (*To Ablabius*, GNO III/1, 56.3-10). In the thirteenth century, the Council of Blachernae (1285), under the leadership of Constantinopolitan Patriarch Gregory II, took further steps to interpret patristic texts that speak of the Spirit's being "through" the Son in a sense consistent with the Orthodox tradition. The Council proposed in its *Tomos* that although Christian faith must maintain that the Holy Spirit receives his existence and hypostatic identity solely from the Father, who is the single cause of the divine Being, he "shines from and is manifested eternally through the Son, in the way that light shines forth and is manifest through the intermediary of the sun's rays" (trans. A. Papadakis, *Crisis in*

Byzantium [St. Vladimir's, 1996], 219). In the following century, Gregory Palamas proposed a similar interpretation of this relationship in a number of his works; in his *Confession* of 1351, for instance, he asserts that the Holy Spirit "has the Father as foundation, source, and cause," but "reposes in the Son" and "is sent—that is, manifested—through the Son" (ibid., 194). In terms of the transcendent divine energy, although not in terms of substance or hypostatic being, "the Spirit pours itself out from the Father through the Son, and, if you like, from the Son over all those worthy of it," a communication which may even be broadly called "procession" (*ekporeusis*) (*Apodeictic Treatise* 1: trans. J. Meyendorff, *A Study of Gregory Palamas* [St. Vladimir's, 1974] 231-232).

The Greek and Latin theological traditions clearly remain in some tension with each other on the fundamental issue of the Spirit's eternal origin as a distinct divine person. By the Middle Ages, as a result of the influence of Anselm and Thomas Aquinas, Western theology almost universally conceives of the identity of each divine person as defined by its "relations of opposition"—in other words, its mutually defining relations of origin—to the other two and concludes that the Holy Spirit would not be hypostatically distinguishable from the Son if the Spirit "proceeded" from the Father alone. In the Latin understanding of *processio* as a general term for "origin," after all, it can also be said that the Son "proceeds from the Father" by being generated from him. Eastern theology, drawing on the language of John 15:26 and the Creed of 381, continues to understand the language of "procession" (*ekporeusis*) as denoting a unique, exclusive, and distinctive causal relationship between the Spirit and the Father and generally confines the Son's role to the "manifestation" and "mission" of the Spirit in the divine activities of creation and redemption. These differences, though subtle, are substantial, and the very weight of theological tradition behind both of them makes them all the more difficult to reconcile theologically with each other.

b. Ecclesiological

The other issue continually present since the late eighth century in the debate over the *Filioque* is that of pastoral and teaching authority in the Church—more precisely, the issue of the authority of the bishop of Rome to resolve dogmatic questions in a final way, simply in virtue of his office. Since the Council of Ephesus (431), the dogmatic tradition of both Eastern and Western Churches has repeatedly affirmed that the final norm of orthodoxy in interpreting the Christian Gospel must be "the faith of Nicaea." The Orthodox tradition sees the normative expression of that faith to be the

Creeds and canons formulated by those Councils that are received by the Apostolic Churches as "ecumenical": as expressing the continuing and universal Apostolic faith. The Catholic tradition also accepts conciliar formulations as dogmatically normative and attributes a unique importance to the seven Councils that are accepted as ecumenical by the Catholic and Orthodox Churches. However, in recognizing the universal primacy of the bishop of Rome in matters of faith and of the service of unity, the Catholic tradition accepts the authority of the pope to confirm the process of conciliar reception and to define what does and does not conflict with the "faith of Nicaea" and the Apostolic tradition. So while Orthodox theology has regarded the ultimate approval by the popes, in the eleventh century, of the use of *Filioque* in the Latin Creed as a usurpation of the dogmatic authority proper to ecumenical Councils alone, Catholic theology has seen it as a legitimate exercise of his primatial authority to proclaim and clarify the Church's faith. As our own common study has repeatedly shown, it is precisely at times in which issues of power and control have been of concern to our Churches that the question of the *Filioque* has emerged as a central concern: held out as a condition for improving relations, or given as a reason for allowing disunity to continue unhealed.

As in the theological question of the origin of the Holy Spirit discussed above, this divergence of understanding of the structure and exercise of authority in the Church is clearly a very serious one: undoubtedly papal primacy, with all its implications, remains the root issue behind all the questions of theology and practice that continue to divide our communions. In the continuing discussion of the *Filioque* between our Churches, however, we have found it helpful to keep these two issues methodologically separate from one another and to recognize that the mystery of the relationships among the persons in God must be approached in a different way from the issue of whether or not it is proper for the Western Churches to profess the faith of Nicaea in terms that diverge from the original text of the Creed of 381.

3. Continuing Our Reflections

It has often been remarked that the theology of the Holy Spirit is an underdeveloped region of Christian theological reflection. This seems to hold true even of the issue of the origin of the Holy Spirit. Although a great deal has been written about the reasons for and against the theology of the *Filioque* since the Carolingian era, most of it has been polemical in nature, aimed at justifying positions assumed by both sides to be non-negotiable.

Little effort has been made, until modern times, to look for new ways of expressing and explaining the biblical and early Christian understanding of the person and work of the Holy Spirit, which might serve to frame the discussion in a new way and move all the Churches towards a consensus on essential matters that would be in continuity with both traditions. Recently, a number of theologians, from a variety of Churches, have suggested that the time may now be at hand to return to this question together, in a genuinely ecumenical spirit, and to seek for new developments in our articulation of the Apostolic faith that may ultimately win ecumenical Christian reception.

Recognizing its challenges, our Consultation supports such a common theological enterprise. It is our hope that a serious process of reflection on the theology of the Holy Spirit, based on the Scriptures and on the whole tradition of Christian theology and conducted with an openness to new formulations and conceptual structures consonant with that tradition, might help our Churches to discover new depths of common faith and to grow in respect for the wisdom of our respective forbears. We urge, too, that both our Churches persist in their efforts to reflect—together and separately—on the theology of primacy and synodality within the Church's structures of teaching and pastoral practice, recognizing that here also a continuing openness to doctrinal and practical development, intimately linked to the Spirit's work in the community, remains crucially necessary. Gregory Nazianzen reminds us, in his *Fifth Theological Oration* on the divinity of the Holy Spirit, that the Church's slow discovery of the Spirit's true status and identity is simply part of the "order of theology (*taxis te-s theologias*)," by which "lights break upon us gradually" in our understanding of the saving Mystery of God (Or., 31.27). Only if we "listen to what the Spirit is saying to the Churches" (Rev 3:22) will we be able to remain faithful to the Good News preached by the Apostles, while growing in the understanding of that faith, which is theology's task.

IV. Recommendations

We are aware that the problem of the theology of the *Filioque* and its use in the Creed is not simply an issue between the Catholic and Orthodox communions. Many Protestant Churches, too, drawing on the theological legacy of the Medieval West, consider the term to represent an integral part of the orthodox Christian confession. Although dialogue among a number of these Churches and the Orthodox communion has already touched on the issue, any future resolution of the disagreement between East and West on the origin of the Spirit must involve all those communities that profess the Creed of 381 as a standard of faith. Aware of its limitations, our Consultation nonetheless makes the following theological and practical recommendations to the members and the bishops of our own Churches:

- That our Churches commit themselves to a new and earnest dialogue concerning the origin and person of the Holy Spirit, drawing on the Holy Scriptures and on the full riches of the theological traditions of both our Churches, and to looking for constructive ways of expressing what is central to our faith on this difficult issue
- That all involved in such dialogue expressly recognize the limitations of our ability to make definitive assertions about the inner life of God
- That in the future, because of the progress in mutual understanding that has come about in recent decades, Orthodox and Catholics refrain from labeling as heretical the traditions of the other side on the subject of the procession of the Holy Spirit
- That Orthodox and Catholic theologians distinguish more clearly between the divinity and hypostatic identity of the Holy Spirit, which is a received dogma of our Churches, and the manner of the Spirit's origin, which still awaits full and final ecumenical resolution
- That those engaged in dialogue on this issue distinguish, as far as possible, the theological issues of the origin of the Holy Spirit from the ecclesiological issues of primacy and doctrinal authority in the Church, even as we pursue both questions seriously together
- That the theological dialogue between our Churches also give careful consideration to the status of later councils held in both our Churches after those seven generally received as ecumenical
- That the Catholic Church, as a consequence of the normative and irrevocable dogmatic value of the Creed of 381, use the original Greek text alone in making translations of that Creed for catechetical and liturgical use

- That the Catholic Church, following a growing theological consensus, and in particular the statements made by Pope Paul VI, declare that the condemnation made at the Second Council of Lyons (1274) of those "who presume to deny that the Holy Spirit proceeds eternally from the Father and the Son" is no longer applicable.

We offer these recommendations to our Churches in the conviction, based on our own intense study and discussion, that our traditions' different ways of understanding the procession of the Holy Spirit need no longer divide us. We believe, rather, that our profession of the ancient Creed of Constantinople must be allowed to become, by our uniform practice and our new attempts at mutual understanding, the basis for a more conscious unity in the one faith that all theology simply seeks to clarify and to deepen. Although our expression of the truth God reveals about his own Being must always remain limited by the boundaries of human understanding and human words, we believe that it is the very "Spirit of truth," whom Jesus breathes upon his Church, who remains with us still to "guide us into all truth" (John 16:13). We pray that our Churches' understanding of this Spirit may no longer be a scandal to us or an obstacle to unity in Christ, but that the one truth towards which he guides us may truly be "a bond of peace" (Eph 4.3) for us and for all Christians.

ORIENTAL ORTHODOX–CATHOLIC

Editors' Note: *The short pastoral note in this section builds on the theological work of earlier dialogues (see BU, 359-370). For background documentation on which this text is based, see Ronald G. Roberson, ed.,* Oriental Orthodox–Roman Catholic Pastoral Relationships and Interchurch Marriages *(Washington, DC: United States Conference of Catholic Bishops, 1995).*

Document 25

GUIDELINES CONCERNING THE PASTORAL CARE OF ORIENTAL ORTHODOX STUDENTS IN CATHOLIC SCHOOLS

Oriental Orthodox–Roman Catholic Theological Consultation in the United States, 1999

The Oriental Orthodox–Roman Catholic Theological Consultation in the United States has discussed at length the increasingly common presence of Oriental Orthodox students in the Catholic schools of our country. Rejoicing in the mutual respect and esteem that characterizes the relationship between our two communions, we issue the following guidelines to promote a more effective realization of that relationship in Catholic schools. They are designed to offer specific suggestions that are consistent with the ecumenical policy of the Catholic Church and pay due respect to the pastoral practice of the Oriental Orthodox Churches.

As Pope John Paul II reminds us, "it is absolutely clear that ecumenism, the movement promoting Christian unity, is not just some sort of 'appendix' which is added to the Church's traditional activity. Rather, ecumenism is an organic part of her life and work, and consequently must pervade all that she is and does; it must be like the fruit borne by a healthy and flourishing tree which grows to its full stature" (UUS, no. 20). Among the primary concerns of Catholic schools, therefore, will be to foster this ecumenical activity and to provide appropriate pastoral care for students who belong to other faith traditions, especially fellow Christians.

The Oriental Orthodox Churches today are the Armenian Apostolic Church, the Coptic Orthodox Church, the Syrian Orthodox Church of

Antioch, the Ethiopian Orthodox Church, the Eritrean Orthodox Church, and the Malankara Orthodox Syrian Church of India. Each of these churches is fully independent with its own hierarchy, but all of them are in full communion with each other. Because of this, it is possible for the clergy of any one of these churches to minister to members of any other Oriental Orthodox Church. In order to assure appropriate pastoral care, it is clear that Catholic pastors, school administrators and teachers should have an adequate knowledge of the churches and traditions of their students. We have indicated below resources that we hope will be helpful in this task.

As a matter of principle, the Catholic Church does not seek converts among the faithful of the Oriental Orthodox Churches. Thus every effort should be made to respect and even promote the participation of Oriental Orthodox students in the life of their own churches and to avoid practices that could appear to constitute an invitation for an Oriental Orthodox student to join the Catholic Church. In particular, it is inappropriate for Oriental Orthodox students to be included in preparation programs for Confirmation or First Communion, especially since they will have received these sacraments at the time of their baptism.

Another practice that can give the impression of seeking converts is the requirement in some places of membership in—and financial contributions to—the Catholic parish where a school is located in order to pay a lower tuition fee. This can appear to be a financial incentive for an Oriental Orthodox family to join the Catholic parish. While the tuition policy of Catholic schools is a complex question and we cannot offer a solution to this problem that would be applicable in all cases, we strongly encourage Catholic pastors to find a way to allow Oriental Orthodox to participate in their schools without appearing to encourage transfer of membership to the sponsoring Catholic parish. It should be kept in mind that dual church membership is not acceptable for either of our communions.

Sacramental sharing is another area of concern. While the Catholic Church allows the Oriental Orthodox faithful to receive its sacraments in many cases (cf. CIC, c. 844 §3, and CCEO, c. 671), the Oriental Orthodox Churches themselves have varying disciplines on the matter. The Coptic and Ethiopian Orthodox Churches do not allow their faithful to receive sacraments in any church outside the Oriental Orthodox communion, but the Armenian and Syrian Orthodox do allow it in some circumstances. Care should be taken to respect the discipline of the church to which an individual Oriental Orthodox student belongs. At the same time, care should also be taken to prevent an undue sense of exclusion among Oriental

Orthodox students. Whenever possible, they should be included as active participants in Liturgies of the Word and other non-sacramental services.

In all these cases, the best solutions can always be reached by direct contact with the local Oriental Orthodox pastors of the students involved. They should be consulted whenever questions arise, and should be invited to participate in the pastoral care of the students who belong to his church by hearing confessions, teaching religious education classes, celebrating liturgical services, etc. Along these lines we recall the statement of the 1993 *Ecumenical Directory*, no. 141, which reads:

> In Catholic schools and institutions, every effort should be made to respect the faith and conscience of students or teachers who belong to other churches or ecclesial communities. In accordance with their own approved statutes, the authorities of these schools and institutions should take care that clergy of other communities have every facility for giving spiritual and sacramental ministration to their own faithful who attend such schools or institutions. As far as circumstances allow, with the permission of the diocesan bishop these facilities can be offered on the Catholic premises, including the church or chapel.

If no Oriental Orthodox pastor is located in the area, it is best to contact the nearest bishop of the church to which the student belongs. This information can be obtained from the local diocesan ecumenical officer or the Secretariat for Ecumenical and Interreligious Affairs at the National [United States] Conference of Catholic Bishops in Washington, D.C.

LUTHERAN-ORTHODOX

Editors' Note: *The following two texts provide reports from the dialogue between the Orthodox churches and the U.S. Lutheran churches. They are part of the larger Lutheran-Orthodox dialogue project. For other texts from the Lutheran-Orthodox dialogues, see John Meyendorff and Robert Tobias, eds.,* Salvation in Christ: A Lutheran-Orthodox Dialogue *(Minneapolis: Augsburg, 1992).*

Document 26

COMMON RESPONSE TO THE ALEPPO STATEMENT ON THE DATE OF EASTER/PASCHA

Lutheran-Orthodox Dialogue in the USA, 1999

1. In March 1997, a consultation sponsored by the World Council of Churches and the Middle East Council of Churches, meeting in Aleppo, Syria, issued a statement "Toward a Common Date for Easter." The members of the Lutheran-Orthodox Dialogue in the USA, assembled in Ligonier, Pennsylvania, on July 12-13, 1999, reviewed this statement, heard a presentation on it by the Rev. Dr. Paul Nelson of the Evangelical Lutheran Church in America, and had an opportunity for discussion. We strongly affirm the basic principles of the Aleppo Statement and urge its careful and pastorally sensitive study.

2. In particular, we affirm the recommendation of the Aleppo Statement that the churches maintain/reappropriate the norms established by the First Ecumenical Council in Nicaea (AD 325). The statement does well to draw attention to the continuing relevance of Nicaea to the faith and life of our churches.

3. Furthermore, we agree that the Aleppo Statement is faithful to the Nicene norms in espousing principles such as the following: Christians should celebrate the Feast of the Resurrection on the same day, so as not to give a divided witness in the world. The calculation of the date of Easter/Pascha is tied to the cycles of sun and moon. This provides a salutary reminder of the cosmic dimensions of Christ's victory over sin and death. Proposals to celebrate Easter on a fixed date should be rejected. There is an "intimate connection between the biblical passover and the Christian

celebration of 'Christ our paschal lamb'" (10[c]), "a link that reflects the flow of salvation history" (AS, 12[a][i]). Faithfulness to the spirit of the Council of Nicaea dictates that the date of the vernal equinox and of the following full moon be calculated by the best scientific means available.

4. The Aleppo Statement notes that in the year 2001 the Pascal calculations presently in use in our churches result in the same date for Easter/Pascha. The statement recommends that, in the interval between now and then, the churches study and consider means to implement its recommendations for achieving a common celebration.

5. Our Lutheran-Orthodox Ecumenical Dialogue in the USA endorses the statement's call to study during the period leading to Easter/Pascha 2001. This study should take place at all levels of our churches, including that of congregations/parishes, where study of the statement may be useful for raising ecumenical awareness; for explaining why Easter/Pascha is a movable feast, and how its date is calculated; for explaining the reason for divergent dates for Easter/Pascha in communities where Eastern and Western Christians live together; and for exploring the cosmic and the salvation historical dimensions of Christ's resurrection.

6. At the same time, our Lutheran-Orthodox Dialogue in the USA recognizes the need for the greatest sensitivity in the discussion of the possibility of change in the traditional means of calculating the date of Easter/Pascha. We pledge to one another and to our other ecumenical partners that we will continue to seek reconciliation between all Christians in this matter.

7. It is our prayer and hope that we all maintain/reappropriate the norms of the First Ecumenical Council and that this faithfulness will lead us, in a future not too far distant, to the celebration of Easter/Pascha on a common date, so that we may give "a common witness to the resurrection of our Lord Jesus Christ, the central mystery of the Christian faith." Our dialogue therefore urges our churches to give the Aleppo Statement serious attention.

Antiochian Village
Ligonier, Pennsylvania
July 13, 1999

Document 27

LUTHERAN-ORTHODOX COMMON STATEMENT ON FAITH IN THE HOLY TRINITY, 1998

1. Our theological dialogue as Orthodox and Lutherans has made clear to us that each of our churches believes in the Father, the Son, and the Holy Spirit, one God. We recognize one another's churches as churches believing in the Holy Trinity. We also recognize that our churches do not simply believe in but worship the Holy Trinity. In our worship we not only confess our faith in the Trinity, but we encounter each of the persons of the Holy Trinity in their distinction from one another and their unity with each other as the one God.

2. In our worship, Lutherans and Orthodox both explicitly confess faith in the Holy Trinity in the words of the Nicene Creed. Our churches are both committed to the Nicene Creed as ecumenically binding dogma, that is, as a statement of the apostolic faith in the Holy Trinity which is permanently normative for all Christians. We may therefore briefly summarize our shared faith in the Trinity by reference to the Nicene Creed.

3. As Lutherans and Orthodox we both confess faith in "one God, the Father almighty, maker of heaven and earth." Confessing faith in God the Father, we together believe in the monarchy of the Father. The Father is the supreme principle, origin, source, and cause of all that exists and has life. He alone is unoriginate, and all that is, uncreated and created, originates from him. The Son and the Spirit are from his very being, whereas everything else is made by him from nothing, through his Son, and by his Spirit.

4. As Lutherans and Orthodox we confess together faith in "one Lord Jesus Christ, the only-begotten Son of God." This eternal Son of God is "begotten, not made." Unlike any creature, he does not come to be out of

nothing by an act of God's will. He is eternally generated or begotten by the Father, receiving from the Father the Father's own divine nature or essence (*ousia*) which is undivided. He is therefore "one in essence [*homoousios*] with the Father." Although he is other than the Father, a hypostasis or person distinct from the Father, the Son is fully the one God, just as the Father is. Therefore, as Lutherans and Orthodox we reject any form of Arianism, according to which the Son of God is less than fully God and entitled to less than fully divine honor and worship.

5. As Lutherans and Orthodox we confess together that this same eternal Son of God "for us and for our salvation came down from heaven, was incarnate by the Holy Spirit from the Virgin Mary, and was made man." Fully God from all eternity, the Father's only-begotten Son became fully human in time, accepting the whole reality of human life and death. We therefore confess together that in Christ two natures, divine and human, are inseparably united in one person, so that there is one Lord Jesus Christ, true God and true human being. The eternal Son of God himself was truly born, suffered, was crucified, and died in the flesh; this same Son was buried in the flesh, rose from the dead on the third day, and ascended to the Father's right hand in heaven. The only-begotten and incarnate Son reveals the Father to us and sends the Holy Spirit into the world.

6. As Lutherans and Orthodox we confess together faith in "the Holy Spirit, the Lord, the giver of life." Like the Son, the Holy Spirit receives his existence from the Father, though the Spirit "proceeds from the Father," while the Son is "begotten" of the Father. Like the Son, he receives from the Father the Father's own divine nature, and so he is one in essence with the Father and the Son. He is other than the Father and the Son, a hypostasis or person distinct from both, yet fully the one God, just as the Father and the Son are. The Creed attests to this not only by calling him "the Lord, the giver of life," attributing to him divine names and actions which belong to God alone, but also by saying that "with the Father and the Son he is worshiped and glorified." Because he is true God, to him belongs that honor and worship which are due to God alone.

7. Our dialogue has discussed extensively the historical and theological issues surrounding the one point in the Creed on which Lutherans and Orthodox have traditionally disagreed with regard to faith in the Holy Trinity: the procession of the Spirit. Together with other churches rooted in Latin-speaking Christianity, Lutherans have traditionally confessed the creedal faith in the Holy Trinity by saying that the Holy Spirit "proceeds from the Father and the Son [*Filioque*]," and Lutheran theologians have

traditionally defended both the addition of the phrase "and the Son" and the truth of the teaching embodied by this addition. Orthodox have traditionally opposed both the addition of the *Filioque* clause to the Creed and the teaching that the Spirit proceeds from the Son. Our dialogue has progressed to the point where we can make the following statements regarding this historic dispute.

8. Lutherans, together with many other Western Christians, now widely recognize that the addition of the *Filioque* to the Nicene Creed, which took place locally by a unilateral action of the Latin Church and without the action of an Ecumenical Council, was illegitimate and contributed to disunity among Christians. Moreover, many Lutherans are now convinced that the original Creed without the *Filioque* addition could and should be restored in their worship. This need not contradict the Lutheran Confessions, which commit Lutherans to "the decree of the Council of Nicaea" (CA I). It is especially important to note that this article commits Lutherans not simply to the teaching of "the synod of Nicaea," but to the decree—that is, the text—of Nicaea, and to the specific doctrinal decisions embodied in that text. But the text of "the synod of Nicaea"—that is, the text of AD 325, amplified by the First Council of Constantinople of AD 381, as reported in the Acts of the Council of Chalcedon of AD 451—does not include the *Filioque*. It simply says that the Holy Spirit is *το εκ του πατροζ εκπορευομευου* ("the one proceeding from the Father"), in line with the Gospel of St. John (John 15:26). On this basis, Lutherans can now acknowledge that the *Filioque* is not ecumenical dogma but has the status of a local tradition which is not binding on the universal church.

9. For this reason, the Lutheran members of this dialogue are prepared to recommend to their Church that it publicly recognize that the permanently normative and universally binding form of the Nicene Creed is the Greek text of AD 381 and that it undertake steps to reflect this recognition in its worship and teaching. This would be a way of enacting in the Evangelical Lutheran Church in America the Lutheran World Federation resolution of 1990, which found it "appropriate" that member churches "which already use the Nicene Creed in their liturgies may use the version of 381, for example in ecumenical services," and further found it appropriate that Lutherans preparing common vernacular texts of the Nicene Creed together with Orthodox churches "may agree to a version without the 'western' *filioque*."

10. At the same time, Lutherans are not prepared to regard the teaching that the Holy Spirit proceeds from the Father and the Son as a

heresy—a teaching against faith in the Holy Trinity. It is part of their confessional documents, and many of the chief teachers of the Lutheran tradition, including Luther himself, taught it vigorously. Lutheran recognition that the *Filioque* is not part of the Nicene Creed in its original and ecumenically binding form is not, therefore, to be equated with Lutheran rejection of all theological teaching which ascribes to the Son a role in the procession of the Holy Spirit, still less with an acknowledgment that all such teaching is heretical. Nevertheless, Lutherans are open to further exploration of the relation of the Spirit to the Son in conversation with Orthodox and in careful dialogue with their concerns.

11. Orthodox very warmly agree with the Lutherans that the *Filioque* does not belong to the normative Creed as recognized by the Council of Constantinople of AD 379/380, which was accepted unanimously by both East and West. At the same time, Orthodox do not regard the teaching that the Holy Spirit proceeds from the Son as well as from the Father to be one which they can accept. This teaching is opposed to the monarchy of the Father and to the equality of the Spirit to the Father and the Son as a hypostasis or person distinct from both, as expressed by the original Creed. On the other hand, Orthodox may accept the teaching of the "double procession" of the Spirit from the Father and the Son in the patristic sense that the Spirit is sent from the Father through the Son in the mystery of our salvation in Christ. The relation of the Son to the Spirit in the context of salvation (*oikonomia*) is not the same with their relation in the eternal Trinity (*theologia*). Thus for Orthodox the dispute over the *Filioque* can be narrowed down to accepting or rejecting the distinction between how the Trinity is eternally in themselves and how they appear in Christ. That the Holy Spirit eternally comes forth from the Son, so as to depend for his being and his possession of the one divine nature on the Son as well as on the Father, is a teaching which Orthodox uniformly oppose.

12. Despite our differences in theological perspective, Lutherans and Orthodox agree on certain basic theological commitments which constitute criteria of acceptable Trinitarian teaching. In particular they agree that any acceptable Trinitarian teaching (a) must affirm the monarchy of the Father; (b) must affirm that the divine essence exists only in the three distinct, equal, and undivided persons of the Trinity, without confusion of their personal properties; and (c) must affirm the consistent Christian teaching of the intimate relation of the Son and the Spirit in the economy of salvation.

13. In our dialogue, we have prayed and worked for fuller and more widely acknowledged unity between our churches in the Trinitarian faith. In

many areas of faith in the Holy Trinity, our dialogue has reached substantial agreement. We look forward to a time when our churches will affirm the Nicene faith through common liturgical usage of the unaltered creed of AD 381. We trust that such common affirmation of faith will lead to the resolution of those theological differences which are still before us.

Bishop Donald J. McCoid, Co-Chair
His Eminence Metropolitan Maximos of Aenos, Co-Chair
November 4, 1998

CHRISTIAN REFORMED–CATHOLIC

Editors' Note: *The Christian Reformed Church (CRC) has only recently become a member of the World Alliance of Reformed Churches and therefore did not participate in the international or U.S. Reformed-Catholic dialogues until 2002. Its own ecumenical history has been somewhat ambivalent. (See Henry Zwaanstra,* Catholicity and Secession: A Study of Ecumenicity in the Christian Reformed Church *[Grand Rapids: Eerdmans, 1991]). However, it has been active in evangelical ecumenism and in Faith and Order, U.S., Canada, and World Council.*

The text excerpted here is unique in that it is the action of one church in its own internal life. However, for the Christian Reformed Church to develop an accurate understanding of the Catholic Church and its confessional evaluation of Catholic sacramental faith and practice, two face-to-face theological dialogues were necessary, in addition to considerable correspondence. The discussion of this issue is an ongoing process in the synod of the CRC. This text represents the report to the 2004 synod of the CRC. (For subsequent texts, see www.crcna.org/whatweoffer/resources/downloads.*) In the context of this dialogue, the CRC is now a full member of the U.S. Reformed-Catholic dialogue. Before this, eight rounds of dialogue have occurred (see BU, 371-448), the last two of which centered on pastoral themes.*

For more on Reformed-Catholic ecumenism, see the Roman Catholic–Presbyterian/Reformed Consultation, Laity in the Church and the World: Resources for Ecumenical Dialogue *(Washington, DC: United States Conference of Catholic Bishops, 1998); and Patrick Cooney and Rev. John Bush,* Interchurch Families: Resources for Ecumenical Hope *(Washington, DC: United States Conference of Catholic Bishops, 2002). For a summary of the dialogues, see* Journey in Faith: Forty Years of Reformed-Catholic Dialogue *(Washington, DC: United States Conference of Catholic Bishops, in press).*

DOCUMENT 28

HEIDELBERG CATECHISM, QUESTION 80: REPORT OF THE INTERCHURCH RELATIONS COMMITTEE CLARIFYING THE OFFICIAL DOCTRINE OF THE ROMAN CATHOLIC CHURCH CONCERNING THE MASS

To the Synod of the Christian Reformed Church, 2002/2004

I. Introduction

A. Background, Mandate, and Structure of the Report

In 1998, the synod of the Christian Reformed Church in North America (CRC) received two overtures concerning question and answer 80 ["Q. and A. 80"] of the Heidelberg Catechism (HC). . . . [*The report reviews the process from 1998 to 2004 in detail, including the members if the Interchurch Relations Committee (IRC) and the Catholic partners.*]

From the beginning, both sides agreed that Q. and A. 80 is organized and the following way:

Question 80: How does the Lord's Supper differ from the Roman Catholic Mass?

Answer:

A1. The Lord's Supper declares to us
that our sins have been completely forgiven
through the one sacrifice of Jesus Christ
which he himself finished on the cross once for all.

B1. It also declares to us
that the Holy Spirit grafts us into Christ,
who with his very body
is now in heaven at the right hand of the Father
where he wants us to worship him.

A2. But the Mass teaches
that the living and the dead
do not have their sins forgiven
through the suffering of Christ
unless Christ is still offered for them daily by the priests.

B2. It also teaches
that Christ is bodily present
in the form of bread and wine
where Christ is therefore to be worshiped.

A3. Thus the Mass is basically
nothing but a denial
of the one sacrifice and suffering of Jesus Christ

B3. and [basically nothing but] a condemnable idolatry.

This way of dividing up the material suggests that the question asked in Q. and A. 80 receives a twofold answer: the doctrines of the Lord's Supper and the Mass differ in the way they understand both the sacrifice of Christ (A) and the presence of Christ (B). Each of these two issues is treated in three subsections: A1 explains the Reformed view of the Lord's Supper as it relates to Christ's sacrifice, A2 the objectionable part of the Roman Catholic view, and A3 the Heidelberg Catechism's response to the Roman Catholic view. B1 explains the Reformed view of the Lord's Supper as it relates to the presence of Christ, B2 the objectionable part of the Roman Catholic view, and B3 the Heidelberg Catechism's response to the Roman Catholic view.

B. Historical Note

Q. and A. 80 did not appear in the text of the first German edition of the Heidelberg Catechism, which probably left the publisher sometime in February 1563. It first appeared in the second German edition (March 1563) and in the official Latin translation of the Heidelberg Catechism (March 1563). It was also included, in slightly expanded form, in the third (April 1563) and fourth (November 1563) German editions, the last of which became the "*textus receptus*" of the Heidelberg Catechism and the basis for the 1975 CRC translation used above.

It is not clear why the first edition of the Heidelberg Catechism did not include Q. and A. 80. One possibility is that Q. and A. 80 was composed and added in direct response to a statement on the Mass adopted by the Council of Trent in September 1562. The first appearance of Q. and A. 80 in the second German edition of the catechism might indicate that the decision of Trent had not reached Heidelberg until after the first edition of the Heidelberg Catechism had already gone to press. This, however, is conjecture. We simply do not know when the statements of Trent first came to the attention of the Heidelberg theologians or whether these statements provoked a confessional rebuttal.

The only documentary evidence we have to work with is a letter dated April 3, 1563, to John Calvin from Caspar Olevianus, one of the contributors to the Heidelberg Catechism. Olevianus writes that "in the first German edition . . . the question on the difference between the Lord's Supper and the papal Mass was omitted" but that "after some urging on my part [*admonitus a me*], the elector decided that it should be added to the second German and first Latin editions" (Calvini Opera, 19:684). It is not clear from this letter whether Q. and A. 80 was intentionally omitted from the first edition, whether its omission was later regarded as an oversight, or whether it was composed in response to Trent. Nor is it clear who exactly was responsible for the wording of this question. The fact that it was Olevianus who urged the elector to add this material and that the language of Q. and A. 80 is reminiscent of that of Calvin (see, e.g., "The Geneva Confession of 1536," no. 16) may indicate that Olevianus, Calvin's protégé in Heidelberg, was himself the composer.

C. Recent Synodical Decisions Regarding Question and Answer 80

Recent CRC synods have on two previous occasions faced the possibility of eliminating or revising Q. and A. 80. On both occasions, synod decided not to proceed in that direction.

Synod 1975 received both an overture and a communication regarding Q. and A. 80. In the overture, a classis asked that Synod 1975 take appropriate steps to delete the part of Q. and A. 80 that describes and rejects Roman Catholic teaching, on the grounds that this section describes and negates the faith of others rather than offering "a confessional expression of the Reformed faith" and that it "unnecessarily gives offense to inquirers of Roman Catholic background before they have had opportunity to gain appreciation for the Reformed faith" (Acts of Synod 1975, 646). In response, Synod 1975 referred the overture to the churches and asked the New Confession Committee to receive responses from the churches and to serve a subsequent synod with advice on Q. and A. 80 (Acts of Synod 1975, 106). In the communication, a minister suggested that the new translation of the Heidelberg Catechism, which was then in progress, should follow the first German edition, thereby omitting Q. and A. 80. Synod did not accede to this request on the grounds that the Synods of 1972 and 1974 did not require that the translators use the first German edition and that other Reformed churches use versions of the Heidelberg Catechism that include Q. and A. 80 (Acts of Synod 1975, 92).

Based on the report of the New Confession Committee, Synod 1977 made no changes in Q. and A. 80, on the following grounds: the responses from the churches were inconclusive, weighty reasons are needed to alter a historical creed, the Roman Catholic church has not repudiated the statements of the Council of Trent that Q. and A. 80 rejects, the sharp language of Q. and A. 80 is rooted in "indignation at the withholding of assurance of salvation from believers," and the main emphasis of Q. and A. 80 is assurance of salvation rooted in complete forgiveness of our sins through Christ's only sacrifice (Acts of Synod 1977, 88-89, 657-58).

D. Outline of the Report

I. Introduction
   - A. Background, mandate, and structure of the report
   - B. Historical note
   - C. Recent synodical decisions regarding Q. and A. 80

- D. Outline of the report
- E. List of documents cited

II. Differences over sacrifice

- A. The teaching of the Heidelberg Catechism
  1. The Lord's Supper: Communication of redemption accomplished on the cross
  2. The Mass: Continual sacrificial mediation of forgiveness
  3. Critique of the Roman Catholic Mass: Affront to the salvation accomplished by Christ
- B. Roman Catholic teaching
  1. One Sacrifice—different forms
  2. The Eucharist: Sacramental representation and perpetuation of the one, unique sacrifice
  3. The eucharistic sacrifice completes the purification of those who die in Christ
  4. The Eucharist: More than sacrifice
- C. Key differences between the Heidelberg Catechism and Roman Catholic teaching
  1. The nature and the direction of the sacrament
  2. The role of the church in the mediation of salvation
     - a. Gift received or sacrifice offered
     - b. Centrality of word or sacrament
  3. The Mass's efficacy for the dead

III. Differences over the presence of Christ in the sacrament

- A. The teaching of the Heidelberg Catechism
- B. Roman Catholic teaching
  1. The bodily presence of Christ in the elements
     - a. Historical statements
     - b. Contemporary statements
  2. Veneration of the consecrated bread and wine
- C. A key difference between the Heidelberg Catechism and Roman Catholic teaching

IV. Conclusions and recommendations
- A. Conclusions
- B. Recommendations

E. List of Documents Cited

Baptism, Eucharist and Ministry. Geneva: World Council of Churches, 1982.

Calvin, John. *Calvin: Theological Treatises*. Translated by J. K. S. Reid. Library of Christian Classics. Philadelphia: Westminster, 1954.

Catechism of the Catholic Church, 2nd ed. Washington, DC: Libreria Editrice Vaticana–United States Conference of Catholic Bishops, 2000.

Documents of Vatican II. Edited by Austin P. Flannery. Grand Rapids: Eerdmans, 1975.

Neuner, J., and J. Dupuis, eds. *The Christian Faith in the Doctrinal Documents of the Catholic Church*, 7th ed. New York: Alba House, 2001. [Contains selections from key documents from the early church to the present. Our references to DS can be found in this volume in the chapter on the Eucharist.]

Thurian, Max, ed. *Churches Respond to BEM: Official Responses to the "Baptism, Eucharist and Ministry" Text*, vol. 6. Faith and Order Paper 144. Geneva: World Council of Churches, 1987.

II. Differences Over Sacrifice

A. The Teaching of the Heidelberg Catechism

The Heidelberg Catechism says little about the sacrificial character of Christ's death in the questions and answers on the Lord's Supper (Q. and A. 75-80). It does, however, address Christ's sacrificial death in its earlier treatment of the Apostles' Creed. There it says that "by his suffering as the *only atoning sacrifice*," Christ has "set us free, body and soul, from eternal condemnation" and has gained for us "God's grace, righteousness, and eternal life" (Q. and A. 37; emphasis added). Then, in the introductory questions on the sacraments, the Catechism emphasizes that we receive forgiveness of sins and eternal life "by grace alone because of Christ's *one sacrifice finished on the cross*" and that through the sacraments the Holy

Spirit teaches and assures us that "our entire salvation rests on Christ's *one sacrifice* for us on the cross" (Q. and A. 66-67; emphasis added).

Then, in Q. and A. 80, the Heidelberg Catechism presents the Lord's Supper as a testimony to the sufficiency and finality of Christ's sacrifice on the cross (A1), contrasts this confession to the Roman Catholic understanding of the Mass as sacrifice (A2), and concludes that the Roman Catholic teaching is nothing but a denial of the one sacrifice and suffering of Christ (A3).

1. *The Lord's Supper: Communication of Redemption Accomplished on the Cross (A1)*

The [Heidelberg] Catechism highlights the finality and sufficiency of Christ's sacrifice in two ways. First, it is at pains to underscore the nature of Christ's sacrifice as a once-for-all event that was completed in the past. The Catechism's fourfold reinforcement of this finality is marked by the italicized phrases: "the (a) *one* sacrifice of Jesus Christ (repeated in the conclusion, A3) which (b) *he himself* (c) *finished* on the cross (d) once for all (see also HC, Q. and A. 66 and 67).

Secondly, having underscored Christ's sacrifice as a completed past event (redemption accomplished), the Heidelberg Catechism seeks to safeguard this once-for-all character by emphasizing a particular way in which the Lord's Supper mediates this finality (redemption applied). The sacrament is a visible sign and pledge that "*declares* to us that our sins have been [present perfect: completed action with continuing effect] completely forgiven" by virtue of the once-for-all event. To this declaration regarding Christ's work in the past, the Catechism joins a declaration regarding our bond to the ascended Christ: the Lord's Supper "also declares to us that the Holy Spirit grafts us into Christ, who with his very body is now in heaven at the right hand of the Father where he wants us to worship him."

2. *The Mass: Continual Sacrificial Mediation of Forgiveness (A2)*

In contrast to its understanding of the Lord's Supper, the Catechism emphasizes that the Roman Catholic Church teaches that sins are forgiven only by the continual offering of the Mass by priests ("*unless* Christ is *still offered* for them *daily* by the priests").

The Heidelberg Catechism's reference to the relation of the Mass to the "dead" is best understood not as introducing a new issue, namely, the state of the dead, but as yet another illustration of how the Mass assumes the inconclusiveness or insufficiency of Christ's sacrifice on the cross: even at death the once-for-all sacrifice does not secure final salvation; to secure the complete forgiveness of those who have died requires the daily sacrifice of the Mass.

3. *Critique of the Roman Catholic Mass: Affront to the Salvation Accomplished by Christ (A3)*

On the basis of its analysis of the sacrificial character of the Mass, the Heidelberg Catechism draws what appears to be an obvious conclusion: "the Mass is basically nothing but a denial of the one sacrifice and suffering of Jesus Christ."

B. Roman Catholic Teaching

Against the background of the Heidelberg Catechism's statements, one of the two main tasks that flow out of the committee's mandate is to determine what the teaching of the Roman Catholic Church is regarding the sacrificial character of the Mass. This section of the report attempts to do just that.

Appealing to documents contemporary with, and subsequent to, the Heidelberg Catechism, the Roman Catholic representatives insisted that Q. and A. 80 misconstrues the Roman Catholic understanding of the Mass. The understanding of the Mass as sacrifice, they explained, in no way detracts from the once-for-all sacrifice of Jesus Christ. This understanding may be summed up in the four points below.

1. *One Sacrifice—Different Forms*

The Council of Trent clearly affirms the unrepeatability of Christ's sacrifice on the cross, a sacrifice which is sacramentally made present in the Mass:

> He then, our Lord and God, was once and for all to offer Himself to God the Father by His death on the altar of the cross, to accomplish for them an everlasting redemption. (Trent, Session 22, ch. 1; DS 1740. In the same section, Trent speaks of "the bloody sacrifice which He was once for all to accomplish on the cross.")
>
> In this divine sacrifice which is celebrated in the Mass, the same Christ who offered Himself once in a bloody manner (cf. Heb. 9:14, 27) on the altar of the cross is contained and is offered in an unbloody manner. . . . the victim is one and the same: the same now offers through the ministry of priests, who then offered Himself on the cross; only the manner of offering is

> different. The fruits of this oblation (the bloody one, that is) are received in abundance through this unbloody oblation. (Trent, Session 22, ch. 2; DS 1743)

The Second Vatican Council (1962-1965) reaffirms Trent's teaching regarding the unity of Christ's sacrifice and the eucharistic sacrifice:

> Through the ministry of priests the spiritual sacrifice of the faithful is completed in union with the sacrifice of Christ the only mediator, which in the Eucharist is offered through the priests' hands in the name of the whole Church in an unbloody and sacramental manner until the Lord himself come (cf. 1 Cor. 11:26). The ministry of priests is directed to this end and finds its consummation in it. (PO, no. 2)

Both in Trent and in the Second Vatican Council, the difference between the sacrifice on the cross and the sacrifice of the Mass is that the one sacrifice is offered in different manners. As a sacramental representation of the *one* unique sacrifice, the Mass is said to be a "true and proper sacrifice" and "truly propitiatory" (Trent, Session 22, ch. 2, and canon 1; DS 1743, 1751; cf. canon 3, DS 1753). In our conversations, the Roman Catholic representatives interpreted "truly propitiatory" to mean that in the Mass the fruits of Christ's propitiation become ours (a transfer that happens only in the context of faith).

On the basis of the Heidelberg Catechism, the committee challenged the Roman Catholic representatives as follows: as a *re-enactment* of the sacrifice of Christ which mediates forgiveness, the Mass detracts from the finality and sufficiency of Christ's sacrifice. To this the Roman Catholic representatives responded: since the sacrifice of the Mass is a re-enactment and representation of the *one final, sufficient, and unrepeatable sacrifice of Christ on the cross*, the Mass by its very nature as sacrament of that once-for-all event cannot detract from the one sacrifice of Christ.

2. The Eucharist: Sacramental Representation and Perpetuation of the One, Unique Sacrifice

The Roman Catholic representatives emphasized that, in Roman Catholic doctrine, the sacrifice of the Mass does not stand in competition with Christ's sacrifice but sacramentally represents it. The duplication of the term *sacrifice* in describing both Christ's gift on the cross and the gift of the Mass presents no problem from the Roman Catholic perspective because of a theology of sacramental representation. The *one* sacrifice, the same victim, is indeed offered but in an entirely different *way*, namely, *sacramentally*. By virtue of this sacramental representation, the Eucharist, far from being "basically nothing but a denial of the one sacrifice," renders present the unique and unrepeatable sacrifice of Jesus Christ. At the Last Supper, Christ left the church with "a visible sacrifice (as the nature of man demands)" that "represents," that is, makes present (see the explanation of "real presence" below), *in an unbloody manner* the bloody sacrifice that was "*once for all*" accomplished on the cross. In this way the "salutary power" of the cross "is applied for the forgiveness of sins" (Trent, Session 22, ch. 1; DS 1740). In the "unbloody oblation" of the Eucharist, the "fruits" of the bloody oblation are "received" (Trent, Session 22, ch. 2; DS 1743).

Similarly, the *Catechism of the Catholic Church* (promulgated in 1992) affirms, "The Eucharist is the memorial of Christ's Passover, the making *present* and the *sacramental* offering of his *unique* sacrifice, in the liturgy of the Church which is his Body" (no. 1362, emphasis added; in no. 1382 the term used is "perpetuated").

In addition to representing Christ's sacrifice, the eucharistic sacrifice perpetuates the sacrifice of the cross:

> At the Last Supper, on the night he was betrayed, our Savior instituted the eucharistic sacrifice of his Body and Blood. This he did in order to perpetuate the sacrifice of the Cross throughout the ages until he should come again, and so to entrust to his beloved Spouse, the Church, a memorial of his death and resurrection: a sacrament of love, a sign of unity, a bond of charity, a paschal banquet in which Christ is consumed, the mind is filled with grace, and a pledge of future glory is given to us. (SC, no. 47)

On this view, the eucharistic sacrifice is not another sacrifice but is the perpetuation and memorial of Christ's sacrifice on the cross.

According to the Roman Catholic representatives, therefore, the Heidelberg Catechism's conclusion that the sacrifice of the Mass detracts from the sufficiency or finality of Christ's sacrifice misconstrues the Roman Catholic understanding of the Mass as standing in competition with the cross—a construal that Trent explicitly repudiates: "By no means, then, does the latter [the unbloody oblation] detract from former [the bloody oblation]" (Trent, Session 22, ch. 2; DS 1743). Trent anathematizes anyone who says that the sacrifice of the Mass "detracts from" Christ's sacrifice on the cross (Trent, Session 22, canon 4; DS 754).

3. The Eucharistic Sacrifice Completes the Purification of Those Who Die in Christ

According to Roman Catholic teaching, the offering of the Mass also for those who have died in the Lord but who "are not yet wholly purified" (Trent, Session 22, ch. 2, and canon 3) does not impugn the finality or sufficiency of the forgiveness accomplished by Christ's sacrifice. The eternal state of those who die in the Lord is not in question. They are simply being purified for the state of full glorification. One might say, therefore, that in Roman Catholic teaching the effect of the Mass on those who die in the Lord lies not in the area of justification but of (final) sanctification.

As to the state of these departed saints, the *Catechism of the Catholic Church* says,

> All who die in God's grace and friendship, but [are] still imperfectly purified, are indeed assured of their eternal salvation; but after death they undergo purification, so as to achieve the holiness necessary to enter the joy of heaven. (no. 1030)

Thus, the Roman Catholic representatives held that ascribing posthumous purifying efficacy to the Mass in no way detracts from the finality of the redemption (as the certainty of forgiveness and of eternal life) accomplished on the cross. Just as the Protestant affirmation of sanctification as a continuing process in the lives of believers does not detract from the finality or sufficiency of the cross, the belief that this process extends beyond death does not detract from the once-for-all sacrifice.

4. The Eucharist: More Than Sacrifice

Except for the teaching on bodily presence, the Heidelberg Catechism focuses solely on the Mass as sacrifice. Although this may be understandable in view of the polemical context, the Roman Catholic representatives pointed out that to describe the Eucharist solely as sacrifice obscures its "inexhaustible richness." The Council of Trent affirmed in the "Decree on the Most Holy Eucharist" (1551) that in instituting this sacrament Christ

> poured out, as it were, in this sacrament the riches of His divine love for men, "causing His wonderful works to be remembered," (cf. Ps. 111 [110]:4), and He wanted us when receiving it to celebrate His memory (cf. 1 Cor. 11:24) and to proclaim His death until He comes to judge the world (cf. 1 Cor. 11:26). His will was that this sacrament be received as the soul's spiritual food (cf. Mt.

> 26:26) which would nourish and strengthen (cf. no. 1530) those who live by the life of Him who said: "He who eats Me will live because of Me" (Jn. 6:57). (Trent, Session 13, chapter 2, DS 1638)

Reflecting this, recent Roman Catholic teaching says that the Eucharist includes elements such as meal, spiritual nourishment, offering of thanksgiving, memorial, sign of unity, bond of love, source of grace, and pledge of future glory (SC, no. 47; CCC, nos. 1328-1332, 1358-1565). Although we acknowledge the many dimensions of the Eucharist, in the following section, we will follow the Heidelberg Catechism in focusing on the main point in dispute, namely the understanding of the Eucharist as sacrifice.

C. Key Differences Between the Heidelberg Catechism and Roman Catholic Teaching

Taking seriously the Roman Catholic self-understanding expressed in official teaching regarding the Mass as sacrifice (presented above) and leaving aside for the moment the Heidelberg Catechism's conclusion ("basically nothing but a denial"), it is instructive to analyze and assess some key differences between the Heidelberg Catechism and Roman Catholic teaching.

1. The Nature and the Direction of the Sacrament

According to Roman Catholic teaching, the Eucharist is the sacrifice of the church in which the church sacramentally re-presents, and joins in, Christ's sacrifice:

> The Church which is the Body of Christ participates in the offering of her Head. With him, she herself is offered whole and entire. She unites herself to his intercession with the Father for all men. In the Eucharist the sacrifice of Christ becomes also the sacrifice of the members of his Body. The lives of the faithful, their praise, sufferings, prayer, and work, are united with those of Christ and with his total offering, and so acquire a new value. (CCC, no. 1368)

In Roman Catholic teaching, the central moment of the Eucharist is Christ's sacrifice to which we are joined. This understanding of the Mass means that, though the entire sacrament and the effects it communicates are gifts of God, the Mass includes as a constitutive element the church's priestly sacrifice to God (LG, no. 10).

The Heidelberg Catechism consistently and exclusively describes the Lord's Supper as God's *gift to us*, which we receive. This does not mean, of course, that the Godward direction is absent. In Reformed worship, the sacrament of the Lord's Supper is surrounded (in anticipation and in response to God's gift) by our doxology and thanksgiving (*eucharistia*). Indeed, the entire event is described as a "*celebration* of the Lord's Supper." This is clearly our celebration. Thus, though in both Roman Catholic and Reformed understandings this liturgical event as a totality is bi-directional, God-ward and human-ward, a significant difference appears. In the Mass, the God-ward direction is part and parcel of the sacrament itself. For this reason it may appropriately be called a *sacrifice*, *our* sacrifice. The Lord's Supper, by contrast, is never spoken of in this way; only our response to this sacramental gift may be called a sacrifice, in the sense of a thank-offering. In his "Catechism of the Church of Geneva" (1545), Calvin sums up his view of this difference:

> Minister: Then the Supper is not instituted with the object that the body of his Son be offered to God?
>
> Child: Not at all. For he himself only, since he is the eternal Priest, has this prerogative (Heb. 5:5). And this his words declare, when he says: Take and eat. For there he commands, *not that we offer his body, but only that we eat it* (Matt. 26:26). ("Catechism of the Church of Geneva," in *Calvin: Theological Treatises*, 137, emphasis added)

2. The Role of the Church in the Mediation of Salvation

Implicit in the difference between the Eucharist as sacrifice and gift is a difference regarding the understanding of the role of the church in the mediation of salvation. It is important, however, to note that the point at issue is not *whether* the church has such a role. Because both traditions have a high view of the church and the sacraments, both ascribe a central role to the church in communicating salvation. Accordingly, the Belgic Confession maintains that outside the church there is no salvation (art. 28). More specifically, this mediating role of the church comes to expression in the common description of the sacraments as "means of grace." The Belgic Confession states that Christ "works in us all that He represents to us by these holy signs." Hence it is not erroneous to say that "what is eaten is

Christ's own natural body and what is drunk is his own blood"—though "not by the mouth but by the Spirit, through faith" (art. 35).

a. Gift Received or Sacrifice Offered

There is no dispute therefore regarding "mediation" as such. The difference concerns the manner of mediation. This can be illustrated by the way in which Christ's command regarding the celebration of his supper is construed. Calvin's argument that Christ's command was not that we "offer his body, but only that we eat it" seems incontrovertible. Of course, the Roman Catholic Church does not pull its teaching regarding sacrifice out of thin air. On the contrary, for Trent, Christ's "institution of the most holy sacrifice of the Mass" (heading of ch. 1, of the twenty-second session) is foundational, but it links Christ's command to a different part of the narrative of the Last Supper. After simply recounting that Christ gave the bread and wine to the disciples, Trent continues, He "ordered them [his disciples] and their successors in the priesthood to offer, saying: 'Do this as a memorial of Me,' etc. (Lk. 22:19; 1 Cor. 11:24)" (session 22, ch. 1; DS 1740). Trent understands the "this," which the disciples are commanded to "do," to refer not to receiving that which Christ gives but to doing what Christ does, namely, offering a sacrifice.

That Trent deliberately and explicitly links Christ's command in a different way to the upper room narrative is evident in the accompanying negations. In canon 2, the Council declares: "If anyone says that by the words, 'Do this as a memorial of Me' (Lk. 22:19; 1 Cor. 11:24) Christ did not establish the apostles as priests or that He did not order that they and other priests should offer His body and blood, *anathema sit*" (DS 1752). Moreover, the previous canon explicitly repudiates a minimalist understanding of "offering," as if it refers simply to the distribution ("offering" in this sense) of the elements to the communicants: "If anyone says that in the Mass a true and proper sacrifice is not *offered to God* or that the offering consists merely in the fact that Christ *is given to us, anathema sit*" (DS 1751, emphasis added). Understanding the words of institution in terms of receiving or offering Christ's body and blood makes a decisive difference in the way in which the Lord's Supper is said to be a "means of grace" (cf. BC, art. 33).

The different interpretations of Christ's words of institution entail a decisive difference in identifying the primary agents of the sacramental action. If Christ commanded us to present a sacrifice, the primary celebrant of the eucharistic offering can be none other than the ordained priests. In Roman Catholic teaching, the priest, in sacramental identification with

Christ, effects this sacrifice: "The ministerial priest, by the sacred power that he has, forms and rules the priestly people; in the person of Christ he effects the eucharistic sacrifice and offers it to God in the name of all the people" (Dogmatic Constitution on the Church, no. 10; cf. Decree on the Ministry and Life of Priests, nos. 2 and 13). In fact, while encouraging the participation of the entire community of the faithful, Vatican II allows for a priest to celebrate the Mass with no one else present (SC, no. 26-27; Decree on the Ministry and Life of Priests, no. 13). Normally, however, the whole congregation celebrates the Eucharist through and with the priest. The ordained priests "unite the votive offerings of the faithful to the sacrifice of their Head" (LG, no. 28). In contrast, Reformed Christians insist that Christ commanded us, not to offer a sacrifice, but only to receive the benefits of Christ's sacrifice by eating and drinking the bread and wine. Thus, the Reformed tradition thinks of the celebrants that Jesus has in view as none other than the entire company of believers.

b. Centrality of Word or Sacrament

The Reformed confessions consistently conceive of sacraments as signs and seals of God's promise. In explaining the nature of the Lord's Supper, therefore, the Heidelberg Catechism underscores its character as testimony: "The Lord's Supper *declares* to us that our sins have been completely forgiven. . . . It also *declares* to us that the Holy Spirit grafts us into Christ" (Q. and A. 80, emphasis added). A minimal understanding of this declarative function would reduce the "sacrament" to an instrument of divine pedagogy, an audio-visual aid. To understand the sacraments as merely pedagogical rituals, however, is to overlook the richness of Reformed teaching, which describes the sacramental action as "pledge," "sign," and "seal."

Thus, the Heidelberg Catechism states that Christ assures us by the "visible sign and pledge" of the Lord's Supper

> that we, through the Holy Spirit's work, share in his true body and blood *as surely as* our mouths receive these holy signs in his remembrance, and that all of his suffering and obedience are as definitely ours as if we personally had suffered and paid for our sins. (Q. and A. 79, emphasis added)

Again, the Heidelberg Catechism teaches, "as surely as I see with my eyes" the bread broken for me and the cup given to me, "so surely his body was offered and broken for me and his blood poured out for me on the cross." Not content with describing the sacrament as a visual demonstration, the Heidelberg Catechism goes on to say,

> *as surely as* I receive . . . and taste with my mouth the bread and cup of the Lord, given me as sure signs of Christ's body and blood, so surely he nourishes and refreshes my soul for eternal life with his crucified body and poured-out blood. (Q. and A. 75, emphasis added)

Similarly, the Belgic Confession insists that God so fully backs up this sacramental declaration that he himself, through his Spirit, in his Son, comes along with the signs, so to speak: "we do not go wrong when we say that what is eaten is Christ's own natural body and what is drunk is his own blood" (art. 35).

The efficacy attributed to the Lord's Supper is therefore by no means less than that attributed to the Mass, but the Lord's Supper has its efficacy as sealed promise, as visibly signified word, as tangible declaration. The sacrament is an extension of and is subservient to proclamation. According to the Heidelberg Catechism, "the Holy Spirit produces [faith] in our hearts by the preaching of the holy gospel, and confirms it through our use of the holy sacraments" (Q. and A. 65; see also Belgic Confession, art. 33).

In the Reformed understanding of the means of grace, the overarching category is proclamation. Accordingly, the Lord's Supper is a specific form of *a declaratory event*.

For the Roman Catholic Church, the Second Vatican Council was instrumental in fostering a renewed emphasis on the word and proclamation. The Council insists that the sermon is an essential part of the liturgy and mandates that it is to focus on the proclamation of "God's wonderful works in the history of salvation, that is, the mystery of Christ, which is ever made present and active within us, especially in the celebration of the liturgy" (SC, no. 35). Indeed, the Council states that "since nobody can be saved who has not first believed, it is the first task of priests as co-workers of the bishops to preach the Gospel of God to all men" (PO, no. 4). Frequently the Scripture is coordinated with the sacrament as worthy of equal honor: "The Church has always venerated the divine Scriptures as she venerated the body of the Lord, in so far as she never ceases, particularly in the sacred liturgy, to partake of the bread of life and to offer it to the faithful from the one table of the Word of God and the Body of Christ" (DV, no. 21). The word and the specifically sacramental action, however, can both be subsumed under the Mass: "The two parts which in a sense go to make up the Mass, viz. the liturgy of the word and the eucharistic liturgy, are so closely connected with each other that they form but one single act of worship" (SC, no. 56).

When the Council describes the specific functions of the priests, however, it becomes clear that the most unique and characteristic expression of the priestly office is the celebration of the Eucharist. The specific power conferred in the sacrament of ordination is that of effecting (by the power of the Spirit and the presence of Christ) the eucharistic sacrifice (see IIB, above); in fact, "the sacred nature and organic structure of the priestly community [i.e., the people of God] is brought into operation through the sacraments and the exercise of virtues" (LG, no. 11). Accordingly, the Council can describe "the nature of priesthood" initially without reference to proclamation: "These men were to hold in the community of the faithful the sacred power of Order, that of offering sacrifice and forgiving sins." Only later in this section does the apostolic mission of spreading the Gospel of Christ come into play (PO, no. 2). The priests are said to "fulfill their principal function" in the Eucharistic sacrifice, for it is there that "the work of our redemption is continually carried out" (PO, no. 13).

In the Roman Catholic understanding of the means of grace, the overarching category is sacrament. The central sacrament is clearly the Eucharist from which "especially . . . grace is poured forth upon us as from a fountain" (SC, no. 10). Although in the Reformed understanding, as we have noted, the church may be said to play a significant role in the mediation of grace, it conveys grace—even in the administration of the sacraments—principally as herald.

In summary, in Reformed teaching the message is the privileged medium of grace, while in Roman Catholic teaching the Eucharist is the privileged medium of grace. This contrast does not mean that what is privileged in one tradition excludes what is privileged in the other. Rather, the center of gravity is located at a different point. The pull exerted by these different centers results in significantly different understandings of church, sacrament, and the mediation of salvation.

3. *The Mass's Efficacy for the Dead*

Although there are significant differences between Rome and the Reformers regarding the state of departed believers and their relationship to the church on earth, this subject need not be treated as an independent topic in our current discussions with the Roman Catholic Church. The reference to "the dead" in Q. and A. 80 is significant only insofar as it reflects the issue of the efficacy attributed to the Mass and the degree to which the Heidelberg Catechism says such putative efficacy detracts from the finality and decisiveness attributed to the cross. In that regard, a difference remains in that the Reformers affirm that at the time of death, sanctification, too, is complete, for by virtue of his completed sacrifice, Christ is our sanctification.

III. Differences over the Presence of Christ in the Sacrament

Against the background of the Heidelberg Catechism's statements, the second main task that flows out of the committee's mandate is to determine what the teaching of the Roman Catholic Church is regarding the presence of Christ in the sacrament of the Eucharist. This section of the report carries out this task.

A. The Teaching of the Heidelberg Catechism

In its predominantly irenic spirit, the Heidelberg Catechism presents its teaching on the Lord's Supper in questions and answers 75 through 79. It describes the feast as nourishment and refreshment of the soul given to the church as a sacramental sign and seal of God's gracious promises, a celebration instituted and designed to assure the believer of salvation in Jesus Christ. It asserts with great clarity that "even though it [the bread] is called the body of Christ in keeping with the nature and language of sacraments," it "is not changed into the actual body of Christ" (Q. and A. 78). Instead, the consistent formula appears to be that of "as surely as":

> as surely as I see with my eyes the bread of the Lord broken for me and the cup given to me, so surely his body was offered and broken for me and his blood poured out for me on the cross. (Q. and A. 75)
>
> as surely as I receive from the hand of the one who serves, and taste with my mouth the bread and cup of the Lord, given me as sure signs of Christ's body and blood, so surely he nourishes and refreshes my soul for eternal life with his crucified body and pouredout blood. (Q. and A. 75)
>
> we, through the Holy Spirit's work, share in his true body and blood as surely as our mouths receive these holy signs in his remembrance. (Q. and A. 79)

At the root of the Catechism's teaching lies the conviction that Christ "is in heaven and we are on earth" (Q. and A. 76), a teaching often referred to by theologians as the "extra-Calvinisticum," whereby the ubiquity of Christ's humanity is denied. The ascended Lord is host of the meal where believers are nourished "through the Holy Spirit, who lives both in Christ and in us . . ." (Q. and A. 76).

Then, in an uncharacteristically polemical manner, the Heidelberg Catechism proceeds—in Q. and A. 80—to single out and contrast certain aspects of its teaching with their counterparts in the teaching of the Roman Catholic Church regarding the Mass. It is the Holy Spirit who "grafts us into Christ." Our Savior and Lord "with his very body is now in heaven at the right hand of the Father," and this is "where he wants us to worship him" (section B1). The Roman Catholic Church, on the other hand, teaches "that Christ is bodily present in the form of bread and wine where Christ is therefore to be worshiped" (section B2). Thus, the Mass is said to be "a condemnable idolatry" (section B3).

B. Roman Catholic Teaching

The Roman Catholic theologians with whom the committee met affirmed that the Heidelberg Catechism is substantially correct in its presentation of the Roman Catholic teaching regarding Christ's bodily presence in the consecrated bread and wine. They expressed a caution that the word bodily should not be misunderstood. When Roman Catholics seek to explain the mystery of the presence of Christ in the bread and wine, we were told, they generally proceed by way of the *via negativa*. Among the steps taken along that way is the denial of a localized or fleshly presence. Externally, the bread and wine retain their appearance even after consecration. Yet, at the same time, the whole Christ is sacramentally present in them—the whole Christ, body and blood, soul and divinity. Thus, he is indeed "bodily present in the form of bread and wine."

The way in which the Roman Catholic Church has explained the bodily presence of Christ in the sacrament is through the doctrine of transubstantiation. The Roman Catholic theologians with whom the committee met emphasized that what is important is affirming the real presence of Christ and the change of the elements of bread and wine. The doctrine of transubstantiation has been used in order to give a theological articulation of Christ's bodily presence in the bread and wine. Although other explanations of this presence would be possible, none has yet been approved by the

Roman Catholic Church. The next section offers a brief summary of important developments and statements in Roman Catholic teaching regarding the change in the elements of bread and wine.

1. *The Bodily Presence of Christ in the Elements*

a. Historical Statements

The question of the bodily presence of Christ in the elements became a significant issue during the Middle Ages. Berengar of Tours (c. 1010-1088) provoked much opposition when he maintained the real presence of Christ in the sacramental meal but denied "that any material change in the elements is needed to explain it" (*Oxford Dictionary of the Christian Church*, 3rd ed., s.v. "Berengar of Tours"). In response, Berengar's opponents introduced a distinction between "material" and "substantial" change. The Council of Rome (1079) required Berengar to swear that "the bread and wine which are placed upon the altar are by the mystery of the sacred prayer and the words of our Redeemer *substantially* changed into the true and real and life-giving flesh and blood of Jesus Christ our Lord" (DS 700; emphasis added). In 1215, the Fourth Lateran Council said, "His body and blood are truly contained in the sacrament of the altar under the appearances of bread and wine, the bread being transubstantiated into the body by the divine power and the wine into the blood" (DS 802). The early reformer John Wycliffe (c. 1330-1384) and his followers, the Lollards, rejected the doctrine of transubstantiation, arguing that the consecration of bread and wine in the Mass is not a sacrifice and that since the elements remain bread and wine, adoration of the Eucharist is idolatry. These views were among the "heresies" for which they were condemned and persecuted.

That Christ is bodily present by virtue of a change in the substance of bread and wine is stated quite clearly in the teaching of the Council of Florence (1439):

> The form of this sacrament is the words of the Savior with which He effected this sacrament; for the priest effects the sacrament by speaking in the person of Christ. It is by the power of these words that the substance of bread is changed into the body of Christ, and the substance of wine into His blood; in such a way, however, that the whole Christ is contained under the species of bread and the whole Christ under the species of wine. Further, the whole Christ is present under any part of the consecrated host or the consecrated wine when separated from the res. (DS 1321)

During the sixteenth century, those who tried to reform the church included the doctrine of the bodily presence of Christ among the teachings that needed reform. In response, the Council of Trent stated,

> To begin with, the holy Council teaches and openly and straightforwardly professes that in the blessed sacrament of the holy Eucharist, after the consecration of the bread and wine, our Lord Jesus Christ, true God and man, is truly, really and substantially contained under the appearances of those perceptible realities. For, there is no contradiction in the fact that our Savior always sits at the right hand of the Father in heaven according to His natural way of existing and that, nevertheless, in His substance He is sacramentally present to us in many other places. We can hardly find words to express this way of existing; but our reason, enlightened through faith, can nevertheless recognise it as possible for God, and we must always believe it unhesitatingly. (Trent, Session 13, ch. 1, DS 1636)

> Because Christ our Redeemer said that it was truly His body that He was offering under the species of bread . . ., it has always been the conviction of the Church of God, and this holy Council now again declares that, by the consecration of the bread and wine there takes place a change of the whole substance of bread into the substance of the body of Christ our Lord and of the whole substance of wine into the substance of His blood. This change the holy Catholic Church has fittingly and properly named transubstantiation. (Trent, Session 13, ch. 4; DS 1642)

> If anyone denies that in the sacrament of the most holy Eucharist the body and blood, together with the soul and divinity, of our Lord Jesus Christ and, therefore, the whole Christ is truly, really and substantially contained, but says that He is in it only as in a sign or figure or by His power, *anathema sit*. (Trent, Session 13, canon 1, DS 1651)

b. Contemporary Statements

The Second Vatican Council initiated a number of significant renewals and reforms in the Roman Catholic Church. Given its pastoral focus, this Council made no significant revisions in the doctrine of the bodily presence of Christ.

The recent *Catechism of the Catholic Church* says:

> At the heart of the Eucharistic celebration are the bread and wine that, by the words of Christ and the invocation of the Holy Spirit, become Christ's Body and Blood. . . . The signs of bread and wine become, in a way surpassing understanding, the Body and Blood of Christ. (no. 1333)

It then proceeds to cite DS 1651 and DS 1642 of the Council of Trent, indicating in the strongest possible terms that "it is by the conversion of the bread and wine into Christ's body and blood that Christ becomes present in this sacrament" (*Catechism of the Catholic Church*, no. 1375). Indeed,

> the Eucharistic presence of Christ begins at the moment of the consecration and endures as long as the Eucharistic species subsist. Christ is present whole and entire in each of the species and whole and entire in each of their parts, in such a way that the breaking of the bread does not divide Christ. (CCC, no. 1377)

Similarly, in 1965, Pope Paul VI rejected seeing the Eucharist as "nothing else than an efficacious sign 'of Christ's spiritual presence and of his intimate union with his faithful members in the mystical Body'" (*Mysterium Fidei*, no. 39, quoting Pope Pius XII). Appealing to Christ's words at the Last Supper, he said, "The very words used by Christ when he instituted the most holy Eucharist compel us to acknowledge that 'the Eucharist is the flesh of our Saviour Jesus Christ which suffered for our sins and which the Father in his loving kindness raised again'" (*Mysterium Fidei*, no. 44, quoting Ignatius of Antioch). Thus Christ is made present in the sacrament by

> the change of the whole substance of the bread into his body and of the whole substance of the wine into his blood. . . . As a result of transubstantiation, the species of bread and wine . . . no longer remain ordinary bread and wine, but become the sign of something sacred, the sign of a spiritual food. . . . For there no longer lies under those species what was there before, but something quite different; and that, not only because of the faith of the Church, but in objective reality, since after the change of the substance or nature of the bread and wine into the body and

> blood of Christ, nothing remains of the bread and wine but the appearances, under which Christ, whole and entire, in his physical "reality" is bodily present, although not in the same way as bodies are present in a given place. (*Mysterium Fidei*, no. 46)

One way to get a sense of current Roman Catholic teaching is to observe that church's response to important ecumenical developments. In its Faith and Order Paper drafted at Lima in 1982, the World Council of Churches sought to articulate a "significant theological convergence," noting that the commission responsible for the text "includes among its full members theologians of the Roman Catholic and other churches which do not belong to the World Council of Churches itself" (BEM, ix). On the meaning of the Eucharist, it made the following assertions:

> Many churches believe that by the words of Jesus and by the power of the Holy Spirit, the bread and wine of the Eucharist become, in a real though mysterious manner, the body and blood of the risen Christ, i.e., of the living Christ present in all his fullness. Under the signs of bread and wine, the deepest reality is the total being of Christ who comes to us in order to feed us and transform our entire being. Some other churches, while affirming a real presence of Christ at the Eucharist, do not link that presence so definitely with the signs of bread and wine. The decision remains for the churches whether this difference can be accommodated within the convergence formulated in the text itself. (BEM, Commentary on Eucharist, no. 13)

The response of the Roman Catholic Church to these assertions is significant:

> A distinction is made in Commentary 13 between churches that "believe" in the *change* of the elements and those which do not link Christ's presence "so definitely to the signs of bread and wine." But the final sentence seems to relativize the word "believe." It asks whether the "difference can be accommodated with the convergence formulated in the text itself." On the one hand, we welcome the convergence that is taking place. On the other hand, we must note that for Catholic doctrine, the *conversion* of the elements is a matter of faith and is only open to possible new theological explanations as to the "how" of the intrinsic change. The content of the word "transubstantiation" ought to be expressed without ambiguity. For Catholics this is a

> central mystery of faith, and they cannot accept expressions that are ambiguous. Thus it would seem that the differences as explained here cannot be accommodated within the convergence formulated in the text itself. ("Churches Respond to BEM," 22)

In response to the statement in *Baptism, Eucharist and Ministry* that the bread and wine "become the sacramental signs of Christ's body and blood," the official Roman Catholic response adds a comment that "the thought that they become sacramental signs is linked to the intrinsic change which takes place, whereby unity of being is realized between the signifying reality and the reality signified" ("Churches Respond to BEM," 22).

It appears, then, that the official position of the Roman Catholic Church on the matter of the presence of the body and blood of Christ in the Eucharist has remained consistent since the Council of Trent. The Heidelberg Catechism's representation of that position as holding that "Christ is bodily present in the form of bread and wine" may omit nuances of Roman Catholic teaching but is substantially correct.

2. Worship and the Consecrated Bread and Wine

What, then, of the Heidelberg Catechism's insistence that Christ "wants us to worship him" as seated at the right hand of God and not "in the form of bread and wine" in the elements of the Eucharist? On these points, the Council of Trent is abundantly clear:

> There remains, therefore, no room for doubting that all the faithful of Christ, in accordance with the perpetual custom of the Catholic Church, must venerate this most holy sacrament with the worship of *latria* which is due to the true God. Nor is it to be less adored because it was instituted by Christ the Lord to be received. For in it we believe that the same God is present whom the eternal Father brought into the world, saying: "Let all God's angels worship Him" (Heb. 1:6; cf. Ps. 97 [96]:7), whom the Magi fell down to worship (cf. Mt. 2:11) and whom, finally, the apostles adored in Galilee as Scripture testifies (cf. Mt. 28:17). (Trent, Session 13, ch. 5; DS 1643)

And again,

> If anyone says that Christ, the only-begotten son of God, is not to be adored in the holy sacrament of the Eucharist with the

> worship of latria, including external worship, and that the sacrament therefore is not to be honoured with special festive celebrations nor solemnly carried in processions according to the praise-worthy universal rite and custom of the holy Church; or that it is not to be publicly exposed for the people's adoration, and that those who adore it are idolaters, *anathema sit*. (Trent, Session 13, canon 6, DS 1656)

In these passages, venerating the holy sacrament means worshiping the body and blood of Christ, who is sacramentally present under the appearances of the consecrated bread and wine.

In their discussions with us, representatives of the Roman Catholic Church acknowledged the polemical tone of these statements, indicating that such may have been more appropriate in the sixteenth century than in the decidedly more ecumenical context of today. They also noted that the primary purpose of reserving (storing) consecrated elements is not to venerate the elements but to make communion possible for the dying (*Eucharisticum Mysterium* [1967], ch. III, I, A). On the main issue itself, however, they insisted along with Trent, first, that the holy sacrament is to be venerated with the worship of latria and, second, that this worship does not constitute idolatry inasmuch as, in the adoration of the consecrated bread and wine, Christ is being worshiped, not the elements.

C. A Key Difference Between the Heidelberg Catechism and Roman Catholic Teaching

With regard to veneration, it is important to remember that the Reformed creedal tradition did not embrace the Zwinglian interpretation of the sacrament. The Belgic Confession (TBC), for example, while recognizing that eating the "living bread" is a matter of appropriating and receiving Christ "spiritually by faith," declares the "manner" of God's working in the sacrament to be "beyond our understanding" and "incomprehensible to us, just as the operation of God's Spirit is hidden and incomprehensible." Or, again, while insisting that the "manner in which we eat" is "not by the mouth but by the Spirit, through faith," it declares that "we do not go wrong when we say that what is eaten is Christ's own natural body and what is drunk is his own blood" and, later, that we must therefore "receive the holy sacrament" with "humility and reverence" (TBC, art. 35). It seems reasonable to assert that the difference between Roman Catholic and Reformed teaching is not whether the sacramental meal should be treated with reverence but the precise manner in which that reverence is expressed. Roman Catholic teaching insists on veneration (with the worship of *latria*) of the consecrated bread and wine because sacramentally they are the body and blood of Christ. Reformed teaching requires believers to receive the sacrament in humility and reverence, since the ascended Lord is spiritually present as the host and substance of the meal. Thus, the Belgic Confession also states—with little ambiguity—the concern that "Jesus Christ remains always seated at the right hand of God his Father in heaven" and that "he never refrains on that account to communicate himself to us through faith" (TBC, art. 35).

IV. Conclusions and Recommendations

A. Conclusions

Based upon the above study, the committee proposes the following statements as summary conclusions of the Roman Catholic Church's teaching concerning the sacrament of the Mass:

1. Although the Eucharist is spoken of as a sacrifice, it is much more than that. It is a meal, spiritual nourishment, offering of thanksgiving, memorial, sign of unity, bond of love, source of grace, and pledge of future glory.

2. The difference between the sacrifice on the cross and the sacrifice of the Mass is that the one sacrifice is offered in different manners.

3. The Eucharist sacramentally represents and perpetuates the one unique and unrepeatable sacrifice of Christ on the cross.

4. In the consecration of the bread and wine, the substance of the bread and wine become, in a way surpassing understanding, the body and blood of Jesus Christ.

5. In the Eucharist, the real presence of Christ means that the risen and glorified Christ is present under the appearances of the consecrated bread and wine and should be worshiped in the adoration of those consecrated elements.

6. The consecrated bread and wine deserve the adoration due to the ascended Jesus Christ. In this adoration, Christ is being worshiped, not the elements.

7. Offering Mass for the dead does not detract from the finality of redemption accomplished on the cross. The effect of the Mass on those who die in the Lord lies not in the area of justification but of (final) sanctification.

If the bishops of the Roman Catholic Church in the United States and Canada endorse the above report as an accurate presentation of official Roman Catholic teaching regarding the sacrament of the Eucharist, that will have significant implications on whether, and how, the Heidelberg Catechism ought to be modified. If Roman Catholic teaching is as it is presented in this report, the committee has serious concerns about the Heidelberg Catechism's conclusion that "the Mass is basically nothing but a denial of the one sacrifice and suffering of Jesus Christ and a condemnable idolatry" (Q. and A. 80). If this report accurately presents Roman Catholic teaching, there are also serious questions about the Heidelberg Catechism's representation, in Q. and A. 80, of what "the Mass teaches." Thus, if this report accurately presents Roman Catholic teaching, significant changes in the Heidelberg Catechism may be warranted.

Given the seriousness of the issues involved, including the possibility of altering one of the church's confessions, the committee believes that Synod 2002 should take every appropriate step to assure the Christian Reformed Church that the report's presentation of Roman Catholic teaching is accurate. Thus, the committee is taking the unusual step of recommending that this report be sent by Synod 2002 to the Roman Catholic bishops of the United States and Canada for their endorsement of its accuracy in presenting the Roman Catholic position. If this endorsement is granted, or even if some other response is given, the Interchurch Relations Committee should be expected to advise a future synod about any further action that may be needed regarding Q. and A. 80 of the Heidelberg Catechism.

Based upon the above study, the committee has also identified the following topics as worthy of further dialogue both within the Reformed churches and bilaterally between the Roman Catholic and Reformed churches:

1. What is the proper understanding of the nature and direction of the sacrament? Is it to be understood primarily as a sacrifice we offer or as a gift we receive?

2. What is the relationship between Word and sacrament as means of grace?

3. What is the role of the church (and its ministers) in mediating God's grace?

4. Given that both Reformed and Roman Catholic believers affirm the real presence of Christ in the Lord's Supper, what is the significance of the differences of understanding about the nature of that presence (i.e., spiritual vs. bodily presence)? How should we understand the presence of Christ in the Lord's Supper?

5. For Christians who do not believe that the bread and wine become the body and blood of Christ, does Roman Catholic veneration of those elements constitute improper worship?

6. What implications do the differences and agreements regarding the Lord's Supper have for the relationship between the Roman Catholic Church and Reformed churches?

B. Recommendations

The Interchurch Relations Committee recommends the following:

1. That Synod receive the report as fulfillment of the mandate given by Synod 1998 to the IRC "to make an attempt to dialogue with the leadership of the Roman Catholic Church to clarify the official doctrine of that church concerning the mass" (Acts of Synod 1998, 427).

2. That Synod submit the report to the United States Conference of Catholic Bishops and the Canadian Conference of Catholic Bishops requesting their agreement that the report gives an accurate presentation of official Roman Catholic teaching regarding the sacrament of the Eucharist.

3. That Synod ask the Interchurch Relations Committee, on the basis of the response received from the Roman Catholic bishops of Canada and the United States, to advise a future synod about any further action that may be needed regarding Q. and A. 80 of the Heidelberg Catechism.

4. That Synod ask the Interchurch Relations Committee, on the basis of the response received from the Roman Catholic bishops of Canada and the United States, to advise a future synod about the value of further dialogue between the Christian Reformed Church and the Roman Catholic Church.

5. That Synod send this report to churches in ecclesiastical fellowship and to the Reformed Ecumenical Council informing them of our study and inviting their response.

Further Action for Synod 2004

I. Background

In 2002, the Interchurch Relations Committee presented to synod [the above report]. . . .

These actions were all fulfilled shortly after Synod 2002 adjourned. To date, the CRC has received responses from the Catholic bishops but has not received any response from churches in ecclesiastical fellowship. The Reformed Ecumenical Council will not meet again until July 2005, when the report will be on its agenda.

Letters have been received from the following Roman Catholic respondents:

A. The Canadian Conference of Catholic Bishops, signed by Thomas Collins, Archbishop of Edmonton, Chair of the Commission for Christian Unity. Archbishop Collins also provided a written response to our committee's follow-up questions regarding the original letter.

B. The United States Conference of Catholic Bishops, signed by its President, Most Reverend Wilton D. Gregory, Bishop of Belleville.

C. The Bishops' Committee for Ecumenical and Interreligious Affairs of the United States Conference of Catholic Bishops, signed by its Chair, Stephen E. Blaire, Bishop of Stockton.

D. A letter to the Canadian Conference of Catholic Bishops from Walter Cardinal Kasper, President of the Pontifical Council for Promoting Christian Unity, who in consultation with the Congregation for the Doctrine of the Faith prepared observations regarding the process and the text of the report.

Although all the responses affirmed the accuracy of our report, Cardinal Kasper stated the conclusion most succinctly: "the Catholic doctrine concerning the Eucharist is stated clearly and accurately in this report." Still, the comments received from the Roman Catholic respondents led the committee to make slight alterations to the original report. In our view, the revised report offers a clearer and more accurate presentation of the Roman Catholic view of the Eucharist than the original did.

In April 2003, the IRC reconvened its subcommittee and asked it to provide advice and recommendations regarding the request of Synod 2002, namely:

3. That synod ask the IRC, on the basis of the response received from the Roman Catholic bishops of Canada and the United States, to advise a future synod about any further action that may be needed regarding Q. and A. 80 of the Heidelberg Catechism. (*Acts of Synod 2002*, 489)

The subcommittee met several times in pursuit of its mandate. . . . The remainder of this report constitutes the committee's analysis, advice, and recommendations.

II. The Heidelberg Catechism on the Mass

A. *Introduction*

If the committee's earlier report is accurate in its presentation of official Roman Catholic teaching about the Mass, then what should the Christian Reformed Church do in response? In comparing the Lord's Supper with the Roman Catholic Mass, does the Heidelberg Catechism in Q. and A. 80 accurately describe and appropriately criticize and condemn the Mass?

The committee struggled to discern whether Q. and A. 80 was written in response to official Roman Catholic teaching, to the practice of Roman Catholics in sixteenth-century Europe, or to some combination of the two. One clue is that the [Heidelberg] Catechism refers—twice—to what the Mass teaches. At the conclusion of the section describing what the Mass teaches, the German edition of the Catechism includes a footnote referring both to the Canon of the Mass, which was the central part of the Mass liturgy in use at the time, and to a section of "Gratian's Decree," an influential but not officially recognized twelfth-century collection of patristic and medieval texts on canon law. The section of Gratian's Decree to which the

[Heidelberg] Catechism refers contains excerpts from texts on the transformation of the bread and wine into the body and blood of Christ. So when the Catechism claims to describe what "the Mass teaches," its footnote includes one reference to a liturgical document that would illustrate what occurs during the Mass and one reference to a document that includes statements about the transformation of the elements into the body and blood of Christ. It therefore appears that the Catechism appeals to Roman Catholic teaching *about* the Mass as grounds for its statement that the Mass teaches that "Christ is bodily present in the form of bread and wine." And the Catechism seems to appeal to a liturgical text that would illustrate what actually occurs *in* the Mass as the basis for its claim that the Mass teaches that "the living and the dead do not have their sins forgiven through the suffering of Christ unless Christ is still offered for them daily by the priests" and perhaps also in its claim that the Mass teaches that "where Christ is . . . to be worshiped" is "in the form of bread and wine." That is, the Catechism seems to base its description of what "the Mass teaches" in part on what the Roman Catholic Church taught about the Mass and in part on the message that was conveyed by what actually happened during Mass.

Another clue to what the Catechism means comes from the commentary on the Heidelberg Catechism by Zacharias Ursinus, one of the Catechism's authors, which echoes the Catechism in several references to what "the Mass teaches." In one such instance, Ursinus quotes prayers from two different canons or liturgies of the Mass, both of which ask God to receive the sacrifice being offered for the salvation of people's souls. He then asks, "What need was there that Christ should offer himself, if the oblation of a sacrificing priest might avail for the redemption of souls?" (*Commentary of Dr. Zacharias Ursinus on the Heidelberg Catechism*, trans. G. W. Williard, 2nd American ed. [Columbus, 1852], 418-419). He seems to suggest that what occurs in the liturgy would lead one to think that salvation comes through the sacrifice offered by the priest, not through the once-for-all sacrifice of Christ. With respect to the sacrificial character of the Mass, Ursinus, like the Catechism, seems to be saying, "When the church performs the actions associated with the Mass in the way that it does, it communicates this message."

Interpreting at least part of Q. and A. 80 in this way receives some support from the broader perspective of the Heidelberg Catechism. The Catechism often focuses on the importance to the believer of various doctrines or practices. It begins with a question that addresses the believer's comfort: "What is your only comfort in life and in death?" (Q. 1). Later, after working through the Apostles' Creed, it asks, "What good does it do you, however, to believe all this?" (Q. 59). When beginning a section on the sacraments, it says, "In the gospel the Holy Spirit teaches us and through the holy sacraments he assures us . . ." (A. 67). Then, regarding baptism it asks, "How does baptism remind you and assure you that Christ's one sacrifice on the cross is for you personally?" (Q. 69). And it begins its treatment of the Lord's Supper by asking, "How does the Lord's Supper remind you and assure you that you share in Christ's one sacrifice on the cross and in all his gifts?" (Q. 75). Given the Heidelberg Catechism's frequent focus on the value or impact of certain teachings or practices for Christian faith, it should come as no surprise that it concerns itself with the impact or teaching of the Mass as practiced in the world inhabited by the Catechism's authors, that is, in northern Europe in the sixteenth century.

B. *The Heidelberg Catechism as Response to Official Teaching*

Although at least part of the Heidelberg Catechism appears to be addressing the teaching that arises from the practice of the Mass, it seems worthwhile to assess what the Heidelberg Catechism says if one takes it to be describing and evaluating official Roman Catholic teaching about the Mass. On this interpretation of the Catechism, it would not be an accurate description of Roman Catholic teaching to say that "the living and the dead do not have their sins forgiven through the suffering of Christ unless Christ is still offered for them daily by the priests." The Roman Catholic Church teaches that the "Eucharist sacramentally represents and perpetuates the one unique and unrepeatable sacrifice of Christ on the cross" (see sections II and IV.A.3 above). Even though the Roman Catholic Church teaches that "Christ is bodily present in the form of bread and wine," when the Catechism adds the statement, "where Christ is therefore to be worshiped," it sets up a misleading contrast between worshiping Christ in heaven and worshiping him in the consecrated bread and wine. The Roman Catholic Church holds that the ascended Christ is to be worshiped *through* the adoration of his body and blood, which is what it believes the consecrated bread and wine have become (see section III above). So if taken as a description of official Roman Catholic teaching, the Catechism's statements about what the Mass teaches are only partly correct.

What about the evaluative judgments that the Catechism offers? If they are taken as directed against official Roman Catholic teaching, do they offer fair criticism? In this context, the Catechism's first judgment, that "the Mass is basically nothing but a denial of the one sacrifice and suffering of

Jesus Christ," seems unwarranted. Official Roman Catholic teaching affirms that Christ offered a final, sufficient, unrepeatable sacrifice on the cross and that the Mass re-enacts or re-presents that sacrifice and suffering in an unbloody manner.

If taken as a criticism of official Roman Catholic teaching, the Catechism's evaluation that the Mass is "a condemnable idolatry" also seems unwarranted. Roman Catholic teaching holds that one is to worship the ascended Christ through the veneration or worship of the consecrated bread and wine, which have become the body and blood of Christ. This teaching arises from taking Jesus' words, "This is my body . . . this is my blood" (Mark 14:22, 24, and parallels) literally and from taking Paul to be referring to sharing in Christ's actual blood and body (1 Cor. 10:16). The Roman Catholic Church has developed the doctrine of transubstantiation in order to describe how it can be that bread becomes the actual body of Christ and wine becomes his blood (even while retaining their appearances as bread and wine). Taking these words literally is an error, in our opinion. Just as Jesus' statement "I am the vine, you are the branches" (Jn. 15:5) must not be taken literally, so too his statement, "This is my body . . . this is my blood," should not be taken literally. Nevertheless, it seems inappropriate to charge Roman Catholics with idolatry when they are worshiping the ascended Christ through the consecrated elements.

Since official Roman Catholic teaching regarding the Mass has remained quite stable from the sixteenth century to now, the Catechism—if taken to be describing and evaluating that official teaching—is either accurate both now and in the sixteenth century or inaccurate in both time periods. The above analysis leads to the conclusion that the Heidelberg Catechism must be regarded as wrong, both now and in the sixteenth century, *if* it is taken as describing and evaluating official Roman Catholic teaching. But, as has been suggested above, the committee believes that, with official Roman Catholic teaching lying in the background, the Heidelberg Catechism seems to focus at least in part on the practice of the Mass, that is, on what the event of the Mass communicates to people. And the practice of the Mass, and thus what the Mass communicates to people, has undergone significant changes from the sixteenth century to today.

C. *The Heidelberg Catechism as Response to Practice*

Since it may be assumed that Q. and A. 80 is not concerned with what "the Mass teaches" in isolation from the way in which the sacrament functioned in that time, it may be helpful to note some significant features of the way in which the Mass was conducted in Northern Europe in the sixteenth century and compare that with the practice of the Mass today.

In the sixteenth century, the Mass was conducted in Latin, a language that very few laypersons knew. In addition, the priest conducting the Mass spoke *sotto voce*, with the result that people in attendance heard mumbling in a language they did not understand. If any proclamation of the Gospel occurred during Mass, it was in Latin and therefore was not comprehensible by the congregation.

Because the people understood little or nothing of what was said during Mass, the event became focused on ringing bells and visual displays. The "Order of Low Mass," the typical liturgy of the Mass in use from the thirteenth century (or perhaps as far back as the ninth century) up to the Council of Trent (1545-1563), included frequent ringing of a bell. As the event of transubstantiation neared, a bell would be rung thrice and then again once. As the priest consecrated the bread in the event of transubstantiation, a bell would be rung thrice, and then three more times when the priest consecrated the wine. As one historian notes, "just before the offering in every Mass a bell was rung to warn worshipers absorbed in their own prayers to look up, because the moment of consecration and elevation was near. . . . In great churches where many Masses were celebrated simultaneously, those at side altars were timed so that their sacrings were staggered, none preceding that at the main Mass at the high altar" (Eamon Duffy, *The Stripping of the Altars: Traditional Religion in England 1400-1580* [New Haven and London: Yale University Press, 1992], 97). The English reformer Thomas Cranmer (1489-1556) described the spectacle that the Mass became. He says that people would run "from their seats to the altar, and from altar to altar, . . . peeping, tooting and gazing at that thing which the priest held up in his hands" because they "worshipped that visible thing which they saw with their eyes and took it for very God" (*Miscellaneous Writings and Letters of Thomas Cranmer*, ed. J. E. Cox [1846], 442). The custom of elevating the host (that is, the bread and the wine that were thought to become the body and blood of Christ) apparently began in the late twelfth century in response to a controversy about when the consecration occurred (Nathan Mitchell, *Cult and Controversy: The Worship of the Eucharist Outside of Mass* [New York: Pueblo Publishing Co., 1982], 186). Both Cranmer and recent historians note that during the Reformation era people would sometimes call out to the presiding priest to "hold up" or "heave higher" the host if they could not readily see it (Edward Foley, *From Age to Age* [Chicago: Liturgy Training Publications, 1991], 111).

In this context, the Heidelberg Catechism's emphasis on visual elements takes on new meaning. For example, the Catechism says, "as surely as I *see with my eyes* the bread of the Lord broken for me and the cup given to me, so surely his body was offered and broken for me and his blood poured out for me on the cross" (Q. and A. 75, emphasis added). Again, "he wants to assure us, by this *visible* sign and pledge, that we, through the Holy Spirit's work, share in his true body and blood as surely as our mouths receive these holy signs in his remembrance" (Q. and A. 79, emphasis added). In contrast to the uninterpreted—and easily misinterpreted—visual displays offered at Mass, the Lord's Supper was presented in a language the people could understand, accompanied by the preaching of the Word of God. In order that people might rightly understand the Gospel and receive the sacrament as a means of God's grace, the Lord's Supper was presented to all of the senses, and thus included the hearing of the Word.

In addition to emphasizing the spectacle of the transubstantiation of bread and wine into the body and blood of Christ, the medieval "Order of Low Mass" with which the authors of the Heidelberg Catechism would have been familiar also included frequent requests to God to accept the sacrifice being brought (by the priest on behalf of the people). Although it is hard to know when one such request stops and another begins, at least twelve times during the liturgy God is asked (typically by the priest) to accept the sacrifice that is being offered in remembrance of Christ's death and for the salvation of those present as well as all faithful Christians, living and dead ("Order of Low Mass," in Bard Thompson, *Liturgies of the Western Church* [Cleveland: The World Publishing Co., 1961], 55-91). This language remained part of the liturgy produced at the Council of Trent, a liturgy that was in standard use in the Roman Catholic Church into the 1970s.

With all the emphasis in the medieval (and even pre-Vatican II) Mass on God's accepting our sacrifice (a sacrifice offered by the priest) and on worshiping the consecrated bread and wine, all done in a language the people did not know, one can understand why the authors of the Heidelberg Catechism came to the conclusions they did about what the Mass itself is teaching and what is wrong with that teaching. The Catechism, at least in part, responds to and criticizes an inappropriate way of conducting and presenting the Lord's Supper or Eucharist.

D. The Heidelberg Catechism and Contemporary Roman Catholic Practice

Insofar as the Heidelberg Catechism was responding to inappropriate practices in the liturgy of the Mass, those who use the Catechism today as their confession of faith must ask whether the inappropriate practices persist even now. The Second Vatican Council (1962-1965) is enormously important in this regard. It brought about or endorsed important changes in the practice or conduct of the liturgy in the Roman Catholic Church. The Mass is now conducted in the language of the people, not in Latin. In a typical service, people hear Scripture read and the Gospel proclaimed in a language they can understand. The Roman Catholic Church has approved new Eucharistic prayers, some of which focus less on God's accepting our sacrifice and more on other important elements of the Eucharist.

Still, Roman Catholic practices regarding the Mass vary considerably today. In North America and in many other parts of the world, the reforms of Vatican II have had a dramatic effect. But the reception of the reforms advocated by Vatican II varies considerably within the Roman Catholic Church. In some places, the Catechism's description and evaluation of what is taught or communicated to people by a certain way of conducting the Mass may yet apply.

III. Conclusion

A. *Summary*

So what should Reformed Christians do with Q. and A. 80? What, in particular, should be done with the description and evaluation of Roman Catholic teaching in Q. and A. 80?

First, although Reformed Christians continue to have genuine and significant differences with Roman Catholics on the sacrificial character of the Eucharist (see sections II.C.1-2 above), the differences are not such that Reformed Christians are warranted in calling either Roman Catholic teaching or the proper expression of that teaching in practice "a denial of the one sacrifice and suffering of Jesus Christ." The Roman Catholic Eucharist may in significant ways obscure the important reality that Jesus' sacrifice and suffering occurred once for all and has been completed. Yet, when the Eucharist is celebrated as approved by the Roman Catholic Church, it does not deny or obliterate this reality.

Second, although Reformed Christians continue to reject the teachings that the consecrated bread and wine have become the body and blood of Christ and that Christ should be worshiped through venerating or worshiping the consecrated bread and wine, they are not warranted in saying that following these teachings is idolatry. By encouraging the worship of Christ through venerating or worshiping the consecrated bread and wine, the Roman Catholic Eucharist may in significant ways detract from proper worship of the ascended Lord, Jesus Christ. Yet, when celebrated as approved by the Roman Catholic Church, it does not constitute idolatry.

In sum, it would be inappropriate for the CRC to continue, by its confession of Q. and A. 80 of the Heidelberg Catechism, to suggest that it accurately describes or fairly condemns either official Roman Catholic teaching or the practices that are in accordance with it. Q. and A. 80 contains a salutary warning against teachings, attitudes, and practices related to the Eucharist that are idolatrous and that obscure the once-for-all sacrifice of Jesus Christ, and it may still apply to Roman Catholic practice in certain parts of the world. Nonetheless, its descriptions and condemnations cannot be said to apply to official Roman Catholic Eucharistic teaching or to practices that are in accordance with it.

B. Recommendations [to the 2004 CRC Synod]

1. That Synod receive the slightly revised report regarding Heidelberg Catechism Question and Answer 80 and the Roman Catholic Mass.

   Ground
   The changes, made in the light of comments from the various Roman Catholic respondents, render the report clearer and more accurate.

2. That Synod declare the following:

   a. The Mass, when celebrated in accordance with official Roman Catholic teaching, neither denies the one sacrifice and suffering of Jesus Christ nor constitutes idolatry.

      Grounds

      1. Official Roman Catholic teaching affirms that Christ offered a final, sufficient, unrepeatable sacrifice on the cross and that the Mass re-enacts or re-presents that sacrifice and suffering in an unbloody manner (see section II.B above and section II above).

      2. The Roman Catholic Church holds that the ascended Christ is to be worshiped through the adoration of his body and blood, which is what it believes the consecrated bread and wine have become. In the adoration of the consecrated bread

and wine, Christ is being worshiped, not the elements (see section II.B above and section III above).

3. The understanding of the Mass underlying this declaration is grounded in a lengthy conversation with representatives of the Roman Catholic Church (see section I above).

b. Q. & A. 80 still contains a pointed warning against any teachings, attitudes, and practices related to the Eucharist that obscure the finality and sufficiency of Christ's sacrifice on the cross and detract from proper worship of the ascended Lord.

Grounds

1. Practices are not always in accord with official teaching. When and where that occurs, Q. and A. 80 serves as a pointed warning.
2. In some places in the world today, practices associated with the Eucharist obscure and distort important Eucharistic teachings, as they did in the sixteenth century.

3. That Synod propose to the churches that, rather than being deleted completely, Q. and A. 80 be retained but printed in a smaller font.

Grounds

1. Q. and A. 80 does not offer an acceptable description or evaluation of Roman Catholic Eucharistic teaching or of practices in accordance with it.
2. In certain contexts. Q. and A. 80 has offered, and will continue to offer, a needed warning against teachings, attitudes, and practices related to the Eucharist.

4. That Synod propose to the churches the following footnote to Heidelberg Catechism Q. and A. 80 as the way to deal with the confessional difficulties it presents:

"Question and Answer 80 was absent from the first edition of the Catechism but was present in a shorter form in the second edition. The translation here given is of the expanded text of the third edition.

"The Synod of 2004 concluded that the Mass, when celebrated in accordance with official Roman Catholic teaching, neither denies the one sacrifice and suffering of Jesus Christ nor constitutes idolatry. The same synod also concluded that Q. & A. 80 still contains a pointed warning against any teachings, attitudes, and practices related to the Eucharist that obscure the finality and sufficiency of Christ's sacrifice on the cross and detract from proper worship of the ascended Lord. Therefore, Q. & A. 80 was not removed from the text but retained in a smaller font."

5. That Synod submit the revised report and the proposed footnote to the Reformed Ecumenical Council for review at its next assembly in July 2005 and also submit the report and recommendations to those churches in ecclesiastical and corresponding fellowship with the CRC.
6. That Synod ask each church council and each classis to review the proposed footnote to Q. and A. 80 and to submit their responses to the general secretary by December 1, 2005, so that they can be considered by the Interchurch Relations Committee along with responses from other denominations and the REC.
7. That Synod instruct the Interchurch Relations Committee to receive the responses and propose any changes to Synod 2006.
8. That Synod instruct the Interchurch Relations Committee to send both this report and the slightly revised earlier report to the Canadian Conference of Catholic Bishops and the United States Conference of Catholic Bishops, thanking them for their participation in dialogue with us, and also to appropriate ecumenical bodies.

[The acts of the 2004 and subsequent synods will need to be consulted for the disposition of these recommendations.]

MENNONITE-LUTHERAN

Editors' Note: *Of all of the churches of the Reformation, the Mennonite, or Anabaptist, tradition was the most widely persecuted by Catholics and Protestants alike. The* Augsburg Confession *of the Lutheran Churches even condemns this movement by name. The following document is among initiatives undertaken by Catholic and Protestant churches to reassess their evaluation of these ecclesial communities and to repair the damage done to the Gospel by a history of persecution.*

Document 29

RIGHT REMEMBERING IN ANABAPTIST-LUTHERAN RELATIONS

Lutheran-Mennonite Dialogue, 2004

Introduction

1. The process leading to this round of conversations of the Liaison Committee of the Evangelical Lutheran Church in America (ELCA) and the Mennonite Church USA (MCUSA) stretches back to informal conversations among denominational leaders since at least 1986. Subsequent resolutions adopted by two ELCA synods urging this church publicly to reject the invectives of Martin Luther and other Lutheran Reformers led the ELCA Church Council in April 1999 to direct the Department for Ecumenical Affairs to establish a liaison committee with the MCUSA.

2. In 2000-2001 the Mennonite Church appointed the Rev. Dr. Thomas N. Finger, Dr. James C. Juhnke, Dr. Gayle L. Gerber Koontz, and Dr. John D. Roth; the Evangelical Lutheran Church in America appointed the Rev. Dr. Janyce C. Jorgensen, the Rev. Russell L. Meyer, the Rev. Paul A. Schreck, and the Rev. Dr. David G. Truemper. The first meeting of the Liaison Committee was scheduled to begin September 13, 2001, but because of terrorist attacks that week was not convened until February 21-24, 2002, at Goshen College in Goshen, Indiana, with subsequent meetings convened October 31–November 3, 2002, at the Lutheran Center in Chicago, Illinois; February 28–March 2, 2003 at Sarasota, Florida; October 16-19, 2003, at Bethel College in North Newton, Kansas; and March 18-21, 2004, at Valparaiso University in Valparaiso, Indiana.

3. The Liaison Committee was charged with the task of reflecting upon ways to heal the memories of sixteenth-century conflict, to examine the condemnations of Anabaptists found in the *Book of Concord* to determine if they apply to Mennonites today, to discuss baptism and church-state relationships, and to identify other theological issues that might divide these two church bodies.

4. A series of papers were prepared and discussed on the following topics: experiences of each church during the Lutheran Reformation; the experience of each church in the North American context; the role and authority of confessional writings; hermeneutics and biblical interpretation; Anabaptist and Lutheran understandings of the state; apostolicity, ecclesiology, and ministry; right remembering of the martyrs' tradition; Christians in the political realm; pacifism and the Gospel of peace; just war theory; baptism; catechism and the catecumenate; and affirmation of baptism (confirmation).

5. In addition to discussing these papers, meetings included visits to historical sites for firsthand experience of elements of each heritage, tours of congregations' social ministries, worship in each other's congregations, and an educational forum bringing together interested members of local Mennonite and Lutheran congregations to discuss the issues that separate the two church bodies and to interact with the members of this Liaison Committee.

6. These educational forums were a unique component for both Mennonites and Lutherans involved in interchurch conversations. Participants at these forums raised questions about the condemnations in the Lutheran confessions, expressed confusion about the divergent practices of baptism and holy communion, and conveyed a desire to cooperate more fully in social ministries. Many reported mutual participation in local ministerial associations and community worship services. In other instances, however, members of Mennonite and Lutheran congregations had never before met, in spite of decades of active participation in their respective churches. There were requests for educational materials that could be used at future gatherings and expressions of appreciation for the divergent gifts each tradition could offer the other. One item raised at every forum was the strong desire for deepening levels of trust, respect, and cooperation among members of our two church bodies.

7. This common statement seeks to articulate in brief form a few of the significant insights that emerged from the conversation and offers recommendations for consideration by each church body to further deepen this fledgling relationship.

Right Remembering

8. The Liaison Committee began with the stated goal of working toward the "Healing of Memories." It became apparent in our first meeting that both churches would be better served by developing a deeper understanding expressed in the term "Right Remembering." The limitation inherent in the concept of "healing memories" was that, as an end in itself, both churches ultimately could find satisfaction for the sins of the past without seeking to live as reconciled sisters and brothers in the future. Right remembering, however, provides an ongoing approach for examining potentially church-dividing issues within a framework of mutual respect and trust. It encourages more accurate understanding of each church's history and teaching. In this sense, right remembering not only leads to the healing of painful memories but also contributes in an continuing way to a deepening relationship between our two church bodies.

9. Mennonite self-identity is so intimately connected with the remembrance of the Anabaptist martyrs of the sixteenth century (witness the presence of *The Martyrs' Mirror*[1] in many Mennonite homes) that no significant conversation between Lutherans and Mennonites would be conceivable without addressing the implications of those memories. Nor is this merely an historical question, a matter of Mennonites' recalling—and Lutherans' admitting—that approximately one thousand Anabaptists were killed in lands governed by Lutheran princes in the sixteenth century. Rather, it also is a contemporary question: What does it mean for today's Mennonites and Lutherans that there once was Anabaptist blood on Lutheran hands?

10. The following questions emerged (informally) for the Liaison Committee and received repeated attention in our discussions:

- What are the actual facts about these killings and Lutheran involvement in them? How shall we parse the question of the responsibility of present-day Lutherans for the actions of sixteenth-century princes? What connections exist between the condemnations of Anabaptists in the *Augsburg Confession* and the execution of Anabaptists in Lutheran lands in the sixteenth century?
- What consequences emerge for relationships between today's Mennonites and Lutherans if we remember rightly these

> relationships between our forebears in central Europe in the sixteenth century? Does the path to better mutual understanding and affirmation lead necessarily through sixteenth-century Europe? If so, how shall we proceed along that path?

11. Most Mennonites are aware at some level of their martyr heritage, but they remember that heritage in blurred and partial ways that make healing of memories very complex. Most Lutherans, however, are unaware of sixteenth-century history, its condemnations and executions, but remember their own heritage as a persecuted and condemned, even outlawed, movement in ways that will make right remembering very complex indeed.

12. The temptation is strong on both sides to project contemporary norms and assumptions onto the sixteenth-century experience. Further, we repeatedly noted that many of our divergent theological perspectives have been shaped by our different historical locations in regard to political power.

13. Right remembering thus became a steady theme for the Liaison Committee. Mennonites pointed out the deep difference between the militant leaders of the "Kingdom of Münster" and the pacifism of earlier Anabaptists and of the subsequent movement under Menno Simons's influence. Lutherans sought to make clear that the condemnations of Anabaptists in the *Augsburg Confession* were not motivated by a desire to eliminate "heretics" within Lutheran territories but were due to pressures placed upon the Lutheran Reformers to demonstrate their own catholicity demanded by the civil imperial laws of the day. Lutheran and Mennonite Liaison Committee participants struggled together to better understand the consequences of the law of the Holy Roman Empire of the German Nation (the Code of Justinian), which prescribed the death penalty for people who either refused infant baptism or declared it to be invalid or wrong. It also was clear that at least some Lutheran princes attempted to avoid or curtail the prosecution of Anabaptists.

14. Since confessional statements function to inform our remembering and our sense of identity, the need became apparent to reflect on their role in our respective church bodies. Mennonites tend to be wary of confessional statements because these sometimes have been used by governments and churches in more powerful social positions (even at times by Mennonite leaders and groups) to critique, exclude, or condemn. Mennonites, however, have often written confessional statements to promote understanding and

unity among themselves. Lutherans tend to place a high value on confessional statements, regarding in particular the documents in the *Book of Concord* as both a true witness to the Gospel (as that came to be understood in the Wittenberg Reformation in the sixteenth century), and as a reference point for the integrity and authenticity of Lutheran churches in subsequent centuries.

15. The question of contemporary response to sixteenth-century actions, however, remained unresolved. If the effect of martyr memories is to enforce a continuing separation of Mennonites from fellow Christians, is an adequate lesson learned from their sacrifice? If the effect of condemnations in the *Augsburg Confession* is that mistaken images of Anabaptists are perpetuated or violence against them justified, how can Lutherans understand that document to be a true witness to the Gospel? We were left with a complicated picture of a multilevel discussion that warrants continued conversation in order that right remembering may become a lens through which issues that continue to divide our two churches may be reconsidered. What follows is the attempt of the Liaison Committee to reflect upon baptism and the relationship between church and state through that lens.

Baptism

Points of Agreement

16. Lutherans and Mennonites view baptism not only as a one-time event, but also as an ongoing process that plays a crucial role in the Christian life, both corporate and personal. For both, baptism is (1) a corporate act of the church, in which a congregation receives those who are baptized and commits itself to their ongoing nurture in the faith. Baptism is the sole sacrament or ordinance which initiates people into church membership.

17. For both denominations, (2) baptism's meaning is appropriated throughout the Christian life. Lutherans emphasize remembering one's baptism, dying, and rising with Christ daily. Mennonites often mention threefold baptism: baptism of the Holy Spirit precedes water baptism, and baptism of blood[2] follows it. The first and third, however, also are processes intertwined throughout the Christian life. Lutherans and Mennonites recognize the importance of nurturing mature, active, articulate Christians and churches in today's world. For both Mennonites and Lutherans, (3) the baptismal act is performed with water and in the name of the Holy Trinity. For both, (4) faith is essential to baptism, and (5) baptism witnesses to salvation's origin in God's initiating grace.

18. Both traditions (6) baptize adult converts. Both utilize a formal period of preparation (known as the "catechumenate" for Lutherans and "adult membership classes" for Mennonites) to provide the candidates with instruction in the basics of Christian faith and life prior to baptism.

Points of Divergence

19. For Lutherans baptism may, and most often does, mark the Christian journey's beginning in infancy or early childhood. In these cases, faith is exercised by the congregation and by the child, parents, and sponsors. The faith of those who are baptized continues to be nurtured through worship and learning, and through a period of formal learning (catechism) culminating in the Rite of Affirmation of Baptism (confirmation). Subsequent to confirmation the baptized are recognized as adult members of the congregation with the responsibility to participate in the decision making of the body. Other services for the renewal of baptism are used throughout the Christian life.

20. For Mennonites, infants and young children are welcomed into the church through dedication. The faith of parents, sponsors, and the congregation is exercised as they commit themselves to the nurture of these children. Children participate vitally in church life and salvation. Their growing faith is nurtured through worship, learning, ethical formation, and catechism. At the conclusion of catechism the church may confirm a request for baptism. Subsequent to baptism believers are recognized as members of the congregation with responsibilities for the life and mission of the church.

21. Additional differences may be linked to the respective understandings of human nature, faith, and the nature and purpose of the church. As noted in the above agreements, both church bodies affirm God's sovereign initiative in salvation, and also active human response. Lutherans, however, tend to prioritize the first and to fear that Mennonite baptism, with its stress on voluntary response, might obscure this. Mennonites tend to prioritize the second and fear that Lutheran infant baptism might obscure the active appropriation of grace and the importance of discipleship. It is not clear to what extent these differences are simply ones of emphasis, and to what extent they might be shaped by different anthropologies and/or ecclesiologies.

Church and State

22. Questions regarding the church and its witness to the world, the relationship of church and state, and the gospel of peace go to the root of our shared denominational histories during the early years of the Protestant Reformation. The Anabaptist-Mennonite commitment to voluntary membership in a church separated from a fallen world, and their general refusal to wield the sword or swear fealty oaths, seemed to threaten the very fabric of European society. On the other hand, Lutherans did not seek to reform the existing medieval church-state relationship and often resorted to torture and execution of people who presented perceived and actual threats to social authority. These historical circumstances shaped our divergent understandings of the relationship of church and state, the role of Christians in preserving unity within the church and order within society, and the use of coercion based on lethal force. Mennonites today reject the violent apocalyptic predictions associated with some parts of the earliest Anabaptist movement, to which Lutherans of that day responded harshly. Lutherans today reject the violence inflicted on sixteenth-century Anabaptists.

Points of Agreement

23. Lutherans and Mennonites understand the church to be the messenger of the Kingdom of God in the world, clearly differentiated from the state and the broader society. Because we confess that Jesus Christ has been exalted as Lord of lords (Eph. 3:10), we acknowledge his ultimate authority over all human authorities (Eph. 1:20-23). The church therefore needs to maintain a critical stance in relation to the state in order to fulfill its prophetic witness and service in the world. As Christians, however, Lutherans and Mennonites acknowledge the legitimate, divinely sanctioned, role of the state to preserve order; we are to respect those in authority and to pray for all people, including those in government (Rom. 16:6ff; 1 Tim. 2:1ff), even in those times when we must obey God rather than human authority (Acts 5:29).

24. Both churches teach that Jesus taught love for one's enemies; he reached out to the oppressed, downtrodden, and rejected of the earth; he prayed for his enemies even while being rejected on the cross. God has redeemed the world through Jesus' death ("for . . . while we were enemies, we were reconciled to God through the death of his Son" [Rom. 5:10]). We bear witness to this free gift of God's forgiveness and grace when we extend that same love to others, especially to our enemies.

25. Lutherans and Mennonites recognize that we are inextricably woven into, and beneficiaries of, modern culture and society. Neither tradition proposes an isolationist relation between church and the world. Both traditions understand the deeply communal nature of human life and seek, in their divergent ways, to nurture communal practices that both reflect and represent the Gospel to the wider world. We embrace the biblical concepts of the church being an "already but not yet" sign of the reign of God, which includes "being leaven" in the world.

26. Although Mennonites have historically embraced Christian pacifism and Lutherans a just-war theory, we share in an "unequivocal rejection of nuclear war."[3]

Points of Divergence

27. Mennonites regard participation in war and coercion based upon the use of lethal force as incompatible with the teachings of Jesus and therefore precluded for Christians. Lutherans also renounce a Christian's exercise of coercion based upon the use of lethal force in personal life but further hold that Christians who serve in public offices or roles have ethical obligations for preserving order and may at times exercise lethal force justly and impartially.

28. Lutherans and Mennonites use the metaphor of "two kingdoms" in very different ways. Lutherans use this metaphor to describe how Law and Gospel are experienced in the "Right Hand" (Gospel) and "Left Hand" (Law) work of God. They understand these polarities to pervade human society, both within the church and the state. Lutherans hold that a Christian can, in good conscience, serve the will of God in using lethal force when upholding the Law through the power of the state. Mennonites, when they speak of the two Kingdoms, more often associate the Kingdom of God with the church in distinction from the Kingdom of this world. While Mennonites cannot in good conscience exercise coercion based upon the use of lethal force, they do ask the state to act according to higher values or to standards which, while less than what God expects of the church, may bring the state closer to doing the will of God.

Recommendations

29. The Liaison Committee of the Evangelical Lutheran Church in America and the Mennonite Church USA affirm the prayer of Jesus recorded in John 17 that his followers might all be one. Divisions in the church of Christ are not new; some even are recorded in the Acts of the Apostles. In the first century, however, divisions were considered abnormal and contrary to

God's will. In this twenty-first century, divisions among Christians too often are considered normal and therefore go unquestioned and unhealed. The Liaison Committee witnessed time and again the ways in which the division between our two church bodies is a wound in the Body of Christ and urge continued efforts toward healing. Specifically, we recommend

- That one representative of the Evangelical Lutheran Church in America and one representative of the Mennonite Church USA be appointed as a delegation from the United States to participate with delegations from Germany and France, coordinated by the Lutheran World Federation and the Mennonite World Conference, in a formal review of the sixteenth-century condemnations contained in the *Book of Concord* to determine if they still apply
- That the Evangelical Lutheran Church in America request that the Lutheran World Federation, in consultation with the Mennonite World Conference, prepare a document that describes the hermeneutic for interpreting the historically limited portions of the *Book of Concord* (such as fealty sworn to the emperor) that permits Lutherans to understand those confessional writings as "true witness[es] to the Gospel" and "further valid interpretations of the faith of the Church"
- That the ELCA Church Council adopt as a message of that church "Declaration of the Evangelical Lutheran Church in America to the Churches of the Anabaptist Tradition," attached as Appendix A
- That the Evangelical Lutheran Church in America and the Mennonite Church USA authorize continuing conversation on the divergent practices of baptism and confirmation identified in this common statement to determine whether they can be understood to be complementary; additional topics worthy of consideration would include the Lord's Supper, human nature, the relationship of church and state, the nature of faith, and ecclesiology
- That the use of educational forums in joint congregational settings be commended as an invaluable and formative model for future dialogues

- That appropriate staff members from each church body identify existing worship resources and collaborate in the preparation of new materials that may be used in joint settings
- That the Mennonite Church USA and the Evangelical Lutheran Church in America identify existing material and authorize the development of educational resources on right remembering of the persecution of martyrs in the sixteenth century, peace and justice issues, and other topics to be used in ongoing Mennonite-Lutheran educational forums sponsored by local congregations
- That specific Mennonite and Lutheran congregations be identified to serve as "pilot sites" to assist in the development and refinement of these study resources
- That congregations of the Mennonite Church USA and the Evangelical Lutheran Church in America be encouraged to develop joint social ministries to the communities they serve
- That the educational institutions of the Evangelical Lutheran Church in America and the Mennonite Church USA initiate faculty- and student-exchange opportunities so that each church body may learn firsthand from the other
- That an official reception, symposium, or service of thanksgiving be convened to receive and discuss this common statement, its implications, and ways to implement these recommendations

Appendix A

Declaration of the Evangelical Lutheran Church in America to the Churches of the Anabaptist Tradition

Introduction

During the sixteenth-century reformation in Central Europe, a variety of statements and pronouncements were made by representatives of the churches of the *Augsburg Confession* regarding the people called "Anabaptists." In our own century, these statements and pronouncements have become highly problematic, not only for our relationships with the contemporary successors of those Anabaptists but also for our own self-understanding as members of the one, holy, catholic, and apostolic Church. Particularly in the light of dialogues between Lutherans and Mennonites in Europe in the latter decades of the twentieth century, and in the light of our current exploratory conversations between the Evangelical Lutheran Church in America (ELCA) and the Mennonite Church USA (MCUSA), it is desirable to clarify those sixteenth-century statements, and it is necessary in most cases to repudiate them.

The Record

The anti-Anabaptist statements made by Lutherans in the sixteenth century fall into several categories, with very different levels of authority for present-day Lutherans.

- Some are nothing more than the personal judgments of individual persons; however, because leaders like Martin Luther and Philip Melanchthon are among those involved, many contemporary Lutherans and Mennonites may regard those statements as having a particular authority or influence. Such statements not only hereticize the Anabaptists of their day but also call upon the state to use its power to extirpate the heresy.
- A second group of statements appear in documents that attempted to resolve disputes among Lutherans, such as the *Formula of Concord* of 1577, where the signatories agree (FC SD XII) that the power of the state should be used to eradicate Anabaptist teachings from Lutheran territories. These statements are particularly problematic, because they suppose that secular authority ought be used to resolve religious differences—a position especially dangerous in the light of much popular discourse since the terrorist attacks in September 2001.
- A third group of statements appear in the *Augsburg Confession* (V, VIII, IX, XII, XVI, XVII, XXVII), where sixteenth-century Anabaptists are singled out as the only contemporary group to be formally condemned in that confession and to be declared beyond the pale of the holy catholic Church. In the light of historical research and recent dialogue, it has become clear that most of these condemnations are in fact based upon

erroneous judgments about what sixteenth-century Anabaptists believed and practiced. For the sake of the truth, it is important to repudiate such erroneous condemnations.

- At least two of those condemnations in the *Augsburg Confession* (IX, XVI), however, point to serious and abiding differences of teaching and practice between our two churches, and we would be true to neither tradition if we were to disregard these condemnations or to repudiate them. These have to do with the theology and practice of baptism and with the propriety of Christian participation in the exercise of the police or military power of the government. The only way forward in these areas is to engage in open and forthright dialogue, in order to ascertain whether the differences to which they point are to be regarded as church-dividing or not.
- One additional consideration is important. In the Holy Roman Empire of the German Nation (the "government" of reformation Germany) it was the inherited law of the empire that anyone who repudiated the validity of infant baptism or insisted on re-baptism was guilty of a capital offense. Accordingly, as the Anabaptist movement gained ground in Germany in the decades following 1525, various groups denounced as Anabaptists were in fact executed for a capital crime. It was an easy move for the drafters of the *Augsburg Confession* to repudiate the capital crimes of the Anabaptists as they sought to establish that the princes and city councils who submitted the *Augsburg Confession* were still catholic Christians. Since this point of imperial law is no longer at issue for today's Lutherans and Mennonites, Lutherans need to make a clear statement about how our differences in faith and practice shall be regarded and addressed.

Our Declaration

- The ELCA repudiates any notion that would call upon the secular authorities to become involved in any way in the discussion and resolution of religious differences. We repudiate the comments of Luther and Melanchthon that called upon the state to punish Anabaptists. This includes our repudiation of the statements in the *Formula of Concord* to the same effect. The modern state is in no way to be made the instrument of any church in the matter of the resolution of differences in belief and practice.

- The ELCA declares that five of the seven condemnations of Anabaptists in the *Augsburg Confession* (V, IX, XII, XVII, XXVII) were either based on erroneous and mistaken judgments by the confessors or involved erroneous generalizations from some Anabaptists to all persons implied by that label; in both cases these condemnations are to be regarded as null and void as far as any application to today's Mennonites is concerned.
- The *Augsburg Confession's* condemnations of the Anabaptists in the matter of baptismal faith and practice (CA IX) and participation in the police power of the state (CA XVI) are properly the subject of free and open dialogue between our churches. We repudiate any call for the exercise of the authority of the state in regard to the Mennonite Church in these matters, and we earnestly desire to ascertain, in free and open dialogue, whether the differences that remain between our two churches in these matters are in fact church-dividing. We have learned from our European sisters and brothers that it has indeed been possible for the Lutheran churches of France and Germany to adopt statements declaring these condemnations not to be church-dividing and declaring further that these condemnations do not apply to today's Mennonites. We earnestly desire the dialogue requisite to coming to a similar conclusion.

NOTES

1. *The Martyrs' Mirror* was first published in 1660 as a collection of martyr stories, beginning with Christ's Apostles, naming confessors of Christ through the ages, and ending with stories of more than 800 Anabaptists martyred between 1524 and the early seventeenth century. The book's author intended to include only Anabaptists who gave testimony to biblical faith and held nonresistant principles. The second edition, published in 1685, included 104 illustrations and has been particularly prized by Mennonites through the centuries.

2. For sixteenth-century Anabaptist-Mennonites, the baptism of blood often did include literal martyrdom or severe physical persecution. More broadly, it referred to what other traditions called "mortification," or the lifelong process of putting to death behaviors and attitudes which oppose "vivification," or God's sanctifying bestowal of new life. Baptism of blood occurred inwardly, through repentance and renunciation, and outwardly, through both disciplining in the congregation and social discrimination due to beliefs and practices.
3. See "For Peace in God's World," a social statement of the Evangelical Lutheran Church in America adopted by its 1995 Churchwide Assembly. See also J. D. Roth, *Choosing Against War: A Christian View* (Intercourse, PA: Good Books, 2002).

PART THREE

Faith and Order Dialogues

Editors' Note: *In contributing to the World Council of Churches study on the Apostolic Faith* (wcc-coe.org/wcc/what/faith/tsof.html *[accessed May 1, 2004]), the United States Commission held fourteen consultations. (The results of some of these consultations can be found in previous volumes: BU, 484-490; GC I, 649-643). Among these were ones focused on the Christological differences between the Oriental Orthodox Churches and the Chalcedonian Orthodox and Western churches, with the U.S. African American churches, and three with the historic peace churches. These texts, along with two other Faith and Order reports, follow.*

Original texts and background essays can be found in Paul Fries and Tiran Nersoyan, Christ in East and West *(Macon: Mercer University Press, 1987); and David T. Shannon and Gayraud Wilmore, eds.,* Black Witness to the Apostolic Faith *(Grand Rapids: W. B. Eerdmans, 1988).*

DOCUMENT 30

CHRISTOLOGICAL CONCERNS AND THE APOSTOLIC FAITH

A Working Paper from the Consultation of the Commission on Faith and Order with the Oriental Orthodox Churches, 1985

Introduction

During the past twenty years, four dialogues have taken place between the Oriental Orthodox Churches and the Eastern Orthodox Churches. In addition, during the 1970s a series of four consultations took place in Vienna at the *Pro Oriente* Foundation between Oriental Orthodox theologians and Roman Catholic theologians. In these unofficial agreed statements and communiqués, remarkably, the divisive issue of the christological statement of Chalcedon is apparently resolved. In these documents Oriental Orthodox, Eastern Orthodox, and the Roman Catholics agree that ancient differences dividing the church following the Council of Chalcedon in 451 have more to do with terminology as well as other disaffections than with theological substance. In each consultation, participants agreed that in Jesus Christ, the invisible Godhead became visible and fully human.

For this consultation, seven representatives of the Reformation traditions were asked to study these documents and to produce working papers for the consultation looking for points of contact and points for further exploration between their own communions and Oriental Orthodoxy. The Oriental Orthodox participants were asked to respond to these papers. These papers, along with the communiqués, agreed statements, and selected papers from the earlier discussions, became the basis of the dialogue.

I. Christological Issues

All groups participating in the New York meeting agreed that in Jesus Christ we encounter God the Word become truly human. Furthermore, it was recognized that historically, for the Oriental Orthodox, it is God the Son who is the subject of the Incarnation, for it is only God who can save us. Some time was spent discussing whether this affirmation of the importance of the single divine subject in Christ was parallel in function to the Reformation churches' insistence upon "justification by faith alone": both deny that human beings are capable of saving themselves by their own efforts; both insist that salvation comes as the free gift of God who loves us and gives us eternal life.

Of the members of the Reformation groups presenting papers, the participants from the Presbyterian Church (USA), Lutheran Church in America, United Methodist Church, and the Episcopal Church stated that their christological traditions were in agreement not just with the content but also with the manner in which the early church councils affirmed them. The Southern Baptists, Disciples of Christ, and Mennonites, while they agreed with the content affirmed by the Councils, found that the way in which the questions were posed and in which the creeds and their language were used was significantly different from their way of experiencing and expressing Christian truths. At other points in the discussions, however, the Reformation groups found themselves in different constellations of agreement and difference. All groups participating agreed that, while we are grounded in the past, our work should be directed toward the life of the church in the modern world, with our vision on the future.

The conversations raised important issues that were only briefly touched. While these may not be church-dividing problems, they can be profitably discussed in the Apostolic Faith Study, should participants in the study see fit. These issues include

1. What does it mean to speak of Jesus Christ as "fully human"? What are the necessary elements of this humanity? How does this way of seeing him challenge the common American understandings about what it means to be human?

2. What does it mean to speak of Jesus Christ as "fully divine"? How does divinity act in the person of Jesus Christ? What does it mean to be God?

3. What is the relation of Christology to soteriology?

4. Is there a substantive issue (and if so, what is it) behind the reluctance of the Oriental Orthodox to speak of Jesus Christ as "fully God and fully human" rather than "fully God and fully man"?

5. What does all this mean for the life and witness of the church?

II. Methodological Considerations Related to the Search for Church Unity

During the course of the discussions, the participants became increasingly aware that they approach issues such as Christology from different ecclesiological perspectives and that these perspectives lead to different priorities in ecumenical dialogue. Some of the participating churches give priority to the preservation of a theologically pluralistic community, while others give priority to the preservation of the tradition as historically articulated. It also became apparent, however, that old stereotypes of these positions are inappropriate. Those concerned with diverse community and participatory authority, for example, are by no means disinterested in the truthfulness of Christian proclamation and witness but argue that truth is discovered through dialogue in community. Likewise, those concerned with fidelity to tradition are not disinterested in diverse community and the relation of revealed truth to the whole life of the church, but insist that such community must be firmly rooted in the truth revealed to the apostles and maintained in the apostolic tradition of the church. This is important since the different emphases help to explain certain "attitudes" that are frequently misunderstood. Some church representatives appear to be "suspicious" or "rigid" when their intent is to affirm the importance of tradition and teaching authority. Others appear "relativistic" (due in part to the absence of authoritative teaching instruments) when their intent is to affirm that we are already part of Christ's body.

With growing trust, some agreements about ecumenical methodology were possible. We could commonly endorse Archbishop Nersoyan's assertion that unity among Christians demands consensus only in essentials, while "for the rest we leave the mind of the Christian free with a freedom that may be guided but not imposed upon." We further agreed with his statement that the mystery of God in Christ is "inexhaustible and ineffable and for the human mind never fully comprehensible or expressible" and that Christians should, therefore, be able to live with "different emphases in the theological and dogmatic elaboration of Christ's mystery." We note with real regret that many apparent divisions have resulted from terminological misunderstandings that have obscured real identity of faith (though this in no way minimizes those genuine differences that must be addressed).

The members of the consultation were quite impressed by the recognized need and increasing willingness of churches divided for fifteen centuries to find new ways of resolving ancient discussions, ways that challenge all of the churches to seek paths towards reconciliation in the development of doctrinal formulations. Finally, Protestants would like to hear issues of church authority and structure discussed in explicit relationship to issues concerning the church's mission, and to explain how their own understandings of church structure are related to their visions for mission. We recognize the need for more study of the amount of theological diversity which the Christian community can tolerate, on our understanding of just what is essential (and therefore demands consensus) and what is secondary (and therefore admits of legitimate diversity).

These issues are treated in the *Pro Oriente* documents and relate to the World Council study of Conciliar Fellowship. The reception process of *Baptism, Eucharist and Ministry* in which the churches are currently engaged should help the understanding of various modes of authority.

III. Future Directions: Christology and Ecclesiology in the Broader Context

In the course of the consultation, the questions raised and difficulties in understanding each other often stemmed from the fact that the traditions and present lives of our various churches are very diverse and often unknown to one another. For this reason, future discussion of issues closely related to Christology and ecclesiology might help set these areas in an appropriate context and enable us to understand the significance of

Christological and ecclesiological affirmations that each of us makes. The purpose of raising these other issues would not be to complicate our discussions but simply to provide the background against which the primary issues might be better focused.

It appears that Oriental Orthodox Christological concerns are linked with the concept of salvation as "divinization," a notion unclear to most Protestants. Contrariwise, the reasons why Protestants have emphasized justification seem somewhat unclear to some Orientals. Second, Protestants would have a deeper appreciation of Orthodox Christology were they to comprehend better its grounding in the sacramental life of these churches. However, it is not always clear to Protestants how the Oriental Orthodox emphasis on "sacraments" is related to the active lives of Christians in the world. Protestants may need to clarify how, for themselves, meaningful christological statements are linked to being Christ's disciples and to hear how the Oriental Orthodox make this connection, particularly through active participation in sacramental life.

IV. Authority

Tradition, we realize, has been understood in many different ways by Orthodox, Anglican, and Protestant Christians. Protestants have generally not given tradition prominence in their ecclesiology, but this does not mean that tradition is not to be found in the churches of the Reformation. One important question, we believe, is where tradition exercises authority within Protestant bodies. The Reformed, as well as the Anglican and Lutheran Churches, appeal to creed, confessions, and liturgies, while free churches locate tradition in commonly accepted practices, hymns, generative histories, and ethos. While many Protestant churches do not afford tradition formal authority, it is nonetheless indispensable for their faith and practice. Participants recognize the importance of examining more carefully the informal and yet powerful place of the authority of tradition in many Protestant churches. At the same time, Protestant participants were brought to appreciate the role of formal authority as found in Orthodox churches. In an age of relativism, the high regard that Orthodox Christians have for the authority of Council, ancient practice, and ministerial office may be valuable for Anglican and Protestant Christians.

We emphasize at this point that when we explore the matter of authority in respective traditions, we are dealing with something more than narrow ecclesiastical issues. At stake here is the question of the faithful proclamation of the church throughout its history and the integrity of its mission to the world. How shall we be certain that the witness of the church is true to the Lord who calls us to service? How shall we know that our acts are faithful to God's purpose? How shall we determine that the hope offered through us is no false hope? Such questions cannot be answered apart from questions of the authority of Jesus Christ as exercised through Scripture and tradition in the church. How do we speak authoritatively in a way that is consistent with the gospel we proclaim?

V. Pastoral Reflections

The convergences on the understanding of Jesus Christ, truly divine and truly human, would challenge the churches, recognizing their faith in these consultations and in the ecumenical movement, to begin to reflect in their life and mission a common witness and supportive collaboration at many levels of church life.

We recommend to the Apostolic Faith Study of the NCCC that it suggest appropriate measures to see that religious education materials be revised to

1. Recognize the measure of reconciliation among Anglican, Protestant, Catholic, Eastern and Oriental Orthodox Churches that has been achieved on the basis of ecumenical dialogue

2. Recount the nontheological factors that have perpetuated the fifth-century divisions throughout the centuries

3. Remove the caricatures which Orthodox and Catholics may have of Protestant Christology, and which Protestants and Catholics may have of Eastern and Oriental Orthodox communities

We encourage the Apostolic Faith Study to reflect on how its progress in common understandings of the faith among our churches may contribute to more sensitive ways of relating to one another with respect and without proselytizing. We encourage Faith and Order to suggest ways of providing common witness among these churches corresponding to the level of common faith represented in this consultation.

We recommend to seminaries and other instrumentalities of clergy/leadership education to use the *Pro Oriente* and World Council sponsored discussions, as well as the papers of this consultation in their published form, to enrich programs of theological education in all churches.

We recommend that the Apostolic Faith Study of the NCCC explore agreements or pastoral arrangements between various Oriental Orthodox patriarchates and Roman Catholic and Eastern Orthodox churches for models of response to the agreed statements on the pilgrimage towards full communion. Since Christ is the center of our faith, and since we can affirm in common that "God was in Christ," we feel it is encumbent upon our churches to explore through Faith and Order ways of giving greater common witness to our constituencies and beyond.

DOCUMENT 31

TOWARD A COMMON EXPRESSION OF FAITH: A BLACK NORTH AMERICAN PERSPECTIVE

Faith and Order Consultation, Richmond, 1984

Introduction

A special consultation on one common expression of the Apostolic faith from the perspective of Black Christians in the United States brought together representatives of several Black denominations at Virginia Union University in Richmond, Virginia, in December 14-15, 1984. The consultation included representatives of the Black constituencies of several predominantly white denominations. In some cases the participants were delegated by denominational administrative headquarters; others were representatives of their communions without official appointment. The content of this document, therefore, stands upon the authority of the consultation alone and does not purport to convey the agreements of an ecclesiastical council of Black churches.

This document, moreover, does not pretend to be an exhaustive response to the Apostolic Faith Study or a formal statement of the major themes of the Black theology movement that has evolved in North America in recent years. The Richmond Consultation, sponsored by the Commission on Faith and Order of the National Council of Churches in the USA, attempted to convey to the World Council of Churches and to other interested organizations what we, a group of Black theologians and church leaders from across the United States, perceive as a general consensus among us concerning a common expression of the faith of the One, Holy, Catholic and Apostolic Church. In the several working papers we discussed and in this report we seek to add to the worldwide ecumenical study of a common expression of apostolic faith the distinctive perceptions and insights that come out of the historic experience of Black Christians in North America.

As Black academics, denominational officials, pastors, and lay leaders, we speak out of more than two hundred years of suffering and struggle as "the stepchildren of church history" who have been ridiculed, ignored, and scorned by the white churches of both Europe and North America. The truth of the Gospel among our people that some have sought to suppress or disregard burns like fire in our bones. In any discussion of one common expression of faith, we have no alternative other than to make certain clear affirmations to those churches that directly or indirectly participated in and benefited from the rape of Africa that resulted in the exploitation and oppression of an African Diaspora wherever Black people are found.

We speak, however, from our own particular locus in the so-called First World, where we are less than 12 percent of the population of what is the richest and most powerful nation in the world. But inasmuch as our churches and people have never truly shared that wealth and power, we speak as a marginated Black community with a unique understanding of White racism and with strong affinities with the so-called Third World.

In this document, from a historic consultation in Richmond,Virginia, we make bold to declare that God, our Creator, has condescended through Jesus Christ, our Liberator, by the power of the Holy Spirit, our Advocate and Comforter, to convey, preserve and enhance the faith of the Apostles among the despised and alienated African American people of the United States. We commend to all who may be concerned the fruit of our prayerful reflection on the themes of the unity, holiness, catholicity, and apostolicity of the Church of Jesus Christ as we join with you in search of a common expression of the faith.

I. Unity

We affirm that the unity of the Church not only expresses the unity of the Triune God, but is also a sign of the unity of humankind that holds together in one family the diversity of all races and cultures. In the economy of God each "tribe," each ethnic group and culture, has its own vocation to bring its gift to the full household of faith. Notwithstanding the effort of some White Christians to disdain the contribution of Black folk to the faith and to its impact upon the institutions of the American church and society, we declare that the meaning of Blackness as cultural and religious experience edifies and enriches the universal message of the Christian faith. Blackness, in the religions of the African Diaspora, is a profound and complex symbol of a diversified yet united experience: servitude and oppression, faithfulness through suffering, identification with the exclusion, martyrdom and exaltation of Jesus as the Oppressed One of God who triumphs over enemies, a passion for justice and liberation, the exuberance of Black faith and life, rejoicing in the Risen Lord in Pentecostal fervor and in service to the "least" of Christ's brothers and sisters.

White Christians have too often treated unity as if it were only a spiritual reality. We believe that unity must not be spiritualized but manifested in concrete behavior, by doing just and loving service to one another. The cost of unity in the Church is repentance and affirmative discipleship (i.e., action). We have, therefore, a profound hermeneutical suspicion about any movement for unity that is dominated by North Atlantic attitudes and assumptions. We have observed that when our white brothers and sisters speak of unity they often mean being together on terms that carefully maintain their political, economic, and cultural hegemony. Unity is frequently confused with "Anglo-conformity"—strict adherence to premises and perspectives based upon the worldview and ethos of the North Atlantic community with its history of racial oppression. Christian unity is, however, based upon the worship of a common Creator who is no respecter of persons, obedience to a common Lawgiver and Judge whose commandment to break every yoke is not abrogated by the gracious justification of sinners, and upon participation in the earthly mission of a common Redeemer, the sharing of whose suffering and ordeal makes us truly one, though of many races and cultures.

Blackness is one of God's gifts for the realization of the unity of the Church and humankind at this critical stage of history. It has been preserved by God as a cultural and religious inheritance of the Black churches of Africa, the Caribbean, and North and South American since the mission of the Ethiopian eunuch to the upper Nile Valley after his baptism by the Evangelist. It is rooted in the divine revelation to our African ancestors who lived before the Christian era. It has traditionally celebrated the goodness of the Almighty Sovereign God and the goodness of creation. It has emphasized the humanity of the historical Jesus, i.e., his earthly life, example, teaching, suffering, death, and resurrection. It confesses belief in the humanity of Jesus together with the oneness with God, the Creator, and the Holy Spirit, but understands that humanity in non-sexist terms rather than being exclusively of the male gender. It identifies with the shadow of death that falls upon the Cross as a symbol of suffering and shame, yet crowned with light inexpressible in the victory of the resurrection.

Thus, the meaning of unity is related to the meaning of Blackness for the Afro-American Church and points to its vocation as a church of the poor and oppressed who claim liberation in the Black Messiah of God and want to share the humanizing experience of suffering and joy in struggle with others who want to work for a world of justice and equality for all. Unity is possible only when there is acceptance of suffering under Christ's work of liberation and when there is commitment to his mission.

II. Holiness

The Black churches of North America made a unique contribution to the Holiness and Pentecostal movements of world Christianity at the beginning of this century. The Black Pentecostal obsession with the text of Hebrews 12:14 ("strive . . . for the holiness without which no one will see the Lord" [RSV]) and Black leadership of the interracial Azusa Street Revival of 1906-1908 in Los Angeles created the groundwork for modern Pentecostalism—the most remarkable religious movement among the oppressed communities of the world since the Awakenings of the eighteenth and nineteenth centuries. Although most African American churches did not originate from pentecostalism or the Azusa Street Revival, most of them have been influenced by the Pentecostal emphasis upon the *ruach/pneuma* of God in their conception of the Person and Work of the Holy Ghost. Their understanding of holiness as a process of moral perfection is rooted in the necessity of a personal encounter with God that is manifested in both the ecstasy of congregational worship and the praxis of social justice.

On the other hand, holiness in the Black Church is not coterminous, as in some expressions of White liberalism, with frenetic social activism. Personal encounter with God as a prerequisite of sanctification and commitment to social transformation are both necessary, but the obligation to "give glory to God," to "glorify the holiness of God," is an essential corollary of the obligation to be engaged in "building the Kingdom" that continues to be frustrated by racism and oppression. The Black Church is sustained by prayer and praise. It exists in and for the glory of God and not the glorification of human institutions. We know that to struggle in the midst of the world is to experience the glory of God that is thwarted by racism and oppression, but we also know that we need to praise God in the sanctuary in order to struggle! One of our spirituals has the refrain "Have you got good religion?" The response is "Certainly, certainly, certainly Lord!" Good religion is, therefore, understood to make worldly things that were formerly dubious better, and bad religion ruins the best of all possible worlds where there is no acknowledgement of God's presence. Without holiness no one shall see the Lord.

Ultimately, the holiness of the Church is a work of the Holy Spirit. We affirm that the One, Holy Church cannot exist apart from ministries of justice and liberation. We also affirm that true liberation is inseparable from deep spirituality. The intimate involvement of Christians with the Holy Spirit is expressed first in worship that celebrates the manifest presence, goodness, and glory of God and moves from the sanctuary to the streets where it empowers the world to goodness, transfigures its wretchedness and need, and creates the quality of life that is symbolized by the nimbus that encircles the throne of God.

III. Catholicity

Although Afro-American Christians have customarily been denied equal partnership in the *koinonia* of Christ, we nevertheless affirm the universality of the Christian faith. Universality in the Black religious experience has to do with the particular reality of people in concrete situations that are dissimilar but inseparable. Afro-American churches share with all who confess Jesus Christ the conviction of the universality of God's love "from each to all in every place." We recognize solidarity in creation, sin, and redemption with all human beings and seek with them to make catholicity visible by overcoming humanly erected barriers between people.

We deplore the fact that the profession of universality has actually meant that the norms of what is considered acceptable to the Church had to originate in the West. For years anything that White Christians in Europe and North America did not interpret as catholic lay outside the realm of true faith and proper order. Such assumptions distorted the truth about Jesus Christ and permitted the Gospel to be used to divide people rather than free them to express the fullness of the faith in their own cultural styles and traditions. It also robbed the White churches of the opportunity to correct their own deficiencies.

In the late eighteenth and early nineteenth centuries, Black preachers were refused ordination, and their congregations were not considered in good order. Not until rebellious white Methodist and separatist Baptist clergy defied custom and accepted them as duly constituted ministers and churches did Black Christianity become legitimate in the eyes of Whites. To this day Black churches have protested any semblance of alienation or exclusion on account of race, class, or discriminatory educational qualifications. Unfortunately, the struggle for sexual equality has lagged behind in many Black churches, and Black women need greater support in their resistance to subordination.

From the perspective of the Richmond Consultation, catholicity has to do with faith in Jesus Christ, baptism, and continuing in "the apostles' teaching and fellowship" and in "the breaking of bread and the prayers" (Acts 2:42). No person, group, or institution that meets these requirements should be excluded from the visible Church or relegated to an inferior status by human authority, ecclesiastical or secular. The sin of racism, sexism, and classism that refuses or discourages the fellowship of African Independent church or Black Holiness and Pentecostal denominations, among others in various parts of the world, must be repudiated as denying the catholicity of the Body of Christ.

Catholicity, in our view, also demands a persistent critique of and challenge to the economic and political status quo; for those churches that benefit from the existing international order too easily assume its normative character and become self-appointed guardians of what is supposedly good for all. Thus, many North American conservatives and fundamentalists speak of American democracy as "Christian" and oppose Christian socialists as irregular at best and heretical at worst. Similarly, the "Moral Majority" in the United States supports "constructive engagement" with apartheid in South Africa as consistent with universal reason and the welfare of "all people of good will." In this view anti-communism becomes the test of universal Christian ethics, and those who do not fall into line are considered sectarian, ignorant, and contrary to the mainstream White American tradition, which is regarded as the universal faith of the Church.

Jesus Christ challenged the assumption that faith in God or salvation was limited to the scribes and the Pharisees, or the rich and powerful. Instead he empowered sinners, the poor, strangers, and women. His demonstration of catholicity was to open his arms to all who would be saved. His Church today can do no more or less.

IV. Apostolicity

We affirm the Apostolic tradition that recognizes the transmission of authentic faith down the centuries by all those who have faithfully lived it, whether or not they have been officially designated as apostles. We believe that "what does not teach Christ is not Apostolic, even if it was taught by Peter or Paul; again what preaches Christ, this is Apostolic, even when preached by Judas, Annas, Pilate and Herod." We recognize, therefore, the apostolicity of what we have received from our slave ancestors who, though "unlearned and ignorant" men and women, reinterpreted the distorted Christianity they received from the slave masters and passed down to succeeding generations of Black believers the story of Jesus who was "the strong Deliverer," "the rose of Sharon, the bright and morning star," "the king who rides on a milk-white horse," "the dying lamb," "the Lord who's done just what he said," "the Balm in Gilead," and "the help of the poor and needy, in this lan'. . . ." But we acknowledge the importance of the Apostolic tradition being engaged and not merely passed on. Apostolicity must be lived out in the context of contemporary events. It is not the recitation of past formulations, but the living of the present commandments of the Risen Lord.

In the final analysis, the test of apostolicity is the experiencing of the life, death, and resurrection of Jesus Christ in our daily struggle against demonic powers that seek to rob us of our inheritance as children of God redeemed by the blood of Jesus Christ. Our deeds, more than our creeds, determine whether we have fully received and acted upon the faith of the apostles.

Jesus said, "If you continue in my word, you are truly my disciples, and you will know the truth, and the truth will make you free" (John 8:31, 32). Afro-American Christians look to the words and acts of the Jesus of history for the Apostolic teaching as well as to the mystery of the Christ of faith. We take seriously the life, ministry, and teaching of Jesus as the One who identified with the marginated of society and continues to identify with them. It is in the Black Church's historic identification with marginality that Jesus is appropriated as the Black Messiah, the paradigm of our existential reality as an oppressed people and the affirmation of our survival and liberation.

Finally, for Black Christians, the search for an expression of the Apostolic faith must be multiracial and multicultural rather than captive to any one race, sex, class, or political ideology. The Church and the ecumenical movement must no longer submit to domination by social, economic, or intellectual elites. The faith once delivered to the apostles by Jesus Christ is for the whole world and must be capable of being transmitted and responded to by all.

Conclusions and Recommendations

1. The Afro-American Christian tradition, embodied particularly in Black Baptist, Methodist, and Pentecostal Churches but continuing also in other Black-led Protestant and Roman Catholic congregations, has been and continues to be an indigenous expression of the faith of the apostles in North America.

2. The Richmond Consultation affirms the World Council of Churches study "Towards the Common Expression of the Apostolic Faith Today" and is committed to work with the WCC and other ecumenical bodies toward the unity we seek.

3. We invite the other churches participating in the Faith and Order movement to give greater study and recognition to how God has maintained the continuity of the Apostolic Faith primarily through the oral character and noncreedal styles of the African American tradition expressed in worship, witness, and social struggle.

4. We urge the other member churches of the National and World Council Commissions on Faith and Order to take note of the unity of faith and practice that the Black Church has historically emphasized and to engage the Faith and Order movement in greater involvement in the struggle against racism and all forms of oppression as an essential element of the Apostolic confession.

5. We call upon Black churches in North and South America, in the Caribbean, and in Africa to confess boldly the faith we received from the Apostles, despite every effort made to distort and falsify it and, joining with us who were a part of this historic consultation in Richmond, to intensify their involvement in the Faith and Order movement by sharing the "gift of Blackness" with those of other traditions.

6. Finally, we urge that this report be published and widely disseminated by the Commission on Faith and Order of the WCC as a study document and that Black Christians all over the world be encouraged to initiate interracial discussion groups for the consideration of its content and

implications for the ecumenical movement; and that the result of such dissemination and discussion be reported back to the Commission on Faith and Order by cooperating national councils.

Document 32

REPORT OF THE BAPTISM, EUCHARIST AND MINISTRY CONFERENCE

Commission on Faith and Order,

National Council of the Churches of Christ in the USA,

Chicago-Area Theological Schools, 1986

Editors' Note: *The 1982 World Council text* Baptism, Eucharist and Ministry *(wcc-coe.org/wcc/what/faith/bem1.html [accessed May 1, 2004]) has been one of the most important texts in the modern ecumenical movement. Faith and Order USA provided three consultations to enhance U.S. church participation in the process: one before the Lima meeting, one immediately after to enable the churches' reception and evaluation, and the third, reported here, reviewing the responses of the U.S. churches.*

This text and other background essays can be found in Jeffrey Gros, ed., The Search for Visible Unity *(New York: Pilgrim Press, 1984); "Baptism, Eucharist and Ministry Conference,"* Midstream *25:3 (July 1986): 322-329; and* American Baptist Quarterly *7:1 (March 1988): 38-49.*

Preface

With the unanimous adoption of the theological convergence text *Baptism, Eucharist and Ministry* (BEM) by the Faith and Order Commission of the World Council of Churches in Lima, Peru, in January 1982, a new day was initiated in the life of the ecumenical movement towards the reconciliation of the divided churches. A process was launched calling for the response and reception of *Baptism, Eucharist and Ministry* which would provide a substantial theological basis moving us toward recognizing one another through baptism as fellow members in the body of Christ, toward recognizing our ministers as true ministers of Word and Sacrament, and toward the time when we can join in common celebration of the Lord's Supper.

The initial stage in the reception process was to invite the churches to respond "at the highest appropriate level of authority" to four questions: (1) the extent to which your church can recognize in this text the faith of the Church through the ages; (2) the consequences for relations and dialogues with other churches; (3) guidance from the text for one's worship, educational, ethical, and spiritual life and witness; and (4) suggestions for ongoing work of Faith and Order in relation to the study on a common expression of the Apostolic Faith today. All responses were requested by December 31, 1985.

The Faith and Order Commission of the National Council of Churches of Christ in the USA has sponsored three conferences related to BEM for the U.S. churches. In partnership with the Chicago Area Theological Schools, this 1986 conference was held to review the responses prepared by the churches in the United States and to identify learnings from those reports in order to assist the next stages of reception. The conference, chaired by Robert K. Welsh (Disciples of Christ), was held at the Divine Word International retreat center at Techny, Illinois, on April 2-4, 1986. It brought together ninety-eight participants representing thirty different communions. Official responses were available from the American Lutheran Church, the Lutheran Church in America, the Lutheran Church–Missouri Synod, the Christian Reformed Church, the Christian Church (Disciples of Christ), the Episcopal Church, the Moravian Church, the Presbyterian Church (USA), the Reformed Church in America, the Seventh-Day Adventist, the Universal Fellowship of Metropolitan Community Churches, and the United Church of Christ. Proposed responses were available from the American Baptist Churches, the United Methodist Church, and the Bishops' Committee for Ecumenical and Interreligious Affairs of the National [United States] Conference of Catholic Bishops. Three reports also served as primary background material from a "Believers' Church Conference," an International Orthodox Symposium, and an American Orthodox Consultation.

The conference design included the preparation of background "synthesis papers" of the responses in relation to the four questions addressed to the churches and of presentations during the meeting to highlight the major learnings and issues identified. The keynote presentation was made by Dr. Günther Gassmann, Director of the Faith and Order Commission of the World Council of Churches. Reports were also presented from the perspectives of the Black Church, local and regional ecumenism, theological education, and the larger context of the Faith and Order agenda in relation to confessing the Apostolic Faith and the study on "The Unity of the Church and the Renewal of Human Community."

The following report brings together the key issues identified in the Conference regarding the "reception process" on BEM beyond official response. It does not attempt to summarize those reports; rather, it seeks to highlight the learnings from that material which point toward a common agenda for the future.

BEM: Its History

Baptism, Holy Communion or Eucharist, and ministry are essential elements of the Church of Jesus Christ. They are not the only elements; neither do they have an existence of their own, apart from the communal life and service of the Church. The fact that there have long been differing theological interpretations of the sacraments and ministry and modes of practicing them does not justify complacency with many of the church divisions identified with these differences. When the New Testament exalts the "one Baptism" (Eph 4:5) and "one loaf" (1 Cor 10:17), while asserting that all the various kinds of ministry are intended to "build up the Church" (1 Cor 14:12) in unity, it implicitly rejects and condemns rupturing the church's oneness because of them. Yet this is what has happened during centuries of church history.

In our century, the Ecumenical Movement exists, in one main sense, to bring divisions to an end. The Commission on Faith and Order of the World Council of Churches has the particular mandate "to assist the churches toward the goal of visible unity in one faith and in one eucharistic fellowship, expressed in worship and common life in Christ . . . that the world might believe" (WCC Constitution, III [I]).

For half a century before 1967, the Faith and Order participants recognized the need to overcome the church divisions—not mere differences—over Baptism, the Lord's Supper, and the general and ordained ministry. Launching plans that year in Bristol, England, they invested their talents and time in study and dialogue on how to move toward a common understanding. By this time, all the Eastern Orthodox Churches, the Roman Catholic Church, and many conservative evangelical churches were officially represented in the Faith and Order Commission. At meetings in Louvain, Belgium, in 1971 and Accra, Ghana, in 1974, the reports of study groups showed an unexpected degree of convergence. This was due also to the growing influence of an informed liturgical movement in many churches, to the formal dialogues between various communions, and to such church union efforts as the Consultation on Church Union in the United States. Thus, a number of factors, like leaven in dough, were causing changes of attitude and openness to new theological reasoning, scholarship, and agreement. Moreover, the uncertainties felt within some churches over the meaning of sacraments and ministry in modern cultures gave members a desire for the coherent views being expressed in ecumenical contexts. Without betraying or surrendering their strong denominational traditions, the churches learned to expect renewing and purifying suggestions from the wider experience.

As defensiveness turned to openness, and suspicion to trust, a new theological atmosphere developed. When churches' responses to the first draft of BEM were reviewed in 1977, this new situation was made evident.

Not surprisingly, however, the serious attention to these issues being given by hundreds and thousands of people enabled them to perceive new complexities and depths of the divisions of the Church. Even if full agreement could be found on sacraments and ministry, the unity which Christ wills for the Church would not be sufficiently manifest. Doctrines and practices of Baptism, Eucharist, and ministry are no more divisive than positions or prejudices held with respect to other races, the status and service of women, major moral questions, and the mission of the Church to all of humanity. The final text of BEM at Lima, Peru, in 1982 took into account these other dimensions of division. It attempted to show the relevance of BEM to the healing of other divisions in the Church and humanity. It demonstrated that, important and popular as it is, BEM is just one aspect of the whole ecumenical effort for justice, peace, and unity.

These were the primary concerns of delegates to the Sixth Assembly of the World Council of Churches in Vancouver, 1983. Many, preoccupied with justice and peace and dubious about unity, have come to see that the churches' witness to justice for the oppressed and to reconciliation of divided peoples is indeed weakened by the lack of integral unity.

Since 1983, numerous conferences and studies on BEM have been held throughout the world. No initiative or document of the World Council of Churches has ever elicited so much wide response.

Learnings from the U.S. Churches

What have we learned in this conference about "reception"? This is, of course, the word classically used for the process by which the work of an ecumenical council becomes part of the living tradition of the Church. Indeed, it is the Church's "reception" of its results which makes a council "ecumenical." In the patristic age that process could take two hundred years or more. Reception, in this sense, is a theological process relating a formulation of Gospel truth to the faith of the whole People of God.

The process of "response" is one moment in a more extended ecumenical process, which may come to be understood as "reception." The internal debates of the churches over their own definition of reception, their mode of response, the theological understanding given to the process and the authority underlying it begin to provide a basis for a theological understanding of reception in the ecumenical movement.

With this understanding there is continuity with the historic understanding of "reception," yet an openness to the contemporary situation in our divided churches. Reception, then, takes account of the action of the Holy Spirit in the different decision-making bodies of our divided churches and challenges our churches to give a theological account of the ecclesiological implications of the response and reception processes. Furthermore, the process of "reception" would apply as much to the lived faith of Christians in other traditions affirming BEM, as to the verbal formulations of the text itself.

The influences of BEM in liturgical life, educational practice, and common mission are integral to an emerging description of reception. BEM has influenced the churches through widespread use of the "Lima Liturgy" (not an official interpretation of BEM and needing further work, but still a medium of "reception"; see *wcc-coe.org/wcc/what/faith/lima-e.html*) reflecting decades of common theological and liturgical research. In one communion BEM has come in time to influence the compilation of a new hymnal. BEM has also found its way into seminary classrooms, not only in courses on ecumenism or even on the sacraments, but also in general introductory courses. Once BEM becomes a basic point of reference in theological education, reception is well underway. Official response is not absent from reception but does not exhaust its theological meaning for the faith of the church. The faith reflected in BEM enters the ethos, the praxis, the spirituality of our churches to the extent it resonates with the faith of the church through the ages. It has been used in lay study groups and also in interchurch discussions.

In seeking to understand this process, we must remember its contexts. The churches themselves, while responding to BEM, have been busy with a multitude of other things, including other ecumenical dialogues. Moreover, the reception of BEM by the churches is part of the process by which they prepare for participation in present and future Faith and Order studies: the study "Toward the Common Expression of the Apostolic Faith Today" and the study on "The Unity of the Church and the Renewal of Human Community." The responses in some cases show the need for the review of the Montreal (1963) work on Scripture and Tradition and the Nairobi formulation of Conciliar Fellowship (1975). These studies, in short, are part of BEM's reception and tests of how well the whole Faith and Order process is accomplished.

The methods and contents of the various "responses" suggest how "reception" has been variously conceived. Polity, spirituality and ethos in the different churches have made a difference. One can draw inferences from style and language. But there are surprises. Our stereotypes are challenged by what we read. Clearly, however, the churches vary in their degree of experience in responding to and assimilating ecumenical convergences. Perhaps the central question is this: how far do process and result embody (not merely describe conceptually) the ecclesiology and authority of the diverse communions? Further theological work will be necessary on these questions of authority, limits of diversity, and ecclesiology.

In all this there has been unexpected value. The challenge of BEM has raised for each church the question how well it is prepared "to give an account of the hope" that is in it or, more formally, to confess the apostolic faith. Is it possible for us today, from "the highest appropriate level of authority" to the grassroots, to respond as one body to this ecumenical initiative? Who really speaks for us? BEM could turn out to be the catalyst we need to consider such questions seriously and thus be prepared for ecumenical initiatives to come.

Issues for Reception

The responses of the U.S. churches surfaced a number of issues that remain to be studied and resolved if Christians are to find the unity they seek and God wills. Among these issues are

1. Authority: Who speaks for Christians, and will they listen?

2. The role of Scripture and Tradition in determining decisions facing the Church today: Are they normative or prescriptive? Interpretation requires an openness to the Spirit in the present situation as well as speaking through Scripture and history.

3. The role of women in ministry is a focal point of present theological discussion, involving, as it does, many other theological issues. Where does the issue of the ordination of women find its place in this important concern of all churches?

4. The ministry of all baptized Christians is an important part of the mission of the Church to the world. What is the relation between the ministry of the whole Church and the ordained ministry?

5. The distinction between *episcopos* (bishop) and *episcopé* (oversight) is useful for ecumenical understanding. Further work needs to be done to spell out this relation between the classical approach to apostolic succession and the understanding found in BEM.

6. How are non-sacramental and Pentecostal Christians to be more intimately involved in these discussions on BEM?

7. There is a concern for inclusive language. What are the theological implications of BEM's masculine language when speaking of God and the Church?

8. BEM does not resolve the different theological understandings of grace, faith, and baptismal practice between churches that baptize only adults and those that also baptize infants.

9. The role of the Holy Spirit in the Church, Reformation insights into the power of God's Word and into the Eucharist as *anamnesis* continue to be important issues that need further work.

10. Finally, holding together the agendas of life and work/faith and order is critical for the mission of the Church to unite the fragmented family of God (John 11:52).

Challenges for Reception

In order to further the reception process of BEM among the churches, as well as to continue the momentum and serious interest which the response process initiated throughout the life of churches in North America, five specific challenges were identified to be addressed both to the churches and to the Faith and Order Commission of the World Council and National Council of Churches:

1. Clearly the focus of the majority of the responses was addressed to Question 1, i.e., recognizing in BEM the faith of the Church through the ages. Modest response or attention was given to Questions 2 and 3 regarding the consequences for ecumenical relations and guidance in areas of worship and educational, ethical, and spiritual life and witness. *The challenge now is to take up these questions with the full attention and seriousness such as that which is evidenced in response to Question 1, while necessarily involving churchwide participation in this necessary process of implementation.*

2. While some churches sought wide involvement among their memberships in the response process, there is still the urgent need that BEM be made known throughout the churches to laity, pastors, congregations, seminaries, and program agencies. *Reception must be aimed at the education and involvement of the whole people of God, as well as the churches' leadership and decision-making structures.*

3. The issues identified earlier in this report (Section III) need to be taken up by the Faith and Order Commission and by the churches if BEM is finally to be received in its full potential. *The challenge is to develop procedures—e.g., involving seminary communities, special consultations related to particular themes—which will address these specific concerns underlying the present inability of churches to claim BEM fully as an expression of the Apostolic Faith.*

4. Many responses identified questions related to an ecclesiology which is implicit in BEM yet not openly expressed or acknowledged. However, it has been a part of the wider Faith and Order discussions for twenty years, especially in the work of the Montreal (1963) World Conference on Scripture and Tradition and from the Nairobi (1975) Assembly of the WCC on Conciliar Fellowship. These are yet to be received by the churches. *The challenge is to begin making explicit that which has been implicit and testing the emergence of this "ecumenical ecclesiology" which gives shape to the BEM text (i.e.,* koinonia: *community, fellowship, communion [WCC and NCC constitutions]).*

5. Reception is a different, more demanding, and even more difficult task than that of response. The debates and clarification of its theological meaning within and among the churches must continue. It is an ongoing pilgrimage which must engage the whole life of the churches. *The challenge is to adopt and teach such an understanding of "the process of growing together in mutual faith" in which the churches "develop doctrinal convergences step by step, until they are finally able to declare together that they are living in communion with one another in continuity with the apostles and the teachings of the universal Church" (BEM, Preface, ix).*

Document 33

THE APOSTOLIC FAITH AND THE CHURCH'S PEACE WITNESS: A SUMMARY STATEMENT, 1991

Editors' Note: *The Faith and Order Study on Confessing the Apostolic Faith Today has taken up the claim of the historic peace churches—Mennonite, Brethren, and Quaker—that the Church's witness to peace is an essential element in confessing the apostolic faith. The two following texts summarize the results of three consultations with these churches. International bilateral dialogues have also taken up these themes.*

For other peace church dialogues, see the following: Mennonite World Conference Catholic Dialogue, "Called Together to be Peacemakers," Information Service, *2003: II/III, nos. 113, 111-148; Ross T. Bender and Alan Sell, eds.,* Baptism, Peace and State in the Reformed and Mennonite Traditions *(Waterloo, Canada: Wilfrid Laurier University Press, 1991); Hans Georg von Berg et al., eds.,* Mennonites and Reformed in Dialogue *(Geneva: World Alliance of Reformed Churches, 1986); Viggo Mortensen, ed.,* War, Confession and Conciliarity *(Geneva, Lutheran World Federation, 1992).*

The October 27-29, 1991, consultation in Douglaston, New York, was the second consultation on the apostolic faith and the church's peace witness sponsored by the Commission on Faith and Order of the National Council of the Churches of Christ in the USA. It continued and built on the deliberations of the first gathering, which was held in March 1990 at Bethany Theological Seminary, Oak Brook, Illinois.

The first consultation focused on peace statements produced by Roman Catholic, Orthodox, Protestant, and historic peace church (HPC) groups in North America during the 1980s. Participants in the March 1990 meeting came with responses to these peace statements. The responses identified points of convergence and divergence among the statements in their use of Scripture, in their theological arguments (including their use of historical, philosophical, or political reasoning), in their primary theological categories (e.g., ecclesiology, christology, creation and its preservation, individual Christian vocation, peace), and in the ecclesial and moral implications of the positions taken.

Participants in the first consultation also served as an initial planning group for the 1991 consultation and commissioned several of their number to complete preparations for it. The group decided that more attention should be given to the biblical bases for the church's peace witness and secondarily to two historical periods that have been crucial for unity and division in Christian peace witness (the period of the early church in the first three centuries, and the time of the appearance of the historic peace churches in the sixteenth, seventeenth, and eighteenth centuries). In preparation for the second consultation, several biblical scholars talked together and wrote papers, which were forwarded to participants prior to the second consultation. The historical studies provided additional background for understanding divergences in the churches' traditions.

Participants in the second consultation discussed these biblical and historical papers and also heard a presentation by Reformed theologian Richard Mouw of Fuller Theological Seminary, Pasadena, California, on dialogue between Reformed and Mennonite theologians on the church's peace witness. Mouw's case study in ecumenical conversation summarized key areas of traditional Anabaptist-Reformed disagreement and noted some signs of hope for further dialogue in the contemporary context.

What follows is a summary statement from consultation participants on common concerns, areas of convergence and divergence, and recommendations for further conversation.

I. Introduction

We acknowledge that those Christian groups historically opposing church involvement with the state and especially with its violent defense have claimed to be doing nothing less than preserving the faith delivered to the apostles. For them, differences among the churches on issues of Christian participation in violence and war stand in the way of confessing a common faith. These divisions are a matter of vital importance, like the church order, sacramental, and creedal differences that have already been widely recognized as separating Christians.

We are aware that movement toward a common expression of the apostolic faith involves much more than resolving a particular ethical issue frequently presumed to have only peripheral theological and confessional significance. Movement toward the Christian unity envisioned in the gospel of Jesus Christ also requires a common understanding of the ecclesiological issues that both inform and derive from the churches' disagreements about what faithfulness in the church's peace witness entails.

II. The Uses of Scripture in North American Church Peace Statements of the 1980s

At the 1991 consultation, with the help of Howard John Loewen's detailed analysis (see chapter 2 [in the] volume [of essays from the conference][1]), we noted similarities as well as wide-ranging differences in the use of Scripture in peace statements produced by the historic peace churches and by Roman Catholic, Protestant, and Orthodox churches or their representatives during the 1980s. Similarities and differences were noted with respect to specific Scripture texts cited, hermeneutical assumptions, use of Scripture in theological argument, and ethical and ecclesial implications drawn from or incorporated into the appropriation of Scripture. The statements generally agree that peace is a central theme in Scripture, that it is rooted in some way in the eschatological reign of God, and that Jesus did not resort to violence. They differ in their estimate of the relevance of biblical views of peace, war, and violence for churches in the contemporary context.

We did not come to clear conclusions on the significance of the hermeneutical practices reflected in the churches' peace statements for the churches' confessional divergence or convergence. It may be that the statements' shared concern for peacemaking is beginning to inform the churches' appropriation of Scripture in ways that relativize the traditional interpretations that have undergirded confessional divisions along just war and pacifist lines. The fact that all these statements have recently been produced by these groups does seem to indicate that concern for peace witness, which had earlier been left largely to the historic peace churches, has now become important for virtually all Christian groups.

We were left with several questions about the churches' peace statements' use of Scripture. First, to what degree do the peace church, just-peace church, and other traditions sufficiently establish the claim that the positions represented in their statements are based on Scripture or in harmony with Scripture? Conversely, to what degree do they either neglect to make that claim or fail to establish it adequately?

Second, is a new paradigm emerging in the churches' assessment of violence and war to supersede the paradigm that has supported traditional divisions between pacifists and just war adherents? The recent church peace statements appear to share several characteristics that may indicate movement toward a new model: a focus on creating conditions for peace and preventing war, a central concern for nonviolence and finding alternatives to war, a presumption that all (not only national leaders) are responsible for making peace and preventing war, and a concern to learn from rather than to ignore or condemn pacifists.

Third, to what degree do the churches' peace statements present a persuasive call to give a biblical vision of peace priority over understandings of peace in postbiblical traditions? Some of us perceived the churches' statements to be granting a biblical vision that kind of priority, while others were less sure that all the statements have done so or have intended to do so.

Fourth, to what extent does the world situation of the 1990s call for a reassessment of the use of Scripture in the church peace statements of the 1980s? The threat of nuclear holocaust arising from massive confrontation between superpowers of the East and West is no longer an issue demanding the churches' reflection. To what degree did that problem condition the churches' use of Scripture in ways that call for critique and reinterpretation?

III. The Old Testament as a Scriptural Base

Our conversations on the Old Testament as a scriptural base for the church's peace witness were informed by the papers provided by Ben Ollenburger ("Peace and God's Action Against Chaos in the Old Testament") and Dianne Bergant ("Yahweh: A Warrior God?"), chapters 3 and 4 in this volume.

We noted that biblical scholars generally, and the biblical scholars contributing to this consultation specifically, differ in their understandings of the relation between confessional and scholarly readings of Scripture, as well as on hermeneutical and theological method. Nevertheless, we agreed that it is as difficult to justify Christians' participation in the wars of our nations on the basis of the Old Testament as it is to justify Christians' refusal to participate in any war on the same basis. Or to put the matter in other terms: the Old Testament renders problematic any confessional reading that claims to ground a just war or crusade or pacifist position in it, though the ways in which it challenges each of these readings may differ.

Several Old Testament texts and passages related to deliverance, war, peace, and creation figured prominently in the presentations and discussion, including (but not limited to) Exodus 14 and 15; Judges 41 and 5; Psalms 24, 68, 89, 104; and Isaiah 17 and 37. Some participants missed sustained attention to the themes of the suffering servant and Cyrus in Isaiah 40-55.

We agreed that affirming the continuity between the Old and New Testaments remains foundational on theological and confessional grounds, as well as for hermeneutical reasons. We also agreed that the Old Testament, in continuity with the New Testament, could provide greater resources than the churches have yet appropriated for the praxis of faithfulness to God in just peacemaking.

IV. The New Testament as a Scriptural Base

It is perhaps ironic that we devoted less time to conversations on the New Testament as a scriptural base for the churches' peace witness than to other aspects of the consultation. Our discussions were informed by Paul Anderson's essay "Jesus and Peace" (chapter 5 in the present volume), an earlier version of the Richard Jeske paper (now titled "Peace in the New Testament," chapter 6 above), and an essay on Romans 13 by Thomas Hoyt (which was not available for this volume).

We acknowledged that the New Testament unambiguously calls the church to accept and proclaim the gospel of peace, to follow the way of Jesus in loving enemies and rejecting violence, to carry out a ministry of peacemaking and reconciliation, and to practice the justice of God's reign. It therefore poses the major confessional problem for just-war proponents, to the extent that they seek to justify their position on the basis of Scripture. Simultaneously, it challenges proponents of pacifism, to the extent that they focus narrowly on rejecting Christian participation in war and violence.

The presentations and our discussions covered a wide range of New Testament themes and passages related to peace, war, nonviolence, and reconciliation. Themes given particular prominence included Jesus' temptations, teachings, and example; Christians' discriminating submission to the demands of the state; and their ministry of peace and reconciliation. Particular attention was given to several New Testament texts, including Matthew 5, Mark 10:42-45, John 14:27 and 16:33, Romans 5 and 13, 2 Corinthians 5, Philippians 2, Ephesians 2, and several passages in Revelation.

V. The Historical and Contemporary Appropriation of Scripture in the Churches' Peace Witness

The historical essays by David Hunter (chapter 7: "The Christian Church and the Roman Army in the First Three Centuries") and by Donald Durnbaugh and Charles Brockwell (chapter 8: here titled "The Historic Peace Churches: From Sectarian Origins to Ecumenical Witness") and Richard Mouw's presentation provided the background and basis for discussing the convergence and divergence of several church traditions on Christian participation in war. Most of the conversation centered on Mouw's description and assessment of similarities and differences between the Reformed and the Anabaptist/Mennonite traditions.

We noted factors that make Christian pacifism both difficult and attractive for nonpacifists. For example, the concern to liberate, defend, or preserve the neighbor from oppression, evil, and death—using the sword if necessary—out of love for the neighbor renders pacifism difficult for nonpacifist Christians. Simultaneously, the desire to be faithful to the New Testament witness and awareness of past abuses of just-war rhetoric and practice make Christian pacifism attractive.

Similar considerations make a nonpacifist stance both attractive and difficult for pacifist Christians. The plight of the neighbor in situations of overwhelming evil makes a nonpacifist approach attractive to pacifists concerned for justice. At the same time, awareness of the church's departure from its pre-Augustinian social ethic and the desire to follow Jesus faithfully make any use of violence difficult for the Christian pacifist to accept.

VI. Major Issues Warranting Additional Attention

In the course of the consultation, we noted several questions related to apostolic faith and the church's peace witness that we believe deserve more sustained reflection than we were able to give them:

1. What is the relationship between our primary identity as Christian disciples and members of a transnational church and our identity as citizens of a particular nation and our exercise of power in that society?

2. Should the influence of national loyalty and identity on the churches' peace witness and on their biblical interpretation be understood in positive or negative terms, as constructive or problematic, or both?

3. What is the role of spiritual formation in nurturing, sustaining, and guiding the church's peace witness?

4. Do the changing language and categories in the churches' biblical interpretation regarding peace fundamentally call into question the traditional paradigms that have contributed to or justified divisions between churches?

5. Should our review of historical traditions in our search for Christian unity involve reexamining confessional condemnations by churches' teaching just-war doctrine of churches rejecting participation in war and violence?

6. According to the non-HPCs, is a Christian pacifist stance (together with participation in war under certain conditions) also compatible with the apostolic faith? Is this still a church-dividing issue for these Christians? According to the HPCs, are churches that accept both Christian pacifism and Christian participation in war under certain conditions acting in harmony with or contrary to the apostolic faith?

VII. Recommendations

1. We recommend to the Working Group on Faith and Order that the study and conversation on the apostolic faith and the church's peace witness be continued during the 1992-1995 quadrennium. Although the consultations to date have taken several steps toward clarifying the biblical bases of the church's peace witness, significant work remains to be done,

particularly on the New Testament basis for this witness and its continuity with the Old Testament. Further, questions about a possible change in paradigm of churchly and scholarly understandings of peace and the significance of such a change for traditionally church-dividing positions merit further examination, clarification, and response (see VI.4 above). Has there been a paradigm shift? If so, what is its character, and what are its implications for significant convergence in the churches' peace witness?

2. We suggest that further attention be given to encouraging and developing recommendations for conversation and reconciliation between the churches whose historic teaching and practice on war and peace have been an occasion for strife, division, condemnation, and persecution.

3. We propose that the Working Group on Faith and Order share the results of this consultation with those in the broader ecumenical conciliar movement seeking a common understanding of what it means to confess the apostolic faith today. We also encourage them to give sustained attention to the apostolic character of the church's peace witness.

NOTE

1 [This text and supporting essays found in] Marlin Miller and Barbara Nelson Gingrich, eds., *The Church's Peace Witness* (Grand Rapids: Wm. B. Eerdmans, 1994), 15-69. [In this statement, "this volume" refers to this book of supporting documents.]

Document 34

THE FRAGMENTATION OF THE CHURCH AND ITS UNITY IN PEACEMAKING

Report of a Consultation of the Commission on Faith and Order Apostolic Faith Study, 1995

Editors' Note: *This text and background essays can be found in John Rempel and Jeff Gros, eds.,* The Fragmentation of the Church and Its Unity in Peace Making *(Grand Rapids: Wm. B. Eerdmans, 2001).*

Background

1. A consultation meeting June 13-17, 1995, at Notre Dame, Indiana, was a third meeting on the pilgrimage toward the unity of the church in a "Common Confession of the Apostolic Faith Today," focusing on the apostolic character of the church's peace witness. This consultation, sponsored by Faith and Order of the National Council of Churches of Christ in the United States and Joan B. Kroc Institute for International Peace Studies of the University of Notre Dame, builds on the work of the World and National Councils in exploring the common ground for a conciliar communion, and specifically on two previous consultations, at Bethany Theological Seminary, Oak Brook, Illinois, in 1990 and in Douglaston, New York, 1991.

2. Previous work on the history of the church's confessional tradition, *Faith to Creed*, and the results of the previous consultations in this series, *The Church's Peace Witness*, provided historical and biblical foundations for the present discussion. This consultation provided a significant opportunity to explore the link between ecclesiology and peacemaking, in dialogue with

the Historic Peace Churches. This report is prepared for the work of Faith and Order of the National Council of Churches of Christ in the United States of America. Members of Orthodox, Anglican, Roman Catholic, and Protestant churches presented a variety of the positions of the churches over the question of peace and the relationship of the church to society, the impulse of the churches' contribution to the quest for visible unity, and the present developments that might place the relationship among these churches in a new context. These studies in the United States take place against the background of the Gospel imperative to peacemaking and the unity of the church. Faith and Order's *Confessing the One Faith* provides an articulation of where some churches are on this pilgrimage at this time.

3. The previous consultation provided an encouraging common ground in the churches' approach to the biblical witness and its use in their contemporary approach to the question of peace and its centrality in the church's confession:

> The statements [of the churches produced during the 1980s] generally agree that peace is a central theme in Scripture, that it is rooted in some way in the eschatological reign of God, and that Jesus did not resort to violence. They differ in their estimate of the relevance of biblical views of peace, war and violence for church in the contemporary context... It may be that the statements' shared concern for peacemaking is beginning to inform the churches' appropriation of Scripture in ways that relativize the traditional interpretations that have undergirded confessional divisions along just war and pacifist lines. The fact that all these statements have recently been produced by these groups does seem to indicate that concern for peace witness, which had earlier been left largely to the historic peace churches, has now become important for virtually all Christian groups. (*The Church's Peace Witness*, 210)

The convergence in ecclesiology was less clear from the earlier consultation; therefore, the present discussion invited papers from Lutheran, Reformed, Roman Catholic, Mennonite, Brethren, Churches of Christ, and Assemblies of God perspectives. Significant responses were incorporated into the discussion from Orthodox, Baptist, Methodist, Anglican, and Quaker perspectives.

4. The divisions in the Body of Christ in the world are a counter witness to the peace sought and proclaimed by the church as the follower of

the Prince of Peace who prayed that his disciples might be one. The movement toward unity among the churches is itself a sign and model of their peacemaking vocation. The consultation considered a wide range of theological, historical, and ethical perspectives on the relationship of the unity of the church, peace among the churches, and the churches' peacemaking vocation in the world.

5. In this consultation the churches have been encouraged to speak out of the specificity of their histories and traditions, seeking common ground in Jesus Christ and the common elements shared in the quest to be faithful to the church's call to be united in peacemaking. As the consultation has looked at the origins of the churches' alienation, their various resources for unity, and witness in peacemaking, hopes have emerged for reconciliation in the apostolic faith, formation in Gospel discipleship, and common witness in the world.

6. We lament that Christians have used their faith to further hate and violence. Nevertheless, events of the last decade have also shown that the peacemaking efforts in the world and the responses of the churches have made a difference in human history. While areas of disagreement continue, peacemaking is an essential element of the apostolic faith is acknowledged by all. We continue to recognize divergences in the approach to this apostolic mandate in our pilgrimage toward full communion.

Learnings

7. We are agreed, on the basis of the Apostolic Tradition, that Christians, following our Lord and Savior Jesus Christ, are called to be peacemakers. We consider this a common confession of the faith once delivered to the apostles, basic to our Christian unity. In a world of violence, be it in the streets or in warfare, churches affirm that peace is the will of God and that peace has been shown to us most clearly in the life, teachings, death, and resurrection of Jesus Christ. Peacemaking is most deeply rooted in Christ and the unity of the church, and such unity is a gift of the Holy Spirit linked to repentance and forgiveness. Through the power of the Holy Spirit, we are enabled to practice peacemaking as a way of participation in the life and death of Christ. A primary vocation of every believer is love, out of which peacemaking flows. Our peace with God impels us toward peace with neighbor and love of enemies.

8. In the face of the fragmentation of the church we are agreed on the importance of spiritual formation for unity in peacemaking. Both pacifist and non-pacifist churches find themselves in a world where evil has become multifaceted in ever more insidious ways, ranging from a hierarchy of violence to the arrogance of power politics, intertwined with economic greed and pervasive military power. In our church communities, we want to train our members for peacemaking, helping them to develop a wider repertoire of responses to evil and violence and to enemies. As Christians, many of us would endorse, instead of "fight or flight," Jesus' way of creative nonviolence which confronts enemies, unmasking sin and injustice. Formation or training in peacemaking is important on an ongoing basis, not just in times of crisis or war. Some participants have recalled the missionary injunction of Jesus "to be wise as serpents and innocent as doves" (Matt. 10:16) as a call for healing and a symbol of sharp discernment and vigilance against the sin of playing God (Gen. 3:5). Others have recalled the many ways of spiritual formation in the past, be it monastic discipline, penitential discipline for those who have killed as soldiers or guardians of the peace, or critical involvement in the affairs of this world.

9. Among many represented at this meeting, criticism of the just-war theory has deepened. Nuclear warfare stretched the capabilities of the just-war theory. Moreover, nation-states seldom use just-war criteria as the basis for deciding whether to enter a war, considering issues in the continuation of a war, or assessing the consequences after a war has finished. For some, the just-war tradition is an unused resource that can enhance peacemaking if seriously taken into account by Christians. Most wars since the close of the Cold War are civil wars.

10. At the Notre Dame meeting, we affirmed the importance of hearing each other's church histories as a means of understanding each other's positions on peacemaking. Repentance of past persecutions of peacemakers, disowning the anathemas of past confessions, and forgiveness will further our future dialogue. We can affirm our common history in the early centuries of the church, including a common history of martyrdom during those first centuries. We recognize that those church traditions that have claimed the first-century church as the primary model of the church have often claimed the first-century church's peace position.

11. We also recognize in the histories of the American churches the difficulties and changes with regard to the peace position that occurred especially during World War I, in many of our traditions. In addition, the shaping impact of World War II, Vietnam, and the Cold War in general has left a greater legacy

of testing and reviewing the churches' capacity for peacemaking and has resulted in renewed attempts to articulate and in greater understanding of our diverse attempts to articulate a theology of peacemaking.

12. We are agreed that some form of critical participation in civil government and in the surrounding society is appropriate. We are interested neither in complete withdrawal from society nor in uncritical absorption into the dominant culture.

13. We are agreed that, at some point, Christians may be called to obey God rather than human authorities. Our ultimate loyalty is to God, and to the church, the people of God. Our primary identity is Christian. At some point, the issue of peacemaking may be a question of allegiances or of idolatry. We saw the relevance of eschatology for sustainable and hopeful peacemaking. Peacemaking is dependent on hope in God's deliverance of the righteous, God's judgment on the unjust, and fulfillment of peace in God's reign.

Points of Contention

14. A. While we are in agreement that all Christians should be striving for peace, there continues to be significant disagreement over the best ways to pursue peace. Some individuals and traditions hold that to follow Jesus is to relinquish all contemplation and taking of violent action toward another human being, created in the image of God, for whom Christ died. Others wonder if the love of neighbor may at times call for effective intervention—even armed intervention—to save innocent parties from hostile aggression. Would this action be an honorable means of action or cause Christians to become what we hate?

15. B. While the various churches may come to embrace clear positions on peace and nonviolence as normative for Christians, churches also struggle with what to do with members who chose another path. What is the significance of this diversity within each church for the unity and healing of divisions among the churches? Should particular strategies and stances toward peacemaking become obligatory, or should churches simply give clear witness to the truth they have received? Then again, how meaningful can a testimony be if it goes unheeded by the church's members? While churches do not want to become dictatorial, they clearly desire to provide accountability for maintaining their convictions, while at the same time providing pastoral care for those who dissent for reasons of conscience.

16. C. Marks of the church are of central concern, but as of yet, we have no full agreement as to what are the necessary marks. Some wonder if they should include gathering in the name of Jesus and Christ-like discipleship—even leading to suffering. This being the case, a clear connection between the death and resurrection with Christ experienced in the eucharist and baptism may be understood to extend to ethical stances in the world. For the Christian, one must be willing that self should suffer for truth, and not that truth should suffer for self.

17. D. Understandings of church and state continue to be matters of concern. On one hand, the responsibility of states to protect and order a society is appreciated; on the other, Christians may feel pressured by the state to go against conscience. We recognize the tensions between the polarities of charisma and institution within the church and affirm at each step solidarity with Jesus and his teachings.

Struggles faced by developing church traditions may include questions of survival and the sense of being disenfranchised. Conversely, the temptations of more established church traditions may include challenges of inertia and the inability to change directions.

As churches accumulate greater influence, governments and powers become more interested in influencing their directions. Within this situation, Christians must be wise as serpents so as not to be co-opted into unholy alliances which threaten our ability to be innocent as doves (Matt. 10:16) and loyal to our common Lord.

18. E. Peacemaking would be furthered considerably if at least Christians could agree not to kill each other. Should not our loyalty to our common Lord supersede our loyalties to family, home, and state? On the other hand, why should Christians be willing to kill or harm non-Christians, for whom Jesus also shed his blood? They too are beloved by God and created in the divine image. How could Jesus' followers commit acts of violence against those he commands us to forgive? Then again, just-war criteria have often been invoked with the specific intention of limiting violence, conflict, and casualties. It is the question of the use or nonuse of force in the common goal of peacemaking that remains unresolved within the churches.

Recommendations

In the face of the increasing complexities of Christian unity and peacemaking, the participants of this consultation make the follow-ing recommendations:

19. A. That definitions of unity, mission, and peacemaking be well grounded in an understanding of the apostolic faith as a source of power to create regional and global ways of peacemaking, with a focus on unmasking the reality of evil and on the church as the community of the meantime between Christ's first and second coming. As the community of the interim (the people of "the way": Acts) the church has been empowered by the Lord to bear his witness in the world, to live as a sign and foretaste of the age to come, and to announce his coming lordship.

20. B. That unity and peacemaking require special programs of faith formation, in and among the churches, that assist in developing the skills of nonviolent Christian living and understandings of the churches and their quest for visible unity.

21. C. That the churches develop programs of prayer for peace, for the unity of the church, and for one another. These prayers nourish communion in Christ and move Christians to the conversion to God's will for the unity of the Church and the peace of the world.

22. D. That the churches provide opportunities for a dialogue of conversion, whereby Christians can encounter one another in their common quest for understanding, deepening their commitment to peace and justice in the world, and growing in their zeal for the unity of the Church.

23. E. That those churches who have condemned one another's positions on pacifism and engagement in the world reconsider whether these condemnations can be put aside through public acts of reconciliation; that those churches which in the past have persecuted the Peace Churches or have contributed to the estrangement of other churches can find occasions for public repentance and petitions of pardon in communal acts of reconciliation, forgiveness, prayer, and confession together.

24. F. That Faith and Order, in the National Council of Churches, explore the relationship of the apostolic character of the churches' faith and order as they develop from traditions of continuity and traditions of restoration.

25. G. That the conciliar work on justice, peace, and integrity of creation consider unity in common confession, sacramental life, and mutual accountability for the process of common witness and action in the world.

26. H. That further study be done in the relationship of the church as the People of God in the context of national and ethnic identity.

Document 35

A RESPONSE TO *UT UNUM SINT*

Report of the Faith and Order Commission, USA,

to the Pontifical Council for the Promotion of Christian Unity, 2003

Editors' Note: *In response to Pope John Paul's 1995 encyclical, with its invitation to dialogue, both World Council and U.S. National Council of Churches Faith and Order Commissions provided a preliminary response. A second invitation was issued after these preliminary responses had been collated for the Catholic Pontifical Council for Promoting Christian Unity. This document is one response to that second, more elaborate, invitation, the text of which (together with supplemental texts) can be found in "Petrine Ministry,"* Information Service *202, 109/I-II: 29-42.*

I. Prefatory Comments

A. Gratitude for the Invitation to Discussion

At the outset of its response to *Petrine Ministry: A Working Paper*, the Commission on Faith and Order of the National Council of the Churches of Christ in the USA acknowledges with gratitude the graciousness and the significance of Pope John Paul II's offering an open invitation, based "on the already existing, though still imperfect communion between all Christian communities," "to discover and to realize together the will of Christ for his Church" (1.4 [in "Petrine Ministry"]). The Faith and Order Commission has worked hard to foster the degree of communion that currently exists among Christian communities in the USA; thus we recognize the invitation as addressed to us and count it a privilege to respond to the invitation. The Commission shares the concern for the unity of the Church and for the *charism* of primacy to be exercised as a ministry of unity and a service of love (1.2). Further, the Commission notes with gratitude the mandate for all to "discover and to realize together the will of Christ for his Church" (1.4). We engage in the process of dialogue in a spirit of deep humility before Christ and in a spirit of willing openness to his will for the whole people of God, recognizing that a fuller exercise of primacy may call for revision or adjustment (1.3) not only in the exercise of papal primacy but also in the manner in which Christian communities respond to and/or receive the exercise of a Petrine ministry.

B. The Desire to Make Common Cause with the PCPCU

This response is offered to the Pontifical Council by the whole Commission on Faith and Order in hopes that its work may further the cause of Christian unity. Where points of tension may surface between what *Petrine Ministry* says and the Commission is able to say at this point, these tensions should be understood as those areas of concern that, when discussed with a desire for mutual understanding and a common desire to discern the will of Christ, may bear rich fruit for the life of the church.

C. Recognition of the Breadth of Concern

The Commission recognizes that issues concerning the nature of primacy and the exercise of the Petrine office have been a widely shared concern from the earliest days of the church, have played a significant role in defining the divisions between churches, and continue to be discussed in a broad spectrum of ecclesial communions today. Questions about primacy, therefore, are of concern to all the churches. We recognize the fact that when the Bishop of Rome speaks, he is understood not only by most Christians but also by the non-Christian world to be the major spokesperson for Christianity. In a world crowded by many voices, we celebrate that the Gospel of Jesus Christ thus receives a hearing. The Commission is pleased to respond in a manner that acknowledges that all churches may benefit from a common understanding of primacy and Petrine ministry, because such common understandings have the potential to enhance the Church's proclamation of the Gospel of Jesus Christ.

D. The Commission's Prior Work on Authority

Prior to the invitation of the PCPCU, the Commission on Faith and Order had begun discussion of some of the issues posed in *Petrine Ministry.* In response to specific requests from its member communions, the Commission's current quadrennium (2000-2003) has devoted two of its three Study Groups to the issue of authority. One Study Group is concerned with the question of how authority is exercised within the Church. Another Study Group has focused its efforts on considering how the Church may speak authoritatively in the pluralistic culture in which it finds itself. A third Study Group is assessing current progress toward full communion in the North American context. While the issue of authority is by no means coterminous with the issue of primacy or of the exercise of Petrine ministry, the Commission notes (concurring with UUS, no. 94) that without power and authority, the office of Petrine ministry would be "illusory." Hence, the studies underway by the Commission may well serve to respond to the invitation for fraternal dialogue (UUS, no. 96).

E. The Process by Which This Response Was Formulated

In June 2002, the Faith and Order Commission of the National Council of Churches of Christ in the USA received *Petrine Ministry: A Working Paper* from the Pontifical Council for Promoting Christian Unity. All members of the Commission have had opportunity to read that document, to consider it prayerfully, and to offer responses to it from their various confessional positions. Responses from commissioners were forwarded to the Study Group considering Authority in the Church, which coordinated those responses and offered a single paper to the Commission for its consideration at its March 2003 meeting in Washington, D.C. Therefore, this response to *Petrine Ministry* includes input from a very broad spectrum of confessional positions.

F. Future Response Expected

The Commission's current quadrennium will conclude in October 2003. The publications of one of the working groups should have been completed by then, and the other should be completed around 2005. The results of these studies will be made available to the PCPCU once they are in completed form. The Commission hopes that the fruits of its labors will serve to clarify those issues of authority and its exercise that continue to be sources of division, as well as those issues upon which the churches are in agreement. Such clarity, we believe, can serve to enhance the process of dialogue concerning the nature and exercise of a Petrine ministry.

II. Statements of Convergence and Divergence

In the meantime, the Commission is already at this stage able to offer to the PCPCU some statements of convergence and recognizable divergence among its members regarding the nature of authority. Following these statements of consensus and divergence, the Commission offers a number of suggestions of issues that may warrant further conversation as the discussions of primacy and the Petrine Ministry continue.

A. "*Petrine ministry*" seems to assume a particular "shape" of primacy, i.e., primacy as a ministry to the universal church (cf. 1.1, 1.2, and 1.3, which speak of the ministry of the Bishop of Rome in terms of "all the churches," and the extensive discussion in 3.3 of the universal jurisdiction of Petrine ministry). In the first instance, the Commission notes that not all communions recognize the category of "primacy" and that, even within communions that recognize the term, "primacy" has acquired several different meanings. Further discussion of the Petrine ministry would be well served by the development of a common language of primacy per se that could be shared by all communions. (See item A below.)

B. The Commission recognizes the foundational work performed by biblical scholars in recent years, work that has surfaced the existence of a variety of understandings of the church and its order within the New Testament itself (WCC Faith and Order Paper 181, hereinafter NPC, 86).

C. That said, the Commission affirms that, in conformity with what is common to that variety of understandings, all authority in the Church is received from Christ, the sole Head of the Church, and is mediated by the power of the Holy Spirit.

D. Many communions believe that authority exercised within the Church is therefore a *delegated* authority, implying a distance and discontinuity between Christ and the Church. Others speak of Christ's authority as *transferred* to the Church, implying an organic unity between Christ and the Church. Still others see the relationship between the authority of Christ and the Church not so much in terms of structure or office but as a function of truth and discernment—a process by which effective church leadership facilitates the ongoing leadership of Christ. This is an area of divergence among the churches, and the PCPCU may encounter this divergence as dialogues concerning primacy continue.

E. While there is convergence on point C above, there remains divergence among the churches regarding the manner in which the Holy Spirit acts within the Church as it responds to the mandate to speak the Word of Christ to the people of God. The issue of primacy, therefore, may bring to the surface significant pneumatological differences among the churches.

F. The Commission concurs with *Petrine Ministry* (4.2) that many "ecclesiological fundamentals still need preliminary ecumenical study and discussion, viz., regarding the sacramental structure of the Church, episcopal ministry and apostolic succession." During the course of our discussions, for example, we encountered vigorous disagreement between, and in some cases within, communions regarding whether the Church itself is a sacrament.

G. We have found, further, that as a consequence of their positions regarding the Church's sacramentality, some assume that the Church itself (not merely individual members of the Church) is constantly in need of renewal and conversion; others will rule out such a notion *prima facie*. This difference not only reflects widely divergent assumptions regarding the nature of the Church; it also has profound implications on how the nature of authority is construed and put into practice.

H. During the course of our discussions, the Commission has discovered that churches differ regarding the interpretations of Matthew 16:17-19, Luke 22:31-32, John 21:15-19, John 20:21-23, Galatians 2, and Acts 15, viz., whether these texts establish a particular form of primacy (e.g., a "Petrine office" distinct from a more functional role of "Petrine ministry" or "Petrine function"; cf. *Petrine Ministry*, 3.1) and, more specifically, whether primacy is to be vested in a single individual. Indeed, some of the churches within the Commission in principle reject the possibility of an earthly primate, believing that it may diminish the uniqueness of the primacy of Christ.

I. The Commission affirms the statements in *The Nature and Purpose of the Church* that the ministry of oversight in the church is exercised "communally, personally, and collegially" (94-106). The Church is, thus, ordered in a fashion that enhances the full and conscious participation of the whole people of God.

J. Different communions recognize different sources of authority as gifts of the Holy Spirit, including but not limited to the following: Scripture, Tradition, traditions, office, creeds, confessions, worship, spiritual experience, reason, and conscience. Not every one of these sources of authority is recognized in every communion, and even in those cases where two or more communions may agree on locating authority in a common source, they may give different weight to one or more than one source of authority compared to other sources.

K. The recognition and reception of an office of Petrine ministry by all would entail revision and alteration of practices not only within the Roman Catholic Church but also within the various communions. The nature and extent of those revisions and alterations are difficult to foresee, but could call forth significant change in the day-to-day functioning of both the Roman Catholic Church and the other communions.

L. We have found that communions differ widely concerning whether authority is more properly understood as a form of power granted to holders of office by a rite of conferral conducted by the Church, or whether the authority of a holder of office is a *charism* that must be recognized by a community of faith and continuously confirmed by the congruity of the office-holder's life and witness with the community of faith's construal of the Gospel. This distinction is not principally a matter of "top-down" vs. "bottom-up," but of how tenure in office and the office-holder's leading of a life that exhibits holiness and integrity are understood to relate to one another.

M. We affirm that because the Holy Spirit is given to the whole Church (1 Cor. 12:7; NPC, 11), authority in the Church should be exercised in such a way that it is open to the participation of all members. While communions may not agree that this implies a democratic or egalitarian church polity, we share a common conviction that consultation with all in decision making is important. Such consultation as a pattern for decision making finds warrant in Acts 15, is echoed in the Ecumenical Councils of the Church, and continues to find successors in the polities of many churches.

III. Suggestions for Further Discussion

During the course of our discussions, we have identified several areas of concern that may be useful for the PCPCU to consider in future dialogues regarding Petrine ministry. We offer the following considerations and suggestions that have arisen from our continuing attention to the study of authority within the church.

A. Given IIA above, the Commission expects that further discussion of primacy and the Petrine ministry could be served by starting with primacy as a local, pastoral, and Eucharistic ministry, in contrast to primacy as a ministry understood primarily in universal and jurisdictional terms. The distinction is not made in order to forestall all possibility of discussion the universal and jurisdictional aspects of primacy, but to recommend a starting point that may welcome all churches to a frank and productive discussion of the Scriptural and experiential warrant for primacy.

B. While the Scriptures put forward many images of the Church, within the United States the Church as the People of God has become a widely shared metaphor. One area of discussion in the future may be an exploration regarding whether further development of an understanding the Church as the People of God in contrast to, while not in contradistinction to, other metaphors for the Church might affect the manner in which primacy and the Petrine ministry are exercised and received.

C. From their beginnings, some communions within the Reformation tradition have longed for the reformation of the Church, not for revolution. That said, even those communions most sympathetic to the possibility of a Petrine ministry may find it difficult to overcome centuries of anti-Roman polemics. That polemical spirit has given rise to differences in the use of language that make it difficult to attain mutual understanding of even the most basic issues involved. (See IIF above; what, for example, is meant by "Church"?) While some churches of the Reformation may find it possible to speak positively of a Petrine office, Petrine ministry, or the functioning of universal primacy in some form, for many the binding of that ministry to Rome is considered to be, at most, a gift from God for the *bene esse* of the church, and not *de iure divino* (*Petrine Ministry*, 3.2).

D. Because churches differ regarding the relationship between the Scriptures and the Tradition, warrants for positions derived principally or wholly from Tradition without sufficient Scriptural support are not likely to be received broadly.

E. While many communions may recognize a pastoral and unifying role for the Petrine ministry and may even be willing to locate that ministry in Rome and to recognize a limited universal jurisdiction for pastoral purposes, they may also insist on a fundamental difference between pastoral authority and magisterial authority.

F. Future dialogues may find it helpful to consider, in a spirit of mutual grace and patience, the extent to which the exercise of the Roman Petrine ministry has been actually received as either a building block or a stumbling block to the expression of *koinonia* within the Church.

G. Dialogues may find it helpful to discuss primacy and Petrine ministry in eschatological terms, particularly with regard to the vision of Paul in 1 Corinthians 15:20-28.

H. Future dialogues concerning the exercise of authority and the Petrine ministry could explore the influence of neo-Platonic/Aristotelian philosophical systems, incorporated into Western thought through the influence of Pseudo-Dionysius and other late antique and medieval thinkers, on presumptions about whether a given practice or understanding is a consequence of the use of that philosophical system rather than *de iure divino*. Because the intellectual foundations of society in the United States were formed within a post-Enlightenment context that granted little authority to any source other than human reason and are today strongly influenced by postmodernism, further discussion with churches in the context of the United States may do well to confront the philosophical difficulty of attaining either a common understanding of primacy and authority or a widely received form of their exercise.

I. Given II-I and II-M above, future discussions of primacy and Petrine ministry would do well to explore what kinds of structures and processes, either at the level of the local or the universal church, enhance the full and conscious participation of the whole people of God in the life of the Church.

IV. Conclusion

The Faith and Order Commission of the National Council of Churches of Christ in the USA looks forward to further dialogue with the Pontifical Council for Promoting Christian Unity. It is our prayer that this response to the working paper *Petrine Ministry* might bear fruit as communions seek to develop a common understanding of the Church's ministry as servants of Christ and of the place of a Petrine ministry within the continuing ministry of Christ to his beloved.

Index

Index

C

D

G

H

Index

K

L

P

Q

R

S

T